COMPARATIVE MEDIA LAW AND ETHICS

Providing practical and theoretical resources on media law and ethics for the United Kingdom and United States of America and referencing other legal jurisdictions such as France, Japan, India, China and Saudi Arabia, *Comparative Media Law and Ethics* is suitable for upper undergraduate and postgraduate study and for professionals in the media who need to work internationally.

The book focuses on the law of the United Kingdom, the source of common law, which has dominated the English-speaking world, and on the law of the USA, the most powerful cultural, economic, political and military power in the world. Media law and ethics have evolved differently in the USA from the UK. This book investigates why this is the case.

In one chapter Tim Crook considers other media law jurisdictions:

- common law – a focus on India – the biggest democracy in the world and the largest middle class
- civil law – a focus on France – the influential founder of the European Union and host country for the ECHR at Strasbourg
- socialist law – a focus on China – the country with the highest economic growth and largest population
- Islamic law – a focus on Saudi Arabia – one of the most influential sources of legal religiosity.

Tim Crook analyses media law, as it exists, the ethical debates concerning what the law ought to be, and the historical development of legal and regulatory controls of communication. Underlying concepts discussed include the subject of media jurisprudence – the study of the philosophy of media law; media ethicology – the study of the knowledge of ethics/morality in media communication; and media ethicism – the belief systems in the political context that influence journalistic conduct and content. Throughout, media law and regulation are evaluated in terms of their social and cultural context.

The book has a companion website – www.ma-radio.gold.ac.uk/cmle – providing complementary resources and updated developments on the topics explored.

If you need to compare different law and ethics systems, are studying international journalism or want to understand the legalities of working in the media in different jurisdictions, then you should find this an important and useful guide.

Tim Crook is Senior Lecturer in Media Law and Ethics and Head of Radio at Goldsmiths College, University of London, as well as being a Visiting Instructor on Media Law to the British Broadcasting Corporation. He has worked professionally in radio, theatre, television and film as a journalist, producer, director, and sound designer for more than 30 years and has won more than 60 awards for drama, journalism and production. His previous publications include *Radio Drama* (1999) and *International Radio Journalism* (1997).

COMPARATIVE MEDIA LAW AND ETHICS

Tim Crook

Routledge
Taylor & Francis Group

LONDON AND NEW YORK

First published 2010
by Routledge
2 Park Square, Milton Park, Abingdon, Oxon OX14 4RN

Simultaneously published in the USA and Canada
by Routledge
270 Madison Avenue, New York, NY 10016

Routledge is an imprint of the Taylor & Francis Group, an Informa business

Typeset in Baskerville by
Bookcraft Ltd, Stroud, Gloucestershire
Printed and bound in Great Britain by
CPI Antony Rowe, Chippenham, Wiltshire

British Library Cataloguing in Publication Data
A catalogue record for this book is available from the British
Library

Library of Congress Cataloging in Publication Data
Crook, Tim, 1959-
Comparative media law and ethics/Tim Crook.
p. cm.
Includes bibliographical references and index.
1. Mass media–Law and legislation. I. Title.
K4240.C76 2009
343.09′9–dc22
2009027136

ISBN 10: 0-415-55157-9 (hbk)
ISBN 10: 0-415-55161-7 (pbk)
ISBN 10: 0-203-86596-0 (ebk)

ISBN 13: 978-0-415-55157-1 (hbk)
ISBN 13: 978-0-415-55161-8 (pbk)
ISBN 13: 978-0-203-86596-5 (ebk)

CONTENTS

ILLUSTRATIONS

Figure

Tables

ABBREVIATIONS

Note on case law citations: In the text UK and US case law citation is simplified into a system of abbreviations for the convenience of people not familiar with the discipline of law. This means there will be an indication of the parties e.g. A v B, a simple acronym for the court, e.g. HL stands for House of Lords, and then the year of the ruling. The table of case law in the Bibliography uses traditional professional and scholarship case law citations.

ABA	American Bar Association
ACLU	American Civil Liberties Union
ADR	Alternative Dispute Resolution
AG	Attorney General – government law officer in UK or USA
AIDS	Acquired immune deficiency syndrome
AP	Associated Press (US news agency)
Appeals Cir US	US Federal Appeals Circuit
ASBO	Anti-social Behaviour Order (British law)
ATE	After the event insurance in English and Welsh legal proceedings
Aust. HC	Australian High Court
BBC	British Broadcasting Corporation
BCE	Before Common Era
BNP	British National Party (far-right political organization in UK politics)
BSC	Broadcast Standards Commission (former regulatory body for broadcasting in UK)
BV	Besloten Vennootschap (Dutch equivalent of Ltd in UK or Inc in USA)
CBS	Columbia Broadcasting System (USA)
CFA	Conditional Fee Agreement
CIA	Central Intelligence Agency
CKB	Court of the King's Bench (higher English court in early nineteenth century)

CMLPC	Comparative Media Law and Policy Centre for Socio-Legal Studies, University of Oxford
CoA Civ	Court of Appeal Civil Division
CoA Crim	Court of Appeal Criminal Division
CoE	Court of Exchequer (higher English court in early nineteenth century)
CPS	Crown Prosecution Service
DC US	US Federal District Court
DNA	Deoxyribonucleic acid
DPP	Director of Public Prosecutions
EC	European Community
ECHR	European Court of Human Rights (Human Rights court based in Strasbourg)
ECJ	European Court of Justice (EU court based in Luxembourg)
Ecofin	The European Council of Economic and Finance Ministers
EU	European Union
Ex p	*ex parte*
FBI	Federal Bureau of Investigation
FCC	Federal Communications Commission
FDC	Federal District Court
FOI	Freedom of Information
FOIA	Freedom of Information Act
FTC	Federal Trade Commission
G8	An annual international forum for the heads of government for eight leading countries in the Northern Hemisphere including Canada, France, Germany, Italy, Japan, Russia, the United Kingdom, the United States and representation from the European Union.
GBP	Great Britain Pounds
HC	High Court
HCJ	High Court of Justiciary (Scotland)
HL	House of Lords
HO	Home Office (UK)
HRH	His/Her Royal Highness (courtesy address for members of the British Royal Family)
ICC	International Criminal Court
ICCPR	International Covenant on Civil and Political Rights
ICHRP	International Council on Human Rights Policy
ICTY	International Criminal Tribunal for the former Yugoslavia
IIPA	Intelligence Identities Protection Act 1982 (US)
IRN	Independent Radio News

Plates

ACKNOWLEDGEMENTS

The completion of this book would not have been possible without the help and encouragement of Marja Giejgo. Its successful commissioning and enthusiastic sponsorship I owe to Associate Editor at Routledge Aileen Storey. I am grateful to Judith Oppenheimer, Stacey Carter, Matthew Brown, Christina Kesisoglou and colleagues for the book's design, copy-editing and production.

I am grateful to all my colleagues at the Department of Media & Communications, Goldsmiths, University of London for encouraging and supporting my development of the teaching of comparative media law and ethics. I am also grateful for the privilege of professional collaboration in devising and providing media law workshops at the BBC through the auspices of Valerie Nazareth, Sarah Fuller, Kevin Steele, Philip Wheeler, Alex Gerlis, Sean McTernan and Míċeál Mylvaganam.

I pay tribute to Geoffrey Robertson QC, Sir Andrew Nicol QC, Heather Rogers, QC John Wadham and Keir Starmer QC for the generosity and skill of their past representation and the quality of their juristic writing. Special thanks to all the fine journalists I have worked with covering London's Central Criminal Court and Royal Courts of Justice and specializing in the coverage of legal affairs, and the support of Liberty, the National Union of Journalists and the *Independent* newspaper.

Anat Balint has contributed to the provision of some of the knowledge tables during her brilliant seminar teaching at Goldsmiths during 2008–2009, and I express my thanks to the Office of Court Administration of Texas for its permission to reproduce Figure 1.1, the legal system of the state of Texas in Chapter 1.

ISP(s)	Internet Service Provider(s)
ITC	Independent Television Commission (former regulatory body for regulating UK independent television)
ITN	Independent Television News
ITV	Independent Television (UK)
JCPVC	Judicial Committee of the Privy Council
LVF	Loyalist Volunteer Force (Northern Ireland)
MEPO	Metropolitan Police (London)
MGN	Mirror Group Newspapers
MI5	British Security Service
MI6	British Secret Intelligence Service
MLRC	Media Law Resource Centre (USA)
MLRJC	Media Law and Restorative Justice Commission (a proposed body to reform retributive media law and regulatory processes)
MOD	British Ministry of Defence
MP(s)	Member(s) of Parliament (UK)
MPS	Metropolitan Police Service
MSBP	Munchausen Syndrome By Proxy
NA	Narcotics Anonymous
NATO	North Atlantic Treaty Organization
N.D. Cal.	North District Court of California in the US Federal legal system
NGO	Non-governmental organization
NHS	National Health Service (UK)
NPC	National People's Congress (China)
NPR	National Public Radio (US)
NSA	US National Security Agency
NSK	Newspaper Publishers and Editors Association (Japan)
NUJ	National Union of Journalists (Great Britain and Ireland)
Ofcom	Office of Communications (UK)
OSA	Official Secrets Act
PCC	Press Complaints Commission (UK)
PhD	Doctor of Philosophy
POW	Prisoner of War
QBD	Queen's Bench Division of the High Court of England and Wales
QC	Queen's Counsel
R v	Regina versus (Latin term representing the King/Queen as prosecutor or taking civil legal action on behalf of the UK state)
RCFP	Reporters Committee for the Freedom of the Press
RIPA	Regulation of Investigatory Powers Act 2000 (UK)

RSF	Reporters Sans Frontières
SC US	US Supreme Court
SCS	Scottish Court of Session
SHJ	Scottish High Court of Justiciary
SIS	Secret Intelligence Service (UK)
SJC	Supreme Judicial Council of Saudi Arabia
SLAPP	Strategic Lawsuits Against Public Participation
SOE	Special Operations Executive (British Second World War foreign intelligence and subversion agency)
TNA	The National Archives (UK)
TRIPS	Trade-Related Aspects of Intellectual Property Rights
UCC	Universal Copyright Convention
UK	United Kingdom
UKIP	United Kingdom Independence Party
UN	United Nations
UNESCO	United Nations Educational, Scientific and Cultural Organization
UNHRC	United Nations Human Rights Committee
UNTS	United Nations Treaty Series
UrhG	Urheberrechtsgesetz (German copyright law)
US (U.S.)	United States
US 2nd Cir.	Second Appeals Circuit of the US Federal courts system
US 4th Cir.	Fourth Appeals Circuit of the US Federal courts system
US 5th Cir.	Fifth Appeals Circuit of the US Federal courts system
US SC	US Supreme Court
USA	United States of America
VAT	Value Added Tax (UK and Europe)
WCT	World Copyright Treaty
WGN	Call sign for radio and television stations based in Chicago USA ('WGN' stands for 'World's Greatest Newspaper' and harks back to the time when the radio service was founded by the *Chicago Herald Tribune*)
WIPO	World Intellectual Property Organization
Wisc. App.	State of Wisconsin Court of Appeal
WPPT	World Performances and Phonograms Treaty

1

PRIMARY MEDIA LAW OF THE UK AND USA

The purpose of this book is to investigate the media law and ethics of the United Kingdom and United States of America with some reference to other legal jurisdictions, primarily France, Japan, India, China and Saudi Arabia. The focus on the UK and USA is justified by the fact that the United Kingdom is the source of common law, which has dominated the English-speaking world and the USA is the most powerful cultural, economic, political and military power in the world. US media law and ethics have evolved differently from the UK. This book tries to investigate why this is the case. The book is supported by a companion website at: www.ma-radio.gold.ac.uk/cmle which aims to complement each chapter, and to provide updated information on the topics and multi-media resources to encourage further research and exploration of the subject.

The international perspective is continued through a brief analysis of other media law jurisdictions: common law (India – biggest democracy in the world and largest middle class); civil law (France – influential founder of the European Union and host country for the European Court of Human Rights [ECHR] at Strasbourg); socialist law (China – country with highest economic growth and largest population) and Islamist law (Saudi Arabia – most influential source of legal religiosity). There is consensus at the time of writing that the media law systems of China and Saudi Arabia operate within the context of authoritarian societies, where the nature of democratic accountability is limited in some proportion to the nature of media freedom enjoyed in those countries. Reference is made to media law in Japan because it is the second largest economy in the world and is considered to have a hybrid/composite system of law influenced by the civil and common law doctrines.

The key difference between the UK and USA is that the First Amendment of the US constitution sets out an absolutist principle asserting an unqualified right to freedom of the press. In history and present-day reality the First Amendment does not have an absolute remit, but it does ensure that freedom of expression and media freedom could be said to be more of a trump card in balancing other rights as compared to the situation in the

United Kingdom. The UK Parliament at Westminster incorporated the European Convention on Human Rights into legislation in 1998 (enacted October 2000), and Article 10 on freedom of expression is substantially qualified. The contrasting principles are set out in Table 1.1.

Article 10(1) of the Human Rights Act is significantly qualified by 10(2) which states:

> The exercise of these freedoms, since it carries with it duties and responsibilities, may be subject to such formalities, conditions, restrictions or penalties as are prescribed by law and are necessary in a democratic society, in the interests of national security, territorial integrity, or public safety, for the prevention of disorder or crime, for the protection of health or morals, for the protection of the reputation or rights of others, for preventing the disclosure of information received in confidence, or for maintaining the authority and impartiality of the judiciary.

The US First Amendment is not qualified in this way. Its absolutist implication prompted the Supreme Court Justices Black and Douglas, in the 1964 case of *Sullivan v New York Times*, to speculate that the statement that 'Congress shall make no law' abridging speech and press freedoms meant Congress could make no law. *Sack on Defamation* suggested 'Nothing short of an absolute prohibition of libel judgments against the press would, in

Table 1.1 The differences in defining UK and US freedom of expression

United States of America	United Kingdom:
Constitutional principle guaranteeing freedom of expression	Legislative principle guaranteeing freedom of expression
'Congress shall make no law respecting an establishment of religion, or prohibiting the free exercise thereof; or abridging the freedom of speech, or of the press; or the right of the people peaceably to assemble, and to petition the government for a redress of grievances.'	Article 10, Freedom of Expression: '1. Everyone has the right to freedom of expression. This right shall include freedom to hold opinions and to receive and import information and ideas without interference by public authority and regardless of frontiers. This article shall not prevent states from requiring the licensing of broadcasting, television or cinema enterprises.'
It is to be noted that the First Amendment guarantees freedom of speech and freedom of the press. It is therefore possible to construct a social and constitutional role for the press/media which is in addition to an individual's right to free speech.	Article 10(1) appears to subsume the idea of freedom of the media within 'freedom of expression'.

Plate 1 The Lady of Justice statue at the top of the dome of the Old Bailey in London does not wear a blindfold, a metaphor for the aspiration to open justice in criminal proceedings.

Plate 2 The Supreme Court building in Washington DC. The Court is responsible for media law rulings that are said to give journalists more freedom to publish than their counterparts in Britain.

their opinion, assure freedom from verdicts based on the unpopularity of defendants or their ideas and from the limitation on free debate that follows upon such verdicts.' (Sack 2003: 1–9)

Professor Eric Barendt contends that free speech utopia engendered by the idea that there can be no laws restricting the conduct of communication was sensibly scotched when Justice Holmes observed in 1919 that the 'most stringent protection of free speech would not protect a man in falsely shouting fire in a theatre and causing a panic.' (Schenck v US, SC US 1919) Barendt believes the Douglas and Black constituency of media jurisprudence is as dead as the dodo:

> The absolutist position is also untenable because the regulation, and on occasion even the prohibition, of speech may be justified to protect the free speech rights of others. Even Meiklejohn, who took a very wide view of the protection to be afforded political speech under the First Amendment, recognized that addresses at public meetings could be limited and cut short on valid speech grounds. Absolutists can try to defend their corner by asserting that 'abridging' does not cover all forms of regulation and that 'the freedom of speech' is not the same as 'speech', so that rightly understood the term does not exclude restrictions on some modes of expression. (Meiklejohn 1960: 19–20) But really the game is up, the poverty of literalism laid bare.
>
> (Barendt 2005: 49–50)

The prospect of restorative justice

But would it be wise to fully subscribe to Barendt's eloquent debunking of media freedom absolutism? What would happen in a liberal democracy if, for example, the law of defamation were abolished? Would political and social institutions and the economic infrastructure fail? If it is accepted that the Information Age has generated bottom-up methods of global media publication through Internet and Twitter etc., can it not be argued that any victim of false and unjustifiable attack on reputation has an equal publication remedy? Invasions and abuses of privacy can be handled socially by the ethic of forgiveness and compassion. When a city's electronic traffic control systems fail, does it necessarily follow that motorists are incapable of socially taking personal responsibility for their driving and avoiding collisions and gridlock? Justices Black and Douglas have left seeds that could develop a much softer body of media jurisprudence and ethics. It is indeed possible and rather exciting to develop a discourse of media power attenuation based on the doctrine of restorative justice. If there were an absolutist First Amendment-style constitutional prohibition against media laws in the UK and the USA, could they not be replaced by a constitutional process of restitution, apology and right to reply?

All of the capitalist disincentives of media legal costs engendering 'chilling effects' and Strategic Lawsuits Against Public Participation could be eradicated. Publishers and claimants, including government and judicial authorities, could consent to a participation in quasi-legal and regulatory rituals of arbitration, understanding and apology, negotiated in supervised conferences. Disputes between publishers and complainants would be solved by discussion and, where necessary, restitution by apology and retraction.

Roots of US media freedom culture

R. Bruce Rich writes that the roots of media freedom have been planted in United States history and culture very deep indeed:

> Underlying these First Amendment guarantees is the belief that the key to effective government is an informed citizenry, one that is not told by the government what is right, but instead makes those determinations itself, through its own education. Armed with the knowledge provided to them in a free 'marketplace of ideas', these citizens elect officials who, with the citizens' informed consent, steer the government on its proper course.
>
> (Rich 1995: 1)

The political philosophical spirit underpinning these words is rich with the heritage of John Locke, Thomas Paine, Jeremy Bentham and John Stuart Mill. In contrast, Nick Braithwaite was writing in 1995 that part of the explanation of media libel defendants having such a hard time in England lies in the nature of Britain's unwritten and disordered constitution:

> – really no more than a set of unwritten conventions, habitually observed. English libel law, unfettered by constitutional constraints or a statutory press code, sets a high value upon the protection of private reputation and has traditionally paid mere lip-service to the social utility in freedom of expression. Above all, it has failed to balance the private right with attention to public interest considerations ...
>
> (Braithwaite 1995: 85)

The debate between the rights of a free media and the reputation and privacy interests of private citizens, public figures, corporations and state bodies is undoubtedly the backbone to the analytical discourse of this book. Both corners have varied and intriguing constituencies of argument and opinion. Rich asserts that the marketplace of ideas should be expected to be rough and tumble, cut and thrust, and should accept the irresponsible in human communication as much as the responsible:

> On the theory that no one, authoritarian voice possesses all wisdom, or the 'truth', it has been our perspective that the truth can only emerge through the clash of conflicting ideas. The result of this process can be very strong and passionate debate. Unpleasant, harsh and unpopular statements can be published, critical of the status quo and of current government officials and policy. Such a policy of rejecting one voice in favour of many, of making room for the minority point of view along-side the majority, of not merely tolerating, but actively encouraging, criticism of government, is the basis of the US system of free speech and press. As one of our distinguished judges, Learned Hand, wrote of this policy some years ago: 'To many this is, and always will be, folly; but we have staked upon it our all.'
>
> (Rich 1995: ibid.)

It remains a fact that there are more people in the world not enjoying the liberties and freedom of democracy experienced by UK and US citizens. My father, Captain John H. Crook, died in 1986 with a copy of Alexander Solzhenitsyn's forensic exposure of the injustice of Soviet persecution of political dissent on his bed. And he once told me in his last days that we should never forget one of the lessons of his life: 'There are only two steps from tyranny: the first is when you deny a journalist the right to ask unpopular questions; the second is when you deny a lawyer the right to defend unpopular causes.' This is what he fought for on the battlefield of Normandy in 1944 and for which many of his fellow officers and soldiers died.

In the USA and UK there has been a battle over just how much supremacy 'freedom of expression' and 'freedom of speech and the press' have over other rights. It would appear that the US First Amendment has been given priority in many Supreme Court rulings. But as the British journalist and media law Professor Marcel Berlins observed, the situation in Britain is a matter of conjecture:

> In 1994, the appeal court judge Lord Justice Hoffmann said: 'It cannot be too strongly emphasised that outside the established excep-tions, or any new ones that Parliament may enact in accordance with its obligations under the Convention, there is no question of balanc-ing freedom of speech against other interests. It is a trump card which always wins.' Hoffmann's card-game analogy has resulted in a contro-versy that still continues and is the crux of the question: is freedom of expression a superior right?
>
> (Berlins 2003: 34)

Media communicators in Britain may argue that Hoffmann's hoped-for ace of spades has turned into something of a joker. Despite a plethora of rhetoric on how important to democracy freedom of expression is, the legal game at the time of writing would appear to operate as a balancing exercise, with the conduct and content of media publication subject to an intense focus and every case being decided on its merits. But it might be argued that the jurisprudential opportunity to make freedom of expression the paradigm in any balancing exercise is provided by the 1998 Human Rights Act legislation. When the proposed act was being debated in Parliament, the then chairman of the Press Complaints Commission, Lord Wakeham, successfully inserted Section 12(4), which states:

> The court must have particular regard to the importance of the Convention right to freedom of expression and, where the proceedings relate to material which the respondent claims, or which appears to the court, to be journalistic, literary or artistic material (or to conduct connected with such material), to –
> (a) the extent to which –
>   (i) the material has, or is about to, become available to the public; or
>   (ii) it is, or would be, in the public interest for the material to be published;
>   (iii) any relevant privacy code.
>
> (Christie and Tugendhat 2002: 629–39)

The legislation appears to give the media in Britain the opportunity to take the initiative on what privacy means. In their professional codes they can nuance and redefine the nature of privacy in the context of media communication. Furthermore, media lawyers can argue much more strongly that this statutory power emphasizes particular regard to the importance of freedom of expression. But the courts argue they have been compelled to recognize a legal right to respect for privacy because sections 2 and 6 of the Human Rights Act 1998 oblige them to take into account ECHR jurisprudence and give effect to convention rights. The right to reasonable expectation of privacy for private information has been grafted onto the existing law of confidentiality. The courts also have to qualify particular regard to freedom of expression in section 12(4) with public interest justification and a balancing exercise with the right to respect for privacy.

It could also be argued that, as Parliament has not statutorily defined 'public interest', media communicators and journalists could wrestle the initiative on the definition from the judiciary through their professional codes. The jurisprudential and journalistic lexicon on defining 'public interest' and 'public concern' is elastic and rich in British and overseas sources. Several senior judges in Britain in Court of Appeal and House of Lords rulings have underlined the concept of public interest lying in a marketplace of ideas that has to recognize popular and entertainment objectives that sustain the viability of journalism. The rhetoric is probably borrowed from the dissenting legal view of US Supreme Court Justice J. Holmes:

> But when men have realized that time has upset many fighting faiths, they may come to believe even more than they believe the very foundations of their own conduct that the ultimate good desired is better reached by free trade in ideas – that the best test of truth is the power of the thought to get itself accepted in the competition of the market, and that truth is the only ground upon which their wishes can be carried out.
>
> (Abrams v US, SC US 1919)

For example, in 2002, the then Lord Chief Justice, Lord Woolf, in his Appeal Court ruling that a Premiership footballer was not entitled to have privacy over the exposure of adulterous relationships in a Sunday newspaper, declared:

> Where an individual is a public figure he is entitled to have his privacy respected in the appropriate circumstances. A public figure is entitled to a private life. The individual, however, should recognise that because of his public position he must expect and accept that his actions will be more closely scrutinised by the media. Even trivial facts relating to a public figure can be of great interest to readers and other observers of the media. Conduct which in the case of a private individual would not be the appropriate subject of comment can be the proper subject of comment in the case of a public figure. The public figure may hold a position where higher standards of conduct can be rightly expected by the public. The public figure may be a role model whose conduct could well be emulated by others. He may set the fashion. The higher the profile of the individual concerned the more likely that this will be the position. Whether you have courted publicity or not you may be a legitimate subject of public attention. If you have courted public attention then you have less ground to object to the intrusion which follows. In many of these situations it would be overstating the position to say that there is a public interest in the information being published. It would be more accurate to say that the public have an understandable and so a legitimate interest in being told the information. If this is the situation then it can be appropriately taken into account by a court when deciding on which side of the line a case falls. The courts must not ignore the fact that if newspapers do not publish information which the public are interested in, there will be fewer newspapers published, which will not be

in the public interest. The same is true in relation to other parts of the media. [...]

In drawing up a balance sheet between the respective interests of the parties courts should not act as censors or arbiters of taste. This is the task of others. If there is not a sufficient case for restraining publication the fact that a more lurid approach will be adopted by the publication than the court would regard as acceptable is not relevant. If the contents of the publication are untrue the law of defamation provides prohibition. Whether the publication will be attractive or unattractive should not affect the result of an application if the information is otherwise not the proper subject of restraint.

(A v B CoA Civ 2002)

Lord Woolf's *ratio decidendi* is the approach to balancing freedom of expression and privacy that most British editors and journalists would like the judiciary to extend from prior restraint hearings to the trial of substantial media law disputes. Baroness Hale, in her speech in the House of Lords ruling that, on a narrow margin of 3 to 2, accorded the model Naomi Campbell a privacy ruling on the tabloid publication of her photograph in a Chelsea street which linked her to her medical treatment for drug addiction, also acknowledged that there was validity in the idea that press freedom needs to breathe in the media marketplace:

Put crudely, it is a prima donna celebrity against a celebrity-exploiting tabloid newspaper. Each in their time has profited from the other. Both are assumed to be grown-ups who know the score. On the one hand is the interest of a woman who wants to give up her dependence on illegal and harmful drugs and wants the peace and space in which to pursue the help which she finds useful. On the other hand is a newspaper which wants to keep its readers informed of the activities of celebrity figures, and to expose their weaknesses, lies, evasions and hypocrisies. This sort of story, especially if it has photographs attached, is just the sort of thing that fills, sells and enhances the reputation of the newspaper which gets it first. One reason why press freedom is so important is that we need newspapers to sell in order to ensure that we still have newspapers at all. It may be said that newspapers should be allowed considerable latitude in their intrusions into private grief so that they can maintain circulation and the rest of us can then continue to enjoy the variety of newspapers and other mass media which are available in this country. It may also be said that newspaper editors often have to make their decisions at great speed and in difficult circumstances, so that to expect too minute an analysis of the position is in itself a restriction on their freedom of expression.

(Campbell v MGN HL 2004 para. 143)

But Baroness Hale did not stop there. She decided that the investigation and intrusion into Naomi Campbell's mental and physical health was no longer a trivial product of popular newspaper coverage of global celebrity. The privacy right in these circumstances deserved to be elevated to a position of sensitivity and consideration:

> I start, therefore, from the fact – indeed, it is common ground – that all of the information about Miss Campbell's addiction and attendance at NA which was revealed in the Mirror article was both private and confidential, because it related to an important aspect of Miss Campbell's physical and mental health and the treatment she was receiving for it. It had also been received from an insider in breach of confidence. That simple fact has been obscured by the concession properly made on her behalf that the newspaper's countervailing freedom of expression did serve to justify the publication of some of this information. But the starting point must be that it was all private and its publication required specific justification.
>
> (Ibid.: para. 148)

In the balancing exercise between Article 10 (freedom of expression) and Article 8 (right to respect for privacy) the Law Lord was driven to investigate a method of jurisprudentially measuring the value and worth of the free speech right being asserted. In the process she came up with a hierarchy and it is implied that publication of intimate and private matters that simply entertain and interest the public as popular newspaper and magazine consumers was at the bottom of the ladder:

> There are undoubtedly different types of speech, just as there are different types of private information, some of which are more deserving of protection in a democratic society than others. Top of the list is political speech. The free exchange of information and ideas on matters relevant to the organisation of the economic, social and political life of the country is crucial to any democracy. Without this, it can scarcely be called a democracy at all. This includes revealing information about public figures, especially those in elective office, which would otherwise be private but is relevant to their participation in public life. Intellectual and educational speech and expression are also important in a democracy, not least because they enable the development of individuals' potential to play a full part in society and in our democratic life. Artistic speech and expression is important for similar reasons, in fostering both individual originality and creativity and the free-thinking and dynamic society we so much value. No doubt there are other kinds of speech and expression for which similar claims can be made.

10

But it is difficult to make such claims on behalf of the publication with which we are concerned here. The political and social life of the community, and the intellectual, artistic or personal development of individuals, are not obviously assisted by poring over the intimate details of a fashion model's private life.

(Ibid.: paras 148–50)

The free press and freedom of expression lobby in UK could argue that there are not enough jurists in case law and academic writing who emphasize that freedom of expression is defined as much by the exercise of irresponsibility as of responsibility. And on both sides of the Atlantic we must be entitled to consider academic texts particularly where the discourse in case law is sparse, lacking in diversity and plurality. In 2005 Professor John Durham Peters jumped into the debate over free speech and the liberal tradition with *Courting the Abyss*. He sought to robustly challenge some of the maxims at the centre of the American marketplace of ideas and free speech toleration that has been fostered through liberal First Amendment Supreme Court rulings during the twentieth century. And he has endeavoured to engage in Anglo-American comparative analysis:

A faith in the power of the airing of ideas to reveal truth over the din of public relations and the dullness of public ignorance still pops up often and in the strangest places. 'I believe in the right of people to judge the truth for themselves in the court of public opinion,' said Mick Hume, editor of *LM* [*Living Marxism*] Magazine, in an important British libel trial on 14 March 2000, whose harsh penalty for libel many interpreted as a symptom of the urgent need for a British equivalent to *Times v. Sullivan*, the 1964 case that raised the bar significantly for defamation suits against the press. Hume invoked all the key terms; the people, enthroned as a judge, autonomously sifting evidence, public opinion as a court. It does not matter that Hume is a Marxist; in a pinch, all the old liberal safety nets still come to the rescue. Liberal rhetoric is a standard default position for people who find their liberty threatened.

(Durham Peters 2005: 17)

However, *Living Marxism* and Mick Hume enjoyed none of the benefits of the old liberal safety nets that Durham Peters suggested he was invoking. In losing the libel action Mr Hume's magazine was liquidated by the damages and legal costs. If *Living Marxism* had indeed been a platform for the Marxist perspective in British periodical journalism, it would no longer be heard in a British media landscape somewhat lacking in left-wing and polemical journalism that challenged the centrist liberal-capitalist consensus. The revisionist and postmodernist viewpoints of

11

academics such as Professor Durham Peters have an important place in the debate covered by this book but, like the statutes and case law jurisprudence of parliaments and judges, they are also texts that need to be analysed, questioned and accepted as the expression of moral and political philosophy.

On the subject of politics it might be argued that Durham Peters' advocacy of ethical and legal restraints in the exercise of the power of speech might well accord with Baroness Hale, particularly on the subject of the need to engage human compassion:

> Defenders of absolute openness might ponder the price we pay for the scope of our minds. How hard must our hearts become? Liberals have no time for tenderness, no regard for faith or folly. If life and death are at stake, who can blame people firm enough to close their eyes? Sometimes simple outrage is a more humane response than rational consideration. The condescending term fundamentalist does not do justice to the impulse to say no to the madness of the world. Must we watch the video of Daniel Pearl being beheaded? Is Hustler publisher Larry Flynt a great hero, as Milos Forman's film suggests? Please.
>
> (Ibid.: 291)

It will be apparent that academics and jurists in the field of media law and ethics are exercising and expressing political power in a public sphere that has become much more global and technologically asymmetrical. At the end of his book, Durham Peters proclaims his virtues as a 'radical centrist' with an ideological call to arms:

> Radical centrists defend liberty and fear for evil. Unlike liberals, they see the constant temptation to corruption in liberty, and unlike conservatives, they see the immense wickedness done in the name of fighting evil. They call for both impersonality and love. They are centrists because they favour fundamentals and distrust the self-certain zealotry of the Left and the Right; they are radicals because of their cheerful readiness to disobey the law and put anything existing in peril. They are serious in their playfulness and light-hearted in their duties.
>
> (Ibid.: 293)

This book intends to analyse media law as it exists, the ethical debates concerning what the law ought to be, and the historical development of legal and regulatory controls of communication. The theoretical underpinning involves a course of learning the subject of media jurisprudence – the study of the philosophy of media law; media ethicology – the study of the knowledge of ethics/morality in media communication; and media ethicism – the belief systems in the political context that influence journalistic conduct and content. The ensuing chapters try to evaluate media law and regulation in terms of their social and cultural context.

It has been indicated that media law and ethics are political phenomena. Consequently, media decision making and law making are likely to be influenced by issues of political philosophy – dealing with the public sphere; and moral philosophy – dealing with private space and consideration.

The book uses the term 'media communicators' in order to include journalists and other media practitioners who do not fall easily into the definition of journalists but publish and express themselves through media communication. They are as liable to ethical and media legal action as people identified as working 'journalists'.

In reading this book, it is hoped that you will be able to acquire most of the learning outcomes set out in Table 1.2.

The first chapter is designed to give you an intense and selective distillation of key UK and US media law and ethics comparisons. The topics covered are not intended to be comprehensive. The purpose of studying the subject is to go beyond a kind of bricklaying knowledge about dos and don'ts and apply a critical evaluation of the why as well as the how of media law. You need to be able to articulate arguments about whether media law is censorship or a justifiable legal attenuation on the abuse of media power. Is UK and US media law a framework of control of journalism by the state through executive, legislature and judiciary, or a system conferring a fair adjudication of rights and wrongs in communication? You may like to consider whether in its historical context the development of mass media journalism has been accompanied by the

Table 1.2 Expected learning outcomes from reading this book

1.	Knowledge of the wider ethical, legal, and cultural contexts of media practice in the United Kingdom and a comparison with the USA and some other countries and genres of jurisdiction;
2.	Understanding of the applications of freedom of expression in varying cultural and political contexts. and understanding the ethical issues in news and general publication and broadcasting;
3.	Knowledge and skills to avoid the transgression of defamation, contempt, privacy and other principal media laws in the UK and the USA;
4.	An appreciation of and ability to critically apply principles of ethical conduct in all fields of the media;
5.	A critical understanding of the cultural, social and political history and context of media law making and of professional regulation;
6.	A critical appreciation of alternative international methods of media law and those factors contributing to self-regulation by media practitioners.

problematizing of journalism and the criminalization of the journalist by various state institutions: therefore the use of law to exercise power over freedom of expression.

It is important to caution the reader that a textbook of this kind cannot be all things to all subjects. The intent and spirit of the writing is to engage the subjects of media law, philosophy and other academic disciplines at introductory level and then increase the level of analysis in the intertwining through comparison. I have in mind the interests of the media practitioner and media student and I endeavour to simplify and explain. It is hoped that the text can operate as an encouraging gateway to read in depth the enriching cascade of specialist textbooks and monographs that have been produced and continue to be updated on the subject of media law and ethics on both sides of the Atlantic and elsewhere.

Media law and ethics phenomena involve debates and discourses that engage oscillating positions, roles and qualifiers. In an avowedly simplistic attempt to map the ground I have set out a table that suggests that there is a constantly changing relationship between the content of media communication and its consequences with performers, defenders and objector/victims. Adjudication varies between adversarial and inquisitorial, positivistic and natural law applications of principles many of which will become familiar concepts early on in the reading: public interest/ concern; national security; privacy; democratic necessity; proportionality; pressing social need; reputation; personal, religious, cultural, ethnic and national honour and dignity. It may become evident that there is no easy way of setting a system of umpiring the expression of human communication in terms of legal and ethical infrastructure. Different societies and cultures do, however, have one fact in common: somewhere they have to decide where to draw the line between the exercise of self-censorship and the application of national and transnational law. When communicators and audiences are not prepared to compromise there are usually emotional and material losers in the ensuing prosecution and litigation of rights and remedies. All societies are forced to confront the paradox that it is difficult to maintain toleration for the Other when the Other is insulting, discriminatory, offensive and uses communication to emotionally, spiritually, ideologically and physically attack and undermine the equilibrium and stability of his or her neighbour. The justice and fairness of the response will often be determined by the former, pre-existing and future power relationships of the parties involved. I have set out a grid in Table 1.3 that aims to map the social, cultural and legal dynamics involved in free speech human communication. Professor Barendt, in the second edition of his seminal text *Freedom of Speech*, categorizes four arguments for a Free Speech Principle: arguments with the importance of discovering truth; free speech as an aspect of self-fulfilment; the argument from citizen participation in a democracy; and suspicion of government.

14

His discourse effectively identifies the key free speech interests as: the speaker's interest in communicating ideas and information; the audience interest in receiving ideas and information; and the bystanders' (or public) interest in speech. (Barendt 2005: 6–23)

Barendt's text is an important landmark in comparative media law scholarship. He analyses the proposition that defenders of legal restrictions on hate speech and misogynist pornography argue their ground from the point of view of equality and dignity rights, particularly in relation to vulnerable and disadvantaged social groups. He also investigates the value of pluralism and freedom of speech and the efficacy and advantages of constitutional protections of free speech. Another valuable contribution to media law scholarship is represented by *Media Freedom Under the Human Rights Act* by the academics Helen Fenwick and Gavin Phillipson. This is a European-centred study of the legal rights revolution in UK media law and its relationship with Strasbourg jurisprudence. My textbook humbly seeks to complement works of this kind as a gatekeeper to an ever-expanding practical and theoretical discipline researched and discoursed in new comparative media law departments and centres at Oxford and Melbourne universities. The large scale of media law and ethics teaching in Britain and America now ventures far beyond the practical knowledge of how to avoid legal transgressions.

Everyday politics of media law and ethics

In 2009 the United Kingdom Parliament at Westminster became embroiled in an expenses scandal that resulted in the resignation of the Speaker of the House of Commons. Revelations about MPs 'working the system' to their financial advantage prompted fury at home and laughter abroad, particularly when a national newspaper, the *Daily Telegraph*, began disclosing the detail of expenses claims for moat cleaning, duck houses, and switching the status of main homes to second homes so that MPs could claim mortgage and maintenance expenses and develop portfolios of property. The Home Secretary had to apologize when it was disclosed that she had mistakenly claimed for the cost of her husband watching porn movies. (Expenses *Telegraph/Guardian* 2009)

Many aspects of this political event have been marked with media law and ethical issues. The pressure to reveal the nature of MPs' detailed expenses claims arose out of an application under the UK Freedom of Information Act 2000, which came into force from January 2005. FOI campaigners, including the American journalist and author of *Your Right to Know*, Heather Brooke, had to contest the matter at the High Court in order to overcome Parliament's assertion that the details of MPs' allowances and expenses should be exempt from disclosure. In May 2008 the High Court in the case of *Corporate Officer of the House of Commons v*

Table 1.3 Social, cultural and legal dynamics of free speech human communication

Social	Cultural	Legal
Free speech expression Content in everyday life and multimedia. Freedom of expression varies according to media infrastructure. Older media, e.g. print, are considered less powerful and are freer in licensing of content and right to publish compared with radio and television. Newest media, e.g. blogosphere, uncensored, but problematized through moral panic. Free speech content will always be qualified by the nature, scale and diversity of media institutional ownership. Freedom value diminishes in proportion to extent of monopolistic and narrow media institutional ownership.	**Author and darer, agent provocateur of taste, decency, political and religious orthodoxy** Taking risks by communication, the expression of artistic and ethical invention and experimentation. Exposing abuse of power, injustice, corruption, hypocrisy, making false and malicious accusations for the purposes of spite, advantage and ideological mischief. Pushing the boundaries of mockery, satire and comedy for the purposes of political attack and entertainment. Expressing prejudice and hatred as a desire to dominate and compensate for insecurities.	**Adversarial system of arbitration through the combat of ideas and evidence** Positivistic liberalism. Resolution by verdict after Platonic, Hegelian and Marxist thesis and anti-thesis, interpenetration of ideas and sides. Derided by feminist analysis for promoting patronymic values, and by Asian subaltern studies for perpetuating Orientalism and post-imperialism, and continually problematizing 'the Other' as alien and extreme. A perpetuation of the Classical, Renaissance, and Enlightenment division between Attics and Asians.
Offence, insult and harm Sedition, blasphemy, and insulting the honour and authority of the state. Encouraging religious and racial hatred. Libel, slander, privacy, contempt of court, malicious falsehood, false light, indecency, and damaging national security.	**Bystander and arbiter/ defender of speech rights** Protecting the principles of free speech in politics, media, public opinion and judiciary. Media institutions, political and moral entrepreneurs and public opinion. Pressure groups and political charities. Applying rules of public interest, democratic necessity, proportionality and pressing social need.	**Inquisitorial system of searching for the truth** Acknowledging the religious imperative where prophets for the word of God adjudicate by natural law. Postmodernist sensibility which is cynical of rationalist progress and no longer confident in the idea of free speech supremacy. Inquisitional enquiry encourages elasticity with regard to truth values, is sceptical about the concept of immutability, giving rise to moral relativism.
Emotional hurt and material destruction Loss of self-esteem and internalized inferiority; material loss through negative social and economic action. Economic and military destabilization. These consequences can be as extreme as suicide, vigilante justice, economic ruin and bankruptcy.	**Objector and victim** Individuals, capitalist corporations with legal personality, associations and interest groups, ethnic and religious communities, minorities defined by race, gender and sexuality.	**Hybrid system of toleration** Legal and ethical mechanisms of attenuation, proportionately balancing the assertion of competing rights, acknowledging the weakness and vulnerabilities of the 'Other' and minorities. Checking the tyranny of public opinion.

Information Commissioner & others ruled that the House of Commons was a public authority subject to FOI legislation, and that the release of MPs' expenses claims did not directly or indirectly infringe parliamentary privilege.

The court ruled that there was no doubt about the legitimate public interest engaged by the requests for information:

> questions whether the payments have in fact been made within the rules, and even when made within them, whether the rules are appropriate in contemporary society, have a wide resonance throughout the body politic. In the end they bear on public confidence in the operation of our democratic system – at its very pinnacle the House of Commons itself.

> (Corporate Officer of the House of Commons v Information Commissioner & others HC 2008)

But it became apparent that many of the files were going to be 'redacted' by the time of their public release in July 2009, because the House of Commons believed it was able to conceal information in order to protect the privacy of MPs' families on a case by case basis. (Tomlinson *Guardian* 2009) There was the risk that there would be a cover-up, particularly where there was suspicion that addresses for which the allowances were claimed were being let or did not exist. It later emerged that some MPs were claiming for mortgage interest payments after the mortgage on the properties had been paid off.

In May 2009 an anonymous whistleblower passed on the uncensored data disks to a retired SAS army major and businessman, John Wick, and the true nature of MPs' claims were leaked to the *Daily Telegraph*. The extent to which many MPs exploited the expenses system to their personal advantage generated an intense media debate about the integrity, honesty and propriety of democratically elected representatives. Some MPs caught in the eye of the storm said allegations published by the newspaper were 'actionable' and they were consulting lawyers to consider suing for libel. The Speaker of the House of Commons, Michael Martin, called in the police to investigate the source of the leak – a political decision which backfired when it appeared that public opinion was calling for a police investigation of MPs over their expenses claims.

Key media law and ethics principles of 'national security' and 'public interest' became engaged, as became evident when the Metropolitan Police made a statement regarding complaints it had received surrounding MPs' expenses (Table 1.4).

The last paragraph of the police statement referred to a previous controversy when the government claimed that leaks of politically

Table 1.4 Metropolitan Police statement regarding complaints about misuse of
MPs' expenses

Officers from the Met's Economic and Specialist Crime Command met
yesterday with senior CPS lawyers on the first panel to assess the allegations of
misuse of parliamentary expenses.

They discussed the range of complaints, established what the assessment process
will be and the nature of information that would be considered by the panel.

There will be further meetings of the panel to take these matters forward. At
this time no decision has been made to start any investigation.

On the connected matter of the alleged leak of information relating to
members' allowances the MPS can today announce its decision not to
investigate.

We have considered a range of offences and although the leak of documents is
not something that the MPS would condone, we have looked at the likelihood
of a successful prosecution and whether a prosecution is appropriate given
other potential sanctions that might be available, such as through employment
related proceedings. Other considerations were the prospect of obtaining
evidence and the best use of resources.

The assessment was informed by a recent published decision from the
Director of Public Prosecutions that was, in part, applicable to this case. From
this the MPS believes the public interest defence would be likely to prove a
significant hurdle, in particular the 'high threshold' for criminal proceedings in
misconduct in public office cases.

Whilst the unauthorised disclosure of information would appear to breach
public duty, the leaked documents do not relate to national security and much
of the information was in the process of being prepared and suitably redacted
for release under the Freedom of Information Act.

Source: Metropolitan Police Service bulletin 0000001287, 19 May 2009

embarrassing information about the asylum and immigration system
threatened national security. The Home Office asked the police to investigate and anti-terrorist detectives formally arrested and interviewed under
caution the opposition Home Affairs spokesman Damian Green MP. They
also searched his home and his office at the House of Commons. The
Speaker, Michael Martin, was criticized for not protecting the privileges of
Parliament, particularly when it emerged that the police officers carried
out their search at the Palace of Westminster without a warrant.

The Director of Public Prosecutions, Keir Starmer QC, later announced
that there was no realistic prospect of a conviction against either Mr
Green or his source, Home Office civil servant Christopher Galley, and
so he decided that charges should not be brought against either of them.
Mr Starmer said the information contained in the leaked documents 'was
not secret information or information affecting national security; it did

not relate to military, policing or intelligence matters. It did not expose anyone to a risk of injury or death. Nor, in many respects, was it highly confidential. Much of it was known to others outside the civil service, for example, in the security industry or the Labour Party or Parliament.' (Crown Prosecution Service 2009)

In the USA the concept of the public interest is sometimes referred to as 'matters of public concern' and the First Amendment constitutional protection of free speech means that public concern is usually what the media regard as newsworthy. As a result, the definition of public concern is not primarily defined and controlled by executive, legislature and judiciary. In the same month as Britain was rocked by its parliamentary expenses scandal, described by US satirist Jon Stewart as 'Scamalot', President Barack Obama announced that the US administration would continue to challenge in the courts moves by the American Civil Liberties Union (ACLU) to release images of US soldiers abusing prisoners in Iraq and Afghanistan. Here was another affair engaging media law and ethics. This controversy related to issues of privacy, freedom of information and national security; namely the safety and lives of US military personnel. The determining conceptual qualifier in the dispute was the American understanding of 'public concern'. The ACLU and US media argued that the First Amendment entitled them to publish the photographs. Publication in 2009 was even a greater matter of genuine public concern because President Obama had departed from his Republican predecessor, George W. Bush, in deciding to close the detention centre for 'enemy combatants' at Guantánamo Bay, Cuba, although there was no clear commitment to end the 'extraordinary rendition' of terrorist suspects to detention centres situated in countries outside the USA. He had also banned the use of 'water-boarding' and other aggressive interrogation techniques used by the CIA and US security forces to extract information from terrorist suspects after the attacks on America that claimed nearly 3,000 lives on 11 September 2001. Such techniques had been condemned as torture.

The US government position was that releasing more photographs of prisoners being abused by American soldiers would inflame passions and put the lives of innocent American citizens in danger all over the world. It had at first argued that publication of the images would breach the privacy of both the victims and US military personnel. In its arguments it cited the extent to which anti-American interests would exploit the images for propaganda purposes and embed media messages of hate directed at the USA. Global media is now considered bottom-up rather than top-down, and media propaganda munitions of the mind are now asymmetric in terms of being disseminated by new media such as the Internet. The images could be edited by jihadist Al Qaeda supporting websites to assist in the brainwashing of young people to take up arms and terrorism against the USA and its allies.

The US administration's position turned on media law and ethics. It considered the consequences of publication of images that could become iconic in the representation of conflict. This morally consequential decision is utilitarian and seeks to override the universalizable standard of adhering to truth and freedom of expression. Specialists at the Pentagon would have evaluated the impact of the leaking to the US journalist Seymour Hersh in 2004 of some of the prisoner abuse photographs taken at Abu Ghraib jail in Iraq and their dissemination in *New Yorker* magazine and on the US broadcast network CBS. In February 2006 the Internet news site Salon uploaded and published the entire collection of 74 photos and three videos taken at Abu Ghraib. (Zarek 2006: 16)

Pentagon experts may have argued that these propaganda messages had a material link to *propagande par le fait* – 'propaganda of the deed' doctrine of terrorism that advocates the deployment of physical violence against political enemies. The ACLU first requested the images of abuse in October 2003 under the US Freedom of Information Act. They were successful at the US District Court in Manhattan in 2005, and in September 2008 the US Court of Appeals affirmed the original ruling that dismissed the government's argument that the privacy rights of the soldiers and detainees in the images would be violated by disclosure. The Court of Appeals decided that the argument about potential damage and risk to American citizens anywhere in the world was far too speculative. (RCFP 2008)

The Reporters Committee for the Freedom of the Press (RCFP) submitted to the Court of Appeals Second Circuit a dossier of iconic images of war and conflict and argued that:

> Discovery of these images has led to citizen discussion on military interrogation techniques, detainment facilities and command structure, and of the need for government accountability. Several members of the military were found guilty of abuse or dereliction of duty and several others have been court-martialed over their suspected involvement; both the military and Congress are conducting investigations on the issue. Releasing the images to allow for meaningful evaluation of their contents would substantially advance the public's interest in knowing 'what its government is up to,' ensuring government accountability for actions it has conceded were wrong.
>
> (RCFP 2009)

One of the arguments advanced was that photography is the closest that many citizens get to viewing military action conducted on their behalf:

> When famed Civil War photographer Matthew Brady received permission from President Lincoln to photograph the Civil War, he set in motion what would be a reliance by the public on visual images to depict important historical events. Photographs completely

Plate 3 First woman jury, Los Angeles, November 1911. US legal and media culture is used to the public and open participation of jurors in criminal and civil trials. Most US states allow jurors to be interviewed by the media and in most cases they are identified as part of a rigorous voir dire enquiry into their background and attitudes by the adversarial parties in a trial. By contrast, identifying and/or photographing jurors in the UK would be a serious criminal offence and this extends to any attempt to discuss their deliberations with them.

changed how Americans view war – they remove the physical barrier of distance and enable the viewer to be an eyewitness to history.

(Ibid.)

Appendix A of the RCFP opinion set out photographs that have become representative symbols of history and include: Walker Evans's image of an American rural family suffering from starvation during the Great Depression; the US Air Force image of the mushroom cloud and aftermath of nuclear explosion over Japan in 1945; the Associated Press photograph by Joe Rosenthal of US marines raising the Stars and Stripes at Iwo Jima; the Associated Press photograph by Jim Pringle of cheering concentration camp inmates; the Associated Press photo by Nick Ut of the naked Vietnamese girl running in terror down a road after being burned by a napalm attack during the Vietnam War; the image by Associated Press photographer Carmen Taylor of a United Airlines jet a split second before crashing into the World Trade Center's South Tower on 11 September 2001; the moment caught by Associated Press photographer Eddie Adams when a South Vietnamese general shoots his Vietcong prisoner in the head; Peter Turnley's photograph of the carbonized face of an Iraqi soldier ambushed on the road to Basra while trying to flee the invasion of Kuwait; and the US Army photograph of the flag-draped coffins of US servicemen killed in Iraq being brought home by transporter plane.

A separate standard for regulating and controlling broadcast media

Radio and television as electronic dimensions of communication can be seen as weapons or mechanisms of power rather than the eyes and ears of the public. Consequently the state can find justifiable reasons for controlling and licensing broadcasting. In the UK the state has invested Ofcom with statutory regulatory laws that police the conduct of broadcast journalists and the content of their journalism. The nature of those controls and the policies formulated from the powers given to it by Parliament can be read at www.ofcom.org.uk. In the USA, the Federal Communications Commission (FCC) performs a similar role in regard to the licensing of radio and television and regulating the content of the broadcasting. The remit of the US First Amendment is thereby compromised in US broadcasting. UK and US broadcasters face huge financial penalties, and the withdrawal of the right to broadcast as the ultimate penalty, if they get things wrong. UK and online print journalists are 'regulated' by a voluntary Press Complaints Commission and the heaviest sanctions that can be applied are dismissal if compliance with the code had been written into their employment contracts and the embarrassment of a critical PCC adjudication being published on the organization's website at www.pcc.org.uk. US journalists have had a long-standing tradition of training and education in ethics and many sign up to voluntary compliance with professional codes. While there is no US federal-style 'Press Council' it would be wrong to assume that there is no ethical culture. It could be argued that US journalism has been much more progressive and proactive in applied ethics through the media institutional role of 'fact-checking' and independent press ombudsmen policing ethical standards on the part of journalistic conduct and content. This book makes a division between primary media law – constitutions, statutes and judge-made case law – and secondary media law – effectively the body of principles and codes that determine the outcome of disputes in applied media ethics. A more detailed breakdown of the distinction is set out in Table 1.5.

Constitutional contexts: written and unwritten

The essential differences between the legal and political cultures of the two countries are that the United States has a written and federal constitution and the United Kingdom has an unwritten and evolving unitary constitution with devolved parliaments and assemblies and a complex constitutional arrangement with Europe. The UK has, through various treaties, relinquished sovereign power and law-making influences to European Union institutions and the European Court of Human Rights.

A breakdown summary of the British and American systems of constitution, law and government is set out in Table 1.6.

Table 1.5 The distinction between primary and secondary media law

Primary media law	Secondary media law
Statutes passed by the United Kingdom Westminster Parliament, treaties, directives and regulations emanating from the European Union; Federal statutes passed by the United States Congress, and any of the fifty state legislatures. The UK does not have a written constitution whereas the USA has a federal constitution and 50 state constitutions.	Broadcasting regulatory codes approved and published by statutory bodies created by legislature, and voluntary code agreements regulated by non-state-constituted organizations. In the UK, the Office of Communications (Ofcom), established by the 2003 Communications Act, performs this role. In the USA, the Federal Communications Commission (FCC), established by the Federal Communications Act in 1934, assumes an equivalent role. (The first regulatory Act in the USA created the Federal Radio Commission in 1927.) Both Ofcom and the FCC have the legal power to fine broadcasters as well as to suspend and cancel licences. Their codes, guidelines and decisions generate what is known as administrative law.
Case law made by judges in the higher courts of England and Wales, Northern Ireland and Scotland; in the USA, in the Supreme Court and Federal circuit as well as the higher legal courts of the 50 constituent states.	
Under section 12 of the Human Rights Act 1998, the United Kingdom Parliament has given UK judges the power to take into account media codes of ethics when presiding over conflicts between Article 10 freedom of expression, and Article 8 right to respect for private and family life. One result of this 'balancing exercise' is that the development of case law by judges has seeded a UK media privacy law based on precedent. The textual content of ethics codes has informed the development of legal restraints on media behaviour and publication. The consultative Assembly of the Council of Europe passed resolutions in 1970 and 1998, designed to protect the individual against interference with his/her right of privacy. In 1970 the Assembly said that 'The phrase "where public life begins, private life ends" is inadequate to cover this situation.' After the death of Diana, Princess of Wales in Paris in 1997 the Assembly issued a further resolution reaffirming 'the importance of every person's right to privacy, and of the right to freedom of expression', but emphasized that 'these rights are neither absolute nor in any hierarchical order, since they are of equal value' (Tugendhat and Christie, 2002: 619–20).	A voluntary body called the Press Complaints Commission regulates print, magazine and online media in the UK. No such nationwide organization exists in the USA but professional working journalists do follow codes published by the Society of Professional Journalists, National Photographers Association, American Society of Newspaper Editors, and the Radio-Television News Directors Association. The UK's largest trade union for journalists, the NUJ, established a code of ethics in the early part of the twentieth century.
	The British Broadcasting Corporation does not have its exact equivalent in the USA in terms of size and funding. The BBC regulates and disciplines its own staff using published 'Editorial Guidelines' enforced by the operationally independent BBC Trust. US National Public Radio (NPR) has a widely respected code of ethics. In the USA, the legal concept of privacy has been developed in states' legal systems since the publication of 'The Right to Privacy' by Samuel Warren and Louis D. Brandeis in 4 *Harvard Law Review* 193 (1890), but 'information privacy has not been recognised by the Supreme Court as a right which can restrict another person's First Amendment right of free speech. In cases involving the news media, freedom of speech almost always prevails on the grounds of newsworthiness' (Tugendhat and Christie, 2002: 64).

Table 1.6 Comparison of the constitutional contexts of UK and US media law

United Kingdom	United States of America
Unitary constitution, but four constituent countries (England, Wales, Northern Ireland and Scotland, and island protectorates of Isle of Man and Channel Islands have separate devolved parliaments/assemblies and some have separate legal jurisdictions. The Isle of Man and the Bailiwicks of Jersey and Guernsey are not part of the United Kingdom and neither are they part of the European Union. They are self-governing British Crown dependencies.	Federal constitution consisting of fifty states each having its own legal authority, laws and constitution, but subject to unified federal law system.
Westminster Parliament: House of Commons (elected representatives from England, Wales, Scotland and Northern Ireland (main source of legislative power); House of Lords (appointed representatives and less power than House of Commons). English and Welsh Legal System: statute and common law precedent. High courts, appeal courts and Supreme Court (in 2009). United Kingdom executive government is constituted from representatives of the Westminster Parliament. UK executive government has supreme sovereign power and if supported with landslide majorities in the House of Commons is capable of passing any law contrary to established human rights and constitutional conventions.	Scottish Parliament at Holyrood, Northern Ireland Assembly, Welsh Assembly, and independent parliaments for Isle of Man and Channel Islands (UK responsible for foreign affairs, but these island protectorates not part of European Union). Scotland and Northern Ireland have separate legal systems with some appeal references to the supreme court. Isle of Man and Channel Islands have separate legal systems with appeal references to Judicial Committee of the Privy Council in Westminster, London (a kind of supreme court for electing commonwealth countries).	The written federal constitution convenes a balance of powers between the executive (President and White House executive administration), legislature (Congress consisting of separately elected House of Representatives and Senate) and judiciary (Supreme Court). The system was designed to build in checks against abuse of power and encourage compromise. Consequently the various bodies that make up the US constitution have much more equivalent power than the constitutional bodies of the United Kingdom. The US Supreme Court has much more power than its equivalent in the UK, as it can strike out state and federal congressional legislation and presidential executive decisions as 'unconstitutional'. This can lead to accusations of judicial autocracy and activism, particularly as there are only nine Justices – including the Chief
The UK judiciary only has power to declare executive decisions and legislation	The most distinct legal system outside England and Wales is the Scottish system, which has been influenced by continental Roman and civil law. The Roman-Dutch traditions derive from the close cultural links between Scotland and France before	

United Kingdom	*United States of America*
as 'being incompatible' with 1998 Human Rights Act. A key disadvantage in the UK is that its largely unwritten constitution creates vagueness in disputes that turn on the liberty and freedom of the individual. Many sovereign powers have been surrendered to European Union institutions and now its legal system is transnationally influenced by the European Court of Human Rights whose decisions must be 'taken into account'. The ECHR is a quasi-European body enforcing a convention on human rights constituted by a representative body called the Council of Europe with many signatory countries from outside Europe and with cultures and legal traditions which are substantially different from those of the United Kingdom. Decisions of the EU Court of Justice in Luxembourg are binding on EU. union with England in 1707. Scottish district courts can be seen as the equivalent of English magistrates' courts. The next level up is the Sheriff court, which hears both criminal and civil cases and combines the role of the Crown and County Courts. The procurator fiscal is the independent official who prosecutes criminal cases and performs a similar role to the English Crown Prosecution Service. The final criminal court in Scotland is the High Court of Justiciary, which operates as both a trial court for serious cases and an appeal court from the Sheriff courts. There is no appeal on criminal issues to the UK Supreme Court. The supreme court for civil appeals is the Court of Session from which there is an appeal route to the Supreme Court in Westminster. The separate legal systems of the Isle of Man and Channel Islands are of less importance to British journalists as they affect smaller populations.	Justice – whose political leanings can be manipulated by presidential nomination. Congress has the power to 'impeach' the US president only on the grounds of misconduct in office. Federal law is a combination of case law made by judges in federal courts, and laws made in Congress. Federal law prevails in any dispute between state law and federal law. A key advantage in the USA is that its written constitution is a fixed and referential authority guaranteeing power and rights in the relationship between those governing and those governed. While the US system has checks and balances it can also be afflicted by the phenomenon of constitutional gridlock, so that in the USA government decision making is more difficult than it is in parliamentary regimes. The US government is divided into three constitutional branches that can cancel out each other's powers.

Media law and ethics: transnational and international law

Media law and ethics in the USA and UK do not operate as self-contained jurisdictions that bask in the glory of legal independence from each other and the rest of the world. The transnational nature of global media law is cross-jurisdictional and the catastrophic wars of the twentieth century have resulted in an increase in the influence and reach of international law and ethical influences that are political and cultural. It would be a mistake to ignore the wider context of the United Nations Universal Declaration of Human Rights. The treaty obligations engendered by any country signing and adhering to the declaration may be easy to ignore, but history indicates that human rights discourse and international juris-prudence have had a positive influence on the relationship between the individual and the state in respect of powers, duties and obligations.

It could be argued that the essential transnational tension in media law and ethics throughout the world is between libertarian and authoritarian tendencies. This book enjoys the indulgence of analysing the comparison between the liberal-capitalist democracies of the UK (estimated population in 2008: 60,943,912) and the USA (estimated population in 2008: 303,824,640). While these two English-speaking G8 and first-order soci-eties, through the phenomena of imperialism and post-imperialism, exercise considerable global power and influence, it has to be recognized that the bright lights of freedom, liberty and democracy do not shine so brightly elsewhere. And there is an ongoing debate that some of the bulbs in London and Washington DC flicker intermittently or lost their elements many years ago. What concepts and values should we use to measure and determine the oscillation between libertarian and authori-tarian genres in media law and ethics jurisdictions? This is a mighty ques-tion and the answer is inevitably complex. However, I have attempted to represent the tension in a grid of vectors set out in Table 1.7.

Both the UK and USA are subject to scrutiny and assessment of their human rights records by the United Nations Human Rights Committee. Periodically the body publishes reports on individual countries and evalu-ates their performances under Article 40 of the International Covenant on Civil and Political Rights. At the Committee's ninety-third session in July 2008, the UK's media laws were severely criticized in terms of using the Official Secrets Act (OSA) to silence the revelation of genuine issues of public interest, the operation of the country's libel laws in discouraging critical media reporting, the phenomenon of 'libel tourism' and the crea-tion of the criminal offence of 'encouragement of terrorism'.

In particular the Committee was concerned with the way the Official Secrets Act of 1989 had been frustrating former 'employees of the Crown' from releasing into the public domain genuine public interest issues. The

Table 1.7 The democratic index in media law and ethics

Libertarian tendency	*Authoritarian tendency*
Freedom of expression, free speech and free press/media set as superior constitutional rights.	Free speech rights qualified by rights of national security, privacy, national reputation and honour on an equal or subsidiary basis.
Independent judiciary. Judges democratically elected or appointed by independent commission. Representation of the judiciary is proportionate to host society's gender and make-up of ethnic communities.	The judiciary is appointed and controlled by executive and legislature and compromised by bribery, intimidation and corruption. Judiciary recruited and populated by narrow representation of gender, class and ethnicity.
Rule of law. Every citizen is equal before the law. Constitutional checks and balances on abuse of power by executive. Independent police infrastructure capable of enforcing laws developed and made by legislature and judges. Equal access to civil and criminal justice. Rights to legal representation. Legal aid scheme for economically disadvantaged. Proportionate and fair policy and prosecution of criminal law.	Disproportionate concentration of power in executive, legislature or judiciary. Lack of constitutional safeguards against abuse of power, persecution of minority opinions, groups and communities. Discriminatory policing, compromised by bribery and corruption. Unequal access to justice. Failure of police and judiciary to prosecute just laws and inability of ordinary citizens to seek remedies for civil wrongs.
Habeas corpus. No detention without trial. Constitutional guarantees and limits on periods of detention before charge and trial by an independent judicial tribunal. Protection from torture and inhuman treatment. Visiting rights for families and relations, inspection rights for the Red Cross.	Detention and/or restriction of civil liberties (e.g. house arrest/curfew) without being brought before an independent judicial tribunal for trial within a reasonable period. Subject to arbitrary powers of arrest, imprisonment and punishment. Secret imprisonment, torture and inhuman treatment.
Freedom of religion. Separation of religious institutions and authority from rule of law, legislative and executive power. Toleration of criticism of religion, but protection against expressions of religious and racial hatred. Reasonable and proportionate judicial remedies and legal sanctions against 'hate speech'.	Theocratic tyranny. Discrimination and persecution for religious belief and worship. Surrender of rule of law and legal authority to religious institutions and authority. Censorship of religious criticism and no legal protection for expressions of religious and racial hatred.

Continued overleaf

Libertarian tendency	Authoritarian tendency
Limited and proportionate civil remedies for publication that damages individual and institutional reputation. Burden of proof on plaintiff/claimant/prosecutor. Need to prove falsity and material rather than emotional damage. High threshold of protection for public interest/concern communication, authorial intentions recognized as a legal defence, need to prove malice and reckless disregard for truth. Caps and restrictions on legal costs and damages. Legal checks and protection against 'legal terrorism' by powerful plaintiffs/claimants.	Criminal prosecution and sanctions, including imprisonment, for publications that damage reputation and challenge individual/institutional honour and feelings. Burden of proof on defendant. Truth only a defence with 'public interest'. Presumption of falsity, reduced standard of media negligence, subjective construction of meaning by audience. Operation of a 'chilling effect' through high legal costs, civil damages, weak defences. SLAPP effect: Strategic Lawsuits against Public Participation phenomenon.
Initiative and discretion on defining public interest and concern by independent media. Public interest based on what interests the public and on legal recognition of freedom to communicate without responsibility. Recognition of public interest in entertainment and diversity of media market.	Definitions of 'public concern' and 'public interest' controlled and defined by executive and judiciary. Public interest structured by high threshold of values and hurdles with a paradigm against entertainment and 'what interests the public'. No promotion of or respect for diversity of the media market.
Guaranteed rights to fair and public trial and a positive culture of open justice. Transparency in the independence and fairness of media jurisprudential justice. Equal rights to appeal. Judges only allowed to control proceedings and denied censorship powers on media publication. Restrictions on publication limited to strictly defined exceptions subject to challenge and appeal. Public identification of defendants and witnesses and all parties to legal proceedings.	Exclusion of press and public from legal proceedings. Arbitrary powers of censorship on reporting legal processes and proceedings. Gagging orders on legal parties, jurors, extending to reporting restrictions and bans beyond courtroom walls. Secret justice through anonymous or pseudonymous witnesses in criminal and civil proceedings. Use of secret evidence/dossiers unknown to defendants. Judicial use of state-appointed 'special advocates' unable to give instructions to their clients on the identity of prosecution witnesses and the nature of evidence. Legal decision making based on secret and/or hearsay evidence. Low standard of proof such as 'mere suspicion' instead of 'beyond reasonable doubt' or 'on the balance of probabilities'. Lack of scrutiny in the use of government witnesses and agents provocateurs. Contempt laws silencing criticism and scrutiny of judicial process.
Constitutional and 'rights' checks on the legal processes of 'prior restraint' that injunct and censor media publication. Case law and statutory rules against *ex parte* legal proceedings held in private/secret where decisions to prohibit or postpone publication are made without legal representation of media parties and without public scrutiny. Freedom of expression for lay jurors post-trial on their justice participation experiences.	

Libertarian tendency	Authoritarian tendency
Self-regulation and ethical reflexivity by media communicators and institutions. Exercise of responsibility through formulation of ethical codes on conduct and content. Media institutional use of fact checkers, press/media ombudsmen, restorative justice remedies through independent regulatory bodies respecting rules of natural justice.	State regulation and licensing of journalism and media institutions. Statutory press/media councils and regulatory bodies with punitive powers to fine, suspend, disqualify and cancel licences, professional membership and rights to work in media. Adjudication *ex parte* or on paper-only submissions without representation and oral hearings and no rights of appeal.
Independent and diverse media with a mixture and balance between commercial and public service broadcasting media, fair remuneration, pay, conditions and secure and long-term career paths for journalists and media communicators. Anti-monopoly laws and regulation limiting cross-media ownership.	State-owned and controlled media monopolies. Private control and buying controlling interests in transnational media and publishing corporations by ruling elites to silence and discourage critical reporting. Censorship by hiring and firing, and self-censorship achieved through a climate of fear and insecurity.
Democratic and transparent elections through universal franchise, checks and balances and separation of powers. Full access to the media with powers of scrutiny for electoral registration and polling. Regulation of broadcasting to ensure balanced and fair reporting of elections.	Limited franchise, cynical and manipulative polling qualifications, rigged elections and corrupt electoral practices. Intimidation of journalists and media groups reporting government opposition. Disproportionate distribution of campaigning media resources and partisan media reporting.
Respect and adherence to United Nations Declaration of Human Rights, international conventions on human rights, International Criminal Court, and Geneva Conventions.	Hypocrisy about and/or open defiance of human rights. Refusal to sign international treaties creating liability for breaching human rights.
Recognition and protection for unilateral journalism during conflict and war. Providing access to conflict and war zones that is both supervised and unsupervised. Advising journalists and media organizations on degrees of safety and risk. Keeping GPS coordinates and information on the location of media crews and briefing military commanders to avoid accidental attacks or cross-fire death and injury to media personnel. Legal accountability for military attacks on journalists.	Indifference and/or hostility to the safety of journalists reporting conflict. Restricting access to or excluding journalists from conflict zones. Giving preference to 'embedded' and accredited journalists. Overt and covert military intimidation and attacks on journalists working for media institutions that publish critical coverage. Using media signs, equipment and disguise for military and intelligence purposes. 'Privatizing' violence and murder against journalists by using irregular militias or mercenaries.

Continued overleaf

Libertarian tendency	Authoritarian tendency
Balanced protection of citizens' privacy rights. Legal and constitutional restrictions on surveillance and data collection on the lives and activities of private citizens; including journalists in the course of their work.	Priority privacy rights for citizens and government investigative officials, civil servants and politicians. Saturated surveillance society matrixes that include DNA registers, exploitation and snooping of government and private databases.
Rigorous freedom of information legislation. Limiting the time period for the disclosure of government information to 30 years or less. Minimizing the categories of FOI exclusions from disclosure. Legislating for a well-resourced and robust independent information commissioner to police compliance with FOI laws. Ensuring that only nominal costs are charged for preparing the release of information.	No FOI or 'sunshine' laws guaranteeing public access to information collected and stored by government/state bodies. Long delays of at least 30 years in the release of government/state papers. Expanded absolute and quasi-qualified exceptions to FOI release. Charging journalists, media organizations and private citizens exorbitant rates for research and preparation of released records.
Effective scrutiny of state intelligence agencies. Avoiding the use of anti-espionage legislation in order to discourage public-interest and 'motivated by conscience' whistleblowers. Not using national security as a means for covering up political and administrative embarrassment when exposure would be in the public interest. Effective resourcing of legislative oversight committees and public disclosure of their legislative reports and findings. Cultural separation of journalism from spying.	Absolute or near total secrecy and suppression of all information relating to intelligence, police and state investigative agencies. Imposing criminal liability on private citizens and journalists who received state information where the classification of confidentiality and secrecy is broad and all-encompassing. Official Secrets Act laws that use the threat of terrorism and espionage to silence and mute exposure and public criticism of political incompetence. Anonymity for police firearms specialists who kill citizens and armed forces personnel accused of killing and assaults on non-combatants.
Protection of journalists' sources. Effective and enforceable shield laws. Making the protection of journalist sources a pressing social need and necessity in any democratic society. Giving the concept priority over other rights and providing for an exceptional circumstances justification for ordering the identification of a journalist's source.	Priority given to executive, legislative, corporate and judicial interests in the exposure of whistleblowers and journalist sources. Heavy penalties for journalists who try to protect their sources. Wide powers for state agencies to tap the communications of journalists and collect surveillance evidence for the purposes of identifying their sources.

Libertarian tendency	*Authoritarian tendency*
Positive culture for education and training of journalists/media communicators in media law and ethics. Celebration and recognition of iconoclastic and public interest journalism.	Social, political and cultural problematization of journalism. Using journalism as a cover for espionage. Higher politico-economic rewards and status given to public relations, marketing and government information workers.
Balanced intellectual property rights through creative commons and preservation and access to media records and archives. Ensuring the ability of authors of creativity and skilled expression to benefit fairly from the commercial exploitation of their work without blocking general access to the information.	Stripping media communicators of all their intellectual property and moral rights during employment. Imposing copyright laws that restrict the dissemination and communication of archives, history and information. Large corporate and state bullying of people making minor copyright infringements. Over-commodification of archives and cultural assets.

Act provides no public interest defence for civil servants and the leaking of public interest information obtained through employment can be penalized even when there is no harm to national security. The Committee devoted much attention to the UK's practical application of libel law, which was condemned for discouraging critical media reporting on serious public interest issues and effectively censoring the ability of scholars and journalists to publish their work. The phenomenon of 'libel tourism' was cited as a clear threat to Article 19 of the Universal Declaration of Human Rights. The UK's 'unduly restrictive libel law' affected freedom of expression worldwide on matters of valid public interest, particularly with the advent of the Internet and international distribution of foreign media.

The Committee recommended a full-scale re-examination of the English and Welsh doctrines of libel law. It was suggested that the UK consider introducing the US 'public figure' defence where the plaintiff/claimant has to prove actual malice on the part of media defendants. The Conditional Fee Agreements and so-called 'success fees' whereby media defendants had to reimburse claimants' lawyers' fees and costs regardless of scale were forcing defendants to settle libel actions without having had the chance to air valid defences. The UN was applying pressure on the UK to adopt US-style legal mechanisms in its libel laws, including the ending of the British presumption of falsity.

The introduction of the 'encouragement of terrorism' offence in section 1 of the 2006 Terrorism Act was criticized for being broad and vague. The UK was advised to reform its wording in order to avoid a potential disproportionate interference with freedom of expression, since it was apparent that it was possible to commit the offence even when there was no intention to directly or indirectly encourage acts of terrorism. Shifting the construction of meaning in political language to a perception by somebody somewhere who might engage in terrorism was seen as anti-democratic and unjust. (UN ICCPR 2008)

The Human Rights Committee turned its attention to the USA in July 2006, when its major concerns related to the measures and policies of the administration under George W. Bush in what was described as 'The War on Terror'. The Committee was highly critical of US counter-terrorism measures, the practice of secret detention facilities, interrogation techniques, allegations of suspicious deaths, torture or cruel, inhuman or degrading treatment or punishment inflicted by its personnel, the position of detainees at Guantánamo Bay, the practice of rendition, the use of the Material Witness Statute and immigration laws to detain persons suspected of terrorism in a largely secret process. As will be apparent later, these human rights concerns cut across the debate about secret justice and the constraints on media reporting in the US between 2001 and 2009. The Committee concentrated on the operation of the Patriot Act that was passed by Congress in the aftermath of the 9/11 attacks.

The Committee focused on the human rights problems arising out of the application and implications of the Patriot Act, which had expanded the delayed notification of home and office searches, increased government accessibility to individual personal records and belongings and the rights of challenge. It was concerned that the National Security Agency (NSA) was still able to monitor phone, email and fax communications of US and non-US nationals without any judicial or independent scrutiny. (UN ICCPR 2006)

It would be understandable at this stage to assess the force and sanction behind the Human Rights Committee reports and the nature of the UN legal power applying to sovereign member states. The influential theorist on jurisprudence Professor H.L.A. Hart questioned the legal status of 'international law'. He argued that:

> the absence of an international legislature, courts with compulsory jurisdiction, and centrally organized sanctions have inspired misgivings, at any rate in the breasts of legal theorists. [...] international law not only lacks the secondary rules of change and adjudication which provide for legislature and courts, but also a unifying rule of recognition specifying 'sources' of law and providing general criteria for the identification of its rules. These differences are indeed striking and the question 'Is international law really law?' can hardly be put aside.
>
> (Hart 2002: 214)

Hart was aware of the obligations states had under the United Nations Charter, but he believed 'any assessment of their strength is worth little if it ignores the extent to which the law enforcement provisions of the Charter, admirable on paper, have been paralysed by the veto and the ideological divisions and alliances of the great powers.' (Hart 2002: 233) He was writing in 1961. Has the situation changed? Francis Pakes, writing in 2004, appears to agree with Hart when he observes:

> there is no such thing as a global constitution, nor is there a universally accepted international criminal code. The nature of international law is more diffuse than that. That is why it is called *soft law*, as opposed to the hard laws of code and constitutions. International law is used, on the one hand, to regulate how states should treat each other, and on the other hand is concerned with how states should treat its [*sic*] citizens.

> (Pakes 2004: 147)

The United Nations Charter on human rights could be regarded as a significant contextual influence on media law systems in UN member states. It has been advocated transnationally since 1948. An international charity and pressure group campaigning for freedom of expression named itself after the relevant value in the Charter: Article 19. It would, therefore, be justifiable in recognizing the Charter as a global reference point for values and concepts in media law and ethics.

The Universal Declaration of Human Rights was proclaimed on 10 December 1948 by the General Assembly of the United Nations and called upon all member countries 'to cause it to be disseminated, displayed, read and expounded principally in schools and other educational institutions, without distinction based on the political status of countries or territories'. The first three paragraphs of the Preamble set out an ethical context for human relations and respect for human rights throughout the world. The lexicon emphasizes the idea of inherent human dignity, inalienable rights to freedom, justice and peace and the importance of freedom of speech and freedom from fear. The Declaration highlights the importance of the rule of law. Article 19 states categorically that everyone has the right to freedom of opinion and expression and that this right should be exercised without interference. Furthermore the right to receive information through any media should be protected regardless of frontiers. Article 19 was contextualized and qualified by the UN International Covenant on Civil and Political Rights in 1966, which emphasized that the positive rights inherent in Article 19 carried with them special duties and responsibilities including certain restrictions provided by law. Those responsibilities included respect for the rights or reputations of others and the protection of national security, of public order, public health or morals. (UN ICCPR 1966)

It is somewhat intriguing that the United Nations has asserted copyright in its human rights documentation. The Charter's reproduction and

distribution, for example, has a price. This may not have been the intention of the British writer H.G. Wells, who can be credited with beginning
the debate on the need for a twentieth-century declaration on the Rights
of Man in correspondence to *The Times* in 1940. He wanted a publication
of principles to explain what people were fighting for. This was the year
when Great Britain and its empire were alone in combating and resisting
Nazi-occupied Europe. The *Daily Herald* newspaper took up the clarion
call for debate and reserved a page a day over one month for the discussion of articles in a draft declaration. A Penguin paperback special *The
Rights of Man: What We Are Fighting For* became a bestseller and was translated into thirty languages. The author of *Values for a Godless Age: The Story
of the UK's New Bill of Rights*, Francesca Klug, says that Wells 'sent a copy to
his friend, President Franklin Roosevelt and on 1 January 1942 the allied
powers belatedly included the protection of human rights among their
official war aims. After some further lobbying, this goal was reflected in
the founding charter of the UN.' (Klug *New Statesman* 2000)

An examination of H.G. Wells' original text makes it clear that the UN
declaration was undoubtedly inspired and seeded from his initiative. He
was determined to identify the need to protect the principle of habeas
corpus (no detention without scrutiny by a judicial tribunal), democratic
law, the right to subsistence, the right to work and to have possessions,
and the importance of a free market and profit seeking. The origins of
Article 19 lie in a clause that sought to address the new tyranny of the
government/state dossier:

> That although a man is subject to the free criticism of his fellows, he shall
> have adequate protection from any lying or misrepresentation that may
> distress or injure him. All administrative registration and records about a
> man shall be open to his personal and private inspection. There shall be
> no secret dossiers in any administrative department. All dossiers shall be
> accessible to the man concerned and subject to verification and correc-
> tion at his challenge. A dossier is merely a memorandum; it cannot be
> used as evidence without proper confirmation in open court.
>
> (Wells 1940: 47–8)

The integrity and clarity of Wells' writing challenges the legally controversial justification advanced in the US and UK for secret evidence to be used
to found a level of proof set at 'mere suspicion' in terrorism detention and
control procedures. Both countries have reckoned with detention without
trial, control orders and deportation of terrorist suspects in the frame of
administrative immigration law. Wells saw freedom of expression and the
right to information in terms of the relationship of the individual to the
state and its capacity to wage tyranny through secret dossier. In London,
British lawyers educated in the traditions of Magna Carta, Blackstone and

Bentham have had to agree to take on the role of 'special advocates' so that they can examine secret dossiers the content of which they are not allowed to disclose to their clients. The delays in introducing freedom of information laws until 1966 for the USA and 2000 for the UK suggest the precision and righteousness of Wells' position took a long time to be understood.

In the wake of the success of the Gestapo and KGB and other spy agencies in authoritarian countries in collecting false and prejudicial information on citizens without challenge or judicial oversight, Wells realised that a developing information age was making the world a smaller place, but subject to much greater and potentially sinister powers of communication and surveillance:

> The enormous change in human conditions to which nearly all our present stresses are due, the abolition of distance and the stupendous increase in power, have flung together the population of the world so that a new way of living has become imperative, have not only made warfare more disorganising and inconclusive but have also made its methods more socially penetrating and disconcerting. The elaboration of methods and material has necessitated a vast development and refinement of espionage, and in addition the increasing difficulty of understanding what the warfare is really about has produced new submersive and demoralising activities of rumour-spreading, propaganda and the like, that complicate and lose contact at last with any rational objective. Any fool can tell a lie and too many fools like doing so.
>
> (Wells 1940: 48)

It could be argued that the United Nations has begun to build an infrastructure of judicial authority. The 1948 Declaration consists of rhetoric that is constitutional in style and all of the articles could form the basis of any first-order national and sovereign bill of rights. Through the Rome Treaty of 1998 the UN has constituted an International Criminal Court that has the principal aim of achieving justice for all. Pakes says its operation will help to secure justice for victims of genocide and crimes against humanity, and by investigations and prosecution generate a global impact of deterrence. (Pakes 2004: 163) It is certainly the case that a free-standing international criminal court with an investigative and case preparation infrastructure was not part of the United Nations profile when Professor Hart wrote *The Concept of Law* in 1961. The Rome Statute has included apartheid and enforced disappearance in its definitions of crimes against humanity. However, *realpolitik* in the global sphere may still remain an obstacle to its effectiveness:

> Many countries felt that the prosecutor should enjoy complete independence, in particular from the UN and its Security Council. Others, most notably the US, felt that these powers should be constrained. The underlying reason is the idea that when a prosecutor has unlimited

freedom in deciding where and when to investigate, this might hamper the maintenance of peace in those regions. It also involves the risk of frivolous or political prosecutions. [...] the US is one of the countries that will not ratify the Statute. Another non-signatory is Israel. It is debatable to what extent a tribunal that lacks the support of the US can have an impact on the reinforcement of human rights on a global scale. After all, the tribunal will not have a police force and will rely on states for funding, information, and the apprehension of suspects.

(Pakes 2004: 165)

The USA is a signatory to a regional convention on human rights in a similar position to the relationship between the UK and the European Convention on Human Rights. The Inter-American Convention on Human Rights was adopted on 22 November 1969 and came into 'force' on 18 July 1978. Article 13 of this Convention sets out a much more detailed assertion and qualification of freedom of expression than the First Amendment and can be examined in Table 1.8

Table 1.8 The Inter-American Convention on Human Rights, Article 13

Article 13 – Freedom of Thought and Expression

1. Everyone has the right to freedom of thought and expression. This right includes freedom to seek, receive and impart information and ideas of all kinds, regardless of frontiers, either orally, in writing, in print, in the form of art, or through any other medium of one's choice.

2. The exercise of the right provided for in the foregoing paragraph shall not be subject to prior censorship but shall be subject to subsequent imposition of liability, which shall be expressly established by law to the extent necessary in order to ensure:
   (a)   respect for the rights or reputations of others; or
   (b)   the protection of national security, public order, or public health, or morals.

3. The right of expression may not be restricted by indirect methods or means, such as the abuse of government or private controls over newsprint, radio broadcasting frequencies, or equipment used in the dissemination of information, or by any other means tending to impede the communication and circulation of ideas and opinions.

4. Notwithstanding the provisions of paragraph 2 above, public entertainments may be subject by law to prior censorship for the sole purpose of regulating access to them for the moral protection of childhood and adolescence.

5. Any propaganda for war and any advocacy of national, racial or religious hatred that constitute incitements to lawless violence or to any similar illegal action against any person or group of persons on any grounds including those of race, colour, religion, language, or national origin shall be considered as offences punishable by law.

The countries that have signed or ratified the Convention are: Argentina, Barbados, Bolivia, Brazil, Chile, Colombia, Costa Rica, Dominica, Dominican Republic, Ecuador, El Salvador, Grenada, Guatemala, Haiti, Honduras, Jamaica, Mexico, Nicaragua, Panama, Paraguay, Peru, Suriname, Trinidad & Tobago, United States, Uruguay, Venezuela.

The key difference to be considered between the UK and USA in relation to regional human rights conventions is that the USA has the world's oldest constitution and that its own Bill of Rights is the supreme source of legal authority. The constitution and its amendments have been politically and legally sustained over two hundred years and have evolved in the conceptualization and definition of civil rights in the context of social and cultural change. The expression of those rights is more in the nature of Natural Law, because the language is absolutist and immutable, though application in practice has been positivistic. Consequently, the US constitution empowers the American journalist with a greater force of freedom as well as the right to bear arms. I have featured what could be described as the civil rights concepts in the US constitution in Table 1.9.

Table 1.9 Civil rights concepts in the US Constitution

Article I – The Legislative Branch
Section 9 – Limits on Congress
The privilege of the Writ of Habeas Corpus shall not be suspended, unless when in Cases of Rebellion or Invasion the public Safety may require it.
No Bill of Attainder or ex post facto Law shall be passed.

Article III, The Judicial Branch
Section 2 – Trial by Jury, Original Jurisdiction, Jury Trials
The Trial of all Crimes, except in Cases of Impeachment, shall be by Jury; and such Trial shall be held in the State where the said Crimes shall have been committed; but when not committed within any State, the Trial shall be at such Place or Places as the Congress may by Law have directed.

Article IV – The States
Section 4 – Republican Government
The United States shall guarantee to every State in this Union a Republican Form of Government, and shall protect each of them against Invasion; and on Application of the Legislature, or of the Executive (when the Legislature cannot be convened) against domestic Violence.

The Amendments
The following are the Amendments to the Constitution. The first ten Amendments collectively are commonly known as the Bill of Rights.

Amendment 1 – Freedom of Religion, Press, Expression. 12/15/1791.
Congress shall make no law respecting an establishment of religion, or prohibiting the free exercise thereof; or abridging the freedom of speech, or of the press; or the right of the people peaceably to assemble, and to petition the Government for a redress of grievances.

Amendment 2 – Right to Bear Arms. 12/15/1791.
A well regulated Militia, being necessary to the security of a free State, the right of the people to keep and bear Arms, shall not be infringed.

Continued overleaf

Amendment 4 – Search and Seizure. 12/15/1791.
The right of the people to be secure in their persons, houses, papers, and effects, against unreasonable searches and seizures, shall not be violated, and no Warrants shall issue, but upon probable cause, supported by Oath or affirmation, and particularly describing the place to be searched, and the persons or things to be seized.

Amendment 5 – Trial and Punishment, Compensation for Takings. 12/15/1791.
No person shall be held to answer for a capital, or otherwise infamous crime, unless on a presentment or indictment of a Grand Jury, except in cases arising in the land or naval forces, or in the Militia, when in actual service in time of War or public danger; nor shall any person be subject for the same offense to be twice put in jeopardy of life or limb; nor shall be compelled in any criminal case to be a witness against himself, nor be deprived of life, liberty, or property, without due process of law; nor shall private property be taken for public use, without just compensation.

Amendment 6 – Right to Speedy Trial, Confrontation of Witnesses. 12/15/1791.
In all criminal prosecutions, the accused shall enjoy the right to a speedy and public trial, by an impartial jury of the State and district wherein the crime shall have been committed, which district shall have been previously ascertained by law, and to be informed of the nature and cause of the accusation; to be confronted with the witnesses against him; to have compulsory process for obtaining witnesses in his favor, and to have the Assistance of Counsel for his defence.

Amendment 7 – Trial by Jury in Civil Cases. 12/15/1791.
In Suits at common law, where the value in controversy shall exceed twenty dollars, the right of trial by jury shall be preserved, and no fact tried by a jury, shall be otherwise re-examined in any Court of the United States, than according to the rules of the common law.

Amendment 8 – Cruel and Unusual Punishment. 12/15/1791.
Excessive bail shall not be required, nor excessive fines imposed, nor cruel and unusual punishments inflicted.

Amendment 11 – Judicial Limits.
The Judicial power of the United States shall not be construed to extend to any suit in law or equity, commenced or prosecuted against one of the United States by Citizens of another State, or by Citizens or Subjects of any Foreign State.

Amendment 13 – Slavery Abolished. Ratified 12/6/1865.
1. Neither slavery nor involuntary servitude, except as a punishment for crime whereof the party shall have been duly convicted, shall exist within the United States, or any place subject to their jurisdiction.
2. Congress shall have power to enforce this article by appropriate legislation.

Amendment 14 – Citizenship Rights. Ratified 7/9/1868.
1. All persons born or naturalized in the United States, and subject to the jurisdiction thereof, are citizens of the United States and of the State wherein they reside. No State shall make or enforce any law which shall abridge the privileges or immunities of citizens of the United States; nor shall any State deprive any person of life, liberty, or property, without due process of law; nor deny to any person within its jurisdiction the equal protection of the laws.

Amendment 15 – Race No Bar to Vote. Ratified 2/3/1870.
1. The right of citizens of the United States to vote shall not be denied or abridged by the United States or by any State on account of race, color, or previous condition of servitude.
2. The Congress shall have power to enforce this article by appropriate legislation.

Amendment 19 – Women's Suffrage. Ratified 8/18/1920.
The right of citizens of the United States to vote shall not be denied or abridged by the United States or by any State on account of sex.
Congress shall have power to enforce this article by appropriate legislation.

Amendment 24 – Poll Tax Barred. Ratified 1/23/1964.
1. The right of citizens of the United States to vote in any primary or other election for President or Vice President, for electors for President or Vice President, or for Senator or Representative in Congress, shall not be denied or abridged by the United States or any State by reason of failure to pay any poll tax or other tax.
2. The Congress shall have power to enforce this article by appropriate legislation.

Amendment 26 – Voting Age Set to 18 Years. Ratified 7/1/1971.
1. The right of citizens of the United States, who are eighteen years of age or older, to vote shall not be denied or abridged by the United States or by any State on account of age.
2. The Congress shall have power to enforce this article by appropriate legislation.

Source: www.law.cornell.edu/constitution/constitution.overview.html

As has been indicated the UK has never had a written constitution. The nearest it comes to having one is in incorporating the regional European Convention on Human Rights into statute law, which is something the USA has not done and is unlikely to do in relation to the Inter-American Convention. It is inconceivable that the US Supreme Court would find itself being obliged to 'take into account' the decisions of a regional human rights tribunal situated in Haiti, Bolivia or Venezuela exercising international treaty powers to adjudicate complaints by US citizens against their government.

In 2009, Britain's then second most senior judge, Lord Hoffmann, discussed the subject of the universality of human rights in the annual lecture to the Judicial Studies Board. He observed that:

> The United States Supreme Court was, I think, the first judicial body required to give practical effort to the abstract terms of a human rights instrument; to act as mediators between the high generalities of the constitutional text and the messy detail of their application to concrete problems.

> (Hoffmann 2009: para. 11)

As a result the Court would rule on the meaning of the words 'equal treatment' in the 14th Amendment in a crucial case of whether an education authority could or should provide buses across a town to make sure its schooling was not racially segregated. In another case the Court would test the words of the Fifth Amendment, 'no person shall be compelled in a criminal case to give evidence against himself' by deciding if a police officer was obliged to warn a suspect that he had the right of silence and was also entitled to a lawyer paid for by the state. The Supreme Court has had more than two centuries of case law to resolve constitutional questions of this kind. As a result the Court's judicial authority is able to influence American society in a way that is unequalled by any other court or tribunal in the world. Lord Hoffmann's analysis of the US constitution and Supreme Court was engaged to evaluate and attack the constitutional legitimacy of the European Court of Human Rights in Strasbourg and what he saw as a trend to go beyond its jurisdiction and to create a federal law of Europe. Geoffrey Robertson and Andrew Nicol had also strongly criticized the ECHR in the fifth edition of their text *Media Law* for an approach to the balancing exercise between freedom of expression and privacy which, in their opinion, was 'poorly reasoned and badly expressed.' (Robertson and Nicol 2008: xi) They used rather dismissive vocabulary in their analysis of the Princess Caroline of Monaco ruling in 2004 and questioned whether the ECHR

> had a right to stop photographers from snapping her in a public place because this in some unexplained way hindered the development of her personality. 'There is therefore a zone of interaction of a person with others, even in a public context, which may fall within the scope of private life', was the incoherent verdict of the Strasbourg court. The court has a backlog of tens of thousands of cases (mainly from Turkey and the former Soviet Union states): its rushed seven judge decisions often lack intellectual rigour and consistency, and even 'grand chamber' decisions come couched in Euro-prosaic generalities. It is regrettable that s. 2 of the Human Rights Act provides that Strasbourg decisions 'must be taken into account', because many are simply not worth the effort.
>
> (Ibid.)

Robertson and Nicol acknowledged the influence of the European Convention in engaging British law with a human rights perspective, but the time had now come for the introduction of a UK written constitution and bill of rights that was more effective in protecting free speech and trial by jury, which incidentally was not specifically guaranteed in the Convention, unlike the US constitution.

Lord Hoffmann argued in his Judicial Studies Board speech that the ECHR's interference with the judicial culture of the United Kingdom was presumptuous and creating jurisprudential mischief. He observed that the US Supreme Court had developed and maintained a large measure of universal respect because of its high quality of judges, their knowledge of American society, and the fact that they presided over an American court, established by constitution, appointed by president, and endorsed by the Senate. He also observed the Supreme Court judges' sociological credibility in that they were 'an essential and historic part of the community which they serve. They have a special constitutional legitimacy for the citizens of the United States.' (Hoffmann 2009: para. 14) In contrast Lord Hoffmann observed that the ECHR

> has no mandate to unify the laws of Europe on the many subjects which may arguably touch upon human rights. Because, for example, there is a human right to a fair trial, it does not follow that all the countries of the Council of Europe must have the same trial procedure. Criminal procedures in different countries may differ widely without any of them being unfair. Likewise, the application of many human rights in a concrete case, the trade-offs which must be made between individual rights and effective government, or between the rights of one individual and another, will frequently vary from country to country, depending upon the local circumstances and legal tradition.
>
> (Hoffmann 2009: para. 24)

Lord Hoffmann explained that the Strasbourg Court has used a doctrine known as the 'margin of appreciation' to 'aggrandize its jurisdiction and to impose uniform rules on Member States. It considers itself the equivalent of the Supreme Court of the United States, laying down a federal law of Europe.' (Hoffmann 2009: para. 27)

Lord Hoffmann honed his attack on the manner in which the Strasbourg Court has imposed alien cultural imperatives on the UK's indigenous system of media law. Like Robertson and Nicol, Lord Hoffmann reserved the sharpness of his criticism for the ruling in the Princess Caroline privacy case where the balance to be struck in the United Kingdom between freedom of the press and privacy should be decided by a Slovenian judge addressing a decision of the German Constitutional Court and expressing a cultural and political observation about US media law:

> I believe that the courts have to some extent and under American influence made a fetish of the freedom of the press ... It is time that the pendulum swung back to a different kind of balance between what is private and secluded and what is public and unshielded.
>
> (Von Hannover v Germany ECHR 2005)

Hoffmann speculated that the famous English writer on jurisprudence, Jeremy Bentham, would have retorted:

> What grandeur [...] What legislative power the judicial representative of Slovenia can wield from his chambers in Strasbourg. Out with this pernicious American influence. What do their courts or Founding Fathers know of human rights? It is we in Strasbourg who decree the European public order. Let the balance be struck differently. I say, and all the courts of Europe must jump to attention.
>
> (Hoffmann 2009: paras. 36–7)

Lord Hoffman argued that the United Kingdom remains an independent nation

> with its own legal system, evolved over centuries of constitutional struggle and pragmatic change. I do not suggest belief that the United Kingdom's legal system is perfect but I do argue that detailed decisions about how it could be improved should be made in London, either by our democratic institutions or by judicial bodies which, like the Supreme Court of the United States, are integral with our own society and respected as such.
>
> (Hoffmann 2009: para. 39)

International media ethics: an influential source of authority

The transnational influences on US and UK media law extend to the rhetoric and content of media ethics. Conventions and symposia, often UN sponsored, agree and publish covenants and resolutions. UNESCO and Reporters Without Borders recognize the Munich Charter on the rights and obligations of journalists as authoritative. It was written and approved in Munich on 24 and 25 November 1971 and adopted by the International Federation of Journalists. This is an example of scores, perhaps hundreds of journalistic ethical codes that have been drawn up in different countries. Ethics codes usually aim to be advisory and not prescriptive. However, the osmosis from guidance to regulatory and legalistic obligation can be traced in many countries, including the United Kingdom.

The Munich Charter

The Munich Charter asserts that the right to information, to freedom of expression and criticism is one of the fundamental rights of man, that all rights and duties of a journalist originate from this right of the public to be informed on events and opinions. The charter seeks to attenuate the power of obligation between the journalist and public and the journalist and employer so that responsibility towards the public exceeds any other responsibility, particularly towards employers and public authorities.

In some respects the charter acknowledges that there is a positive engagement of self-censorship, not through fear but through a sense of ethical responsibility. But a journalist can only respect these ethical duties while exercising his profession if conditions of independence and professional dignity effectively exist.

The main difference between the UK NUJ and Munich convention codes is that the latter is almost equally balanced between duties and rights. The European declaration sets out journalistic expectations of the employing journalistic institutions and contextual societies. It implies that the exercise of journalistic duties requires the respect and provision of rights that go far beyond those currently expected in liberal market democracies.

The Munich convention represents idealistic goals for the virtuous journalist. But it would be fair to raise the question: why should it be assumed that 'virtuous journalism' should be the only goal of media communication? It could also be argued that the freedom of journalism, speech and communication is more effectively measured and confirmed by the breach of these aspirations as much as by their compliance. The Munich Charter is set out in pages 14–18 of the joint UNESCO and Reporters Without Borders publication *Practical Guide for Journalists* (2002) and is downloadable as a pdf file from www.rsf.org.

Human Rights Act and European Union

The Human Rights Act 1998, which was enacted (came into force) in October 2000, has radically changed the nature of UK law. It compels the courts and public authorities to apply and 'give effect to' the articles of the European Convention on Human Rights. There have been a substantial number of new cases where publications and media practices have been judged according to Article 10 – Freedom of Expression – and Article 8 – The Right to Privacy.

In addition to the Human Rights Act, the UK's closer integration into the European Union has resulted in European Community and Union law influencing matters. This means that the rulings of the European Court of Human Rights in Strasbourg and the Court of Justice of the European Communities in Luxembourg have a significant bearing on British law.

Furthermore, the United Kingdom has become embedded in a confederated European constitution, where a growing number of decisions relating to economic and employment issues, police and judicial affairs, foreign and defence policy are being taken outside the sovereign jurisdiction of the Westminster Parliament.

It is argued by politicians opposed to Britain's membership of the EU that Britain's absorption into a European constitution could be seen as one of the most extraordinary political deceptions applied to UK citizens in the history of their country. It is said that the debate about the proposal for a new European constitution failed to appreciate that the cumulative effect of previous European Union treaties since 1959 had already established a complex constitutional structure that the United Kingdom became a part of from 1972. This political consideration has been reflected in the popularity of the United Kingdom Independence Party (UKIP), which has succeeded in sending elected representatives to the European Parliament in several elections by proportional representation. Christopher Booker and Dr Richard North analysed the pro-European integration theory of the French politician Jean Monnet in their 2003 book *The Great Deception: The Secret History of the European Union* and acknowledged Monnet's unique achievement of inspiring

> the nations of Europe to an unprecedented degree of peaceful cooperation. [...] He instinctively knew he could only achieve his goal by working towards it crabwise, step by step, and by concealing the real nature of that goal behind a pretence that it was something less than what it was. There were heady moments when he was tempted to burst out into the open; most notably in the early 1950s when, carried away by his coup in setting up the Coal and Steel Community, he spoke of it as 'the first government of Europe,' and then, two years later, launched his plan for a 'European Political Community.' But ... he soon learned from these mistakes. Thus emerged what was perhaps his most influential bequest to the 'European project', that strategy which came to be known as *engrenage* or 'the Monnet method.'
>
> (Booker and North 2003: 427–8)

Booker and North contend that a 'gradual assembling of a European government has amounted to a "slow motion coup d'etat", based on a strategy of deliberate deception, into which Britain's leaders, Macmillan and Heath, were consciously drawn.' (Booker and North 2003: vi–viii) In conclusion, they state that the political project to achieve a federal Europe has overreached itself because it was a gamble that was doomed to fail:

> All that was wrong with Le Corbusier's tower blocks became obvious when real people had to live in them, to discover that they defied human realities and human needs. It was the same with the tower blocks created by Monnet's technocrats. The nation state and democracy were too fundamental to human needs and human nature simply to be eliminated by technocratic diktat. Just as when people woke up to the soulless inhumanity of Le Corbusier's utopian [*sic*] dream they

hankered for all the warmth and vitality and human reality of old cities they had lost, so the same has become true of all that had been swept away by the Utopian dream of M. Monnet. Only when people discovered that they had lost their democracy and the power of their countries to govern themselves did they begin to appreciate in a new way just how valuable was that which had been taken away from them without their knowing it. They had become victims of one of the greatest collective acts of make-believe of the 20th century: fit in that respect to rank alongside the self-deceiving dreams of Communism.

(Booker and North 2003: 454)

Negative understandings and representations of European Union Law

The lack of knowledge and understanding of how the European Union works is fairly widespread. There also seems to be a 'yawn factor' whenever the question of European Union stories arises in newsrooms. There appears to be a culture that stories from and about Europe are boring and of no interest to British audiences unless they involve sensational scandals proving the decadence of 'foreigners', concern the shenanigans of UK celebrities, or represent dramatic disasters and natural catastrophes. The European Commission has felt itself compelled to campaign against British media myths about Europe that are often recycled in so-called 'funny' stories about Brussels' directives on straight bananas and toys in pigsties.

Over many decades the EU executive institutions have been issuing regulations and directives that have had substantial and binding effects on the laws and legal obligations of people in the UK as EU citizens. The law of copyright has been transformed way beyond the terms legislated nationally in 1988. Copyright in literary and artistic works was extended by EU law from a term of 50 years after the death of an author, artist and composer to 70 years.

Photographs published prior to 1945 were generally perceived to be in the public domain until EU law provided the opportunity for copyright to be asserted by descendants of identifiable photographers whose work could be argued to be artistic. The authors' rights concept developed in the French and German legal jurisdictions began to merge with the English and American common law substantial skill/labour doctrine. It is not widely known that the reason British courts are obliged to recognize the interests of foreign libel litigants in Internet-defamation disputes has more to do with 'EU Council Regulation 44/2001 of 22 December ("the Brussels Regulation"), and the Brussels and Lugano Conventions ("the Conventions"), on jurisdiction and the enforcement of judgments in civil and commercial matters'. (Collins 2005: 5)

There are signs though of the mainstream media attempting to explain the significance of European integration beyond the long-standing debate about whether the British should give up their pound for the euro currency. The BBC has made some efforts to improve journalistic coverage and understanding. The BBC has tried through its College of Journalism to increase training for its personnel about the importance of the European Union and increase reporting resources in Brussels. In 2005 the BBC appointed the charismatic and skilled broadcaster, political journalist, Mark Mardell, as European Editor in an effort to popularize the coverage and understanding of European politics and Britain's role in the European Union, particularly in the year when Britain had assumed the role of the European Presidency. Mr Mardell successfully increased the profile of the European news agenda and in 2009 was appointed chief US correspondent.

The EU constitution

The European Commission is the EU's civil service. At its head are the president and a cadre of twenty-seven European Commissioners. The Commission oversees the enforcement of EU laws and proposes new ones. It cannot enact legislation. That is the job of the Council of Ministers. Ministers from each member state attend when their subject is under discussion (e.g. the Chancellor of the Exchequer attends meetings of the council of economic and finance ministers, known as Ecofin). It is important to avoid confusing the Council of Ministers with the European Council, which is a meeting of EU heads of government and usually happens twice a year. It is also important to appreciate that a separate body called the 'Council of Europe' is not part of the EU. That body was set up to promote European cultural values and gestated the European Convention on Human Rights and European Court of Human Rights situated in Strasbourg.

The European Parliament sits in Brussels and Strasbourg. It examines proposed legislation. Any amendments are sent to the Council of Ministers. This Parliament has the final say on the Commission's budget and on applications from countries seeking EU membership. (Allen 2003: 42)

This is just a nutshell description of a union that could consolidate as a significant superpower in the twenty-first century. In 2005 the EU expanded to 25 member states, and the political implications of this enlargement involving many states from the old Iron Curtain area of Eastern Europe may well have been the stalling factor in the 'No' vote for the new European constitution through referendums in France and the Netherlands in 2005. In 2007 the EU enlarged to a membership of 27 states with the addition of Romania and Bulgaria.

In the same year the EU agreed the Lisbon Treaty though it was criticized for being similar to the rejected constitution. The Irish electorate voted 'Yes' to the treaty in 2009. In ratifying this treaty, a new Charter of Fundamental Rights will be legally binding on all EU member states. The UK opted out of the Charter that defines rights in different ways to the ECHR. Article 11 on freedom of expression states 'The freedom and pluralism of the media shall be respected.' Article 52.3 also empowers the EU Court of Justice to provide more rights protection than is currently provided by the Strasbourg court. The existing arrangement of treaties, elections to the European Parliament, EU-wide administrative infrastructure and EU judicial system and constitution appears to retain the nature of a constitutional confederation. It is similar to that in Switzerland, where the cantons have much more independence than do the US states.

Since the Single European Act of 1986, the Treaty on European Union in 1993 that followed the Maastricht Treaty, and the Treaties of Amsterdam 1997 and Nice 2000, the UK has become much more inextricably involved in the federal processes of pan-European government. While economic integration has become more consolidated as the first pillar, the second and third pillars on Common Foreign Policy, and Security Policy and Police and Judicial Cooperation have been developed largely through secret and private processes of intergovernmental consultation and negotiation. Most of the decisions have been made behind closed doors.

EU legal system: lack of transparency and open justice

The UK organization Statewatch argued that the EU had not been very effective in honouring the citizen's right of access to documents. Tony Bunyan stated in *Secrecy and Openness in the EU* (1999) that the 'Amsterdam era has inherited a European state, composed of definable agencies and practices, that has been developed largely in secret with minimal democratic input.' (Bunyan 1999: xiv) Bunyan believes that 'we are witnessing the emergence of a European state – in particular of the coercive, "hard", state functions and practices covering internal security.' (Ibid.)

Robertson and Nicol write that although the EU has paid lip service to rights of access to documents, the published codes are inevitably followed by exceptions:

> The first category is mandatory (i.e. the Council or Commission must deny access.) This applies where disclosure could undermine the protection of the public interest (public security, international relations, monetary stability, court proceedings, inspections and investigations), the protection of the individual and of privacy, the protection of commercial and industrial secrecy, the protection of the Community's financial interests, the protection of confidentiality as

requested by the legislation of the Member State that supplied the information. The second exception is discretionary and allows the Council or Commission to refuse access 'to protect the confidentiality of [the Council's or Commission's] proceedings'.

(Robertson and Nicol 2002: 583)

Identifying and clarifying the ECHR

The European Court of Justice is based in Luxembourg and applies and interprets EU law. It is a very powerful court and its decisions are binding on the legal systems and parliaments of member states. The European Court of Human Rights is based in Strasbourg and applies the principles contained in the European Convention on Human Rights. It was set up by the Council of Europe and is not an institution of the EU. The pressure and backlog of cases meant that a filtering tribunal called 'the European Commission' that heard applications at first instance, and decided whether they should be heard by the full Court, was abolished in 1998. The ECHR was transformed into a full-time judicial panel. The Court can now sit in chambers of seven or three judges, or in a grand chamber of seventeen judges. The ECHR at Strasbourg has judges from signatory countries beyond the European Union. They include Albania, Turkey and Russia. A summary of the European Convention on Human Rights and Fundamental Freedoms is set out in Table 1.10.

The International Court of Justice and the International Criminal Court sit at The Hague, in the Netherlands, and are constituted by the United Nations. The Court of Justice has often been called the World Court and it seeks to resolve disputes between states. (Allen 2003: 43) The Criminal Court was created by the 1998 Statute of Rome and has been given global jurisdiction to try 'War Crimes' and 'Crimes against Humanity'.

The ECHR is a much more open and transparent process, compared to EU institutions and judicial proceedings. Robertson and Nicol observe that:

> The European Council of Ministers and the European Commission both sit in private. There is no public right of access to their meetings. The European Court of Justice and the European Court of First Instance [a smaller EU court set up to cope with widening jurisdictional responsibilities as well a growing case load] sit in public for the oral part of their procedure. By English standards, these hearings are very brief. Most of the argument is presented in written form. At least in the Court of First Instance, there is no right for the public to have access to the court file.

(Robertson and Nicol 2002: 585–6)

Article 1 – Obligation to respect human rights – 'The High Contracting Parties shall secure to everyone within their jurisdiction the rights and freedoms defined in Section 1 of this Convention.'

Article 2 – Right to life – 'No one shall be deprived of his life intentionally save in the execution of a sentence of a court following the conviction of a crime for which this penalty is provided by law.'

Article 3 – Prohibition of torture – 'No one shall be subjected to torture or to inhuman or degrading treatment or punishment.'

Article 4 – Prohibition of slavery and forced labour – 'No one shall be held in slavery or servitude. No one shall be required to perform forced or compulsory labour.'

Article 5 – Right to liberty and security – 'Everyone who is deprived of his liberty by arrest or detention shall be entitled to take proceedings by which the lawfulness of his detention shall be decided speedily by a court and his release ordered if the detention is not lawful.'

Article 6 – Right to a fair and public trial – '… everyone is entitled to a fair and public hearing within a reasonable time by an independent and impartial tribunal established by law. Judgment shall be pronounced publicly … Everyone charged with a criminal offence shall be presumed innocent until proved guilty according to law.'

Article 7 – No punishment without law – 'No one shall be held guilty of any criminal offence on account of any act or omission which did not constitute a criminal offence under national or international law at the time when it was committed.'

Article 8 – Right to respect for private and family life – 'Everyone has the right to respect for his private and family life, his home and his correspondence.'

Article 9 – Freedom of thought, conscience and religion – 'This right includes freedom to change his religion or belief and freedom, either alone or in community with others and in public or private, to manifest his religion or belief, in worship, teaching, practice and observance.'

Article 10 – Freedom of expression – 'This right shall include freedom to hold opinions and to receive and import information and ideas without interference by public authority and regardless of frontiers.'

Article 11 – Freedom of assembly and association – 'Everyone has the right to freedom of peaceful assembly and to freedom of association with others, including the right to form and to join trade unions for the protection of his interests.'

Article 12 – Right to marry – 'Men and women of marriageable age have the right to marry and to found a family, according to the national laws governing the exercise of this right.'

Article 13 – Right to an effective remedy – 'Every one whose rights and freedoms set forth in this Convention are violated shall have an effective remedy before a national authority notwithstanding that the violation has been committed by persons acting in an official capacity.'

Continued overleaf

Article 14 – Prohibition of discrimination – 'The enjoyment of the rights and freedoms set forth in this Convention shall be secured without discrimination on any ground such as sex, race, colour, language, religion, political or other opinion, national or social origin, association with a national minority, property, birth or other status.

Article 15 – Derogation in time of emergency – 'In time of war or other public emergency threatening the life of the nation any High Contracting Party may take measures derogating from its obligations under this Convention to the extent strictly required by the exigencies of the situation, provided that such measures are not inconsistent with its other obligations under international law.'

Media law and the Internet

The Internet and World Wide Web represent a revolution in human communications. The technology is global, interactive and can switch between top-down broadcasting transmission to one-to-one and bottom-up vectors of distribution. It is argued, particularly by Internet Service Providers (ISPs), that the Internet is impossible to control. This is not the case with the telephone system, where interception and monitoring is as straightforward as listening to any call between two people on a closed circuit. It is said the Internet is an open system and has no centralised connection facility. Furthermore the sheer volume of traffic and the availability of encryption software mean that random monitoring is not viable. It can be regarded as the digital equivalent of the needle in the haystack. As a result the Internet is to some extent jurisdictionally borderless. In 2008 and 2009 the Internet spawned another dimension of rapid and asymmetrical communication that was branded as 'Twitter'. This involved the streaming of instant messaging limited to 140 characters or less each time to facilitate easy reading and transmission on wireless Internet networks via mobile phone. The mobile phone connected to the Internet/World Wide Web also performs the role of citizen journalist with the instant capability of camera use for still and moving pictures. This outmanoeuvres the power and grip of mainstream media news organizations to be the cultural conduits of journalism and public records.

Yet there is the clearest evidence that the Internet can be controlled. It is not a lawless virtual landscape. Countries with totalitarian and authoritarian governments have not found it difficult to block and filter content and prosecute individuals judged to be a threat to the state. The Internet channels and retains the traffic of data from transmitters to consumers albeit on a hyper-scale. Electricity can be powered on and powered off. Wireless communications can be jammed, interrupted, diverted, monitored and archived. Cable communications through which most Internet traffic sluices around the world can be filtered and blocked. And it is also clear that existing media law bites on the data-stream of the superhighway as on any other kind of publication.

There appears to be a free-flow debate on whether and how Internet content should be regulated. Attempts are being made to censor and litigate. These defy the claim that blocking or removing material is impossible because authorship and 'hosting' can be thousands of miles away, beyond the jurisdiction of a country that judges the content to be unlawful. Many states have passed laws that enable the police to prosecute the consumers and receivers of unlawful content. This is feasible particularly because computer hard drives retain a data trail.

Media content is vulnerable to legal action for intellectual property infringement, defamation and contempt. In 2001 the Court of Appeal in London ruled that an international businessman, Grigori Loutchansky, was entitled to sue *The Times* for an article containing allegations against him that could be downloaded from the newspaper's archive over the Internet. The single publication was judged to be whenever anyone was able to view it and was not based on the idea that the time of publication was restricted to the date and time of posting. (Loutchansky v Times Newspapers Ltd HC 2002) It is known as the Duke of Brunswick Rule, which dates back to the year 1849, when the eponymous aristocrat was able to sue a newspaper for libel after dispatching his butler to buy an old back copy. (Duke of Brunswick v Harmer HC 1849)

This rule is not followed in the USA, where the limitation rule on libel action runs from the time any document is put online. British media editors look with envy on the US one-publication-only rule and regard their own situation as a recipe for injustice – particularly when an old archive article will be difficult to defend when notebooks have been lost or discarded, witnesses's memories become unreliable and key personalities may be dead or untraceable. The one-publication rule has been sustained by state court rulings so that the legal defence applying to traditional print publications now extends to Internet sites. Golden and Vogel state that the courts found that 'failure to extend this rule would subject Web publishers to almost perpetual liability and would seriously inhibit the exchange of free ideas on the Internet.' (Golden and Vogel 2006: 58–9)

On the issue of jurisdiction, the federal courts are reluctant to recognize the right of claimants to sue across US state boundaries, let alone national borders, unless the effects of a publication can be proved and, in the case of Internet publication, a sliding scale of interactivity demonstrates that the publication was intended to have an impact in the state where the writ has been issued. (Young v New Haven Advocate 4th Cir. UC 2002 and Revell v Lidov 5th Cir. US 2002)

The New Haven Advocate case turned on the issue of the target of the newspapers' journalism. Even if Connecticut papers could be read online in Virginia this did not mean a claimant could sue them in the Virginia courts. There was no intention on the part of the papers' journalists to serve the interests of Virginia readers.

The logic of this approach is not always appreciated by British, European and Australian judges. In 2001 the US ISP Yahoo! was sued in France by two pressure groups that campaigned against anti-Semitism. An auction site hosted by Yahoo! traded in Nazi and Third Reich memorabilia. Such activity amounted to a criminal offence in the French legal jurisdiction, where there are laws prohibiting the dissemination of Nazi propaganda and race-hate literature. Their existence can be explained by the historical trauma of German occupation of France during the Second World War and the deportation to the concentration camps and death of a large proportion of its indigenous Jewish community. The French court imposed an accumulating fine for every day Yahoo! failed to block access to French citizens trading in the online Nazi regalia. (Zelezny 2004: 24)

Yahoo! fought back with a lawsuit in a federal court in California and obtained a declaration that the French court's order was not enforceable because it conflicted with US First Amendment constitutional protection. (Yahoo! v La Ligue Contre Le Racisme Et l'Antisemitisme, N.D. Cal. 2001)

The Times newspaper appealed its Internet archive libel case with Loutchansky to Strasbourg and argued that the application of the Duke of Brunswick Rule was redundant in a post-modernist information age of the Internet and global media village. The republication rule for libel was established in the Victorian Age, when aristocrats could direct their butlers to iron their newspapers as well as track down libels about their masters. More particularly the ruling meant that national newspapers could not maintain a publicly accessible Internet archive, provided another dimension to the chilling effect on freedom of expression, and left managers of Internet services with the risk of ceaseless liability, since the one-year limitation period in which a claimant could sue started every time an article was accessed.

But the ECHR was unsympathetic. It decided that the finding of the London High Court and appeal court that the newspaper had libelled the claimant again by continuing to publish two news articles on the Internet, previously subject to libel litigation, was a justified and proportionate restriction on the right to freedom of expression. (*Media Lawyer* May 2009: 41–2) The ruling left one small note of comfort to British media institutions publishing on the Internet:

> The Court would, however, emphasise that while an aggrieved applicant must be afforded a real opportunity to vindicate his right to reputation, libel proceedings brought against a newspaper after a significant lapse of time may well, in the absence of exceptional circumstances, give rise to a disproportionate interference with press freedom under Article 10.
>
> (Times Newspapers Ltd (Nos 1 and 2) v UK ECHR 2009)

Both the UK and US courts accept that the Internet is not a defamation-free zone. In Britain the academic Dr Laurence Godfrey successfully sued Demon Internet because it had failed to remove a fake defamatory message in a news-group allegedly written by him. (Godfrey v Demon Internet Ltd HC 2001) The ISP was unable to use the section 1 'innocent dissemination' defence from the 1996 Defamation Act because it had kept the message on the Internet for ten days after his request for removal.

In 1997 Norwich Union Healthcare paid £450,000 in libel damages to Western Provident for damaging email rumours about its financial status that had been circulated on its intranet. (*Media Lawyer* September 1997: 22) The claimant company had obtained the emails through interlocutory injunction prior to issuing the writ for libel. In 2003 a teacher from Lincoln recovered damages in the Small Claims Court from a former pupil who left a libellous message about him on the popular Friends Reunited site. (Dunlop *Yorkshire Post* 2002)

The Shetland Times newspaper sued an electronic publisher 'Shetland News' for breach of copyright in relation to unauthorized hypertext links. (Bonnington et al. 2000: 341) The music and movie industries have been proactive in the policing of copyright infringement on the Internet. And there seems to be a pattern emerging that copyright protection increases in step with the profit potential of e-commerce.

The UK judiciary has no difficulty dealing with the risks posed by Internet journalism and archiving in relation to court proceedings. As early as 1995 a Stipendiary Magistrate (now known as a District Judge) directed that ISP Compuserve should block the distribution into the UK of foreign reports of the committal proceedings of alleged serial murderer Rosemary West. (Cathcart *Independent* 1995) In 2005 the Attorney General successfully prosecuted a father for contempt of court after he posted the contents of a confidential family law case judgment on a website and in a journal. (Attorney General v Pelling HC 2005)

The socializing dimension of the Internet through web forums is attracting actions for libel and breach of privacy. In 2008 Deputy Judge Richard Parkes awarded damages for libel and privacy in a case where somebody had created a false Facebook profile and group in the name of a former friend that breached privacy and was also libellous. (Firsht v Raphael HC 2008)

However, in a more globalized media world the draconian approach to *sub judice* issues represented by Britain may be somewhat unrealistic. In 1992/93 the Canadian judiciary struggled to maintain a blanket reporting ban on the guilty plea of, and twelve-year jail sentence imposed on, Karla Homolka for the sexual abuse and homicide of teenage children. Her plea bargain to manslaughter and agreement to give evidence against her husband, Paul Bernardo, in a later trial were clearly an intense matter of public interest. The court order did not apply to US media. The electronic media border between the two countries was obviously porous. The synthesis of a media legal border seemed absurd and unworkable. The Internet was not as pervasive as it is now, but nothing could be done about the flouting of the ban through emailing and consumption of non-Canadian news services.

Cyberspace defamation law in the US has grown and developed with the exponential expansion of Internet communications as a social utility. There is also a recognized socio-economic migration of the source of journalistic publication moving from old print/magazine technology to online multimedia platforms. There is no shortage of cases where claimants have sued the originators of defamatory content, whether in traditional newspaper online sites or on electronic bulletin boards. The chain of liability has been predictable. But many US states have retraction statutes which, in relation to traditional media publication, mean that a claimant cannot take legal action until the defendant has had a chance to consider publishing a correction or retraction. Litigation in Wisconsin suggested that such retraction laws may not be applicable to web communications. (It's in the Cards v Fuschetto Wisc. App. 1995) In 1996 the US Congress decided to intervene when libel suits began to hit ISPs who had little or no editorial control over web postings.

Section 230 of the Communications Decency Act is seen as a 'Good Samaritan' provision and states that 'No provider or user of an interactive computer service shall be treated as the publisher or speaker of any information provided by another information content provider.' In some respects it is similar to the innocent dissemination defence under section 1 of the UK Defamation Act 1996. Dr Matthew Collins observes that Section 230 is broader than statutory defences in the UK and Australia because it applies to all providers and users of interactive computer services. (Collins 2005: 442)

The issue of Internet defamation liability is somewhat more complicated than a binary opposition in terms of where the content is uploaded and where it is downloaded. The Australian High Court decision in Dow Jones & Co Inc v Gutnick in 2002 generated considerable global debate about freedom of speech online; particularly because the Australian judges decided that a resident in the state of Victoria was entitled to sue an American publisher in the Victoria Supreme Court for an alleged libel that could be downloaded on his terminal in Victoria. Collins argues that the contractual relationship between Dow Jones and its subscribers means that there was a quality of commercial activity that could have had the same result in an American court according to the effects rule of publication. (Collins 2005: 461–3)

The key approach of the American courts in Internet jurisdiction is to look at how the publication has been deliberately and knowingly targeted into the legal jurisdiction/forum that the claimant wishes to use for litigation. In UK law the intention of publishers is irrelevant. And Collins asserts that the British courts 'have no discretion to decline to exercise jurisdiction on *forum non conveniens* grounds' because EU law is binding in respect of the Brussels 2000 regulation on jurisdiction and enforcement of judgments in civil and commercial matters. (Collins 2005: 459)

Moore and Murray are convinced that Internet defamation and privacy are likely to be a fertile hunting ground for litigation in US jurisdictions:

> The battle ground for future libel and other torts, such as invasion of privacy, is the Internet. As more users come on board, it is inevitable that more and more libellous information will appear, as subscribers become, in effect, gatekeepers and publishers.
>
> (Moore and Murray 2008: 451)

Zelezny observes that many other issues and problems need to be resolved in cyber-libel:

> Just what kind of Internet sites do come under the domain of state retraction statutes? What does it take for someone to become a 'public figure' in cyberspace? On the Internet, which communication is 'a matter of public concern' and which is purely private communication?
>
> (Zelezny 2004: 163–4)

In some respects the Internet should be evaluated with some jurisprudential creativity and scepticism. It could be argued that by its very nature Internet content lacks the credibility and authority of traditional media. Its global nature means that it is impossible for any Internet user to know and abide by all the laws of the countries that will receive the communication.

Just as it is very difficult for ISPs to have any prior or current knowledge of what is being said, written and depicted on their sites, it can also be said that the authors of Internet content are bound by more limited concepts of responsibility. The digital simulacrum involves the infinite copying and reproduction of information in all its forms. The concept of copyright becomes meaningless and unenforceable. This must surely mean the death of originality and authenticity. If Internet content is beyond trust and credibility how can there be any liability for defamation? Likewise, how can there be any risk of Internet publication creating serious prejudice in the minds of potential jurors?

Holding Internet communicators accountable for their utterances in the same way as speakers at public meetings, writers of books and newspapers, and live television and radio broadcasters seems to misunderstand the cultural and socio-psychological nature of the medium. There is no adequate time for second thoughts. It is easy to publish defamation, contempt and other unlawful content by mistake. In 2008 the English High Court did discuss whether alleged defamation on Internet bulletin boards was more akin to spontaneous slander than libel. It is also easy to accidentally transmit to batched email addresses. The informal, anonymous and uninhibited culture of the Internet is not served by the nature of its technology. In reality it is a hyperactive digipanopticon or, to use the words of the academic Oscar H. Gandy Jr., 'The Panoptic Sort', the name he assigned to

> complex technology that involves the collection, processing and sharing of information about individuals and groups that is generated through their daily lives as citizens, employees, and consumers, and is used to coordinate and control their access to the goods and services that define life in the modern capitalist economy. [...] a system of disciplinary surveillance that is widespread but continues to expand its reach.
>
> (Gandy 1993: 15)

The technology strips the Internet user of all privacy and immunity from responsibility. But the spirit of human interaction on the Internet is the very opposite of the technological reality. Any Internet immunity from existing media laws would depend on the law deciding that it was an irrelevant medium of communication. However, there are no signs of this happening. If anything, the legal web is entwining in ever-increasing ways with the World Wide Web.

The British legal practice of court-reporting censorship orders was unable to control the challenge of the expression of public opinion on the Internet during 2008 and 2009. In the case of the three adults convicted of causing the death of 19-month-old Peter Connolly, judges tried to keep secret the identity of the child, his mother and stepfather, but a viral email and Internet campaign consistently outmanoeuvred the court orders. One Facebook site of 68,000 members revealed the full name of the child victim, described in the media as 'Baby P,' his mother Tracey Connelly, stepfather Steven Barker and Barker's older brother Jason Owen, and called for the defendants to be tortured and hanged. An Old Bailey judge's decision to try Connelly and Barker under pseudonyms in a second trial over an allegation that Barker had raped a 2-year-old girl and Connelly had criminally neglected her was also frustrated by cyberspace communications. By August 2009 Mr Justice Coleridge decided to allow the mainstream media to fully identify the adult defendants and child victim in 'order to maintain public confidence in the judicial system.' (Laville *Guardian* 2009)

Libel tourism

In 2005 Mr Justice Eady decided that the English and Welsh courts did have libel jurisdiction in a claim by Saudi Arabian businessman Sheikh Khalid Bin Mahfouz and others against Dr Rachel Ehrenfeld and her US publisher, Bonus Books. The book was published only in the USA, but the judge stated in his ruling that 23 copies had been sold in the UK and 200,000 people had accessed the first chapter, which had appeared on a website. (*Media Lawyer* July 2005: 31–2) Mr Justice Eady said the allegations that the Bin Mahfouz family had been one of the main sponsors of Al Qaeda and other terrorist organizations were of 'the most serious and defamatory kind'.

The judge was able to make a declaration that the book contained false and defamatory statements and award damages and costs even though the defendant refused to respond to the litigation. The UK litigation was possible under a process of 'summary disposal.' (Defamation Act 1996: sections 8–10) Dr Ehrenfeld sought a declaration in the US courts that Mr Justice Eady's ruling was unenforceable in the US and her book was not defamatory in American law. (O'Neill *Press Gazette* 2005) When the US courts were unable to do this, the state of New York passed legislation to protect writers and publishers working there from the enforcement of defamation judgments made by other courts, unless those courts accorded the same freedom of speech protection as New York and US federal law. The statute was given retrospective effect in order to protect Dr Ehrenfeld's position. This has been followed by legislation in the state of Illinois and bills are being tabled in Congress for a federal statute shielding US citizens from what are seen as illiberal British libel laws and counter to the spirit of the First Amendment. The states of Florida and California were in the process of legislating similar laws as this book went to press.

In 2006 the *Sunday Times* reported that American stars were queuing up to sue in 'libel friendly' Belfast because Northern Ireland has similar libel laws to England, but waiting lists are shorter and the costs can be 75% lower. (Clarke *Sunday Times* 2006) Reference has already been made to the UN's Committee on Human Rights criticizing the phenomenon of 'libel tourism' of foreign businessmen and millionaires using the High Court in London to sue foreign publishers under claimant-friendly defamation laws. (Verkaik *Independent* 2008) There is no shortage of articles reporting a campaign being run by the Open Society Justice Initiative that includes the writers' group English PEN, the Media Legal Defence Initiative and non-governmental organizations Global Witness, Human Rights Watch and Index on Censorship. The term 'libel tourism' is pejorative and trivializes the agony, struggle and remedies sought by overseas libel claimants who choose to litigate for publication within the UK in the global information age, whether the output is traditional old media of newspaper, magazine and book or new media cyberspace.

It is more than likely that the freedom to communicate across frontiers with immunity from legal sanctions will continue to be curtailed as the world comes to terms with the implications of near-instant global messaging. Reference has already been made to the Australian High Court decision in December 2002 that gives authority to the principle that you can sue where you download rather than where the person libelling you uploaded. Businessman Joseph Gutnick was able to bring a libel action against the Dow Jones international news agency over website allegations concerning his tax affairs even though the article was originally published and uploaded in America. (*Media Lawyer* March 2003: 29–30) The Australian judge Justice Kirby was sending out a message to the global American media that dominates film, international journalism, satellite broadcasting, the Internet and most cultural industries:

> Where a person or corporation publishes material which is potentially defamatory of another, to ask the publisher to be cognisant of the defamation laws of the place where the person resides and has a reputation is not to impose on the publisher an excessive burden. At least it is not to do so where the potential damage to reputation is substantial and the risks of being sued are commensurately real. Publishers in the United States are well aware that few, if any, other jurisdictions in the world observe the approach to the vindication of reputation adopted by the law in that country.
>
> (Dow Jones & Co Inc v Gutnick Aust HC 2002 para. 151)

Justice Callinan in the same case warned: 'If a publisher publishes in a multiplicity of jurisdictions it should understand, and must accept, that it runs the risk of liability in those jurisdictions in which the publication is not lawful and it inflicts damage.' (Ibid.: para. 192; also Collins 2005: 460)

Can it not be argued that in a global world of communications, the English and Welsh legal system with its satellite jurisdiction in Northern Ireland is providing global justice to individuals trading internationally and depending on their good name? If the most powerful country in the world, the USA, defaults on providing a remedy, why should not London fill the vacuum and provide the justice remedy? It could also be argued that international libel and privacy claimants use London media law specialists because they are among the best in the world. The London libel arena balances the power of transnational media corporations with that of the individual.

The British MP Andrew Pelling told the House of Commons on 17 December 2008:

We just have to think about what happened to Kate and Gerry McCann [the parents of missing Madeleine McCann]. Four newspapers thought it appropriate and responsible to suggest that the McCanns had been responsible for the death of Madeleine and the disposal of her body. It is important to remember that it was the courts [in London] that brought the libel to an end, and the newspapers had to publish, on their front pages, in an unprecedented way, apologies to Kate and Gerry McCann.

(Hansard 17 December 2008 col. 74WH)

A similar high-profile apology and settlement for libel damages was achieved in relation to the British citizen living in Portugal, Robert Murat, who had been subject to equally damaging allegations concerning the disappearance of the four-year-old girl when he had gone out of his way to help in the search and assist the global media descending on the resort in Portugal.

The battle lines over 'libel tourism' were sharply drawn in a debate on the English and Welsh libel laws in the Westminster Parliament at the end of 2008. The former Europe minister and president of the NUJ Denis MacShane endeavoured to explain what was at stake:

As in the 18th century, the British establishment is seeking to silence Americans who want to reveal the truth about the murkier goings-on in our interdependent world. I speak not, I am glad to say, about the government but about the English legal system. Lawyers and courts are conspiring to shut down the cold light of independent thinking and writing about what some of the richest and most powerful people in the world are up to.

The practice of libel tourism as it is known – the willingness of British courts to allow wealthy foreigners who do not live here to attack publications that have no connection with Britain – is now an international scandal. It shames Britain and makes a mockery of the idea that Britain is a protector of core democratic freedoms. Libel tourism sounds innocuous, but underneath the banal phrase is a major assault on freedom of information, which in today's complex world is more necessary than ever if evil, such as the jihad ideology that led to the Mumbai massacres, is not to flourish, and if those who traffic arms, blood diamonds, drugs and money to support Islamist extremist organisations that hide behind charitable status are not to be exposed.

I put it to the House that it is unthinkable that the state legislatures of New York, Illinois, and Congress itself, are having to pass Bills to stop British courts seeking to fine and punish American journalists and writers for publishing books and articles that may be freely read in the United States but which a British judge has decided are offensive to wealthy foreigners who can hire lawyers in Britain to persuade a British court to become a new Soviet-style organ of censorship against freedom of expression. [...]

It is worrying that 30 non-governmental organisations recently met human rights lawyers to express concern that libel tourists come to London to prevent the publication of NGO reports on parts of the world and individuals that, of course, rarely get much coverage in our newspapers. NGOs are an important source and conduit of information that is of interest to public policy and to the broader public, telling us what is going on and who is doing what to whom in parts of the world. These things need exposure. The NGOs are meeting lawyers because, thanks to libel tourism, some of the individuals mentioned in their reports can come here and attack those publications, seeking redress against distinguished organisations such as Human Rights Watch.

(Hansard 17 December 2008 cols 59WH–71WH)

The debate raised highlights how the differences in approach to libel have pitted two friendly countries against each other and spawned the intriguing question: which system of libel law is superior? The media law specialist Paul Tweed, a partner in the Belfast-based firm Johnsons Solicitors, addressed the New York Bar Association and wrote to the US Senate Judiciary Committee to make the point: 'There is one law in the UK and one law in the United States. If you start having States demanding changes in each others' law, where will it end?' (*Media Lawyer* January 2009: 29) Mr Tweed argued that publications needed to be factually true and properly researched before publication. He advised against US federal and state moves to pass 'libel tourism' statutes, as they would suppress free speech rather than support it. US citizens unfairly libelled in the UK would be deterred from taking action because of the block on enforcing judgments. Their only recourse to protecting their reputations would be shut down. The situation would lead to people wrongly believing that unchallenged defamatory allegations were in fact true. Mr Tweed warned that the 'people who will suffer most from this draconian legislation will be US citizens with international reputations who will be left totally vulnerable to the whims of the tabloid press in Europe'.

In 2009 the House of Commons Culture, Media and Sport Select Committee held an enquiry into 'Press Standards, Privacy and Libel'. A consortium of US publishers and media law bodies submitted written evidence that stated that US 'libel tourism' and 'libel terrorism' bills had been stoked up by a real and justified grievance:

we do not think, however, that such laws satisfactorily address a problem that has arisen between two friendly nations. US/UK co-operation in communications is vitally important to both countries: indeed, 'freedom of speech' was the first of the four freedoms enumerated by President Roosevelt after America entered the Second World War on the side of the UK and of liberty. We respectfully suggest that the problem caused by libel law – and sometimes, by libel lawyers – could be addressed by the UK government and parliament so that it will no longer threaten to damage US/UK relationships.

(H of C Select Committee 2009, Advance Publications, Inc et al)

The US media organizations made a scathing attack on the nature of English and Welsh libel law and strongly urged parliamentary reform of the burden of proof:

What US courts find repugnant about UK law is that it places the burden of proving truth on the defendant and holds him liable to pay damages for statements he honestly believed to be true and has published without negligence. In every other area of tort law the burden of proof is on the claimant: why should libel be any different? The reason, of course, is that the English common law disfavours free speech. It does so by use of two absurd presumptions: that defamatory (i.e. critical) statements are always true, and that defamations always do significant damage. These two presumptions – of falsity and damage – are both in terms illogical, but are in law irrebuttable and further proof that English law disfavours free speech.

(Ibid.: para. 5)

Navigating the legal systems

There is no shortage of excellent textbooks that can elucidate the complexities and nuances of the US and UK legal systems. The present book could not possibly replicate the wisdom and learning contained therein. However, to give the reader context for the debates in comparative media law, Table 1.11 attempts to provide a diagrammatic representation of the legal system of England and Wales within the United Kingdom and Europe. Figure 1.1, by kind permission of the state of Texas, sets out the structure of civil and criminal law from Justice Courts dealing with civil actions of no more than $10,000 to the Court of Criminal Appeals, which is the final state appellate jurisdiction in appeals of death sentences. Table 1.12 provides a simplistic charting of the US Federal Legal System, which has parallel jurisdiction in the state of Texas. Such concomitant legal provenance does not operate in Scotland, which has an independent legal system whose structure is set out in Table 1.20.

Table 1.11 Legal system of England and Wales within the United Kingdom and Europe

From County Court to European Court of Justice	From Magistrates' Court to the European Court of Human Rights	From Crown Court to the International Criminal Court
European Court of Justice	European Court of Human Rights	International Criminal Court, the World Court and other international tribunals and juridical bodies
Applications for preliminary rulings (Art. 234). Actions against member states etc. 27 judges advised by 8 advocates-general. A Grand Chamber of 13 judges, in chambers of 3 or 5, or rarely in full plenary session in cases of exceptional importance.	Actions for advisory opinions or rulings against Contracting States for breaches of Convention rights. President, Vice Presidents and judges. Appeal from chamber of seven to Grand Chamber of seventeen.	
European Law references can arise in any English court.	Appeals to the ECHR take place when all legal remedies in the English courts have been exhausted.	The instigation of proceedings in international courts depends on the protocols agreed by treaty. Remedies may be restricted to state governments or available to its citizens.
Supreme Court (from 2009)	Judicial Committee of the Privy Council	
Appeals from Court of Appeal and High Court, Scotland and Northern Ireland. Final appeals on devolution from Scotland, Wales and Northern Ireland. President and Deputy President and twelve Justices of the Supreme Court.	Appeals on law from the Commonwealth, General Medical Council and other professional bodies etc., ecclesiastical appeals. Lord President, Supreme Court Justices, Privy Councillors (Lords of Appeal) etc.	

From County Court to European Court of Justice	From Magistrates' Court to the European Court of Human Rights	From Crown Court to the International Criminal Court
Court of Appeal Civil Division Appeals from the High Court and County Courts, Master of the Rolls and Lord Justices of Appeal. Minimum of one. Appeals on law and fact. Leave/permission usually needed.	Appeals of general public importance. Permission/leave needed. Leapfrog appeals from the High Court on a legal point of general public importance. Consent of Supreme Court, HC and parties required.	Court of Appeal Criminal Division Appeals from the Crown Court and Queen's Bench Division. President of the Courts of England and Wales, Lords Justices of Appeal and High Court Judges. Appeals from the Crown Courts on law/fact/sentence. Leave needed.
'Employment Appeals Tribunal' hears appeals from Employment Tribunals that deal with disputes in employment law such as racial and gender discrimination, sexual harassment and unfair dismissal. SIAC (Special Immigration Appeals Commission) hears appeals from Immigration Tribunals that deal with increasing complexity of immigration law, including 'control orders' under terrorism legislation.	'Court of Protection' – an office where Chancery judges manage property of the mentally ill. 'Technology and Construction Court' – one High Court Judge plus circuit judges try technical and scientific cases on construction and computer disputes. 'Restrictive Practices Courts' – High Court Judges and lay people hear restrictive practices and fair trading cases.	'Coroners' Courts' – A coroner and/or jury deal with cases of sudden death. The Coroner's system of inquests dates back to the early Middle Ages and investigates, through an inquisitorial rather than adversarial process, the cause of death for any citizen of the United Kingdom dying suddenly at home or abroad, and any individual who dies in England or Wales.
High Court Chancery Division Exceptional multi-track claims over £15,000 in tax, bankruptcy, property, trusts, Patents Court, Companies Court. Vice Chancellor and High Court Judges.	High Court Family Division Divorce, family property, proceedings under the Children's Act. President and High Court Judges. Hears appeals on family law issues from county and magistrates' courts.	High Court Queen's Bench Division Exceptional multi-track claims over £15,000 in contract, tort, etc. Admiralty Court, Commercial Court, Administrative Court President of the Courts of England and Wales and High Court Judges.

Continued overleaf

From County Court to European Court of Justice	From Magistrates' Court to the European Court of Human Rights	From Crown Court to the International Criminal Court
Divisional Court Appeals in bankruptcy	Divisional Court Appeals from magistrates' courts	Divisional Court Appeals by case stated from Crown Court and magistrates' courts, and Judicial Review of Coroners' inquests.
County Court Most multi-track cases (over £15,000 civil cases). Fast track cases (£5,000 to £15,000). Small claims under £5,000. Family proceedings, patents. Equity limit £30,000. Appeal from District Judge is normally to Circuit Judge. Circuit Judges and District Judges and Recorders	Magistrates' Court Civil: family proceedings; criminal: trial of summary offences and triable either way. Penalties £5,000 and up to 6 months' imprisonment. (Power to jail up to 1 year not yet enacted.) Youth Court: maximum 2 years' detention and training. Two or three lay justices or one District Judge (magistrates' court), advised by a justices' clerk or court clerk (legal advisor).	Crown Court (can be seen as a High Court of Crime) Jury trials of indictable offences and offences triable either way: appeals from magistrates' courts on fact and sentence. Divided into 3 tiers. High Court Judges, Circuit Judges, Recorders, Magistrates.

Note:
Method of appeal and position in the legal hierarchy of *stare decisis* is indicated by the text rather than strict position in the table.

Broadcasting the courts

Victories on freedom of expression won by US and UK print journalism in the nineteenth century were denied to broadcasting in the twentieth century. As a result it took more than fifty years for the microphone and camera to be allowed into the Westminster Parliament. It has taken longer in the case of UK courtrooms. There was a short-lived experiment in Scotland in the 1990s that faded away when the judges took fright at what was described as 'a media circus' surrounding the global televising of the murder trial of O.J. Simpson in Los Angeles. There has been closed-circuit televising of the Hutton Enquiry, the inquest into the death of Diana Princess of Wales and Dodi Fayed, and a few murder trials attracting significant media interest. But the English judges continue to restrict the potential to merely cabling into 'overspill' media and public

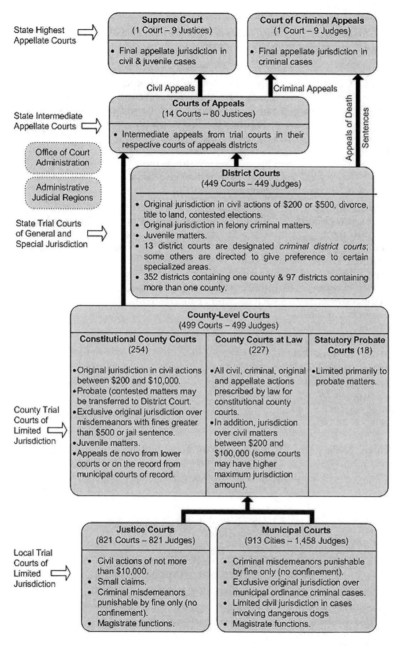

Figure 1.1 Legal system of the state of Texas

Source: Reproduced by permission of the Office of Court Administration of Texas, published at Texas Courts online www.courts.state.tx.us/

Table 1.12 US federal legal system

Main spine of federal courts structure	Route of appeal for specialist federal courts	Route of appeal for state legal system and armed services courts
Nine Justices and a Chief Justice of the United States chosen/ nominated by the President and approved by the Senate. Appointment and service for life or until retirement.	Supreme Court of the United States. The oldest federal court. *Stare decisis* operates in the sense that this is the final superior court and lower courts have to follow its decisions. In *Marbury v Madison* 1803 it asserted that it has the power to overturn laws passed by Congress.	Referrals of test cases by Supreme State Courts that believe a federal law may be unconstitutional.
Regional Courts of Appeal: Twelve circuits. Eleven circuits cover the fifty constituent states of the Federation and US territories (unlike Great Britain they are not referred to as colonies). For example, the second circuit represents the states of Connecticut, New York and Vermont. The 12th circuit is not officially known as such, but is usually understood as the US Court of Appeal for the District of Columbia. This DC court hears appeals from federal regulatory agencies and commissions such as the FCC and FTC.	Court of Appeal for the Federal Circuit. This court is sometimes referred to as the '13th circuit' and has jurisdiction for specialist areas of the law and will take appeals from district courts in intellectual property disputes such as patents and trademarks.	Court of Appeal for the Armed Forces
US District Courts: Ninety-two.	US Court of International Trade US Court of Federal Claims US Court of Veteran Appeals	Army, Navy-Marine Corps, Air Force, Coast Guard Courts of Criminal Appeals.
US Tax Court	International Trade Commission The Merit Systems Protection Board Patent and Trademark Office Board of Contract Appeals	
Federal judges are appointed and not elected – unlike state judges. The federal courts tend to resist TV broadcasting of proceedings, Athough two Court of Appeal Circuits are exceptions.		

gallery tents and annexes. In fact the only actual form of broadcasting in England from the Royal Courts of Justice may have been in 1982, when the author negotiated the sound recording and transmission of the ceremonial valedictory speeches of Master of the Rolls Lord Denning, in the Lord Chief Justice's Court. My predecessor as IRN Old Bailey correspondent, Ken Dennis of the Press Association, had previously recorded and broadcast the valedictory ceremony on the retirement of the Recorder of London in a courtroom of the Central Criminal Court. However, the UK's new Supreme Court, inaugurated the televising of English court proceedings in October 2009 with a media open justice application as one of its first hearings. This court replaces the Judicial Committee of the House of Lords and is part of a reform of the British legal system set out in the Constitutional Reform Act 2005.

In contrast, the US Supreme Court, along with the Federal Circuit, at the time of writing, continues its general prohibition on TV broadcasting of court proceedings, unlike many of the state courts, which for more than two decades have encouraged the development of a 'Court TV' culture.

US judicial proceedings and the electronic media have not always been happy bedfellows. The American Bar Association effectively prohibited US judges from allowing the broadcasting of court cases after the circus surrounding the 1935 trial in Flemington, New Jersey of Bruno Hauptmann – convicted and executed for the murder of the young child of Charles Lindbergh. In 1981 the US Supreme Court in the case *Chandler v Florida* ruled that the presence of cameras did not inherently render a trial unfair. Properly controlled use of cameras inside the courtroom could avoid the deprivation of a defendant's constitutional right to a fair hearing. (Zelezny, 2004: 280–2) The absence of broadcasting of court proceedings in most of the UK legal system is perhaps the most tangible and obvious distinction in the media law culture of the two countries. In 2009 cameras in the courtroom seem to be part of the fabric of US court reporting. There are fewer instances when state legislation enables judges to close their courts to electronic news media when they are convinced there would be a threat to the defendant's Sixth Amendment rights.

In high-pressured trials of celebrities, or of defendants accused of criminal responsibility for notorious terrorist incidents, a withdrawal from broadcasting can give the judges greater power over the conduct of their proceedings. They feel better able to maintain the discipline of due process, as was the case in the trials of individuals connected with the bombing of the Oklahoma federal building and the Los Angeles trial of the late singer Michael Jackson on child abuse charges. Only live radio broadcasting of the jury's not guilty verdicts was permitted.

The more bashful federal system has by no means locked the door on broadcasting. In the dispute over the election count in the state of Florida in 2000 (*Bush v Gore*) the Supreme Court in Washington DC released the audio transcripts of its proceedings. It is suggested that judicial and political confidence in court broadcasting in the UK could be achieved through a radio/audio step in broadcasting experimentation; the same process by which microphones and cameras were eventually allowed into the Palace of Westminster. A partnership between a public broadcaster such as the BBC and the Ministry of Justice could lead to the setting up of a court radio digital channel whose costs and risk would be substantially less than an entrée with television. By 2009 the US Supreme Court and most federal appeal circuits were releasing audio recordings of oral argument to the media. The 2nd and 9th Circuit Courts of Appeal permitted television coverage on a case-by-case basis. Radio can be seen as a bridge towards television in the courts. The contrasting narrative of broadcasting the courts in the USA and UK is set out in Table 1.13.

The critical perspective in media law

Media communicators have an opportunity to recontextualize the nature and development of media law and critically appreciate their status and purpose within British and American liberal-capitalist societies. In trying to understand how the systems work, some journalists believe their function in a democratic society is to question the justification of such censorship in every case. A debate endures about whether the proper role of the journalist is that of a lapdog or of a bloodhound. It has not gone unnoticed that former British Prime Minister Tony Blair characterized the media as behaving like 'feral beasts'. Was this the attitude of a politician flinching from the pain of media scrutiny, or criticizing abuse of media power that crosses the boundary from public interest analysis to abuse of private space and dignity?

The media communicator is faced with three key areas of control: contempt/protecting fair trial; defamation; and privacy. Parallel to and empowering these factors in the US and UK is the way that powerful state and corporate institutions control journalistic sources and define the concept of the public interest. What constitutes the public interest is not a matter of consistent agreement between judges, politicians and journalists. In the USA the executive and judiciary do not control the notion of 'the public interest'. Americans prefer also to use the expression 'public concern' and the initiative and determination of what is a matter of 'public concern' is the prerogative of the media; not the presumption of judges and politicians.

Some journalists argue that a number of aspects of US and UK media law could be argued to be against the public interest because they fail the key tests of justice and legal validity. It is argued that punishments and disincentives that include imprisonment and huge amounts in damages and legal costs are disproportionate to the harm that mere journalism

Table 1.13 Television and radio access to court proceedings

United Kingdom	United States of America
The 1925 Administration of Justice Act prohibits the use of cameras or live sketching during court proceedings in England and Wales. The English and Welsh statutory prohibition was introduced after newspaper circulation wars encouraged the market for surreptitious still images of defendants in notorious murder cases. Press photographers would conceal cameras in their top hats and cough loudly when operating the camera. The legislation does not apply in Scotland. Scottish judges, therefore have discretion to permit photography, filming or sketching, although they became reluctant after the global coverage of the murder trial of O.J. Simpson in Los Angeles in 1994. Another disincentive is the fact that consent of all parties involved must be obtained, and judicial permission sought; consent may be withdrawn up to 24 hours after filming has taken place; and proceedings can only be broadcast when the judge can be sure this can take place without risk to the administration of justice. Television access to Scottish courts was applied for during the Lockerbie bombing trial and appeal, which were held in the Netherlands under Scottish law. The application to televise the trial was refused, but the appeal was shown unedited on the Internet, and shown in television news broadcasts and documentaries. In 2004, a television pilot scheme was tried out at the Royal Courts of Justice in the Strand, London in order to demonstrate to senior judges that modern television technology was not a disruption to proceedings.	The first trial ever broadcast over radio occurred in 1925 during the sensational prosecution of teacher John Thomas Scopes at Dayton, Tennessee, who was accused of violating a law against teaching the theory of evolution in schools. Chicago Station WGN obtained exclusive broadcasting rights after rigging up five loudspeakers to transmit the proceedings to Dayton townsfolk. Judge John Raulston also allowed in newsreel and still cameras to take pictures. He relished the media attention, declaring: 'My gavel will be heard around the world.' This initial enthusiasm for extending the public gallery to radio and cinema newsreels ended with the carnival atmosphere of the 'Lindbergh Circus' at Flemington, New Jersey in 1935 and the murder conviction and execution of Bruno Hauptmann. The American Bar Association decided that the trial had been in the nature of a 'Roman Holiday' and in 1937 passed a resolution on professional ethics known as 'Canon 35', which stated: 'Proceedings in court should be conducted with fitting dignity and decorum. The taking of photographs in the courtroom during sessions of the court or recesses between sessions, and the broadcasting of court proceedings are calculated to detract from the essential dignity of the proceedings, degrade the court and create misconceptions with respect thereto in the mind of the public and should not be permitted.' Canon 35 was amended in 1952 to ban TV cameras, and Congress legislated against radio and photographic coverage of federal criminal cases.

Continued overleaf

United Kingdom	United States of America
It is also an offence to photograph and film people entering and leaving 'court precincts'. It would be advisable to find out what constitutes the precincts at specific court complexes so that camera/tripod positions are not challenged by the police. In April 2009 the European Court of Human Rights at Strasbourg ruled that the conviction and fine imposed by the Norwegian courts on two journalists for unlawful publication of photographs under section 131A of Norway's Administration of Courts Act 1915 of a person while leaving a court building did not give rise to a violation of Article 10 of the Convention (Egeland and Hanseid v Norway [2009] ECHR (no. 34438/04).	The American judiciary does not go as far as applying censorship powers beyond the courtroom walls. The idea of imposing restrictions on the use of radio or camera equipment outside the courtroom but on 'the court precincts', particularly to record people arriving and leaving, would be regarded as somewhat alien to the tradition of a free press and media. However, by 1965 the suspicion and prejudice surrounding the alleged dangers of television led to the Supreme Court ruling in *Estes v Texas* that photographic and broadcast coverage of the prosecution of a friend of President Lyndon Johnson had deprived him of a fair trial. In 1977 the state of Florida Supreme Court consented to a one-year pilot scheme of electronic media coverage of all state courts without the consent of trial participants.
Section 9 of the 1981 Contempt of Court Act makes it an offence to use a tape recorder or bring into a court a tape recorder for use without leave of the court. There is also a practice direction from the Lord Chief Justice of England and Wales prohibiting the broadcasting of tape recordings of court hearings. It might be argued that this was a missed opportunity to experiment with relatively non-obtrusive radio coverage, as had been the case with Parliament from 1978 before a decision was made to let in television cameras.	The green light to widespread televising of court proceedings was given by the US Supreme Court in the case of *Chandler v Florida*, when the justices ruled that 'consistent with constitutional guarantees, a state may provide for radio, television and still photographic coverage of a criminal trial for public broadcast, notwithstanding the objection of the accused.' The Supreme Court justices and federal judges remain largely opposed to televising the proceedings, despite some successful pilot studies involving civil cases in the 1990s.

and media publication can cause. In 2009 both countries still had criminal libel laws, although they were largely redundant in practical application.

It is also argued that media law sanctions are negative remedies against journalism in a free and democratic society, and in relation to the UK there has been very little transparency, publication, notification and consultation with the media during the last thirty years over an exponential rise in primary and secondary media law legislation. On the other hand, critics of the media argue that the law needs to check the catastrophic damage to the emotional and economic well-being of individuals and companies (which in UK and US law have legal personality) caused by lies and negligent publication. The purpose of media law is to ensure that a fair trial takes place through due process of legal proceedings, and not in the media. Vulnerable witnesses need to be protected from vigilante reprisals and intimidation, and state investigators and security forces need to be protected from revenge attacks and damage to national security. The purpose of media law is to ensure that media communicators exercise powers of communication with responsibility and respect the dignity of the human individual. Public interest is not simply what interests the public in terms of prurience, voyeurism, gossip curiosity and entertainment.

Consequently, in your study of media law you have the right to formulate your own opinions about whether journalists have too much or too little power. Has the balancing exercise by judges diminished the right to freedom of expression to the point of subordination against other rights such as national security, privacy, along with the exaggeration of the imperative of such fundamental rights as life, and fair trial? Is there not a tendency for judges to take particular merits and sets of circumstances and turn these into moral and political crises of media abuse of power? In essence, are the media becoming increasingly infantilized, as if they are children that have to be controlled, or as a counterargument, does media law educate the media into the maturation of a constitutional role that avoids freedom without responsibility? In a democratic society, how much moral discretion should be given to journalists when they wield their mighty pens or tap away on their keyboards when editing digitally across multimedia platforms?

Contempt – the law against reporting legal proceedings

The profession and academic discipline of media law encourages a concentration and evaluation of the latest precedents decided by the highest courts. But a more investigative and journalistic approach seeks to understand how the power in the UK to censor the media 'to protect the administration of justice' with judicial injunctions and statutory prohibitions (the breach of which is a criminal offence) came about.

British legal culture has constructed a power to protect juries from prejudice, based on a case from 1820. However, an examination of the archives relating to the prosecution of the *Observer* newspaper for contempt, known as *R v Clement*, demonstrates that the case was a decision to protect the state's embarrassment in using paid agents provocateurs to give evidence against political activists opposed to the government of the day. (R v Clement CKB 1821; and In the Matter of W.I. Clement CoE 1822) The editor of the *Observer* was fined £500 for reporting a series of

71

Old Bailey trials of the Cato Street conspirators accused of being involved in a plot to blow up the British Cabinet in London. It is the foundation precedent of the all-embracing power to postpone the reporting of an entire trial because evidence will prejudice a following trial.

The Cato Street conspiracy case was part of a government campaign to suppress political discontent. It was a year after the massacre by armed militia of demonstrators at Peterloo, Manchester. The inquest into the deaths of men and women who had been sabred to death had been adjourned without any conclusion. Arthur Thistlewood had been jailed for involvement in another flashpoint known as the Spa Fields riot. He and thirteen other men met in a stable loft of a house in Cato Street, off the Edgware Road in London. It was alleged that they planned to murder Cabinet members during a dinner in Grosvenor Square (the present location of the US Embassy) and then intended to seize key buildings in London and declare a revolutionary republic.

One of the five defendants executed was a black man, William Davidson. He was the illegitimate son of the Attorney General for Jamaica. It would seem that the conspiracy had been originated and led by a government agent provocateur, George Edwards, who disappeared from the scene once the trials commenced. He was employed and paid by a police official at Bow Street. The aims of the conspirators were vague and lacked unity of purpose until Edwards arrived on the scene and began to urge violent action. He produced the newspaper cutting announcing the location of the first Cabinet dinner since the late king's death. When the police converged on Cato Street just as arms were being distributed, Edwards had absented himself. One police officer was shot dead in the exchange of fire. Thistlewood escaped, only to be arrested at a hideout that Edwards had found for him.

Edwards was never seen again even though defence lawyers repeatedly insisted that the Crown produce him as a witness. The defendants pleaded not guilty to high treason and elected to be tried separately in a sequence of four trials. Lord Chief Justice Charles Abbott said that the evidence in each trial would be very similar, and feared that if each trial was contemporaneously reported it would give witnesses an opportunity to alter their evidence in the next trial. (R v Clement CKB 1821)

In fact the suppression on reporting only served to cover up the growing scandal of entrapment and the payment and inducements to government informers. It was obvious that the main witness, Robert Adams, had learned his evidence by rote, and he reproduced it word for word before each jury. He had been one of the original conspirators, but turned 'King's evidence' and was effectively working for the government as a supergrass of the Georgian age.

In trial after trial defence counsel demanded that the Crown produce the missing agent provocateur, George Edwards. This exhortation by defence counsel in the third trial fell on deaf ears:

There is a witness in the list of the name of Edwards, who has been not only present, but a material adviser, and active agent in every thing done, and Edwards stands the most prominent man in the whole transaction. You see 'him first, him last, him midst, him without end'. Whatever is said, Edwards has a share in; whatever is done, Edwards has a hand in; and yet the incredible Mr Adams alone is called. Edwards, as Adams has expressed himself, had the title of aide-de-camp, and yet he is not called to support Adams.

(Stanhope 1962: 117–8)

The *Observer* breached the judge's direction by publishing what it described as 'a fair, true and impartial' account of the proceedings and the evidence heard by the court. It was fined £500 for contempt in disregarding the judge's order. This was the origin of the power of a British court to censor the reporting of proceedings by publication outside the courtroom until the trial or other trials had been completed. The justification was 'the interests of truth and justice', although this would appear to be a contradiction in terms. The allegedly cynical and questionable tactics of the prosecution merited publicity. Each defendant was on trial for his life. The banning of the reporting of these succeeding trials until the end of the last one was untenable and a bias against democracy, the public interest and justice. It was absurd that the public gallery was open but the newspapers were silent. Separating the indictment so that each conspirator was tried separately may have been fair to the defendants. Suppressing publicity for each trial was not.

The *Observer*'s editor, William Innell Clement, was tried for contempt and fined £500 in his absence and without any legal representation. The judges presumed that he had deliberately left London so that he could not be served the summons. But the Courts of King's Bench and Exchequer that heard his appeals in 1821 and 1822 was composed of panels including some of the very judges, Lord Chief Justice Abbott, Chief Baron Richards and Mr Justice Best who had originally fined him. It is not surprising that they dismissed his appeals. The situation substantially breached the natural justice principle, *nemo judex in causa sua*, that no one shall be a judge in his own case. It would have been recognized as an irregularity in the 1820s. Nowadays it would be unconscionable.

Clement had an arguable case about whether there had been a recognizable court order postponing reporting of the trials. It was not written down or recorded by the court, was not available for inspection, and there were conflicting accounts of whether Lord Chief Justice Abbott had said he 'expected that all persons, therefore, will attend to this admonition' or 'will observe this injunction.' (In the Matter of W.I. Clement CoE 1822)

Baron Garrow in the 1822 appeal claimed that the *Observer* was 'the only paper in which the account had been published, all the other papers in the kingdom preferring the observance of an honourable propriety, by submitting to the prohibition of the court.' (Ibid.) But an examination of reports in *The Times* indicates that this was not necessarily the case. Although *The Times* did not provide detailed reports of the evidence, it did summarize the first and second trials and provided a list of witnesses and the gist of what they said between 18 and 23 April 1820. The newspaper even stated that in the second trial of the defendant James Ings, the former soldier and prosecution informer Robert Adams 'gave nearly the same evidence which he had already detailed in Thistlewood's trial.' (*The Times* 22 April 1820: 2)

It would seem the entire purpose of Lord Chief Justice Abbott's reporting ban was vitiated by the decision on Monday 25 April to allow the foreman of the jury in the first trial of Thistlewood, Alexander Barclay of Teddington, and five other men who had served on the jury of the previous trial to try the last case of James Thomas Brunt. Mr Barclay had 'begged to be excused on account of his former services' but he was not challenged by either the prosecution or the defence, whose leading counsel declared he 'wished him to be on the jury because having been on the first trial, he would be enabled to see the distinction between the two cases, and to discover the difference in the evidence.' (*The Times* 25 April 1820: 3) It could never be said that *R v Clement* was a credible precedent justifying the postponement of reporting criminal trials in order to prevent prejudice to juries in following cases. This would have been impossible when six jurors deliberated in two of the succeeding cases. If anything, *R v Clement* is a testament to the principle of trusting juries to try their peers without prejudice and solely on the basis of the evidence before them.

The Cato Street conspiracy defendants were convicted and subjected to the grotesque sentence of 'hanging, drawing and quartering' in a public execution outside the Old Bailey. It was decided to omit the barbaric practice of mutilation by quartering, but they were still hanged and beheaded before silent, brooding crowds that uttered the occasional cry of 'Bring out Edwards'. It could be said that the prosecution of the *Observer* for contempt, cited in the law books as *R v Clement*, created a flawed and discredited precedent that has attacked and undermined the principle of open justice and compromised what should be a constitutional right to provide contemporaneous reports of criminal trials.

This historical precedent can be contrasted with the 1807 US case of former Vice-President Aaron Burr, who was placed on trial for charges of treason. He was accused of trying to solicit revolution by seeking the secession of the western United States from the rest of the federal union. Burr was a controversial character in the politics of the time and, despite being one of the founding fathers of the USA, he had no shortage of enemies, particularly after he had dispatched the popular Alexander Hamilton in a fatal duel a few years before. Thomas Jefferson, the then President of the United States and author of the Constitution, wanted revenge. In his message to Congress in January 1807 Jefferson boldly asserted that Burr was guilty, and the address caused a frenzy of newspaper allegations and counter-allegations. What jury could not be influenced by the overwhelming and demonizing clamour for a guilty verdict against Aaron Burr? He was a traitor to the constitution, an insurrectionist and seditious libeller. He wished to become the Napoleon and Emperor of America.

In law Burr argued that he could not obtain a fair trial in any American jurisdiction, but the then Chief Justice, John Marshall, gave the opinion that it was acceptable for jurors to have some advance knowledge of a case, provided they kept their minds open to a fair consideration of the testimony. The eventual 'not guilty' verdict provided a foundation stone for the idea that the due process of law can triumph over sensationalist media comment and gossip and the case of *US v Burr* is cited as a historical precedent on the separation of powers between Supreme Court and Presidential executive.

Later in the nineteenth century, a newspaper industry serving the growing literacy of working people through the 'penny press' developed the phenomenon of 'yellow journalism' (in Britain aka the 'gutter press') – an entertaining and sensationalistic style of reporting in a competitive market of high-circulation newspaper conglomerates owned by powerful 'barons' such as Hearst and Pulitzer. A similar development occurred in Britain, where the competition in the early twentieth century would be between the newspaper groups owned by Lords Northcliffe and Beaverbrook. In both countries the tradition of court reporting was a significant part of the product and service to readers. The nature and style of court journalism would be at the centre of debates over 'trial by newspaper' and whether the coverage of 'indecency' could 'deprave and corrupt' readers.

The political class would continually express caution about any potential interpenetration or collapsing of the function of politics and fourth-estate media. Any party political monopoly between media and politics would attack and suffocate the nature of democratic debate, plurality and competition between opinion which, in the words of the American academic Alexander Meiklejohn, 'give to every voting member of the body politic the fullest possible participation in the understanding of those problems with which the citizens of a self-governing society must deal.' (Meiklejohn 1948: 89) When Lords Beaverbrook and Rothermere joined forces in Britain in the 1930s to form a New Empire Party to challenge the political mainstream in elections, backed by the campaigning force and power of their newspaper ownership, the then British Prime Minister, Stanley Baldwin, provided a warning of the social and political consequences: 'What the proprietorship of these papers is aiming at is power, and power without responsibility – the prerogative of the harlot throughout the ages.' (Margach 1978: 30–1) Baldwin was responding to libels against him, but he was not prepared to sue in the courts even though he had been advised that an apology and heavy damages were inevitable: 'The first is of no value and the second I would not touch with a barge pole.' (Ibid.)

It could be argued that UK legal culture has exaggerated the impact of media prejudice and avoided taking measures adopted in the USA to promote jurors' consideration of the evidence in trials before them. The UK law against interviewing jurors about their deliberations (section 8 of 1981 Contempt of Court Act) could be seen as another example of the process of protecting the mythology of media prejudice. The proposal to bar communication by jurors of their deliberations arose out of interviews conducted with the jurors in a conspiracy to murder case at the Old Bailey in 1979 featuring a former leader of the Liberal Party as one of the defendants. In 2009 the Attorney General successfully prosecuted *The Times* newspaper and the jury foreman of a manslaughter trial over a published interview with jurors expressing anxiety over the role of complicated evidence given by expert medical witnesses during the trial. The newspaper was fined £15,000 and the jury foreman £500. (Attorney General v Seckerson and Times, HC 2009) *The Times* intended to appeal the case on the grounds that Article 10 rights of freedom of expression for the jurors and media made the prohibition on interviewing members of a jury after the case incompatible with the Human Rights Act:

> there had been no damage to the administration of justice, no individual juror was identified, no individual's opinions were disclosed and the articles were written in good faith, after taking legal advice, on a matter of public importance – the heavy reliance placed on expert medical evidence in 'shaken baby' cases.
>
> (Ford *The Times* 2009)

In the USA such prosecutions would be unconstitutional, and culturally it is accepted practice in most states for jurors to have the right post verdict to talk to the attorneys in the case about their deliberations as well as to engage in interviews with members of the media. The relaxed and engaging participation of Los Angeles jurors with the media in after-trial interviews in the Michael Jackson case was seen as confirming the value and integrity of the criminal justice process and the endorsement of citizen participation through jury service.

However, in the United Kingdom there is a legal cultural view that the confidentiality of jury deliberations must be sacrosanct in order to protect the confidence and robust independence of the jury's status as an independent tribunal. This position was explained by Lord Justice Pill in the 2009 *Times* newspaper ruling:

Jurors should not be constrained by fears a juror would legitimately have if his friends and neighbours, and the general public, may come to know of his views, which could be unpopular views. If views were expressed in the hope of their being disclosed, or with an intention to disclose, that would also have a deleterious effect on the quality of deliberations. It is the principle of the secrecy of the jury room which is at stake and which is central to the proper administration of justice in this jurisdiction, as stated in the authorities. It is not necessary to establish that the disclosure has led to injustice in the case concerned. [...] Disclosures found to be in breach of the section do not obtain cover by being interwoven, whether intentionally or unintentionally interwoven, with expressions of general concern, which may legitimately be made by a juror. They do not obtain cover by the addition of favourable comments about how the jury functioned, as some of the disclosures in this case may have done. Indeed, disclosures incorporating favourable comment about other jurors could constitute a breach.

(Attorney General v Seckerson and *Times*, HC 2009 paras 51–2)

It should also be appreciated that the difference in geography means that the UK media are more homogeneous in their coverage compared to a more heterogeneous media in the USA. British courts have greater difficulty in moving trials away from towns and cities where feelings are running high, and do not have the same powers as judges in many US states to investigate the influence of media prejudice on jurors, and sequestrate jurors from media influence.

Most British media contempt law is determined by the 1981 Contempt of Court Act that enabled judges to issue specific bans on court reporting. Orders under Section 4(2) postpone reports of court proceedings and orders under Section 11 prohibit reports of information withheld from the public before the proceedings. The Act was criticized for creating an opportunity for judicial activism. Judges could now use formal statutory powers of censorship in situations where there was no media representation. This disparity in power would be disastrous for the protection of the open justice principle in British courtrooms. The consequences were witnessed directly by the author, who at the time was a legal affairs specialist journalist covering cases day by day at the Central Criminal Court and Royal Courts of Justice. In a matter of a few weeks in 1982 I was able to compile a dossier of direct censorship bans that would have been seen as unlawful or improper before the passage of the 1981 legislation. The report was distributed to politicians and media organizations. The Contempt of Court Act had been approved by Parliament without any machinery for appealing the reporting ban powers given to courts. Journalists in courtrooms had to consider taking on freedom of press advocacy as well as reporting court cases when judges were prepared to give them a hearing, a concept known as *locus standi*.

But the disparity in the power relationship between journalists and judges and lawyers would increase. From 1980, monetarist economics in UK media corporations would seek the increase in profits by rationalization of news-gathering costs, since the threshold on increasing turnover through advertising and circulation/audience was effectively capped by the nature of media markets. In the period between 1980 and 1997 the demand for court-reporting services in broadcasting and print media collapsed. I had built a news agency that specialized in providing reports for the UK's independent radio and television organizations. Weekly retainers would be cancelled and eventually the UK's independent radio network would have no interest in taking voice reports or originated news packages on judicial stories on a day-by-day basis when the actuality could be copied from television recordings and 'voiced up' in the newsroom from Press Association agency copy. Saving editorial costs was more important than benefiting from contacts, knowledge and grassroots journalism from the very arenas where important legal, social and political decisions affecting the public interest were being made.

In an idealistic hope that the situation would change I continued to maintain a full professional broadcasting studio with digital studio transmission lines at the Royal Courts of Justice until 2001. The financial costs were mine. But eventually it had to close through apathy, indifference and constitutional negligence. The trend in deracinating reporting and journalistic resources in the British legal system has been systematically diagnosed and analysed by the award-winning investigative journalist Nick Davies in his popular text *Flat Earth News* (2008). Davies rightly observes that the courts 'are the most productive single source of stories in the country, not just of human interest but of all the unseen tensions in a community's life which come bubbling up through crime and civil actions.' (Davies 2008: 77) Davies has been able to measure a massively reduced coverage of the Central Criminal Court and Royal Courts of Justice, 'the two most important courthouses in the country', and he reported that across the country 'most of the work of the eighty-two regional Crown Courts, more than two hundred other county courts and more than 350 other magistrates' courts is invisible ....' (Ibid.: 78)

Like a ghost, I sometimes forlornly wander the courtrooms of London and elsewhere, hearing cases that twenty years ago would justify front-page coverage and the lead item in broadcast bulletins. But the absence of journalists in courtrooms means that court staff and courtroom protagonists are no longer cognizant of media and public scrutiny. Time and time again I am challenged to produce my press pass and justify my presence. There has been an increasing tendency for student journalists sent to develop experience in covering court cases to be ordered not to take notes and frequently to be excluded from courtrooms that should be open to the public and media. Incidents have occurred in London and Cardiff. Public galleries are sometimes unofficially sealed, when security guards are directed to allow admittance only if visitors can produce passports to prove identity, and then they will only be given a chance to experience 'open' court proceedings after their details and passport numbers have been recorded in a database.

The issuing of prior restraint reporting bans on public proceedings is so arbitrary, summary and routine that on one visit to the pressroom of the Central Criminal Court I found a pile of court reporting orders lying on a desk as though somebody had jammed the 'copy' key of a photocopying machine. The British courts have even conjured up the Kafkaesque achievement of issuing court reporting bans on the content and existence of court reporting bans themselves. It should be stated, however, that the British media have not been slow in or averse to challenging the practice. A high-water mark in setting out the limit of judges' powers to make reporting bans in criminal trials is the Court of Appeal case in 2001 brought by the *Daily Telegraph* and other media groups. They failed to persuade the court to overturn a ban which postponed the reporting of a trial of police officers until after the conclusion of a second, related trial. Lord Justice Longmore set out a three-stage test that British judges should adopt:

1. The first question was whether reporting would give rise to a not insubstantial risk of prejudice to the administration of justice in the relevant proceedings. If not, that would be the end of the matter.

2. If such a risk was perceived to exist, then the second question arose: would a Section 4(2) order eliminate it? If not, there could clearly be no necessity to impose such a ban. Again, that would be the end of the matter.

On the other hand, even if the judge was satisfied that an order would achieve the objective, he would still have to consider whether the risk could satisfactorily be overcome by some less restrictive means. If so, it could not be said to be necessary to take the more drastic approach.

3. Suppose that the judge concluded that there was indeed no other way of eliminating the perceived risk of prejudice; it still did not follow necessarily that an order had to be made. The judge might still have to ask whether the degree of risk contemplated should be regarded as tolerable in the sense of being the lesser of two evils. It was at that stage that value judgments might have to be made as to the priority between competing public interests.

It was the duty of the Court of Appeal when exercising the present jurisdiction not merely to review the decision of the trial judge but to come to its own independent conclusions on the materials placed before it.

(R v Sherwood, ex parte The Telegraph Group & others, CoA Crim. 2001, Times Law Report, 12 June 2001)

The British judiciary has not grasped the fact that the British media can ill afford to maintain reporting resources in courtrooms for cases they cannot report contemporaneously, cases that sometimes continue for many months. The American judiciary and media would have found it astonishing to read a *Guardian* news report in 2005 about the sentencing of Kamel Bourgass to 17 years' imprisonment for taking part in a terrorist plan to destabilize society when he had been previously convicted of stabbing to death a police officer who had tried to arrest him: 'that conviction, for which he was jailed for life last year with a recommendation that he serve a minimum of 22 years, can only now be reported after the lifting of restrictions.' (Campbell, Dodd, Norton-Taylor and Cowan *Guardian* 2005) The delay in reporting this information had lasted an entire year. But his second trial had also been smothered by a reporting ban so that all of the evidence that unfolded over nine months and that led to the acquittal of his eight co-defendants was telescoped into only one day of reporting.

This situation was highly controversial. It had been complained about by the Commissioner of the Metropolitan Police Sir Ian Blair, who had written to the Attorney General stating that the reporting bans on terrorist trials were undermining the confidence of the Muslim community in the police. They were preventing public dissemination of successful police enquiries and prosecutions. (Travis *Guardian* 2005) Four postponement orders on the reporting of trials involving Bourgass and others suspected of terrorist offences meant that for more than two years the public could not be informed that the evidence backing government claims of a plot to poison the London underground with ricin were scientifically groundless. One of the witnesses in the trial, Duncan Campbell, wrote in the *Guardian* in April 2005 that the court's verdicts on five of the defendants and the dropping of charges against the other four proved that there had been no ricin ring:

nor did the 'ricin ring' make or have ricin. Not that the government shared that news with us. Until today, the public record for the past three fear-inducing years has been that ricin was found in the Wood Green flat occupied by some of yesterday's acquitted defendants. It wasn't.

(*Media Lawyer* May 2005: 14)

The USA has not been spared the market economics of rationalization in journalistic reporting resources. But I have yet to find evidence of the collapse in court reporting that is occurring in the UK. The idea that an American judge has the power to regularly and routinely censor beyond his or her courtroom walls is culturally and constitutionally untenable. In *Bridges v California* in 1941 the Supreme Court ruled that the courts did not have any contempt powers to penalize out-of-court publications unless there was a 'clear and present danger' of serious and imminent threat to the administration of justice, a much higher threshold of justification than the language of the UK 1981 Contempt of Court Act, which speaks of 'a substantial risk of prejudice.' (Denniston 1992: 271) In *Pennekamp v Florida* 1946 the Supreme Court directed that out-of-court reporting bans on media criticism of conduct by judges were unlawful unless it could be shown there was a clear and imminent threat of obstructing the fair and impartial trials of pending cases. (Ibid.) In *Craig v Harney* in 1947 the Supreme Court asserted that trials are public events and court-room proceedings are public property. Out-of-court and prior restraint reporting bans were again strongly discouraged. The line of authority guaranteeing First Amendment rights to public access to court proceedings as well as circumscribing the power of US judges to control only the proceedings before them and not the content of media published outside their courtrooms continues to the landmark case in 1980 of *Richmond Newspapers, Inc v Virginia*. The depth and jurisprudential power of Chief Justice Burger's opinion in giving priority to media access rights has not been matched by UK court rulings. This is a profound irony, as Burger based his ruling on research into and reading of English and Welsh common law as well as United States constitutional law. Burger made it abundantly clear that any common law-based legal system was capable of adopting numerous mechanisms to avoid the shutting of its doors to the media and public through *in camera* proceedings. Furthermore the jurisprudential resonance of his opinion and those of the other Supreme Court Justices in their ruling shatters the legal legitimacy of prior restraint reporting bans on open court proceedings:

> the historical evidence demonstrates conclusively that at the time when our organic laws were adopted, criminal trials both here and in England had long been presumptively open. This is no quirk of history; rather, it has long been recognized as an indispensable attribute of an Anglo-American trial. Both Hale in the 17th century and Blackstone in the 18th saw the importance of openness to the proper functioning of a trial; it gave assurance that the proceedings were conducted fairly to all concerned, and it discouraged perjury, the misconduct of participants, and decisions based on secret bias or partiality. [...]

81

Jeremy Bentham not only recognized the therapeutic value of open justice but regarded it as the keystone:

'Without publicity, all other checks are insufficient: in comparison of publicity, all other checks are of small account. Recordation, appeal, whatever other institutions might present themselves in the character of checks, would be found to operate rather as cloaks than checks; as cloaks in reality, as checks only in appearance.' J. Bentham, *Rationale of Judicial Evidence* 524 (1827). [...]

The right of access to places traditionally open to the public, as criminal trials have long been, may be seen as assured by the amalgam of the First Amendment guarantees of speech and press; and their affinity to the right of assembly is not without relevance. From the outset, the right of assembly was regarded not only as an independent right but also as a catalyst to augment the free exercise of the other First Amendment rights with which it was deliberately linked by the draftsmen. [...]

... a trial courtroom also is a public place where the people generally – and representatives of the media – have a right to be present, and where their presence historically has been thought to enhance the integrity and quality of what takes place. [...]

Free speech carries with it some freedom to listen [...] What this means in the context of trials is that the First Amendment guarantees of speech and press, standing alone, prohibit government from summarily closing courtroom doors which had long been open to the public at the time that amendment was adopted. [...] We hold that the right to attend criminal trials is implicit in the guarantees of the First Amendment; without the freedom to attend such trials, which people have exercised for centuries, important aspects of freedom of speech and of the press could be eviscerated.

(Richmond Newspapers Inc v Virginia SC US 1980)

On the other hand, the UK 1981 Contempt of Court Act was welcomed in providing a simple rule that media contempt was a publication that tended to 'create a substantial risk of serious prejudice'. It was clear that the rule should apply when reporting crime or legal stories after an arrest had been made, warrant for arrest had been issued, or when a civil case had been 'set down for trial'. It was clear that substantial risk related to size and timing of publication. Serious prejudice related to the nature of the content and how it could 'seriously' influence jurors or potential jurors. It was common sense that the key risk areas were publishing the previous convictions of accused people, accusing them of more serious offences by mistake, saying they have confessed, publishing details of police evidence, or commenting on the honesty of the defendant or witnesses.

However, there may have been a discernible shift in the application of media contempt strict liability in Britain. 'Strict liability' in law involves criminal liability for the criminal act i.e. publication (known as *actus reus*) with a diminishing application of mental intention (known as *mens rea*). Consequently media contempt in the 1981 Contempt of Court Act excludes a lack of intention to commit contempt as a defence. Much more seriously, prejudicial content is being tolerated after arrest and before charge on the basis that the fade factor in 'substantial risk' means that jurors do not hold memory of the material that could prejudice their minds.

The contemporary problem of terrorism and the extension of detention limits for terrorist suspects for up to 28 days has meant a longer period between arrest and charge, where the media vacuum has been filled with intense speculation and reporting in the 24/7 rolling news world. It would appear that the government has recognized the need to provide information to the public about the disruption of alleged terrorist conspiracies. In one major enquiry the Home Secretary and senior Scotland Yard officers held a press conference after the arrest to explain the overall nature of the investigation and outline the main allegations.

It is not clear if the judges are happy about this. The leading UK jurists on contempt law, Sir David Eady (a High Court Judge) and Professor A.T.H. Smith (academic and barrister), have written:

> according to some commentators, the strict liability rules have continued to be honoured more in the breach than the observance ... it would seem to indicate either a need for more determined enforcement of the existing law or the desirability of introducing reform with a view to bringing practice into line with principle.
>
> (Eady and Smith 2008: vii)

In a speech in 2007, the former Attorney General Lord Goldsmith said there was a perceived need for greater openness in terrorism cases, and a huge public interest in information being available about the progress of police investigations and the steps being taken to protect the public and bring dangerous offenders to justice. (Ibid.)

In addition, the Court of Appeal ruled against the Attorney General over an injunction he had obtained against the BBC, who wished to report a leaked memo concerning the Scotland Yard enquiry into loans for peerages. The Court decided that Article 10 freedom of expression trumped an evaluation of the risk of a fair trial being undermined (Article 6). This means that the application of strict liability after arrests had been an unjustifiable restriction on the freedom of information guaranteed by the Human Rights Act 1998. (Attorney General v BBC CoA Civ 2007)

The nature of this 'more liberal' climate for the British media appeared to be confirmed by the content of a letter that the Attorney General

Baroness Scotland wrote to the *Times* in response to publication of background reports at the end of a terrorist trial where there was the prospect of a retrial, which is set out in Table 1.14.

There has also been a limited move towards *voir dire* style enquiries into jury panels to exclude the risk of media prejudice. In 2008 the trial judge at Ipswich Crown Court in the case of Stephen Gerald James Wright, accused of murdering five women who worked as prostitutes, directed

Table 1.14 The Attorney General's letter to *The Times*, September 2008

Sir, Recent correspondents (letters, Sept 11, 15) have suggested that the law on contempt of court is not being effectively enforced. As Attorney-General this responsibility falls to me and I take it extremely seriously.

The law on contempt involves a delicate balance between two vital public interests – on the one hand freedom of speech and of expression, and on the other hand the right of an accused person to a fair trial. Not every public comment about a particular case, however outspoken, will seriously interfere with the rights of the accused. That may be so, for example, where there is likely to be a long gap in time between the publication and any future trial, so that it is unlikely to weigh heavily in the minds of the jury by the time they come to hear the case (the 'fade factor'). It may also be so where what is published in the media amounts to no more than the evidence that will be put before the jury in any event.

Compliance with the law is, in the first instance, the responsibility of individual editors and journalists. The fact that I do not routinely advise the media on their responsibilities under the law is not a sign of leniency or any lack of concern. I and my office will carefully review media comment about active proceedings to ensure it does not fall on the wrong side of the line. In those cases where I consider that contempt proceedings are justified I will not hesitate to bring them. This year, contempt proceedings have been successfully concluded against the editor and publisher of the Sunday World and against ITV Central. The Sunday World action resulted in record fines of £50,000 against the paper and £10,000 against the editor. It would be wrong to assume that no further proceedings are in prospect. But I emphasise that decisions to bring proceedings are made case by case, after careful consideration, and applying the tests which have been articulated by the courts.

As part of my wider contempt responsibilities, my office provides guidance and assistance to prosecutors where prosecutions are brought against editors and publishers for breach of statutory reporting restrictions relating to proceedings. We have also provided assistance to courts and members of the judiciary in the resolution of contempt issues.

Journalists and commentators should be in no doubt that I will continue to enforce the law on contempt fairly and robustly.

Baroness Scotland of Asthal

Attorney-General

Source: Scotland (*Times* 2008)

jurors to excuse themselves if they had any involvement with and knowledge of the victims and enquiry, to avoid reading and consuming media about the case and indulging in Internet research. In addition, 'reserve jurors' were empanelled. (Dixon *Express* 2008) This was very much in the US style of encouraging jurors to concentrate on the evidence and 'put out of their minds' the influence of prior or contemporary media coverage. It was also an extension of the practice of Old Bailey judges in terrorist trials asking people on jury panels to excuse themselves if they or their relatives had any involvement or experience of terrorist incidents and membership in the security forces.

Confusion over UK contempt of court precedents

Unfortunately the British judicial interpretation of media publication that constitutes a substantial risk of serious prejudice swings between the posts of conservative and liberal judicial opinion. This has been a recipe for confusion, ambiguity and uncertainty. On the one hand a divisional court will decide that the publication of a previous murder and terrorist conviction for an Irishman arrested for the murder and attempted murder of British policemen is not a substantial risk of serious prejudice several months before trial. (Attorney General v ITN CoA Crim 1995) On the other hand media coverage of a defendant's previous criminal record in a libel hearing and the publicity following arrest for assaulting a taxi driver will lead a trial judge to decide that the boyfriend of a television soap opera star could not receive a fair trial. Yet the High Court judges trying the newspapers accused of contempt later decided that there had not been a substantial risk of serious prejudice. (Attorney General v MGN Ltd HC 1997)

An appeal court will decide to quash the murder conviction of two London sisters, citing the prejudicial nature of trial coverage as being partly responsible for the miscarriage of justice. Yet a later High Court panel will rule that the Attorney General was correct in not prosecuting the newspapers for contempt of court. (R v Solicitor General ex p. Taylor HC 1995) A previous Attorney General, Lord Goldsmith, made a practice of pre-empting the adjudication of media contempt issues by issuing edicts of what he believed would be contempt in the media coverage of developing crime investigations.

The 2004 prosecution of the *Daily Star* for identifying two Premiership soccer players arrested in a rape enquiry to some extent changed the rules of crime reporting. (Attorney General v Express HC 2004) The paper had rejected advice from Lord Goldsmith not to name the suspected footballers. The then Attorney General's decision to issue the warning and then pursue the subsequent prosecution for contempt has been a source of controversy. (Sanders *Guardian* 2004) The contempt was to the mechanics of the police enquiry rather than the potential damage to the fair trial of the suspects before jury. This is because the Crown Prosecution Service (CPS) decided not to proceed with charges and the decision had nothing to do with the newspaper's coverage of the enquiry. The fine of £60,000 could be considered harsh in the context of punishments for media contempt.

The contempt conviction was based on the argument that the complainant had not known the identities of the players prior to their publication. But it was accepted that if she had scrutinized all of the press published before the *Daily Star*'s article she would have been able to identify the men being questioned. Furthermore, the value of her identification evidence would surely have been her ability to pick out the suspects whether in an identification parade or by recognizing their faces in a media publication. Jo Sanders, a solicitor for media law firm Olswang, said:

> Now that the *Star*'s refusal to comply with the attorney general's guidance not to reveal the identities of the two footballers has been taken to be an aggravating factor in contempt proceedings, many will think this has crossed the line into unacceptable state influence on the media.
>
> (Ibid.)

Contrasting lights in open and secret justice: the USA and UK

The essential differences in UK and US media contempt law are set out in Table 1.15. A selective summary of additional UK court reporting laws is set out in Table 1.16. The prohibitions and prescriptions directed at UK media communicators for the most part simply do not exist in the USA. Coverage of the US justice system is seen as fundamental to American journalism, but judicial/media culture has found a completely different approach to ensuring a criminal defendant's right to a fair trial.

Judges presiding over trial courts achieve this purpose through the regulation of the proceedings before them and not by extending *ultra vires* powers to gag the media with prohibition and postponement orders, as frequently used by British judges under the 1981 Contempt of Court Act. Where it is established that media publicity has generated a risk of prejudice against any criminal defendant, US judges can seek to eradicate prejudicial attitudes through a more detailed process of jury selection; admonitions and directions to the jury to focus on evidence given under oath in court; or changing the venue of the trial. Where the media prejudice is overwhelmingly oppressive, US judges also have the power to delay the trial until the furore and memory of publicity have died down

Table 1.15 Comparison of UK and US media contempt law (protecting the fair trial)

United Kingdom	United States of America
Strict Liability rule 'Substantial risk of serious prejudice'. Applies when a case is active: time of arrest, issuing warrant for arrest, issuing of a summons, oral charging, or when a civil case is set down for trial. (Contempt risk in civil cases is only relevant to libel, false imprisonment and malicious prosecution cases sitting with juries.) There is a defence under Section 5 of the 1981 Contempt of Court Act to protect newspapers, radio/ TV programmes and news online sites that report on public interest subjects that are 'merely incidental' to ongoing trials. The 28-day detention period in terrorist cases, lengthening the period between arrest and charge, combined with the intensity of 24/7 media coverage is shifting observance of the strict liability rule to the time when a charge is made. Campaigning programmes with a partial position could be liable under common law contempt if there is an intention to prejudice a future trial.	The First Amendment makes criminal liability for publication unconstitutional. The US judiciary has much greater confidence in American jurors following directions to strike media prejudice from their minds.

In the case of Nebraska Press Association v Stuart 1976 the Supreme Court ruled that prior restraints that directly infringe media First Amendment rights must be avoided where there are alternative measures that judges can adopt in order to protect an accused person's fair trial rights. In the 1980 case of Richmond Newspapers v Virginia, Chief Justice Burger asserted that the public and media have a strong First Amendment right to attend criminal trials and the courts should do everything possible to avoid closing courtroom doors when Sixth Amendment fair trial rights are threatened. He based his ruling on English and Welsh common law. |
| Section 4(2) orders under the 1981 Contempt of Court Act give judges the power to postpone the reporting of part and whole trials. Such orders need to state clearly what the media is postponed from reporting (extent) and the exact time when the order ceases to apply (usually return of all verdicts). Section 4(1) of the 1981 Contempt of Court Act states that no person can be guilty of contempt for publishing/broadcasting fair, accurate and contemporaneous reports of court proceedings in good faith where no orders have been made. | Ordering the postponement of reporting would be regarded as unconstitutional under the First Amendment.

Prior restraint 'gagging' orders against the media of this kind were effectively outlawed by the US Supreme Court in 1976 in the case of Nebraska Press Association v Stuart. The Justices ruled that pre-trial publicity, even if pervasive and adverse, does not inevitably lead to unfair trials: 'prior restraints on speech and publication are the most serious and the least tolerable infringement'. US judges are expected to deploy 'alternative measures': |
| These orders are usually issued to cover parts of jury trials heard in the absence of the jury where arguments about inadmissible evidence are ventilated. The freedom of expression Article 10 of the Human Rights Act places a legal obligation on courts to minimize the derogation from the open justice principle. | (a) Continuance – delaying trial until prejudicial publicity has died down

(b) Change of venue

(c) Intensive voir dire – questioning members of the jury panel to determine whether they have been prejudiced by media coverage. |

Continued overleaf

Courts have the power to prohibit media publication of matters withheld from the public before the proceedings under section 11 of the 1981 Contempt of Court Act. This relates to anonymous witnesses who fear reprisals, or complainants of blackmail where the threatened menaces are embarrassing. The orders should only be used where the courts had a previous common law power to conceal the information.

These orders are occasionally made in relation to information revealed to the public in open court and this is strictly not empowered by the legislation. Orders that prohibit media reporting should be constructed from the legislation providing the power to do so.

Excluding press and public through 'in chambers' or 'in camera' orders. The practice is common in the British legal system and is almost invariably followed in many Official Secrets Act prosecutions. More recently the appeal court ruled that Crown Court bail applications should be in open court (Malik v Central Criminal Court 2006). Youth courts bar the public, but not accredited journalists. Most family proceedings used to be held in secret, but media campaigning has improved journalist access with plans to allow reporting.

Interviewing/soliciting information from jurors about their deliberations over a verdict is a criminal offence in the UK under section 8 of the 1981 Contempt of Court Act. The contempt offence should not prevent jurors being interviewed about their experiences outside the deliberation process or for their opinions about many aspects of the trial, such as the judge, conduct of lawyers and outcome of the case in terms of verdict and/or sentence. However, the judiciary is very sensitive to media approaches to and dialogue with jurors.

There is a tendency for judges to create a cordon sanitaire around jurors

(d) Jury admonitions – instructing jurors not to read or listen to media coverage.

(e) Sequestration – providing for a supervised location for the jurors throughout the trial to shield them from news reports.

Judges have been allowed to gag trial participants such as lawyers, witnesses, jurors and parties.

The US legal system does not believe in cost and administrative convenience diluting the significance of media rights. Consequently witnesses must be identifiable to the pubic and defendants in criminal trials. These are express constitutional rights. The UK practice of secret witnesses, use of intelligence service dossiers, and 'special advocates' is regarded as authoritarian and unlawful.

The US regards media access to proceedings as vital to First Amendment rights and in 1980 the Supreme Court in Richmond Newspapers v Virginia ruled this to be the case. Any overriding justification would have to be extreme.

However, the open justice constitutional protection does not extend to proceedings that by tradition, practice and custom have been conducted in private. Consequently the protection of juvenile offenders and media access to legal processes involving youth offenders can be as restrictive as in the UK.

It is common practice throughout the USA for jurors to be interviewed about their experiences and deliberation of verdicts. In fact it is a significant right exercised by attorneys in many US states following a verdict in order to assess the nature of their case presentation and the impact of evidence. US judges sometimes maintain dignity and control through gagging orders on jurors during trials when there is high media interest in a case. On rare occasions federal judges trying sensitive 'terrorist' in terms of their identity. Sketching, photographing and filming of jurors could be considered 'impeding' the administration of justice. This is despite the fact that jurors answer to their names when sworn and are rarely concealed in public proceedings.

Sexual offence complainants in the UK have lifetime anonymity and journalists who breach this face criminal investigation under the Sexual Offences Amendment Acts 1976 and 1992. Other 'vulnerable witnesses' are given anonymity protection under various acts of Parliament and common law precedents and these include blackmail complainants and witnesses who fear reprisals, state investigators and firearms specialists. UK anonymity restrictions also extend to the deceased victims of crime and defendants in situations of 'jigsaw identification'. The British judiciary are also prepared to issue gagging injunctions to protect notorious criminals from vigilante reprisals and undermining of health as a result of media identification and publicity.

Under the Children and Young Person's Act 1933 there are restrictions to ensure secrecy and anonymity for children/ youths involved in adult criminal and civil legal proceedings. The London High Court has begun to use Section 11 and inherent jurisdictional powers to confer anonymity to witnesses in civil proceedings on the basis of developing media privacy law. In two civil trials women employed in the sex industry were protected by anonymity provisions. One of the women employed to participate in sadomasochistic sessions by the head of Formula 1 racing, Max Mosley, was referred to throughout the case as Witness E. Although unable to give evidence during the privacy hearing, she was visible and identifiable in a post-trial interview with Sky News.

crimes where jurors are in fear of reprisals have concealed the identification of sworn jurors. The more liberal and freedom of expression participation of lay jurors means that criminal justice academics have access to a wide range of qualitative and quantitative surveys on the impact of media publicity on juries trying criminal and civil cases.

Journalists cannot be held liable for revealing the name of a rape victim whose identity was obtained through open court records: 'Once true information is disclosed in public court documents open to public inspection, the press cannot be sanctioned for publishing it' (Cox Broadcasting Corporation v Cohn, SC US 1975). In Florida Star v BJF 1989 the Supreme Court held that a newspaper could not be held liable for negligence where it published the name of a rape victim whose identity was obtained from a police report. US journalists have a tradition of exercising ethical discretion in relation to sex offence complainants. The US judiciary and media bodies also liaise through committees and voluntary discussion panels to moderate policy on the impact of publicity.

In Oklahoma Publishing Co v District Court 1977, the Supreme Court ruled that the First Amendment barred a judge from prohibiting the media from printing the name of a juvenile murder suspect who had been identified at a court hearing open to the media. In Smith v Daily Mail Publishing Co in 1979 the Supreme Court ruled that a newspaper could not be held liable for publishing the name of a juvenile charged with murder, in violation of a state statute requiring the permission of the juvenile court prior to publication. These cases demonstrate that federal law and the First Amendment trump any case law or statutes passed in the US states themselves.

Table 1.16 Selective summary of additional UK court reporting laws

Reporting of preliminary Magistrates' Court hearings for offences tried by jury at the Crown Court or 'either way' offences

Under section 8 of the 1980 Magistrates' Court Act journalists should limit their reports to:

(a) the identity of the court and the names of the examining justices
(b) the names, addresses and occupations of the parties and witnesses and ages of the accused and witnesses
(c) the offence(s) or a summary of them with which the accused is charged
(d) the names of the legal representatives engaged in the proceedings
(e) any decision of the court to commit/transfer the accused or any of them for trial and any decision of the court on disposal of the case of any of the accused not committed
(f) the charge(s) on which the accused, or any of them have been committed/ transferred and the court to which they have been committed/transferred.
(g) the date and place to which committal proceedings have been adjourned, if adjourned
(h) any arrangements as to bail on committal or adjournment
(i) whether a right to representation funded by the Legal Services Commission as part of the Criminal Defence Service was granted to the accused or any of the accused
(j) whether the court has decided to lift or not to lift these reporting restrictions.

These restrictions have been known in many media law textbooks as 'the 10 points'. In practice, the UK media have found that any factual report respecting these criteria will not face prosecution when it includes an element of uncontroversial colour. For example, describing how the accused is dressed and the presence of relatives or newsworthy people in the public gallery is unlikely to create prejudice or attract prosecution. Avoid reporting objections to bail, the previous convictions of the accused and prosecution or defence allegations.

Reporting hearings at the Crown Court prior to or at the beginning of a trial

'Preparatory' hearings are sometimes held at the beginning of long and complex criminal trials to resolve evidential/case management issues and applications by the defence that there is no case to answer. Under the 1996 Criminal Procedure and Investigations Act reports of such hearings are restricted to: 1) name of the court and the judge; 2) names, ages, home addresses and occupations of accused and witnesses; 3) charges or a summary of them; 4) names of lawyers; 5) date and place to which proceedings are adjourned; 6) arrangements as to bail; 7) whether legal aid was granted. The vast majority of pre-trial hearings at the Crown Court are not covered by these restrictions. These include 'plea and direction' hearings. Obviously, guilty pleas that will be followed by sentence hearings should be reportable. Care should be taken not to report matters that could create a substantial risk of serious prejudice to a future trial in situations where the judge has not made a section 4(2) postponing order under the 1981 Contempt of Court Act.

Reporting bail applications

Bail applications at Magistrates' Courts have always been held in open court, but this was not the case at the Crown Court, where they were held 'in chambers' in other words in private. However, in Malik v Central Criminal Court 2006 Mr Justice Gray ruled that such applications should normally be held in public.

Reporting Youth Courts

Nothing should be reported that could lead to identification of the youth or the school that an accused youth or witness attends. Only reporters are permitted access to Youth Court proceedings. Breaches of Anti-Social Behaviour Orders (ASBOs) are brought before Youth Courts. The blanket anonymity applying to these courts is empowered from section 49 of the Children and Young Persons Act 1933. In 2005 the law was amended so that Youth Court justices have to make an order if they wish ASBO breaching youths to retain their anonymity.

Reporting Family hearings

At Magistrates' Courts on the occasions when these proceedings are in open court you can only report: names, addresses and occupations of the parties and witnesses, a concise statement of the charges, the defence and counter-charges in support of which evidence has been given, submissions on any point of law arising in the course of the case, and the decision of the court, the judgment of the court and the observations of the judge. Under section 69(2) of the Magistrates' Court Act 1980, journalists cannot be excluded from family proceedings unless the court is dealing with adoption arrangements or with evidence involving indecency. At County Court and Family Division High Court level from April 2009 only accredited journalists have access to the proceedings. Judges have discretion to exclude reporters if it is in the interest of any child related to the proceeding, for the safety and protection of parties, witnesses or persons connected, and for the orderly conduct of the proceedings, such as a situation where there is no space to accommodate the journalist(s). Under Section 12 of the Administration of Justice Act 1960 when the private hearing is in respect of minors, or proceedings under the 1989 Children Act, it will be a contempt of court to publish any information about the hearing. A rule under the 2006 Court of Appeal case known as Clayton v Clayton means that the restrictions applying from the Children Act 1989 do not apply when the proceedings have ended. This means the ban on identifying the child concerned in the proceedings ends with the termination of the court case. However, judges can and do issue separate court orders preserving confidentiality for children until they are 18. In 2009 Justice Minister Jack Straw said he intended to relax reporting restrictions of family proceedings to make them equivalent to those applying to reporting of the Youth Court.

Continued overleaf

In camera/in chambers

These expressions normally mean that the court hearing has been in private with the press and public excluded, but the Administration of Justice Act 1960 states that publication of a report of a hearing in these circumstances will not be a contempt, unless the case concerns the 1989 Children Act, wardship proceedings involving children, proceedings under the 1959 Mental Health Act, national security issues relating to the 1989 Official Secrets Act, or secret processes and confidential matters such as disputes involving patents, inventions or the financial viability of banks or building societies. It is unlikely that fair and accurate reports of private hearings will carry qualified privilege unless the information emerges from a press conference held by one of the parties to the hearing.

---

and to sequestrate jurors from family, social and media influences. The US federal and state governments, through constitutional obligation and Supreme Court scrutiny, cannot sacrifice First Amendment rights for the purpose of economic convenience.

Judicial precedent from the Supreme Court has established that criminal trial judges have a constitutional obligation to use tools for combating media prejudice that do not infringe First Amendment media rights. The line of authority from *Stroble v California* in 1952 to *Press Enterprise v Superior Court I and II* in 1986 was clear. Gag orders and secret hearings represent unlawful prior restraints on the right of the media to report criminal proceedings. They would only be countenanced in the most rare of circumstances and the weight of evidence that the courts would need to show that such draconian remedies were necessary has to be very high.

Socially and culturally, the spectre of court television confirms that the USA is a country where the media have a constitutional right of access to criminal court cases (*Richmond Newspapers v Virginia* 1980) and this right extends to other kinds of proceedings with a tradition of openness and where it has been shown historically that public access serves a significant function. In *Press Enterprise v Superior Court I and II* in 1986 this related to attending preliminary hearings of criminal prosecutions and having access to the record of what took place.

Consequently the UK Contempt of Court Act strict liability rule on active court cases, restrictions on use of television and radio, prohibition on interviewing jurors about their deliberations, and formalized media gagging orders on reporting trials set out in Table 1.15 are alien concepts and practices in the USA. The same can be said for the top three categories of additional UK court reporting laws in Table 1.16. However, the restrictions set out in relation to reporting youth/juvenile courts, family hearings and any other legal forum that has a tradition of confidentiality do not clash with First Amendment rights, and state privacy laws and legislative statutes justifiably bite on the information that American journalists can legally use in their reports.

Lyle W. Denniston relates that the US juvenile court system is the only branch of law that 'almost complete from start to finish, goes forward under a regime of secrecy.' (Denniston 1992: 147) The cloak of confidentiality is perpetuated by a combination of law and media ethics. American jurisprudence fully recognizes the privacy of the child and the idea that exposure of the errors of youth can have lasting consequences. But Denniston advises that the juvenile system, as with any other dimension of law enforcement, is an important function that requires scrutiny and observance. However, he accepts that 'in reality, the system has been left largely to govern itself.' (Ibid.: 151) It is an area of society that has the attention of sociologists and criminologists, and in 1974 two scholars, Paul Nejelski and Judith LaPook, concluded that the mainstream and local media needed to play a greater role in giving the complex and non-integrated system of US juvenile justice some method of accountability:

> Individual components of the juvenile justice system have not been required either to give reasons for their decision making or to give accounts of their performance. Consequently, their activities often are not observed and the impact of their programs is rarely measurable. [...]
>
> ... each system – law enforcement, education, social service and mental health – has the power to reject cases, divert them to nonjudicial process or arrange for court hearings and judicially mandated treatment. As a result, large numbers of children may be dealt with by the various systems with little external control.
>
> (Ibid.)

The US divorce or 'Domestic Relations' legal system is primarily state based. The power to legislate in the area of family law is deferred by the federal government to the state legislatures. Consequently the method of litigation and legal administration varies from state to state and there will be varying frameworks of privacy laws affecting the journalists' reporting and access rights. Denniston advises that special judicial proceedings involving the adoption of children and commitment of mentally ill people to treatment are customarily conducted in 'closed proceedings, and thus are not open to press coverage.' (Ibid.: 206)

The difficulties that secret justice in family law can generate, which have been so vividly amplified in the United Kingdom, have had a similar debate in America, though on a much more local scale. Ashley Gauthier, in a 2001 article 'Are Secret Courts in the Best Interest of the Child?' investigated cases in New Mexico where parents had been complaining about social workers taking their three-year-old child from them on the grounds she was overweight. Gauthier reported that childcare experts believed children are traumatized by media coverage, but that on the other hand 'children can be harmed if the public is denied access to information about certain cases.' (Gauthier 2001: 15) The states of Minnesota and Michigan allowed journalists access to child protection hearings, and Judge Heidi Schellhas, in an article for the *William Mitchell Law Review*, reflected that the open hearing policy had brought about benefits, as compared to the traditional secrecy that usually accompanied this area of the law:

> my experiences suggested that such secrecy did not protect the children, but rather served only to protect stakeholders in the system and parents accused of child abuse or neglect. Such parents could use closed courtroom proceedings to exclude any relatives, friends or neighbors who had information about or were interested in the child's welfare. Later, parents could depict [child protection agencies], the court and other stakeholders as the oppressors.
>
> (Ibid.)

Defamation – protecting reputation

English and Welsh law in this area can be accused of being constructed to protect the rich and powerful, and as a result it is argued that it has become a major chilling effect on freedom of expression. It is an unusual area of negligence law in that every other aspect of the negligence civil wrong has a much higher threshold of protection for the defendant. In the USA media defendants do not have the burden of proof on truth or justification and damages are only awarded when it can be proved there has been harm. In the UK the practice of uplifting winners' legal costs in conditional fee agreements means that the advice of insurance companies is likely to determine the battle lines in defending libel proceedings and there is the risk that their decisions are based on profit and loss rather than truth/justice and freedom of expression.

The British MP Andrew Pelling wished to clarify misconceptions on how Conditional Fee Agreements (CFAs) actually operated, in a debate in the House of Commons in 2008:

> If the case is lost, the lawyer gets nothing. If the case is won, the lawyer is entitled to be paid his basic charges in addition to a success fee, which is a percentage uplift on the basic charges. The winning client is entitled to seek to recover from the losing opponent his reasonable costs, which are assessed by the court if not agreed, and which may include a reasonable success fee and a reasonable after-the-event insurance premium.
>
> Both the level of the success fee and the amount of the premium are also subject to assessment by the court if the costs cannot be agreed.

Success fees are typically staggered. If a case is settled before proceedings are issued, the success fee will normally be capped at 25 per cent. It only increases to 100 per cent if the case looks like it will progress to trial, where the risks are much higher. The availability of ATE insurance means that if a client loses, the insurance will cover – up to a maximum of the indemnity in the original policy – the newspaper defendant's cost. It is clear that libel lawyers under CFAs act for many people who are on income support, including individuals who may well have been falsely accused of extremely serious crimes.

(*Hansard* 17 December 2008 Column 76WH–77WH)

It is argued that if libel in the UK is a form of gambling, the dice are loaded against journalists. It is also argued that the UK has been less enthusiastic, and late in recognizing a no fault public interest defence for journalism in *Reynolds v The Times* (1999) and *Jameel v Wall Street Journal* (2006).

US defamation law, by contrast

An attempt to map the essentials of English and Welsh defamation law is set out in Table 1.17. The USA established a much higher protection of freedom of speech in libel through the case of *Sullivan v New York Times* (1964). Public interest plaintiffs/claimants have to prove actual malice or a reckless disregard for the truth. Reference has already been made to the postulation by Supreme Court Justices Black and Douglas that perhaps there should not be a defamation law at all; an interesting and Utopian idea that would work were it not for the fact that human beings appear to have an unlimited capacity to fabricate and spit poisonous lies and gossip about other people and pay handsomely for the entertainment in reading, hearing and watching it.

US defamation law shares with Britain a twin civil wrong for written libel and spoken slander but in practice and across the fifty states of the union the definitions and applications are more or less the same. They tend to include the phrasing of subjecting people to public 'hatred, contempt or ridicule'. The broad objective is to protect the right to reputation. Individual persons and companies can sue.

The paths of US and UK defamation turned away from each other at the crossroads of 1964. The US Supreme Court in *Sullivan v New York Times* began to create a bifurcation between the public interest and private individual plaintiff. In order to succeed in an action against a media communicator in the USA the plaintiff, whether public interest or private, has to prove to the court that a defamatory message tending to injure reputation has been published to a third party, that the message is false (unlike in England and Wales, where there is a presumption of

Table 1.17 The essentials of English and Welsh defamation law

---

Libel factors

Libel is lowering the estimation of right-thinking members of society generally, exposing somebody to hatred, ridicule or contempt, causing somebody to be shunned or avoided, or damaging them in their trade, profession, work, or office. Libel can be by innuendo, depends on the natural meaning of words, and can also involve the expression of language that arouses extreme pity. TV journalists must be careful of sound track commentary libelling individuals identifiable in visual footage. This is libel by association.

Libel has to be published to a third party (an audience of one will do), involve defaming somebody who is alive and not dead, and the person defamed has to be referred to and can be identified by implication. The libel writ must be issued within a year of publication. Groups of defamed people can sue together. It seems the group factor does not exceed twenty-five.

Public authorities and government bodies cannot sue. There is a continuing debate among media law jurists over whether trade unions and associations can sue for libel per se.

Private and public companies can sue. Lifting or following up libellous stories from one medium to the next means that you are in danger of repeating the libel. If you review or use a libellous story in radio/television from newspapers you are still liable.

Judges decide whether words are capable of a defamatory meaning. Juries decide the facts. Sometimes judges sit alone to decide meaning and facts, as in the McDonald's libel case – the longest running in British legal history.

Fair comment

An expression of an honestly held opinion, based on true facts, on a matter of public interest and without malice. The comment should be recognizable as comment based on facts that are true or protected by privilege and the comment should be made by an honest person however prejudiced he might be, and however exaggerated or obstinate his views.

Innocent dissemination

This is available for live broadcasters and Internet publishers. When a libel comes out of the blue from a guest or radio/TV participant you will have a defence if you took reasonable steps to prevent the publication and did all you could to mitigate the sting of the libel when it was uttered or written.

Justification

The story needs to be true in substance and fact. In England and Wales, the burden of proof is on the media defendant and not the claimant. You need credible witnesses and evidence to persuade a jury on the balance of probabilities. This is expensive to defend. The current nature of the justification defence does not assist investigative journalism.

Absolute privilege and qualified privilege

Court reporting if fair, accurate and contemporaneous (published to nearest deadline) will be absolutely privileged. This defence applies to publications by Parliament and the words of parliamentarians. The point about absolute privilege is that it is a defence to report libels expressed by people in court that they know to be untrue. Malice cannot undermine the defence of absolute privilege.

Qualified privilege – 'subject to explanation or contradiction'. This defence applies to fair and accurate reports of public meetings, local authority meetings, and statements from government bodies (including the police). It is useful to remember that firefighter, ambulance/paramedic, and coastguard bulletins are not privileged.

'Subject to explanation or contradiction' means that if somebody accused of something wants to put their side of the story you should report it within a reasonable amount of time. Press conferences and the press releases connected to the conferences are covered by this category of qualified privilege but they need to be held for 'a lawful purpose'.

Qualified privilege – This defence applies to fair and accurate reports of past court hearings, and parliamentary proceedings. Only the malice of the reporter or publishing organization can undo this defence.

Public interest qualified privilege

The Jameel/Reynolds defence arises out of two House of Lords cases: *Albert Reynolds v Times Newspapers* 1999 and *Jameel v Wall Street Journal* 2006. In the first case Lord Nicholls set out a ten-point framework for responsible journalism that could in certain circumstances mean that journalism produced in the public interest that had wrongly defamed individual(s) should not be liable for libel action.

The Nicholls pointers on responsible journalism: 1) the seriousness of the allegation. The more serious the charge, the more the public is misinformed and the individual harmed, if the allegation is not true; 2) the nature of the information, and the extent to which the subject is a matter of public concern; 3) the source of the information. Some informants have no direct knowledge of the events. Some have their own axes to grind, or are being paid for their stories; 4) the steps taken to verify the information; 5) the status of the information. The allegation may have already been the subject of an investigation which commands respect; 6) the urgency of the matter. News is often a perishable commodity; 7) whether comment was sought from the claimant. He may have information others do not possess or have not disclosed. An approach to the claimant will not always be necessary; 8) whether the article contained the gist of the claimant's side of the story; 9) the tone of the article. A newspaper can raise queries or call for an investigation. It need not adopt allegations as statements of fact; 10) the circumstances of the publication, including the timing. The list is not exhaustive. It is important for broadcast journalists to maintain a neutral and impartial approach to reporting. The *Daily Telegraph* lost the Reynolds defence argument in its libel dispute with George Galloway MP because the edition carrying reports of allegations based on documents found in Baghdad included editorial comment that appeared to be hostile and biased against Mr Galloway.

Continued overleaf

Despite the initial optimism that the 'Reynolds Defence' would strengthen freedom of expression as a paradigm in the law of defamation, subsequent cases demonstrated the opposite. The media complained that the High Court had a tendency to apply all ten criteria as the test of responsible journalism particularly when the allegations were judged to be very serious. Editors were beginning to describe the 'Reynolds Defence' as a false dawn perpetuating the impression that English libel law was claimant friendly.

In the Jameel 2006 case the Law Lords decided the defence should turn on two issues: whether an article was on a matter of public interest and whether it was the product of responsible journalism. They said Lord Nicholls' ten factors should be useful pointers and not tests to be satisfied or hurdles to be jumped. The Law Lords emphasized the importance of revitalizing freedom of expression by ensuring that journalism in the public interest should not be undermined by libel laws. They also warned judges not to second-guess the professional decisions that editors have to make under the pressure of deadlines. As a result of the Jameel ruling, in 2007 investigative journalist Graeme McLagan, who had lost on a Reynolds libel defence over his book on police corruption *Bent Coppers* in the High Court, succeeded in his appeal. Mr McLagan was a widely respected investigative journalist who had specialized in reporting police affairs for more than twenty years. He used court reports of trial proceedings in his book. However, the Court of Appeal supported the High Court judge's view that he was not entitled to the 'neutral reportage' defence.

'Neutral reportage' is being recognized as a dimension of the Reynolds public interest/qualified privilege defence. In a nutshell, it extends a defence to the attributed and neutral reporting of allegations and counter-allegations by parties to a political dispute in which the public has a legitimate interest. In the 2006 case *Roberts v Searchlight* two members of the British National Party sought to sue the anti-fascist magazine *Searchlight*, its editor and journalist. Mr Justice Eady ruled that the 'neutral reportage' defence could be available even where the journalists had not been neutral. The key test was the manner of reporting. The magazine argued that it had merely reported allegations against the BNP members without adopting or endorsing them. The judge highlighted the importance of reporting both sides in a disinterested way.

falsity), that the message has identified the plaintiff (as in England and Wales, identification can be by implication and the defamatory meaning by innuendo) and there has been fault on the part of the communicator (a requirement in negligence common law, but excluded in English and Welsh defamation law). In the case of public interest plaintiffs the fault proved has to be at the high standard of 'actuated by malice' or a demonstration of 'reckless disregard for the truth'. The proof of the negligence has to be up to the standard of 'clear and convincing'. In the state of Ohio this standard of proof also applies to private plaintiffs. The state of New York has developed a 'gross irresponsibility' standard of care to cover situations involving private plaintiffs involved in matters of legitimate public concern. In the majority of other states the plaintiff usually only has to prove negligence or a lack of 'reasonable care' on the part of the defendant, which is still a situation considered more favourable than in the UK, where the burden of proof in justification is always with the defendant.

In a series of cases the Supreme Court has tried to provide guidance on how the distinction between public interest and private plaintiffs is achieved. In the 1985 libel case of *Gertz v Welch*, Justice Lewis Powell endeavoured to define two genres of public figures: all-purpose public figures who are widely known and have prominent positions in society, such as politicians and celebrities, and who clearly exercise power, patronage and influence; and limited or 'vortex' figures who voluntarily step into the public gaze and are actors endeavouring to change the outcome of a public interest controversy. The elements of voluntary entrance and intending to change the outcome of public controversy must be shown in order to qualify for the status of limited public figure. Justice Powell also made it clear that such people reverted to their private status after leaving the limelight of the news event or controversy. (Sadler 2005: 157)

The USA has similar libel defences to the UK and the most effective are truth and constitutional privilege. In constitutional privilege public officials and public figures have to adduce clear and convincing evidence of actual malice. Truth is an absolute defence. Clearly the constitutional privilege means that defaming a public official or figure by mistake is also a defence so long as there was no provable intention to defame and the conduct of the media communicator was so incompetent and negligent that it could be shown he/she was reckless as to whether the plaintiff were defamed or not.

The private plaintiffs need only show negligence on the part of a media defendant to win their case and the burden of proof is on the balance of probabilities. As in England and Wales, there are other similar defences such as fair comment, the privilege of reporting fairly and accurately the content of public proceedings and documents, and neutral reportage, which was a US origination. US states support defences not available in the UK and these include, anti-SLAPP (see below), the news wire defence and the defence of public retraction. Broadcasting or publishing a retraction in many states can place a ceiling and block on damages and costs.

Neutral reportage developed from a federal appellate case *Edwards v National Audubon Society, Inc* in 1977 and the principle established was that the media would be shielded from libel judgments if they had reported defamatory content in a fair, neutral and accurate fashion in the context of newsworthy allegations made by others about public officials or public figures. No official or public setting would be required. (Zelezny 2004: 154) However, in 2006 Kyu Ho Youm reported that recent federal court rulings had demonstrated a fair amount of hostility among judges toward claims of neutral reportage, leaving media lawyers hesitant to pursue it as a libel defence. (Kyu Ho Youm 2006: 58) The US wire service defence is unknown in the UK and offers an element of justice to media organizations that have unknowingly republished defamatory news stories from reputable news agency sources without substantial change and without having any reasonable suspicion that the articles might be legally problematical.

Another key difference in libel between the UK and USA is that the American courts generally require plaintiffs to prove that they have suffered damage or injury as the result of defamatory publication. Presumed damages are prohibited unless the public interest plaintiff can demonstrate that the defendant acted with actual malice. Proof of actual injury is required in all cases that involve matters of public concern and where actual malice has not been shown. Special damages can only be awarded to compensate a plaintiff if he can prove the actual pecuniary loss. Punitive damages cannot be recovered without a showing of actual malice. And some states have raised the threshold of demonstrable malice to the level of 'common law malice, i.e. ill-will, spite or vengeance'. (Rich 1995: 20–1)

Private plaintiffs have to offer solid evidence of their injuries and this must be tangible and intangible. Some states block the award of even presumed damages to private plaintiffs in matters of public concern unless they can prove actual malice.

Why are the British so different?

This disparity in media legal culture between the apparent sunshine of the USA and arctic climate of the UK requires explanation. It might be argued that the slow move to a no fault defence in Britain was sabotaged by a more widespread anti-journalism cultural prejudice that included politics and the law. It could be argued that the balance of justice is against the interests of journalism in the operation of many aspects of English and Welsh defamation law. The phenomenon of libel tourism, so that foreign nationals can sue in the English courts even if only a few copies of the magazine, book or newspaper have been sold in the English jurisdiction, has already been analysed as an allegedly unfavourable infringement on freedom of expression.

These disincentives to journalistic freedom are exacerbated by those rare cases of well-known claimants convicted of perjury to gain an advantage in adversarial litigation and exploiting the contingency of prejudiced juries who tend to be overenthusiastic in awarding damages designed to punish the mythology of intrusive and harmful journalism.

The McLibel case demonstrates that perhaps only the impecunious and determined, who have nothing financial to lose, and with a political/ideological cause that fits in with a fashionable consensus (pro-environment and anti-fast food) are likely to be able to effectively challenge the rich and powerful in the libel arena and partly win with a justification defence. The verdict was that Helen Steel and David Morris were not able to justify all of the defamatory meanings contained in the original leaflet and McDonald's were awarded £60,000 though took no action to enforce judgment. The defendants' advocacy in person had been Herculean. They successfully appealed against some of the justification findings and the damages were reduced by £20,000. Prior to the litigation McDonald's private detectives attending London campaign meetings equalled the number of anti-fast food activists. It should be mentioned that London Greenpeace had no connection with the global Greenpeace pressure group. Denied legal aid, Ms Steel and Mr Morris had their lives taken over by the case for a period equivalent to some life sentences. They stubbornly refused to give in and eventually the ECHR ruled that the case was a breach of the right to freedom of expression and the right to a fair trial. (Steel & Morris v United Kingdom ECHR 2005)

Hooper writes 'McDonald's had won on points, but their victory was a public relations disaster.' (Hooper 2001:174) Had the corporation sued in the US courts, its action may have had a different course in US law and it is possible that it would have been blocked by an emerging defence to civil defamation claims known as 'anti-SLAPP'. By 2004 nineteen US states had enacted statutes to provide protection against 'strategic lawsuits against public participation'. Anti-SLAPP laws provide:

> specific statutory protection against law suits of questionable merit that are filed to stifle political expression. Generally the statutes provide for an early dismissal of the claim and recovery of legal fees. The laws originate from a study that found that libel, slander and other suits were being filed against people who would testify, protest or speak out on certain public issues such as zoning, land use issues.
>
> (OSCE 2005: 173)

There are many aspects of English and Welsh defamation law that could be reformed. Unlike contempt, there is no standard phrase or sentence of definition. The benchmark maxims that libel is lowering the estimation of right-thinking members of society generally, exposing somebody to hatred, ridicule or contempt, causing somebody to be shunned or avoided, or damaging them in their trade, profession, work or office, appear to belong to an age when the aristocracy and bourgeoisie were anxious about what their servants were reading and the only people travelling on the top deck of the Clapham Omnibus were male, middle-aged and heterosexually married. The fact that libel can be by innuendo depends on the natural meaning of words and can also involve the expression of language that arouses extreme pity means that the author is effectively dead à la Roland Barthes. Roland Barthes was a French structuralist/

post-structuralist philosopher who argued that the author should not be regarded as the origin of his/her text or the authority for its meaning; hence the title of his well-known essay 'The Death of the Author', first published in 1968.

Can there really be freedom of expression if the law decides that the construction of meaning is always by audience and that authorial intention is irrelevant? In fact, in most disputed libel cases the potential libel meaning is decided by judges. And it is the judges who have set out the ideological frame of what should be permitted as 'responsible journalism'. Lord Nicholls, in the Reynolds ruling of 1999, with good intentions, set out ten criteria as some kind of journalistic Decalogue, and for the media defendants trying to sustain the defence they could have been forgiven for thinking it was an Old Testament ethical code of immutable and universal laws set out in the Ten Commandments collected from Mount Sinai by Moses. The libel judges, whose discretion it was to decide whether the media defendants should be availed of the qualified privilege, had a tendency to require that serious defamations required most if not all of the Law Lord's criteria for responsible journalism. It is somewhat ironic that the Law Lords decided that the *Sunday Times*, in its reporting of the allegations connected to the resignation of Irish Taoiseach Albert Reynolds, did not merit the public benefit of qualified privilege defence. This is because the journalists had not complied with enough of the criteria set out by Lord Nicholls. It was also arguable whether this ruling created a new qualified privilege defence. It may have been a case of changing the threshold for the long-standing common law legal, moral or social duty to publish material and a corresponding duty or interest in receiving it.

As a result, journalists who made honest mistakes could only be protected from libel actions if they effectively jumped ten hurdles of conduct that included proving they gave a right to reply, reported it fairly, properly evaluated the credibility of their sources, avoided sensationalism, and selected a story in the public interest.

The *Daily Telegraph* lost the 'Reynolds defence' argument in its libel dispute with the MP George Galloway because he was not given a fair chance to comment on allegations unsupported by documents found in Baghdad combined with hostile and biased editorial comment.

It may be unfortunate for journalists that only judges can decide whether a publication is entitled to this class of qualified privilege defence. It depends on whether you prefer the journalist's fate to be at the mercy of judicial or jury adjudication. The effect of this situation is that judges have been cast into the role of legal regulators on what will be regarded as 'responsible journalism'. It was also unfortunate that, despite the initial optimism that the 'Reynolds defence' would strengthen freedom of expression as a paradigm in the law of defamation, subsequent cases demonstrated the opposite. High Court Judges such as Mr Justice Gray and Mr Justice Eady tended to apply the criteria too strictly or elevated and prioritized criteria such as 'the seriousness of the allegation' to the point where 'the gravity of the allegations "permeates through and affects most, if not all, of the other tests".' (Butterworth *Guardian* 2004) This was the fate of the *Wall Street Journal* at the first High Court hearing of the Jameel libel action. Siobhain Butterworth, Head of Legal Affairs at the *Guardian*, argued at the time that the High Court ruling in *Jameel v Wall Street Journal* and Lord Hutton's report gave cold comfort to news organizations hoping to rely on the 'Reynolds defence' for reports based on unidentified sources. She stated:

> In these cases Reynolds privilege should perhaps be seen as an umbrella which a journalist may struggle to open out when an allegation he has published turns out to be either untrue or impossible to prove – and which is easily blown inside out and rendered a useless form of protection.

> (Ibid.)

Jameel v Wall Street Journal, House of Lords 2006: the US fighting to improve British libel law

In 2006, the UK House of Lords heard the appeal in the case of Jameel, a Saudi Arabian businessman and his company against the *Wall Street Journal*. In their ruling the Law Lords sought to create a more liberal climate for media libel defendants. Lord Nicholls' ten criteria were no longer deontological commandments from the Old Testament, meaning the imposition of duties or obligations on journalists in order to qualify for the defence, and judges should not second-guess editors who had to make decisions under the pressures of intense deadlines and where the opportunities to investigate, check and verify are limited. It is important to realize that this 'public interest' defence for honest mistakes is granted by judges and not by jury verdict; and by judges who are appointed from a very narrow ethnic, gender and class base.

It has been argued that the House of Lords' ruling has nuanced the Reynolds defence in favour of journalists. Lord Bingham said Lord Nicholls' famous list of circumstances for responsible journalism should be interpreted as pointers, not hurdles. He said: 'The publisher is protected if he has taken such steps as a responsible journalist would try to take and ensure that what is published is accurate and fit for publication.' (Jameel v Wall Street Journal HL 2006) Lord Bingham added:

> consideration should be given to the thrust of the article which the publisher has published. If the thrust of the article is true, and the public interest condition is satisfied, the inclusion of an inaccurate

103

fact may not have the same appearance of irresponsibility as it might
if the whole thrust of the article is untrue.

(Ibid.)

The Reynolds case emphasized the importance of realizing that it is
good journalistic practice to put a damaging story to the subject before
publication. But in the *Jameel* case the Law Lords accepted and supported
the view that an approach to the claimant is not always necessary. Lord
Hoffmann argued: 'It might have been better if the newspaper had delayed
publication to give Mr Jameel an opportunity to comment in person. But
I do not think that their failure to do so is enough to deprive them of the
defence that they were reporting on a matter of public interest.' It may
be obvious to every journalist trying to absorb the complexities of this
defence that media law in this area of defamation is twisting and turning
on subtle principles and a sophisticated combination of circumstances. It
is a reminder of how much critical and investigative British journalism is
becoming reliant on a framework of legalized evaluation and approval
where the stakes are high in terms of costs and time if challenged in the
courts through the libel laws.

So the Jameel case was an example of so-called 'libel tourism' that
actually benefited British journalism and improved the prospect of UK
media groups and any foreign media publishing by old media or new
media within UK borders to enjoy a much more tolerant libel by mistake
defence. The strident criticism of UK libel by the consortium of US media
in their written submission to the House of Commons Select Committee
on Culture, Media and Sport declared:

> The Wall Street Journal in *Jameel v Dow Jones* put up the money
> and won a major victory in refurbishing the *Reynolds* public inter-
> est defence. However, Dow Jones only received part of its costs.
> Nonetheless the case exposed how libel judges from libel chambers
> had been sabotaging the *Reynolds* public interest defence since 1999,
> when it was developed by the House of Lords. Is it not a matter of
> some embarrassment to UK legislators that freedom of speech in the
> UK is dependent on the long purse of foreign news organisations?

> That long purse is no longer available. Several major US papers are
> now in receivership, and the drying up of the advertising market with
> consequent loss of journalistic jobs means there is little money avail-
> able for improving media law in Britain. Leading US newspapers are
> actively considering abandoning the supply of the 200 odd copies they
> make available for sale in London – mainly to Americans who want
> full details of their local news and sport. They do not make profits out
> of these minimal and casual sales and they can no longer risk losing

millions of dollars in a libel action which they would never face under US law. Does the UK really want to be seen as the only country in Europe – indeed in the world – where important US papers cannot be obtained in print form?

(H of C Select Committee 2009, Advance Publications, Inc et al: paras 12–13)

The essential philosophical weakness of English and Welsh defamation law is that intention is no defence. Furthermore, it will operate as a mechanism of censorship and controlling freedom of expression, sometimes in an authoritarian way, as long as the construction of meaning is based on a false belief of 'objectivity' in audience perception. Another way of understanding the jurisprudential flaw in defamation is that the subjectivity of authorship is shifted to the subjectivity of readership. The injustice lies in the judgment of subjectivity by readership.

English and Welsh law could be criticized for being inconsistent in maintaining a much higher standard of liability and proof for negligence compared to that of defamation. In negligence there is a need to recognize duty of care, breach of duty, causation of damage and the concept that damage was a reasonably foreseeable consequence. In libel defamation no damage has to be proved at all. It many respects it is a law depending on the upholding of the power of human ego, and compensating people for damage to their feelings. It is a remedy for the body emotional. As a result it can be argued that, in many cases, defamation serves to make truth a casualty by narrowing the horizon of freedom of expression.

Neutral reportage

'Neutral reportage' in England and Wales is being recognized as a dimension of the Reynolds public interest/qualified privilege defence and it was clearly inspired by the development of the defence in America. In a nutshell, it extends a defence to the attributed and neutral reporting of allegations and counter-allegations by parties to a political dispute in which the public have a legitimate interest. In the case of *Al-Fagih v HH Saudi Research & Marketing* in 2001 the London Court of Appeal ruled that where a newspaper had reported in an entirely objective way an allegation about someone made in the course of a political dispute by one of his opponents, it was entitled to the Reynolds defence. Furthermore, the newspaper did not lose its defence merely because it had not verified the allegation. A further case in 2006, *Roberts v Searchlight*, involved two members of the British National Party who sought to sue the anti-fascist magazine *Searchlight*, its editor and journalist. In this case Mr Justice Eady ruled that the 'neutral reportage' defence could be available even where the journalists had not been neutral. The key test was the manner of reporting. The magazine argued that it had merely reported allegations against the BNP members without adopting or endorsing them. The judge highlighted the importance of reporting both sides in a disinterested way. The advantage of this defence is that reviewing newspaper and media coverage of a dispute that involves libellous allegations should not attract a libel action in itself, provided that the reportage does not endorse the allegations in any way.

False light (USA) and malicious falsehood (UK)

In England and Wales the law of malicious falsehood is damaging a person in their work by publishing inaccurate information. The information may not be defamatory. The information has to be untrue. The claimant has to prove that the statement was published maliciously. Its equivalent in the USA is 'false light', a state-based tort which is available to plaintiffs who have been damaged by inaccurate information that again does not have to be defamatory. It could be seen as a quasi libel/privacy tort and the plaintiff is required in most states, where the tort is available, to prove that the publication presented him in a negative way, that the 'false light' would be offensive to a reasonable person, and that the publisher had been guilty of acting with actual malice.

Criminal libel: a plague on both their houses

In 2009 both the UK and USA still had criminal libel on their statute books, though its practical prosecution seems to have become redundant and anachronistic. However, in the global context it is seen as doing harm in countries that seek to justify more oppressive measures against media communication. NGOs argue that it is a poor example for the mother and father of liberty and democracy in the world, if that is how the UK and USA are perceived, to continue to retain criminal libel in their respective canons of law. It is a fact that countries such as Japan and India operate civil and criminal libel alongside each other. Most defamation actions in France are taken through the criminal jurisdiction. The UK had, up until 2009, retained the criminal offence of seditious libel, a law used in the Enlightenment age to persecute opponents of King George III and sympathizers of American colonists. As a result of pressure from the campaigning groups PEN, Index on Censorship and Article 19, the British government announced in July 2009 that it would abolish the laws of criminal and seditious libel. (Gibb *The Times* 2009)

British criminal libel required leave of a High Court Judge. The publication needed to be so serious that it was deemed capable of creating a breach of the peace and therefore required the intervention of the state. In 2008 the UK government took measures to abolish the criminal offence of blasphemous libel. In the report on *Libel and Insult Laws: A Matrix On*

Where We Stand and What We Would Like To Achieve, the Organization for Security and Cooperation in Europe reported in 2005 that nineteen US states and territories still had criminal libel statutes and in the period between 1992 and August 2004 there had been forty-one attempted and actual criminal defamation prosecutions:

> six defendants were convicted under criminal defamation statutes. In three cases, the statute in question was declared unconstitutional on appeal.
> From 1965 through August 2004, 16 cases ended in final convictions. Nine of these included jail sentences, with an average sentence of 173.6 days.
>
> (OSCE 2005: 172)

In a debate in the British House of Lords in July 2009 Lord Lester revealed that there were records of two criminal libel convictions in England and Wales up until the end of 2006: 'Across Europe and the Commonwealth, similar offences exist and are used to suppress political criticism and dissent.' (Gibb *The Times* 2009)

Privacy – emotional identity and human dignity and the private interest of the state

The USA has had a long-standing independent civil wrong or 'tort' in privacy and has fully recognized the legal right of its citizens to be left alone. But the law operates within state jurisdictions and the Supreme Court rarely originates or develops media privacy jurisprudence. It has, however, employed the *New York Times* 'actual malice' standard as a constitutional limitation on the ability of the states to compensate plaintiffs in 'false light' invasion of privacy cases. Justice Brennan ruled that where there was a discussion of public interest issues not even the plaintiff's private status mattered. He argued that guarantees for speech and free press are not quarantined by the purpose of political expression and comment on public affairs. Everyone in a civilized community risks exposure to publicity and in crystal-clear language he declared that the risk 'is an essential incident of life in a society which places a primary value on freedom of speech and of press.' (Time, Inc v Hill, SC US 1967)

It could be said that Justice Brennan may have been treading carefully in any move to balance privacy rights with the First Amendment because privacy deals with truth and factual reality and the mistaken expression of facts that can have no bearing on reputation:

> In this context, sanctions against either innocent or negligent misstatement would present a grave hazard of discouraging the press from

exercising the constitutional guarantees. Those guarantees are not for the benefit of the press so much as for the benefit of all of us. A broadly defined freedom of the press assures the maintenance of our political system and an open society. Fear of large verdicts in damage suits for innocent or merely negligent misstatement, even fear of the expense involved in their defense, must inevitably cause publishers to 'steer [...] wider of the unlawful zone' [...] and thus 'create the danger that the legitimate utterance will be penalized.'

(Sack 2003: 1–10 and Time, Inc v Hill, SC US 1967 para. 389)

US privacy law encompasses the false light statutes, media intrusion, disclosure of embarrassing private facts and commercial or political misappropriation of personality. It is generally assumed that private citizens have a greater right to a legitimate expectation of privacy than do public officials and figures such as politicians and international celebrities. But state courts recognize that boundaries can be drawn in the relentless intrusion into the private worlds of celebrities, whether in the hunt for interviews or in the application of intrusive long-lens photography into private property. The state of California operates an anti-paparazzi statute in order to prevent the overbearing harassment of the concentration of global celebrity in Los Angeles. Privacy statutes also originate in states on the East Coast, such as New York, another key location for the US cultural and entertainment industries.

The concept of intrusion can accommodate the developing tort of intentional infliction of mental distress. The most celebrated example was the action by the religious evangelist Jerry Falwell against the publisher of *Hustler* magazine, Larry Flynt, that has become somewhat mythologized in Hollywood film. Mr Falwell claimed emotional distress in a spoof Campari advert that mockingly implied an indecent encounter with his mother in an outhouse. The parody is reproduced on page 205 of Zelezny's 2004 edition of *Communications Law* and page 407 of Moore and Murray's 2008 edition of *Media Law and Ethics*. Mr Falwell was unsuccessful in his action because the Supreme Court wished to limit the remedy to circumstances of highly offensive communication, alleging facts and not fantasy, that were published with provable actual malice.

In a nutshell, US privacy law is available for US citizens if private information is published when it does not have a legitimate news purpose, and there is media intrusion into private homes or hotel rooms with the use of surreptitious recording devices. The remedy is also available where individuals are portrayed in misleading and highly objectionable contexts without their consent and their names or identifiable images are used in a commercial message or political campaign without consent. Unlike European privacy jurisprudence, there are no recoverable torts available in the USA for photography and filming in locations open to public view or for the publication of information derived from public records.

The recognition of inherent personality rights means that in US privacy law the citizen is entitled to determine the use of name, image and likeness in public communication. Privacy law is rather dynamic in the sense that the social concept of celebrocracy is a relatively recent phenomenon and rapid technological changes in media technology raise new issues of the boundary lines between public and private zones of existence.

UK privacy law: an unhappy story

The development of UK media privacy law has been an unhappy one, full of controversy, argument, accusations of political deceit, judicial sleights of hand, and sensational and tragic case histories. The British media are beginning to argue that 'the chilling effect' is being added to by the development of media privacy law. Yet when Article 8 of the European Convention of Human Rights became UK statute law in 1998 many people seemed to have had a collective amnesia about the accumulating criminal and civil privacy restrictions directed at journalists for nearly a hundred years. They simply had not been defined as 'privacy'. Examples include the statutory and judicial restrictions on identifying sexual offence complainants, children/youths in criminal proceedings, 'vulnerable witnesses' and the parties involved in divorce and child custody proceedings. The contrasting scope and origins of US and UK privacy law are set out in Tables 1.18 and 1.19.

It could also be argued that the Official Secrets Act has been a mechanism of protecting a notion of 'privacy' for the state in relation to politically sensitive information. 'National security' is the all-embracing mantra to justify the secrecy. The concept tends to be defined by the executive and legislature and confirmed by the judiciary. The media can be persuaded to agree to secrecy where there is a real threat to life, but when this overlaps political and propagandist sensitivities the ethical and legal position becomes much more ambiguous. The self-censorial media blackout in 2007/2008 on Prince Harry's deployment to Afghanistan brokered by the Society of Editors is an example of this.

In 2008 a large proportion of a murder trial at the Central Criminal Court was held in secret as the judge was bound by the terms of the Official Secrets Act. He made his decision in a secret hearing and for secret reasons. In 1994 the author and another journalist, Caroline Godwin, challenged the reasons for holding an entire drugs trial in secret, but the appeal at the Royal Courts of Justice was held in secret and the ruling was given in secret, and the issue of whether the appeal was successful or not will have to remain secret. The law professor and media affairs journalist

Table 1.18 Media privacy law in the United Kingdom

Protection for sexual offence complainants
All sexual offence complainants (male and female) have media publication anonymity for all time after they have made a complaint of a sexual offence. This statutory prohibition remains even when they can be seen giving evidence and their names are disclosed in the public courtroom. They can waive their anonymity to help a police enquiry or for some other personal or public interest reason. It is important that their permission is in writing. Broadcasters need to be alert to properly disguising distinctive voices, dress codes and hairstyles when interviewing complainants with anonymity, as allowing identification by anyone who can recognize a complainant would be a criminal offence. In exceptional situations a criminal court can lift the anonymity if it is judged that the restriction presents a substantial block to the reporting of the case. Child sex offence complainants (aged 15 and under) can never waive their anonymity. Bear in mind that the range of sexual offences for which complainants have anonymity has been considerably expanded.

Protection for children/youths
Youths (aged 17 and under [in Scotland 16 and under]) can have anonymity if an order is made under the Children and Young Persons Act 1933 – known as 'Section 39 Orders'. This applies to witnesses and defendants. They should not be made if the victim is a baby or so young as not to be conscious of the effect of publicity, i.e. under 4. They should not be made if the child victim is deceased. Children who are wards of court and in local authority care cannot be identified as the subject of matrimonial/Children Act proceedings, or any other custody disputes. It may be possible to give publicity to a child that is a ward of court where the event or issue bears no relation to the proceedings.

It is important to avoid the risk of jigsaw identification, e.g. when one media organization reports the case of a father raping his daughter and another reports it as a named man accused of raping an unnamed young woman. The audience could put two and two together. Anti-Social Behaviour Orders (known as ASBOs) are applied for by local authorities with the support of the police. These are technically civil proceedings. Youths being dealt with should be identified in order to comply with the spirit of the legislation, although the courts should take into account the welfare of the youths when balancing privacy with freedom of expression. Publicity supports the principle of 'naming and shaming' and warning people in the community that troublesome youths should not be at large in shopping centres or banned areas. If youths breach ASBOs they are dealt with by Youth Courts in criminal proceedings. There is normally default anonymity for youths in these courts under section 49 of the Children and Young Persons Act 1933, but on 1 July 2005 the law was amended so that Youth Court justices have to make an order if they wish ASBO breaching youths to retain their anonymity. The situation has been complicated by the fact that Parliament has also given Youth Courts the power to impose ASBOs on young offenders at the same time as they are convicted of criminal offences. In this situation journalists have to use their initiative to persuade the justices to lift the default reporting restrictions to identify the ASBO youths in these circumstances.

Media privacy arising out of Article 8 of the Human Rights Act
In Britain there has been rapid progress in establishing a media privacy law through case law based on Article 8 and ECHR jurisprudence from decisions in Strasbourg. In

2004 a narrow majority of Law Lords in Britain's then supreme court (the Judicial Committee of the House of Lords) affirmed a right to privacy for the model Naomi Campbell in a news article published in the *Daily Mirror* newspaper. Campbell had lied to the general public when she denied taking drugs. The *Daily Mirror* published a photograph of her which proved the lie. But Campbell said her privacy had been invaded because she was photographed leaving a Narcotics Anonymous meeting in the affluent Chelsea area of London. The *Daily Mirror* newspaper said the photograph was taken in a public street and there was a public interest in publishing it. The Law Lords' decision was by a majority of three to two. The majority of the Law Lords emphasized that the privacy being protected related to Ms Campbell's medical treatment for addiction. In 2004 Princess Caroline of Monaco won a case at the European Court of Human Rights on the basis that taking her picture with or without her children while in a public place was an invasion of her privacy. In 2007/8 the *Harry Potter* author J.K. Rowling sought a similar remedy in relation to photographs taken of her with her young son and partner in Edinburgh. The Human Rights Act also requires the courts to take into account any relevant privacy codes issued by the PCC, BBC and Ofcom when considering restrictions that prevent broadcasts or print publication occurring. Many lawyers and judges in the UK now concede that the UK has a clear and developing law of privacy. The trend was confirmed in December 2006 with two appeal court rulings. In Loreena McKennitt v Ash the judges upheld a High Court ruling that a book by McKennitt's former friend *Travels with Loreena McKennitt: My Life as a Friend* revealed personal and private detail that the singer was entitled to keep secret. In HRH Prince of Wales v Associated Newspapers, the Court of Appeal decided that the *Daily Mail* was not entitled to publish substantial extracts from eight hand-written journals kept by Prince Charles to record his impressions and views in the course of overseas tours made by him to Hong Kong between 1993 and 1999. During this period the colony was handed over to China (1997). In a balancing exercise the judges decided that it was necessary to restrict freedom of expression in order to prevent disclosure of information received in confidence. The court had to decide whether it was in the public interest that the duty of confidence should be breached.

Protection for 'vulnerable witnesses'
Section 11 of the Contempt of Court Act 1981, and the Youth Justice and Criminal Evidence Act 1999, give protection to 'vulnerable witnesses'. Blackmail victims (where the menaces are of an embarrassing nature) are entitled to anonymity whether or not an order has been made. When 'vulnerable witnesses' are giving evidence the judge can clear the court and leave only one journalist present. It is an offence to report this exclusion before the end of the trial or to report the special measures taken to protect the vulnerable witness. The courts can ban identification of adult witnesses (aged 18 and over) if satisfied that the quality of the evidence or level of cooperation will be diminished by fear or distress. Under the 2005 Serious Organised Crime and Police Act it is an offence to disclose new identities of witnesses who are under police protection because of violence or intimidation, or any details of other arrangements for their protection. Under the right to life provisions of the Human Rights Act, the High Court can make injunctions on media identification of the identity and whereabouts of notorious convicted criminals such as the child killers Mary Bell, Jon Venables and Robert Thompson, and Ian Huntley's partner Maxine Carr. (She was convicted of perverting the course of justice and feared violent reprisals after her release from prison.)

111

Table 1.19 Privacy law in the USA

The foundation for US discussion of privacy as a legal concept	Influence of the First Amendment	Privacy law in state legal systems and recognized remedies available to plaintiffs
'The Right To Privacy', by Samuel Warren and Louis D. Brandeis, originally published in 4 *Harvard Law Review* 193 (1890).	The First Amendment is the trump card.	The majority of the fifty US States have recognized four civil torts that could be considered 'privacy': Appropriation and misuse of personality rights; Disclosure of private facts; False light; and Intrusion.
The press is overstepping in every direction the obvious bounds of propriety and of decency. Gossip is no longer the resource of the idle and of the vicious, but has become a trade, which is pursued with industry as well as effrontery. To satisfy a prurient taste the details of sexual relations are spread and broadcast in the columns of the daily papers. To occupy the indolent, column upon column is filled with idle gossip, which can only be procured by intrusion upon the domestic circle. The intensity and complexity of life, attendant upon advancing civilization, have rendered necessary some retreat from the world, and man, under the refining influence of culture, has become more sensitive to publicity, so that solitude and privacy have become more essential to the individual; but modern enterprise and invention have, through invasions upon his privacy, subjected him to mental pain and distress, far greater than could be inflicted by mere bodily injury.	Thus far state torts have been kept under control by the US Supreme Court and by narrow application in the lower courts, even to the extent that state laws prohibiting the naming of sexual offence complainants and juveniles in court cases have been ruled unconstitutional.	In some states there are criminal statutes that in effect protect privacy, similar to the UK Protection of Harassment Act 1997, Data Protection Acts 1984 and 1998, and Regulation of Investigatory Powers Act 2000. In most cases the US states' statutes are concerned with the use of electronic eavesdropping devices.

The foundation for US discussion of privacy as a legal concept	*Influence of the First Amendment*	*Privacy law in state legal systems and recognized remedies available to plaintiffs*
If we are correct in this conclusion, the existing law affords a principle which may be invoked to protect the privacy of the individual from invasion either by the too enterprising press, the photographer, or the possessor of any other modern device for recording or reproducing scenes or sounds. For the protection afforded is not confined by the authorities to those cases where any particular medium or form of expression has been adopted, nor to products of the intellect. The same protection is afforded to emotions and sensations expressed in a musical composition or other work of art as to a literary composition; and words spoken, a pantomime acted, a sonata performed, is no less entitled to protection than if each had been reduced to writing. The circumstance that a thought or emotion has been recorded in a permanent form renders its identification easier, and hence may be important from the point of view of evidence, but it has no significance as a matter of substantive right. If, then, the decisions indicate a general right to privacy for thoughts, emotions, and sensations, these should receive the same protection, whether expressed in writing, or in conduct, in conversation, in attitudes, or in facial expression.	In recent years US plaintiffs have alleged intentional infliction of emotional distress against the media. It is possible for such a claim to be viable, but at the Supreme Court in 1988 *Jerry Falwell v Larry Flynt and Hustler Magazine* has limited the tort so that public figures, at least, must show that the highly offensive communication of alleged facts was published with actual malice. Inevitably the Internet is raising privacy concerns. Legislation and court decisions are wrestling with the question of when it is a legal violation to access personal email, access secure websites and collect consumer data without consent.	Five general guidelines on privacy laws in state jurisdictions: 1) Scenes open to public view can be photographed, and information in public records may be reported, without consent. 2) Private information about an individual, once you have it, may always be published or broadcast if a legitimate news purpose exists. 3) In areas specifically intended for privacy, such as private homes and hotel/motel rooms, you may not secretly snoop, tape-record or photograph, even if a newsworthy motive exists. 4) Written consent must be obtained before using a person's name or picture in a commercial/political campaigning message. 5) People should not be represented in a misleading and highly objectionable context without consent (potential false light).

Marcel Berlins was one of only a few observers who thought this situation was somewhat disturbing:

> Now there may or may not have been perfectly good reasons for the secrecy of the whole thing, and if there were, I can understand that revealing those reasons might give the whole game away. What makes me uneasy is that the process makes it impossible to test that reasoning, or the scope of the ban. The experienced Crook and Godwin only stumbled across this secret trial by a combination of nous, good digging and luck. How many 'in camera' orders are being made by judges, perhaps wrongly, without anyone knowing about them at all?
>
> (Berlins *Guardian* 1994)

It was rare then for criminal cases to be closed, i.e. *in camera*, but it is being increasingly reported that secret hearings and secret witnesses in 2009 are becoming more common. Successful campaigning on our part had resulted in Parliament legislating for section 159 of the Criminal Justice Act 1988, where the parties to British criminal trials had to give notice of an application for *in camera* hearings. The prosecutor or defendant who seeks a secrecy order 'on the grounds of national security or for the protection of a witness' must give seven days' notice before the start of the trial and a prominent notice must be posted on the court precincts. If the application is successful, the hearing must be postponed for twenty-four hours to allow for an appeal. Criminal and other courts can also go 'in chambers' at the discretion of the judge. This also involves excluding the press and public. But where there is a public interest in open proceedings and it becomes clear to the court that there is no justification for remaining in private, the press and public should be allowed back in. This latter rule was established after an appeal by the author against in chambers hearings at the Central Criminal Court in 1989 (Re Crook CoA Crim 1989)

In the UK, there has been a tendency, recognized by the UN's Human Rights Committee, to prosecute and convict people who work for government and wish to be whistleblowers on the grounds of conscience. Dr David Kelly was driven to suicide or, on the basis of a book written by a Liberal Democrat MP, he may have been murdered. Katharine Gunn and Derek Pasquill had OSA charges against them dropped; Cabinet office communications officer David Keogh and House of Commons researcher Leo O'Connor were prosecuted, convicted and imprisoned. They went to jail for six and three months respectively and when their trial accidentally remained in open court to discuss part of the 'secret' memo they had passed on to each other, a gagging order on the media not to report the information was sustained at the Court of Appeal.

There is a risk that the culture of 'national security' will lead to an increase in the extent of courtroom secrecy and reporting bans. In 2007 the details of a legal action accusing British soldiers in Iraq of murdering and abusing civilians remained secret for several months. However, it could also be argued that these instances of secrecy represent rare and exceptional circumstances and constitute a response by the UK state and judiciary to unprecedented threats to security by international and domestic terrorism and the consequences of the country's military deployment in conflict zones abroad.

Privacy is direct censorship of truth in the sense of operating as prior restraint on the publication by the media of accurate information, whereas libel is a remedy against publication of untrue allegations and imputations. Generally, privacy applies pre-publication and libel post-publication. Both areas of the law trade on human emotions: libel in terms of honour, self-esteem and status; privacy in terms of personal security, dignity and familial duties.

Critics of developing UK media privacy law fear it is designed to protect the celebrocracy elite from media examination of the use and abuse of economic and political power. This power is dependent on the social currency and exchange value of media representation. The consequences: the development of a media privacy tort by non-elected judges; the creation of new criminal offences under legislation that include protection from harassment, regulation of investigatory powers and data protection. There is a risk that these laws criminalize long-established techniques of journalistic practice, and favour the rich and powerful at the expense of the poor and disenfranchised. The moral panic of 'invasion of privacy' has been constructed as a mischief perpetrated by media when there is scant scrutiny of the state's invasion of personal privacy by surveillance, covert investigation, collection and misuse of data.

From the late 1980s a political campaign for a specific 'privacy law' to control the ethical excesses of tabloid media gathered momentum around a discernible moral panic centring on the harassment of popular celebrities; in particular, the harassment of the dying television chat show host Russell Harty in 1988 and the intrusion by journalists into the hospital room of the seriously injured actor Gordon Kaye in 1990.

Martin Wainwright's feature article in the *Guardian* in June 1988 headlined 'The haunting of Harty – Russell Harty's last days brought out the press pack in full cry, but their tactics could put them on a tighter leash' (Wainwright *Guardian* 1988) revealed ethically questionable tactics deployed by journalists and photographers to acquire pictures and information about Mr Harty when he was dying from hepatitis in St James's University Hospital in Leeds.

The legend of the tabloid hunting of Russell Harty was developed further at Mr Harty's memorial service in October 1988, when the playwright Alan Bennett lamented that the broadcaster had been set up by a 'gutter press' revelling in sexual indiscretions, and harassed by reporters in the months leading up to his death:

115

Reporters intermittently infested his home village for more than a year, bribing local children for information about his life, forcing their way into the school, even trying to bribe the local vicar. Now, as he fought for his life in St James's Hospital, one newspaper took a flat opposite, and a camera with a long lens trained on his ward. A reporter posing as a junior doctor smuggled himself into the ward, and demanded to see his notes. Every lunchtime, journalists took the hospital porters across the road to the pub, to bribe them into taking photographs of him.

(Bennett quoted by Fiddick *Guardian* 1988)

The Gordon Kaye saga involved a reporter and a photographer for the *Daily Sport* newspaper intruding into the actor's private hospital room after he was critically injured in a freak accident when driving his car in bad weather conditions. He was photographed and interviewed when he was in no state to give informed consent. The journalists refused to leave after being challenged by nurses and were eventually ejected by security guards. At the time, the newspaper said it was proud of its scoop, but the appeal court condemned the behaviour and Lord Justice Bingham said Mr Kaye had suffered a monstrous invasion of his privacy:

If ever a person has a right to be let alone by strangers with no public interest to pursue, it must surely be when he lies in hospital recovering from brain surgery and in no more than partial command of his faculties. It is this invasion of his privacy which underlies the plaintiff's complaint. Yet it alone, however gross, does not entitle him to relief in English law.

(Kaye v Robertson HC 1991)

Bingham and his fellow judges bemoaned the lack of a legal privacy remedy in English law to award damages to Mr Kaye and block the newspaper from publishing its story. Both sagas gave rise to public outrage and disapproval. No photograph of the dying Russell Harty surreptitiously obtained by long lens photography was ever published and the public condemnation of his hounding by the popular media may have had a restraining influence. Although Gordon Kaye could not win on privacy, the appeal court was able to use the existing law of malicious falsehood to ensure that the *Daily Sport* could not claim that he had consented to the photographs or interview. Tony Livesey, a later editor of the newspaper, acknowledged that it was 'the greatest invasion of privacy in journalism. [...] Lessons were learned. We are never doing that again.' (Flintoff *Independent* 1998) Media texts published during this period reveal an intensity of political and public opinion calling for the creation of a privacy law.

116

However, the UK Parliament has resisted actually legislating for an explicit 'privacy law'. Instead, Article 8 of the Human Rights Act 1998 has obliged the courts to convert the law of confidentiality as a contract between powerful celebrities and their employees into a privacy duty that also binds the media as a third party. In cases involving public figures such as Naomi Campbell, Loreena McKennitt and Prince Charles the jump from confidentiality to privacy was achieved by creating a legal block or remedy against the media for the publication of confidential/private information where public interest was not deemed to be what may simply interest and entertain the public.

This has meant that a mother on income support, Mrs Mary Wainwright, had to go to Strasbourg to secure a privacy remedy for unjustifiable strip-searching when she tried to visit her son in prison. (Wainwright v United Kingdom ECHR 2006) This is the difference between material/physical breach of privacy – an intrusive strip-search – being given less prominence and validity than an emotional/psychological breach of privacy – publishing the fact that Naomi Campbell was undergoing NA therapy for drug addiction after she had wrongly stated publicly that she did not take drugs.

The post-modernist reach of privacy is now expanding into new areas of censorship:

a) There is an increasing phenomenon of extending the principle of the vulnerable witness into the vulnerable defendant and convicted criminal. The perpetual gagging order on the whereabouts and activities of Maxine Carr has created the disturbing phenomenon of twenty-first-century witch-finding and persecution. Women seen as outsiders or moving into neighbourhoods without any known history are being harassed, attacked and driven out by the vigilante suspicion that they must or might be Maxine in disguise. Maxine Carr's partner Ian Huntley was convicted in 2003 of murdering two 11-year-old girls in Soham. Carr was convicted of perverting the course of justice by lying to the police after the girls had been killed. She obtained a general injunction against media coverage of her identity and whereabouts after her release from prison. This could be considered as something of an ironic boomerang, as the original purpose of the court injunction was to protect Maxine Carr herself from vigilante intimidation and violence.

b) There is an ideological framing of journalism as the cause of moral/social and political instability, an incitement and invitation to criminal behaviour and threat to the right to life. As a result there is growing anonymity and partial anonymity for armed services personnel in courts-martial, soldier and police officer marksmen who kill civilians in security operations, notorious criminals facing vigilante justice, undercover state investigators, and all kinds of witnesses to serious crimes. The identities of the police marksmen who shot Jean Charles de Menezes at Stockwell underground station in 2005 remain a secret despite the successful prosecution of the Metropolitan Police under health and safety legislation and a high-profile public inquest at which they gave evidence with their identifying features concealed from the public. It is argued that public identification of police firearms specialists would render them vulnerable to reprisal and undermine their effectiveness in future operations. In 2008 a man extradited from Morocco on charges relating to the £50 million Securitas robbery in Tonbridge appeared at Maidstone Magistrates' Court and was 'not named for legal reasons'. He was identified after making his first UK court appearance, but no explanation was given as to why he had been anonymized during the extradition process. This raises the question of whether it can ever be right that adult individuals accused of involvement in the biggest robbery in British criminal history should be arrested, extradited and appear in court anonymously.

c) There is the increasing phenomenon of terrorist suspect detainees and individuals subject to 'control orders', asylum seekers and political/economic refugees in the immigration legal process being deracinated in media coverage to the point that they are only referred to as A, B, C, Y or X. The Special Immigration Appeals Commission (SIAC) has the power under SIAC Rule 39(5)h 'to make provision to secure the anonymity of the appellant or a witness. Most cases are under anonymity orders. Several individuals from Algeria accused of being involved in a terrorist plot to release ricin in the London underground were named in relation to their trial at the Central Criminal Court (although most of their year-long trial was not reported because of a Contempt of Court Act reporting ban), yet were anonymized when detained after their jury acquittals and dealt with by SIAC hearings. They had the public support of two of the jurors who acquitted them, who coincidentally insisted on and were granted anonymity in the subsequent media coverage.

In March 2004 SIAC decided that a 37-year-old man from Libya had been imprisoned on evidence that was 'wholly unreliable and should not have been used to justify detention.' (Gillan *Guardian* 2004 and Verkaik *Independent* 2004) The Court of Appeal heard an appeal from the Home Secretary, partly in secret, and confirmed the original decision to release him. However, the man at the centre of the case continued to be known only as 'M'. The Lord Chief Justice, Lord Woolf, said:

While the need for society to protect itself against acts of terrorism today is self-evident, it remains of the greatest importance that, in a society which upholds the rule of law, if a person is detained as M was detained, that individual should have access to an independent tribunal or court which can adjudicate upon the question of whether the detention is lawful or not. If it is not lawful, then he has to be released.

(Home Office v "M" CoA Civ 2004)

In December 2004 a panel of Law Lords, by a majority of 8 to 1, decided that this detention procedure was incompatible with the Human Rights Act. Many of the detainees at the centre of this case retained their anonymous identities, a vista which would be intolerable in US First Amendment culture. Subsequent terrorist events in London have gestated further legislation to substitute detention with 'control orders' that amount to house arrest and to extend this power to include British citizens as well as foreign nationals. There are no guarantees of open justice provisions in relation to the full judicial scrutiny of these procedures. In 2009 the legal rights research organization Justice published a detailed report into the use of secret evidence in the British legal system:

The core principle of British justice has been undermined as the use of secret evidence in UK courts has grown dramatically in the past 10 years.

Secret evidence can now be used in a wide range of cases including deportations hearings, control orders proceedings, parole board cases, asset-freezing applications, pre-charge detention hearings in terrorism cases, employment tribunals and even planning tribunals. Defendants in some criminal cases are now being convicted on the basis of evidence that has never been made public. Criminal courts have issued judgments with redactions to conceal some of the evidence relied upon. Evidence from anonymous witnesses has also been used in hundreds of criminal trials and is widespread in ASBO hearings.

Since they were first introduced in 1997, almost 100 special advocates – lawyers prohibited from communicating with those they represent – have been appointed. [...]

This report calls for an end to the use of secret evidence. Secret evidence is unreliable, unfair, undemocratic, unnecessary and damaging to both national security and the integrity of Britain's courts.

(Metcalfe 2009: 5)

The 238-page Justice report is sobering and salutary reading. In 1993 the author and Caroline Godwin put in papers for an appeal against secret witnesses at an Old Bailey murder trial on the basis that it was an affront to open justice as well as to the justice to defendants, who should be able to know the identity of their accusers. We were advised by leading criminal QCs to withdraw as it was thought our action on media rights would provoke wholesale engagement of secret witnesses into the criminal justice system. It would seem we would have made no difference had we proceeded or not.

In an article for *The News Media & the Law*, Rory Eastburg suggested that after the terrorist attacks on 11 September 2001 the general presumption that US courts had been open was turned on its head and 'secrecy has been the norm for proceedings that dealt, however tangentially, with terrorism or national security.' (Eastburg 2008) The problem identified by British civil rights lawyers in dealing with secret immigration and deportation procedures and detention and control orders was mirrored in the USA though on a much greater scale. Journalists had limited access to military tribunals dealing with the hundreds of detainees transported to Guantánamo Bay in Cuba. Eastburg reported that the federal courts accommodated the Bush administration's wish to promote secrecy in the prosecution of terrorism cases. An Algerian-born Florida resident was secretly jailed for five months in 2001 and his application for habeas corpus was kept secret. Eastburg charted the administration's use of national security to assert a dormant 'state secrets' privilege in civil law cases. As in the UK, administrative immigration proceedings were swathed in secrecy:

> Ten days after the September 11 attacks, Chief Immigration Judge Michael Creppy issued a memorandum to all immigration judges and court administrators, directing judges to close all terrorism-related immigration hearings and avoid 'disclosing any information about the case to anyone outside the Immigration Court.'
>
> (Ibid.)

Just how the state secrets privilege concept could be used in the US legal system was explored by Susan Burgess in her 2006 article 'Cases without courts: the state secrets privilege keeps some claims from ever being heard'. She investigated the pattern of plaintiffs who had been losing their day in court because the government had invoked the state secrets privilege to withhold information needed to prove their case. This was an intriguing echo of a scandal in Britain from the 1990s when a group of executives working for an engineering firm, Matrix Churchill, faced possible prison sentences in a customs prosecution for breaching sanctions by selling arms-making equipment to Iraq. Government 'public immunity certificates' had sought to suppress the fact that they had been encouraged to do so by another government department and with the knowledge of Britain's Secret Intelligence Service, MI6. Without disclosure it is difficult to know whether US state secrets privilege is placing people in a similar jeopardy:

> Kahled el-Masri thinks he deserves $75,000 from the US government for what he alleges was five months of beatings, sodomy and imprisonment in the 'Salt Pit,' a CIA-run facility in Afghanistan.

US District Judge T.S. Ellis agrees el-Masri should be compensated if his allegations are true. But Judge Ellis, of the US District Court in Alexandria, Va., dismissed el-Masri's case against the government in May, ruling that further litigation would jeopardize national security. Judge Ellis did not consider the validity of the allegations, but ruled that the government properly sought to dismiss the case under the state secrets privilege.

(Burgess 2006)

d) There is an increasing development of the anonymous concept in British communications culture. The notion of the non-person designated as X or Y, a given identity of oblivion, is spreading throughout many aspects of journalistic coverage of legal issues and legal proceedings. It includes myriad areas of civil litigation, such as the identities of individuals in persistent vegetative state cases, their doctors, relatives, and health professionals. It has been propagated primarily in the family area of law, where it could be argued that there has been a collapse in public confidence as a result of the secrecy. The paradox of the British cult of anonymity may be effectively illustrated by the unsuccessful attempt by the *News of the World*'s chief investigative reporter, Mazher Mahmood, to obtain a High Court injunction in 2006 against the distribution of his photograph on the grounds of privacy. He argued that it would expose him to danger and undermine his ability to continue undercover stings of alleged criminals. Another paradoxical case in 2009 involved a policeman blogger known as Nightjack who failed to secure an injunction under privacy law to maintain his anonymity. His lawyer, Hugh Tomlinson QC, had argued that:

thousands of regular bloggers who communicated nowadays via the Internet, under the cloak of anonymity, would be horrified to think that the law would do nothing to protect their anonymity if someone carried out the necessary detective work and sought to unmask them.

(The Author of a Blog v Times newspapers HC 2009)

Mr Justice Eady decided that *The Times* should be free to unmask him as, although 'there would be no reason to publicise genuinely private matters about police officers, such as their domestic arrangements or personal relationships, [...] blogging is not a wholly private activity.' (Ibid.) Nightjack's position was vigorously defended by Professor Jean Seaton, who wrote in the *Guardian*: 'This decision damages our capacity to understand ourselves just when we need new forms to develop. After Tuesday's ruling, would you blog about your workplace?' (Seaton *Guardian* 2009)

121

Secrecy in the family courts – a dimension of UK privacy

On 27 April 2009 English and Welsh family courts were finally opened to the media after decades of sitting in secret. But as the Press Association's *Media Lawyer* reported, despite the hopes of campaigning journalists, 'rule changes allowing reporters into court were not accompanied by any changes to reporting restrictions – meaning that most cases, particularly those involving children remain unreportable.' (*Media Lawyer* May 2009: 1) The government had agreed to compel the judges to open their doors after a long-standing campaign by *The Times* and *Daily Mail* newspapers. The investigative journalism of Camilla Cavendish was recognized as having impressed politicians of the need for change.

But there was a problem. In an editorial, *Media Lawyer* argued that it was pointless opening the family courts unless there was also proper reporting:

> The judges of the family courts have what one of their number once described as the most Draconian powers available to any court since the abolition of the death penalty – a judge has it within his or her power to order that a child should be removed from the care of one or both its parents and be adopted by another couple, with the strong possibility that they might never see each other again.
>
> (*Media Lawyer* May 2009: 21)

Unfortunately, journalists were subject to section 12 of the Administration of Justice Act 1960, which makes it a contempt of court to report hearings sitting in private that exercise jurisdiction in respect of minors and custody disputes. *Media Lawyer* constructively suggested the government engaged to family hearings the same restrictions that apply to youth courts, which were open to the media but not the public and had a default prohibition on identifying youths or their schools: 'That system has been in place since 1933, and has worked well ever since.' (Ibid.)

By July 2009 successful lobbying by the UK Newspaper Society and Society of Editors, ITN and the Press Association had resulted in the government pledging itself through the Minister of Justice to introduce a system of reporting restrictions similar to youth courts that provides for reporting the substance of cases without identifying the parties, and giving the Family Court judges a discretion for identification when it was in the public interest. (*Media Lawyer* July 2009: 1–2) The government would have been assisted by the expert advice of *Media Lawyer* editor Mike Dodd, who, in his mature years as a Press Association legal affairs journalist, qualified as a barrister (UK attorney) after obtaining first and Master's degrees in law.

Previous to April 2009 UK Family Division judges, such as Mr Justice Munby, had occasionally released 'no names' judgments in open court.

In one case he stopped social workers controversially removing a baby from its mother without a court order. That ruling actually emanated from the Administrative Court sitting in open session and in the presence of a reporter from the Press Association. It was unlikely to have reached the public domain had it been subject to an emergency application in the Family Division. Bubbling beneath the surface of this secret culture were allegations that social workers had been persecuting socially and mentally vulnerable parents so that their children could be taken into care to meet central government adoption targets, that expert witnesses were providing suspect scientific evaluations, and that the system was institutionally discriminatory against fathers. This amounted to an appalling libel on a profession populated with hard-working and well-meaning people.

Polemical criticisms of family law are part of an ongoing debate about the extent to which media power needs to be controlled and regulated by the legal system. For every criticism of family law secrecy there is a valid argument that such confidentiality is imperative for the interest of children in custody disputes. What justification is there for media exploitation of the private agony and distress experienced in family breakdown? Where this involves any public interest in global celebrity, Family Division judges do respond with the public release of their rulings. This occurred at the conclusion of the divorce of Paul and Heather McCartney in 2008. It was apparent that many aspects of the dispute had been leaked to the media. The proceedings remained in private. Heather Mills McCartney was not successful in an appeal to prevent the judge from making his ruling public. When the government engaged in a consultation exercise on opening family proceedings to the public on a no names basis, a survey in 2007 with young people involved in such cases revealed opposition to such a move.

But it was becoming apparent that these areas of secrecy were beginning to be socially counterproductive, or at the very least subject to some controversy. Whereas there is always a good argument that matrimonial and child custody disputes should remain private to protect children from embarrassment, the lack of journalistic scrutiny could hide any evidence of trends of fathers being discriminated against in custody arrangements and vice versa. The justice of expert evidence and social worker intervention in the lives of families leading to children being taken into care and forced adoption would not be open to public scrutiny and evaluation.

An enquiry headed by the President of the Family Division looked into thousands of cases where the disputed medical evidence from experts may have resulted in parents losing their children to local authority care, fostering or adoption. Despite the background of criticism it concluded no cases had been wrongly decided. Family Court judges make their decisions on the balance of probabilities, rather than the higher criminal standard of beyond reasonable doubt.

There had been reports that erroneous diagnosis of Munchausen Syndrome By Proxy (MSBP) was responsible for serious miscarriages of justice as far back as 1996. (Doward *Observer* 2004) The parents who believed they had been unjustly separated from their children had been prevented from being identified and complaining to the media because of the risk of being held in contempt of court. The media had no access whatsoever to the private court hearings making these decisions. The totalitarian nature of Family Division injunctions that seemed to be worded to protect social services departments and other professionals from controversial publicity could be perceived as an abuse of legal power and serious challenge to the democratic tradition. The BBC *Panorama* series and investigative journalist John Sweeney made a number of significant programmes which helped to bring out these issues into the public domain.

The author had warned as far back as 1997 that the secrecy attaching to the coverage of family proceedings and youth justice would only undermine public confidence in the system and corrode the quality of justice delivered behind closed doors. In evidence given before the Child Exploitation and the Media Forum in Westminster it was reported that:

> As a court reporter he criticised the Family Division of the High Court which uses secret hearings in which judges, with the involvement of social workers, permit 'unsubstantiated allegations of child abuse' to be made by mothers in adversarial child custody proceedings against fathers and the partners they are living with.
>
> Mr Crook said censorship of journalists in reporting children's affairs is never in the interests of children but is in the interests of adult professionals abusing or neglecting their responsibilities. A free press is the last resort of the abused, oppressed, vulnerable and disadvantaged members of society, he insisted.
>
> (Mediawise 1997)

It is important to emphasize that judges, lawyers and professionals working in family courts are and were not choosing to work in secret. The exclusion of the press and public and confidentiality attaching to the process was a matter of law. Judges did not have discretion to admit journalists to family proceedings dealing with children as they were bound by statutory restrictions. There was only a possibility in rare cases involving important principles they could release redacted and anonymized rulings for public reporting. Specific and general criticism of family courts and law could not be rebutted or balanced as the judges, lawyers and professionals involved were legally prohibited from publicly discussing case histories.

The cloak of secrecy inherent in family legal proceedings had the effect of masking scientific fashions in the medical diagnosis of physical and sexual abuse. Decisions that could condemn children to years of living in council care or enforced separation from their biological parents would have been excluded from any public process of verification or monitoring. Years later, when the credibility of expert witnesses and their theories were thrown into doubt, the damage to individual lives was judged to be irreparable and irreversible. The Family Courts were and still are involved in the ethically controversial process of approving the withdrawal of medical care from long-term coma patients.

On 19 January 2004 the appeal court judge Lord Justice Judge said medical science was 'still at the frontiers of knowledge' about unexplained infant deaths when giving his reasons for quashing the conviction of Angela Cannings for murdering her two baby sons:

> Experts in many fields will acknowledge the possibility that later research may undermine the accepted wisdom of today. 'Never say never' is a phrase which we have heard in many different contexts from expert witnesses. That does not normally provide a basis for rejecting the expert evidence, or indeed for conjuring up fanciful doubts about the possible impact of later research. [...] In cases like the present, if the outcome of the trial depends exclusively or almost exclusively on a serious disagreement between distinguished and reputable experts, it will often be unwise, and therefore unsafe, to proceed. [...] Unless we are sure of guilt the dreadful possibility always remains that a mother, already brutally scarred by the unexplained death or deaths of her babies, may find herself in prison for life for killing them when she should not be there at all. In our community, and in any civilised community, that is abhorrent.
>
> (R v Cannings CoA Crim 2004 and Dyer *Guardian* 2004)

The idea that the exclusion of journalistic scrutiny in the family courts had been a contributing factor to this injustice had formed part of a debate about lives being ruined in secret. (Cohen *Observer* 2004) There was also a growing body of credible research indicating that lay magistrates were taking the decisions in up to 70 per cent of local authority applications for Emergency Protection Orders (known as EPOs) to take children into care. (BBC Radio 4 2004) Parents were neither given notice, nor even represented at many of these secret hearings. The magistrates were given only part-time and very limited legal training. They represented the lowest rung on the ladder of judicial experience and authority. Family Court proceedings that have resulted in children being taken from their natural parents had also attracted strong criticism from the European Court of Human Rights. (P. C. and S v United Kingdom ECHR 2002)

On the very rare occasions when these Magistrates' proceedings are in open court journalists are only permitted to report: names, addresses and occupations of the parties and witnesses, a concise statement of the charges, the defence and counter-charges in support of which evidence has been given, submissions on any point of law arising in the course of the case and the decision of the court, the judgment of the court, and the observations of the judge.

There was evidence that Magistrates' courts were unreasonably applying a blanket exclusion of reporters from family proceedings. In 2004 the *Middleton & North Manchester Guardian* successfully resisted an attempt by Rochdale Magistrates' Court to exclude its reporters from attending family proceedings. (Slattery *Press Gazette* 2004) Under section 69(2) of the Magistrates Court Act 1980, journalists cannot be excluded from family proceedings at Magistrates' courts unless the court is dealing with adoption arrangements or with evidence involving indecency.

In February 2007 the then Attorney General, Lord Goldsmith, launched a review of criminal cases over the previous ten years in which a controversial paediatrician acted as a prosecution witness. In 2007 Sally Clark, a solicitor wrongly accused of killing two of her three children, died after being jailed and later cleared and freed on appeal. Her family said she had not recovered from the miscarriage of justice arising from a trial which the Court of Appeal had decided had been presented with flawed evidence by two expert prosecution witnesses.

When the BBC sought to investigate the adoption system through a series of half-hour documentaries in 2007, the High Court was persuaded to give privacy rights to an 18-year-old mother with learning difficulties whose child was taken away from her. The programme included the last contact session between mother and daughter, which was tearful and distressing, and also included a scene when the impression was given that she was sometimes rough with her daughter and had problems with anger management. (T v BBC HC 2007)

In newspaper reports at the time of the injunction the BBC said the young mother had agreed to be filmed and the adoption agency and her social worker had agreed for the programme to be broadcast. But Mr Justice Eady, having heard evidence from the mother's doctor, decided that 'The broadcast itself would constitute quite simply a massive invasion of T's privacy and autonomy, and would undermine her dignity as a human being.' (Dyer *Guardian* 2007b)

The UK courts have sought to place the dividing line between where the privacy interests in family law matters should stop and where the interests of criminal open justice should begin. In *Re S* in 2004 the Law Lords ensured that open justice in the criminal system would not be undermined by privacy restrictions arising from family proceedings. Lord Steyn said:

> the ordinary rule is that the press, as the watchdog of the public, may report everything that takes place in a criminal court. I would

add that in European jurisprudence and in domestic practice this is a strong rule. It can only be displaced by unusual or exceptional circumstances.

(Re S HL 2004)

Lord Justice Potter, President of the Family Division, ruled in 2005 that there were such exceptional circumstances in the case of a woman convicted of knowingly infecting the father of her second child with HIV. This was another situation where the British courts were not prepared to leave the situation to the ethical discretion of journalists. The judge decided that open justice in the criminal case should give way to the need to protect the mother's two children caught up in a situation over which they had no control, where they were in a delicate and vulnerable state and the subject of care proceedings of uncertain outcome. (A Local Authority v W.L.W. and T & R HC 2005; also *Media Lawyer* September 2005: 37–8)

What enabled the gestation of British privacy law?

A leading influence in the movement to develop British privacy law and apply new laws to control journalistic conduct and content was the lawyer Sir David Calcutt QC whose 'Review of Press Self-Regulation' in 1993 gave jurisprudential rocket-boosters to the view that self-regulation by the print media had failed and that regulation should now be administered by a statutory body.

He advocated the creation of criminal offences for journalistic misconduct and suggested that there should be a new civil remedy for the invasion of privacy. (Christie and Tugendhat 2002: 520) This would box in the print media between the pressure of defamation tort and a new privacy tort.

Some politicians did not conceal their delight in the introduction of the 'Privacy' Article 8 of the European Convention on Human Rights into British legislation. On 2 July 1998 Martin Linton MP addressed the House of Commons, stating:

> According to opinion polls, almost 90 per cent of the public favour a privacy law. As *The Guardian*, my former employer said, this is a type of privacy Bill: it is not solely about privacy, but while Lord Wakeham, as the watchdog, has been guarding the patio doors, a privacy Bill has slipped through the cat flap. I am very glad that it will be on the statute book.

(Ibid.)

The case law value of journalistic codification had been further enhanced and drawn into the authority of precedent through section 32 of the Data Protection Act 1998. This had directly linked a media defence that publication of stored data information is in the public interest if it complies with relevant codes on journalistic ethics and conduct. As Michael Tugendhat QC and Iain Christie, the authors of *The Law of Privacy and the Media*, recognized:

> the regulatory codes have achieved a greater significance than they might otherwise have had. They are now intimately linked into the question of whether it is appropriate for a court to grant a legal remedy for alleged invasions of privacy by the media.
>
> (Ibid.: 521)

The Human Rights Act 1998 (came into force October 2000)

This legislation made UK judges consider the European Convention on Human Rights when deciding cases. The legal world seemed to have a confusing attitude as to whether the Act incorporated, integrated or gave effect to Convention rights.

Whereas some legal writers insisted that the act did not 'incorporate' the Convention into British law, at the very least it did make British courts and public authorities 'give effect' to Convention rights. Hugh Tomlinson QC was categorical in stating that the Human Rights Act was designed to 'give further effect' to the Convention and 'does not directly incorporate the Convention into English law'. (Crone et al. 2002: 269) This may well amount to the same thing as incorporation. Christie and Tugendhat used the word 'incorporated' advisedly and stated: 'The rights set out in Schedule I to the Human Rights Act are not made part of English law rather the HRA provides a mechanism for enforcing those rights in English courts and for obtaining remedies for their violation.' (Christie and Tugendhat 2002: 30)

British media privacy law by paparazzi

In 2004 a slim majority of Law Lords in Britain's supreme court (the Judicial Committee of the House of Lords) affirmed a right to privacy for the model Naomi Campbell in a news article published in the *Daily Mirror* newspaper. Campbell had lied to the general public when she denied taking drugs. The *Mirror* published a photograph of her proving that lie. But Campbell said her privacy had been invaded because she was photographed leaving a Narcotics Anonymous meeting in the affluent Chelsea area of London, and this related to her therapeutic medical treatment.

The *Daily Mirror* said the photograph was taken in a public street and there was a public interest in publishing it. The Law Lords' decision was by a majority of three to two and a clear consequence for journalism was that it considerably weakened the importance of freedom of expression when investigating any hypocrisy of public figures that overlapped with matters concerning their health. The future balancing exercise would mean a clash of principles. For example, there had been considerable debate over whether former Prime Minister Tony Blair and his wife Cherie should have revealed whether their baby son Leo had or had not been given the MMR vaccine. It was government policy that children in the UK would have the vaccine and parents would only be able to obtain separate inoculation for their children privately. On the other hand, a decision by any parent on the health of their young children was considered a private issue intrinsic to the dignity and enjoyment of family life.

The House of Lords' decision in the Naomi Campbell case was groundbreaking in elevating the privacy right over freedom of expression, and this move by the Law Lords was supported by the legal victory one month later in June 2004 by Princess Caroline of Monaco at the European Court of Human Rights, where the mere taking of her picture in a public place, without any linkage to health issues or her children, was judged to have been an invasion of her privacy. The President of the Court, Cabral Barreto, stated:

> The Court considers that a fundamental distinction needs to be made between reporting facts – even controversial ones – capable of contributing to a debate in a democratic society relating to politicians in the exercise of their functions, for example, and reporting details of the private life of an individual who, moreover, as in this case, does not exercise official functions. While in the former case the press exercises its vital role of 'watchdog' in a democracy by contributing to 'impart[ing] information and ideas on matters of public interest' (Observer and Guardian, cited above, ibid.) it does not do so in the latter case.
>
> (Von Hannover v Germany ECHR 2004)

Barreto observed that the context in which the photos were taken, without Princess Caroline's knowledge or consent, and the harassment endured by many public figures in their daily lives could not be fully disregarded. Barreto added:

> The Court reiterates the fundamental importance of protecting private life from the point of view of the development of every human being's personality. That protection … extends beyond the private family circle and also includes a social dimension. The Court considers that anyone, even if they are known to the general public, must be able to enjoy a 'legitimate expectation' of protection of and respect for their private life.
>
> (Ibid.)

The cultural departure from the Anglo-American tolerance for media coverage of the private lives of celebrity was further highlighted in the concurring opinion of Judge Zupančič. As his speech in the ruling has been heavily criticized by British judges and jurists it would be fair to give more space to his reasoning:

> I nevertheless believe that the balancing test between the public's right to know on the one hand and the affected person's right to privacy on the other hand must be adequately performed. He who willingly steps upon the public stage cannot claim to be a private person entitled to anonymity. Royalty, actors, academics, politicians etc. perform whatever they perform publicly. They may not seek publicity, yet, by definition, their image is to some extent public property.
>
> Here I intend to concentrate not so much on the public's right to know – this applies first and foremost to the issue of the freedom of the press and the constitutional doctrine concerning it –, but rather on the simple fact that it is impossible to separate by an iron curtain private life from public performance. The absolute *incognito* existence is the privilege of Robinson; the rest of us all attract to a greater or smaller degree the interest of other people.
>
> Privacy, on the other hand, is the right to be left alone. One has the right to be left alone precisely to the degree to which one's private life does not intersect with other people's private lives. In their own way, legal concepts such as libel, defamation, slander etc. testify to this right and to the limits on other people's meddling with it. The German private-law doctrine of *Persönlichkeitsrecht* testifies to a broader concentric circle of protected privacy. Moreover, I believe that the courts have to some extent and under American influence made a fetish of the freedom of the press.
>
> (Ibid.)

The ECHR conferred the privilege of privacy to a wealthy international celebrity and member of a European royal family in a stated reaction against the 'fetish of the freedom of the press'. It was now clear that the effect of developing media privacy law had resulted in freedom of expression no longer being the trump card. Now the two principles are 'balanced' by judges who are empowered by the Human Rights Act to refer to the ethical and regulatory codes published by the Press Complaints Commission, BBC and Ofcom. This has been a back-door route to developing media privacy law or a right to respect for privacy without the process of parliamentary legislation.

In a 2004 ruling, the Law Lord Lord Steyn explained the nature of the judicial balancing act:

First, neither article has precedence as such over the other. Secondly where the values under the two articles are in conflict, an intense focus on the comparative importance of the specific rights being claimed in the individual case is necessary. Thirdly, the justifications for interfering with each right must be taken into account. Finally, the proportionality test must be applied to each. For convenience I will call this the ultimate balancing test.

(Re S (Identification: Restriction on Publication) HL 2004)

Developments in the law of privacy in photographs taken in a public place

In 2007 the *Harry Potter* author J.K. Rowling challenged the English and Welsh legal system to reconcile the different approaches to celebrity privacy between the UK and Europe. The Law Lords in the Naomi Campbell case argued that nobody has the right to prevent themself being photographed when they are in a public place with no reasonable expectation of privacy. The specific facts of the Campbell case turned on the belief that the judges felt the photographs revealed too much information about her private medical health treatment, and that when she was leaving Narcotics Anonymous in the King's Road, Chelsea she had a reasonable expectation of privacy. But in the Princess Caroline case, the Strasbourg judges argued that images of the Princess playing with her children, shopping and dining with a friend, and simply being out on her own in public should not have been published as they related to her private life and not to any public interest debate.

J.K. Rowling sought to extend the notion of expectation of privacy in the situation where an unpixelated photograph was published of her and her husband pushing their son in a buggy along an Edinburgh street. But the High Court judge ruled against J.K. Rowling on the basis that there was nothing in the photographs that raised any of the special circumstances in Campbell. He argued that if there was a risk that the child's security might be compromised, if taking the pictures caused the child distress, a higher degree of protection would apply. He also observed that while the Princess Caroline case indicated that a person's private recreation might now be protected even if it took place in public, there was still a basic area of innocuous public activity where no right to privacy exists. Baroness Hale had explained in her speech in the Naomi Campbell case that had she been photographed going out to buy a bottle of milk she would have had no remedy for breach of privacy. In conclusion, J.K. Rowling and her family had no reasonable expectation of privacy and the photographs of them could be published.

When this ruling was made, the media lawyer Michael Hales said the situation meant 'there is an increased and indistinct range of private

131

activity that takes place in public and cannot be photographed.' (Hales *Press Gazette* 2007)

Guardian media lawyer Korieh Duodu suggested the multi-millionaire author had a good chance of succeeding in the higher courts:

> The English courts are now using the von Hannover ruling to give wings to our fledgling privacy law. Last year, in McKennitt v Ash, the court of appeal drew on von Hannover in order to find that a Canadian folk singer's rights of privacy had been infringed by an author who had published various matters that she contended were already in the public domain.
>
> (Duodu *Guardian* 2007)

And this lawyer was proved right in 2008 when the Court of Appeal reversed the High Court judge's ruling in J.K. Rowling's litigation. She and her husband had taken the action on behalf of their son David Murray against the picture agency that employed the photographer. The legal issue to be decided was whether the young boy (18 months old when the pictures were taken) had an arguable case that he had a reasonable expectation of privacy. The Court of Appeal decided that his parents should be permitted to take his claim for breach of Article 8 to trial on his behalf. The Master of the Rolls, Sir Anthony Clarke, in giving the court's decision, said:

> To hold that the child has a reasonable expectation of privacy is only the first step. Then comes the balance which must be struck between the child's rights to respect for his or her private life under article 8 and the publisher's rights to freedom of expression under article 10. This approach does not seem to us to be inconsistent with that in Campbell, which was not considering the case of a child. [...] we have little doubt that, if the assumed facts of this case were to be considered by the ECtHR, the court would hold that David had a reasonable expectation of privacy and it seems to us to be more likely than not that, on the assumed facts, it would hold that the article 8/10 balance would come down in favour of David. We would add that there is nothing in the Strasbourg cases since von Hannover which in our opinion leads to any other conclusion.
>
> (Murray v Big Pictures CoA Civ. 2008)

The tension over Britain's developing media privacy law is bringing into focus the political and social dilemma of who defines the notion of the public interest. Is it a simple case of what interests the public? That would appear to be the democratic paradigm, yet such a path, if taken, risks damaging the interests of national security, public safety, due legal process and the right to reputation in defamation and privacy. Inevitably state institutions and elites, e.g. Parliament and the judiciary, along with those people in society who have the money and power to enforce 'public interest' values dominate the process of definition. In a sense they are the primary definers. As a result it could be argued that judicial decisions and legislative definitions of public interest are inconsistent and lack clarity. In the context of the Official Secrets Act, the former MI5 agent David Shayler was not entitled to run a defence in his criminal trial on the basis that he thought he was acting in the public interest. In *Jameel v Wall Street Journal* it could be argued that the public interest paradigm was in the interests of journalism because the defence of qualified privilege permitted a media defendant to publish defamatory material if the court decided it referred to matters of public interest and the media defendant had served the duty of informing the public by complying with responsible standards of journalism (previously codified by judges).

In *A v B plc and another*, known as the Gary Flitcroft case, the Court of Appeal argued that the public had a legitimate interest in being told that a Premiership footballer was having extramarital relationships because, as law lecturer Steve Foster suggests, 'the test of public interest would be led by the public's desire to access that information, irrespective of its political and social importance.' (Foster *Press Gazette* 2007) The subsequent precedents have weakened this proposition.

Von Hannover v Germany at the ECHR clearly stated that the public did not have a legitimate interest in the harassment and photographing of Princess Caroline and her family in public places. In a no names England and Wales case in 2007, *CC v AB*, Mr Justice Eady determined there was no public interest in permitting publication of the details of adultery for no better reason than spite, money making or for spreading 'tittle-tattle'.

This is a clear example, perhaps, of the judiciary exercising value judgments about how the popular media pursues its idea of 'public interest'. The 2006 High Court and appeal court rulings in *McKennitt v Ash* undoubtedly resisted the idea that a person's popularity did not place his/her private life in the public domain and justify disclosure of private-life details in the public interest. The judiciary can be criticized for presuming, as a state elite, what the public should be interested in rather than what in reality and in terms of the media market they are actually interested in. Foster rightly emphasizes that 'between a judge and the general public there is little common ground over what the public interest actually means.' (Ibid.)

The media might argue that there was no clear declaration or sign-posting that a British media privacy law was being introduced by way of either legislation or a green light to the judges to create it through case law. This is in direct contrast to the way the privacy tort was developed in the USA. The actual construction of the Article 8 'right to respect for private and family life, home and correspondence' in the European Convention suggests that Article 10 'freedom of information' takes precedence. This is because Article 10 is not qualified by the right of 'everyone to respect for private and family life, home and correspondence'. Furthermore, the qualification for Article 8 is stated as 'There shall be no interference by a public authority with the exercise of this right …'. This suggests that the original authors of the Convention did not intend that the privacy remedy should be available on a horizontal citizen-to-citizen basis, i.e. between a citizen and media publisher. The legal remedy was intended to be solely available to citizens in a vertical citizen-to-public authority basis. The original purpose of the right had been to protect the citizen against 'Big Brother' – in other words, the surveillance and intrusion of the state into private and family life etc.

The citizen-to-citizen (media publisher) horizontal remedy for privacy is only achieved by imagining that the judiciary is a public authority that should intervene to protect the citizen from any denial of rights by the media. Council of Europe resolutions and ECHR case law compel the British courts to observe that neither Article 10 freedom of expression nor Article 8 privacy should have precedence over the other.

The balancing exercise makes any communication of accurate and truthful information about a person's private life vulnerable to censorship. This is also the case when any citizen can be said to have a reasonable expectation of privacy. The judges become the referees or censors. The leading litigants become those individuals with the power and wealth to use the courts. Consequently the British media now fear that freedom of expression has been surrendered to the contingency of those who object to the emotional hurt of having the truth published about anything in their private zone of interaction.

Case law in these circumstances invites British judges to take on the role of arbiters of taste and decency and moral authority. Where does the exercise of political power end and that of judicial power begin? When British judges decide that media exposure of hypocrisy in drug abuse, adultery and sexual peccadilloes or of the indulgence of greed and privilege in private is 'mere title-tattle', they risk being seen as politicians, not independent judges.

Some of the leading cases could be criticized for confusing the boundaries between privacy and libel. For example, the majority Law Lords in *Campbell v Daily Mirror* in 2004 decided that the newspaper was justified in exposing the supermodel as a liar when she denied taking drugs. But they also ruled that the newspaper could not support its story by proving the accusation with a photograph of her emerging from a therapy session with Narcotics Anonymous. If the newspaper was denied the right to publish this information on the grounds of privacy, would they not need it if Ms Campbell had sued for libel on the basis that the newspaper had accused her of being a hypocrite?

In 2008 Mr Justice Eady presided over the privacy action taken by the president of Formula One racing, Max Mosley, against the *News of the World* who had filmed him taking part in a sado-masochistic session. The court ruled that the paper had no evidence he had been involved in Nazi role-play which would have been a matter of public interest. In the balancing exercise Mr Mosley's right to respect for privacy defeated the paper's assertion of freedom of expression. The woman who filmed the session for the News of the World had owed Mr Mosley a duty of confidence. There was no public interest in the media intrusion or exposure of this private activity. The newspaper was motivated by the fact that Mr Mosley was a powerful global figure in motor racing and the son of Sir Oswald Mosley, the notorious twentieth-century leader of the British Union of Fascists.

One of the women being paid by Mr Mosley had approached the newspaper with the story. It could be argued that the only method by which the newspaper could obtain the evidence to support the allegation was by surreptitious filming. But when Mr Justice Eady decided that the newspaper was wrong to allege that the rituals filmed could be associated with the Nazis or a concentration camp theme, he rendered the method of acquiring the evidence an intrusion and breach of Mr Mosley's privacy rights.

The Mosley case is hardly in the same league as the legendary 1972–3 Pulitzer Prize-winning *Washington Post* Watergate probe that immortalized its reporters, Carl Bernstein and Bob Woodward, through the Hollywood film *All The President's Men*. The *News of the World*'s pursuit of what it saw as the public interest is not likely to be perceived as the 'respectable' investigative journalism admired by the BBC, the *Guardian, Independent* and *Observer* newspapers. Unless there is a real public interest in exposing the sexual behaviour of public figures, Britain's media will face an interpenetrating risk of being sued for privacy in relation to news gathering conduct and libel for news publication content.

The Scottish media law system

Just under one tenth of the population of the United Kingdom, in Scotland (5,168,000 estimated in 2008), is subject to a separate legal system, which was not fused with that of England and Wales after the Act of Union in 1707. It would be wrong to draw many analogies between Scotland's relationship with Westminster and the position of the state of Texas in relation to Washington DC. Geographical size and scale of population are vastly different. Texas is the fourth-largest state of the USA, with 24 million citizens. It may have had a short-lived period of independence, but it does not have the background of many centuries of independence and history enjoyed by Scotland prior to the eighteenth century. Although Texas has its own legal system and state parliament, unlike Scotland, it also has the presence of the federal legal system of District courts and the remit of the fifth Appeals Court Circuit. Scotland's legal system is much more independent and no appeals on criminal matters can go beyond the High Court of Justiciary.

Contrasting legal cultures north and south of the border

Scottish law is a blend of Continental civil law, Roman law influences and English and Welsh common law. The Phillimore Committee's enquiry into the law of contempt in 1974 reported that 'the procedural and theoretical differences which exist between the two systems do not obscure the wide similarity of substance in the law of the two countries.' (Phillimore 1974: para. 23) The committee recommended uniformity with England and Wales. A summary outline of the structure of the Scottish legal system is set out in Table 1.20.

Table 1.20 The Scottish legal system

Criminal jurisdiction	Civil jurisdiction
No appeal to any other court, although matters of human rights law can be taken to ECHR in Strasbourg and EU law to the European Court of Justice.	Appeal on points of law to the UK Supreme Court in London, on human rights issues to the ECHR in Strasbourg and on EU law to the ECJ.
High Court of Justiciary. Trials before a single judge of serious crimes such as murder, rape, armed robbery and terrorism. Sitting with a jury of fifteen with three possible verdicts: guilty, not guilty and not proven, and with majorities of up to 8:7. The more serious crimes are known as 'solemn' cases and prosecuted in the High Court by the Lord Advocate, Solicitor General or one of the Advocate Deputes. The Crown Office is the equivalent of the English Director of Public Prosecutions and Crown Prosecution Service. High Court trials sit with juries and the trial judges impose the highest prison sentences and unlimited fines. The head judge of the Scottish criminal system is known as the Lord Justice General, with the Lord Justice Clerk next in precedence who also sits in the Court of Session.	Court of Session, which is the supreme civil court in Scotland and sits in Edinburgh. Can hear civil litigation at first instance and also deal with appeals on civil matters from courts of session and the Sheriff courts. It is divided between the Outer House, which deals with first instance cases and is staffed with twelve judges called Lords Ordinary who sit alone or with juries; and the Inner House, which deals with appeals; further divided between the first division, presided over by the Lord President with four judges, and a second division presided over by the Lord Justice Clerk. The head judge of the Scottish civil system is known as the Lord President of the Court of Session.

Criminal jurisdiction	Civil jurisdiction

Sheriff courts sitting with a judge known as a Sheriff who can try criminal cases with or without a jury. The solemn cases tried here can impose prison sentences as long as 3 years. The vocabulary of Scottish criminal procedure can be different; for example 'fire-raising' is used for the English crime of arson, 'culpable homicide' for manslaughter and 'house-breaking' for burglary. The defendant in Scottish criminal trials is known as 'the panel'. In Scotland the accused, as well as the Lord Advocate, can bring a charge of contempt against the media.

The Sheriff courts deal with lesser financial civil claims and family cases. Scottish legal terminology uses the terms 'pursuer' for the English and American claimant and plaintiff, and 'defender' for defendant. The concept of prior restraint injunctions is represented by the word 'interdict'. In both civil and criminal courts lawyers are known as advocates, not barristers. Instructing lawyers, as in England, are known as solicitors.

District Courts presided over by a Justice of the Peace or a Magistrate and dealing with minor criminal cases with maximum penalties of 60 days' imprisonment or £2,500 fine.

In Scotland there is no equivalent system of Coroner's courts and inquests. Instead, sudden deaths that relate to public safety are investigated by 'Fatal Accident Enquiries' presided over by Sheriffs.

The Office of the Procurator Fiscal is responsible for investigating (with assistance of the police) and prosecuting crime in Sheriff court districts under the supervision of the Crown Office. The Procurator Fiscal directs the police in criminal law, decides on whether the accused is held in custody or the case should continue. He questions the accused at a private hearing before a Sheriff within 24 hours of any arrest. Solemn cases should be tried within 12 months of the accused person's first court appearance. In other cases where the accused is in custody they should be tried within 110 days.

Scottish land law is dealt with by the Lands Tribunal for Scotland, Land Valuations Appeal Court and Scottish Land Court. The obscure Court of Lord Lyon deals with disputes over heraldry. Other legal institutions in Scotland performing important functions include the Office of the Public Guardian, Office of the Social Security Commissioners, the Pensions Appeal Tribunals for Scotland and VAT and Duties Tribunal for Scotland.

There is no youth or juvenile court system in Scotland: it was abolished in 1968. Instead, young people accused of crimes are dealt with by Children's Panels in private hearings with an official known as a 'reporter' investigating the child's circumstances. The age of criminal responsibility in Scotland is 8, rather than 10 in England and Wales, and the laws on identifying children in relation to legal proceedings are much stricter.

The Scottish legal system has a more restrictive approach to the concept of media contempt of court and it also has a law of defamation, though there are a number of differences from the system in England and Wales: the libel/slander does not have to be published to a third party, pursuers have 3 years in which to issue a writ for libel, justification is known as *veritas* and damages can be substantially reduced by the publication of an immediate apology.

Continued overleaf

Criminal jurisdiction	Civil jurisdiction

Children in adult courts

In criminal proceedings section 47 of
the Criminal Procedure (Scotland) Act
1995 bans identification of children
aged under 16 if they are the accused,
victim or witness. Deceased child victims
are usually identified. Criminal courts
have discretion to lift the reporting
ban. In adult courts children appearing
as witnesses where the defendants are
not under 16 could be identified in the
absence of any reporting ban. There is
discretion to allow the media to attend
children's hearings, but identification of
any children involved in the proceedings
is not allowed and this includes any kind
of photography. Reporting bans can also
be imposed on children aged 16 and
under involved in fatal accident enquiries.
Scottish judges also have the power to
ban identification of children under 17
involved in custody disputes.

But case law and custom do indicate that the Scottish judiciary is more
protective of the concept of legal authority and dignity and the Scottish
media may be more conscious of the need to protect the emotional integrity and dignity of the victims of crime; particularly of sexual offence
complainants. The Scottish judges are more protective of the concept
of fair trial against trial by media. For example, Lord Justice General
Cooper made it clear in 1954 that a guillotine on media reporting came
down once a person had been committed for trial and that

> public dissemination thereafter of insinuations or suggestions capable
> of prejudicing the public mind and the minds of prospective jurors
> with regard to a pending prosecution cannot be tolerated, for it is in
> our view prejudicial to the interests of justice.
>
> (MacAlister v Associated Newspapers SHJ 1954)

Six years later Lord Justice General Clyde stated:

> it is not part of our system that there should be a sort of preliminary
> trial of the case conducted in public by a newspaper, feeding to its
> readers pieces of evidence which the newspaper has unearthed, and
> which may ultimately be brought out in their proper setting at a trial
> in Court. Anything of the kind strikes at the very basis of the principle

that in Scotland an accused is entitled to a fair trial by an unbiased and unprejudiced jury.

(Stirling v Associated Newspapers SHJ 1960)

This harsher approach to media freedom has always posed difficulties for publishers wishing to distribute in England and Scotland. The Scottish police are not as free as the forces south of the border to make disclosures in press releases and press conferences after a suspect has been detained. They are guided by the Procurator Fiscal, who on very rare occasions may authorize the release of information to encourage members of the public to come forward. But the Scottish police have a long-standing policy of not releasing the details of a suspect or accused person who would be appearing before the Sheriff's court on serious matters (always in private session), and even then only the barest facts are made available, i.e. name, address, age and the fact he/she has been remanded for further examination. There is, therefore, an ever-present problem of potential contempt for editors supervising the reporting of a case with a Scottish legal process, and the police south of the border following a more open practice of media communication and sourcing background information.

The Scottish judiciary have never had any enthusiasm for American-style *voir dire* vetting of the jury: 'it is not part of our practice in Scotland to examine the antecedent knowledge of potential jurors before the ballot is held.' (Spink v HMA SHJ 1989)

The Scottish legal system could claim to have been more progressive in approaching criminal offending by children as a social problem, rather than as a penalizing process with a continuation from the nineteenth century of what Michel Foucault described as 'carceral culture' and the 'culture of spectacle'. As an extreme metaphor Scottish legal culture could be said to have decided that a more compassionate policy was needed toward youth offending than one of corporal punishment and placing 8-year-old children in public and adult criminal courts. Scotland also inaugurated the first United Kingdom televising of court proceedings through the issuing of a practice direction 'Television in the Courts' by the Lord President in 1992:

Requests from television companies for provision to film proceedings, including proceedings at first instance, for the purpose of showing educational or documentary programmes at a later date will be favourably considered. But such filming may be done only with the consent of all parties involved in the proceedings, and it will be subject to approval by the presiding Judge of the final product before it is televised.

(Eady and Smith 2005: 1246)

139

From 1999 Scotland was able to reinstitute its own parliament with the power to legislate on Scottish affairs. It has its own Minister of Justice with Scottish law officers, the Lord Advocate and Solicitor General, consulting the legislators in the Edinburgh Parliament. The taking into account of the European Convention on Human Rights from May 1999, about 18 months before England and Wales, has softened the country's rather dour approach to balancing the free media/fair trial issue, which tended to be more judicially conservative than the approach of the senior judges in London. The situation has changed from senior Scottish judges advising counsel not to quote bad English precedents to an element of harmonization. In an unobtrusive way it would seem that senior Scottish and English judges identify and compare more of what their legal systems have in common than how they are different. A brief comparison of the law of defamation in Scotland and in England and Wales is set out in Table 1.21.

The Scottish judiciary were more severe in punishing media contempt than their southern counterparts because of a separate procedure of visual dock identification and a different process of detention and arrest. A criminal suspect in Scotland can be detained for up to six hours before being formally arrested. This gives the police time to evaluate whether there is sufficient evidence to proceed further. Although the 1981 Contempt of Court Act strict liability rule (contempt being a substantial risk of serious prejudice) does not apply until the arrest stage is reached, the Scottish media are advised to proceed with great caution, as publication 'of information which creates a serious risk of prejudice to any future trial before an arrest is made or a warrant issued may be regarded as contempt at common law.' (Bonnington et al. 2000: 19)

There was also an obligation on the Crown to bring prosecutions to trial within 110 days of the first appearance in court at full committal. This limited the application of the fade factor in 'substantial risk' of prejudice. However, the Scottish system now allows for exceptions and extensions to the 110-day requirement in serious and complicated 'solemn' cases. Prejudicial reporting is, of course, more likely to stay in the minds of potential jurors over a three- to four-month period. Arlidge, Eady and Smith observe:

> It seems that Scottish and English courts have more recently been coming closer together in their application of public policy considerations relevant to these varied and difficult problems. It would be surprising if this were not in large measure due to the need to take account of the priorities of the European Convention on Human Rights.
>
> (Eady and Smith 2005: 1212)

Table 1.21 Distinctive differences between Scottish law of defamation and that of England and Wales

There is no distinction between libel and slander and both words are used as synonyms for defamation.

Exemplary damages form no part of Scottish law.

A cause of action does not die with the defamer and where a suit has commenced it does not die with the death of the person defamed.

Defamation in Scotland does not depend on publication to a third party. Publication to the person defamed is sufficient for a cause of action.

The pursuer of a defamation action in Scotland can sue within three years of any publications, whereas the limitation in England and Wales is one year.

There has been no criminal law of libel in Scotland.

The defence of justification is known as *veritas* and defamatory words can be defended as being 'justified'even though not in fact true.

Vulgar abuse known as *rixa* is a defence and covers intemperate expressions used in argument.

Scottish law allows a separate defence of 'fair retort' that intends to cover situations where someone repudiates defamatory statements by other people.

In Scotland statements in legal pleadings and instructions to counsel attract qualified legal privilege, unlike absolute privilege in English law.

Scottish defamation law has more similarities to than differences from the law in England and Wales.

Scottish defamation actions tend to be less frequent, with damages on a rather lower scale than in England and Wales.

The pursuer must in summons or initial writ state the sum of damages which is claimed and this is the maximum figure that can be awarded.

Actions for defamation can also be raised in the Sheriff Courts (equivalent of English County Courts), so there is an opportunity for fast-track and low-cost justice.

Scottish law retains the concept of a verbal injury civil wrong, known as *convicium*. To succeed, the pursuer has to prove that the defender has maliciously expressed an idea that creates public contempt or ridicule and causes the pursuer hurt feelings. The concept may be redundant. One of the last notable cases was *Sheriff v Wilson* in 1855 where a newspaper ridiculed the pursuer for being a glutton.

Scottish judges have been following their English counterparts in deciding that the robustness of jurors and their willingness to follow the evidence presented to them in court did not require their discharge after prejudicial media coverage, the order of a retrial and, at worst, an acceptance that the accused could never receive a fair trial. Lord Justice Clerk observed in 1999:

The administration of justice has to be robust enough to withstand criticism and misunderstanding. It would, of course, be an entirely different matter if the court were faced with conduct intended to impede or prejudice the administration of justice. The court could be well justified in making an order to prevent a deliberate affront to the administration of justice, for example, where a publication was regarded as impugning the integrity of the court or attacking its authority.

(Al-Megrahi v Times SHJ 1999)

This position was buttressed by the comment of Lord Cameron in 1982:

I think it may be assumed that jurors, having taken an oath to return a true verdict according to the evidence and having received clear direction from the presiding judges to put from their minds everything except the evidence which they have heard in court will be faithful to that oath and obedient to the directions of the judge.

(X v Sweeney SCS 1982)

Criticizing the system: legal authority and dignity

The Scottish judges can be seen as being more sensitive to criticism of their trial processes. Lord Skerrington expressed the view in 1918 that 'anyone is entitled to criticize the law, provided that he does so in a manner which is not disrespectful to the court and which is not calculated to interfere with the administration of justice.' (Kemp v Glasgow Corporation SCS 1918) This background of jurisprudential protectiveness sets the Scottish judiciary apart from that of England and Wales, where there is a greater tolerance of media attack and an acknowledgement that:

The path of criticism is a public way: the wrong headed are permitted to err therein: provided that members of the public abstain from imputing improper motives to those taking part in the administration of justice, and are genuinely exercising a right of criticism, and are not acting in malice, or attempting to impair the administration of justice, they are immune. Justice is not a cloistered virtue: she must be allowed to suffer the scrutiny and respectful, even though outspoken, comments of ordinary men.

(Ambard v AG for Trinidad & Tobago JCPVC 1936)

Gone are the days when a Birmingham newspaper in 1900 would be held in contempt for 'scurrilous abuse of a judge' in publishing the editorial opinion that Mr Justice Darling was:

an impudent little man in horsehair ... a microcosm of conceit and empty headedness ... No newspaper can exist except upon its merits, a condition from which the Bench, happily for Mr Justice Darling, is exempt. Mr Justice Darling would do well to master the duties of his own profession before undertaking the regulation of another.

(Borrie and Lowe 1973: 154)

The *Birmingham Daily Argus* was angry that the judge had warned the press not to publish any obscene matter arising out of a prosecution for obscene libel.

The last English and Welsh contempt prosecutions for abusing and impugning the impartiality of judges occurred in the 1920s and 1930s. One example, in 1928, involved the political weekly the *New Statesman*, which was held in contempt for attacking the judge presiding in a libel case involving Dr Marie Stopes, the pioneer of birth control:

We cannot help regarding the verdict given this week in the Libel action brought by the Editor of the *Morning Post* against Dr Marie Stopes as a substantial miscarriage of justice. We are not at all in sympathy with Dr Stopes' work or aims, but prejudice against those aims ought not to be allowed to influence a Court of Justice in the manner in which they appeared to influence Mr. Justice Avory in his summing up ... The serious point in this case, however, is that an individual owning to such views as those of Dr Stopes cannot apparently hope for a fair hearing in a Court presided over by Mr. Justice Avory and there are so many Avorys.

(R v New Statesman HC 1928)

In 1930 the socialist newspaper the *Daily Worker* was found to have scandalized the court with the observation:

Rigby Swift, the Judge who sentenced Comrade Thomas, was the bewigged puppet and former Tory member of Parliament chosen to put the Communist leaders away in 1926. The defending counsel, able as he was, could not do much in the face of the strong class bias of Judge and Jury.

(R v Wilkinson HC 1930)

It is in this historical context that there was some surprise in 2008 when solicitor Aamer Anwar had to answer for public media comments he had made after his client Mohammed Atif Siddique had been convicted of possessing terrorism-related material, circulating inflammatory materials and setting up websites showing how to make and use weapons, and jailed for eight years. Mr Anwar found himself before the High

Court of Justiciary on a 'remit by a trial judge of an issue of possible contempt of court'. Lawyers for Mr Anwar and the UK civil rights pressure group Liberty argued on a point of law that holding him in contempt for comments made after the conviction and sentence of his client was not compatible with the freedom of expression rights in Article 10 of the European Convention. This was the first time a solicitor had faced a contempt of court accusation in the UK for comments made outside the courtroom.

In a press conference outside the Glasgow High Court in September 2007 Mr Anwar had stated:

> Atif Siddique was today found guilty of doing what millions of young people do every day, looking for answers on the Internet. This verdict is a tragedy for justice and for freedom of speech and undermines the values that separate us from the terrorist, the very values we should be fighting to protect. This prosecution was driven by the state with no limit to the resources used to secure a conviction and it was carried out in an atmosphere of hostility after the Glasgow Airport attack and ending in the week of 9/11. Atif Siddique states that he is not a terrorist, and is innocent of the charges, and that it is not a crime to be a young Muslim angry at global injustice. In the end, Atif Siddique did not receive a fair trial, and we will be considering an appeal. The family now wishes to go home and to consider what has happened today.
>
> (re: Aamer Anwar SHJ 2008 para. 2)

The trial judge, Lord Carloway, objected to a combination of comments made by the solicitor in the press conference, in a press release, and during an interview on BBC *Newsnight* because they misrepresented the events of the trial, appeared to show disrespect for the court and jury, appeared to criticize his own conduct of the trial, and appeared to criticize the prosecutor and a witness.

The judges in Edinburgh were briefed on the latest Canadian case involving possible contempt through criticism of a judge in 1987. In Ontario a lawyer called Kopyto had said of a decision by Judge Zuker:

> This decision is a mockery of justice. It stinks to high hell. It said it is okay to break the law and you are immune so long as someone above you said to do it. Mr Dowson and I have lost faith in the judicial system to render justice. We're wondering what is the point of appealing and continuing this charade of the courts in this country which are warped in favour of protecting the police. The courts and the Royal Canadian Police are sticking so close together you'd think they were put together with Krazy Glue.
>
> (Ibid.: para. 25)

Kopyto's conviction for contempt was quashed. This was put forward as an example of how the courts should be able to weather trenchant criticism without permanent and significant damage to the administration of justice.

Lord Osborne, in giving the opinion of the Scottish high court, rejected the idea that Article 10 of the European Convention on Human Rights meant that public criticism of judges and court decisions could not be held to be in contempt of court:

> It is quite possible to conceive of language which would be of such an extreme nature that it did indeed challenge or affront the authority of the court or the supremacy of the law itself, particularly perhaps where the integrity or honesty of a particular judge, or the court generally, is attacked. [...] We believe that what we have just said is wholly consistent with the terms of Article 10 of the Convention. In paragraph 2 of that Article it is said specifically that: 'The exercise of these freedoms, since it carries with it duties and responsibilities, may be subject to such restrictions or penalties as are prescribed by law and are necessary in a democratic society ... for maintaining the authority and impartiality of the judiciary.'
>
> (Ibid.: para. 37)

Lord Osborne concluded that while Mr Anwar's statements 'embody angry and petulant criticism of the outcome of the trial process and a range of political comments concerning the position of Muslims in our society, we believe that the authority of the courts and the supremacy of the law have not been challenged or damaged by this criticism.' (Ibid.: para. 45) Lord Osborne described some of the comments made by the solicitor as being entirely unfounded and misleading, but not contempt of court. He added: 'This court is entitled to expect better of those who practice [sic] before it.' (Ibid.) It goes without saying that any American reading the account of this case would find the narrative alien and the application of legal concepts unreal in the context of their First Amendment traditions of robust free speech in the marketplace of ideas. Unlike in Scotland, where judges are appointed and accorded with an inherent aura of judicial authority, many US state judges have to stand for election and their authority is sustained by democratic mandate as well as by the context of federal and state constitutional authority. The imperative of judicial independence is therefore driven by contrasting factors that seek to achieve the same result.

The voluntary code on protecting sexual offence complainants:
a Scottish and English comparison

It is a fact that the Scottish Judiciary has never had to problematize the media in Scotland in respect of identifying the victims of sexual offences. As the authors of *Scots Law for Journalists* have said: 'The law in England on rape reporting has a much more chequered history, perhaps illustrating the wisdom of a voluntary code.' (Bonnington et al. 2000: 25) As a matter of custom, convention and practice, judges of the High Court of Justiciary usually close the doors of their courtrooms whenever victims of sexual offences give evidence, with the purpose of encouraging the giving of evidence. Reporters covering the cases would be allowed in court to take notes on the understanding that they would not publish anything that could lead to the complainant's identification. In 1983 Lord Avonside explained:

> In our courts a victim alleged to have been raped almost invariably gives evidence behind closed doors. In such a situation the public is not permitted to hear her evidence. It has been the practice, particularly in Glasgow, to allow the Press reporters to remain. They are asked to exercise a wise discretion, and, in my experience, this they do admirably. The trial judge could, of course, if he thought it desirable, exclude the Press and clear the court completely.
>
> (Ibid.)

It is, therefore, apparent that Scottish journalists have exercised ethical discretion in protecting the feelings and social dignity of sexual offence complainants with such discipline and consideration that there is no recorded case of any Scottish media publication or journalist being accused of breaching the practised anonymity, or being prosecuted for defying the implicit wish for the courts to give such witnesses confidentiality both in the courtroom and outside.

The Scottish position contrasts starkly with the situation in England and Wales, where Mrs Justice Rose Heilbron presided over a committee in 1975 that took evidence about many rape victims being traumatized by the publicity exploited in popular newspaper reports of their cases, where there seemed to be a language of entertainment associated with the coverage rather than fair and accurate reportage of serious and unpleasant crime.

The Heilbron Committee recommended legislation to give English and Welsh courts a statutory power to grant anonymity to complainants in rape cases:

> public knowledge of the indignity which [the complainant] has suffered in being raped may be extremely distressing and even positively

harmful, and the risk of such public knowledge can operate as a severe deterrent to bringing proceedings ... The balance of argument seems to us to be in favour of anonymity for the complainant other than in quite exceptional circumstances. While fully appreciating that rape complaints may be unfounded, indeed that the complainant may be malicious or a false witness, we think that the greater public interest lies in not having publicity for the complainant. Nor is it generally the case that the humiliation is anything like as severe in other criminal trials: a reprehensible feature of trials of rape ... is that the complainant's prior sexual history ... may be brought out in the trial in a way which is rarely so in other criminal trials.

(Heilbron 1975: paras. 153–7)

Parliament legislated for the Sexual Offences Amendment Act in 1976 and decided to extend the anonymity to the defendant in rape cases in order to ensure equality in law between complainants and defendants and protect potentially innocent defendants from the social stigma of the rape allegation. This exceptional provision for defendant anonymity was repealed in 1988.

A tragic case in 1984 may have been an influential reason for the reversal on defendant anonymity. The police in the north of England had not been able to fully publicize the escape from police custody in Yorkshire of a man accused of rape because of the anonymity restriction extending to the defendant. While a fugitive, he went on to break into a house in Sheffield where the occupants were sleeping after a wedding reception. He murdered two parents, their adult son, and raped the family's 18-year-old daughter. At his trial for the three murders, the trial judge agreed to lift the anonymity on the rape complainant because of a provision in the legislation which gives the court discretion if there is a substantial block to the reporting of the proceedings. The judge hoped that the media would show some restraint and sensitivity in reporting the case. Unfortunately, one popular newspaper gave front-page prominence to the cross-examination of the rape victim.

An attempt to map the main reporting restrictions facing journalists covering the Scottish courts is represented in Table 1.22.

English and Welsh reporting restrictions in relation to sexual offence complainants have been substantially extended by legislation since 1976. Statutory powers of anonymity apply to all kinds and degrees of sexual offences, and the anonymity provision applies from the time a complaint is made in perpetuity. (Sexual Offences Amendment Act 1992 and Sexual Offences Act 2003) Complainants can waive their anonymity, though they do so only rarely. English and Welsh judges also have formal powers to adopt special measures for the protection of witnesses and this can involve clearing the public gallery and leaving only one pooled reporter

Table 1.22 Media reporting restrictions in the Scottish legal system

Sexual offence complainants	By tradition the High Court of Justiciary closes its doors to the public when rape and attempted rape complainants give their evidence, with reporters allowed to be present but implicitly agreeing not to publish anything leading to the identification of the alleged victims. This ethical practice combines with legal custom to suggest that any identification of alleged sexual offence victims in Scotland would be regarded as a contempt of court. No Scottish media publication has ever been prosecuted for breaching this ethical/customary understanding.
Photography and televised coverage of accused persons	The Scottish legal process of dock identification means that it has generally been considered contempt of court to publish photographs or film of anyone arrested for a criminal offence in Scotland, or during the trial proceedings. '[T]here will be circumstances in which the identification of the accused will not give rise to a risk of prejudice. To give one example, if a celebrated television chat show host appeared on a speeding charge there would be unlikely to be any objection to his picture being published. His identity would already be well-known and a speeding case would not be tried by a jury' (Bonnington et al 2000: 169).
Injunctions in courts of England and Wales	Media law injunctions granted in the High Court of England and Wales do not apply in Scotland and if 'interdicts' are applied for, the issues will be evaluated according to Scottish law. As a result, the Scottish media were not bound by a London court ruling that the son of a British Home Secretary involved in a cannabis supply incident could not be identified because he was 17 years old. The bar in Scotland on identifying youths in criminal matters was 16. The situation also applies to injunctions involving the Official Secrets Act, as in the case of the book *Inside Intelligence* by MI6 intelligence officer Anthony Cavendish in 1989. The Scottish courts are not prepared to issue England and Wales style *contra mundum* (against the world) interdicts. Lord Eldon in *Iverson v Harris* 1812 held that a court could not 'hold a man bound by an injunction who is not a party in the cause'.
Children in Children's Panel system	Default anonymity for all children, a ban on photography, including pixellation, and on any references to their schools. Reporters are allowed to attend the hearings by discretion, unlike their counterparts in England and Wales who have a right to attend Youth Courts. Anonymity is achieved by the Social Work (Scotland) Act 1968 and the Children (Scotland) Act 1995. Children dealt with for criminal offences are asked to accept or deny a statement of fact. If the child's legal representative denies the statement, the case is transferred to the Sheriff for a 'Referral hearing'. These procedures take place in the Sheriff's private chambers. If the Sheriff decides that the child has committed a crime the matter is sent back to the Children's Panel for adjudication.
More severe application of 1981 Contempt of Court Act	After the arrest of a suspect, or the issue of a warrant (when the case becomes active) the Scottish courts expect a more stringent adherence to the strict liability rule. No photographs of any accused person likely to be tried by jury are permitted, and the kind of background and speculation tolerated in England and Wales on the basis of the 'fade factor' in a trial taking place many months later is likely to be treated as a contempt of court. Judges are also more sensitive to public and media criticism of their conduct and trials.

present and directing the provision of video-link facilities or screens to assist complainants who feel intimidated by the public courtroom environment. (Youth Justice and Criminal Evidence Act 1999) Yet there has been neither an accompanying increase in the number of victims reporting sexual offences nor any increase in the number of prosecutions leading to conviction. In fact the very reverse has been the case. This would suggest that the social difficulties and inhibitions of sexual offence complainants extend beyond the issue of potential media reporting of their cases. The media construction of sexual crime and its social and criminological understanding are complex issues.

The appropriate degree of open justice and privacy protection relating to the criminal prosecution of sexual offences remains a live and heavily debated issue in the United Kingdom. The House of Commons Select Committee on Home Affairs in 2003 recommended that the reporting restriction preserving the anonymity of complainants be extended to persons accused of those offences for the limited period between allegation and charge 'as an appropriate balance between the need to protect potentially innocent suspects from damaging publicity and the wider public interest in retaining free and full reporting of criminal proceedings.' (Fifth Report 2003: para. 80)

It had been impressed by the experience of a television celebrity arrested as he came off stage from a pantomime performance as Captain Hook. Lurid media coverage included headlines with such expressions as 'held over child sex', 'accused of sex attacks on boys', 'camp entertainer with an unconventional marriage', 'the weird life of Mr Saturday Night TV', yet a month later the police 'decided to take no further action on the grounds that there was insufficient evidence to charge.' (Ibid.: note 122)

The Committee was reluctant to extend the anonymity to a later time such as criminal conviction or sentence after its attention was drawn to the example cited by Professor Jennifer Temkin in her book *Rape and the Legal Process*. In 1986 the Wiltshire police had been constrained by anonymity rules from publishing the name of a man wanted for rape, who subsequently raped another woman before being arrested. (Temkin 2002: 308)

Neither the Scottish nor English and Welsh courts have considered the fullest option in the protection of sexual offence complainants in court proceedings – the hearing of their evidence in much more private and protected environments, with a restriction on the reporting of details to the briefest of summaries or, as expressed in the 1926 Judicial Proceedings (Regulation of Reports) Act 1(i)(b): 'a concise statement of the charges, defences and counter charges in support of which evidence is given'. This would have been a comfort to the complainant in a trial held at the Central Criminal Court in 2004 before Mr Justice Aikens. The witness explained that many of her work colleagues had already identified her and she was acutely embarrassed by the existing and potential reporting of intimate details connected with the event provided by both prosecution and defence. She asked the judge for further reporting restrictions on the evidence:

> If the details for which I am asking for a reporting restriction are published, there is a large number of people (those who work with me; and those who work in supporting roles e.g. security around the buildings) who I see on a daily basis and who will know those details about me.
>
> If that happened I would not be able to face returning to work and I would lose not only my income, but what has been till now a successful and satisfying career.
>
> As a result of this, without the benefit of the restrictions sought, I believe that I will be unable to give evidence in this case. Should they be granted I believe that they will maximise the quality of my evidence and give me the confidence I need to enter the court.
>
> (R v Burrell Central Criminal Court 2004 para. 11)

Counsel for the press resisted the applications for these further restrictions on the grounds that the media were an extension of the public gallery and the two were indivisible; there were the prosecution interests of upholding open and public justice in the role of minister of justice so that the public could say that purpose was pursued properly and fairly; there were the defendant's interests in having an open trial that the public could see was fair; there were the court's interests in an open trial showing the world that there had been no undue pressures on it; and there were the interests of the public in having access to open proceedings so that they could have confidence in the independence of judges and the administration of justice from the Executive. (Ibid.: para. 22) Mr Justice Aikens was persuaded that between the competing public interests, he could not impose the restrictions that the anonymous complainant had asked for. After giving evidence over two days, a medical practitioner experienced in dealing with complainants of sexual assault reported that she was too unwell to continue her evidence. The defendant had denied the rape allegation, saying that the woman had consented, and he was formally acquitted.

Would the complainant have obtained more protective legal measures from the Scottish Judiciary and media? Certainly the closing of the public gallery at the High Court of Justiciary in Glasgow or Edinburgh would have given her an additional shield of protection. The cooperative tradition maintained by Scottish judges and journalists could have extended to an understanding on how much of the evidential detail should have been released into the public domain. Journalists usually discard much of the detail in cases of this kind on the grounds of taste and decency.

The compassionate approach seemed to be evident in the case presided over by Lord Hodge in 2007, where he had issued reporting restrictions in order to preserve the anonymity of a woman infected with HIV and hepatitis C by her former lover. The defendant denied culpably and recklessly failing to tell her that he carried the infections, having unprotected sex with her, and endangering her life and health, but he was convicted by the jury. Lord Hodge explained that he, like other Scottish judges, had the power under section 92(3) of the Criminal Procedure (Scotland) Act 1995, to remove everyone from the court during the taking of a sexual offence complainant's evidence and, in the context of common law powers to regulate the proceedings, he could also allow a name or other matter to be withheld from the public in proceedings before the court. He added an order under section 11 of the Contempt of Court Act 1981 to effectively copper-bottom the restriction and make it apply to the media beyond the courtroom.

Lord Hodge said that a consultant clinical psychologist's reports indicated the victim was devastated by what had happened to her and that her mental health would be seriously undermined if members of the public were to discover her identity. Lord Hodge explained:

> I was satisfied that there was no counterbalancing public interest in the disclosure of information which would lead to her being identified. The order did not prevent open justice. Members of the press remained in court throughout this trial and the order which I made did not restrict the ability of the media to give a balanced report of the sad events which these proceedings have disclosed. [...] I recognise the benefits of accurate reporting of court proceedings and the very valuable role of a free press in informing the public of the administration of justice. There are cogent reasons why as a general rule court proceedings are conducted in public and can be reported by the media. But exceptional circumstances can arise where it is necessary to restrict the publication of matters in relation to court proceedings in the interest of the administration of justice.
>
> (*Media Lawyer* March 2007: 39)

The ethical position of the media was that it was intending to make representations against the judge's order but decided to withdraw after learning about the nature of the case and the complainant's predicament. The judge returned the courtesy by explaining his legal approach in a written and open court explanation.

This is an interesting demonstration of respect between media and judiciary and not unlike the position I experienced in 1982 when, with other journalists at the Central Criminal Court, we decided to challenge the early use of Section 11 to ban reporting the identity of a young woman who had been the principal prosecution witness in a kidnapping case. There was a newsworthy element to the case because of the prominent nature of her family. The woman's father instructed counsel to apply for the order on the basis that she was a recovering heroin addict and publicity would undermine her treatment. My position, and that of the other journalists, was that we would be prepared to exercise our discretion in not identifying her in court reports, but had to challenge the unprecedented nature of the court order. It sought to be retrospective, as she had already been named and her photograph had been widely published in relation to the case. She was named before the public during the open court proceedings and we had also discovered that the media had not been given any right of appeal against reporting bans issued by judges in the 1981 legislation. She herself had also indicated in cross-examination that she thought her father was more interested in the problem of publicity than she was.

From a personal point of view I admired the young woman's family for doing everything in their power to protect her and I had already decided that I would be prepared to exercise my ethical discretion in not continuing to name her. I was influenced by the fact that someone close to me had been fighting a desperate battle against addiction illnesses from which she would eventually die and so I had personal knowledge of the situation. It was most disappointing that editors of some national newspapers were persuaded to criticize in writing our decision to challenge the judge's misuse of powers which, unlike Lord Hodge in Scotland, he did not have at that time.

The situation was resolved by the NUJ's funding an appeal to the Divisional Court, and an application to the ECHR in Strasbourg. (R v Central Criminal Court 1984) Any potential harm to the prosecution witness, known as 'Miss X', that might be caused by the overturning of the ban was deftly side-stepped by joining the case with another Crown Court reporting ban that did not involve the issue of witness vulnerability. Another judge had banned a television company from using actors to simulate contemporaneous reports of a celebrated official secrets prosecution while the case was being heard before a jury. After the European Court application had been ruled admissible, the British government negotiated a settlement by introducing legislative machinery for appealing Crown Court reporting restrictions.

Although the First Amendment will usually protect US journalists from publishing matters of public record, it cannot be said that they are not willing to follow ethical traditions in protecting the privacy and dignity of alleged crime victims. The nature and style of reporting sexual offence crimes in US states is often negotiated and influenced by joint judicial and media bench committees and this may be another positive model illustrating the wisdom and virtues that emerge from all sides committing themselves to a voluntary code of ethical conduct.

Conclusion

The focus in the comparison of primary media law and ethics of the USA and UK has been on the areas of contempt of court or 'free press/fair trials', defamation and privacy. There has also been an exploration of the differences in the approach to media law issues in Scotland, a constituent country of the UK, which for reasons of history has had an independent judicial system since union with England and Wales in 1707.

A fundamental difference between British and American media law is that in the USA a long-standing and legitimate written constitution has evolved with the history and developing power and confidence of the country. A strong constitutional protection for freedom of speech and freedom for the media, operating as a priority in relation to other constitutional rights, has again in the context of historical events given American media communicators more freedom to make mistakes and not be penalized by criminal or civil sanctions. The crystallization of the democratic and libertarian potential of the First Amendment did not happen, though, until the USA had to politically, socially and culturally bring about an end to the systematic structure of apartheid and discrimination applying to its African-American population. The significance of the defining or 'liminal' Supreme Court case that catalysed a genuine revolution in US media law in 1964 will be analysed in Chapter 3.

In the area of free press/fair trials, prior restraint powers exercised by UK judges and criminal sanctions through contempt prosecution have severely restrained the range and depth of media coverage of crime and law stories. This approach is clearly different from the situation facing the US media. The British policy would have validity if it could be shown to inhibit miscarriages of justice and promote the impartial and fair adjudication of citizens sitting in judgment of their peers. The policy could be investigated by reliable and empirical research, yet the country's contempt laws make it a criminal offence to interview jurors on the extent to which media influences affected their deliberation of verdicts. Is it possible to identify specific factors indigenous to British society and culture that require such a stringent approach to the censorship of court reporting? An analysis of two case histories, one British involving an American defendant, and the other an American case involving a doctor who lost everything but his faith in the American constitution, will be the subject of Chapter 4.

In the third area of analysis it would seem that America has been settled in its approach to the development of a law of media privacy for a good hundred years. Jurisprudence was seeded with academic analysis by the jurists Brandeis and Warren, privacy laws were developed through statute

Table 1.23 Sources of Scottish media law

Scots Law for Journalists, by Alistair Bonnington, Rosalind McInnes and Bruce McKain, 2000, 7th edition, Edinburgh: W. Green/Sweet & Maxwell Ltd. An 8th edition is planned for 2010.

'Scotland', in *Arlidge, Eady & Smith on Contempt*, by Sir David Eady and Professor A.T.H. Smith, 2005, 3rd edition, London: Sweet & Maxwell Ltd.

'Scottish Legislation', in *Media Law for Journalists*, by Ursula Smartt, 2006, London, Thousand Oaks and New Delhi: Sage. (Summaries on Luke Mitchell murder trial [2004–2005], naming of the Home Secretary's son [1997], Orkney child abuse cases [1989–1993] and Cox and Griffiths – *Daily Record* case [1998].)

'Law of Defamation in Scotland', in *Carter-Ruck on Libel and Slander* by Peter F. Carter-Ruck and Harvey Starte, 1997, 5th edition [6th edition due in August 2009], London: Butterworths, pp. 415–17. Contempt of Court in Scotland, by Rosalind M.M. McInnes with J. Douglas Fairley, 2000, Welwyn Garden City: CLT Publishing Group.

Scottish Legal system: structure, sources and rulings at www.scotcourts.gov.uk/about.asp

The Scottish Law Commission at www.scotlaw.com.gov.uk/

---

and case law in the various state jurisdictions, and the Supreme Court ensured that First Amendment rights were not crippled. The narrative in Britain is rather more chaotic and unhappy. Parliament has claimed that it has not and will not legislate for a privacy law. But at the same time it has been accused of allowing the judges, through judicial activism, to develop privacy law 'by the back door' after the European Convention on Human Rights was incorporated into British statute law and included a clearly defined right to respect for privacy. The mischief or justice of this move, without written constitutional context and correction has been leading to media law developments set out in Chapter 5 that might be regarded as intolerable, unconstitutional and jurisprudentially flawed in the USA. In our consideration of the nature of Scottish media law a focus on the case history of a lawyer having to answer to a charge of contempt for seeking to represent the views of his client post conviction demonstrates a greater sensitivity to criticism of judges, juries and trial participants than we would find in the English and American jurisdictions. However, the mutual respect, voluntary engagement of journalism ethics and use of judicial devices to protect sexual offence complainants in Scotland suggests that the relationship between judiciary and media does not have to be one of enduring tension, distrust and antipathy. Contemporary sources and explanations of Scottish media law are set out in Table 1.23.

2

MEDIA JURISPRUDENCE, MEDIA ETHICOLOGY AND MEDIA ETHICISM

Media jurisprudence investigates the philosophy of making media laws. Media ethicology enquires into the discourse on the ethics of media communication, in particular the private space for individual moral decisions. Media ethicism is the study of the doctrines of media communication, and concentrates on the political-philosophical context. Media jurisprudence looks into how and why laws are made to control media messaging. Media ethicology invites a study of the debate on how media communicators should behave from a moral point of view. Media ethicism investigates the belief systems or doctrines of media communicators. These belief systems are ideological, religious or political. They are sometimes spiritual and, at the very least, are always philosophical.

This chapter seeks to bring clarity and logic to the study of the broader subject area of linking journalism, media, law and ethics. The subject is clearly located at the conjunction of moral and political philosophy. It is a subject area that at the time of writing appears to be expanding and developing in universities throughout the world. It has been taught in the Department of Media & Communications at Goldsmiths, University of London since 1991 and is now established in the syllabus for undergraduate and postgraduate courses. It is a complex subject because the object of this enquiry is complex. Furthermore, ideas, concepts and methodologies overlap between the spheres of media jurisprudence, ethicology and ethicism.

Media jurisprudence

Media jurisprudence requires an analytical and descriptive process in determining the nature of media laws and a normative discourse on what media laws ought to be. This bifurcation is sensible. The English jurist Jeremy Bentham talked about the expositional and the censorious. Another English jurist, John Austin, defined the division as between the analytical and the normative. Any observation of human society reveals that this is the tendency of social human discourse. There are always

155

those who want to understand things by analysis, and there are always those who want to make judgments on what is right and wrong. And there are always the people who wish to do both. In America and Britain it is possible to identify three broad traditions of media ethicological discourse: the deontological; the consequential; and the virtuous. These are summarized in Table 2.1

It is possible to go so far as to say that media jurisprudence is the scientific enquiry into media legal phenomena. What is the nature of the reality

Table 2.1 The three traditions of media ethicological discourse

Deontological (duty-based)	*Consequential (utilitarian and teleological)*	*Virtue (human flourishing)*
Christian ethics	Utilitarianism	Neo-Aristotelianism
Duties apply regardless of the consequences. Influence of the Decalogue (Ten Commandments). Absolute duties. Word of God sets absolute values of right and wrong. Essentially a system of dos and don'ts; similar to other monotheistic religions such as Islam and Judaism. Whilst 'Thou shalt not kill' is supposed to be universalizable, complex variations of the Christian doctrinal tradition can justify killing in the context of 'a just war', an exceptional circumstance. The Christian moral code is an objective and infallible guide to correct behaviour because the code is regarded as an expression of God's will.	The right and wrong of human speech and actions are determined not by intentions but by consequences. Leading advocates included Jeremy Bentham (1748–1832) and John Stuart Mill (1806–73). The doctrine sought to establish a secular morality by calculating probable consequences in terms of human happiness. It is hedonistic in nature because the ends are articulated in terms of 'pleasure'. Bentham saw happiness as a blissful mental state and the absence of pain. He coined the term 'felicific calculus' as an objective method of applying his moral formula. Mill sought to categorize higher and lower forms of happiness, the former being intellectual and idealistic; the latter being sensorial and materialistic.	Virtue ethics are inspired by Aristotle's ethical theory set out in Nicomachean ethics. These ethicists stress the importance of character and conduct over the course of a person's life. The moral question is dependent not on the rights and wrongs of motives, actions and consequences, but rather on the virtues that guide the way an entire life is lived. Human flourishing rather than happiness was encapsulated in the ancient Greek word *eudaimonia*. Human virtue was the pattern of behaviour and feeling of an individual's life, and includes emotions as well as an intelligent judgment in responding to situations.

Deontological (duty-based)	Consequential (utilitarian and teleological)	Virtue (human flourishing)
Kantian ethics	**Negative and rule utilitarianism**	**The Golden Mean**
Actions are motivated by internal moral duty rather than purpose or goal. Essential obligation, over being obliged. Emotional feelings are not good enough in terms of moral motivation. There has to be a sense of moral duty, not the self-interest of personal feelings or the gratification of an objective or goal. Intentions are defined by maxims. Morality is a system of categorical imperatives, or commands. The first and basic maxim is 'Act only on maxims which you can at the same time will to be universal laws'; similar to a Golden Rule of Christianity: 'Do unto others as you would have them do unto you'. Everybody should be treated as ends in themselves rather than means to an end. Hence the maxim 'Treat other people as ends in themselves, never as means to an end' represents an important categorical imperative.	Negative utilitarianism determines that the best speech/action in any set of circumstances is not the one producing more happiness than unhappiness for the greatest number of people. It would be speech that produces the least overall amount of unhappiness. Rule utilitarianism avoids the unhappy consequences of act utilitarianism, where an evil motive and action produces aggregate happiness for the greatest number of people. It adopts rules and principles that tend generally to produce more happiness for the greatest number. It is a method of combining the deontological with consequential ethics. It is also regarded as altruistic rather than hedonistic utilitarianism.	Virtue ethics guide people not to always take the middle ground, but rather to make the right decisions in any set of circumstances. In terms of communicating, the virtue ethicist speaks appropriately in relation to the context. This involves good motives, and determining good actions to achieve good consequences. Aristotle saw the virtuous individual harmonizing all his/her virtues in order to live a worthwhile life. Virtues are to be distinguished between intellectual and moral. Moral virtues are acquired through training and are habit forming. Intellectual virtues are conscious decisions. It is the difference between the emotional and the rational. They fall between two extremes, i.e. 'The Golden Mean', but *phronimos*, or practical wisdom, is expressed according to the shifting extreme polarities of any situation.

of media laws? What is the structure of the system of media laws that apply to media communication? This is a metaphysical enquiry because it searches for evidence in the same way that traditional sciences test theories about how the world works. *Meta* in Greek means beyond or after. So the etymological meaning of metaphysical is after or beyond the study of physics. It searches for a definition and explanation of the reality of

Plate 4 W.T. Stead in 1889, the editor of London evening newspaper the *Pall Mall Gazette*, who, in his zeal to campaign against child prostitution went to jail for breaking the law.

media laws. It is an aspiration to objectivity. In reality, scholarship in this area is likely to clutch at the straws of subjectivity. *Juris* in Latin means 'of law' and *prudens* means 'skilled'. This means that we aim to be skilled in our approach to explaining what media law is and what it ought to be.

When we ask what media law ought to be we are inevitably invited to consider what constitutes good media law and we should consequently have a view on what constitutes bad media law. This enquiry is a search for knowledge. How can we be certain that a media law is right or wrong? Are there any absolute truths about the moral validity of media laws? This is an epistemological enquiry. It is an investigation into the theory of the knowledge of media laws. John Austin effectively set out this distinction between the analytical and the normative approach in his 1832 book *The Province of Jurisprudence Determined*.

It would be useful to explain the intellectual and academic expectations of media jurisprudence. Fundamentally, the general approach involves the study of legal rules for journalists. As the definition of journalism is elastic and open to debate, it would be more helpful to talk about the laws that apply to media communicators. This will enable us to embrace people who communicate in the media industries beyond those roles associated with journalistic programmes and institutions.

The existence of a body of legal rules for media publication tends to be a feature of the more developed legal systems. The analysis of these legal rules oscillates between a general approach and a particular approach. When the media laws of more than one legal jurisdiction are analysed this would be a general approach in media jurisprudence. When the structure and elements of media laws in a single legal system are analysed the media jurisprudential approach would be particular.

When analysing the media laws of any jurisdiction there is an academic aspiration to be scientific and empirical in the process of discovering and explaining the elements of media law. Language is essential to defining and explaining media law. This means that media jurisprudence must analyse, challenge and probe the limitations of language used and how statements can be proved or falsified.

When studying the normative values of media law every effort is made to define the standard of perfection and criteria for what constitutes 'good media law'. The normative as opposed to analytical approach concentrates on what media laws ought to be. This understandably leads on to a critical approach to media jurisprudence. When we criticize the moral values inherent in media laws it is likely that we will be invited to offer proposals to change them. We can be prescriptive in our process of criticism. In this process of prescription we are likely to recommend what the media laws that we propose should prohibit, censor and limit in terms of behaviour and content. We will be deciding on what kinds of communication and media behaviour we wish to make unlawful.

Most interdisciplinary and multidisciplinary subjects require either a parallel or intertwining of methodology from different academic disciplines. Since media laws exist within the context of human societies and cultures and can be described as responses to or linked to social and cultural phenomena, it would be logical to acknowledge the sociological and cultural studies references in media jurisprudence. In reality the multidisciplinary nature of the subject embraces a variety of disciplines including traditional philosophy, psychology, sociology, anthropology and cultural studies.

Media jurisprudence engages a debate between first order and second order language. First order language makes bold jurisprudential assertions. Second order language seeks to clarify the thinking that lies behind these jurisprudential and ethicological assertions. For example, we want to know why people think a particular media law is right or wrong.

The contextual approach to studying media jurisprudence also requires considering the historical development and growth of media law systems. Economic as well as social phenomena affect the creation and application of media laws. This is particularly the case in respect of treating information as intellectual property.

Media jurisprudential, ethicological and ethicist concepts

Conceptual terms are, unfortunately, not fixed with assured transferable meanings. In one academic discipline they may mean one thing, and in another something else. In media and cultural studies the word 'ontology' seems to restrict itself to a science of being or the real nature of things. In Greek the word *ont* means 'being' and *ology* relates to 'discourse on'. But the word in traditional philosophy embraces more than the study of ideas in being and belief systems. In the mainstream subject of philosophy, ontology involves a study of the idea of God in being. The ontological argues for the existence of God, based purely on a proposed definition of God, and independent of evidence. The ontological is anterior to human experience. It is *a priori* and not *a posteriori*. The ontological is therefore a clear attitude about the nature of being rather than a position in a debate about whether being is a matter of God's existence or not.

This leads us on logically to another regularly used concept and word in the study of media jurisprudence and ethicology. Deontology is the discourse on duty or moral obligations. The word is based on the Greek *deont* meaning 'it is right'. You will frequently be presented with the word 'deontological', meaning that there is an immutable duty to comply or follow the moral and legal prescription.

Academic writing on journalism and communication can be subject to intellectual vagueness and potential misunderstanding. We need to be open minded and appreciate cross-cultural, cross-disciplinary, cross-temporal changes and differences in meaning.

We have accepted that the intellectual journey that we undertake is not a simple one. Media jurisprudence is predicated within the rich debates present in political philosophy. What is the relationship between media law and the individual? What is the nature of justice in media law? How is the application of media laws reconciled with the understanding of individual freedom, the idea of the general will, the sovereign power of the state and the debates concerning the nature of the social contract?

Media jurisprudence has to be considered in the context of ethics and moral philosophy. Are media laws created and applied from facts, values or choices? Media laws have to be evaluated in terms of the tension between recognizing the absolute or the relative in morality. Are media laws the product of moral values or of a political and cultural construction by society? How can media laws be reconciled with the notion of individual freedom and determinism?

The methodology of media jurisprudence has to be considered in the context of the philosophy of science. What is the difference between theory and observation? How do we determine whether a media law is right or wrong? The key concepts are also determined by what we understand as the relationship between personal identity and individual consciousness. This is because morality is rooted in conscience. We cannot ignore the philosophy of religion, which determines the nature of mind and body within a wider understanding of the existence of God, the meaning of God, religious experience and the problem of evil. These issues have to be considered within the wider context of theories of knowledge, our understanding of appearance and reality, and the uses and function of language.

The dominant intellectual metaphor in a significant area of academic study is the idea of the binary opposition, or the dialectical. We can be forgiven for thinking that it originates from Marxist dialectical materialism; but in fact it hails from a mental template that Plato formulated almost three thousand years ago.

Plato's writing, and in particular the setting out of his Socratic dialogues, provides an early inspiration for the idea that the world and reality are characterized by contradictions between opposites. The dialogues use Socrates (470–399 BCE), probably as Plato's vicarious character who, continually interrogated, established ideas of natural science, ethics and politics. In fact the absolutist *a priori* philosophical position adopted by Plato contrasts creatively and conveniently with his pupil Aristotle's desire to embrace a more relativist approach. The eternal contradiction between objectivism and subjectivism could be said to have seeded from these schools of scholarship. Plato was the master and Aristotle was his pupil. Plato (427–347 BCE) founded a school of philosophy called the Academy. Aristotle (384–322 BCE) founded a school called the Lyceum.

Plato and Aristotle became key sources for dichotomies in philosophy. These include the oscillation between rationalism and empiricism and between idealism and materialism. Plato believed that forms or ideals are most important, with a perspective from top to bottom. Aristotle believed that the particulars of life are most important, with a perspective from the bottom up.

Another way of distinguishing these two giants of ancient Greek philosophy would be to cast Plato in the role of the mathematician. Truth resides in the purity of an equation by Euclid. Aristotle is the biologist, where truth resides in the creativity of human experience. Plato's position advocated an assignation of specificity in meaning. This excludes deviant interpretation and prescribes the same meaning in every case where the media law rule is applicable. It underlines the pre-eminence of certainty and predictability in extracting the meaning of media law rules. Formalism is an established intellectual approach of analysis in media jurisprudence. It seeks to minimize the element of choice in interpreting the terms expressed in legal rules.

However, both Plato and Aristotle believed that we strive towards a goal of goodness. Aristotle believed that the highest teleological objective for man was encapsulated in the word *eudaimonia*, which can be translated as 'full of good spirit' or happiness. Another way of translating the word is to consider the idea of a lifetime of human flourishing. The pursuit of happiness would be the teleological goal enshrined in the American constitution and the purpose of nineteenth-century utilitarianism. The notion of the good is the value associated with key social objectives such as equality, human dignity and liberty.

The word *dialectic* is derived from the Greek verb for debate or discourse, *dialego*. Dialectical debate, or the struggle between two opposing binary positions, is supposed to result in newer and higher forms of resolution which are, in turn, challenged by more opposing arguments. The German philosopher Georg Hegel is credited with arguing that existence is the product of reason or pure thought in the context of a collective consciousness that he described as the *Volksgeist*.

Hegel's dialectic involves the interpenetration between thesis, an existing or established idea, and antithesis, an opposing or contradictory idea. This intercourse between the two opposites will produce synthesis, a newer and higher form of idea that will have generated qualitatively superior notions. Progress is, therefore, defined as a continuing cycle of dialectical struggle and resolution between new opposites, gestated by the interpenetration of thesis and antithesis. There is a curious similarity between this process of conceptualizing thesis and antithesis into synthesis, and the explanation for biological reproduction and evolution.

Karl Marx borrowed Hegel's philosophical model of the dialectic discourse. Marx's interpenetration would be between materialistic phenomena rather than abstract noumena. He saw the dialectical struggle between the physical realities of social class and economic circumstance as opposed to a struggle between mental ideas. Phenomena are those things that can be perceived by the senses and noumena are those things that are in themselves. Noumena can be imagined, but not experienced by human senses. Marx postulated an interpenetrative struggle between social and economic classes. Reality was therefore a dialectical tension between natural and social phenomena, and he called this dialectical materialism.

A close examination of the political debates that take place before media law legislation is enacted in Parliament reveals dialectical communication and resolution. This is also true of the adversarial jousts in courtrooms before judge-made law is created in the process of media law litigation. It is a discernible pattern of discourse in media jurisprudence.

Plato believed that it was possible for people to know the absolute truth about things. Plato would have been certain that he could set out an explanation of justice as truth. This confidence in being able to rely on absolute truths is known as cognitivism. It is an unfashionable position. Many professors in the world of academia will be wholly resistant to the idea that journalism or media communication is capable of expressing pure objectivity and absolute truth. However, in the field of media jurisprudence it would be prudent to acknowledge that there are many people in the world who sincerely believe in notions of absolute truth. It could be described as an emotional aspiration. Journalists and writers continually seek to write the truth about an event or story. It cannot be ignored as a humanistic intellectual objective. Sometimes academics confuse the use by professional journalists of the word 'objectivity' as a conceited belief in expressing absolute truth when it is usually deployed as an aspiration to disclosing a narrative explanation through analytical investigation.

We should also be aware that media laws might develop as a result of contractarian agreements. Individuals agree on the terms, rules and etiquette by which they communicate with each other. Does such a social contract exist as a matter of genuine historical fact? Or is it a case of logical presumption based on the empirical observation that there are established and maintained ties of social civility? The contractarian approach envisages that media laws evolve as a result of agreement rather than conflict.

Another way of evaluating media law is to consider the role of the command or imperative authority. The analysis therefore emphasizes that the nature of law is based on the constitution of orders, commands and coercive actions from identifiable sources of legal power in any society. Jeremy Bentham and John Austin believed that law is a set of general commands by a sovereign power reinforced by the threat of sanctions. The Austro-American jurist Hans Kelsen believed that law was a system of conditional directives that he described as primary norms. The primary norms are applied by officials, with specific sanctions for law breaking.

Some theorists have adapted the idea of the primary norm to take on the pre-eminence of proto-norm in media ethics. The word 'proto' is derived from the Greek word *protos* for 'first' in contrast to *meta*, meaning 'over or beyond'. Again, this binary approach to analysis seems to be parallel to the distinction in meaning between the Latin terms *a priori* and *a posteriori*.

Media laws can be divided between primary and secondary laws. The terminology could also switch to a division between 'hard' and 'soft' law. It could be argued that primary laws are those passed by legislatures as statutes and case law decisions, or legal precedents made by judges. Secondary laws are regulatory rules created and policed by delegated bodies or disciplinary organizations. The formulation of primary or secondary media law can be the result of discretion in judicial decision making.

This envisages that judges make decisions that are based on their own personal and individual conceptions of right and wrong, or what they believe is the best course to take in terms of public policy and social interest. In this way they are exercising a quasi-legislative function. It is argued that when judges make decisions in these hard cases they are creating new media law. This is likely to happen when there is no clear rule of law that can be applied to the facts of the case under consideration, or where there is an irreconcilable conflict between existing rules.

The jurisprudential philosopher Ronald Dworkin disagrees with the proposition that judges are exercising discretion when deciding these cases. He argues that in such cases there is always a right answer and the person or organization who wins had a right to win the case.

Judges and politicians often judge the merits of media laws in terms of their efficacy. What is the capacity of a certain measure to achieve a particular goal or objective? The jurist Hans Kelsen argues that efficacy is a specific requirement for the operation of any legal system. Media laws are to be evaluated on their capacity to apply sanctions regularly and efficiently. The media jurisprudential approach to epistemology is divided between empiricism and rationalism. In rationalism all knowledge is appreciated mentally. In empiricism all knowledge is appreciated by the senses. Therefore, the rationalist approach is based on the mental knowledge of ideas and interpretation of experience. The application of the mind happens first and the evaluation of sensory experience is secondary. The empirical approach prioritizes a study of the world based on observation by senses.

In media jurisprudence empiricism rejects all judgments based on value. True propositions about the nature of media law can only depend on objectively verifiable statements. The process of reasoning is therefore inductive because it requires an empirical observation of facts and the formulation of a hypothesis that is applied to these facts. This empiricist process must take place before any attempt is made to advance a theoretical explanation of any media legal phenomena. This is the opposite of a deductive process of reasoning, where the argument is based on logical and mentally thought-out principles, not on any assessment of observable evidence.

It will be apparent that the analysis and normative debates in media jurisprudence are often predicated on a point of view. The morality perspective starts from a position where there is certainty on what is good and bad, right and wrong, acceptable and unacceptable. It is deontological. The values are judged by an *a priori* standard. The materialist perspective is derived from the Marxist doctrine and assumes that changes and developments in media law are based on the material conditions of human social interaction. Dialectical and historical materialism determines the historical development of media laws in society. This is achieved through an ongoing struggle within associations and contradictions between economic, political, technical and social phenomena. The libertarian perspective predicates the development of media law on the concept of liberty. All the legal and social arrangements for media law must protect, attain and specify the particular freedoms inherent in liberty. The intuitionist perspective emphasizes the possession of human conscience that intuits an understanding of right and wrong, good and evil.

Media ethicology

It can be argued that media laws and media ethics are created as the result of moral judgments. Moral philosophy can be divided between the formalist approach and the content theoretical approach. Again, the difference can be attributed to the distinction between Platonic and Aristotelian theory. Form is about personal value judgments. Content is about experience and observation. The characteristics of formalist moral philosophy are: prescriptive, overriding and universalizable. The universalizable factor means that the moral judgment has a wide application that transcends applicability to single issues or problems. The overriding factor means that it is the trump card in any balancing issue between one moral question and another. The prescriptive factor means that the moral judgment is a specific recommendation directed to the self and others. It is the ethical directive on how to behave in a particular set of circumstances.

Again, the twin approaches of formalist and content offer a binary opposition in meaning and analysis. Content theorists regard the morality of media laws and ethics as having a specific content that can be objectively defined, identified and empirically analysed. This means that the morality of media laws and ethics consists of definite social phenomena that have been developed over time to help people deal with the recurring problems of trying to live together and communicate with each other. Content morality is therefore all about those principles that regulate the human condition in terms of balancing the social relationship between individual interests and protecting those values considered vital for the survival and maintenance of human society.

As a result of this approach some media laws will be considered invalid if they substantially deviate from these key moral principles. A leading legal writer on content theory was the London University Law Professor H.L.A. Hart, whose seminal book *The Concept of Law* (1961) argues that morality must contain a specific content of prioritized principles. These must recognize that survival is the pre-eminent objective of law. Consequently laws must begin by protecting life, property and promises. He called this his 'minimum content theory'. Hart was concerned about the identification of rules as generally accepted standards of behaviour. He believed that law is constituted by a systematic interaction between specific types of social rules. These rules have particular characteristics and can be divided between primary rules, which impose duties on citizens to act or forbear in certain situations, and secondary rules, which are power conferring and which determine how the primary rules are properly created, applied and changed.

Media jurisprudence and media ethicology are concerned with the influence and provenance of natural law theory. Natural law jurists argue that laws are a social necessity and based on universal principles that can be understood and revealed through rational contemplation. Therefore, media laws and ethics are eternal and immutable because they are based on the nature of human beings. It follows that any law that violates the natural moral code is invalid.

Aristotle, in *Nicomachean Ethics Book 1*, argued: 'Every art and every investigation, and similarly every action and pursuit, is considered to aim at some good. Hence the good has been rightly defined as "that at which all things aim". Clearly, however, there is some difference between the ends at which they aim: some are activities and others are results distinct from the activities. Where there are ends distinct from the actions, the results are by nature superior to the activities.' (Aristotle 2003: 3) Natural law therefore asserts that there is supreme good for human beings to aspire to. Plato, in his articulation of the 'Form of the Good', argues that the good purpose has a permanent reality that is beyond our own minds and perceptions.

Natural law is not the same as the law of nature. It is the rational consideration of the final purpose of everything in nature and the conscious shaping of action to bring it in line with that purpose.

Natural law is also concerned with considering media laws and ethics as having some teleological purpose. Teleology is the view that existence has an ultimate purpose or end and those media laws will inevitably help us to reach this goal. The objective is an ultimate state of perfection. Media ethics and laws must therefore strive to precipitate this end. Law must be a teleological device to advance us on our road to perfection.

Hans Kelsen preferred to think in terms of norms. These are generally accepted standards of social behaviour that in their primary form stipulate sanctions for contravention and can relate to conditional directives given to officials to apply sanctions under certain circumstances. A particular person usually regards sanction as a negative or harmful formal consequence of a specific act. Sanction involves an exertion of legitimate power by state and society.

John Austin, in his book *The Province of Jurisprudence Determined* (1832), stipulated that sanctions constituted harm, pain or evil. These sanctions are a necessary element of the law. He saw the law as being made up of the general commands of the sovereign power backed by sanctions that were the negative consequences that followed non-compliance with the sovereign authority. Hans Kelsen, in his book *General Theory of Law and the State* (1945), regarded sanctions as both positive and negative. Some constituted punishments. Others could be rewards that officials mete out to non-compliant citizens in certain circumstances.

The notion of the obligation is often considered fundamental to understanding the nature of media laws and ethics. The German Enlightenment philosopher Immanuel Kant probably inspired H.L.A. Hart to make the distinction between being obliged to act or forbear in accordance with a media law and being under an obligation to do so. Being obliged involves being motivated by fear of some sanction that occurs as an external pressure. Being under an obligation involves an internal as well as an external pressure to obey a media law. It is the consent by conscience.

This internal element can be described as the subject feeling a sense of duty to act or forbear (abstain or refrain from action). Kant placed a higher moral value on the internal element rather than the external influence. He recognized that the social consequences are the same, but the sense of moral being within the individual is clearly not. Kant's sense of moral obligation was termed the 'categorical imperative'. It is a deontological concept in that the moral obligation is absolute rather than based on any consideration of particular circumstances or the expected results of utilitarianism. The categorical imperative applies to all situations. It is a maxim that invokes a duty that is universal and obliges the individual to treat people as ends and never as means. Whatever one wishes to do, one should be prepared for everyone else to do it as well. You should act as if you were following a universal rule. The categorical imperative clearly mirrors the Christian concept of doing unto others only that which you would wish them to do unto you.

Kant's deontological categorical imperative is based on his distinction between the unknowable things that are in themselves and the things that we know and understand through human experience. The human mind perceives and understands space, time and causality. Freedom exists through the ability to make moral choices. However, Kant argues that the human individual is noumenally free, but phenomenally conditioned. People are free in themselves but all their actions have causes. Kant adhered to the Christian belief in God because, if God did not exist, there could be no guarantee that living rightly would ultimately lead to the highest good. As it might not be possible to achieve the highest good in the temporal existence of a human life, then Kant assumed immortality must exist in some form beyond death.

A key factor in formulating media laws and asserting media ethics is policy. Policy is the assertion of a social or community objective that seeks to improve the cultural, political, social or economic well-being of any society. The jurist Ronald Dworkin sought to set out the difference between policy and principle in law making. Matters of principle set out the rights of individuals. A principle is a statement or proposition that describes the rights which an individual may hold, as opposed to a policy that serves the interests of the wider community. Matters of policy could be determined even though this would lead to a restriction of the rights of individuals. But Dworkin stressed the importance of considering justice and fairness when making a choice between policy and principle.

The binary opposite of natural law in media jurisprudence and ethicology is positivism. This approach to scholarship emphasizes the importance of validating laws on the basis of those that have been posited. This means laws that have been established and advocated by people in positions of power in society. Positivism wishes to deny the link between law and morality. This genre of philosophical discourse has been inspired by the work of David Hume, who, in his *Treatise on Human Understanding*, argued that there can be no valid and logical connection between the *is* and *ought* in moral philosophy. Positivism recognizes only matters of fact and experience. The concept is based on the Latin word *posit* meaning to 'lay down'. This is the concrete rather than the abstract approach to analysis.

Positivism rejects the allegiance of natural law theory to the link between law and morality. However, this does not mean that positivists refuse to adopt or support moral principles. Professor H.L.A. Hart was a committed positivist in the way he analysed laws. In his view the law is effectively defined by positivism as an expression of human will. The command of the sovereign power is a positivist phenomenon and not the manifestation of divine power or will.

He also saw positivism as an intellectual method of analysing the meanings of legal concepts. Positivism was therefore analytical jurisprudence. Professor Hart talked about positivism being a theory of the judicial process in the sense that it was a closed logical system. He believed correct judicial decisions are deduced by considering the relevant legal rules and then evaluating the facts of a particular case. Hart did not believe there was any connection between law as it is and law as it ought to be. He therefore subscribed to the positivist separation thesis.

Hart did not support the idea of cognitivism in ethics. In his view, moral judgments cannot be established as the result of rational arguments or the presentation of evidence and proof. Hart also believed that positivism required acquiescence to the obligation to uphold the rule of law. He stated that the obligation to obey the law was unconditional, no matter what the content.

Moral consequentialism

In our broad sweep of the field of ideas and concepts in media jurisprudence and media ethicology we have become familiar with systems of thought that set out a paradigm or objective that always or infrequently takes priority in the constitution and operation of legal power and ethical judgment. Theorists talk about balancing policies with principles. These theories often involve a rule of measurement in this balancing exercise. It may be deontological and without qualification. Or it may be variable according to specific circumstances.

The idea that the end justifies the means is an example of the variable rule. Niccolò Machiavelli advocated the variable rule of moral consequentialism. He argued that both a prince and a republican state must contemplate morally reprehensible actions in order to ensure survival. An evil exercise of legal power would, therefore, be justifiable in exceptional circumstances.

Utilitarianism is another form of moral consequentialism. Its variable rule regards an act, measure, social or legal arrangement as being good or just if its overall effect advances the happiness or general welfare of the majority of persons in society. This paradigm is sometimes expressed as the greatest good for the greatest number. Utilitarianism is clearly a goal-based formula for solving the problem of distributing justice, fairness and the social and economic benefits and burdens of society. But the rule of measurement is predicated on giving precedence to the advancement of collective good and welfare. As the paradigm lies with the interests of the wider community or state, it is inevitable that the political and libertarian rights of individuals may be liquidated.

Utilitarianism involves several different branches of thought on how best to achieve the just operation of social and legal measures through the exercise of power by institutions. The calculus that determines the method of achieving the greatest good for the greatest number varies in the balance between the rights and interests of the individual and the wider society. Classical or total utilitarianism serves to maximize aggregate happiness or welfare. Aggregate means the sum total or greater mass. Average utilitarianism serves to maximize average happiness or welfare per capita. Average means 'mean value' and per capita means for each person. Act utilitarianism involves acts or measures that on the whole have the best consequences. Actual rule utilitarianism involves the application of a rule which, if generally followed, will on the whole have the best consequences. Professor Michael Slote explains that the indirect consequentialism implied means 'that an act is right if it accords with a set of rules whose being accepted, or followed, would have consequences as good as those that would result from any other set of rules being accepted.' (Slote 2005: 937–9) Ideal rule utilitarianism is the application of a rule which, if generally followed, will on the whole have as good or better consequences than any other rule governing the same act. (*Jurisprudence* 2008: 15)

John Stuart Mill sought to categorize happiness/pleasure into a distinction between higher and lower pleasures, with higher pleasures including mental, aesthetic and moral dimensions. It is better to be a human being dissatisfied than a swine satisfied and it is preferable for a human being to be a dissatisfied Socrates than a satisfied fool. Mill sought to identify the deeper dimensions of human experience when defining happiness as a higher goal: love of honour, freedom and beauty. He seeded the future discourse on balancing human rights by arguing that justice is different from other areas of morality, because it includes those duties to which others have rights. Justice can be an action that is right and wrong and something that an individual person can claim as his or her moral right. Mill's general approach to utilitarianism can be summarized as seeking to promote qualitative altruism instead of quantitative hedonism. (Warburton 2006: 153–4)

The scope of media jurisprudence, ethicology and ethicism

It should be clear that this subject area is broad and complex. The issues and topics covered are wide and varied and touch on many academic disciplines and subjects. The focus of the subject should be clear. What are the incidence, existence and consequence of media laws and media ethics as a social phenomenon? What are the origins and sources of media laws and media ethics in any society under consideration? What is the historical development of media law in general and the emergence and evolution of specific legal systems, traditions and practices? What is the historical development of ethical discourse and the nature and evolution of ethical doctrine?

What is the meaning of specific media law concepts and the construction of the various media legal structures and processes that seek to control media communication? What is the meaning of media ethical discourse? What is the link between media laws and media ethics and other social phenomena such as political ideology, economic interests and imperatives, social class, race, morality and religious conventions?

We are also committed to studying the operation of media laws and media ethics as a method of social control. We want to investigate the effects media laws and ethics have on the individuals to whom they are applied. We seek to evaluate the extent to which such laws and ethics are perceived in terms of justice and any notion of political, cultural, social or economic progress.

Media ethicology – the classical ground, Plato's legacy

The theoretical position of Plato (427–347 BCE) is a primary foundation of ethics and political philosophy. His thinking and writing influence morality and politics through several thousand years of human society. It is important to understand how Plato would embody his understanding of how human beings functioned in his advocacy of how society and government should be organized and structured. In essence Plato's legacy is the authoritarian tendency. He believed that government was for the people and not by the people, because they had to be ruled by an educated elite who would determine the laws and policies in the best interests of the great majority. Plato was a young follower of Socrates, whose public dialogues in the marketplace inspired and enlightened the young radicals of ancient Athens. It is possible to consider Socrates as the first journalist, because he was somebody who questioned the everyday nature of justice and state authority in the marketplace. By provoking the ire of the rulers, he paid the ultimate price of prosecution, state trial for agitating and radicalizing young people, and he was effectively executed by being forced to take hemlock. It is an early recorded example of the manifestation of intolerance by political consensus, what John Stuart Mill would describe as the potential tyranny of democracy against minority opinion that is perceived to threaten political, economic and emotional stability. While it can be said that Plato's political philosophy is historicized as the antithesis of the liberal democratic tradition in the West, it continues to match the structure of hierarchy and leadership in the companies and corporations of global capitalism. Plato's political philosophy essentially places social goals ahead of individual needs.

Aristotle (384–322 BCE) set out a political philosophy which could be interpreted in the modern age as placing an emphasis on individual self-fulfilment and personal happiness. Aristotle has been described as an empiricist and relativist. He is associated with the idea of the Golden Mean, where happiness is achieved through moderation. Plato on the other hand is considered authoritarian and absolutist. The good is fixed, anterior even to the gods. For Plato, justice was a thing in itself – superior to man-made law, that was a mere shadow of real justice. Ideal Justice can only be realized in an Ideal State ruled over by philosopher kings. For Aristotle there was a distinction between natural justice and conventional justice. Natural justice is based on the fundamental end, or purpose of human beings as social and political beings who are trying to attain a state of goodness. Conventional justice varies from state to state and is dependent on the history and needs of particular human communities.

Hedonism and Epicurus (341–270 BCE)

Hedonism as a moral philosophy can be interpreted as the essential root of the value of entertainment. It justifies communication to amuse and satisfy the desire for gossip. Epicurus believed in attenuating the drive for pleasure. He recognized that pursuing pleasure too arduously leads to pain. He made a distinction between psychological hedonism and ethical hedonism, which could be interpreted as the difference between the biological drive versus the rational anticipation that to pursue pleasure relentlessly brings unhappy consequences.

Cynicism and Diogenes (412–323 BCE)

Cynicism is a product of social context. It is a philosophy of consolation in times of despair. If the world is fundamentally evil, in order to live properly cynicism suggests we must withdraw from participation in it. It is founded on the belief that we should not trust happiness to the possession of material pleasures. There is, however, a clear risk of being anti-social through indifference. Diogenes was perhaps a living metaphor for the doctrine of practising such a frugal and miserable life. He was likened to an animal and provided the Greek root word *kuno* to cynicism, which means 'dog-like'. Cynicism holds that all the products of civilization are worthless: 'If salvation is to be found it is to be found in a rejection of society and in a return to the simple life – to a life of ascetic living.' (Popkin and Stroll 1998: 19) There are many anecdotes about Diogenes, including the occasion when Alexander the Great visited him while he was living in a barrel, having denied himself all the material pleasures of life. When Alexander asked what he could do to help him, he is said to have replied that the young man could stand out of the light and let him enjoy the sun. (Ibid.) Denyer writes that his desire to live by *praxis* (theory in action) and collapse 'the distinction between public and private, Greek and barbarian, raw and cooked, yours and mine' led to the flamboyant display of disgusting actions and savage repartee; hence the acquisition of his nickname 'Dog'. (Denyer 2005: 215–16)

Stoicism and Epictetus (55–135)

Stoicism is a moral philosophy that involves attaining salvation in a crumbling world. It is a guide to learning to be indifferent to external influences. Good or evil depends upon oneself. Virtue resides in the will. As the world is predestined, stoicism argues that we should learn to accept what happens and thereby free ourselves from the burden of desires and passions. Place the responsibility for good or bad directly upon the individual rather than upon society. The doctrine asserts that 'one is virtuous if one can learn to accept what happens and if one can understand that all this is part of a divine arrangement which one is powerless to alter.' (Popkin and Stroll 1998: 22) Epictetus had been a slave owned by one of the Emperor Nero's freed men. He is said to have put up with his master's physical abuse without protest, on the grounds that he should treat his body as a mere garment. Professor Stephen Clark writes that Epictetus saw philosophy as becoming 'indifferent to bodily comfort, or social applause, in order to think and act as a citizen of the world, a part of a larger whole – which should not make us forget that we are also members of families and ordinary cities, with more particular duties.' (Clark 2005: 256)

Christian ethics – St Thomas Aquinas (1225–74)

Pastoral Christian ethics encompass the Decalogue – more popularly known as the Ten Commandments from the Old Testament, and the moral teachings of Christ from the New Testament. In analytical Christian ethics it is understood that there is a doctrine of immortality in which the Divine being lays down the rules for moral behaviour. Christian ethics are primarily divided between studying divine theory and casuistry, more readily understood as applied ethics.

St Thomas Aquinas is one of the most influential philosophers of Christianity and he reflected on and analysed what should be the nature of law in Christian society. He articulated four categories of law: Eternal Law – God's Rational Guidance for all created things; Divine Law – revealed in the scriptures; Natural Law – discovered through human reason; Human Law – essence is to be just. The Latin maxim coined by Aquinas, *lex injusta non est lex* – an unjust law is not law – became a significant maxim of human ethics in the context of state and society. It means that disobedience to an unjust law becomes a duty and can be justified unless this would lead to social instability. 'Law is a necessary institution in such a community, and just laws will reflect directly (*specificatio*) or indirectly (*determinatio*) the universal morality of natural law.' (Guest et al 2004: 68) Cicero (106–43 BCE) also believed in the view that an unjust law is not law and the test of good law is whether it accords with the dictates of nature.

Baruch Spinoza (1632–77)

Spinoza was a rigid determinist and a relativist. He argued that nothing is good or bad in itself, but it is only so in relation to someone. The individual will only be happy when he/she realizes that there are limits to human power. Everything that happens must happen necessarily. He recommended that the individual should not waste energy on struggling against fate.

Niccolò Machiavelli (1469–1527)

Machiavelli represents the rational tradition of pragmatic ethics, where moral conduct in many respects is determined by the desire for success. This means that Machiavelli was a moral consequentialist and his ethical outlook was teleological. It means that ends are more important than means, but that does not necessarily mean that the ends always justify the means. Machiavelli was a political philosopher and diplomat during the Renaissance, and is most famous for his political treatise *The Prince* (1513), which has become a cornerstone of modern political philosophy.

Machiavelli has been widely demonized and misinterpreted, largely because of his pragmatic view of the relationship between ethics and politics. The adjective 'Machiavellian' has become a pejorative used to describe a politician who manipulates others in an opportunistic and deceptive way. It can be argued that the way journalism and media political power are explored in popular films retains a Machiavellian approach to analysis and justification for minor wrongs being committed to achieve greater goods. It is the principle of venial behaviour; that is, pardonable conduct in order to expose and prosecute greater evils.

The philosophy lecturer Nigel Warburton summarizes Machiavelli's understanding of human psychology: 'Machiavelli has a low view of human nature. Based on his own observation, and his knowledge of Florentine history and classical texts, he declares that people behave in a predictably bad way. They are fickle, they lie, they shun danger, and they are greedy. In these circumstances, a prince needs to use fear to achieve effective rule; being loved isn't a reliable source of power, since people break bonds of gratitude when it suits them to do so. If you have a choice it is best to be both loved and feared: but if you have to choose one above the other, choose to be feared.' (Warburton 2006: 38)

Bertrand Russell focused on the core of Machiavelli's political philosophy in *The Prince*:

> A ruler will perish if he is always good; he must be as cunning as a fox and as fierce as a lion. There is a chapter (XVIII) entitled: 'In What Way Princes Must Keep Faith'. We learn that they should keep faith when it pays to do so, but not otherwise. A prince must on occasion be faithless:
>
> 'But it is necessary to be able to disguise this character well, and to be a great feigner and dissembler; and men are so simple and so ready to

obey present necessities, that one who deceives will always find those who allow themselves to be deceived. I will mention only one modern instance. Alexander VI did nothing else but deceive me, he thought of nothing else, and found the occasion for it; no man was ever more able to give assurances, or affirmed things with stronger oaths, and no man observed them less; however, he always succeeded in his deceptions, and he knew well this aspect of things. It is not necessary therefore for a prince to have all the above-named qualities [the conventional virtues], but it is very necessary to seem to have them.'

He goes on to say that, above all, a prince should *seem* to be religious.

(Russell 2004: 486)

Russell's evaluation of Machiavelli was written during the 1930s and 1940s and as a result, the moral cynicism of the Renaissance thinker's theory on the ethics of political power is equated with the totalitarian menace of twentieth-century dictatorships:

In Russia and Germany new societies have been created, in much the same way as the mythical Lycurgus was supposed to have created the Spartan polity. The ancient lawgiver was a benevolent myth; the modern lawgiver is a terrifying reality. The world has become more like that of Machiavelli than it was, and the modern man who hopes to refute his philosophy must think more deeply than seemed necessary in the nineteenth century.

(Russell 2004: 490)

These sombre echoes have given us the pejorative adjective 'Machiavellian'. And it is these tactics that characterize the pursuit and maintenance of power in authoritarian and liberal-democratic countries as well as the vertically structured global and public media corporations that provide the immediate social and economic environment for most journalists in the world.

It is always important to think of the pragmatic in Machiavellian philosophy, and this is apposite in the quotation from his book *The Art of War*: 'No enterprise is more likely to succeed than one concealed from the enemy until it is ripe for execution.' (Machiavelli 1990: 202) Machiavelli was a sophisticated thinker and writer whose work needs to be contextualized by the politics and culture of his time. In many respects his discourse on *Virtù* – the skill and prowess in exercising power in service of the state – and *Fortuna* – an acceptance of the reality of the world where an individual's fate is as much determined by the actions of others and the fortunes of the state – are the foundation of a realistic approach to politics. Warburton is most eloquent in explaining Machiavelli's discourse on *Virtù* and *Fortuna*:

Machiavelli believes that half of our lives are governed by chance events over which we have no control; no matter how well-prepared he may be, a prince's projects can still be thwarted by misfortune. Fortune is like a river which floods its banks: once it is in full flood, there is nothing anyone can do to control it. But this doesn't stop us from taking action before the river floods, so that the damage caused will be less severe. Chance events usually cause most damage where no precautions have been taken. Machiavelli does, however, believe that fortune favours the young and the bold. In a disturbing metaphor, fortune is a woman who responds to the advances of an audacious young man who beats and coerces her. *Virtù* is the manly quality he uses to subdue her.

(Warburton 2006: 39)

Bertrand Russell warned against being preoccupied with the sensation of being shocked by Machiavelli's exposure of the dark interior of human selfishness and greed:

he certainly is sometimes shocking. But many other men would be equally so if they were equally free from humbug. His political philosophy is scientific and empirical, based upon his own experience of affairs, concerned to set forth the means to assigned ends, regardless of the question whether the ends are to be considered good or bad. When, on occasion, he allows himself to mention the ends that he desires, they are such as we can all applaud.

(Russell 2004: 483)

It is this balanced and open-minded approach that Nigel Warburton brings to Isaiah Berlin's more considered evaluation of Machiavelli's political writings:

On his interpretation, Machiavelli's great originality and appeal lies in the fact that he recognized the shortcomings of classical and Christian morality when applied to the situation of a prince. A prince who displays the traditional virtues, such as honesty and compassion, is likely to play into the hands of his enemies, who are unlikely to be so scrupulous. Berlin's point is that, far from being amoral, Machiavelli, perhaps unwittingly, introduced the notion that there could be more than one morality and that these moralities might not be compatible with one another. It's not that one morality is the true one and all others false. Rather there are genuinely incompatible moralities that are each consistent from within.

(Warburton 2006: 41)

Machiavelli is often appropriated as a metaphor for the dark side or 'dirty hands' in journalistic practice and pragmatics. John C. Merrill, in *Journalism Ethics: Philosophical Foundations for News Media*, tabulated that Machiavellianism is the frame for a creed of values that advises media communicators to:

> Share power carefully; never apologize or admit error, unless it's expedient; always tout Truth – 'your truth'; justice follows power – might is right; obey laws if they don't harm your success; normal morality: sign of weakness & timidity; extol craftiness and cunning; keep ahead of the lazy masses; it's better to exploit than to be exploited; people will believe almost anything.
>
> (Merrill 1997: 59)

This interpretation and historicizing of Machiavelli underlines the fact that the paradoxical tension in media ethics lies in political and academic discourse expecting public journalism operating in the social and political philosophical context to be judged by private moral philosophical precepts. When Jean-Paul Sartre wrote his 1948 play *Dirty Hands* he was attempting to investigate the distinction between public and private morality. When his character Hoederer describes his hands being fouled up to the elbows because they had been plunged in filth and blood, he asks rhetorically: 'So what? Do you think one can govern innocently?' If the principle applies to politicians, can it not be applied to those who govern the representation of public opinion – the fourth estate of journalism? A forensic study of history appears to suggest that public opinion in the liberal-democratic tradition tolerates the violation of ordinary moral values on the grounds that they are abnegated for the sake of the greater good. Professor Sissela Bok observes that in the practice of politics the dirty hands symbolism

> is often invoked by public officials hoping to brush aside accusations of wrongdoing by claiming to have acted strictly in the public's best interest. Some take a more categorical stand: they argue that it would be naïve to imagine that politicians could ever truly serve the public's best interests without violating fundamental moral principles.
>
> (Bok 2005: 216)

Perhaps it could be argued that journalists as media communicators in the public sphere are entitled to the same pleading? Media communicators who operate professionally by the principle *damnum sine injuria*, afflicting damage without breaking the law, could be accused of being Machiavellian, particularly if such behaviour is self-serving. The concept is a reminder that journalists who only obey the law cannot escape the charge of conduct and content that is arguably immoral.

Baldassare Castiglione (1478–1529)

Castiglione was born in Casatico, near Mantua and died in Toledo, Spain. He reinforces the Renaissance tradition of coming to terms with the pragmatics of power and ambition. Throughout his life he lived mostly in Milan and Urbino. When he was 18, in 1496, he was sent to the court of Lodovico at Milan. At this court Castiglione pleased everyone with his good manners and excellence in athletics, letters, music and art. During his stay at the court of Urbino he wrote a book called *The Book of the Courtier*. This book defined the behaviour expectations of the courtier in terms of his relationship to the prince and survival and success in an authoritarian environment.

The book became the popular manual for would-be courtiers in Renaissance Europe. Ceri Sullivan observes that it defined the *uomo universale*, who was supposed to display the talents of what the historian Jacob Burckhardt described as:

> 'private man, indifferent to politics, and busies partly with serious pursuits, partly with the interest of a dilettante'. (Burckhardt, 1990: 99 and 100) This display of effortless superiority was labelled as *sprezzatura* (careless grace) by Baldassare Castiglione in *Il libro del cortegiano* of 1528 (translated into English by Sir Thomas Hoby as *The Book of the Courtier* in 1561). The courtier was advised to work hard in private to acquire accomplishments but never to allow such effort to appear when using them.
>
> (Sullivan 2000: 234)

In understanding the historical context of the Renaissance *The Book of the Courtier* defines the political power relationship in the princely state as based on patronage and patron–client relations; not on democracy, liberty and representative government with an independent rule of law expressed through incorruptible judiciary. The courtiers, or aspirational elite, would get on through attending to the concerns over style and appearance and the function and promotion of the arts in court; not politics. Virtuoso displays of creative genius would be tolerated as long as they did not challenge the ego or insecurity of the arbitrary sensibility of the authoritarian ruler. It is possible for the contemporary journalist in China to appreciate this context, as would any media communicator seeking advancement in an authoritarian society.

As George Bull so rightly states:

> It is hard, indeed to think of any work more opposed to the spirit of the modern age [in Britain or the United States]. At an obvious level, its preoccupation with social distinction and outward forms of polite

behaviour creates an intense atmosphere of artificiality and insincerity (when James Joyce first read *The Courtier* his brother told him he had become more polite but less sincere).

The great virtues it proposes for a gentleman are discretion and decorum, nonchalance and gracefulness. As Luigi Barzini comments in his satirical book on the modern Italian, quoting Castiglione as the model, the 'show' is all. The courtier must watch his dress, his speech, his gestures chiefly because of their effect on his reputation. If he fights well in battle, he must make sure his commander sees him do so. He has to consider earnestly whether it is correct behaviour to take part in sport with the common people or even to perform in front of them. In love, he must conquer where he can; whereas the women he most admires are those who regard dishonour as a fate worse than death.

(Bull 1976: 15–16)

How does the philosophy of the courtier translate into modern and postmodern experience? Piers Morgan's story of Rupert Murdoch and peach brandy could be an example:

Tonight I had dinner with Rupert Murdoch in a private room at the Stafford Hotel in St James, opposite his London flat ... Dinner was fun. I was in a good mood, drinking his wine more enthusiastically than I thought he might, and the conversation was relaxed but challenging. I could sense him probing the table for the next creative genius, and coming up woefully short, I suspect. But we all gave it a good go. Some were too clever-dick, throwing all their great views on life at him like over-excited Jehovah's witnesses [*sic*]. Others were a bit too quiet and reverential, forgetting that he likes his executives to be confident leaders, not meek little mice. I just couldn't believe I was there, felt I'd got nothing to lose, and simply tried to engage in what I knew about and keep out of the stuff I didn't. Anything financial, for example – his area of undisputed global expertise – and my lips might as well have been stapled to the floor.

(Morgan 2004: 19–20)

It could be argued that Morgan is describing in his entertaining memoirs how the art of *sprezzatura* had been revived in the twentieth- and twenty-first-century world of international media corporations:

The key moment, though I didn't realize it at the time, came when the waiter asked if we would like a liqueur. Kelvin [MacKenzie] went first, saying no – because he's on the wagon. The others followed his lead, forgetting the crucial fact of his self-imposed month-long abstinence. When my turn came, I asked the waiter what he would recommend and he said, 'Peach brandy, sir.' I flashed a look at Murdoch, who seemed totally uninterested in whether I had one or not, and said 'OK, one of those then, please.' Stuart Higgins next to me added chirpily, 'Make that two.' Then a loud Australian growl emanated from the head of the table: 'Make that three.' It emerged later that this was one of Murdoch's favourite after-dinner drinks. I finished the evening glugging my peach brandy contentedly.

(Ibid.)

It may or may not be significant that shortly afterwards Piers Morgan was made editor of the *News of the World* and Stuart Higgins was appointed editor of the *Sun*.

Peter Burke's analysis *The Fortunes of the Courtier* suggests Castiglione's courtiers may not have survived in the court of Machiavelli's prince:

> The courtier portrayed in the urbane dialogues of Urbino was too outspoken and too much concerned with self-cultivation to have suited the needs of a prince whose chief thought was maintaining or extending his power. This discrepancy may suggest that Castiglione's portrait was unrealistic, or that it was a true likeness only of small courts, or even courts effectively ruled by women.

> In any case, in the sixteenth and seventeenth centuries, European political theory and practice alike moved in Machiavelli's direction. In the age of 'absolute power', it was increasingly assumed that a prince should rule his state alone, without the aid and advice of his nobility, just as the Roman emperors had ruled without a senate.

(Burke 1995: 119–20)

Other handbooks for courtly survival began to be published which advised against the idea of Castiglione's 'autonomous individual who was advised to speak frankly to his prince. In Giraldi's monologue, on the other hand, the keywords are "accommodation", "simulation" and "dissimulation", whether the motive for these disguises is self-defence in a hostile environment, or the manipulation of the prince to fit in with one's own desires.' (Burke 1995: 121)

Bull confers with Burke in the observation that:

> When Machiavelli wrote *The Prince*, in all innocence he shocked the world for several hundred years because he set out to 'represent things as they are in real truth, rather than as they are imagined'. [...] As a handbook for gentlemen, *The Courtier*, conceals the most shameless opportunism under the cloak of a tiresome refinement.

(Bull 1976: 17)

Immanuel Kant (1724–1804)

Kant argued that a moral law requires that people are rewarded proportionately to their virtue. Morality should be defined as acts done from
inclination and acts done from a sense of duty. He is credited with dominating the deontological tradition of ethics and somewhat simplistically
he has been categorized as an absolutist in the Platonic genre of thinking
with an adherence to universal *a priori* values. A brief summary of Kant's
deontological maxims is provided in Table 2.2.

Kant argued that the internal morality of being is more important
than external obligation. A person is acting morally only when he/she
suppresses feeling and inclinations, and follows duties and obligations.
He emphasized that it is the motive that matters. He explained that the
difference between prudential action and moral action is doing what has
to be done and doing what you believe you have a duty to do.

He is credited with conceptualizing the categorical imperative: 'Act only
on that maxim whereby thou canst at the same time will that it should
become a universal law.' (Popkin and Stroll 1998: 46) Another of his
famous maxims stresses the moral purposefulness of human actions and
words: 'So act as to treat humanity, whether in thine own person or in

Table 2.2 Immanuel Kant's ethics (A)

Immanuel Kant born in Königsberg, Prussia 1724 (died 1804)

Deontological ethics
Kant advocated universal maxims:
'Act only according to that maxim by which you can at the same time will that it
should become a universal law.'
'Act so that you treat humanity, whether in your own person or in that of
another, always as an end and never as a means only.'
'Act as though the maxim of your action were by your will to become a universal
law of nature.'

Like all classical and Enlightenment philosophers Kant investigated the realms
of metaphysics (nature of reality and the natural world), epistemology (human
knowledge) and ontology (nature of God and/or being).
a priori = what we know independently of experience
a posteriori = what we know by experience (empirical knowledge)
The weakness of Kant's ethics theory is that in his argument for universal moral
laws he cannot deny that he is evaluating consequences e.g. 'I can by no means
will that lying should be a universal law. For with such a law there would be
no promises at all, since it would be in vain to allege my intention in regard
to my future actions to those who would not believe this allegation, or if they
over-hastily did so, would pay me back in my own coin.' The construction of
the universal maxim therefore depends on a measurement of the consequences
(McCormick 2006).

---

that of any other, in every case as an end withal, never as a means only.'
(Ibid.) Further maxims by Kant and recommended further reading are
to be found in Table 2.3.

Kant believed that the categorical imperative can be utilized to legitimize and support the essential principles of human duties, and Oneill
writes that:

> we can show by a *reductio ad absurdum* argument that promising
> falsely is not universalizable. Suppose that everyone were to adopt
> the principle of promising falsely: since there would then be much
> false promising, trust would be destroyed and many would find
> that they could not get their false promises accepted, contrary to
> the hypothesis of universal adoption of the principle of false prom-
> ising. A maxim of promising falsely is not universalizable, so the

Table 2.3 Immanuel Kant's ethics (B)

Publishes Groundwork of the Metaphysic of Morals, *1785*	*Publishes* The Critique of Practical Reason, *1787*
'Search for and establishment of the supreme principle of morality.'	'Every other rational being thinks of his existence by means of the same rational ground which holds also for myself; thus it is at the same time an objective principle from which, as a supreme practical ground, it must be possible to derive all laws of the will.'
'It is not sufficient to do that which should be morally good that it conforms to the law; it must be done for the sake of the law.'	'Nothing can be conceived in the world, or even out of it, which can be called good without qualification except a good will.'

Sources and recommended bibliography
Acton, H.B. (1976) *Kant's Moral Philosophy*, London: Macmillan.
Olafson, F.A. (1973) *Ethics and Twentieth Century Thought*, Englewood Cliffs, NJ: Prentice-Hall.
Wilkerson, T.E. (1998) *Kant's Critique of Pure Reason: A Commentary for Students*, London: Thoemmes.
Paton, H.J. (1991) *The Moral Law*, London: Routledge.
Scruton, Roger (1982) *Kant*, Oxford: Oxford University Press.
Körner, Stephen (1955) *Kant*, Harmondsworth: Penguin.
Gardner, Sebastian (1999) *Kant and the Critique of Pure Reason*, London: Routledge.
O'Neill, Onora (1998) 'Kantian ethics', in E. Craig (ed.), *Routledge Encyclopedia of Philosophy*, London: Routledge. Retrieved 26 May 2009 from www.rep.routledge.com/article/L042.
McCormick, Matt (2006) 'Immanuel Kant (1724–1804) Metaphysics', *The Internet Encyclopedia of Philosophy*, www.iep.utm.edu/k/kandmeta.htm.

categorical imperative requires us to reject it. Parallel arguments can be used to show that principles such as those of coercing or doing violence are not universalizable, and so that it is a duty to reject these principles.

(O'Neill 1998: 2)

Thomas Hobbes (1588–1679) and John Locke (1632–1704)

Thomas Hobbes chose the evils of absolute power rather than the problems of life in a society that did not contain authority. He said a person is by nature selfish and egoistic. He is famous for stating that the life of man is by nature 'solitary, poor, nasty, brutish and short.' (Popkin and Stroll 1998: 78) Society has to be a compromise to avoid chaos. The covenant is an agreement among people to abide by rules. Subjects must respect the authority of sovereignty. This is the authoritarian version of the social contract.

In contrast, John Locke argued that no one ought to harm another in his life, health, liberty or possession. He stressed that law, not force, is the basis of government. He is associated with the focus on the rule of law in constitutional equilibrium, and in many respects Locke has been described as the architect of democracy. He defined democracy as government by laws arrived at after long deliberations by properly chosen representatives of the people and which are promulgated so that all men may become acquainted with them. He emphasized the need for equal treatment before the law and due process in the application of law. These would be the essential safeguards against the abuse of power.

Karl Marx (1818–83)

Marx's ethical theory is founded on the idea of fairness and justice being privileged over materialistic and class-based deprivation. He observed that industry and technological discoveries develop much more rapidly than do the techniques for controlling them. His ethical outlook is very much based on the principle of avoiding self-alienation and fetishism. He argued for the avoidance of the impact of capitalism because the market free trade system had the effect of cutting people off from each other, and made them fearful and insecure. He said human communities should also avoid the worship of the products of labour, and side-step the tendency for capitalism to depersonalize human relations. He believed that capitalism made people more like machines and machines more like people. Marxist morality is morality based on human values, not upon machine values.

John Stuart Mill (1806–73) and Jeremy Bentham (1748–1832)

Bentham and Mill are described as key founders of the strand of philosophy known as utilitarianism. This continued the teleological tendency in ethics whereby the architects of government and the authors of communication are asked to consider the consequences so that the greatest happiness for the greatest number of people is achieved.

The ethic of utilitarianism asks the individual to consider the objective principle for determining whether speech and action is right or wrong. Communication or action is right insofar as it tends to produce the greatest happiness for the greatest number. If speech produces an excess of beneficial effects over harmful ones, then it is right; otherwise it is not. As a moral theory, utilitarianism separates the rightness or wrongness of speech and action from the goodness or badness of the individual who speaks or performs. It entails democratic government as a political institution. John Stuart Mill sought to attenuate and adjust utilitarianism in order to protect minorities from the tyranny of the majority. Mill can be credited with founding the legal and regulatory harm principle in media communication and this, along with a recommended bibliography on his moral and political philosophy, is set out in Table 2.4.

Mill developed a theory of qualitative altruism as an antidote to Jeremy Bentham's quantitative hedonism by refining utilitarian theory to maximize the value of individual liberty, evaluate justice in terms of a harm principle, and acknowledge social goals. Essentially, he defined utility as qualitative altruism. Mill's ideas, and those of his wife Harriet Taylor, are set out in the famous essay 'On Liberty' published in 1859. He argued that the liberty of the individual could be maximized by promoting specific freedoms such as liberty of expression and publication, liberty of thought and feeling, freedom of opinion, liberty of conscience, liberty of tastes and pursuits, and liberty to unite for purposes which did not harm others.

The idea of rights provides an important distinction between the concept of liberty and the notion of justice. He said that

> the only purpose for which power can rightfully be exercised over any member of a civilized community against his will is to prevent harm to others. His own good, either physical or moral, is not a sufficient warrant. He cannot rightfully be compelled to do or forbear because it will be better for him to do so, because it will make him happier, because, in the opinion of others, to do so would be wise, or even right.

> (Mill 1859: 223–4)

Table 2.4 John Stuart Mill's ethics

John Stuart Mill born in London 1806. Published 'On Liberty' in 1859
Died at Avignon, France in 1873

Nigel Warburton, Senior Lecturer in Philosophy at the Open University,
encapsulates the essence of Mill's political philosophy with the lively aphorism:
'My freedom to swing my fist ends where your face begins' (Warburton 2006:
142). In his text 'On Liberty' Mill sought to articulate a manifesto that would
eliminate the threat posed by the tyranny of the majority over minority groups.

Mill defined the tyranny of the majority in any democracy as pressure on
executive government to adopt laws that oppress idiosyncratic, non-conformist,
dissenting individuals when these individuals are harmless (though what
they say and what they do might be regarded as offensive to the values and
opinions of the majority), and the overwhelming pressure of public opinion.
Public opinion may be dominated by superstition, tradition and prejudice
and, as a result, may be so strong that it deprives the individual of the usual
benefits of civil liberty. In many respects Mill was discoursing on the sociological
phenomenon of 'the moral panic' in media communication that has the effect of
silencing and constraining non-conforming individuals as well as precipitating
legislation that leads to legal discrimination. Mill observed that public opinion
is notoriously susceptible to error. Mill wrote: 'Protection against the tyranny
of the magistrate is not enough: there needs to be protection also against the
tyranny of the prevailing opinion and feeling; against the tendency of society
to impose by other means than civil penalties, its own ideas and practices as
rules of conduct on those who dissent from them; to fetter the development,
and if possible, prevent the formation of any individuality not in harmony with
its ways, and compel all characters to fashion themselves upon the model of its
own' (Popkin and Stroll 1998: 90–1).

In 'On Liberty' Mill conceptualized the 'harm' principle which lies at the heart
of most primary and secondary media law in the Western world. He stated:
'That the only purpose for which power can be rightly exercised over any
member of a civilized community, against his will, is to prevent harm to others.
His own good, either physical or moral, is not a sufficient warrant. [...] In the
part which merely concerns himself, his independence is, of right absolute.
Over himself, over his own body and mind, the individual is sovereign.' In
all modern nations all citizens have arrived at the state of being mature and
rational persons. Mill's essay set out a three-point approach to the definition of
the purpose of free speech which is repeatedly re-articulated in key freedom
of expression precedents in the UK and USA. First, it is wrong to suppress
an opinion which the majority does not approve of because the suppressed
opinion may be true, and a false opinion is frequently corrected through open
discussion. Second, by reflecting on all the arguments against a true opinion,
and by thus being forced to think of ways of rebutting them, we actually come
to understand our opinion more fully. The third reason for requiring that the
opposite opinion to our own should not be suppressed without being heard
first is that even if it is neither wholly true nor wholly false, it may contain
elements of the truth (Heydt 2007).

Sources and recommended bibliography
Crisp, Robert (1997) *Mill on Utilitarianism*, London: Routledge.
Glover, Jonathan ed. (1990) *Utilitarianism and its Critics*, New York: Macmillan.
Berlin, Isaiah (1969) *Four Essays on Freedom*, Oxford: Oxford University Press.
Ryan, Alan (1997) *Mill*, New York: Norton.
Capaldi, Nicholas (2004) *John Stuart Mill: A Biography*, Cambridge: Cambridge University Press.
Skorupski, John (1989) *John Stuart Mill*, London: Routledge.
Skorupski, John (1998, 2005) Mill, John Stuart. In E. Craig (Ed.), *Routledge Encyclopedia of Philosophy*, London: Routledge. Retrieved May 26, 2009, from www.rep.routledge.com/article/DC054SECT12
Heydt, Colin (2007) 'John Stuart Mill', *The Internet Encyclopedia of Philosophy*, www.iep.utm.edu/m/milljs/htm

Skorupski contends that

> Mill remained more of a democrat than other liberals of the nineteenth century, such as de Tocqueville or Burckhardt, but like them he saw how moral and cultural excellence and freedom of spirit could be endangered by mass democracy. Like them, his attitude to the immediate prospect of democratic politics was decidedly missed. What he wanted was a democratic society of freely developed human beings; he did not think it a proximate or certain prospect, and he thought that bad forms of democracy could themselves pose a threat to it by drifting into 'collective despotism' – a danger to which America had already succumbed.
>
> (Skorupski 2005: 2)

It therefore followed that the maximum exercise of freedom of expression could undoubtedly guard against collective despotism that ordinarily feeds off ignorance, secrecy and the limited dissemination of information.

Friedrich Nietzsche (1844–1900) objected to the clumsiness of the utilitarian moral equation in simply counting up the units of happiness and unhappiness. He believed some people were inherently more important than others and their pleasure or lack of it had more ethical significance. He condemned J.S. Mill as an intellectual blockhead:

> I abhor the man's vulgarity when he says 'What is right for one man is right for another.' Such principles would fain establish the whole of human traffic upon mutual services, so that every action would appear to be a cash payment for something done to us. The hypothesis here is ignoble to the last degree; it is taken for granted that there is some sort of equivalence in value between my actions and thine.
>
> (Popkin and Stroll 1998: 39)

Non-rational and emotional ethics – the personalist approach

This genre of moral philosophy situates the human ethic within a subjective, situational and spiritual frame. It is driven by love for the other – one's neighbour. An existential strand of ethics is associated with the philosopher/writers Jean Paul Sartre and Albert Camus.

Karl Jaspers (1883–1969) and Hannah Arendt (1906–1975)

Jaspers and Arendt bridged the rational and the emotional in moral philosophy and organized a meeting point between Eastern and Western philosophical traditions. Jaspers postulated that an existential equilibrium or *humanitas* could be achieved by seeking: courage without self-deception; personal responsibility for the consequences of actions; respect for the personal freedom and self-realization of the Other; the avoidance of exploitation; and intellectual integrity and open-mindedness. (Salamun 1998)

Charismatic voices of ethical conscience

Human history is characterized by charismatic voices of ethical conscience that are also in the religious tradition. Karl Jaspers was intrigued by how monotheistic religions emerged in different parts of the world at about the same time. These ethical voices obviously must include sources of religious inspiration such as Jesus Christ, the Prophet Mohammed and Buddha. In the modern age we could cite Mahatma Gandhi and Nelson Mandela as significant forces in a post-colonial genre of moral and political philosophy. Both are admired and each had a different approach to the mobilization of pacifism and violence as a method of protest and resistance.

Martin Heidegger (1889–1976)

Heidegger is admired and reviled at the same time. He is admired for the power of his thinking in the phenomenological tradition. He is reviled for how he surrendered to the power of his conclusions on time and being, to the point that human ethics were rendered irrelevant. Heidegger in his life was pro-Nazi and did not resist the persecution of Jewish academics. He also failed to politically explain his support for Hitler's Third Reich or acknowledge responsibility for neglecting to reappraise his failure of moral conscience during this period. Heidegger's thinking can be seen as a collapsing phenomenon of philosophical discourse when the interpenetration of binary forces such as idealism and materialism become one and the same. Idealism reified into materialism can have a frightening totalitarian impact on the human condition. It is the force of being predominating over ethical values and it represents the black hole in Heidegger's significance as a moral philosopher of the twentieth century.

Modern analytical ethics as opposed to classical normative ethics

Subjectivist modern ethics

A naturalistic theory is that moral judgments are true or false and such judgments are reducible to natural science such as psychology. An emotivist theory requires that moral judgments are neither true nor false, but are merely expressive of the feelings of the individual.

In motivist ethical theory the rightness or wrongness of human communication depends upon the motive. Consequence theory holds that rightness or wrongness of human communication depends entirely upon the effects of the communication. Subjectivism involves prescriptions of morality and is an argument based on human sentience. It is the class of egoistic argument.

Objectivist modern ethics

In objectivist ethics there can be no dispute between moral matters and factual matters. We have to acknowledge the things that we have to do even though we do not wish to. Our morality has to be rooted in objective references. This position is reminiscent of the tension in jurisprudence between natural law and positivist law.

Feminist ethical and legal theory

This theory concentrates on the premise that codes of ethics and systems of law are often the product of a patriarchal society. Feminist theory has its roots in the women's movement as it developed and flourished in the late 1960s and the 1970s. The general feminist approach analyses ethics and laws in terms of constructing, maintaining, reinforcing and perpetuating patriarchy. It also looks at the ways in which this patriarchy can be undermined and ultimately eliminated.

Undoubtedly the media approach to reporting crimes against women, such as rape, is a key area for analysis. Similarly the nature of intrusions into privacy and how they strip women of their dignity as well as sustain values of patriarchy generates debate and relevant analysis.

Feminist theory justifiably concerns itself with a critique of the inherent logic of media laws, the indeterminacy and manipulability of ethical

doctrines and the role of law and ethical regulation in legitimating particular social relations and the illegitimate hierarchies created by law and
legal institutions.

The feminist theoretical approach involves asking the 'woman question'. This is determining and recognizing the experience of women in
relation to media law and ethics. How do media law and media ethics fail
to take into account the experiences and values that seem more typical of
women than of men and how do existing legal and regulatory standards
and concepts disadvantage women?

Furthermore, feminist practical reasoning employs an intellectual *modus
operandi* arising from context. Rather than fetishizing the text of law and
ethical doctrine, feminist theory appreciates the differences between
persons and values the experience of the disempowered. Feminist theory
also considers itself to be consciousness raising. This involves elevating
individual awareness of the collective experience of women through
sharing their experiences of media conduct and media law, and regulatory enforcement.

Undoubtedly feminist theory is drawn to focusing on issues of media
indecency and pornography as the graphic sexually explicit subordination and exploitation of women. The reporting and media narrative of
rape, domestic violence, sexual harassment and their treatment by media
law and regulatory agencies are relevant issues for feminist analysis.

The feminist perspective can raise interesting debates about women's
experiences of ethical decision making within media institutional environments as journalist performers as well as the perspective of the female
sensibility in being on the receiving end of media law doctrine, process
and institutional remedies. There would be merit in investigating any
mismatch, distortion or denial of women's actual experiences with media
law's assumptions or imposed structures. To what extent are patriarchal
interests served by this mismatch? The ensuing debate can generate ideas
for reform that could have a socially transformative impact on the ideological frames of media ethical and legal doctrine. (*Jurisprudence* 2002:
145–7)

Feminist theorists sometimes seek to define and distinguish masculine
and feminine values. The discourse on masculine values includes identifying patriarchy as characterizing the law in terms of notions of right and
wrong and structuring legal outcomes in terms of victory, predictability,
objectivity, deductive reasoning, universalism, notion of the abstract,
rights and principles.

The discourse on alternative female values includes identifying notions
of interaction, cooperation, caring, mediation and the preservation of
relationships. The male ethic of justice can be characterized as a process
of separation and exclusion, the logic of justice approach, the balancing of
abstract rights and duties, individual achievement and the selection of the

victor or winner. An illustration of this analysis could apply to the efforts by the BBC news presenter Anna Ford to seek a privacy remedy after a popular newspaper took photographs of her topless-bathing on a public beach, where she claimed she had a reasonable expectation of privacy. Both the High Court and the Press Complaints Commission denied her a legal or regulatory 'victory'. The adversarial context of law channelled her grievance into an either/or resolution that was ideologically unsatisfactory. The female ethic of care discourses the values of attachment and inclusion, conciliatory alternatives, standards of care and nurturance, collective responsibility, and the ethic of inclusion. (*Jurisprudence* 2008: 124–57) Feminist media jurisprudence is a valuable source for restorative justice remedies that avoid the application of aggressive retributivist remedies that can have a chilling effect on freedom of expression.

The hybrid in media jurisprudence, ethicology and ethicism: virtue

It could be argued that the ethical concept of the virtuous represents the compromise or hybridization of the morally consequentialist and deontological in varying measures. Judging morality according to the value of the person rather than the action represents a *teleos* or goal of many modern creeds of human conscience. By deciding on a virtuous being and then practising virtue in terms of action, the good life may be lived, and this life combines sensitivity and appreciation of universal principles and maxims as well as the consequences of human speech and actions. This approach is regarded as primarily Aristotelian, and in the modernist tradition is being acknowledged as neo- or New Aristotelian. There is a purpose or goal of happiness common to all human beings. Natural justice would be achieved by the attainment of a state of goodness. Conventional justice varies from state to state in the context of the history and imperatives of their respective societies. The ultimate meaning of all things can be understood from an examination of their different ends. (Warburton 2003: 54–6)

By avoiding extremes we learn to discover what is morally right for us in each problematical situation. Aristotle seemed to suggest that ethics was more of an approximate science determined by context. The doctrine focuses on the cumulative harmony of an individual's morally good traits. It requires the experiencing of proper desires and emotions at the right times, towards the right people, with the right motive and in the right way, rather than badly. The purpose of virtue theory in ethics is to answer the question 'What is the good person?' rather than 'What should I do in order to lead the good life?' An action would therefore be judged as right or wrong if it can be determined as an action which a virtuous person would do. (Ibid.)

The New Aristotelians attempt to leave the internecine and proverbial warfare between deontologists and utilitarians and investigate issues of community, moral health and welfare. This move from individualism and private moral dilemmas to discuss the people we ought to be is known as 'virtue theory' and has been advanced by the philosopher Alasdair MacIntyre and others. He argues that instead of following Classical, Renaissance, Enlightenment, modernist and postmodernist debates that deracinate the certainties and confidence in subjectivist and objectivist moral values, we should recognize the unstoppable communitarian tradition of human society. Hope lies in Aristotle's central idea that people should be habituated into good dispositions towards each other, so that moral behaviour becomes instinctive rather than determined by systems of ethical doctrine. (Ibid.)

H.L.A. Hart seems to embrace the positivist tradition as well as deontological maxims with his adherence to minimum content principles of respect for life, property and the keeping of promises. Karl Jaspers seems to embrace a harmony of deontological maxims and morally consequentialist precepts. He argued for existential equilibrium or *humanitas* that can be achieved by seeking courage without self-deception, personal responsibility for the consequences of actions, respect for the personal freedom and self-realization of the Other, the avoidance of exploitation, and intellectual integrity and open-mindedness. In the process of analysis, it is apparent that the tools of evaluation consistently involve an identification of objectivism, subjectivism, motivism, consequentialism and emotivism.

In all the traditions there is a commonality of codifying principles, norms and evaluative formulae for human flourishing. A model twentieth-century example would be John Finnis, who articulated what he described as key objectives for human flourishing. As a jurisprudential theorist, in his 1980 text *Natural Law and Natural Rights* he argued that there were normative conclusions to be derived from natural law and that these represent a reflective grasp of what is self-evidently good for all human beings. He set out seven principles of practical reasonableness that should be used to order human life and community: 1) Respect for life as a proto basic value; 2) Knowledge – a preference for true over false belief; 3) Play – performances for the sake of it; 4) Aesthetic experience – the appreciation of beauty; 5) Friendship or sociability – acting for the sake of one's friend's purpose or well-being; 6) Practical reasonableness – using personal intelligence to choose actions, lifestyle and character; 7) Religion – the ability to reflect on the origins of the cosmic order and human freedom and reason. (*Jurisprudence* 2008: 26)

Another twentieth-century jurisprudential writer, Lon Fuller, created a code by which the construction of media laws could be evaluated and ethically determined. Fuller believed there should be principles for procedural morality in law making. He argued that the purpose of law was the governance of human conduct through rules formulated by eight key principles of law making. Procedural morality in law creation required a legal system that was characterized by a morality of aspiration: 1) There must be rules; 2) The rules must be prospective and not retrospective; 3) The rules must be published; 4) The rules must be intelligible; 5) The rules must not be contradictory; 6) Compliance with the rules must be possible; 7) The rules must not be constantly changing; 8) There must be a congruency between the rules as declared and published and the actions of officials responsible for the application and enforcement of such rules. (*Jurisprudence* 2008: 60–2; Morrison 1997: 389–90)

Friedrich Nietzsche argued for an intellectually revolutionary challenge to normative shibboleths by discoursing on the genealogy of morals as a narrative of moral relativism; in essence, recognizing morals as political, social and cultural constructions based on power and ideological consolation in the context of materialist alienation. The notions of good and bad, right and wrong therefore had no universal validity because God was dead. In his *Genealogy of Morality* he wrote about the power and strength of resentment experienced by the oppressed. He applied the French word *ressentiment* as meaning an imaginary revenge visited upon the powerful by the powerless as their idealistic way of fighting oppression. Consequently, the powerless suffer a false consciousness or fallacy of bad conscience. He pre-dated Freud by theorizing on the damage that a sense of guilt from frustrated instincts and inward self-torture can have on an individual. Bad conscience can manifest itself through asceticism and self-denial as a way of existence, and altruism in being helpful to other people for their own sakes.

Fairness is frequently cited as one of the common goals of ethical creeds situated in the humanitarian tradition. Fairness is often a critical multiplier in ethical evaluation and similar to the notions of power and toleration. Fairness can be seen as a value that encompasses ideas of social and economic justice and equality. It is central to John Rawls's twentieth-century 'Theory of Justice'. Most of the great philosophers have interpolated the idea of fairness with justice. Aristotle stated that doing injustice is getting more than one ought and suffering injustice is getting less than one ought. Justice was therefore equity. To do justly was simply to be fair. This is transcending the idea of luck and social status and undermines the trite contemporary proverb articulated by many people who exercise power in the capitalist world that 'Life is unfair'. Whilst positivists can rationally argue that you cannot derive an ought from an is, it is certainly possible to derive an is from an ought. To do unfairness is a choice and is not acquiescence to an obligation in nature.

The American political philosopher John Rawls authored two texts, *A Theory of Justice* (1971) and *Political Liberalism* (1993), that constitute a sophisticated theory of social justice in a capitalist world that is both contractarian and libertarian. Rawls argued that the most important quality of human beings is not their sentience but their rationality, their ability to make choices. He said the capacity to make choices is what determines the individual as opposed to the community. He suggests that we should imagine a group of a-historical human beings who come together to agree on a future society by engaging in a 'veil of ignorance'. The process ensures the least privileged members of society will be protected, since everyone wishes to secure themselves from a future life of poverty. A well-ordered society must be characterized by structures and institutions, which allow maximum scope for the individual to make choices. He said that it is only in a situation where individuals are capable of improving themselves under conditions of equality of opportunity that the rational person may flourish. He saw the need to neutralize negative self-interest and at the same time recognize that human beings are also moral persons with a sense of justice. The first principle of justice was the idea of greatest equal liberty, and these liberties include political liberty, freedom of speech and assembly, liberty of conscience and freedom of thought, freedom of the person along with the right to hold personal property, and freedom from arbitrary arrest and seizure as defined by the concept of the rule of law. The second principle of justice was the regulation of the distribution of other primary goods in society, including material wealth and social, economic and political opportunities. He said social and economic inequalities should be arranged so that they are to the greatest advantage of the least advantaged (that is, the representative worst-off person – the difference principle) and attached to offices and positions open to all under conditions of fair equality of opportunity – the principle of fair equality of opportunity. (*Jurisprudence* 2008: 89–97; Popkin and Stroll 1998: 109–11)

Professor Nick Couldry is one of the more original and pioneering 'New Aristotelians' theorizing on media ethics. In his 2006 monograph, *Listening Beyond The Echoes: Media, Ethics, and Agency in an Uncertain World*, he stated:

> Media practice *matters* for how humans flourish more broadly in an era where we depend on the circulation of vast amounts of socially relevant information, and media are vitally involved in that exchange. It follows that a general ethics of media practice is relevant to all of us.
>
> (Couldry 2006: 125)

Couldry asks the question, how can we live, ethically and through media? This is an issue that judges and politicians in any society may well benefit from asking of themselves, rather than continually demanding it of media communicators. Couldry argues that 'ethics is a shared necessity, not simply an individual obligation,' (ibid.: 140) and in the conclusion to his book advises people engaging with the media ethics discipline that 'media ethics, like all ethics, starts from where we find ourselves, not from where we would like to be. Ethics is a framework for building consensus, even where none seems available.' (Ibid.)

The ethics of responding to terrorism

At the beginning of the twenty-first century the catastrophic attack on New York City's World Trade Center and the Pentagon in Washington DC on 11 September 2001 raised the issue of the moral justification for the concept of 'the just war'. The debate over the degree of proportionality to be deployed in a military response to war is as old as Ancient Greece. In Book III of *History of the Peloponnesian War* by Thucydides, the state of Athens, then the equivalent of the USA in terms of being a super-power in the region, debated whether it should exterminate the smaller but terror-sponsoring state of Mytilene.

Terrorism is a tactic of extreme political action that deliberately avoids making any distinction in the targeting of combatants and non-combatants. Western politicians have been advancing, some would say fallaciously, that terrorism equates to an ideology or belief system, when in the historical context it is merely a tactic of war using violence to generate social fear, anxiety and insecurity. Terrorism used to be discussed as force of violence used by states and insurgency groups to wage war and conflict. It can be argued that 'the war on terror' is a meaningless idea. In the absence of a concrete individual or collective identity that can be charged with terrorism in state or international jurisdictions, it is a war that has the potential for being one without end. The construction of 'a war on terror' led British television essayist Adam Curtis to develop a thesis that the phenomenon's rhetoric represented the outcome of an ideological struggle between the politico-religious doctrines of neo-conservatism and radical Islamism.

In the three-part BBC television documentary series *The Power of Nightmares: The Rise of the Politics of Fear*, shown in late 2004, Curtis argued that the US political ideology of neo-conservatism emanated from the University of Chicago's political studies faculty, inspired by the academic Leo Strauss. It is said to be the antithesis of twentieth-century liberalism. Curtis stated that neo-conservatives prescribe the export of US democracy globally through the use of force; that neo-conservativism condemns the destructive force of liberal individualism for inevitably leading to nihilism, a world where nothing is true and everything is permitted. He argued that neo-conservatism approves the use of deceptive propaganda if it is the only way of securing and maintaining the goals of US global dominance. This is achieved by the assertion of powerful myths and illusions that may not be true and include the idea of a national destiny to battle against the forces of evil throughout the world. (Curtis 2004)

This idea of propagandizing a mythology that could effectively be based on lies appears to be heavily borrowed from Plato's myth of the metals. Plato argued that loyalty in the ideal state could be encouraged by a magnificent myth or noble lie about the origins of life. He described the legend of every citizen emerging from the earth fully formed so that residual memories of childhood and education were just a dream. The myth of Mother Earth making all citizens brothers and sisters, and God establishing the hierarchy of metal composition by which gold was added to Rulers, silver to Auxiliaries and bronze and iron to the Workers, would foster a culture of contentment in relation to the social stratification. Class membership would be an eternal given and not a positivist choice. The noble lie thereby engenders false consciousness that serves the interests of the ideal state.

Curtis explained that neo-conservatives were known as 'the crazies' during the administration of US President George Bush senior and took the reins of power during the administration of his son, President George W. Bush. US Defence Secretary Donald Rumsfeld and Vice President Dick Cheney have been described as neo-cons who were the architects of the invasion of Iraq in 2003. Curtis said neo-conservatives see unbridled individual freedom as the source for chaos in society because egoism cuts away at the bonds of national pride and unity. It is permissible to propagate noble lies and mythologies in order to promote social stability. He reported that neo-conservatives utilize techniques of black propaganda and psychological warfare to exaggerate and distort reality and conjure controversial fantasies with an indifference to the deployment of mendacity. In short, they are advocates of political mischief in the social and political discourse. They see religion, such as Christian fundamentalism, as a means of redeeming the moral integrity of the country. In foreign policy the communist Soviet Union has, post-war, been replaced by 'an axis of evil' of rogue states such as Iraq, Syria, Iran and North Korea that threaten the world with an ideology of global terrorism.

It is argued that neo-conservatives were actually allies of radical Islamists in Afghanistan during the 1980s, when they joined in common cause to resist the presence of Soviet military power. (Ibid.)

Curtis's theory contends that the political motivation for the global terrorist war against the USA and its allies lay in the ideology of radical Islamism. This is a genre of radical religious politics articulated by the Egyptian Sayed Kotb and based on the idea that US liberal democracy is a decadent, imperialist and perverted doctrine centred on vulgarity, corruption, selfishness, lustful materialism and immodesty. His writing and activism in Egypt inspired the Islamic Brotherhood and later informed the ideology of Ayman al-Zawahiri, Osama Bin Laden and Al

Qaeda. Kotb argued that the Islamic world was in a state of false consciousness or Jahaliya, and that Western secular barbarism was an external and internal threat to the Muslim world. Islam is being insulted on all fronts and any way of fighting this has existential weight because it is God's will on earth. Kotb was put on trial for treason by Egyptian President General Abdul Nasser in 1965, and he was executed in 1966. The ideology sanctions the killing of corrupt civilians and political leaders (who cease to become real Muslims). Non-believers are demonized and reduced to the status of kafirs/kuffars. The killing of kafirs/kuffars would be acceptable if it shocked the populace into seeing the truth. The means of killing can exceed the bounds of decency, since the purpose is to achieve the sublime objective.

The unpleasant and potentially racist use of the pejorative name-calling 'kafirs/kuffars' is represented in the findings of investigative documentaries produced in the UK Channel 4 series *Dispatches*, 'Undercover Mosque', broadcast on 15 January 2007, and 'Undercover Mosque: The Return', broadcast on 1 September 2008. Unlike the BBC series *Power of Nightmares*, the Channel 4 programmes can be viewed online at www.channel4.com/4od/index.

Curtis's theory as set out in his three one-hour documentaries is clearly partisan and open to the criticism that it simplifies the conflict between the USA and jihadist terrorism generated by Al Qaeda. The method of setting up neo-conservatives and Al Qaeda as a binary dynamic, each perpetuating and sustaining the other in its conflict, over-simplifies a much more complex series of events and political influences. The election of the Democratic President Barack Obama in 2009, substantial changes in US foreign policy, as well as the abandonment of the 'war on terror' rhetoric and tactics, begins to render the discourse out-of-date and wrong. While Curtis sources his opinions to authoritative studies such as Gilles Kepel's *Jihad: The Trail of Political Islam* (2009) and Professor Shadia B. Drury's *Leo Strauss and the American Right* (1999), his documentary series could be accused of having a partial approach to the representation of neo-conservatism. The writings of Irving Kristol, for example, are much more complex than is set out in the simplified language of a polemical television programme. In *Neo Conservativism: The Autobiography of an Idea* (The Free Press 1995), Kristol argues that the neo-conservative is much like a liberal who has been mugged by reality and that the survival of modern democracy requires economic ideas that are expanded by political, moral philosophy and even religious thought.

Bin Laden and his followers argue that their war is a just one, and the collateral deaths of non-combatant civilians are justifiable. They are motivated by a religious fundamentalism that is a minority creed. Controversially, it could be argued that the ethical paradox of their position is that the indifference they have for the fate of non-combatant civilians is as morally or immorally consequentialist as the total war ethics inherent in the atomic bombing of Hiroshima and Nagasaki, and the carpet bombing of German cities and towns during the Second World War. The avowed objectives involved killing women and children and the deployment of military force as a form of terrorism. On the other hand, in the context of the ethics of war studies, other philosophical factors can be brought into the debate. They include concepts of retaliation, revenge and a wider contextual application of the notion of necessity, utility and the humanitarian goal of survival. However, the universal maxims of respecting the right to life and applying the principles of fairness, justice, toleration and forgiveness cannot be excluded from the ethical discourse, and these principles are central to the ethical creed of monotheistic religions that include Islam, Christianity and Judaism.

Case history: W.T. Stead, the *Pall Mall Gazette* and white slavery – applying the ethics of natural law, the Christian moral code, utilitarianism and Kant

W. T. Stead pioneered popular and sensationalist campaigning journalism on moralist grounds. The cultural critic Matthew Arnold described it as 'New Journalism' in the May 1887 issue of the *Nineteenth Century* magazine:

> It has much to recommend it [...] it is full of ability, novelty, variety, sensation, sympathy, generous instincts, its one great fault is that it is feather-brained. It throws out assertions at a venture because it wishes them true; does not correct either them or itself, if they are false; and to get at the seat of things as they truly are seems to feel no concern whatever.
>
> (Griffiths 1992: 434)

W.T. Stead was the focus of this polemic from the author of *Culture and Anarchy* (1867–9) because Stead was the veritable apostle of New Journalism. On becoming editor of the London evening newspaper *Pall Mall Gazette*, Stead redesigned the paper and introduced illustrations, larger headlines and crossheads to break up the previous drab columns of grey type. He introduced the concept of the interview into the English newspaper, and the first celebrity to be featured in this way was the author E.M Forster, the biographer of Charles Dickens. He pioneered the concept of the supplements, which were called *Pall Mall Gazette* extras. Stead pioneered a new style of journalism to a readership that was largely elitist and male, since the *Pall Mall Gazette* had a readership dominated by middle-class and aristocratic men used to picking up their late-afternoon and evening paper in their central London gentlemen's clubs. (Örnebring 2006: 855)

Stead was also the seeker of sensational scoops, with a moral twist. He was, according to his assistant editor Lord Alfred Milner, a compound of Don Quixote and Phineas T. Barnum. What he sought to do was bring an element of performance to the style of popular journalism. A.G. Gardiner, editor of the *Daily News* (1902–19), observed:

> English journalism had, at the end of the 19th century, reached a stage in which some sweeping change was imminent. It had remained essentially what it had been for more than a century – the vehicle of the thought, the interests and temper of the leisured and educated middle class, relatively small in numbers but great in influence.
>
> (Griffiths 1992: 532)

The historian G.M. Trevelyan explained: 'The number of people who can read is enormous; the proportion of those who are educated is small. The printing-press, following the law of supply and demand, now appeals to the uneducated mass of all classes.' (Ibid.)

It was in this context that Stead challenged the snobbery and prejudices of a society which condemned thousands of children to prostitution in the brothels of the East End of London. The practice was known as white slavery. Stead combined the language of the penny dreadful with moralistic conviction. He was described as a deeply religious nonconformist. Cardinal Manning once said to Stead: 'When I read the *Pall Mall* every night it seems to me as if Oliver Cromwell had come to life again.' (Ibid.)

Stead saw journalism as a mechanism for changing society for the good and as being the agent for God's work. By the time he published the series *The Maiden Tribute of Modern Babylon* in July 1885 he had cut his campaigning teeth with stories about Bulgarian atrocities in 1876–77, the plight and poverty of the poor of London, the need to send General Gordon to the Sudan, the castigation of Prime Minister Gladstone for not preventing Gordon's murder, and a campaign to modernize and strengthen the Royal Navy. His journalism had biblical zeal and the verve of moral sensationalism:

> Even in the worst days of American slavery, a Negro could always call his soul his own. [...] But into the prison-house of Prostitution glares no ray of hope athwart the darkness of despair. Its only light is the lurid glare of Hell. Perhaps even that is better than the un-revealed blackness of the lot from which its inmates can only escape by ceasing to live. The doors of their dungeon, locked, bolted and barred by the State, can only be opened by death.
>
> (Stead *Northern Echo* 1876)

The social problem of child prostitution

The circulation of the *Pall Mall Gazette* had increased by 30 per cent in a highly competitive market for the press. The Education Act of 1870 had extended literacy and the popular market for the press to a much greater proportion of the working classes. Circulation meant that income and advertising revenue increased significantly. The issue of child prostitution would be central to the class and cultural tensions between bourgeois middle-class West London and the poor districts of working-class East London.

The East End supplied the sexual products for the affluent men of the West. The bourgeois men of West London had the disposable income to pursue sexual desires which were exploitative and thereby attacked the dignity of the poor. The age of consent was so low that it was not against the law to have consensual intercourse with young teenage girls. Despite a background of iconoclastic reports and campaigns for legislation to check the effective selling of 13-year-old girls to brothels, the passage of the Criminal Law Amendment Bill through the Westminster Parliament was being delayed and likely to be sacrificed in the pressure of other legislative business thought to have greater priority.

Anti-child prostitution campaigners Josephine Butler and Benjamin Scott, the Chamberlain of the City of London, approached Stead. He responded by agreeing to engage in performance journalism. He planned to buy a girl of just over 13 as if for an immoral purpose and then expose the transaction in the *Pall Mall Gazette* (*PMG*) so that the 'public might know at last how simple a matter it was to debauch the innocent.' (Odle 1938: 712)

The campaign by the Pall Mall Gazette

Stead enlisted the support and cooperation of respectable religious bodies. The Archbishop of Canterbury tried to dissuade him. Dr Temple, the Bishop of London, and Cardinal Manning, the Roman Catholic Prelate, urged him to go ahead with his project. Bramwell Booth of the Salvation Army introduced him to a reformed brothel-keeper, Rebecca Jarrett, who agreed to purchase a girl for Stead. Mrs Jarrett claimed that she had acquired 13-year-old Eliza Armstrong from her mother for the sum of £3. Stead was unaware that Mr and Mrs Armstrong had neither given their consent for the girl's ruin nor had even 'sold' her. They were under the impression that she was being introduced into domestic service. He had made fatal assumptions in his pursuit of a sensationalist narrative in order to stir the moral indignation of his readers.

Eliza was taken to a brothel where she was put straight to bed. Since she had been told she was going into service with a kind gentleman she had no idea of the character of her surroundings. As soon as she was asleep, Stead entered her room and called the woman Salvation Army officer who was waiting outside. She entered, told Eliza to dress, and drove her straight to a nursing home where a doctor examined her and pronounced her to be *virgo intacta*. The following morning she was taken to Paris and put into the care of the Salvation Army.

For five days a campaign of articles headlined 'The Maiden Tribute of Modern Babylon' succeeded in reviving the legislation and supporting the political lobby to raise the age of consent to 16. The press had therefore successfully brought about a change in the law so as to alter social conditions. Stead's campaign also inaugurated the phenomenon of sensationalist competition between newspapers and it was one of his competitor evening papers, *Lloyd's Illustrated*, which exposed the fact that Eliza had in fact been technically abducted. Popular journalism, which seeks to expose the hypocrisy of those in power, has a tendency to invite its own prosecution if the original charge is found to have an unlawful context.

Örnebring highlights that Stead's 'Maiden Tribute' campaign was unusual and socially provocative because he gave voice to prostitutes and their keepers:

> A large portion of the 'Maiden Tribute' articles is taken up by interviews. The majority of those interviewed are denizens of the world of prostitution: prostitutes, brothel-keepers, procurers and other criminals. All of the five articles in the series contained lengthy interviews in which the persons involved in various ways in the underage prostitution racket got to speak in detail about their own activities and their feelings (or lack of feelings) on these activities.
>
> (Örnebring 2006: 861)

It is also probable that Stead made himself vulnerable to prosecution for any suspicion of unlawful behaviour on his part by allowing the *PMG* to challenge the Victorian newspaper taboo of never criticizing the police and forces of law and order:

> it criticized the police for their complicity in the business of prostitution, and it did [so] in such a way as to highlight issues of power and class [...] This clear and unequivocal criticism of the police force (and, in other articles, of the justice and penal systems in general) made the *PMG* and the 'Maiden Tribute' campaign different from many other Victorian newspapers.
>
> (Örnebring 2006: 863)

Stead was making a moralistic clarion call for reform with the cutting edge of iconoclastic and judgmental journalism:

The power of police over women in the streets is already ample, not merely for the purposes of maintaining order and for preventing indecency and molestation, but also for the purpose of levying black-mail upon unfortunates. I have been assured by a chaplain of one of Her Majesty's gaols, who perhaps has more opportunities of talking to these women than any other individual in the realm, that there is absolute unanimity in the ranks that if they do not tip the police they get run in [...] A girl's livelihood is in a policeman's hand, and in too many cases he makes the most of this opportunity. To increase by one jot or tittle the power of the man in uniform over the women who are left unfriended even by their own sex is a crime against liberty and justice, which no impatience at markets of vice, or holy horror at the sight of girls on the streets, ought to be allowed to excuse.

(Stead *Pall Mall Gazette* 1885)

Prosecution and trial

A high-profile trial at the Central Criminal Court in November 1885 continued the journalism as performance, although now with risks that few members of the acting profession would be prepared to take. Prosecution and trial heightened the public sphere of his moral crusade and the rhetoric of his evidence to the jury had all the hallmarks of Renaissance flourish:

When I walked the streets of London and heard church bells clang-ing to prayer to a Christian God it seemed to me too cruel to be borne to think that in this and that house of ill-fame there was some poor child, as innocent as any of your daughters, who had been ruined for life. Oh, I seemed to see, written up in letters of fire, that ghastly parody of Christ's words: 'Suffer the little children [...] for of such is the Kingdom of Hell' [...] What I tried to do was, not to abduct a girl, but to raise up sufficient sentiment in this country to render abduc-tions more dangerous. That was my purpose. You know now how I succeeded. I admit I made many blunders, many mistakes, but all men are fallible. You know why I did all this, you know why Jarrett did it, and Booth did it, and we all did it. By your verdict, I stand or fall, and if in the opinion of twelve men, twelve Englishmen, born of English mothers, and possibly fathers of English girls, if you say to me: 'You are guilty', I take my punishment and do not flinch.

(Odle 1938: 707–20)

Stead and some of his co-accused were convicted of child abduction and indecent assault arising out of the doctor and midwife's confirmation of Eliza's virginity, but these were perceived as technical rather than moral offences. The foreman of one jury declared:

201

We find him guilty of being deceived by his agents, we recommend him to mercy, and wish to put on record our high appreciation of the services he has rendered to the nation by securing the passage of a much-needed law for the protection of young girls.

(Ibid.)

It seems that Stead had little doubt that the law would not be on his side when he took his place in the dock of the Central Criminal Court:

I had absolutely no chance of an acquittal, for I had admitted in the clearest possible terms that I had taken away the child, believing that I had purchased the consent of the mother, but I had not the consent of the father. The judge ruled that the consent of the mother was nothing, that the consent of the father was everything, and as I had admitted that I had never even asked for the consent of the father, the case against me was so clear I wanted to plead 'guilty' the moment that the judge ruled that the consent of the father was essential. I was prevented from doing this by my very good friend and lawyer, Sir George Lewis, who through the whole of that memorable time rendered me invaluable service.

(Whyte 1925: 184)

Stead's larger-than-life career ended in death on the *Titanic* in 1912. He was still carrying the last shilling of a dying prostitute, sent to him as a donation to his legal defence fund in 1885. The former prostitute Rebecca Jarrett, who had organized the purchase of Eliza Armstrong and had lied and contradicted herself under the Attorney General's cross-examination lest she should incriminate some of her old friends in vice, lived out her days in the Salvation Army, where she was 'loved and esteemed by those around her.' (Whyte 1925: 186) Eliza contacted W.T. Stead in later years. 'She had a good husband, she wrote, and was the proud and happy mother of a family of six.' (Ibid.)

Applying the ethics of natural law and the Christian moral code

Freedom of expression has depended on the power or force of *natural law* being over and above *positive* or man-made law. This metaphysical dynamic, driven largely by the Stoics, was shouldered on through the works of Roman philosophers such as Cicero to embody the pragmatic idea of *rule of law*. The process of jurist writing accompanied the adoption of Christianity by the Roman Empire and culminated in the jurisprudential work of Emperor Justinian in 533.

The idea that natural law would be beyond the will of king or legislature and an unchanging framework within which man could live persisted as the bulwark against abuse of power in human thinking. St Thomas Aquinas (1227–74) maintained the concept of a Christian God implanting in men knowledge of natural law and a will to obey it. The Doctrine of Two Swords defined the dichotomy of secular power being separate from spiritual power, as developed by Pope Gelasius I in the fifth century. Gelasius counselled against the same body or individual holding both powers and enthused about the advantages of the two spheres working in harmony with each other.

The common factor in the dynamic of power being developed at this time was the idea of balance, or countervailing authority to the temporal presence of tyranny or injustice in the everyday world. The Christian church interpreted the word of God on the basis that all earthly powers were subject to divine law and that in cases of conflict the spiritual authority of the Pope must be supreme over the secular power of any emperor or king. (Morrison 1997: 64–74)

Separating secular from religious authority

St Augustine (354–430) distinguished between the City of God and the City of the World. The foundation stones of human equality were being fashioned through the belief of the universal brotherhood of mankind, with all men being equal in the sight of God.

The concept of God's universal law provided the ethical imperative for Christian heresy or unorthodoxy when power struggles concatenated between church and state, and religious revolts against the Roman Catholic church itself. Key figures in the Reformation, such as Martin Luther, Jean Bodin and John Calvin, wished to transfer the authority of supreme law making away from the Roman Catholic church in Rome.

Sometimes the sovereign power of statehood, or residual natural law powers invested in a new interpretation of the Bible scriptures, provided the source of resistance. The right of resistance became a key issue in the concept that a monarch derived power from the people and could be called to account if the monarchy no longer deserved the allegiance of the people.

Followers of John Calvin rejected his theory of passive obedience when they found themselves in opposition to state policies on spiritual grounds. This was the basis upon which John Knox (1505–72) sought to maintain the Protestant faith against the Catholic monarchy of Mary Stuart.

In France the Protestant Huguenots, and in England the Catholics, sought resistance authority from the notion of natural law in reaction to the exercise of the divine right by French and English monarchies to pursue religious persecution. In 1579 *Vindiciae Contra Tyrannos* represented the first written text to attempt to build a philosophy around the inalienable rights of man.

It stated that a king or queen was answerable for the upholding of the *natural law* and the people had the right to resist any monarch who abused it. The text was adopted as a justification for the trial and execution of Charles I in England and the Glorious Revolution against James II in 1688. (Popkin and Stroll 1998: 25–30)

W.T. Stead and natural law

W.T. Stead takes as his moral authority a deeply held belief that there is a divine being who has laid down certain rules for moral behaviour and that incorrect conduct consists in violating them. The moral code is complex and varied and it is apparent that there is no homogeneous philosophy that can be found in one volume, but there are common factors, which have been influenced by Plato through the interpretation of St Augustine in the fourth century, and then by Aristotle through the interpretation by St Thomas Aquinas in the thirteenth century.

Christian ethics have developed from the absolutist proscriptions of the Decalogue (Ten Commandments). The Christian church developed its social and political role through history. The doctrine of immortality, the respect for asceticism, the preachings of Christ as the expression of divine will, the establishment of Christian ethical theory, followed by casuistry or codes on conduct conducive to goodness and conduct conducive to badness, led to an overall creed which was objective and authoritarian.

The exhortations on what was good and bad were infallible because the code was regarded as the expression of God's will. The identification of God's will would depend on whether the emphasis was on the written scriptures of the Bible, the proclamations of the church as the vicar of God, or the consultation of the individual with God through conscience. (Ibid.)

The moral imperatives of W.T. Stead were derived from a body of ethics which can be regarded as pre-eminent in the two-thousand-year history of Western civilization. Furthermore, its influence has spread around the globe through missionary work, trade and evangelism. Stead's position was that although the law as it stood in his time did not prohibit prostitution by girls aged between 13 and 15, the activity was a moral defiance of God's will. He was equating immorality with spiritual disobedience.

However, could Stead's reliance on God's will be sustained by the argument that it was ordained from a God who was *sui generis* good? If the world represented God's will, how could it be good when it tolerated such evils as young girls being sold by their parents into white slavery to be used as sex commodities by paedophiliac men riddled with venereal diseases? Surely the goodness of God was not unqualified? Notwithstanding this theological paradox, who was to decide the conscience that really expressed God's will? Would it be the conscience of W.T. Stead? Would it be the conscience of the Director of Public Prosecutions, the judge, or the jury?

Stead abandoned ethical constraints of moderation and indifference to campaign by public accusation and moral condemnation. In doing this he behaved dramatically and cast himself in the role of an actor within the plot of the inhuman and immoral activity he sought to expose and outlaw. Whether or not he knew that the 13-year-old girl had been sold to him without her parents' permission, he had willingly proceeded to buy a young girl by pretending to be an agent in the trade of child prostitution.

Even though he was acting with the approval of two Christian church leaders for the overall purpose of changing the law by *agent provocateur* journalism, he was buying another human being through a performance of deceit, subjecting the young girl to an intimate medical examination, reckless as to whether her parents approved or not, and removing her to another country, reckless as to whether her parents approved or not.

W.T. Stead and Spinoza

The carelessness and rashness of his desire to manipulate public opinion and political consensus to bring about a change in the law for the benefit of young children lays him open to the charge of using unethical means to achieve an ethical end. Furthermore it can also be argued that his goal could not be isolated as a spiritual/ethical fulfilment because the process of sensationalist new journalism involved the commercial profits of record sales of the *Pall Mall Gazette*.

W.T. Stead may be able to derive moral justification for his tactics from the philosophy of Baruch de Spinoza, otherwise known as Spinoza (1632–77). Spinoza's position on ethics could be held to be contradictory. He was both rigid determinist and relativist. This means that the key to moral happiness in Stead's conduct is relating the means of action to the circumstances. Certainly the reports of W.T. Stead's acceptance of the inevitable fate that his actions brought upon him demonstrates strong aspects of Spinoza's belief that the happy life consists in recognizing that all events are determined, and emotionally accepting this fact.

Riches, fame and sensual pleasure may not be inherently worthwhile, but they may be a means to make life happier. In the course of the campaign 'The Maiden Tribute of Modern Babylon', was it the case that W.T Stead understood the limits of human power and did he emotionally accept that all events are determined? If this were the case, then Spinoza would have probably concluded that Stead had led the good life. His attitude had accepted that events had been determined by natural laws. Humanity is not free, and at the same time things are not good or bad in themselves, but only in relation to someone or circumstances.

Far from being ruined by what the law, parts of the establishment and public opinion regarded as his legal and ethical mistakes, W.T. Stead liberated himself from fear, anxiety and unhappiness by making his own decisions, shared by many, about the relative goodness or badness of what he had done.

For Stead, the wrong was realized through hindsight and retrospective knowledge. Whatever punishment his society meted out was more than compensated for by the ultimate goal of changing the law and outlawing a practice that brought misery and degradation to thousands of children. W.T. Stead was effectively liberated from the emotional slavery afflicting his critics. The manner of his death on the *Titanic* is perhaps another aspect of his Spinozan dignity.

The ethical weakness of Spinoza's philosophy is that the broad view of deciding good and bad in the context of eternity on relativist terms is the lack of certainty about human judgment. W.T. Stead may have been certain about the relativist goodness and badness of the tactics by which he sought to expose evil through journalism for the purpose of parliamentary reform for a greater good. However, others may be justifiably concerned about the extent to which unlawful behaviour in the quest for a perceived greater good, on balance, creates a greater badness through the means adopted.

Applying utilitarianism

The utilitarian approach established by Jeremy Bentham and John Stuart Mill sets out an objective principle for determining when a given action is right or wrong. How does the Stead case fare when scrutinized by the principle of utility that an action is right insofar as it tends to produce the greatest happiness for the greatest number? The criterion for evaluation is undoubtedly the importance of consequences from the actions determining rightness or wrongness, and not the motive. Bentham had even gone so far as to establish a hedonistic calculus to measure the amount of pleasure and pain that an act causes. In the end, the utilitarian equation should separate the rightness or wrongness of an action from the goodness or badness of the agent performing the action.

In the case of W.T. Stead the distress and humiliation to the parents of the 13-year-old girl bought by the newspaper editor in his campaign, and the potential harm caused to the young girl from being inside a brothel for less than a night and then intimately examined by a doctor, were minor social infractions compared to the greater social good of Parliament passing a law which raised the age of consent and criminalized the selling of children into prostitution, the people who ran the brothels, and the men who sought to make a sexual commodity out of girls aged between 13 and 15.

It could be argued quite strongly that W.T. Stead would have merited a utilitarian acquittal. When 13-year-old Eliza Armstrong had grown up and had become a mother herself she wrote to him expressing thanks for his actions and absolving him of any suggestion that his actions had done her any harm.

One weakness of utilitarian evaluation is that it is difficult to assess all the consequences of an action. If the effects cannot be taken into account, the morality of applying utilitarian concerns is practically useless. If moral judgment is then qualified by determination of probable effects, then the principle becomes subjective rather than objective.

Another flaw of utilitarianism is that it violates the common-sense value that morality can only be determined by consideration of motive or, to use the Latin legal phrase, *mens rea*. The question posed by the case history analysed is this: If W.T. Stead was deriving perverted and sexual pleasures by acting out the role of pimp and commissioning the intimate examination of a 13-year-old girl, utilitarianism establishes a world where everybody acts out reverse and evil motives and yet their acts turn out to be socially desirable because the consequences are more beneficial than harmful. Would not this kind of world be repugnant? The paradox of utilitarianism is that it encourages a social environment made up of people whose actions are good but whose motives are evil.

A more feminist reading of 'The Maiden Tribute' narrative, by Judith Walkowitz, suggests that it is more than possible that W.T. Stead's motives and interests developed a moral ambiguity:

> In most of these interviews, young girls appear as innocent inform-ants, simpleminded in their storytelling. Yet every now and then Stead reversed the direction of erotic energy, presenting himself as unnerved by the presence of a little 'brazen-faced harlot' masquerad-ing as a *femme fatale*.
>
> Disequilibrium and excess shaped Stead's account of the double life and took its toll on the investigator. For he seems to have gone over the edge in his attempt to authenticate and document criminal vice. Two eerie features of his narrative soon become apparent: the readers were shown London's inferno through Stead's elite gaze, and exploration led Stead into actual impersonation of a Minotaur. In order to prove to the public how easy it was to procure a young girl, Stead obtained one himself.
>
> (Walkowitz 2000: 101)

Walkowitz argues that Stead's journalism 'ushered in a new epoch of mass-market fantasies and desires. [...] he had metamorphosed into a compulsive voyeur and chronicler of sexual commerce. [...] This meta-morphosis demonstrates the affinity between the two literary genres of melodrama and pornography.' (Walkowitz 2000: 96–7) A close reading of Stead's account of buying his 13-year-old virgin, whom he called 'Lily', can elucidate the suspicion that Stead's ardour for the campaign was driven by an excess of erotic enthusiasm. His account is set out in Table 2.5.

Table 2.5 Pall Mall Gazette 6 July 1885

A child of thirteen bought for £5

Let me conclude the chapter of horrors by one incident, and only one of those which are constantly occurring in those dread regions of subterranean vice in which sexual crime flourishes almost unchecked. I can personally vouch for the absolute accuracy of every fact in the narrative.

At the beginning of this Derby week, a woman, an old hand in the work of procuration, entered a brothel in _ St., M_ kept by an old acquaintance, and opened negotiations for the purchase of a maid. One of the women who lodged in the house had a sister as yet untouched. Her mother was far away, her father was dead. The child was living in the house, and in all probability would be seduced and follow the profession of her elder sister. The child was between thirteen and fourteen, and after some bargaining it was agreed that she should be handed over to the procurers for the sum of £5. [...]

The next day, Derby Day as it happened, was fixed for the delivery of this human chattel. But as luck would have it, another sister of the child who was to be made over to the procurers heard of the proposed sale. She was living respectably in a situation, and on hearing of the fate reserved for the little one she lost no time in persuading her dissolute sister to break off the bargain. When the woman came for her prey the bird had flown. Then came the chance of Lily's mother. The brothel-keeper sent for her, and offered her a sovereign for her daughter. The woman was poor, dissolute, and indifferent to everything but drink. The father, who was also a drunken man, was told his daughter was going to a situation. He received the news with indifference, without even inquiring where she was going to. The brothel-keeper having thus secured possession of the child, then sold her to the procurers in place of the child whose sister had rescued her from her destined doom for £5 – £3 paid down and the remaining £2 after her virginity had been professionally certified. The little girl, all unsuspecting the purpose for which she was destined, was told that she must go with this strange woman to a situation. [...]

The first thing to be done after the child was fairly severed from home was to secure the certificate of virginity without which the rest of the purchase-money would not be forthcoming. In order to avoid trouble she was taken in a cab to the house of a midwife, whose skill in pronouncing upon the physical evidences is generally recognized in the profession. The examination was very brief and completely satisfactory. But the youth, the complete innocence of the girl, extorted pity even from the hardened heart of the old abortionist. 'The poor little thing,' she exclaimed. 'She is so small, her pain will be extreme. I hope you will not be too cruel with her' – as if to lust when fully roused the very acme of agony on the part of the victim has not a fierce delight. To quiet the old lady the agent of the purchaser asked if she could supply anything to dull the pain. She

Continued overleaf

---

produced a small phial of chloroform. 'This,' she said, 'is the best. My clients find this much the most effective.' The keeper took the bottle, but unaccustomed to anything but drugging by the administration of sleeping potions, she would infallibly have poisoned the child had she not discovered by experiment that the liquid burned the mouth when an attempt was made to swallow it. £1 1s was paid for the certificate of virginity – which was verbal and not written – while £1 10s more was charged for the chloroform, the net value of which was probably less than a shilling. An arrangement was made that if the child was badly injured Madame would patch it up to the best of her ability, and then the party left the house.

From the midwife's the innocent girl was taken to a house of ill fame, No. _, P_ Street, Regent-street, where, notwithstanding her extreme youth, she was admitted without question. She was taken up stairs, undressed, and put to bed, the woman who bought her putting her to sleep. She was rather restless, but under the influence of chloroform she soon went over. Then the woman withdrew. All was quiet and still. A few moments later the door opened, and the purchaser entered the bedroom. He closed and locked the door. There was a brief silence. And then there rose a wild and piteous cry – not a loud shriek, but a helpless, startled scream like the bleat of a frightened lamb. And the child's voice was heard crying, in accents of terror, 'There's a man in the room! Take me home; oh, take me home!' [...]

And then all once more was still.

That was but one case among many, and by no means the worst. It only differs from the rest because I have been able to verify the facts. Many a similar cry will be raised this very night in the brothels of London, unheeded by man, but not unheard by the pitying ear of Heaven –

For the child's sob in the darkness curseth deeper

Than the strong man in his wrath.

Sources: Eckardt et al. 1988: 254–5; transcript and facsimile of original newspaper at www.attackingthedevil.co.uk/pmg/tribute/mt_page2.php

At the trials held in the Central Criminal Court, Walkowitz suggests,

> The most unsensational and uncontroversial witness was the muted child victim of the "Maiden Tribute,' Eliza Armstrong. Overall, Eliza showed remarkable self-possession in recounting her story, which largely paralleled the 'Maiden Tribute,' even to the point of casting the brothel scene in a matter-of-fact manner very different from Stead's voyeuristic perspective.

(Walkowitz 2000: 107)

One of the tragic ironies of Stead's campaign is that although it was instrumental in securing the passage of the Criminal Law Amendment

Act and raising the age of consent for young women, another muckraking journalist was able to take advantage of the intense moral panic of sexual morals. Henry Labouchère waged an equally successful campaign to persuade Parliament to make homosexual relations in a public or private place a criminal offence. As Eckardt, Gilman and Chamberlin so rightly observed, 'it was recognised only later that the phrase "or private" was an invitation for blackmail.' (von Eckardt et al. 1988: 259) Parliament's reforming zeal would also seal the fate of Oscar Wilde and condemn him to two years on the treadmill of Reading Gaol. These consequences highlight a reverse issue about immorally motivated utilitarianism. The proverb 'the pathway to Hell is paved with good intentions' applies to situations where good and honourable motives can be combined with actions and words producing consequences that bring more unhappiness to a greater number of people.

Stead's melodramatic adventures in London's twilight zones, and sensationalist rabble-rousing mixing classical mythology with the sleaze of the penny dreadful had hardly brought good fortune and prosperity to the Armstrong family. Walkowitz observes that Stead's wanderings among the denizens of London's brothels may well have awakened a dimension of his psyche that would not accord with the Kantian 'Kingdom of ends':

> Despite his self-justifications, considerable evidence exists that Stead had confused his part as well, both by misrepresenting what Jarrett had told him and by identifying too closely and enthusiastically with the villain role. By his own admission, he was in an extreme state of excitement the weeks he was exploring the London inferno. 'I had been visiting brothels and drinking champagne and smoking, which I was not used to, and was very excited' [...] he seemed to be 'playing with fire' – inventing scenarios that implicated him in illicit sexuality yet masked his involvement and permitted him to draw back at the last minute.
>
> (Walkowitz 2000: 113)

Kant and the deontological

The application of Kantian ethics introduces a fundamentally different framework of moral evaluation. The individuals being considered have to be rewarded proportionately to their virtue. Moral value is determined by distinguishing acts done from inclination and acts done from a sense of duty; otherwise known as deontological obligations. Kant's position on ethics is complex and subtle, but the imperative at the heart of his approach is that a person acts morally when feelings and inclinations are suppressed for the overall purpose of fulfilling obligations. The obligation or duty is the ought and the inclination is the taste or like.

An example of the exact subtlety in Kant's approach to ethics is the importance of the difference in preposition between acting in accord *with* duty and acting done *from* duty. The latter is moral. The former is not. The essence of morality lies in the motive from which the act is done. As Kant said: 'Nothing can possibly be conceived in the world, or even out of it, which can be called good without qualification, except a good will.' (Popkin and Stroll 1998: 44) Kant distinguishes between prudential action and moral action:

> There are duties, therefore to which life is much inferior, and in order to fulfil them we must evince no cowardice in regard to our life. The cowardice of man dishonours humanity, and it is very cowardly to set too much store by physical life. The man, who on every trifling occasion is exceedingly fearful of his life, strikes everyone as very ridiculous. We must await our death with resolution. There is little worth in that which there is greater worth in treating with disdain.
>
> (Kant 1997: 150)

For Kant, free actions are good in the virtue of the intention:

> Small will and great capacity is less morally good even in great benefactions. Great will and small capacity is morally better, even in benefactions that are small. We also esteem moral acts, not by their physical effects, but for their own sake, even when they are self-interested, and not always when disinterested [...] cultivation of the moral feeling takes precedence over the cultivation of obedience.
>
> (Kant 1997: 4, 7)

The Kantian approach to W.T. Stead would probably conclude noble and moral motives. Whilst Kant's absolutist position would question any financial acquisition of a human being, there is enough evidence to perceive that Stead's motives were predicated on moral action, goodwill and a moral respect for duty.

When subjected to the standard of his actions being judged in the light of how they would appear if there were universal laws, again, there is an argument that Stead acquits himself. Has he lied for expediency? There is little evidence that he has. According to the Kantian categorical imperative, the stricture on honesty in human communication and behaviour means that the journalist should never lie, since if lying were to become a universal law, all human relations based upon trust and the keeping of promises would become impossible. Journalists should only 'act on that maxim whereby thou canst at the same time will that it should become a universal law.' (Popkin and Stroll 1998: 46)

The aphorism 'Do unto others as you would have them do unto you' is echoed in Kant's declaration: 'So act as to treat humanity, whether in

211

thine own person or in that of any other, in every case as an end withal, never as a means only.' (Ibid.) Kant's approach to ethics provides philosophical bedrock for the principle that everyone is created equal and should not be discriminated against before any law. In every dispute in the courts each individual must be accorded equal value in the adversarial battle. Kant's *Lectures on Ethics* provide a route of justice so that morality is predicated by motive and at the same time morality is more objective than subjective inclination or preference. Consequences are contextualized by respect for duty. W.T. Stead made a mistake, but he was motivated by deontological imperatives and his behaviour throughout had been universalized by consistency.

Discursive debate: media decision making when 'terrorists' use the Internet to torture and execute their 'enemies' and the problem of broadcasting human suffering and death

How would you apply the Kantian deontological and John Stuart Mill utilitarian ethical positions in relation to the debate over whether UK broadcasters should have censored the terror videos of Iraq kidnap victims Kenneth Bigley and Margaret Hassan in 2004? How would other ethical doctrines support this analysis? Media ethicology, media jurisprudence and media ethicism are large subjects and the question invites the concentration and focus on two contrasting ethical doctrines articulated by the major philosophers: Immanuel Kant, who is regarded as a deontologist, and John Stuart Mill, who is regarded as an altruistic utilitarian. The debate invites you to imagine you are the editorial decision makers for global television news services on how much material you are prepared to broadcast, or whether to broadcast any of the material at all.

It is very apparent that applying these doctrinal positions brings little respite in the thoroughly uncomfortable ethical decisions that news broadcasters had to take when the kidnappers of Kenneth Bigley and Margaret Hassan tortured their victims and filmed their terror for release on the Internet. The moral discourse engaged when the media is obliged to engage in the making and breaking of news about violence has been eloquently explored by Jean Seaton in *Carnage and the Media* (2005). Seaton sought to celebrate news rather than attack it and recognize that 'principled, honest reporting is not an incidental, but an essential, part of a free society.' (Seaton 2005: 296) She acknowledged that news is not a cold and mechanical reproduction of the ciphers of violence, but 'hot and living – a great artistic backcloth to twenty first century life, the substance of which determines the choices we make and how we live our lives.' (Ibid.)

Mr Bigley's execution by beheading was filmed and transmitted on the Web. Mrs Hassan was shot to death and the event was also filmed. How should the decision to publish these victims' pleas, torture and deaths be determined ethically? Should the journalist evaluate and give priority to the consequences of publication in terms of any good that could be achieved, i.e. keeping the hostages alive, exposing any political injustice brought about by British involvement in the invasion and occupation of Iraq; or in terms of the harm that would arise, i.e. the humiliation and indignity to the victims, the emotional agony and distress to their families, giving the terrorists 'the oxygen of publicity' and serving their propaganda objectives?

The UK Conservative government under Prime Minister Margaret Thatcher imposed a broadcasting ban in 1988 on the inclusion of sound from members of proscribed terrorist organizations in Northern Ireland. As a result, anybody from the Provisional IRA or its political wing, Sinn Fein, could be shown in vision on television but could only be heard by way of actors' ventriloquism. The ban had the effect of substituting the voices of politicians such as Gerry Adams and Martin McGuinness, who have become part of Northern Ireland's political establishment following the Good Friday Agreement peace process. David Pannick QC represented six broadcast journalists and a viewer who attempted a legal challenge that was unsuccessful in the House of Lords and the then in European Commission of Human Rights at Strasbourg. The European judges considered that the ban was a limited extent of interference with free speech and gave weight to the importance of measures to combat terrorism. Mr Pannick argued that there was no logic behind gagging terrorists' empty rhetoric:

> Margaret Thatcher wished to deny terrorists 'the oxygen of publicity'. The case against the ban was, and remains, overwhelming. If broadcasters cannot question the supporters of violence on camera, with the sound turned on, the public is denied information which will assist it to understand the intricacies of political debate, and the poverty of the political thinking of the terrorist cannot easily be exposed to the viewer. The ban was based on an assertion which the Home Secretary was unable to substantiate in fact: that the apologists for terrorism had previously been given easy access to the airwaves to intimidate others. The directives to the broadcasters unacceptably implied that those who watch television and listen to the radio need protection from free speech because they are unable to exercise their critical faculties to reject the feeble attempts of terrorists and their supporters to justify their evil conduct.
>
> (Pannick *The Times* 1994)

Should the journalist evaluate and give priority to the truth of the reality of what the hostage videos represent, and investigate the motivation of

213

the auteurs of these macabre and shocking productions? The risk of censoring the content of the videos was that the broadcasters would be effectively covering up, or lying about, the reality of what was happening to the captives and the impotence and ineffectiveness of British military security in Iraq. They represented graphic evidence that the British and United States military presence in Iraq was powerless to effectively protect their own citizens working in the country.

Such censorship could be considered meaningless in the context of a generally unregulated and uncensored Internet, where all the terror videos could be seen by anyone. It is important to appreciate that the Internet is capable of being censored. Countries with authoritarian governments, such as China, Cuba and Saudi Arabia, apply laws and technology controls to block access to urls and servers. The media messaging by Internet, and the willingness of Middle East satellite news broadcasters to use more of the content of videos than do their Western counterparts, were further indications of the powerlessness of the West to censor and control the representation of the fates of Mr Bigley and Mrs Hassan. Even though it could be argued that ISPs had an ethical as well as legal duty to ensure that any sites providing this footage were blocked and removed electronically, the censorial reach of the British government was not fully transnational. The Internet can be said to have no borders, but the writ of national regulatory and legal jurisdiction extends no further than the end of the Channel Tunnel.

Furthermore, any decision to broadcast the footage could have been motivated by the desire to exploit the voyeuristic sensationalist/entertainment value of the horror content and, as this motive is immoral/amoral, it is arguable that there can be no justification for publication. How does the virtue ethical doctrine apply in these circumstances? Does the journalist believe that the best approach would be a morally consequentialist position in which the editor endeavours to reconcile the reporting of the story in terms of responsible news values, without giving victory to the propaganda objectives of either the hostage takers or the United Kingdom government?

Any decision by media organizations to cooperate with governments in media 'black-out' arrangements is fraught with moral philosophical and political philosophical dilemmas, as was evidenced in the row over Prince Harry's deployment as a young British Army officer to Afghanistan in 2007–8. Whose interests were being served? While nobody in the media wished to be responsible for putting at risk the lives of Prince Harry and any of his fellow soldiers, was it a case of the media being subtly or coincidentally manipulated by the British Ministry of Defence through offers of special access and coverage when the news was eventually released? As it happened, the information first leaked to an Australian magazine whose publication was overlooked by the world's media, and then blown on the

US news website The Drudge Report, whose pervasiveness and global reach inevitably resulted in the Prince's premature recall to Britain.

On close analysis, the subject is rather similar to the debate over media decision making in relation to hostage videos. The ethics are bound up with ambiguities and dilemmas rooted in differing and unequal power relationships.

Hugh Miles poignantly observes that there has been an exponential growth of Arab-speaking media, but no concomitant diminution in the democratic deficit of ordinary Arab citizens:

> Power in the Arab world remains concentrated in the hands of the same individuals and small elite groups who have handled matters of state for decades. Not one leader of an Arab nation has been fairly and freely elected; indeed, no other region in the world – not even sub-Saharan Africa – has such a poor record. Most Arab governments still regard the media as a handy tool for packaging and falsifying information for their public. By evoking emergency state laws they can shut down dissenting newspapers and arrest journalists as they like. Arab press unions, like Arab opposition political parties, are prevented from growing strong. 'The media,' wrote the Arab poet Ahmad Matar, 'is a means of torture.'
>
> (Miles 2005: 329)

Jason Burke, the author of *Al Qaeda: The True Story of Radical Islam* (2007), has explored the issues of propaganda and power raised by the jihadist torture and execution videos through his book, a BBC television documentary *Channel Terror* (Burke 2005) and a feature newspaper article in the *Observer* 'Theatre of Terror' (Burke 2004). In his book Burke analyses the use of postmodernist media culture by the Jordanian Abu Musab al-Zarqawi, who 'showed a combination of unrivalled brutality – executing several hostages by knife – and a talent for media manipulation – rapidly and effectively ensuring the broadcast of the atrocious images of the executions by internet and video.' (Burke 2007: 274–5) In his *Observer* article Burke breaks down the complex cultural motives and objectives in creating information terrorism as a genre of propaganda of the deed. The productions, sometimes highly sophisticated in their use of digital software and editing, are addressing different spheres of audience reception:

> A kidnapping obeys the classical tragic dramatic structure, with a startling opening scene, a series of well-defined, almost ritualized passages, and then a cathartic dramatic ending. Last year [2003] Chechen terrorists actually took over a theatre, acting out their drama on a real stage. In Mrs Hassan's case, the stage is a house in Falluja and the

proscenium arch is our television screen. Mrs Hassan's killers imagine the audience for their carefully constructed drama in two parts: the Muslim world in the stalls, the West in the cheap seats. The aim is to challenge both parts, provoking a different response in each.

(Burke *Observer* 2004)

It can be argued that the ethics behind the making of the execution videos and their transmission on the asymmetric World Wide Web has no relevance at all to the religion of Islam. Islam is a religion steeped in the ethics and grace of mercy, forgiveness, human compassion and hospitality. The Muslim Council of Britain unreservedly condemned the kidnappings, stating that these actions were contrary to all the teachings of the Qur'an. The Council sent a delegation to Iraq to try to negotiate Mr Bigley's release. Yet the television documentary *Channel Terror*, filmed at the Shatila Palestinian refugee camp in Beirut, a place described by Jason Burke as 'wired', where the people are 'switched on, clued up and very much plugged into the digital multi-media age' (Burke 2005), offered up a symbol of the moral ambiguity generated by a material and imaginative construction of war between the West and the Arab world. A young Muslim man dressed in military fatigues talked about Islam and stated: 'It is not allowed to kill innocent people, but the Americans are not innocent people. They are thieves and rapists.' (Ibid.) Burke said he found an intense and enduring debate throughout the Muslim world about the rights and wrongs of terrorism, suicide bombs, hostage and execution videos, and television channels that provided the first and explicit conduit for terrorist digital propaganda. It was engaged with a far greater complexity of ethical and political discourse than was being represented in the West.

Miles argues that the media is:

> too often an agent of recrimination and hate. In serving its viewers, the media on both sides aggravates the differences between two cultures, while significant communication between the two camps remains minimal. When Americans and Arabs meet one another, they shake hands, do business and interact, but they do not communicate in any meaningful way. The most famous Arab Muslim in America [and the same could be said in Britain] is probably Osama bin Laden.
>
> (Miles 2005: 389)

The purpose and context of the debate was and remains power and the extreme use of information as terrorist power. The dissemination on the Internet invades Western space in a manner that cannot be controlled or censored:

What the execution videos have done is take our technology, the spearhead of our invasion, and turned it back on us – exactly as the high-tech passenger jets that so epitomize the modern world were turned on New York. And we don't like it. We are used to controlling the output on our screens. Indeed every development with the media in recent years has been aimed at increasing our control over the material we watch. Now, suddenly someone else is manipulating us, placing material in our way that is deeply challenging and won't just go away.

(Burke *Observer* 2004)

Another BBC television documentary series, *The New Al-Qaeda*, written and presented by Peter Taylor in 2005, argued that the Internet was now the opportunity for 'jihad.com'. The BBC said his series discovered 'how bloodthirsty videos are made in Iraq and circulated by webmasters in the UK and elsewhere, in an underground broadcasting network [...] the web has become a secret and safe means of communication, as well as an inexhaustible online library of training manuals and information on how to carry out terrorist attacks.' (Taylor 2005). The assistant producer of the series, Matt Cottingham, wrote:

The Internet is swarming with websites that triumph al-Qaeda's propaganda. And if you dive beneath the surface of the rhetoric you quickly find its online caliphate – a virtual safe haven for al-Qaeda that allows it to recruit, train, fund, raise and mobilize. Here is the lifeblood that is driving the new al-Qaeda after the US razed its training camps in Afghanistan. Videos showing how to make suicide vests, build mortar bombs, carry out hijacking, build homemade explosives – the list of resources online is endless. It is now possible to learn how to prepare for jihad (Holy War) against the West from the safety and security of your own bedroom.

(Cottingham 2005)

Jason Burke's documentary *Channel Terror* presented an array of broadcasting news executives who reflected on the difficulties of using the terrorists' propaganda videos. All were aware of how inclusion on their broadcast services added to the exploitation of the suffering of Mr Bigley and Mrs Hassan. Professor Stewart Purvis, a former editor and chief executive of ITN, acknowledged the uncomfortable reality of television news often being entertainment through excitement:

The slightly uncomfortable feeling for television journalists is that at the heart of television journalism is excitement and the excitement in part comes from graphic images which create emotional responses

amongst viewers and even, of course, amongst the journalists themselves. So it's always a slightly embarrassing moment to be in a newsroom when somebody says: 'There's a train crash,' and somebody
replies 'Oh, that's very interesting, that's very exciting. How many
dead?' Something you would not do in polite society.

(Burke 2005)

The veteran Channel 4 newscaster Jon Snow was anxious that British
television journalism was too censorious:

Who are we to say 'We've seen it, but you can't. And it's not good for
you to see it. It's not right because you've been manipulated just as
we have been manipulated.' [...] Yes we are too timid and we do keep
the worst of it from people. [...] And I think we do sanitize war. But
we have a real problem. One is that where in the old days, even when
I started reporting, you were one pair of eyes in the field on behalf of
the viewer and you could take them through what had happened in
that immediate instance; now you are getting it straight off the global
media village. And so in a sense it is almost voyeuristic.

(Ibid.)

Roger Mosey, head of BBC television news between 2000 and 2005,
observed:

There's a big ethical debate among journalists about whether we were
doing the terrorists' work for them. [...] It is one of the liberations of
the digital age that there is no censorship and people can essentially
seek out material they want. But what we are doing is deciding what
we show to 30 million viewers in the UK and what we put on their TV
screens at six o'clock when kids are watching or at ten o'clock as the
considered news of the day. And we have to take a different decision
from simply material you can seek out on the Internet if you absolutely have got the will to do so.

(Ibid.)

Ahmed Sheikh, editor-in-chief of Al Jazeera television explained:

We have a different perspective. We treat things differently. We have
the courage to put out the sort of pictures, the explosions and attacks
against US forces because no one else does that. And we do it because
we believe that without this component the picture would not be
complete.

(Ibid.)

Burke's programme demonstrated the nuances of different representations by world broadcasters in the coverage of the online execution of American Nick Berg, who was forced to dress in an orange jumpsuit similar to that worn by detainees at Guantánamo Bay. David Rose was one of the first journalists to investigate the idea that in responding to Al Qaeda's campaign of terrorism against the USA, America had effectively declared war on human rights. In his book *Guantánamo*, Rose highlights the problem of a world power responding disproportionately to an attack made upon it by a smaller and weaker force:

> On Islamist websites and in the Arab press, Guantánamo is cited time and again as a rallying point for jihad, as a justification for creating more suicide 'martyrs'. At the time of writing, terrorism has discovered a new vogue: the decapitation of western hostages in Iraq and Saudi Arabia, videotaped before and during their executions in orange costumes, in deliberate imitation of the detainee uniform at Gitmo.
>
> (Rose 2004: 134)

ABC, BBC News, Chinese Television, and Channel 4 News made different decisions on how much of the execution video they included in their news programmes before the moment of death. The judgment by editors would turn on issues of taste and decency and a desire to avoid allowing their networks to become part of a terrorist propaganda exercise.

The US media first had to grapple with the ethics of representing the execution of one of its citizens in terrorist Internet video in 2002, when this gruesome fate befell the *Wall Street Journal* reporter Daniel Pearl. CBS news obtained a copy of the videotape created by his captors and labelled 'The Slaughter of the Spy-Journalist, the Jew Daniel Pearl'. *The News Media & The Law* reported that CBS faced opposition from the US administration as well as from Mr Pearl's widow:

> Prior to airing a 30-second excerpt of the video on May 14 [2002], CBS News received appeals from officials in the State and Justice departments requesting that they refrain from airing the videotape.
>
> Jim Murphy, executive producer of CBS Evening News, told the Associated Press that 'the government called to tell us that what we were doing was helping to spread the terrorists' word, and I don't think that's the case.' Anchor Dan Rather defended the broadcast as necessary to 'understand the full impact and danger of the propaganda war being waged.'
>
> (*The News Media & The Law* 2002b: 44)

In 2004, as more and more hostages were kidnapped and beheaded and the scenes posted on websites, ISPs began to report record numbers of hits by Internet surfers who wished to consume the material. Professor Purvis indicated regret about learning from a television debate on the hostage videos that:

> a number of phone-in callers said that they went out of their way to find the websites, to watch these beheadings. These were average members of the British public. So if there is an appetite among them for seeing these videos, clearly the beheaders are tapping into a worrying trend amongst our own society.
>
> (Ibid.)

Burke poignantly observed:

> Our favourite, friendly non-threatening medium has suddenly been subverted and we are yet to reassert control. Turning off the TV is no answer. Refusing to broadcast the video doesn't make any difference. The videos exist. We feel compelled to watch them even when we'd rather not. We are in the unwilling audience.
>
> (Burke *Observer* 2004)

What was the moral difference of showing somebody being killed and a second or two before being killed? UK broadcasters are guided by the Ofcom regulatory rule 1.11: 'Violence, its after-effects and descriptions of violence, whether verbal or physical, must be appropriately limited in programmes broadcast before the watershed or when children are particularly likely to be listening and must also be justified by the context.' (Ofcom 2005: 12) This means that there is not an absolute prohibition on broadcasting the moment of death. Yet British and American news broadcasters have generally balked at holding the shot on the image of any human individual being seen to die through violence. The depiction of deceased bodies has also been a matter of intense self-censorship. The BBC in its training courses shows footage of the filming of an African man being killed by a mob wielding machetes. The purpose of the workshop is to ask editorial decision makers when it would be correct to cut from the sequence.

The distance shots of killing are, however, frequently recycled. It is easier to transmit the collapsing Twin Towers in the nihilistic destruction of an iconic metropolitan skyline when the viewer cannot immediately visualize the snuffing out of over two thousand individual lives.

British mainstream broadcasters eventually agreed to work together in the announcement of Kenneth Bigley's death, but Jon Snow of Channel 4 News said that at the beginning the response to the British hostage-video releases was somewhat ad hoc:

It was governed by the usual constraints; the deal with pornography, the deal with blood, the deal with war. But there was the added issue that this thing was being drip-fed. We were getting these videos and it was clearly part of an exacerbating tactic; wind up the family, build up the pressure; alarm and frighten the population.

(Burke 2005)

The editor of Sky News, Nick Pollard, outlined a framework of deonto-logical and utilitarian considerations in his network's evaluation of how to use the hostage videos featuring Mr Bigley:

There was the right of the public to know what was going on; our duty to tell people; that is what we are here for. After all, there is the journalistic imperative to let people know what is going on; the duty to put things in context. Clearly people addressing a camera while held under threat of their lives are not behaving as they would in the free world. There is also the issue potentially of their families watching; the issue of taste and decency in offending viewers. All these things come into play all of the time.

(Ibid.)

When Mr Bigley's death was followed by the kidnapping of Mrs Margaret Hassan, British news network editors re-evaluated their policy on what they would broadcast. Roger Mosey of the BBC described how:

We asked how new was this material and how much did it inform us about what was going on versus the level of distress of the hostage. In some cases you found that nothing new had emerged by the second or third video and the hostage was even more distressed. So the rationale for broadcasting that became less. Sometimes the hostage was not in a particularly distressed state and we were genuinely learning more. In that case we would show very short extracts. [...] The BBC took a more conservative view [...] I've no doubt there were times when we showed less than our rivals did. I'm really happy with that. I think where they ended up, interestingly was in a very similar place to where we were. So, in fact, the policy on Sky and ITN became more conservative.

(Ibid.)

Mr Sheikh of Al Jazeera justified his network's policy of showing much more explicit footage from the hostage videos. The network showed more of Mrs Hassan's early videos: 'We felt that if we showed the appeal that might help save her life. And it worked out in previous situations. We helped secure and save the life of the Filipino hostage, [Angelo] de la Cruz. Because of the appeal the President then decided to withdraw her troops from Iraq.' (Ibid.)

Mr Sheikh said he did not derive any journalistic excitement when receiving hostage videos because it put him in a dilemma: 'I wish I did not receive them in the first place. [...] Then we agreed to deal with this as follows. And I am talking about the Bin Laden tapes. We said "This is a news story. [...] We are showing news. Real news."' (Ibid.)

Hugh Miles believed that Al Jazeera had no reason to be churlish about the way it provided a global editorial platform for Al Qaeda:

> Let's not kid ourselves. Al Jazeera has a working relationship with Al Qaeda and they are very proud of that relationship. They've been careful to nurture that relationship. But this is not something to be ashamed of. The network is rightfully proud of its ability to get information from a terrorist organisation that everybody wants to know about. Al Jazeera has got no sympathy for Al Qaeda's point of view. And it's no different from when the BBC, for example, has run documentaries on the IRA. No one accuses the BBC of being complicit with the IRA. But they've interviewed killers.
>
> (Ibid.)

Hugh Miles, as the author of a leading text analysing how Arab television news has challenged the world, emphasizes that:

> The information age is upon us and in the decades ahead we can expect only more Al Jazeeras, adding to an ever-greater torrent of information, as regional ideas spread around the world and become global. Things will never be how they were before. 'Freedom is like death,' Yosri Fouda once told me. 'You cannot visit death and then come back from it.' And that is what has happened in the case of Al Jazeera. The door has opened, and now no one can close it.
>
> (Miles 2005: 426)

The ethics of publishing death: media ethics in extremis

Images of life-taking in the history of mainstream electronic media are rare; particularly in the context of terrorist spectacle. The first may have been the assassination of King Alexander I of Yugoslavia in Marseilles in 1934. Newsreel cameras recorded his dying moments in the back of his open-top limousine as a French police horseman applied his sabre to the assassin and the crowd set about beating him to death. The black and white film captures the panic and confusion and was graphically replayed in cinemas throughout the world. Today it can be viewed on YouTube – in one version, underscored with a patriotic folk song immortalizing the heroism and sacrifice of the assassin.

222

NBC filmed the moment General Nguyễn Ngọc Loan shot a hand-cuffed Vietcong prisoner in the head during the Tet offensive in Saigon on 1 February 1968. The graphic depiction of the executed man's terri-fied grimace, the collapse of his body to the ground and the fountain of blood spurting from his ruptured temple has been cited as iconic moving imagery that began to change the American public's views on the Vietnam War. The footage continues to be used in documentaries. In the same year ITN reporter Michael Nicholson was present when his crew filmed a Nigerian army officer executing a young Biafran man, also prostrate and defenceless, having been assured he would come to no harm. ITN broadcast the seconds leading up to his death, but did not broadcast his final cry, as AK 47 bullets were pumped into his body, until 30 years later, when Channel 4 television produced a documentary on the history of ITN's flagship news programme *News At Ten*.

Historical documentaries do not flinch in including the colour footage of the assassination of President John F. Kennedy in Dallas, Texas on 22 November 1963. The killing was missed by the great crowd of profes-sional news media in and around the scene on the day of the killing. The moment of death was recorded by amateurs using non-professional cameras. Abraham Zapruder captured the entire sequence of the killing with his ciné camera. The whole sequence lasted twenty-two seconds, it was in colour and graphically presented the impact of what is believed to have been the third bullet, which effectively blew off the back of the president's head.

None of the US media ran the film footage or published stills from this source in the days, weeks, months and for several years after the shooting. CBS correspondent Dan Rather reported what the film contained shortly after the murder and, controversially, claimed that the president's head 'fell forward with considerable violence'. *Time Life* magazine outbid national news agencies and rival magazines for the rights to the Zapruder film, paying $150,000. The film remained in its vaults until stills from it were published in November 1966 in an article entitled 'A Matter of Reasonable Doubt'.

The film was not actually shown/broadcast in terms of its moving image nature until 1974 and 1975 when, on national television, an optics tech-nician demonstrated through certain frames the theory that Kennedy was the victim of crossfire. (Zelizer 1992: 113–14) Whereas there was a cultural and ethical time delay in the publication of Kennedy's moment of death, no such inhibition was applied to the demise of his alleged assassin, Lee Harvey Oswald.

The moment Jack Ruby fired into his stomach and Oswald doubled up and collapsed in excruciating pain was captured live by radio and television broadcast stations and recordings of the event were recycled across the world's news media. Perhaps because it was the credentialized and professional media that covered the moment, there arose afterwards a considerable discourse on the media ethics surrounding Oswald's murder. To what extent did the professional media carry some degree of complicity or responsibility? Barbie Zelizer stated that the 'Warren Report concluded that partial responsibility for Oswald's death "must be borne by the news media," and it called on journalists to implement a new code of professional ethics.' (Zelizer 1992: 92) The detail of the Warren Commission's findings in this area indicate a media fault factor similar to that cited as contributing to the death of Diana, Princess of Wales in 1997. An extract of the 1963 report is given in Table 2.6.

Table 2.6 The Warren Commission on the killing of Lee Harvey Oswald

---

When Oswald and the escorting detectives entered the basement, the transfer car had not yet been backed into position, nor had the policemen been arranged to block the newsmen's access to Oswald's path. If the transfer car had been carefully positioned between the press and Oswald, Ruby might have been kept several yards from his victim and possibly without a clear view of him. Detective Leavelle, who accompanied Oswald into the basement, testified:

'... I was surprised when I walked to the door and the car was not in the spot it should have been, but I could see it was back, and backing into position, but had it been in position where we were told it would be, that would have eliminated a lot of the area in which anyone would have access to him, because it would have been blocked by the car. In fact, if the car had been sitting where we were told it was going to be, see – it would have been sitting directly upon the spot where Ruby was standing when he fired the shot.'

Captain Jones described the confusion with which Oswald's entry into the basement was in fact received:

'Then the change – going to put two cars up there. There is no reason why that back car can't get all the way back to the jail office. The original plan would be that the line of officers would be from the jail door to the vehicle. Then they say, "Here he comes." ... It is too late to get the people out of the way of the car and form the line. I am aware that Oswald is already coming because of the furore, so, I was trying to keep everybody out of the way and keep the way clear and I heard a shot.'

Therefore, regardless of whether the press should have been allowed to witness the transfer, security measures in the basement for Oswald's protection could and should have been better organized and more thorough. These additional deficiencies were directly related to the decision to admit newsmen to the basement. The Commission concludes that the failure of the police to remove Oswald secretly or to control the crowd in the basement at the time of the transfer were the major causes of the security breakdown which led to Oswald's death.

Source: Warren Commission 1964: 230–1

Zelizer writes that the leader of the American Society of News Editors (ASNE) Herbert Brucker

> held broadcasting equipment responsible for creating the sense of intrusion around Oswald's murder. [...] Brucker's comments suggested a link between the legitimation of news media and the boundaries separating public from private space, boundaries that the journalistic community saw as being altered by television's active presence.
>
> (Zelizer 1992: 92)

In April 2008 a London inquest jury ruled that Diana, Princess of Wales and Dodi Fayed had been unlawfully killed due to the 'gross negligence' of the driver of their car, Henri Paul, and the paparazzi who were following by car and motorcycle. The discourse over media responsibility for the deaths had been raging intensely for the eleven years after the fatal accident in Paris on 31 August 1997, and the jury's decision was the first to legally implicate the photographers who had followed the Mercedes car from the Ritz Hotel. An earlier French investigation had cleared the photographers of any legal responsibility under French law. French Judge Hervé Stephan's decision to clear the photographers of manslaughter charges in 1999 had been upheld by France's supreme court of appeal. The London Coroner, Lord Justice Scott Baker, presided over an inquest in 2007–8 where the photographers had refused to give evidence, and he had had no powers to compel them to appear.

The coroner had explained that the verdict of unlawful killing should be left to the jury on the basis of gross negligence manslaughter by the driving of the following paparazzi:

> The Ritz Hotel submits that it should, while the Metropolitan Police disagree. [...] I consider that the driving of certain paparazzi could be regarded by the jury as criminally negligent. [...] On one view of the evidence, the conduct could be fairly characterized as participating in a race through the centre of Paris at twice the speed limit. Some statements of the paparazzi themselves could lead to this conclusion. In addition, the cross-examination of M Darmon provided some support for a conclusion that, after the crash, the paparazzi continued to seek the best picture without regard to helping the injured. This could be relied upon by the jury as indicative of their state of mind before the crash.
>
> (Scott Baker 2008: paras 4(ii)–31)

The Diana death narrative contains a legend of action implicating the visual media in empowering her global celebrity and at the same time threatening the dignity and privacy of her existence as a human being.

None of the British media has been prepared to publish any photographs taken of Diana in the wreckage of the car, even though she was alive at the time. This was a consensus decision based on ethics. The situation at the time of writing and some twelve years after the event remains the same. The issue of political and cultural distancing may be a factor in respecting the notion that photographs of her distress and injury in the hours leading to her death should remain self-censored, since it is the case that a few images have been published in Italy and the United States. Other factors being brought into play undoubtedly include the issue of consent on the part of Diana's family. Her brother, Earl Spencer, had angrily declared that the world's media had blood on their hands. Her sons, the Princes William and Harry, repeatedly condemn any attempt at or question of media organizations considering the publication of their mother's photographs in these circumstances.

This contrasts with the decision by Queen Alexandra to give permission for the photographing of her husband, King Edward VII on his deathbed and the publication of the controversial picture on the front page of the *Daily Mirror* in the issue of 16 May 1910. It was both scoop and scandal, but the obvious difference was that publication had been by the consent of the Royal widow of an image of the dead king at rest. The concealed images of Diana are of a fatally wounded princess in the aftermath of a violent and catastrophic event; their dissemination is not by consent.

From time to time a debate continues in the USA over the ethics of potential media representation of the process of capital execution, continued by the federal government and 37 states and not considered unconstitutional if provided for through 'guided discretion' as set out in rulings by the Supreme Court in 1976. The European Convention on Human Rights ensures that in peacetime capital punishment is unlawful in all signatory countries. The last camera to capture death in an American execution chamber was surreptitious, following the sensationally covered trial of Ruth Snyder (dubbed the 'Bloody Blonde') and her lover, Judd Gray (christened by the popular press 'Lover Boy'), who had murdered Snyder's husband to collect money on his life assurance policies. A photographer from the *New York Daily News*, Thomas Howard, used a hidden camera strapped to his ankle at Sing Sing Prison to capture the rather blurred moment when Ruth Snyder was electrocuted. The image has become notoriously iconic, particularly as it was published on the paper's front page with the single-word headline 'Dead'.

In 1994 a death row inmate wanted his execution in the North Carolina gas chamber videotaped by talk-show host Phil Donahue. The prison's warden objected, and the Supreme Court upheld lower court rulings that such media presence would disrupt the proper operation of the prison. (Lawson v Dixon SC US 1994) Independent radio producer David Isay used the sounds of the death chamber in Georgia for a radio programme distributed on public radio stations. Deborah Potter, in an article titled 'Witnessing the Final Act', reported that an academic thought the programme was pornographic and catered to the lowest appetite. Potter ruminated on the fact that in 2001 the Justice Department had provided a camera relay of the execution of Oklahoma terrorist Timothy McVeigh to an audience of survivors and relatives of those killed. Potter suggested:

> The next time, you can almost predict that it's going to be broadcast. [...] Lots of people might want to watch a televised execution. It could draw big numbers. But that's not a sufficient reason for a station or network news division to put it on the air.
>
> (Potter 2001)

The authoritarian regime in Saudi Arabia did not hesitate in broadcasting live on Saudi television the public beheadings of sixty-three rebel followers of the religious extremist Juhaiman ibn Muhammad al-Otaibi. This followed the provocative seizing of the Great Mosque in Mecca in November 1979. As it is the holiest site in the world for Muslims, they could not have attacked a greater symbol of the Saudi Kingdom's authority and religious integrity. Trevor Mostyn states that the decision to ensure graphic media coverage of the executions was a political one, in the sense that the spectacle of state *lex talionis* served the principle of *pour encourager les autres*. (Mostyn 2001: 2148)

However, the cultural taboo in the West concerning mainstream televising of the moment of death in news and current affairs cannot be held as an absolutist position, and the development of new and alternative media in the Information Age challenges the efficacy of broadcast regulation in this area. In June 2009, 26-year-old philosophy student Neda Salehi Agha Soltan was shot through the heart while taking part in demonstrations against the conduct of the presidential election in Iran. Her killing, allegedly by the hand of a pro-government militia known as the Basij, was captured by so-called 'citizen journalism'. Another protester used a mobile phone to show her falling backwards, a pool of blood collecting on the tarmac, her eyes rolling sideways. As she loses consciousness, men are heard to cry 'Don't be afraid, Neda dear, don't be afraid, Neda stay with me, stay with me', until blood starts gushing from her nose and mouth and it is clear that she has died. The sequence has been distributed and signposted by YouTube and Twitter communications throughout the world, and this has been linked to by newspaper multimedia websites that are not regulated by state broadcasting bodies such as Ofcom in the UK. In Britain, what Joe Joseph in *The Times* described as the 'single event that puts a human face on history [...] the moment when Iran's repression emerged from the forest of newsprint and became personal.' (Joseph *The Times* 2009) has been self-censored by mainstream broadcasting media on the grounds of taste and decency. The moment of Neda Soltan's death has been consumed globally by millions of viewers of all ages and backgrounds through the redundancy, obsolescence and anachronism of old media's framework and rules of newsgathering and censorship, and the outmanoeuvring realities of new media's multidimensional asymmetry. The professional media had no role at all in the recording and distribution of what had happened to Neda. The Iranian state has been powerless to prevent her death becoming a symbol of martyrdom. The professionalized global media infrastructure and Iranian regime became impotent and irrelevant bystanders.

The significance of Neda Soltan's death is that mainstream media platforms no longer hold the privilege of monopolizing the presentation of news. And, as Professor Jean Seaton observes, the representation of violence in news should be 'about recording our perception of the world, not fitting news events into a matrix of the familiar. Above all it should be a stimulus to new thinking, not an anaesthetizing escape from it.' (Seaton 2005: 296)

Privacy law in media representations of violence

It is apparent that the media ethical debate surrounding issues of human feelings and dignity, and the dispute over the boundaries of private and public space concerning individuals caught up in violent and catastrophic news events, have given rise to media law making. The moral panic and public anger surrounding the paparazzi harassment of Diana during her lifetime, linked with their pursuit of the Mercedes car driven by her drunk chauffeur at high speed into the pillar of a Paris underpass, changed the balancing exercise between Article 8 (privacy) and Article 10 (freedom of expression) of the European Convention on Human Rights. Previously, it was argued that freedom of expression was applied by the Strasbourg court as more of a trump card.

The importance of the *Sunday Times* newspaper's victory in 1979 at the ECHR in the notorious thalidomide case was underlined by human rights lawyers Geoffrey Robertson and Andrew Nicol in the first edition of their influential textbook *Media Law: The Rights of Journalists and Broadcasters*:

> The Court has adopted a general approach to the interpretation of Article 10 which is favourable to the media. It has said that Article 10 should not be seen as requiring a 'balance' between, on the one hand, the value of freedom of expression and, on the other, the value of national security, crime prevention and the other exceptions in Article 10(2). These are not competing principles of equal weight: the

values listed in Article 10(2) are simply 'a number of exceptions which must be strictly interpreted'.

(Robertson and Nicol 1984: 5)

It was a fact then and is now that Article 10(2), which qualifies the positive and standing right of freedom of expression, did not include the notion of privacy as a qualifier. The clamour for greater public-figure privacy in the aftermath of Diana's death was overwhelming. Article 8 on Privacy could always be applied as an equal standing right. The influence on decisions of the transnational European Court of Human Rights and how they have been taken into account by the higher British courts is the subject of more detailed analysis in Chapter 5.

There was no reporting in the British mainstream media of Resolution 1165 of the Council of Europe, which was adopted by the Assembly on 26 June 1998. It is included here in Table 2.7, as it is apparent in any close reading that many of the articles in the resolution have underpinned and driven case law and statute reform to increase the regulation and policing of media publication and, in Britain, to gestate a judge-made media privacy law. There is more than a sub-textual ideology in the resolution's language, giving it the appearance of a manifesto for legal control and regulatory enforcement against media institutions. Is it not the case that the media are being cast in the role of criminogenic offenders assaulting the human rights of their audience as victims? Or can it be argued that the assembly for the Council of Europe is simply seeking to attenuate abuse of power by media institutions, whose pressing social need and necessity in a democratic society continues to be sustained by Article 10 – freedom of expression.

There may be some justification in questioning the democratic credibility of the assembly for the Council of Europe. Representation is not, nor was it in 1998, by direct election. Country representatives were appointed from the parliaments of the signatories to the European Convention on Human Rights. A search of mainstream media texts for 1998 does not provide any evidence that there was any recorded and significant media scrutiny or interest in the debates and resolutions of the assembly. On 21 June 1998 the Hungarian News Agency MTI reported that a delegation of the new Parliament in Budapest had left for Strasbourg to attend the assembly's session, which would be discussing the right to privacy, among many other topics. The media correspondent for the *Irish Times* reported from a committee hearing on justice, equality and law reform in the Dail in October 1998 that a witness had referred to a web of privacy law, most of which worked, but the Council of Europe 'had said this summer that where there was a problem laws should be strengthened and introduced "as a matter of priority."' (Foley 1998: 6) In November 1998, Frances Gibb, the legal editor of *The Times*, reported on the reconstruction and

Table 2.7 Resolution 1165 (1998) of the Council of Europe

Resolution 1165 (1998)[1] Right to privacy

1   The Assembly recalls the current affairs debate it held on the right to privacy during its September 1997 session, a few weeks after the accident which cost the Princess of Wales her life.

2   On that occasion, some people called for the protection of privacy, and in particular that of public figures, to be reinforced at the European level by means of a convention, while others believed that privacy was sufficiently protected by national legislation and the European Convention on Human Rights, and that freedom of expression should not be jeopardised.

3   In order to explore the matter further, the Committee on Legal Affairs and Human Rights organised a hearing in Paris on 16 December 1997 with the participation of public figures or their representatives and the media.

4   The right to privacy, guaranteed by Article 8 of the European Convention on Human Rights, has already been defined by the Assembly in the declaration on mass communication media and human rights, contained within Resolution 428 (1970), as 'the right to live one's own life with a minimum of interference'.

5   In view of the new communication technologies which make it possible to store and use personal data, the right to control one's own data should be added to this definition.

6   The Assembly is aware that personal privacy is often invaded, even in countries with specific legislation to protect it, as people's private lives have become a highly lucrative commodity for certain sectors of the media. The victims are essentially public figures, since details of their private lives serve as a stimulus to sales. At the same time, public figures must recognise that the position they occupy in society – in many cases by choice – automatically entails increased pressure on their privacy.

7   Public figures are persons holding public office and/or using public resources and, more broadly speaking, all those who play a role in public life, whether in politics, the economy, the arts, the social sphere, sport or in any other domain.

8   It is often in the name of a one-sided interpretation of the right to freedom of expression, which is guaranteed in Article 10 of the European Convention on Human Rights, that the media invade people's privacy, claiming that their readers are entitled to know everything about public figures.

9   Certain facts relating to the private lives of public figures, particularly politicians, may indeed be of interest to citizens, and it may therefore be legitimate for readers, who are also voters, to be informed of those facts.

10 It is therefore necessary to find a way of balancing the exercise of two fundamental rights, both of which are guaranteed in the European Convention on Human Rights: the right to respect for one's private life and the right to freedom of expression.

11 The Assembly reaffirms the importance of every person's right to privacy, and of the right to freedom of expression, as fundamental to a democratic society. These rights are neither absolute nor in any hierarchical order, since they are of equal value.

12 However, the Assembly points out that the right to privacy afforded by Article 8 of the European Convention on Human Rights should not only protect an individual against interference by public authorities, but also against interference by private persons or institutions, including the mass media.

13 The Assembly believes that, since all member states have now ratified the European Convention on Human Rights, and since many systems of national legislation comprise provisions guaranteeing this protection, there is no need to propose that a new convention guaranteeing the right to privacy should be adopted.

14 The Assembly calls upon the governments of the member states to pass legislation, if no such legislation yet exists, guaranteeing the right to privacy containing the following guidelines, or if such legislation already exists, to supplement it with these guidelines: i. the possibility of taking an action under civil law should be guaranteed, to enable a victim to claim possible damages for invasion of privacy;
ii   editors and journalists should be rendered liable for invasions of privacy by their publications, as they are for libel;
iii   when editors have published information that proves to be false, they should be required to publish equally prominent corrections at the request of those concerned;
iv   economic penalties should be envisaged for publishing groups which systematically invade people's privacy;
v   following or chasing persons to photograph, film or record them, in such a manner that they are prevented from enjoying the normal peace and quiet they expect in their private lives or even such that they are caused actual physical harm, should be prohibited;
vi   a civil action (private lawsuit) by the victim should be allowed against a photographer or a person directly involved, where paparazzi have trespassed or used 'visual or auditory enhancement devices' to capture recordings that they otherwise could not have captured without trespassing;
vii   provision should be made for anyone who knows that information or images relating to his or her private life are about to be disseminated to initiate emergency judicial proceedings, such as summary applications for an interim order or an injunction postponing the dissemination of the information, subject to an assessment by the court as to the merits of the claim of an invasion of privacy;
viii the media should be encouraged to create their own guidelines for publication and to set up an institute with which an individual can lodge complaints of invasion of privacy and demand that a rectification be published.

15 It invites those governments which have not yet done so to ratify without delay the Council of Europe Convention for the Protection of Individuals with regard to Automatic Processing of Personal Data.

Continued overleaf

16 The Assembly also calls upon the governments of the member states to:
  i   encourage the professional bodies that represent journalists to draw
       up certain criteria for entry to the profession, as well as standards for
       self-regulation and a code of journalistic conduct;
  ii   promote the inclusion in journalism training programmes of a course
       in law, highlighting the importance of the right to privacy vis-à-vis
       society as a whole;
  iii foster the development of media education on a wider scale, as part of
       education about human rights and responsibilities, in order to raise
       media users' awareness of what the right to privacy necessarily entails;
  iv   facilitate access to the courts and simplify the legal procedures
       relating to press offences, in order to ensure that victims' rights are
       better protected.

[1] Assembly debate on 26 June 1998 (24th Sitting). See Doc. 8130, report
of the Committee on Legal Affairs and Human Rights (rapporteur:
Mr Schwimmer), Doc. 8147, opinion of the Committee on Culture
and Education (rapporteur: Mr Staes) and Doc. 8146, opinion of
the Social, Health and Family Affairs Committee (rapporteur: Mr
Mitterrand).

Text adopted by the Assembly on 26 June 1998 (24th Sitting).

Source: http://assembly.coe.int/main.asp?link=/Documents/AdoptedText.ta98/
ERES1165.htm. Also Christie and Tugendhat 2002: 619–20.

reform of the European Court of Human Rights, which would now have
'jurisdiction over 800 million people from Greenland to Russia. The court
will have 40 judges, one from each member state of the Council of Europe,
and it is likely to receive about 5,000 cases a year.' (Gibb *The Times* 1998)
Resolution 1165 was not mentioned in the article.

A resolution that has had an important bearing and influence on the
media jurisprudence of the United Kingdom and other countries would
appear to have been debated and passed without any public notice in
Britain. The resolution was passed by a body that, in the words of Britain's
second most senior judge in 2009, 'lacks constitutional legitimacy'. In his
annual lecture to the Judicial Studies Board of England and Wales, Lord
Hoffmann stated that the ECHR:

  now has 47 judges, one for each member state of the Council of
  Europe. One country, one judge; so that Liechtenstein, San Marino,
  Monaco and Andorra, which have a combined population slightly
  less than that of the London Borough of Islington, have four judges
  and Russia, with a population of 140 million, has one judge. The
  judges are elected by a sub-Committee of the Council of Europe's
  Parliamentary Assembly, which consists of 18 members chaired by
  a Latvian politician, on which the UK representatives are a Labour

politician with a trade union background and no legal qualifications and a Conservative politician who was called to the Bar in 1972 but so far as I know has never practised. They choose from lists of 3 drawn by the governments of the 47 members in a manner which is totally opaque.

It is therefore hardly surprising that to the people of the United Kingdom, this judicial body does not enjoy the constitutional legitimacy which the people of the United States accord to their Supreme Court.

(Hoffmann 2009: paras 38–9)

It might be argued that when Parliament decided to legislate for the 1998 Human Rights Act politicians and jurists had not anticipated the degree to which convention rights and ECHR jurisprudence would amend and morph the interpretation of the original text and intentions of the drafters. Article 8.2 was drafted with the words 'There shall be no interference by a public authority with the exercise of this right' but case law made the judiciary the mechanism by which the right to respect for privacy could be enforced against media publishers. Article 10 was drafted so that the right to reputation stated in 10(2) gave free speech presumptive authority over defamation. Yet at least four Strasbourg rulings have generated ambiguity about whether the right to reputation should be recognised as an aspect of the equal standing right to privacy. Fenwick and Phillipson note that two of these cases from France involved high value speech and the 'convictions for defamation were found justified, despite the fact that the speech was of the highest public interest'. (Fenwick & Phillipson 2006: 1069)

It would be reasonable to raise questions about the potential impact of the ratification of the 2007 EU Treaty of Lisbon. The UK legal system is bound by the decisions of the European Court of Justice in Luxembourg. A UK opt out means the Charter of Fundamental Rights will not be justiciable in the British courts. But if the UK decides to opt in some time in the future the charter may become a source of rival rights jurisprudence as it includes the declaration under Article 1 that 'Human dignity is inviolable,' and 'it must be respected and protected.' Article 3 states that 'Everyone has the right to respect for his or her physical and mental integrity.' Furthermore, the Charter's approach to freedom of expression under Article 11.2 goes further than the convention and Human Rights Act by asserting a separate and specific right for the freedom and pluralism of the media to be respected. The Charter states that where its rights correspond with the European Convention nothing will prevent the Court of Justice providing more extensive protection.

3

DEFAMATION LAW

The social and cultural need for defamation law

William Shakespeare reminds us continually in his plays about the paradox of defending honour and reputation. In *King Henry IV Part I* the famous English playwright creates a speech for Falstaff that many an attorney could make to dissuade a rattled plaintiff from suing for libel:

> Well, 'tis no matter; honour pricks me on. Yea, but how if honour pricks me off when I come on? How then? Can honour set to a leg? No: or an arm? no: or take away the grief of a wound? no. Honour hath no skill in surgery then? no. What is honour? Air. A trim reckoning! Who hath it? He that died o' Wednesday. Doth he fell it? no. Doth he hear it? No. 'Tis insensible, then? Yea, to the dead. But will it not live with the living? no. Why? Detraction will not suffer it. Therefore I'll none of it. Honour is a mere scutcheon: and so ends my catechism.
>
> (Falstaff, *Henry IV Part 1*: V, i)

Defamation law in the USA and UK has the same roots in common law. It is played out in the adversarial tradition of juridical combat. And if Shakespeare can be included in the common law of England, the protection of reputation is the struggle to protect something more precious than any jewels and riches upon the earth, and is powerfully expressed in the words of Thomas Mowbray, the Duke of Norfolk in *King Richard II*:

> My dear dear lord,
> The purest treasure mortal times afford
> Is spotless reputation: that away,
> Men are but gilded loam or painted clay.
> A jewel in a ten-times-barr'd-up chest
> Is a bold spirit in a loyal breast.
> Mine honour is my life; both grown in one;

Take honour from me, and my life is done:
Then, dear my liege, mine honour let me try;
In that I live and for that will I die.

(Mowbray, *King Richard II*: 1, i)

The cry of the inconsolable libel plaintiff through the ages can be no more heartfelt than that of Cassio in *Othello*: 'Reputation, reputation, reputation! O, I have lost my reputation! I have lost the immortal part of myself, and what remains is bestial.' (Cassio, *Othello*: II, iii) But before the inchoate litigant, tired and emotional, rushes to the law courts it would be a wise plaintiff who remembers that the advice given to Othello on the subject of the value of a good name was offered by Iago, hardly a paragon of virtue, honesty and honourable motives:

Good name in man and woman, dear my lord,
Is the immediate jewel of their souls:
Who steals my purse steals trash; 'tis something, nothing;
'Twas mine, 'tis his, and has been slave to thousands;
But he that filches from me my good name
Robs me of that which not enriches him
And makes me poor indeed.

(Iago, *Othello*: III, iii)

Tables 3.1 and 3.2 set out the varying advantages of defamation law for British and American media communicators and Tables 3.3 and 3.4 set out the varying disadvantages. Table 3.5 endeavours to select, for argument's sake, case histories justifying the abolition of defamation law and those demonstrating that libel can be a righteous remedy.

Constitutional authorities: USA and UK

The leading authorities in libel law arose out of case histories rooted in political controversy and social conflict. The leading American case is *New York Times v Sullivan* and sets constitutional principles because the Supreme Court decided that there was a need to establish a First Amendment defence for a freer speech standard buttressing and protecting democratic discourse for all US citizens in all the states and territories of the USA. The highest court in the UK is unable to assert constitutional standards on free speech law because Great Britain has neither a federal legal system nor a written constitution, and its line of *stare decisis* is muddied by interference and influences from the European Court of Human Rights in Strasbourg and Court of Justice of the European Communities in Luxembourg. But the jurisprudential rhetoric on free speech in UK House of Lords rulings in *Reynolds v Times* 1999 and *Turkington v Times*

Plate 5 The façade of the Central Criminal Court in London, bearing the inscription 'Defend the children of the poor and punish the wrongdoer'. In the case of the unfortunate American Dr Hawley Crippen in 1910, it is argued that an innocent man was framed, tried by media and wrongly hanged after a trial riddled with police and lawyer corruption, flawed forensic evidence, concealment of evidence and dishonest cheque-book journalism.

Plate 6 The Royal Courts of Justice in the Strand, whose number 13 court is famed for hosting libel trials involving international plaintiffs/ claimants suing US media groups and publishers for small-circulation distribution in Britain.

Table 3.1 Advantages of defamation law for US journalists

1   The First Amendment provides a constitutional guarantee of freedom of the press and blocks abuse of power by federal executive and legislature. Public official/public interest plaintiffs have to prove through direct or circumstantial evidence that media defendants published with knowledge of falsity or with serious doubts about accuracy.
2   The burden of proof in justification is on the plaintiff. The US public figure plaintiff always has to provide evidence of an injured reputation. The private figure plaintiff must offer solid evidence of the injury to reputation, both tangible and intangible, when publication is a matter of public concern.
3   There is a more positive culture for freedom of expression and the rights of a free press in the USA.
4   As it is a more heterogeneous country, with state-based media rather than federal-orientated homogeneous media, libel cases are contextualized locally rather than nationally.
5   There is a high threshold of evidence to undermine the no-fault First Amendment defence, i.e. actuated by malice and showing a reckless disregard for the truth.

Since *Sullivan v New York Times* 1964 the following Supreme Court judgments could be considered advantageous:

a   1967 *Curtis Publishing Co v Butts*. University of Georgia athletic director Wally Butts had successfully sued the *Saturday Evening Post* over an allegation that he was guilty of conspiring to fix a football game. *Walker v Associated Press*. General Edwin Walker had won a libel ruling for an agency report which had erroneously accused him of participating in racial disturbances at the University of Mississippi. The Sullivan rule was extended to include 'public figures' as well as 'public officials'. Butts won at the Supreme Court because the *Evening Post* had had more time to check its information and had been proved to show a reckless disregard for the truth. In *Walker* the Justices found that the incident was news which required immediate dissemination and Associated Press had received the information from a previously regarded trustworthy and competent correspondent present at the scene of events.
b   1971 *Rosenbloom v Metromedia* expanded the actual-malice test. George Rosenbloom, a distributor of pornography in Philadelphia, had been arrested and charged with an obscenity violation. A local radio station owned by Metromedia called him a 'smut peddler'. He was later acquitted and sued the station and obtained $750,000 judgment. By a vote 5–3 the Supreme Court said the actual-malice standard should be extended to matters of public or general interest, even if they involve neither a public official nor a public figure.
c   1988 *Hustler Magazine v Falwell*. The Rev. Jerry Falwell tried to recover damages from *Hustler* and its publisher Larry Flynt for 'intentional infliction of emotional injury'. Falwell said he suffered emotional trauma after reading a vicious cartoon parody about himself in the sex magazine and the cartoon implied that he had had sex with his

Continued overleaf

mother in an outhouse. *Hustler* defended the case on the basis that he was clearly a public figure, and rather than have to prove actual malice and loss of reputation it was clear that the parody was so ridiculous and extreme that no sane person could have believed it. Chief Justice Rehnquist wrote that 'in public debate our own citizens must tolerate insulting, and even outrageous speech in order to provide adequate breathing space to the freedoms protected by the First Amendment'. The case bridged libel and privacy issues.

6 US journalists have a wider ambit of general defences compared to their UK colleagues. In addition to fair comment (publishing an opinion on a matter of public concern, based on true facts, and representing the sincere evaluation of the speaker), fair report, or public record privilege, the concept of neutral reportage of libellous allegations about public figures without the requirement of an official or public setting is well established. A number of states have recognized a 'wire service' defence when a media organization republishes material from a reputable news service without substantial change and without suspecting the content to be false. A large number of US states have also enacted 'retraction statutes' providing media defendants the opportunity to resolve libel lawsuits outside court. Published retractions discourage libel litigation and reduce the costs in fees and damages.

Table 3.2 Advantages of defamation law for UK journalists

1   Responsible journalism is now protected through effective defences, i.e. innocent dissemination for broadcasters and Internet Service Providers and the 1999 Reynolds 'for public benefit criteria' from Lord Nicholls. The 'Reynolds defence' was updated and liberalized in 2006 by the House of Lords in *Jameel v Wall Street Journal*. The Law Lords said it was no longer a form of qualified privilege but a standing 'public interest' defence. This was seen as moving towards the US *Sullivan v New York Times* defence. Judges were advised not to second-guess deadline decision making by editors and not to regard Lord Nicholls' ten criteria for 'responsible journalism' as hurdles that had to be overcome.

2   Absolute and qualified privilege provides useful shields for defamatory allegations in order to serve the dissemination of allegations which are in the public interest. This can be achieved at the Westminster Parliament, in local authority meetings and in the parliaments/assemblies in Wales, Scotland and Northern Ireland.

3   Culturally the UK is a less litigious society and people are more reluctant to take action because of cost, stress and the risk of enabling the repetition of the libel. However, the no win, no fee opportunity with contingency/ conditional fees goes some way to democratizing access to defamatory litigation for non-wealthy people.

4   The high awards in damages and the greater risks of being sued lead to more ethical journalism. The Reynolds/Jameel standard encourages responsible and fair journalism in the public interest and provides a reasonable defence to journalists who make honest mistakes.

5   The risks and consequences of losing libel actions for English claimants
     are a deterrent against unfair libel litigation, e.g. Jeffrey Archer, Jonathan
     Aitken cases.
6   Winners who are awarded damages less than the amount of money paid
     into court are penalized by having to pay both sides' costs. This encourages
     the settlement of libel actions. Examples of plaintiffs/claimants who have
     lost out in this way:

a   The actor William Roache, who played the character Ken Barlow in
     the British television soap opera *Coronation Street*, sued the *Sun* for
     implying that he was such a boring personality when working as a
     professional actor and that people found it difficult working with
     him. The jury found that the article was defamatory but the award
     in damages of £50,000 was equal to an amount the *Sun* had paid into
     court. Consequently Mr Roache was liable for a large amount of the
     defendant's costs even though he had won the case.
b   Dr Wladislaw Dering, who was an inmate at the Nazi-run Auschwitz
     concentration camp situated near Krakow in Poland, sued Leon Uris
     and his publisher over the novel *Exodus* which alleged that Dering had
     performed experimental sterilization operations without anaesthetic
     on other inmates. Although the jury found for him, they awarded
     damages that amounted to no more than the lowest coin in the realm
     (Carter-Ruck and Starte 1997: 595).

Table 3.3 Disadvantages of defamation law for US journalists

1   The different state and federal legal systems mean that it can take a long
     time for First Amendment protection to kick in and the *Sullivan v New York
     Times* public official/interest defence does not apply to all libel actions.
2   The states have developed a separate 'false light' tort which is a low-grade
     form of defamation and liability for inaccuracy.
3   US First Amendment protection in *Sullivan v New York Times* has been
     narrowed through cases in the 1960s and 1970s. This means that when it is
     decided that a plaintiff is not a public official or involved in a public interest
     issue, England and Wales-style common law defamation defences apply.
     However, in the USA the private plaintiff still has to prove justification on
     the balance of probabilities and also has to prove economic damage when
     the article complained about is a matter of public concern.
4   Well-established 'no win and no fee actions' can harass and pursue
     journalists. Also, large corporations can use huge financial resources in
     litigation to exhaust and pummel media organizations.
5   The power of private capital and corporations has generated the
     phenomenon of SLAPPs – 'Strategic Lawsuits Against Public Participation'.
     This is using financial power to fund any and every kind of legal action
     against a target to effectively disable its public/private and social operation.
     It could be viewed as a form of 'legal terrorism'.

George W. Pring and Penelope Canan wrote in *SLAPPS: Getting Sued for
Speaking Out*: 'there was virtually no recognition – by the legal profession,
courts, academia, government or the public – of their similarity or linkages.

Continued overleaf

The tendency was (and often still is) to view them as unrelated and to apply conventional legal labels: a "libel" case, a "business interference" case, and a "conspiracy" case. Looking deeper, we found what they have had in common: every case was triggered by defendants' attempts to influence government action' (Pring and Canan 1996: 8–9).

Professor Lawrence Soley wrote in *Censorship Inc*, 'Today the term is used much more broadly by attorneys, activists, courts and legislators to describe civil suits lacking merit, but which are nevertheless filed against speakers and the press for criticizing corporations, executives and even public officials' (Soley 2002: 88).

6   The First Amendment does not extend to the regulation and licensing of broadcasting and other electronic media – primarily radio and television. This means the FCC can regulate unfair/inaccurate broadcasts that may overlap with defamation issues.

7   The First Amendment can be undermined by prejudicial social and political consensus that determines US Supreme Court decisions. Surveys indicate that the status of journalists and journalism in the USA is declining.

After *Sullivan v New York Times* 1964, the following cases could be said to have narrowed and limited the First Amendment defence to libel:

a   1974 *Gertz v Welch*. Elmer Gertz, a well-known Chicago law professor and civil rights lawyer, was wrongly accused of being a Communist and Marxist and of being involved in a national plot to discredit local police forces in order to establish a national police force that would trample the rights of right-thinking people. Gertz sued the news magazine *American Opinion* and won £50,000. The Supreme Court overruled the award and ordered a retrial and established the principle that the actual malice standard had to be reduced in cases where people had not thrust themselves into a public controversy. Gertz had simply accepted a private client even if the cases were controversial – he had been representing the family of a 17-year-old boy shot by a Chicago police officer. In the retrial he won much higher damages.

b   1976 *Mary Alice Firestone v Time Magazine*. The Supreme Court ruled that Firestone was in the public spotlight because of a divorce action. She had done nothing to thrust herself into a public controversy. She was not a public figure. Therefore the allegation that she had committed adultery was defamatory and did not have First Amendment protection.

c   1985 *Dun & Bradstreet v Greenmoss Builders*. It was established that employment references and private communications were not protected by the First Amendment.

8   US journalists and authors can be caught by the libel tourism permitted in the UK, whereby claimants can sue under English and Welsh libel laws if the publication can be obtained in however small quantities within the British jurisdiction. As a result, in 2005 Roman Polanski successfully sued *Vanity Fair* for issues sold in Britain and he was permitted to give evidence via video-link from Paris. In 2000, the House of Lords gave the Russian émigré Boris Berezovsky permission to sue *Forbes* magazine after the US magazine had wrongly characterized him as a brutal thug and crook. The House of Lords ruled 3–2 that *Forbes* was widely available on the Internet

and Mr Berezovsky had sufficient business interests in Britain to have been damaged. American researcher Dr Rachel Ehrenfeld was successfully sued in London by a Saudi businessman and his two sons over a book which was not published in the UK, although twenty-three copies were sold into the country via the Internet, and one chapter was available on the web. This prompted the state of New York to pass legislation to protect writers and publishers working there from the enforcement of defamation judgments in other courts, unless the New York courts were satisfied that the foreign courts accorded the same protection for freedom of speech as New York and US federal law.

9   The *Sullivan v New York Times* Supreme Court case of 1964 does not provide a carte blanche for US journalists in respect of libel. US defamation retains many of the characteristics of English and Welsh libel law. The US plaintiff has to prove that the message tended to injure reputation, that it was false, published to a third party, identified the plaintiff and, in the case of public interest/officials, that there was actual malice and negligence on the part of the media publisher. US publishers have UK-style defences, e.g. relaying accurately the contents of public proceedings and documents, neutral reporting of newsworthy allegations made about public officials or public figures.

Table 3.4 Disadvantages of defamation law for UK journalists

1   Burden of proof for journalism in justification is on the defendant (balance of probabilities higher when defamation alleges criminal conduct).

2   Defending libel actions is very expensive and inevitably the rich and powerful will be more litigious to protect attacks on reputation. Legal costs vastly outstrip eventual awards of damages and conditional fee agreements involving up to 100 per cent uplift in costs are charged if the case is won, leaving the media defendant sometimes with hundreds of thousands of pounds, even millions, to pay in total legal costs.

3   General social prejudice against the media means that the odds for journalists are not good in front of juries. There has been a history of high awards against the media though judges now have the power to advise juries on the level of damages.

4   Casino-style awards of damages increase the risks of fighting libel actions and increase the pressure on media defendants to settle, even where they believe they had a reasonable chance of winning.

5   Most decisions to defend libel actions are taken by insurance companies, which means that most writs are settled in the claimant's favour.

6   The introduction of contingency arrangements and conditional fee agreements (CFAs), limited forms of no win, no fee, means that more people can sue for libel. It has been reported that 75 per cent of cases taken on by London libel law firms are now in this category.

Table 3.5 Debating the justice and injustice of the libel system for claimants and defendants

Cases justifying abolition of libel	*Cases justifying retaining libel*
Consider the spectre of the bisexual Liberace winning damages against a British newspaper columnist whose language might have implied effeminacy. The *Daily Mirror* columnist Cassandra had constructed a purple prose that was not defended on the basis of justification. The paper's lawyers lost the battle over ordinary meaning before a jury in 1959. Liberace collected a fortune in tax-free damages (£8,000) for the perpetuation on his part of a lie, the truth of which emerged when he died from AIDS contracted as a result of homosexual relations. David Hooper observed, 'As he later faced a palimony action from a male live-in lover, the verdict that he had been unjustly accused of being homosexual was evidently wrong' (Hooper 2000:11).	It is instructive to concentrate on the importance of libel law for writers and artists persecuted by the Un-American Activities Committee and the witch-hunt that was continued by Senator Joseph McCarthy. In Joseph Julian's case a biased judge unjustifiably stopped his libel action and prevented a jury bringing back a verdict in his favour in 1954.
A libel action by Lord Boothby in 1964 led to the resignation of the editor of the *Sunday Mirror*, Reginald Payne. The allegation that Boothby had a liaison with the homosexual figure of organized crime, Ronald Kray, was later established as fact. Boothby enjoyed the benefit of a £40,000 libel settlement for a publication that was actually true in substance and fact, but could not be proved. It also meant that the Krays were virtually untouchable for several years from the point of view of legal forensic trial and police enquiry. In those years brutal murder and extortion visited the people of London. Boothby basked in the hypocrisy of being the innocent victim of gutter journalism. The libel settlement had been part of an elaborate cover-up by Britain's political establishment. The libel settlement included an apology from Mirror Group Newspapers to Ronald Kray and a confidentiality clause	In the case of John Henry Faulk, he pursued a libel action against AWARE, one of the sinister blacklisting organizations, that lasted 6 years. By 1963 the paranoia of the Cold War was beginning to melt into the counter-culture liberality of 'the swinging sixties'. A jury awarded him 3.5 million dollars. Although the bankruptcy of the defendants meant he never received compensation, the verdict broke people's fear of the blacklisters and their grip on American life. In 2002, the case of two nursery nurses from the north-east of England provided a poignant justification for libel protection. Despite their unequivocal acquittal in the criminal courts, a published local authority report continued to accuse them of child abuse. They faced ostracism, ignominy and threat of violent vigilante attacks, as their accusers used the privilege of a local authority enquiry report to give credibility to discredited allegations. Defamation law was the only way the two could be rehabilitated and their names cleared. Mr Justice Eady ruled that Newcastle City Council had lost its qualified privilege because the report's authors included 'a number of fundamental claims which they must have known to be untrue and which cannot be explained on the basis of

prohibiting the Mirror papers from referring to or discussing the case in any way. £40,000 was the equivalent of half a million pounds in today's money. This could not have been a more discouraging message to Fleet Street about the merits of investigating organized crime and its links to well-known politicians.

The libel action brought by Jeffrey Archer against the *Daily Star* in 1987 led to the resignation of the newspaper's editor, Lloyd Turner. His widow wrote later in the UK's *Press Gazette* magazine that she believed the injustice of the verdict broke his heart and contributed to his premature death.

Archer's later perjury prosecution proved he arranged a fake alibi for his case. He had to repay the half a million pounds in damages and additional legal costs with interest. Archer's perjury related to a witness statement that purported to provide an alibi for him on an evening when he was alleged to have liaised with prostitute Monica Coghlan. The sworn statement was not in fact used in evidence, as the date for the allegation changed. Archer and his wife, Mary, continued to deny the charge that he had paid Ms Coghlan for sex, or had ever met her. The trial judge, Mr Justice Caulfield, said of Mrs Mary Archer: 'Remember Mrs Archer in the witness box. Your vision of her will probably never disappear. Has she elegance? Has she fragrance? Would she have, without the strain of this trial radiance? What is she like in physical features, in presentation, in appearance, how would she appeal? Has she had a happy married life? Has she been able to enjoy rather than endure her husband Jeffrey? Is she right when she says to you, you may think with delicacy – Jeffrey and I lead

incompetence or mere carelessness'. Each claimant was awarded £200,000 in damages. Their solicitor said after the case: 'This is an appalling story … It is hoped that lessons will be learnt from this appalling tragedy, by councils, social workers and all others involved in the protection of children.' (Lillie & Anor v Newcastle City Council HC 2002)

The American actor and singer David Soul decided that a review of his 1998 West End play *The Dead Monkey* went beyond fair comment and presented damaging untruths about the show. Soul is still best known for portraying detective Ken 'Hutch' Hutchinson in the 1970s TV show *Starsky and Hutch*. The *Daily Mirror* review had been purportedly written by its former showbusiness columnist Matthew Wright.

The article, written under Wright's by-line, described the play – in which Soul starred with his wife, Alexa Hamilton – as the worst West End show the author had ever seen. It alleged only 45 people attended a Monday evening performance and said the audience laughed derisively at Soul.

Soul's lawyer, Graham Atkins, told the High Court judge, Sir Charles Gray, that Wright had not attended the play but had sent a freelance journalist on his behalf. The freelance journalist, Henrietta Knight, attended the play on a Thursday but, crucially, Wright referred to a Monday staging of the play. The play did not run on Mondays and when Knight saw the play on the Thursday, the theatre had been more than half full. This case is somewhat illustrative of how *not* to sustain the fair comment defence to defamation in reviews. 'Unfair' comment needs to be based on true facts, which the article on *The Dead*

Continued overleaf

a full life?' (Jack *Independent* 1994)

Jeffrey Archer was not the first leading Conservative Party politician to be jailed for perjury in a libel action. Jonathan Aitken, a former British Defence Secretary, had unsuccessfully sued the *Guardian* newspaper and claimed he was going to fight 'the cancer of bent and twisted journalism' with 'the simple sword of truth'. (Engel *Guardian* 1999)

But a statement he used in his case resulted in criminal prosecution and imprisonment. Jonathan Aitken was not a stranger to the world of media law controversy. As a defendant journalist in 1968 he had been involved in a cause célèbre Official Secrets Act prosecution that gave him a reputation for batting for media freedom rather than attacking it.

He had tried to cover up the fact that the Saudi royal family had paid the bill for a weekend stay at the Paris Ritz. He was caught out through a complicated manoeuvre of investigative journalism by the *Guardian*'s then editor Peter Preston, who had been shown Mr Aitken's bill by the hotel's proprietor, Mohammed Al Fayed. Mr Al Fayed did not want to be revealed as the source, so a 'cod fax' was mocked up using a letter sent to the *Guardian* by Mr Aitken, then sent to Mr Al-Fayed [...] who used it to arrange personally with an unknowing member of the Ritz hotel staff that a copy of the bill should be faxed back to the paper.' (Elliott *Guardian* 1994)

Monkey clearly was not.

In the case of George Galloway MP, his steadfast opposition to the Anglo-American invasion and occupation of Iraq had led to his demonization in many mainstream newspapers, expulsion from the Labour Party, and a vicious smear campaign. The *Daily Telegraph* in the UK and *Christian Science Monitor* in the USA used documents unearthed at the time of the fall of Baghdad to accuse him of being a paid agent of Saddam Hussein's regime. The libel laws have been the only way to legitimize his claims of innocence.

Mr Justice Eady described the *Telegraph*'s allegations as 'dramatic and condemnatory'. In an editorial Galloway had been branded as 'Saddam's little helper'. The judge observed that in accusing Galloway of being in the secret pay of Saddam Hussein, the paper had made 'a rush to judgment' in 'a classic case of publishing and being damned'.

The judge said the MP had been seriously defamed. He was also not given a 'fair or reasonable' opportunity to comment on allegations that he had secretly and traitorously received money from the Iraqi regime for his own benefit.

The McLibel Trial is known as the extraordinary and marathon legal battle between McDonald's and a former postman and a gardener from London (Dave Morris and Helen Steel). It ran for two and a half years and became the longest-running trial in English legal history. The judge had to be given special life assurance. Its length even defied the mythology of Jarndyce versus Jarndyce in Charles Dickens's novel *Bleak House*. The defendants were denied legal aid and their request for a jury to adjudicate. The case concerned the distribution of an ironic campaigning leaflet outside the London Holborn branch of McDonald's and involved the global food giant employing several private detectives to infiltrate the campaigning group to collect evidence against Steel, Morris and other defendants. The entire trial was heard by a single judge, Mr Justice Bell, who delivered his verdict in June 1997.

The judge ruled that Steel and Morris had justified their claims that McDonald's 'exploit children' with their advertising, produce 'misleading' advertising, are 'culpably responsible' for cruelty to animals, are 'antipathetic' to unionization and pay their workers low wages. But the two defendants had failed to prove all the points and had libelled McDonald's on other issues and were ordered to pay £60,000 pounds damages, which they obviously could not afford to provide. McDonald's never took legal action to enforce the award. In any event, in March 1999 the Court of Appeal made further rulings that it was fair comment to say that McDonald's employees worldwide 'do badly in terms of pay and conditions', and true that 'if one eats enough McDonald's food, one's diet may well become high in fat etc., with the very real risk of heart disease.' The damages were reduced by £20,000.

The libel action turned out to be a spectacular public relations own goal for McDonald's. As the targets for their litigation were two impoverished and principled individuals with no corporate or material assets to lose, the use of the libel laws became self-defeating. There was no large-scale media libel insurance company that would have insisted on their media client settling. As a result of the court case, the anti-McDonald's campaign mushroomed, the press coverage increased exponentially, and much evidence embarrassing and damaging to McDonald's was disseminated on a globally popular website. A feature-length documentary was broadcast round the world.

The legal controversy continued. Steel and Morris took the British government to the European Court of Human Rights to defend the public's right to criticize multinationals, claiming that UK libel laws are oppressive and unfair, and that they had been denied a fair trial. The court ruled in their favour by declaring that the case had breached their rights to freedom of expression and a fair trial (Steel & Morris v United Kingdom ECHR 2005)

2000 are reminiscent of *New York Times* and would appear to be inspired by transnational influences in free speech precedent. It is somewhat ironic that *New York Times* was not about journalism but about a political advertisement, and in *Reynolds* the newspaper appellant lost against the negligence standard of responsible journalism set by the Law Lords.

The social and political backdrop of *New York Times* was the struggle and progress of the Civil Rights movement in the USA during the late 1950s and early 1960s. Civil Rights activists had accused the police commissioner of Montgomery, Alabama of failing to prevent and properly investigate racist attacks and of intimidating Dr Martin Luther King and his family. The newspaper had a circulation of less than four hundred in the state of Alabama. The civil rights campaign bought a page of advertising in order to support the efforts of thousands of black students from the South and, under the title 'Heed Their Rising Voices' it alleged:

> Again, and again, the Southern violators have answered Dr King's peaceful protests with intimidation and violence. They have bombed his home almost killing his wife and child. They have assaulted him seven times – for 'speeding', 'loitering', and similar 'offences'. And now they have charged him with 'perjury' – a felony under which they could imprison him for 10 years.
>
> (New York Times v Sullivan SC US 1964)

The advertisement also alleged that truckloads of police officers armed with shotguns and tear-gas had intimidated students and demonstrators in Montgomery, had padlocked dining rooms to starve the protesters into submission and directed violence against Dr King Jr. But though it might have been fair comment to state that some of the repression of protests had involved an element of police complicity, many of the advert's claims were exaggerated or wrong. Any examination of the *New York Times* cuttings library would have revealed the factual inaccuracies. L.B. Sullivan was the commissioner of public affairs in Montgomery, and he sued because he believed that the newspaper advert had accused him of dereliction of duty, since he was responsible for the performance and conduct of the police in the city. He received half a million dollars in damages from the Alabama jury. By the time the case came to be decided by the Supreme Court in 1964 another Montgomery city commissioner had obtained a half-million-dollar libel verdict against the same newspaper and there was a queue of eleven libel actions by other plaintiffs claiming $5,600,000 against other US news organizations situated outside the state of Alabama. The Supreme Court judges were faced with the alleged scenarios of chilling effect, strategic law suits against public participation and 'libel tourism' or 'forum hopping'. Libel suits were being launched in many other Southern states in an attempt to censor the news coverage of civil rights demonstrations. CBS was defending actions involving damages of two million US dollars.

One of the key issues to be decided in *New York Times* was whether L.B. Sullivan was being fairly compensated for the measured loss of his reputation in Montgomery, Alabama or whether the *New York Times* had been punished for being a newspaper from the North that had published, in fewer than four hundred copies distributed in the state, a deeply unpopular political expression that also happened to be wrong in part and mistakenly defamatory.

Justice Brennan gave the opinion of the court and, in Sack's, 'struck deep and swept broad' (Sack 2003: 1– 5):

Like insurrection, contempt, advocacy of unlawful acts, breach of the peace, obscenity, solicitation of legal business, and the various other formulae for the repression of expression that have been challenged in this Court, libel can claim no talismanic immunity from constitutional limitations. [...]

Thus we consider this case against the background of a profound national commitment to the principle that debate on public issues should be uninhibited, robust, and wide-open, and that it may well include vehement, caustic and sometimes unpleasantly sharp attacks on government and public officials. The present advertisement, as an expression of grievance and protest on one of the major public issues of our time, would seem clearly to qualify for the constitutional protection.

(New York Times v Sullivan SC US 1964)

The Supreme Court ruling reversed the $500,000 libel award given in Alabama against the *New York Times* and four black ministers. The ruling declared:

The constitutional guarantees (the First and 14th Amendments) require, we think, a federal rule that prohibits a public official from recovering damages for a defamatory falsehood relating to his official conduct unless he proves that the statement was made with 'actual malice' – that is, with knowledge that it was false or with reckless disregard of whether it was false or not.

(Ibid.)

This case established that in relation to the criticism of public officials the media had recourse to a no fault defence unless the publication could be proved to be actuated by malice and a reckless disregard for the truth. This did not give the media carte blanche against libel suits by public officials who were criticized. But it created a shield so that when journalists published information about public officials without malice, they could be spared a libel suit even though some or all of the information turned out to be wrong.

It was the first of a series of decisions that established important First Amendment protections for the press in the libel area. Subsequent Supreme Court cases sought to narrow the definition of a public figure and develop a two-step private plaintiff and public interest plaintiff libel liability.

The British media have been frustrated that they have not shared in the fortune of their American cousins in enjoying the liberation of a *New York Times* ruling. A substantial handicap was that British courts were not interested in taking into account US authorities and Supreme Court precedent. I myself enthusiastically collected Supreme Court rulings to support open justice challenges to English court reporting restrictions in the 1980s and early 1990s, only to be told that precedents from Commonwealth countries such as Australia, New Zealand, Canada and South Africa had more persuasive authority.

The clearest break from Commonwealth influence to a more internationalist approach arose in *Reynolds* in 1999. *The Times* was fighting for a defence much more narrowly defined than that created by the Supreme Court in 1964. The newspaper wanted libellous statements of fact made in the course of political discussion to be free from liability if published in good faith. Lord Nicholls established a new defence for mistaken defamatory publication that went wider than had been asked for, but was much narrower than *New York Times*, though he began his analysis of relevant international authorities with the American case history:

> In the United States the leading authority is the well-known case of New York Times Co. v. Sullivan 376 U.S. 254. Founding itself on the first and fourteenth amendments to the United States Constitution, the Supreme Court held that a public official cannot recover damages for a defamatory falsehood relating to his official conduct unless he proves, with convincing clarity, that the statement was made with knowledge of its falsity or with reckless disregard of whether it was false or not.
>
> This principle has since been applied to public figures generally. In Canada the Supreme Court, in Hill v. Church of Scientology of Toronto (1995) 126 D.L.R. (4th) 129, rejected a Sullivan style defence, although that case did not concern political discussion. The Supreme Court has not had occasion to consider this issue in relation to political discussion.
>
> In India the Supreme Court, in Rajagopal v. State of Tamil Nadu (1994) 6 S.C.C. 632, 650, held that a public official has no remedy in damages for defamation in matters relating to his official duties unless he proves the publication was made with reckless disregard of the truth or out of personal animosity.
>
> In Australia the leading case is Lange v. Australian Broadcasting Corporation (1997) 189 C.L.R. 520. The High Court held unanimously that qualified privilege exists for the dissemination of information, opinions and arguments concerning government and political matters affecting the people of Australia, subject to the publisher proving reasonableness of conduct.
>
> As a general rule a defendant's conduct in publishing material giving rise to a defamatory imputation would not be reasonable unless the defendant had reasonable grounds for believing the imputation was true, took proper steps, so far as they were reasonably open, to

verify the accuracy of the material and did not believe the imputation to be untrue.

Further, the defendant's conduct would not be reasonable unless the defendant sought a response from the person defamed and published the response, except where this was not practicable or was unnecessary.

Press publication of defamatory statements of fact will not be regarded as unlawful if, upon consideration of all the circumstances, it is found to have been reasonable to publish the particular facts in the particular way and at the particular time.

In considering the reasonableness of the publication account must be taken of the nature, extent and tone of the allegations. Greater latitude is usually to be allowed in respect of political discussion.

In New Zealand the leading case is the Court of Appeal decision in Lange v. Atkinson [1998] 3 N.Z.L.R. 424. The Court of Appeal held that members of the public have a proper interest in respect of statements made about the actions and qualities of those currently or formerly elected to Parliament and those seeking election. General publication of such statements may therefore attract a defence of qualified privilege. The exercise of reasonable care by the defendant is not a requirement of this defence.

(Reynolds v Times HL 1999)

It could be argued that the speech of Lord Nicholls does provide a compelling and powerful legal foundation for giving Article 10 freedom of speech priority over competing Articles, such as privacy. He said his starting point was freedom of expression:

> The high importance of freedom to impart and receive information and ideas has been stated so often and so eloquently that this point calls for no elaboration in this case. At a pragmatic level, freedom to disseminate and receive information on political matters is essential to the proper functioning of the system of parliamentary democracy cherished in this country. To be justified, any curtailment of freedom of expression must be convincingly established by a compelling countervailing consideration, and the means employed must be proportionate to the end sought to be achieved. [...]
>
> Without freedom of expression by the media, freedom of expression would be a hollow concept. The interest of a democratic society in ensuring a free press weighs heavily in the balance in deciding whether any curtailment of this freedom bears a reasonable relationship to the purpose of the curtailment. In this regard it should be kept in mind that one of the contemporary functions of the media is investigative journalism. This activity, as much as the traditional activities

of reporting and commenting, is part of the vital role of the press and the media generally. Freedom of speech does not embrace freedom to make defamatory statements out of personal spite or without having a positive belief in their truth.

(Ibid.)

The Law Lords in *Reynolds* set out a much more detailed manifesto or negligence standard for responsible journalism, and it has become known as the 'Reynolds criteria', set out in Table 1.17 of Chapter 1. It is somewhat humiliating for British journalism that the basic ethics of journalistic practice are effectively prescribed to editors by judges, something the US Justices of the Supreme Court have always been reluctant to do. The expressions 'actuated by malice' and 'reckless disregard for the truth' are principles, and not specifically defined duties and responsibilities for media conduct in the construction of media content and guidance for the conduct of media investigation. On the other hand, Lord Nicholls observed that in making every allowance for honest mistakes 'the sad reality is that the overall handling of these matters by the national press, with its own commercial interests to serve, does not always command general confidence.' (Ibid.)

However, the author believes that Lord Nicholls provided a speech in this seminal ruling that could justify seeing freedom of expression and freedom of the media as a trump card when in competition with the other rights of the European Convention. His legal language invested the social process of journalism with a priority and constitutional status, albeit in a country lacking a bill of rights and written constitution:

> Further, it should always be remembered that journalists act without the benefit of the clear light of hindsight. Above all, the court should have particular regard to the importance of freedom of expression. The press discharges vital functions as a bloodhound as well as a watchdog. The court should be slow to conclude that a publication was not in the public interest and, therefore, the public had no right to know, especially when the information is in the field of political discussion. Any lingering doubts should be resolved in favour of publication.
>
> (Ibid.)

The tragedy for *The Times* and British journalism is that the Law Lords in *Reynolds* were not so tolerant in their assessment of the negligence shown by the newspaper in the facts of the case before them. In the facts of *New York Times* it should be remembered that the Justices forgave the newspaper the incompetence and negligence of not bothering to check the content of the advertisement that they were being paid a large amount of money to publish against their news information department. An intern looking at the cuttings file would very likely have spotted the defamatory mistakes. Fundamentally, the setting of a 'reckless disregard for the truth' meant that the higher burden of proof set by the court did not demonstrate an indication of 'actual malice' at the time the advertisement was published:

> The mere presence of [...] stories in the files [of the *Times* indicating the falsity of the advertisement] does not, of course, establish that the *Times* 'knew' the advertisement was false, since the state of mind required for actual malice would have to be brought home to the persons in the *Times*'s organization having responsibility for the publication of the advertisement.
>
> (New York Times v Sullivan SC US 1964)

Can it not be argued that British Law Lords have continued to write opinions and speeches in media litigation since 1999 that cumulatively underline the jurisprudential value of priority, particular regard and a superior right status for Article 10 of the Human Rights Act? Consider the words of Lord Bingham of Cornhill in his speech in *Turkington* that extended the public meeting genre of qualified privilege to media press conferences and press releases. His rhetoric offered constitutional style assertions of the free speech and the free media principle:

> The majority can participate only indirectly, by exercising their rights as citizens to vote, express their opinions, make representations to the authorities, form pressure groups and so on. But the majority cannot participate in the public life of their society in these ways if they are not alerted to and informed about matters, which call or may call for consideration and action. It is very largely through the media, including of course the press that they will be so alerted and informed.

> The proper functioning of a modern participatory democracy requires that the media be free, active, professional and enquiring. For this reason the courts, here and elsewhere, have recognized the cardinal importance of press freedom and the need for any restriction on that freedom to be proportionate and no more than is necessary to promote the legitimate object of the restriction.
>
> (Turkington v The Times HL 2000)

Summer sunshine USA, winter chill UK

In March 2009, the Media Law Resource Centre reported that in the USA 'long-term trends of declining numbers of trials on libel, privacy and related claims, and increasing defence victory rates, continued in 2008.' (MLRC 2009) This not-for-profit media law defence organization had analysed 595 libel trials and appeals against media defendants between 1980 and 2008, and it reported that media defendants had 'increasingly won a higher percentage of cases [...] with the defense win rate at trial rising from 36.8 percent of verdicts in the 1980s to 40.4 percent in the 1990s and 53.6 percent so far in the 2000s.' (Ibid.) MLRC also reported a marked decline in the level of libel damages: 'while punitive damages constituted 56.3 percent of the trial awards in 2008, the long-term trend is that the percentage of cases that had punitive damage awards has declined significantly.' (Ibid.) Another intriguing statistic was that total damage awards in the cases tried from 1980 to 2008 'were reduced 88.1 percent overall from the amounts awarded at trial to the amounts ultimately awarded after post-trial motions and appeal.' (Ibid.)

Any British defence media lawyer and editor/journalist reading these statistics could justifiably say that in libel the USA basks in summer sunshine while they shiver in the chill of a libel winter that is almost arctic in proportions. In December 2008 the Programme in Comparative Media Law and Policy Centre for Socio-Legal Studies at the University of Oxford published a comparative study of costs in defamation proceedings across Europe.

The study was commissioned by Associated Newspapers, the publishers of the *Daily Mail* and *Mail on Sunday*, and concluded that the high level of legal costs that media defendants have to bear under the system of conditional fee agreements (CFAs):

> acts as a catalyst, forcing media outlets to settle claims, resulting in a self-imposed restraint on media outlets who are otherwise faced with the risk of being sued by a claimant on a CFA. Such restraint is imposed irrespective of journalistic standards and shackles the media outlets' important role as a 'public watchdog'.
>
> (CMLPC 2008: 3)

The centre reported that in the context of their European-wide study on defamation legal costs, 'England and Wales is seen to be around 140 times more costly than the average.' (Ibid.) The report summarized the case of *Martyn Jones MP v Associated Newspapers Ltd*:

> which revolved around which offensive term the MP had used in front of a security guard who had asked to see the MP's security pass. Martyn Jones brought the case on a CFA basis and won 5,000 GBP in damages along with costs recovery from the unsuccessful party. In addition to the claimant's costs, which were set at 387,000 GBP, including a 100% success fee, insurance and VAT, the defendant had to pay its own costs.
>
> (Ibid.: 12)

In written evidence to the UK House of Commons Select Committee on Culture, Media and Sport in 2009 the Society of Editors submitted the summary details of examples of CFA cases leaving regional newspapers with huge legal bills:

Case 1

A weekly newspaper was sued by three senior officers of a borough council. They used a London solicitor on a CFA. The issue concerned electoral law after postal votes were not counted in a close-fought borough election. The paper won substantially at the High Court and the council officers (actually the council, which backed the officers) were ordered to pay 80 per cent of costs and the paper 20 per cent of theirs. Two of the three took it to appeal. One dropped out because he was convicted of criminal charges. The other won on appeal, even though he had not been named in the article. The costs order was turned around and the paper had to pay 80 per cent of costs. Costs of £700,000 were doubled under the CFA to £1,400,000. With the paper's costs the bill came to £2 million, even though damages awarded were £25,000.

Case 2

A teacher was sacked in 2005 for gross sexual misconduct and sued the paper for reporting the story after obtaining a 'private' letter. The case was thrown out at the preliminary stage but the paper's costs still came to £15,000 which the litigant could not pay, leaving the paper to foot the bill. The paper recovered £5,000, which was all he owned.

(H of C Select Committee 2009, Society of Editors)

The committee has also heard from firms of solicitors specializing in libel law and libel litigants who do not support the campaign by media groups and civil rights organizations to introduce US-style libel reforms and mitigate the effects of CFA legal cost agreements. Russell Jones & Walker provided evidence that the current British libel regime was just and fair:

The reporting of Madeleine McCann's disappearance and the subsequent police investigation is just one prominent example which shows the freedom of the press has not been significantly inhibited by the use of CFAs. While newspapers might choose to make a commercial exit from a claim rather than risk litigation, the evidence suggests it does not dissuade them from publishing often quite startling defamatory material. In fact, the libel laws now provide greater protection

for defendants, particularly through the defence of Reynolds qualified privilege (which protects responsible journalism). This has led to
fewer cases being brought by claimants, particularly those on a CFA.

Claimants have as much right to protect their reputations as media
defendants have to protect their freedom of speech and CFAs are the
only way of providing access to justice for claimants of modest means,
putting them on an equal footing with the financial might of a media
defendant. One of our successful CFA cases provides a good example
of how access to justice in defamation can be so vital. A community
nurse was accused by a national tabloid in two consecutive front-page
articles of hastening the deaths of 17 terminally ill children. Her life,
career and family were devastated, and without CFA funding she would
have been unable to take any action. We represented her on a CFA,
and secured for her damages of £100,000 and a page 2 apology. This
public vindication enabled her to re-enter the profession she loved.

(H of C Select Committee 2009, Russell Jones & Walker:
paras 17–18)

It was reported by Jaron Lewis and Leah Alpren that the number
of libel writs being issued in London had begun to fall and cases were
being resolved much earlier. In 2006, 213 libel actions were instituted
compared with highpoints of 452 in 1997 and 560 in 1995. (CMLPC 2008:
53) Compared with the US, UK media defendants lose a much greater
proportion of libel cases. In 2007–8, 61 per cent of libel cases ended in
settlement and a statement in open court (36 out of 59) and the proportion of defamation cases featuring celebrities continued to rise. (*Media
Lawyer* November 2008: 3; Sweet & Maxwell 2008) In view of the fact that
a far larger proportion of defended actions that go to trial are usually won
by libel claimants, it can be assumed that the media win rate in the UK for
defamation is likely to be less than 20 per cent.

Jaron Lewis from the firm Reynolds Porter Chamberlain reported:

The number of libel cases continues to fall, even though there is now
more media content published than ever before. The media is now
much more used to interacting with its audience and dealing with
complaints as they arise. Also, media companies are now under much
more pressure than ever before to settle a case because of the potential costs of fighting a case through to trial.

(Ibid.)

The perception of a 'chilling effect' in 2009 appears to be no different to
the situation reported ten and fifteen years before. Examination of texts
published in those years reveals a consistent reporting that the law of libel
impacts upon all media 'from three different angles: as a normal business

cost; as an obstacle to be got round; or as an effective deterrent to the publication of certain material.' (Barendt et al. 1997: 75–6) The authors of the 1997 research published as *Libel and the Media – The Chilling Effect* argued that, were the national press to show greater regard for factual accuracy and confine what it wrote to what it could prove to be true:

> It would require certainty that in every case there were witnesses willing and able to appear in court on the paper's behalf, or that conclusive and legally admissible documentary evidence be in the editor's hands. If such certainty were required for everything contro-versial, there would be no newspapers worth reading.
>
> (Ibid.)

In their study of regional newspapers in Britain it was concluded that editors were worried about the potentially 'significant financial conse-quences of libel proceedings, and for that reason feel vulnerable. It does seem that they are reluctant to cover stories, unless they are absolutely sure that a plea of justification will be upheld in court.' (Ibid.: 99) The researchers decided there was a significant difference in the impact of defa-mation between the broadcasting and on print media. There was a greater culture of control in radio and television. The journalists were subject to statutory as opposed to voluntary regulation. The high costs of making television programmes led to some degree of caution in terms of investi-gating risky stories. However, there were fewer writs against broadcasters, probably because claimants were 'more sensitive, in short, to defamation in a newspaper article than on the audiovisual media.' (Ibid.: 125)

The study reported a much more profound 'chilling effect' in the field of book publishing. Every non-fiction publisher said it was in the libel business and even two university presses said that libel problems had resulted in heavy editing or withdrawal of some books. The effect of libel was described as 'wider, deeper and more insidious.' (Ibid.: 140) Publishing companies were making policy decisions not to commission 'high risk' projects.

The conclusion for this sector of media publication was most alarming: 'The result is pervasive self-censorship for which no person or office is directly responsible, but which is just as powerful as direct prohibitions in stifling publication.' (Ibid.) The chilling effect clearly derives from imagi-native and psychological perception.

The discourse on ethics must, therefore, explore how the machinery of media law and regulation internalizes a process of self-censorship. A culture of self-censorship involves making the avoidance of controversy an aspiration and positive social value, to the extent that it feels emotion-ally and ideologically 'natural'. In this way self-censorship can be reified into statutory law.

The 1997 study concluded that 'We found no evidence for the view that the media are sometimes prepared to fight "poor" cases to defend press freedom.' (Ibid.: 188) This means that defamation law operates as a nexus of capitalist decision making, and it is inevitable that issues of cost and profit are likely to be given greater importance than the principle of freedom of expression.

The 1997 survey highlighted concern about the propensity of police officers to sue for libel. The trend had reached the point where regional newspapers 'had more or less abandoned writing stories with allegations of excessive force or brutality on the part of the police.' (Ibid.) David Hooper described this trend in litigation, funded by the Police Federation and Scottish Police Federation, as 'producing a chilling effect ... even weaker cases in which officers are not named tend to be settled because of the expense of fighting them and the difficulty of contesting the identification evidence.' (Hooper 2001: 137)

In the period between 1995 and 2000 only 150 of the 1,200 complaints to the Police Federation had resulted in proceedings. But the number of successful writs resulted in such cases becoming 'jokingly known in police circles as "garage actions" for the enhancement they brought to the officers' suburban homes.' (Ibid.)

Serial libel litigants also had the effect of stifling media scrutiny of their activities. Hooper described the late Robert Maxwell as an effective exponent of 'libel terrorism'. (Ibid.: 43, 62) Maxwell harassed media organizations over a period of thirty years for anything remotely critical of his activities in publishing, politics, newspapers and football. In 1969 he had been branded by a Department of Trade and Industry investigation as somebody who was unfit to run a public company. Yet he prospered as a business tycoon, launching and buying newspapers, running football clubs, and eventually stealing from the *Daily Mirror*'s pension fund to shore up his bankrupt global business, before his mysterious death in November 1991.

By 2001 Hooper reported that the trend in UK libel damages since 1997 had become somewhat deflationary. There were fewer actions brought by police officers against media organizations. There had been changes in libel law. Judges could give directions on the amount of damages. The appeal court had been substantially reducing large awards to sums proportionate to damages awarded to compensate for personal injuries.

The jurisprudential breakthrough in the *Reynolds* case in 1999 introduced no-fault criteria for UK publications motivated by public benefit and duty. The incorporation of Article 10 of the European Convention on Human Rights into British statute law in 1998 bolstered the privilege available to public interest criticism of politicians, government employees and other citizens and organizations. In 1992 a ruling in the European Court of Human Rights in Strasbourg over media criticism of police behaviour in Iceland enhanced the underpinning of freedom of expression in this area. (Thorgeirson v Iceland ECHR 1992)

George Galloway, Saddam Hussein and the *Daily Telegraph*

George Galloway had been a member of the Labour Party since he joined in 1967 at the age of 13 and at the time of the invasion of Iraq in March 2003 he was the MP for Glasgow Kelvin. He attracted a good deal of public and media attention in the context of his activities and public statements over Iraq and the Middle East. His vocal opposition to New Labour government policy became more controversial once British service personnel were heavily engaged in fighting. Just over a month after the invasion the Daily Telegraph published articles on 22 and 23 April said to be based upon documents found in badly damaged government offices in Baghdad and headlined 'Galloway in Saddam's pay, say secret Iraqi documents,' and 'Memo from Saddam: We can't afford to pay Galloway more.' Two days later the US Christian Science Monitor published similar allegations.

Mr Galloway always stated that the documents found in Baghdad were forgeries and he set about suing both newspapers in the English libel arena to clear his name. On 23 October 2003 Mr Galloway was expelled from the Labour Party.

In June 2003 the US *Christian Science Monitor* apologized and later settled a libel action brought by Galloway in relation to an article published on 25 April of that year. It had accused Galloway of accepting payments totalling $10m in return for promoting Saddam's interests in the West, and the paper admitted that the documents that formed the basis for its story appeared to have been forgeries. An 'extensive investigation' by the *Monitor* revealed that the six papers, dated between 1992 and 1993, had in fact been written within the previous few months. This was proved by chemical analysis of the ink.

Paul van Slambrouck, the editor of the *Monitor*, published a fulsome apology:

> At the time we published these documents, we felt they were newsworthy and appeared credible, although we did explicitly state in our article that we could not guarantee their authenticity. It is important to set the record straight: we are convinced the documents are bogus. We apologize to Mr Galloway and to our readers.
>
> (van Slambrouck *Christian Science Monitor* 2003)

When he was telephoned by a Daily Telegraph reporter Mr Galloway was not told that the newspaper intended to publish its story the next day or given any inkling of the tone or extent of the coverage. Critical to Mr Galloway's case was the fact that he had no warning of the suggestion that he was 'in Saddam's pay,' or would be accused of treason.

Galloway sued Boston-based *Christian Science Monitor* in the English and Welsh libel system because the paper's allegations had been published in the UK via its Internet site. He received an apology in open court and undisclosed damages. He sued the *Daily Telegraph* and won damages of £150,000 in December 2004. Legal costs were estimated at around £1.2 million. Galloway had been branded in an editorial as 'Saddam's little helper'. Mr Justice Eady decided that in accusing Galloway of being in the secret pay of Saddam Hussein, the paper had made 'a rush to judgment' in 'a classic case of publishing and being damned.' (Galloway v Telegraph HC 2004) Also, Galloway had not been given a 'fair or reasonable' opportunity to comment on allegations that he secretly and traitorously received money from the Iraqi regime for his own benefit. In a concluding paragraph to his ruling Mr Justice Eady said:

> It seems to me that Mr Galloway is entitled to be compensated for the manner in which the newspaper chose to put the Iraqi documents into the public domain and the spin which the Defendants chose to put upon them. As he said, *The Daily Telegraph* chose not to confine itself to reporting the documents. He complains of the effect upon his reputation and hurt feelings brought about by the 'blizzard' of comment and inference with which the publication of the documents was surrounded. Moreover, the 'blizzard' came out of the blue without any opportunity to refute their inferences. This again illustrates how unrealistic it would be for me to try to compensate Mr Galloway for the 'blizzard' but not for the content of the underlying documents.
>
> (Ibid.)

Galloway said in an open press conference outside London's Royal Courts of Justice that the newspaper had been given a judicial caning:

> All those people, the old regime of *The Daily Telegraph* – Lord Black, Barbara Amiel, Charles Moore – were amongst the chief trumpeters for the disastrous decision to go to war with Iraq. In aid of their case they said many things, which turned out to be wholly false, bogus, counterfeit, forged and utterly wrong. So, *The Telegraph* has been held to account. I am glad and somewhat humbled to discover that there is at least one corner of the English field which remains uncorrupted and independent and that corner is in this courtroom.
>
> (Press conference 2 December 2004, Channel 4 News, UK)

The *Daily Telegraph* described the judgment as a blow to the principle of freedom of expression in this country. In an appeal before the Master of the Rolls Sir Anthony Clarke and Lord Justices Chadwick and Laws, the newspaper's lawyer, James Price QC, argued that it had never intended to prove that Mr Galloway had taken money from a charitable programme set up to help Iraqis disadvantaged by trade sanctions: 'What is true and established is that the documents which we found are genuine Iraqi Government documents found in closed files on government property. That makes them a matter of public interest.' (*Media Lawyer* November 2005: 11) He said the newspaper was entitled to the *Reynolds* qualified privilege and a newspaper could comment on a privileged story even if its views were provocative, offensive, biased or wrong. (Ibid.)

Mr Justice Eady had decided that the newspaper was not entitled to the responsible journalism privilege established in *Reynolds* because it had not given Galloway a chance to consider the documents and the newspaper's accompanying editorial had not demonstrated a balanced and fair attitude toward the MP. The newspaper's editorial criticism was tantamount to accusing him of treason. Although Mr Galloway was interviewed by telephone, he was not given an opportunity to read the Iraqi documents beforehand, nor were they read to him. The judge observed: 'Allegations of "treason" are not part and parcel of the knocks one expects to take in the course of everyday political debate.' (Galloway v Telegraph HC 2004)

The Court of Appeal upheld Mr Justice Eady's judgment and explained why the newspaper was not entitled to the *Reynolds* qualified privilege, fair comment/neutral reportage defences:

> It appears to us that the newspaper was not merely reporting what the Baghdad documents said but that, as the judge held, it both adopted and embellished them. It was alleging that Mr Galloway took money from the Iraqi oil-for-food programme for personal gain. That was not a mere repeat of the documents, which in our view did not, or did not clearly, make such an allegation. We agree with the judge that, although there were some references to allegations, the thrust of the coverage was that The Daily Telegraph was saying that Mr Galloway took money to line his own pockets. In all the circumstances we answer the question whether the newspaper adopted and embellished the statements in the Baghdad documents in the affirmative.
>
> (Galloway v Telegraph CoA Civ 2006: para 59)

The Galloway case arose from the eye of one of the biggest political storms in post-war British history. It can be argued that Galloway has been politically vindicated by the fact that weapons of mass destruction were never found in Iraq, the Saddam Hussein/Al Qaeda connection has been entirely discredited and the regime change and occupation in Iraq have not brought about the promises of liberty, prosperity and security for Iraqis made by Anglo-American political leaders such as President George W. Bush and Prime Minister Tony Blair. In 2003 George Galloway faced political and social annihilation. Is it the case that the English and Welsh libel laws protected what had become a marginalized political voice from professional and financial oblivion? Mr Galloway might argue that, had he not won his libel actions after being driven out of the Labour Party and forming a new political movement called Respect, the stigma of treason and dishonesty would have meant he would not have been able to unseat a sitting Labour MP in the London constituency of Tower Hamlets in the 2007 General Election.

Galloway sued the *Christian Science Monitor* in the London libel courts rather than using the libel laws in Boston, Massachusetts. Since the paper's defamatory mistakes had more impact in the country of the article's target, where it was published by Internet, Mr Galloway cannot be accused of 'libel tourism'. Furthermore, there is no evidence to suggest that had Mr Galloway sued the Daily Telegraph in the more media friendly US libel system he would have been any less successful.

In the US Mr Galloway's legal team would have had to succeed against media defendants by demonstrating that they showed reckless disregard for the truth and/or had been actuated by malice, and damaged him financially. This means the defendant had been negligent to a reckless extent in disregarding the falsity of their evidence. Mr Galloway would have had to prove falsity; not the media defendant. As a public interest plaintiff Mr Galloway would have to prove through direct or circumstantial evidence that the media defendants published with knowledge of falsity or with serious doubts about accuracy. The proof of the negligence would have to be up to the standard of 'clear and convincing.' The English Appeal Court ruling stated that the Baghdad documents did not allege that Mr Galloway took money for himself, whereas the Telegraph articles complained of did make that allegation unequivocally. The articles were not fairly, neutrally and disinterestedly reporting the contents of the documents. They went beyond assuming the contents of the documents to be true and drew their own inferences as to the personal receipt of funds diverted from Iraq's oil for food programme, which was something that was not alleged in the documents themselves. (Galloway v Telegraph CoA 2006)

It would be interesting to speculate if Mr Galloway could have survived politically had there been no libel laws to enable him to clear his name. The US developed its constitutional First Amendment defence for honest mistake in journalism, so that its media would not be vulnerable to libel actions from people who had the power and ability to protect themselves in the cut and thrust of allegation and counter-allegation. Any assessment on whether Mr Galloway would have survived not being able to achieve libel vindication might take into account his bold and powerful performance before the US Senate's Permanent Subcommittee on Investigations on 18 May 2005, when he declared:

> Senator, I am not now, nor have I ever been, an oil trader and neither has anyone on my behalf. I have never seen a barrel of oil, owned one, bought one, sold one – and neither has anyone on my behalf.
>
> Now I know that standards have slipped in the last few years in Washington, but, for a lawyer, you are remarkably cavalier with any idea of justice. I am here today, but, last week, you already found me guilty.
>
> You traduced my name around the world without ever having asked me a single question, without ever having contacted me, without ever having written to me or telephoned me, without any attempt to contact me whatsoever and you call that justice.
>
> *(Morning Star* 2005)

Mr Galloway's performance can be viewed on YouTube and it might be argued that this was clear evidence of his ability to match the power of negative media coverage. As George Galloway was an experienced and influential politician was he not powerful enough to give his rebuttal in the media and leave the general public to decide for themselves the veracity and reliability of the *Telegraph's* coverage?

The Human Rights Act means that since 2000 the UK courts have been influenced by the media law of civil law-based continental jurisdictions. This is hardly surprising when the British courts have a statutory obligation under sections 2 and 6 of the Act to give effect to convention rights and take into account the jurisprudence of the ECHR at Strasbourg. One impact of this trend is that freedom of expression is not only going to be equally balanced with a respect to the right for privacy. Defamation is being telescoped into the right to privacy in ECHR case law. One consequence of this position is that freedom of expression will have to be equally balanced with the right to reputation. Since 1964 the US Supreme Court has consistently given constitutional priority to the First Amendment when the right to freedom of expression conflicts with the right to privacy or reputation. The UK media are therefore in a much weaker position to defend public interest stories compared to the media in the USA.

4

CONTEMPT/PROTECTING
FAIR TRIAL LAW

Measuring and defining the moral panic and prejudice

The free press/fair trial subject invites a consideration of notorious case histories that capture the *Zeitgeist* of mass media interest and, when they are accompanied by a perception of hysteria and viral reverberation of prejudice against a defendant or defendant(s), may result in miscarriages of justice. Media studies theorists like to engage the phenomenon of the moral panic as a relevant concept, which was discoursed by Stanley Cohen in his seminal 1973 text *Folk Devils and Moral Panics: The Creation of the Mods and Rockers*. The idea was developed by Stuart Hall in *Policing the Crisis: Mugging, the State, and Law and Order* (1978), given extended analysis by Critcher in *Moral Panics and the Media* (2003) and some original philosophical evaluation by Zylinska in her chapter 'Ethics and Moral Panics' in *The Ethics of Cultural Studies* (2005). In the American context, Jon Bruschke and William E. Loges have bridged criminology with media studies in *Free Press vs. Fair Trials: Examining Publicity's Role in Trial Outcomes* (2004).

In this chapter we focus on an analysis of the trial of an American, Dr Hawley Harvey Crippen, in London in 1910. This qualifies for the cliché of being the 'trial of the century' of its time, whose associations with media publicity were clearly problematic and, in all probability, resulted in a most tragic and irreversible miscarriage of justice. The other case covered in this chapter was a miscarriage of justice that could be righted: the case of another American doctor, Sam Sheppard. The Supreme Court judgment in *Sheppard v Maxwell* (1966) is an indicting example of the most damaging impact of media prejudice on criminal proceedings.

Both cases involved public rage and a discourse on infidelity. Crippen had an affair with his secretary, Ethel le Neve. Sam Sheppard had the misfortune that his affair with a work colleague was unearthed early on in the police investigation, and he did not help his situation by lying about it to a coroner's enquiry. The Crippen case seemed global for its time. The Sheppard case was more local to the Cleveland area of Ohio and only became more widely amplified as the campaign to clear him gathered pace and his case reached the Supreme Court. They were twentieth-century cases where the media became one-sided and lacked any kind of plurality in the representation of the defence. What they also had in common is that the prosecuting authorities, media and public opinion appeared to have prejudged the defendants.

The theory of moral panic may not be a relevant theory because the Crippen and Sheppard cases were about individuals, not groups, being identified as a threat to social safety. But the theory might be relevant if, as individuals, they were demonized into a dramatic and representative role. They were certainly put up as recognizable symbols of evil for the mass media, and the developing narrative through investigation, hunt, arrest, trial, verdict and sentence involved an intense build-up of public concern, with identifiable primary and secondary definers constructing and exaggerating the outrage and moral panic.

The gruesome discovery of eviscerated human remains in the cellar of Dr Crippen's house in North London turned him into an Edwardian Jack the Ripper. The Metropolitan Police issued a graphic poster headlined 'Wanted for Murder and Mutilation'. The very idea that he had disappeared with a young woman, presumed to be his mistress, and could be at large anywhere was a considerable source of anxiety, exploited by the competitive popular newspaper market.

Media discourse that was preoccupied with what could and might still happen if justice were not achieved by arrest, conviction and sentence was present in the newspaper coverage of both cases. There was also an accompanying drive of media commentary, seeking to raise the issue that 'something needs to be done'. There were calls for legal reform and social action to resolve the anxiety and fear engendered. And there were tangible signs of response and change recommended by the legal authorities. Somewhat ironically for the media, that change involved the development of stringent reporting restrictions on the coverage of criminal cases in Britain and, in the USA, a set of Supreme Court recommendations on how judges could improve the control of their trial proceedings and nullify the effects of prejudicial media.

In both cases it was as though the legal system and human society ethically turned in on itself in a ritual of moral shame and identified the messenger as a new symbolic defendant who had to be held responsible for the indecent rush to judgment and morbid and almost pornographic enjoyment of gazing upon crimes and criminals.

Interest in real-life crime cases, particularly murder, seems to pander to the voyeuristic and *Schadenfreude* instincts of the audience. Judges, lawyers and sociologists frequently express the desire to evaluate whether media coverage of trials, particularly where the verdict is decided by jury, contributes to injustice, the expression of prejudice and a distortion of reality. The media reporting of trials inevitably involves an exploitation of

Plate 7 Doctor Hawley Harvey Crippen, 1910, probably taken when he was standing in the dock of the Number One Court of the Old Bailey for his trial. His case is illustrative of everything that can go wrong when criminal justice and biased media decide an innocent man must hang for a crime he did not commit. The image appeared in the memoirs of Crippen's prosecutor, Sir Richard Muir, published in 1927. It is unlikely that the trial judge, Lord Chief Justice Alverstone, would have approved of the taking of this photograph, and legislation in 1925 would make such photography in court a criminal offence.

the infotainment dimension of journalistic narrative. Vicarious curiosity is an essential component in the delivery of open justice and in public interest in relation to the reporting of criminal trials.

The UK has a confused attitude toward the jury system: the state is allowed to vet jurors secretly; the defence has no such privilege. Sometimes potential jurors are asked to excuse themselves if they have a connection with the security services, or are victims and relatives of victims of terrorist incidents. Reference has already been made to the 1981 Contempt of Court Act, which made interviewing jurors about the deliberation process a criminal offence. The road is blocked for serious academic research as well as for general journalism. The situation could not be more different in America, which has had the benefit of investing in many laboratory and real-life research studies into the role of publicity in jury deliberation.

Bruschke and Loges reported that, in twelve studies examining pretrial publicity in the absence of trial information, the respondents 'will generally be biased against defendants prior to the introduction of trial evidence, and that the more information that respondents retain, the more likely they are to prejudge guilt.' (Bruschke and Loges 2004: 30)

Eight studies into the issue included trial evidence and found a pretrial publicity effect, but 'virtually all of these studies have been conducted under circumstances that differ from actual trials in very important ways.' (Ibid.: 32) The studies also showed that if pre-trial publicity did emerge as a biasing factor, the influence was much less than the influence of the trial evidence. In laboratory studies that partially supported the existence of a pre-trial publicity effect the results were equivocal and 'affirmed the effectiveness of one remedy or another.' (Ibid.: 47) Bruschke and Loges found seven published studies that offered data 'indicating the absence of any pretrial publicity effect.' (Ibid.: 58)

R v Hawley Harvey Crippen and Ethel le Neve 1910

The Crippen murder case has assumed mythical proportions in terms of the representation of crime mystery and Edwardian culture. Madame Tussaud's has immortalized the middle-aged American purveyor of quack remedies, with the kiss-curl hairstyle, who was convicted and hanged for poisoning and dismembering his wife, Cora, at their home in Hilldrop Crescent, North London. Crippen's relationship with his secretary, Ethel le Neve, with whom he fled the country after Scotland Yard detectives had visited asking questions about Cora's disappearance, also sparked the sensationalist curiosity of the public. This was whipped up by a powerful circulation war. The decision to dress up Ethel as a young man posing as Crippen's son was not at all convincing, and the captain of their transatlantic liner, the SS *Montrose*, alerted by the bloodthirsty clamour for Crippen's arrest, soon suspected that the two passengers calling themselves Mr Robinson senior and Mr Robinson junior were the two fugitives. But he used the ship's Marconi wireless facility to contact the editor of the *Daily Mail* to negotiate the terms of a series of eye-witness accounts and updated reports on the conduct of the suspects before cabling Scotland Yard with the information.

The Crippen case became a landmark in the enforcement of contempt law against mass newspaper publication. Britain's most senior judge, the Lord Chief Justice, held contempt of court trials for newspapers that had been judged to create prejudice during the trial. In *R v Clarke ex parte Crippen* 1910 it was decided that the *Daily Chronicle* had committed contempt of court when it alleged that Crippen had made a confession after his arrest in Newfoundland, because a warrant had been issued for his arrest and the case was pending. The newspaper report was a complete fabrication. Mr Justice Darling observed: 'Anything more calcu-lated to prejudice the defence could not be imagined.' (Borrie and Lowe 1973: 41) Along with his alleged eve-of-execution confession, it was one of a plethora of reports that had more do with fantasy than with reality.

Detective Chief Inspector Dew sued a number of national newspa-pers for the libel that he had told reporters in Canada that Crippen had confessed to the murder. This was the beginning of the tradition of multiple libel actions by police officers.

The surreptitious taking of photographs of Crippen and le Neve at Bow Street Magistrates' Court and of Crippen in the dock of the Number One Court of the Old Bailey began to mobilize the judiciary and government to consider legislation outlawing in-court photography and sketching. This was achieved by 1925. The senior judges were also unhappy about the spectre of cheque-book journalism and the macabre scrambling for the rights to Crippen's pre-execution confession. His solicitor, Arthur Newton, was later suspended and castigated by Mr Justice Darling for the incompetent and inadequate defence of his client. Newton had arranged for the fabrication of a confession from Crippen, which was published in the *Evening Times* when Crippen had in fact gone to his death still proclaiming his innocence. The Law Society found that the solicitor had fabricated other letters and documents purporting to be from his client to the *John Bull* and *Daily Chronicle* newspapers. Newton lost most of his client's income by paying it into a bank which went bankrupt on the first day of the trial. (Morton 2001: 49–53) Legal commentators say that Crippen had poor representation by both his solicitor and his counsel in court.

It is suggested that Newton should have advised Crippen and le Neve to force the British authorities to extradite them from Canada, as the case against them was circumstantial and there was an even chance that they would never reach the dock of the Central Criminal Court. But such an outcome, while it would have been favourable to Crippen and le Neve, would not have been lucrative for Arthur Newton, who had already nego-tiated newspaper retainers to represent the couple in England and barter their life stories and potential confessions, were they to be convicted of the capital crime. (TNA HO 144/1718/19542/sub-file 38) There is also evidence that the clerk to the most celebrated defence QC of the time, Sir Edward Marshall Hall, turned down the chance to take the brief because Newton refused to advance any of the fees, presumably because he wanted to profit from the bulk of the newspapers' provision of legal defence costs. (Morton 2001: 50)

The prosecution and Home Office papers relating to the Crippen case were not released until more than eighty-two years after his trial and execution. Long-standing investigative analysis by the American forensic poisons specialist John Trestrail demonstrates that the anxieties of England's senior judges about media prejudice and solicitor miscon-duct should have gone deeper and wider. Documentaries by Channel 4 television, *The Last Secret of Dr Crippen* (Maltby 2004), and Channel 5 tele-vision, *Was Dr Crippen Innocent?* (Webb 2008), have revealed a catalogue of concealed evidence, suspected malpractice, misrepresentations, and mistakes in forensic science. The director of the Channel 5 documentary, Andy Webb, said 'it seems to me the Crippen case should be required reading for media students.' (Webb *Guardian* 2008a)

Present-day forensic DNA analysis indicates that the human remains found in the cellar of Dr Crippen's home did not belong to his wife, Cora, and that they were not those of a woman. (Hodgson *Guardian* 2007). Mr Trestrail, the author of *Criminal Poisoning: An Investigational Guide for Law Enforcement, Toxicologists, Forensic Scientists and Attorneys* (2007), argues that there has never been a case of hyoscin being used in any other murder case and it is hard to find a poison murder where the victim's body was gutted, eviscerated and buried at the scene of the crime. (Hodgson *Guardian* 2007). This was the trial that established the reputation of the forensic pathologist Dr Bernard Spilsbury, but contemporary standards and prac-tice question the reliability and scientific credibility of his conclusions and confident assertions that a piece of skin found in the remains had the mark of a scar and was thereby linked to the existence of a similar scar observed on Mrs Crippen. Similar doubts have been cast on the evidence about the poisoning. A forensic analysis of scientific and legal doubts about the credibility of his evidence in the Crippen trial is contained in the book *Lethal Witness: Sir Bernard Spilsbury, Honorary Pathologist* (2007) by British lawyer Andrew Rose. His critical views about the quality of legal services provided to Dr Crippen were also expressed in the television documentaries.

Examination of the papers from the case, released to the national archives, reveals the existence of a letter written by somebody claiming to be Mrs Cora Crippen to her husband while he was awaiting execution at Pentonville Prison. (TNA HO 144/1718/19542/sub-file 86) It was retained by the prison governor and not passed on to the defence. Another letter purporting to have been written by Mrs Crippen was given to the then Home Secretary, Winston Churchill. It was last seen going into his pocket and has disappeared. (Maltby, 2004). Perhaps it was still in his pocket when he joined the ranks of other celebrity spectators in the Number One court of the Old Bailey to see Crippen's lover successfully defended by the barrister F.E. Smith. Ethel le Neve was acquitted of being an accessory to murder. It was reported in 2007 that a woman using Mrs Crippen's stage name, 'Belle Elmore', was 'registered as living with Cora's sister in New York. Records show that the same woman entered the US through Ellis Island from Bermuda in 1910 shortly after Mrs Crippen disappeared.' (Hodgson *Guardian* 2007)

The archive papers also revealed that the Director of Public Prosecutions had paid $450 for the US private detective agency, Pinkertons, to bring Mrs Cora Crippen's friend, Bruce Miller, from Chicago to deny being the alleged victim's lover. Evidence that a woman bearing Mrs Crippen's description had tried to withdraw savings and arrange for the removal of large quantities of furniture and belongings from Hilldrop Crescent before her disappearance was not disclosed to the defence. (TNA MEPO 3/198; DPP 1/3)

There is now a suspicion that the presence of Dr Crippen's pyjama jacket with the mysterious human remains in the cellar might have been the result of police planting and fabrication. (Webb 2008). Detective Chief Inspector Walter Dew (1863–1947) retired from the police the day after Crippen's trial, became a high-earning private detective, and collected tax-free libel damages by suing nine national newspapers that had reported him as the source of Crippen's non-existent confession in Canada and other speculation. His autobiography, published in 1938, was titled *I Caught Crippen*. However, the commentator David Aaronovitch is unconvinced by the growing campaign to assert Dr Crippen's innocence. He argued that every aspect of the new evidence can be challenged and that the totality of original evidence demonstrates that Crippen did commit murder. (Aaronovitch *Times* 2008)

The jury in Crippen's trial took twenty-seven minutes to find him guilty. When he was asked if he had anything to say, he replied: 'I still protest my innocence.' Lord Chief Justice Alverstone's peroration in sentencing now seems hollow in the light of the facts that have emerged:

> you have been convicted upon evidence, which could leave no doubt on the minds of any reasonable man, that you cruelly poisoned your wife, that you concealed your crime, you mutilated her body, and disposed piece-meal of her remains; you possessed yourself of her property, and used it for your own purposes. It was further established that as soon as suspicion was aroused you fled from justice, and took every measure to conceal your flight. On the ghastly and wicked nature of the crime I will not dwell. I only tell you that you must entertain no expectation or hope that you will escape the consequences of your crime, and I implore you to make your peace with Almighty God.
>
> (Young 1920: 183)

Crippen's surviving family want his body disinterred from unconsecrated ground and returned to the US. There have been reports that the UK Criminal Cases Review Commission has been examining the safety of the conviction and that it may refer the case to the appeal court with a recommendation for ruling the guilty verdict unsafe and posthumously quashing the result of the trial. (Townsend *Observer* 2009). If this were to happen, the Crippen case would go down in British criminal history as one of the most disastrous miscarriages of justice. Perhaps the culpability should be shared on a historical basis between the media, the police, the legal profession, forensic science and the judiciary.

Sam Sheppard and another 'trial of the century'

Dr Sam Sheppard's wife Marilyn was bludgeoned to death in Bay Village, four miles from Cleveland, Ohio in 1954. From the outset, investigating officers focused suspicion on the doctor and he was arrested on a murder charge, was indicted about a month later, and his trial in October terminated in his conviction four days before Christmas. During the entire pre-trial period virulent and incriminating publicity about him and his wife's murder made the case notorious, and the news media saturated their coverage with charges and counter-charges, including crimes and misdemeanours with which he was never charged.

Three months before the trial he was examined for more than five hours without counsel in a televised three-day inquest conducted before an audience of several hundred spectators in a gymnasium. Over three weeks before his trial the newspapers published the names and addresses of prospective jurors, causing them to receive letters and telephone calls about the case.

The trial began two weeks before a hotly contested election in which the chief prosecutor and the trial judge were candidates for judgeships. Newsmen were allowed to take over almost the entire small courtroom, hounding Sheppard and most of the other key trial participants. Twenty reporters were assigned seats in the courtroom near the place where Sheppard was sitting with his attorney, and also very close to the jury and counsel. He therefore had no privacy and everything he said to his attorney could be heard by the journalists in court.

The movement of the reporters in the courtroom caused frequent confusion and disrupted the trial; and in the corridors and elsewhere in and around the courthouse they were allowed free rein by the trial judge. A broadcasting station was assigned space next to the jury room. Before the jurors began deliberations they were not sequestered, and they had access to all news media, though the court made 'suggestions' and 'requests' that the jurors not take part in interviews in which they were tempted to comment about the case. Though they were sequestered during the five days and four nights of their deliberations, the jurors were allowed to make inadequately supervised telephone calls during that period.

Intensive and sensational media coverage attended every day of the case, including incriminating issues not allowed to be put before the jury. The jurors were thrust into the limelight and asked to perform the role

269

of celebrities. The trial judge was asked to do something about it and his only response was that neither he nor anyone else could restrict the prejudicial news accounts. Despite his awareness of the excessive pre-trial publicity, the trial judge failed to take effective measures against the massive publicity which continued throughout the trial or to take adequate steps to control the conduct of the trial. Twelve years after he was found guilty and sentenced to life imprisonment, Sam Sheppard filed a habeas corpus petition contending that he did not receive a fair trial. The Supreme Court issued an opinion which set the seal on what should be considered the dividing line between fair trial and trial by media in the USA:

> The massive, pervasive, and prejudicial publicity attending petition-er's prosecution prevented him from receiving a fair trial consistent with the Due Process Clause of the Fourteenth Amendment. Though freedom of discussion should be given the widest range compatible with the fair and orderly administration of justice, it must not be allowed to divert a trial from its purpose of adjudicating controver-sies according to legal procedures based on evidence received only in open court. [...] The trial court failed to invoke procedures which would have guaranteed petitioner a fair trial, such as adopting strict-er rules for use of the courtroom by newsmen as petitioner's counsel requested, limiting their number, and more closely supervising their courtroom conduct. The court should also have insulated the witness-es; controlled the release of leads, information, and gossip to the press by police officers, witnesses, and counsel; proscribed extra-judicial statements by any lawyer, witness, party, or court official divulging prejudicial matters; and requested the appropriate city and county officials to regulate release of information by their employees.
>
> (Sheppard v Maxwell SC US 1966)

If the skeleton description of the legal narrative does not hint at the intensity of the injustice, the wider facts make it much worse. Although the prosecutors never considered anybody else a suspect, it was obvious that Dr Sheppard had also been injured and he had given a credible account of a 'bushy-haired' intruder who had attacked his wife and who had gone on to attack him when he disturbed him.

A footnote in the Supreme Court case cited the observation that the celebrity journalist Dorothy Kilgallen, who had been reporting the trial, had been taken aside by the judge and informed that he thought Sheppard was 'guilty as hell.' (Sheppard v Maxwell, SC 1966: note 11 at 358) While Sheppard was mourning the murder of his pregnant wife and facing the accusation that he was the murderer, media intrusion into his private life revealed an affair he had had with a work colleague. He lost both parents within a year of the trial: his mother through suicide; his father prematurely from gastric ulcer.

Sheppard was acquitted at the second trial, held in 1966. The alcoholism he developed as a result of stress meant that the resumption of his medical career resulted in a malpractice suit. He turned to wrestling – his favourite sport at college – and died shortly after appearing before a Senate committee enquiry when he affirmed his faith in the American constitution and was not inclined to demand any blunting of the free press privilege under the First Amendment that had caused him so much harm:

> The wheels of justice grind slowly. But in this country it took ten years to vindicate me. And I hope by testifying here that I can justify the fact that the Supreme Court and the people of the United States have made a wrong right. They can't give me back my parents and the other things but they have attempted. And this is what this free country is all about. I'm proud of my country. I want to make it better in the future which is what you people are doing. And I hope to justify the fact that a guy who was wrongfully convicted was finally released.
>
> (Nugus/Martin Productions 1992)

His attorney, F. Lee Bailey, explained that the problem with the media coverage was not that it had happened, but that it had been all one way:

> if there is one powerful organ of the news media who go overboard in using its strength to persecute one man, there should be another equally powerful organ somewhere to step in and contest. I've studied all the clippings. I never saw anybody come out for Sam Sheppard. It isn't the reporting ability of the news media that is frightening. It is the editing ability. The newspapers had the power to put in the good evidence for the state. It also had the power to leave out the bad evidence.
>
> (Ibid.)

The Crippen and Sheppard case histories inform us that the failure in media ethics and transgression of media law are part of a nexus of complex factors contributing to miscarriages of justice. Trial by media should not be considered as an isolated issue and problem. Indeed Bruschke and Loges argue that 'expensive pretrial publicity research should not be conducted at the expense of quality defense representation.' (Bruschke and Loges 2004: 156) They say that, as a society, we should be embarrassed if millions of dollars are spent each year for such social science legal research 'when public defense programs are so desperately underfunded.' (Ibid.) The ethical obligation on the part of media communicators to avoid partiality in adversarial legal proceedings tried by jury should be obvious. Plurality and fairness of representation appear to be the surest antidotes to trial by media.

Whilst the adverse consequences of unfair media coverage on the administration of justice may be common to both US and UK jurisdictions, the chasm in the approach to open justice is wide. As indicated in Chapter 1, in the USA open justice, media reporting and access rights to the criminal courts are given constitutional priority through the First Amendment. This is evident in the ruling of Chief Justice Burger in *Richmond Newspapers Inc v Virginia* in 1980. Furthermore, the Sixth Amendment guarantees open justice provisions for criminal defendants in respect of 'a speedy and public trial, by an impartial jury' and 'to be informed of the nature and cause of the accusation; to be confronted with the witnesses against him'. The UK has compromised all of these principles.

The fundamental differences in the approach to criminal open justice between the US and UK are highlighted in the series of essays edited by Professor Eric Barendt published in 2009 in *Media Freedom and Contempt of Court*. Professor Joseph Jaconelli, in his 2002 text *Open Justice: A Critique of the Public Trial*, observed that in English law 'there is no fundamental constitutional text embodying the right to an open trial' (Jaconelli 2002: 6) or to the procedural safeguards articulated in the US Sixth Amendment. But Chief Justice Burger in *Richmond* derived the constitutional right in the historical practice of the criminal courts of England and Wales.

British jurisprudence on open justice constantly avers to the House of Lords ruling in 1913 in *Scott v Scott*. Jaconelli observes correctly that Lord Shaw 'extolled the open conduct of trials as "a sound and very sacred part of the constitution of the country and the administration of justice."'(Ibid.; Scott v Scott HL 1913) But the *Scott* case in its *ratio decidendi* never dealt centrally with the issue of media and public access to proceedings. It was a divorce case where one of the parties had been prosecuted for contempt when she sent shorthand transcripts of her private hearing to relatives to counter allegations being made by her ex-husband. The fact remained that in practice in England and Wales during most of the nineteenth and twentieth centuries open justice and media reporting of criminal trials had constitutional priority.

The Rubicon on open justice was crossed on very rare occasions. *R v Clement* in 1820, as explained in Chapter 1, was a flawed and discredited jurisprudential source of the power to prior restrain the reporting of criminal proceedings. In an editorial in *The Times* the judges were accused of arbitrarily ordering the editor of the *Observer* to pay a fine of £500 for failing to observe a court reporting ban based on no previous statute or precedent: 'We confess we know not the law of the case, where it is written, where to be found, or from whence derived; [...] Nothing like it exists on the records of any British court.' (*The Times* 29 April 1820: 2) Clement was fined in his absence, without an antecedent trial where he could be represented, and the punishment was upheld in two appeal court hearings heard by the very judges who had punished him. As *The Times* observed in 1820: 'The whole is in the clouds.' (Ibid.)

The Rubicon was further crossed in 1925 and 1926 when Parliament legislated to ban sketching and cameras from courtrooms and the reporting of indecency and detailed evidence in domestic proceedings. Parliament gave judges discretionary powers to prohibit the naming of juvenile witnesses and defendants in adult proceedings in 1933. Judges gave themselves the power to order the withholding of the identity of homosexual victims of blackmailing gangs during the 1930s. This practice led to the 1974 case of *R v Paul Foot and Socialist Worker* where Lord Chief Justice Widgery crossed the Rubicon again and formalized a common law right to anonymity for blackmail complainants threatened by menaces that were embarrassing. Paul Foot was a legendary investigative journalist who had been seeking to expose senior members of the British establishment for visiting an illegal brothel. He was also anxious that the anonymity would protect people in positions of intelligence and military sensitivity whose private sexual peccadilloes exposed them to the risk of compromising national security. Parliament abandoned open justice as a constitutional paradigm in the Sexual Offences Amendment Act 1976, when it legislated for defendant and witness anonymity in rape trials, and in the 1981 Contempt of Court Act, when it gave judges formalized prior restraint and prohibition powers on reporting criminal cases without any right of appeal for media organizations. Since then the British media have been struggling through litigation costing tens, perhaps hundreds, of millions of pounds to secure the basic right to have freedom of expression simply balanced with the concepts of privacy, fair trial, right to life, administrative convenience and national security.

The first ruling of the UK's Supreme Court in October 2009 was an open justice application by a group of media organisations seeking to identify the names of men appealing against an order freezing their assets because they were suspected of funding terrorism. Geoffrey Robertson QC submitted that the court's first term docket read like alphabet soup because the appellants were referred to only by letters of the alphabet after the lower courts had granted them pseudonym orders. This was a fight to establish the concept that everyone who commenced a legal action should expect to have his or her name published. The Supreme Court agreed to the identification of a man who had previously been known only as 'G' but had used the media to criticize the effect of the financial freezing orders, had been referred to in a terrorist trial and on a Bank of England website.

5

PRIVACY LAW

The British media privacy right is developing a creativity and dynamism that has crossed the line of anything that would be envisaged and tolerated by the US Supreme Court. Despite the protestations of Paul Dacre, the editor of the British newspaper the *Daily Mail*, UK privacy rights now protect the dignity, intimacy and personal family space of private and public individuals. The British courts are taking on the Strasbourg jurisprudence set out in the Princess Caroline von Hannover case of 2004, that public figure status in terms of character *par excellence* does not result in the surrendering of performance of private being in public space. The zone of interaction of a person with others, even in the public context, which may fall within the scope of private life, has expanded. (Clayton and Tomlinson 2009) Private life is personal identity, physical and psychological integrity. The horse has long bolted from the stable and Mr Dacre's attack on the decisions of High Court Judge Sir David Eady has not fully understood that key decisions had already been taken by other judges in courts before him and above him:

> inexorably, and insidiously, the British Press is having a privacy law imposed on it, which – apart from allowing the corrupt and the crooked to sleep easily in their beds – is, I would argue, undermining the ability of mass circulation newspapers to sell newspapers in an ever more difficult market. This law is not coming from Parliament – no, that would smack of democracy.
>
> (Dacre 2008)

Mr Justice Eady became associated with cases the media were losing that engaged in a balancing exercise between freedom of expression and privacy because he was one of a few QBD specialist media law judges in London. Journalism is inclined to personalize the decision of courts by the name of the judge presiding. However, judges have a legal duty to decide cases according to the evidence and existing law of statute and precedent. Their personal beliefs and attitudes are excluded from the decisions they have to take. The Human Rights Act requiring a balancing act between Article 8 and 10, *Campbell v MGN* in 2004 giving individuals a horizontal remedy to sue media publishers over their right to a respect for privacy, and the ending of the constitutional priority for freedom of expression is having the social consequence of blocking media exposure of infidelity and private sexuality in the absence of a provable public interest. Dacre told the House of Commons Select Committee on Culture, Media and Sport in 2009 that Mr Justice Eady was a brilliant judge, but he had been wrong in his approach to media rights.

The irony may well be lost on Mr Dacre and his fellow editors that the UK privacy right has gestated largely through the healthy and lucrative commerce in media exploitation rights. Hollywood celebrities Catherine Zeta-Jones and Michael Douglas came to London to seek a privacy remedy over unauthorized publication of wedding photographs snatched at a ceremony in the USA because they were worth a million pounds. In 2001 the High Court granted an injunction preventing the *Manchester Evening News* from publishing images of a surviving conjoined twin that had been taken on the steps of a hospital. The court agreed to publication by another newspaper that had entered into an exclusive arrangement with the parents. (Attard v Greater Manchester Newspapers HC 2001) These cases suggested that a 'hybrid privacy right of private and commercial information can be a commodity that can be sold, without "the owner" losing the right to protect their privacy.' (Melville-Brown 2006: 399) The Press Complaints Commission complained that in this case privacy should not have been treated as a commodity that could be sold on one person's terms. (PCC Adjudication 15 June 2001 Report 55)

The House of Commons Select Committee's enquiry into 'Press Standards, Privacy and Libel' elicited the submission of two significant memoranda of written evidence from key individuals in the English and Welsh judiciary. Sir David Eady, the High Court judge who was the target of Paul Dacre's attack on judges creating a media privacy law by the back door, released the copy of his speech on privacy to the Intellectual Property Lawyers' Association in February 2009. It provides a narrative of how the media privacy right was established. Eady confirmed that the common law constitutional priority of freedom of expression in relation to privacy and other rights ended as a result of a number of steps taken by Parliament and judiciary between 1998 and 2004. This 'overwhelming priority that the common law had given to it' (H of C Select Committee 2009, Eady) was articulated by Lord Chief Justice Coleridge in *Bonnard v Perryman* in 1891:

> The right of free speech is one which it is for the public interest that individuals should possess, and, indeed, that they should exercise without impediment, so long as no wrongful act is done; and, unless

Plate 8 Media cranes for television cameras covering a serial murder investigation in Suffolk in late 2006. Erected in a suburban street, television media have the potential to use long-view cameras to peer into the gardens and through the windows of a suspect in a sensational murder enquiry. In the US a buzzing swarm of news helicopters normally gathers above the scene of a news event. The technology and style of news gathering becomes a matter for ethical discussion and, in some countries, for litigation for breach of privacy.

276

an alleged libel is untrue, there is no wrong committed; but, on the contrary, often a very wholesome act is performed in the publication and repetition of an alleged libel. Until it is clear that that an alleged libel is untrue, it is not clear that any right at all has been infringed; and the importance of leaving free speech unfettered is strong reason in cases of libel for dealing most cautiously and warily with the granting of interim injunctions.

(Bonnard v Perryman CoA Civ Div 1891)

Eady explained that the priority ended when Parliament, in the 1998 Human Rights Act, legislated for the British courts to take into account Strasbourg jurisprudence, and the Law Lords, in *Campbell v Mirror Group Newspapers* in May 2004, established 'a citizen's reasonable expectation of privacy in respect simply of personal information [...] enforced horizontally by reference to Article 8, as between citizens.' (Eady 2009)

This account was confirmed in the memorandum of the head of the Court of Appeal Civil Division, Master of the Rolls Sir Anthony Clarke, who firmly placed responsibility for the establishment of 'a generalised right to respect for privacy' on Parliament. (H of C Select Committee 2009, Clarke) He pointed out to the House of Commons Select Committee's enquiry that it was the then Lord Chancellor, Lord Irvine, who in November 1997 had stated that through the Human Rights Act it was 'expected that the judges would develop the law appropriately having regard to the requirements of the convention.' (Ibid.) Furthermore, Clarke asserted that the then Lord Chief Justice, Lord Bingham, had warned Parliament of the consequences:

it seems very likely that difficult questions will arise on where the right to privacy ends and the right to free expression begins. The media are understandably and properly concerned that the conduct of valuable investigative journalism may be hampered or even rendered impossible. It is very difficult, and probably unwise, to offer any opinion in advance about where the line is likely to be drawn.

(Ibid.)

In 2002 the *Economist*, in an editorial entitled 'Whose life is it anyway?' had warned:

Six years ago, Lord Bingham, then Lord Chief Justice, warned that if the government failed to legislate on privacy, 'the courts will not be found wanting.' During the passage of the HRA (Human Rights Act), the Lord Chancellor, Lord Irvine, said that the judges were 'penpoised' to develop a privacy law.

(*Economist* 9 March 2002)

The Department for Culture, Media and Sport confirmed in an additional memorandum to the House of Commons Select Committee on Culture, Media and Sport that the government had deliberately passed legislation to create offences that would amount to criminal sanctions against the media for breach of privacy through the Protection from Harassment Act 1997, the Regulation of Investigatory Powers Act 2000, and the Data Protection Act 1998. Some of these offences had no public interest defences. (H of C Select Committee 2009, DCMS)

Sir David Eady's speech outlined the history of significant public disquiet about tabloid intrusion into private lives during the 1980s and early 1990s. The right to respect for privacy had been created in a context. He said that he had been one of the three lawyers on the committee of enquiry into privacy set up in 1989 under the chairmanship of the late David Calcutt QC. He said he was the lawyer representing the Duchess of York in 1992 instructed to seek an injunction to prevent the publication of intrusive photographs featuring the Duchess lying by a pool with a Texan accountant 'taking a particularly close interest in her toes.' (Eady 2009) In recognizing that judges were in the front line of making the legal decisions Eady stated: 'the media have nowhere to vent their frustrations other than by abusing the referee in the particular case. Some of you may know that certain judges have come under increasingly hysterical attack in the media.' (Ibid.)

The expanding protection included intimate and personal information, and it was not for judges to refuse a remedy on grounds of distaste or moral disapproval. Protection extended to 'kiss and tell stories' when they encroached on another person's reasonable expectation of privacy. This includes the increasing phenomenon of general *contra mundum* (against the world) injunctions against all media, prohibiting publication of secret information that the public will never be permitted to know about:

> I cite it simply because the name of the case is one of my favourites: *X & Y v Persons Unknown* [2007] HRLR 4. It has become quite common for celebrities to seek an injunction urgently of the John Doe variety – against persons unknown. Typically, they will have got wind from a journalist of a story in the offing, based on revelations by an unidentified friend or acquaintance. If his John Doe injunction is then served on any newspaper he suspects of involvement, that can be an effective way of spiking the plans of the unknown culprit. That is because of the *Spycatcher* doctrine, whereby even though the newspaper is not a party, it can still be liable for criminal contempt if it publishes the story knowing of the prohibition against the 'persons unknown'. In *X v Y* a procedure was worked out of giving notice to potential media respondents to give them a chance to be heard on the scope of the order. That is appropriate because their Article 10 rights are

potentially involved. They are notified of the information which is to be subject of protection by means of a confidential schedule attached to the order or draft order. So far that seems to be working pretty well.

(Ibid.)

Tessa Mayes, in her report 'Restraint or revelation? Free speech and privacy in a confessional age', argues that it is not that public discussion of private matters is viewed as a problem per se – it is seen as a problem if the subject of the discussion feels hurt or offended. Mayes states that if the issue is seen in terms of balancing the right to freedom of expression with the right to privacy, this effectively means that there is no such thing as a right to free speech or, indeed, a right to privacy. She concludes that the right to privacy has been redefined as a state protection from hurtful public discussion; and the right to free speech has been qualified by restricting speech that may cause offence. (Mayes 2002: 2)

In a comparative context it should be realized that British privacy law is moving in directions that would be considered unconstitutional and unconscionable in US law. The Americans would not have allowed privacy anonymity to settle on witnesses in civil and criminal cases and then migrate to defendants burdened with media notoriety. The privacy right is morphing into a right of oblivion, and the right to live under the deceit of a false identity.

US constitutional barriers limiting the privacy tort

US journalists cannot be held liable for revealing the name of a rape victim whose identity was obtained through open court records: 'Once true information is disclosed in public court documents open to public inspection, the press cannot be sanctioned for publishing it.' (Cox Broadcasting Corporation v Cohn, Supreme Court 1975) In *Florida Star v BJF* 1989 the Supreme Court held that a newspaper could not be held liable for negligence where it published the name of a rape victim whose identity was obtained from a police report.

In *Oklahoma Publishing Co v District Court* 1977 the Supreme Court ruled that the First Amendment barred a judge from prohibiting the media from printing the name of a juvenile murder suspect who had been identified at a court hearing open to the media. In *Smith v Daily Mail Publishing Co* in 1979 the Supreme Court ruled that a newspaper could not be held liable for publishing the name of a juvenile charged with murder, in violation of a state statute requiring the permission of the juvenile court prior to publication. These cases demonstrate that federal law and the First Amendment trump any case law or statutes passed in the US states themselves.

Justice Brandeis is recognized as one of the founding authors of the US privacy tort. Apart from the famous article he co-wrote for the *Harvard Law Review* in 1890, he used his later role as a Supreme Court Judge to develop the principle as evidenced in his 1928 dissenting opinion in *Olmstead v United States*:

> The makers of our Constitution undertook to secure conditions favourable to the pursuit of happiness. They recognised the significance of man's spiritual nature, of his feelings and of his intellect. They knew that only a part of the pain, pleasure, and satisfactions of life are to be found in material things. They sought to protect Americans in their beliefs, their thoughts, their emotions and their sensations. They conferred, as against the government, the right to be let alone – the most comprehensive of rights and the right most valued by civilised men.
>
> (Olmstead et al. v US, SC US 1928)

A basic normative moral precept of American journalism, underlined in most published codes and stylebooks, is that when a person becomes involved in a news event, voluntarily or involuntarily, he forfeits the right to privacy. American news culture also expects that a person somehow involved in a matter of legitimate public interest, even if not a *bona fide* sport or news event, normally can be written about with safety.

The US First Amendment is the key to why celebrities cannot get the same degree of privacy protection now available in the English courts and in Continental jurisdictions such as France and Germany. Generally in the USA, if you are a public figure, or involved in a public interest event, truth will override privacy considerations.

The global US news agency Associated Press quotes the words of Paul P. Ashley, a former president of the Washington State Bar Association:

> The essence of the wrong will be found in crudity, in ruthless exploitation of the woes or other personal private affairs of private individuals who have done nothing noteworthy and have not by design or misadventure been involved in an event which tosses them into an arena subject to public gaze.
>
> (Goldstein 1998: 292)

The significant difference between developing privacy law in the UK and existing privacy law in the USA is that in America the trump card is freedom of the press and expression. In January 1967, Supreme Court Justices decided that the constitutional guarantee of freedom of the press applied to states' invasion of privacy cases involving news reporting. They were reviewing a complaint about the publication of photographs in *Life* magazine in a review of a play. The New York state courts operated a legislated privacy law and provided a privacy remedy to a family who objected to the reconstruction of a traumatic event in their lives.

It was known as the 'Desperate Hours' case. The play had dramatized the story of a couple who had been held hostage in their house. *Life* asked the actors to pose for pictures in the actual house where the real-life family had been kept prisoners in their own home. The privacy claim was based on the assertion that the article implied that the stage drama was a true representation of what had taken place.

The Supreme Court decided to give the magazine the same free press constitutional protection as the *New York Times* in the famous libel judgment of 1964. There would be no licence for deliberate defamation and reckless disregard for the truth, and privacy actions will be successful if the facts of a story are deliberately or recklessly changed, or fictionalized. The Court's approach contrasts with that of the UK Law Lords in model Naomi Campbell's 2004 case against the *Daily Mirror* newspaper. The *Daily Mirror* had published the truth, had fictionalized nothing and had explored somebody who was newsworthy on an issue of public interest; namely, a global celebrity lying when she denied taking drugs, while at the same time being treated for drug addiction problems.

At the time that the High Court originally found for her and awarded her £3,500 (roughly $5,000) in 2002, *The News Media & The Law* reported that if the case had been tried in the USA she would have probably lost:

> American courts grant celebrities a lower expectation of privacy than non-celebrities, which makes proving an invasion of privacy claim difficult. 'Public figures here have much less protection regarding details about their private lives, and Naomi Campbell would certainly be considered a public figure,' said Robert D. Lystad, a media attorney with Baker & Hostetler LLP in Washington DC. In addition, US court rulings allow photographers to take pictures of people from a public place as long as the subject is also in a public place.
>
> (*The News Media & The Law* 2002a: 30)

In the 'Desperate Hours' case the Supreme Court gave freedom of expression the benefit of the doubt in the journalistic and public interest context:

> The line between the informing and the entertaining is too elusive for the protection of [freedom of the press]. Erroneous statement is no less inevitable in such case than in the case of comment upon public affairs, and in both, if innocent or merely negligent, it must be protected if the freedoms of expression are to have the 'breathing space' that they 'need to survive.' [...] We create grave risk of serious impairment of the indispensable service of a free press in a free society if we saddle the press

with the impossible burden of verifying to a certainty the facts associated in a news article with a person's name, picture or portrait, particularly as related to non-defamatory matter.

(Time, Inc v Hill SC US 1967)

Life anonymity for Maxine Carr: 'The nonce bitch deserves to die'; 'I would glass her if she was in my local' (anonymous threats to Maxine Carr)

On 24 February 2005 Mr Justice Eady issued a groundbreaking order, which effectively made Maxine Carr one of the most invisible criminals in Britain. He was in fact making permanent a temporary court order banning the media from reporting any details that could identify her whereabouts after her release from prison, under a probation order, with a new identity. The *Times* law editor, Frances Gibb, observed: 'It also marks a further step towards what some lawyers see as a new privacy law by stealth that protects high-profile criminals from media exposure.' (Gibb *The Times* 2005) What made the case so groundbreaking was that such an overwhelming level of secrecy was accorded to a convicted adult who had not committed murder but had been convicted of a relatively minor criminal offence – conspiracy to pervert the course of justice. The anonymity order was not indefinite. It was possible for a media organization to make an application to the High Court to challenge it in the future. Regrettably, the judge was unable to hear any submissions from media organizations because they were not prepared to instruct counsel. It is possible that they saw the case as a no-win situation, largely due to the fact that the judge was being asked to protect her 'life and limb' as well as her psychological health.

Anonymity trend for terrorist suspects, defendants and convicted criminals

The ruling was the latest in a series of all-embracing injunctions that had 'in perpetuity' nature and were *contra mundum* – applying to every media communicator everywhere and at all times in the legal jurisdiction. Similar kinds of orders were being sought in relation to security forces informants coming to the end of their sentences in Northern Ireland. In May 2009 Mr Justice Silber prohibited media identification of a prisoner being considered for parole who had committed killings which he described as 'by far the most serious and sadistic category of murder cases which I have tried or read of.' (*Media Lawyer* May 2009: 7) The judge said that 'M' was entitled to anonymity because, after being 'outed by the press' when seen in public after being assigned to an open prison he had had to be returned to more secure custody for his own safety. (Ibid.)

The 'threat to safety' argument is used to justify the anonymity of British and foreign nationals subject to detention and control orders under terrorism legislation passed since 2001. The irony is that the government, usually through the intelligence services, has secretly identified the suspects as potential threats to public safety. An attempt was made to challenge the anonymity of terror suspects known only as 'AD' and 'LL' who had disappeared while under control orders, but the move by a consortium of newspapers was rejected by the High Court in October 2006 (*Media Lawyer* November 2006: 9)

The Times launched another challenge to the anonymity relating to a terrorism suspect known only as 'AY' in October 2008. He was subject to a control order, a controversial form of house arrest which involves restrictions on civil liberty and continual surveillance by the security authorities. The High Court made it clear that cost, convenience and anticipated vigilante action against the individual outweighed freedom of expression:

> Such public identification may lead to harassment of and the risk of violence to the individual and his family by groups or individuals. The individual may continue to live where he was living already, and may remain in his job which would be put at risk. A media thirst for detailed and accurate news, in the public interest, may generate persistent investigative reporting alongside highly intrusive watching and besetting. There may be a risk of disorder in any given local community. The knowledge that he is subject to a Control Order may conversely make him attractive to extremists in the area where he lives. It may make the provision of a range of services, including housing, to the individual or his family rather more difficult. If the individual believes that he faces these sorts of problems, he has a greater incentive to disappear, to live elsewhere in the UK or abroad. All of this can make the monitoring and enforcement of the obligations more difficult, and increase significantly the call on the finite resources which the police or Security Service have to devote to monitoring the obligations.
>
> (Times v Home Office Re: AY, HC 2008)

It can be argued that there has been a pattern of applications and litigation seeking to use right to life, fair trial, reputation, privacy, and prohibition on torture to curtail and compromise the principle of open justice in relation to defendants. Reference has already been made to *Re S (a child) identification: restriction on publication* at the House of Lords in 2004. It seemed that the Law Lords, by ruling that the mother charged with murdering one of her children, while another was in care, should be identified in court reports, were drawing a line in the sand. But shortly afterwards the President of the Family Division did make an exception in relation to another mother on trial for criminal offences for knowingly infecting her partner with HIV. This time the court did decide that the potential damage to health and well-being of her children in local authority care outweighed freedom of expression in naming her in reports of the criminal trial.

In 2009 the Law Lords decided that a man acquitted of rape should not continue to have anonymity in a BBC documentary investigating why DNA obtained from the victim, which matched his profile, was ruled inadmissible at his trial. (Re: D and the BBC HL 2009) D previously obtained anonymity because the Attorney General had challenged the legality of the judge's decision to exclude the evidence. The Law Lords' ruling was obtained by brilliant advocacy on the human rights of media freedom on behalf of a public service broadcaster often willing to fight for a legal principle that would be a basic publication right in the USA. In this case the BBC wanted to argue, through a carefully researched investigative documentary, that a man believed guilty of the appalling rape of a 66-year-old woman in her own home should be named and prosecuted. The legal editor of *The Times*, Frances Gibb, observed: 'A rare combination of legal loopholes meant that, for the past 12 years, Wendell Baker has enjoyed both his freedom and an anonymity scarcely ever granted to defendants in criminal trials.' (Gibb *The Times* 2009) The BBC's documentary *Double Jeopardy* was in the campaigning tradition. It set out the case that even though the DNA evidence linking Wendell Wilberforce Baker to the crime was ruled inadmissible when he was acquitted in 1999, subsequent legislative and case law changes ending the rule of double jeopardy and enabling the use of DNA evidence in criminal trials justified a new prosecution. However, Frances Gibb warned that 'there may be one further hurdle for the prosecution to overcome – the possibility that Wendell Baker may now be able to argue that all the publicity given to the case has denied him the right to a fair trial.' (Ibid.) There are other cases where the High Court has ruled that embarrassment and shame to members of a defendant's family, even in the context of allegations of possessing child pornography, will not justify secrecy and anonymity. But the context is in a state of flux. Unlike in the USA, the constitutional position is not fixed. And a media industry suffering from the effects of recession in 2009 finds it expensive and exhausting to marshal the millions of pounds in legal costs needed to fight for free media and free speech principles.

Precedents protecting privacy of notorious criminals

In 2003, the then President of the Family Division, Dame Elizabeth Butler-Sloss, amended an effective all-embracing anonymizing 'media privacy order' on Mary Bell, who killed two toddler boys when she was aged 11. The original injunction issued to protect Mary Bell's identity after she was released from prison was known as 'a Mary Bell Order'. The new injunction issued by Dame Butler-Sloss was designed specifically to protect the privacy of her daughter, whose life could have been destroyed by her mother's exposure as a child killer. This was an application of the balancing act between right to life (Article 2), right to privacy (Article 8) and right to freedom of expression (Article 10).

Previously, Dame Butler-Sloss had granted lifelong anonymity in 2001 to the child killers Robert Thompson and Jon Venables, when they reached the age of 18 and had been released back into the community with new identities. They were convicted of murdering toddler James Bulger in Merseyside, at a controversial trial parts of which were ruled by the European Court of Human Rights to have been breaches of the convention. The difference between Maxine Carr's case and that of Thompson and Venables was that the two boys had been given a partial anonymity under the Children and Young Persons Act 1933 after their conviction for murder. While the trial judge allowed the media to publish their names, in an unprecedented injunction, he prohibited publication of the nature and whereabouts of their detention.

The application to revisit their privacy rights on their release back into society was that there would be a substantial risk to their lives by any removal of the original order when they reached age 18. Dame Butler-Sloss was provided with evidence that identification would expose them suddenly to the risk of really serious harm, possibly murder, and also destroy any benefits accruing from the extensive programme of rehabilitation they had received while in custody.

Unlike in the Maxine Carr case, the news media were represented in Venables & Thompson. Counsel for the media argued that hard cases make bad law; there was a presumption in favour of freedom of expression, which was a primary right in a democracy; to restrain the freedom of the press there must be a pressing social need for the restriction, convincingly established by proper concrete evidence, and the restrictions must be proportionate to the legitimate aim pursued; he questioned whether there was continuing evidence of genuine threats, and if there were truly threats it was the responsibility of the authorities to deal with the threat, and not by way of injunction against the press; he submitted that if either of the boys were tracked by a journalist it should be left to the judgment of the editor whether or not to publish the information; he argued that if injunctions were granted in the present case, they would become a precedent for the future, affecting other notorious criminals campaigning for parole and there would even be applications to restrain publication of the identity of paedophiles; open justice would be imperilled and the right of the public to know about killers would be frustrated; famous people did not generally get protection; an injunction ought not to be *contra mundum* (against the world at large) in a case not involving children. (Venables & Thompson v News Group et al. HC 2001)

In 1998 media interest in the child killer Mary Bell and her daughter had been reawakened by the publication of a book by Gitta Sereny – *Cries Unheard: The Story of Mary Bell*. The author had collaborated with Mary Bell and Bell's assistance had been rewarded by the payment of 'a substantial sum'. But the media speculation about her current life and whereabouts meant that Mary Bell, known as X, and her daughter, known as Y, had 'relocated under compulsion, prompted by press intrusion and harassment, on five separate occasions.' (X and Y v O'Brien et al. HC 2003) The judge cited 'exceptional circumstances' in granting a life-time protective injunction to Mary Bell, and these are set out in Table 5.1. The judge also extended the protection to her adult daughter because the 'positions of the mother and the daughter are so intertwined that it is effectively impossible to look at either of them in isolation.' (Ibid.)

The arguments presented by legal counsel on behalf of the newspapers opposing the *contra mundum* secrecy orders on the identities and whereabouts of Robert Thompson and Jon Venables, the killers of James Bulger, appeared to make little impression on Professor Roy Greenslade, writing editorial comment for the *Guardian* in January 2001. In an article headlined 'Filthy rags: the reaction of some newspapers to the judgement on Venables and Thompson's future is deplorable', Greenslade, a former editor of the *Daily Mirror*, was excoriating in his attack on rival newspapers. He alleged that they:

> showed a streak of veniality, even barbarism, which besmirches Britain's press. Let us name and shame the worse offenders: the *Sun* and *Daily Mail*, as one would expect, and sadly, the *Times*. […] As

Table 5.1 Dame Butler-Sloss: reasons for lifetime anonymity injunction for child killer Mary Bell

The young age at which she committed the offences.

The finding by the jury of diminished responsibility based upon solid evidence of her abusive childhood and the damage she had suffered as a child.

The length of time which has expired since the offences were committed.

The need to support rehabilitation into society and the redemption of the offender.

Her semi-iconic status and the effect of publicity on her rehabilitation.

The serious risk of potential harassment, vilification and ostracism, and the possibility of physical harm.

Her present mental state.

Her concerns for the welfare of her daughter.

Butler-Sloss pointed out, it is newspapers who 'provide the information that would lead to the risk that others would take the law into their own hands.' That, surely, is the key point. These papers are not neutral purveyors of information. While proclaiming the public interest, they are inciting the mob, both feeding off the understandable grief of the Bulger family and taking every opportunity to stoke the embers of hatred.

(Greenslade *Guardian* 2001)

Greenslade seemed confident in 2001 that the unprecedented lifetime injunction would be an exceptional curb on freedom of the press: 'It clearly isn't, as they claim, the thin end of the wedge.' (Ibid.)

The vituperative nature of his rhetoric is representative of the internecine warfare between so-called 'quality' newspapers such as the *Guardian* and *Observer*, both owned by the Scott Trust, and the 'tabloids' such as the *Sun*, *News of the World* and *Daily Mail*. The *Guardian* welcomed the Human Rights Act and the development of a British media privacy law and has been a persistent critic of the style of content, methodology and conduct of 'tabloid' journalists. In the summer of 2009 further angry words were exchanged between the *Guardian* and the *News of the World* when investigative journalist Nick Davies alleged that the tactic of telephone hacking that led to the jailing in 2007 of the *News of the World*'s royal editor Clive Goodman and private detective Glenn Mulcaire was much wider than had been revealed in open court. The House of Commons Select Committee's enquiry into 'Press Standards, Privacy and Libel' was diverted into questioning witnesses in order to investigate the claims. The *News of the World* denied the allegations and Scotland Yard declared that their enquiry had not collected any evidence of further offences meriting prosecution.

The tension between so-called 'quality' and 'tabloid' journalists, so evident in this dispute, reflects the inability of the British media to present any kind of united front on what is meant by 'the public interest' and to campaign for an effective constitutional protection and priority for freedom of expression and freedom of the media.

Anonymity for Maxine Carr and unforeseen consequences

The Soham killings shared the social and cultural notoriety of Mary Bell's offences and the killing of James Bulger. Maxine Carr had provided a false alibi for her boyfriend, Ian Huntley, by lying to the police about her whereabouts at the time the 10-year-old girls were killed by him in his house in Soham. The police did not allege that she had any knowledge of the crimes that he had committed. The summary timetable of events is shown in Table 5.2. Frances Gibb reported that: 'So far all the cases that have attracted such orders have been exceptional. The danger, lawyers say, is that each time they have been a little less exceptional and the boundaries of freedom of expression pushed back a little more.' (Gibb *The Times* 2005)

Mr Justice Eady concluded that granting the injunction was the only effective means available to the court to protect Carr's rights under Article 2 of the Human Rights Act 1998. The three pillars of his approach were that:

(i) The written evidence before the court indicated a risk of serious physical and psychological harm; [The evidence adduced in support was persuasive: a persistent threat from a specific source, actual

Table 5.2 Timeline of events in Maxine Carr case

4 August 2002	Holly Wells and Jessica Chapman, both 10 years old, go missing in Soham, Cambridgeshire.
10 August 2002	Reconstruction of Holly and Jessica's last known movements
17 August 2002	Bodies of the girls are found in a ditch at Lakenheath, Suffolk. Ian Huntley, 28, and Maxine Carr, 25, arrested on suspicion of murder. Huntley was a caretaker at a local school and Carr, his partner, had been a teaching assistant at the girls' school.
21 August 2002	Huntley charged with murder. Carr charged with attempting to pervert course of justice for providing a false alibi to the police for Huntley, and assisting the offender. The alibi was that she was with him at home at the time the girls disappeared, while she was actually in Grimsby and had had a fight with Huntley over the phone.
3 November 2003	Trial begins at Old Bailey.
2 December 2003	Huntley admits he was responsible for death of Jessica Chapman.
17 December 2003	Huntley found guilty of murdering Jessica and Holly. Carr found not guilty of helping him in relation to deaths, guilty of conspiring to pervert the course of justice. Huntley given two life sentences. Carr sentenced to three and a half years' imprisonment.
25 July 2004	In a media interview, Carr says: 'I was stupid and I lied, but I never had any idea what he had done.' The jury's opinion was that Carr was not guilty of assisting an offender and had not known that Huntley had committed the murders.
24 February 2005	Judge in High Court grants indefinite order to protect Carr's anonymity.

Source: Fresco, *Times* 2005

incidents of harassment and expressions of intention by the public to attack or kill Carr, and actual attacks on innocent members of the public by individuals who thought their victims looked like Carr.]

(ii) The existing injunction had been effective in reducing that risk and aiding Carr's treatment and rehabilitation. The real risk to her already fragile psychological health and failure to protect her against that risk would amount to a breach of her rights under Article 8 of the Human Rights Act and ECHR; [This was supported by medical evidence. The judge also took the view that if the injunction were not continued the task of the police and the probation service would be more difficult or impossible.]

(iii) The lack of a challenge by the media to the application was not a reason to grant the application but it showed that they did not believe there had been a significant inhibition of the exercise of their rights under Article 10. In any event, it was open to the media to apply to have the injunction lifted at any time.

(Maxine Carr v News Group Newspapers HC 2005)

The judge accepted that any order which affects Convention rights to freedom of expression must be proportionate and necessary. Public debate over matters of legitimate interest to do with the case, such as the cost of providing a new identity and police protection, would still be possible if the order were continued, as they did not require the revelation of her new name, location and work.

Nick Armstrong, a partner in the Media Group of City Solicitors Charles Russell, argued in *Press Gazette*: 'But how could the result have been any different when certain members of the community are prepared to maim or even kill individuals like Carr who are associated with certain kinds of crime? And in so far as that brutal and moronic reaction is fuelled by inflammatory journalism, the media should maybe look to certain elements within their own ranks before complaining too loudly about erosions of freedom.' (Armstrong *Press Gazette* 2005)

Mr Justice Eady concluded his ruling by saying: 'I am satisfied that the only effective means of discharging the court's protective duty is to grant the injunction in the terms sought. It is necessary to protect life and limb and psychological health.' The injunction bans publication of any details that could reveal her new identity, including any description of where she lives and the nature of her work.

Her QC, Edward Fitzgerald, had argued that the order was 'amply justified' on the grounds laid down in the previous cases of the child killers Jon Venables and Robert Thompson, and Mary Bell, where similar permanent injunctions had been granted. He said: 'There is a real and significant risk of injury or of worse – killing – if the injunction is not granted.' (Rozenberg *Daily Telegraph* 2005; Dyer *Guardian* 2005) Mr

Fitzgerald outlined examples of people mistaken for Carr who had been assaulted or threatened, and read out comments from Internet chat-rooms that included: 'The nonce bitch deserves to die'; 'I would glass her if she was in my local'; and 'I hope she gets what's coming to her and there are some nutters out there who will probably harm her if they recognise her.' (Ibid.) Mr Fitzgerald submitted: 'These are just examples taken in conjunction with the numerous attacks and threats on people mistaken for Maxine Carr. Those expressions of intent to kill or attack indicate there is, as police believe, a very real or significant risk of harm if this injunction is not maintained until further orders. [...] There is a very real risk to her mental health if her whereabouts, identity and details of her care and treatment are published.' (Ibid.)

Mr Fitzgerald listed incidents in which women who had been mistaken for her had been threatened, harassed and abused. A woman was attacked in daylight in Grimsby, Carr's home town; a mob in Leicester threatened to firebomb the home of a family they believed to be sheltering Carr; a woman in Derbyshire who looked like her was harassed and threatened; a woman was spat at in a supermarket in Chepstow; and a woman in East Kilbride became the victim of a hate campaign, with a mob gathering outside her home and death threats on the Internet. Mr Fitzgerald emphasized: 'Those matters indicate the level of risk that there is to her if her identity and whereabouts become known.' (Ibid.) His client had been given a new identity since leaving Foston Hall women's prison in Derbyshire in April 2005, after serving half of a 42-month sentence.

He said there was also evidence of a very real risk to Carr's own mental health. The evidence supporting the application was overwhelming. The ruling and media reports of the case do not disclose whether the police had been able to fully investigate all of the threats made against her to the extent of tracing and identifying the authors and then prosecuting them.

This course of action could be argued as a process of maintaining the rule of law and the protection necessary in any society for an individual to be able to go about her business in her original identity, without fear of reprisal. The continuation of an injunction permitting Maxine Carr to live in the shadows absolved the wider community of their responsibility to enable her to be rehabilitated into the community having served her punishment, and discharged the criminal justice process of deterrent. Courts are obliged to preserve the right to life, and society is obliged to respect the rule of law by not harassing discharged prisoners.

The hearing lasted only forty-five minutes and the judge also received a submission from Anthony Hayden QC, representing the police and Probation Service, who argued that there was a 'cogent and significant and sustained risk' to her life. (Ibid.) Carr had received a number of threatening letters from someone who, detectives said, was forensically aware and organized. It was reported that she had to wear a bullet-proof vest when she went out. These submissions clearly indicated real and cogent evidence that the threat to life was real.

Mr Fitzgerald conceded that the press and the public had a right to communicate and receive information on matters of legitimate public concern. However, he pointed out that:

> The press have clearly felt free to publish many matters about her; most of them have been untrue. [...] She has not been in a position to defend herself against the many allegations that have been made without sacrificing the protection of the limited anonymity granted to her on which the protection of her life and limb depend. [...] It is not true that she told Ian Huntley to burn the bodies of Holly and Jessica, nor that she sought to conceal the physical evidence of that crime. It is not true that she has been writing love letters to Ian Huntley. She has had no contact with him since the trial.
>
> (Ibid.)

He added that she had also not negotiated a book deal and was not seeking in any way 'to profit by selling her story for publication.' (Ibid.) She had not, as suggested in some publications, been living a pampered, luxurious lifestyle. She had not gone for a 'drink-fuelled weekend in a caravan with a boyfriend as alleged.' (Ibid.) She had not been rescued by a helicopter from a baying mob, at a cost of £15,000 to the taxpayer. He concluded: 'I stress that the press are free, if they consider there are legitimate matters of public concern which cannot be published because of the injunction, to make an application to the court, and obviously at such time the merits would be considered.' (Ibid.)

The *Independent* newspaper published an editorial holding the popular media fully responsible for this abrogation of freedom of expression, as well as for the agony and suffering Maxine Carr was being forced to endure:

> It is a sad reflection on the viciousness of certain sections of British society that Mr Justice Eady felt it necessary to issue a court order yesterday granting Maxine Carr anonymity for life. Ms Carr has paid her debt to society and is not a danger to anyone. In a rational world, she would be allowed to get on with her life, like any other normal person without needing extra protection from the law.
>
> (*Independent* 2005)

The newspaper supported the legal measure being taken to injunct the media in order to contribute to her protection:

> The reason why such extreme measures are necessary is because Ms Carr has good reason to believe that if her whereabouts are published,

she will be hunted down by a lynch mob. The Soham case led to an intense outpouring of grief and anger in this country. Much of this anger has been directed towards Ms Carr. And despite the fact that almost three years have passed since the murders, threats to Ms Carr's safety have actually intensified.

(Ibid.)

The *Independent* charged the popular press, generally known as 'tabloid newspapers', with being a party to mob justice: 'Populist newspapers must bear a heavy burden of responsibility for this. Ever since Ms Carr was first implicated in the murders, they have attempted to build her up into a national hate figure.' (Ibid.)

The Channel 4 television documentary *Witch-hunt: First Cut: Being Maxine Carr: Whispering Campaign*, broadcast on 14 December 2007, provided disturbing evidence that the risks to Maxine Carr remain and that there was a manifestation of a social phenomenon generated by the intensification of hatred and demonization, as well as the possibility of a boomerang effect caused by the secrecy impact of the injunction. As the media cannot identify the real Maxine Carr, communities everywhere have no assurance or guarantee that somebody they believe to be Maxine Carr is not a case of mistaken identity. An example of the witch-hunt mentality facing regional police forces was reported in *The West Briton* in January 2007:

Police have issued a statement denying rumours that Maxine Carr, who was the girlfriend of Soham killer Ian Huntley, is living in Penryn. There have been claims of sightings of her and feelings in the town have been running high. Out of their concern that the situation was 'getting out of hand', Cornwall and Devon police have released a statement quelling speculation. [...] Car stickers have appeared and residents have put up posters in a demonstration that Maxine Carr would not be welcome in Penryn. Concerned parents had contacted a local school and a petition was being organised.

(*West Briton* 2007)

The Channel 4 documentary's investigation confirmed a pattern of Maxine Carr lookalike witch-hunting throughout the United Kingdom, including Northern Ireland. One of the victims was Carol Symington, a single mother who had moved to Redcar in Teesside and who was seventeen years older than the person local people believed her to be. Whispers spread quickly that she was Maxine Carr. A small mob gathered outside her little terraced house, called her out and threw a brick through one of the windows. Then, later, an angry vigilante wrestled her to the ground and started tugging at her blonde hair, believing that she was Maxine

292

Carr wearing a wig. Ms Symington told the Channel 4 researchers: 'I'd just been given the house by the local housing association. [...] We'd been looking forward to having a new home, a fresh start to our lives. [...] It was that first evening, you know – we'd only been in the house a few hours. It had got dark, and suddenly they were calling "Maxine. Come out, Maxine. You can't live here. We're not going to leave you alone. We're not going to give you any peace."' (Ginnane 2007)

Carol Symington even tried to show her vigilante group her passport in a bid to stop the attacks. But this constructive and, some would say, more than reasonable and conciliatory response, provoked a second round of abuse. She told the programme: 'Bricks at the windows, things being lobbed into the garden, bottles, calling. The constant calling of my name; my name as Maxine Carr, not as Carol.' (Ibid.)

A year after moving into her new home in Redcar, Symington was forced to move out.

The programme reported that more than a dozen British women had been forced to move home after being mistaken for Maxine Carr. The photo of Holly Wells and Jessica Chapman in their Manchester United jerseys had become an iconic image in Britain, one people would never forget. And so had the police photograph of Maxine Carr. Its notoriety became equal to that of Myra Hindley, the Moors Murderer. The phenomenon of Maxine Carr lookalikes being attacked has snowballed into a twenty-first-century, postmodernist manifestation of witch-hunting.

Karen Meek, a 32-year-old woman originally from Sussex, received death threats after moving from Brighton to Coleraine, in Northern Ireland. As the attacks continued, police informed her that it was because of rumours she was Maxine Carr in hiding. She stated during the documentary: 'I was sick and angry. [...] If I move to the moon it would not be far enough. I still feel angry.' (Ibid.) When rumours swirled so thickly that Maxine Carr had moved into town, the local paper, the *Coleraine Times*, sought legal advice on whether it could run the story. Eventually the paper published on the front page that Maxine Carr was in town, after receiving legal advice that the injunction did not apply in Northern Ireland. But the report was completely wrong and, as a consequence Ms Meek said, the pressure and distress led her to take an overdose towards the end of 2006.

Implications for privacy law and cultural studies

The witch-hunting of Maxine Carr raises a considerable range of cultural, social and feminist issues and is clearly fertile ground for empirical and textual content analysis in a variety of academic disciplines. It seems that in a post-industrial and postmodernist information age of porous trans-national multimedia boundaries, the combination of speed with viral media properties and ancient/medieval social paranoia and prejudice has the potential to reach everywhere. The 'Is my new neighbour Maxine Carr?' whispering phenomenon has even reached the Australian media, largely because of speculation she had been relocated there. (Kent, *Herald Sun* 2007) However, in the field of media law and ethics, Britain is developing a stark departure in its application of privacy and human rights protection to trial participants and acquitted and convicted defendants in its criminal justice system, which would be alien and bizarre in any American legal forum. There is no evidence in any of the British authorities that the courts have any confidence in the media exercising compassionate and ethical discretion in cases where, in the USA, there might be an ethical discretion to avoid identification. The consistent policy is to assume that the rule of law cannot protect vulnerable and sensitive individuals from psychiatric nemesis or vigilante and terrorist reprisal if, to use the words of Mr Justice Ouseley, 'the media thirst for detailed and accurate news in the public interest' (Times *v* Home Office re: AY 2009) is engaged.

American jurists could well argue that the British courts risk sacrificing freedom of expression and open justice because it is too expensive to protect trial participants from violent reprisals. What kind of indictment of British society and its indigenous communities is engendered when there is no confidence or even hope that individuals tried and punished by the legal system cannot be expected to resume their lives and rehabilitate themselves into the community, having served their sentences? A fair question to ask is: where is the rule of law if freedom of expression must be extinguished because neither the judges nor the police have the financial resources, power and support to deter the harassment, intimidation, reprisal and threat to life of people involved in legal proceedings? There is no shortage of assertion and eloquent statement of US concepts about the media being the watchdogs of democracy. But for every step forward in precedent there seems to be a distinguishing compromise of principle that then becomes fertile ground for further confidentiality, secrecy and anonymity based on rights jurisprudence. In 1993 it was argued that the need for the identities of witnesses and of defendants in some cases to be secret from the public would be a rare exception. In 2009 it is a common and systematic practice, discouraged by the occasional precedent, but legalized by legislation. Is it at all inconceivable to predict that in another fifteen years visiting American journalists, lawyers and judges will be pondering the wide and regular phenomenon of the anonymous criminal?

6

MEDIA REGULATION

There is a consistent recurrence in any historical study of critical texts on the ethical performance of the media in either the USA or UK. This is a discourse on 'journalism crisis'. There never was a time when lawyers, politicians, academics, and journalists themselves were not condemning the evils of the 'Fleet Street of Shame' or the 'yellow press.' Even the first historian of the UK and Irish National Union of Journalists, F.J. Mansfield, was writing in 1943:

> Within the last few years the methods of sensational journalism have become invested with a sinister significance. This kind of journalism is far from new; in fact it is as old as the Press itself. Some of those who have studied our earliest papers will agree with Mr R.D. Blumenfeld when he says that sixteenth century journalists were adept in the arts of yellow journalism, and that 'no modern newspaper could rival the news records of that time for sensationalism.'
>
> (Mansfield 1943: 523)

In 2008 Mike Farrell, in the third edition of Roy L. Moore and Michael D. Murray's *Media Law and Ethics*, explained that in the USA where there is no national or local system of press councils and press complaints commissions, and journalists do not have to be members of professional bodies such as the Radio-Television News Directors Association or Society of Professional Journalists:

> The absence of these responsibilities and the performance of the media have undermined public support for the First Amendment and for journalists. A seemingly unending list of public opinion surveys has found that the public holds journalists and the press in low regard. [...]
>
> Stupidity and arrogance, however, are not the most troubling issues for journalists. The too-frequent lapses of ethical practice by those who call themselves journalists undermine confidence in the news

media. Obviously, when the public has little trust in the media, the effort to publish news the public finds credible becomes much more difficult.

(Farrell 2008: 106, 108)

The existing ethical codes of the main US media associations are available online and in leading American media law textbooks. (Moore and Murray 2008: 733–48)

In a detailed researched submission to the UK House of Commons enquiry into libel, privacy and media regulation in 2009, media lawyer Jonathan Coad of Coad & Swan Turton solicitors observed:

> In his book '*The Insider*' Piers Morgan (who edited both *The News of the World* and *The Mirror*) told us that the press was becoming progressively more powerful and aggressive. In his evidence to the Culture Media and Sport Committee on 25 September 2003, Max Clifford stated that '*Paul Dacre* [Editor of *Daily Mail*] *is virtually a law unto himself.*' A feral press is not a new problem; the military dictator Napoleon Bonaparte observed that '*Four hostile newspapers are more to be feared than 1000 bayonets.*' The great campaigner for the abolition of slavery, William Wilberforce was concerned about the press of his époque misleading its readers over the key political issues of the day.
>
> (H of C Select Committee 2009, Swan Turton Solicitors)

In the US John C. Merrill, in his 1997 text *Journalism Ethics: Philosophical Foundations for News Media*, declared: 'Criticism of the media is crashing in from all sides. Journalism and its practitioners increasingly are being cast as social villains, dispensing superficial, negative, and sensational information harmful to the health of society.' The Hutchins Commission studied the US Press during and after the Second World War and its 1947 report is often cited as historical evidence of the US media's socially irresponsible past. However, historicist treatments of the report often fail to contextualize the fact that the commission was criticized at the time for having no experienced journalists or editors, and in the words of Frank Hughes in his 1950 vituperative polemic, *Prejudice and the Press: A Restatement of the Principle of Freedom of the Press with Specific Reference to the Hutchins-Luce Commission*:

> it is propaganda and not scholarship. [...] None of the members have more than a remote acquaintance with the industry the 'commission' sought to investigate, and they made no moves, in three years, to get acquainted with it, unless by hearsay. Objectivity may be a virtue, but the objectivity of ignorance has never produced anything socially useful, nor is it considered to be scholarly.
>
> (Hughes 1950: 24–5)

Plate 9 Capitol Hill, Washington DC. This photograph, taken in 1913 and showing preparations for the swearing-in ceremony of President Woodrow Wilson, illustrates a confident neoclassical architecture accommodating judiciary and legislature delineated by written constitution.

Plate 10 The Palace of Westminster in London is the seat of British parliamentary power, but how much of it is ceded to the 'confederated' European Union and a transnational European Court of Human Rights in Strasbourg that, critics say, has the pretensions of trying to be a Supreme Court for Europe?

There has never been any shortage of complex, sincere and systematic analysis and advocacy of journalism media ethics in the UK and the USA. Mansfield sets out the first British code of ethics agreed by the National Union of Journalists in 1936. (Mansfield 1943: 527–28) The original code emphasized journalists' economic context and disadvantages in the middle of a decade when Great Britain and other countries were trying to recover from global recession. The leading early twentieth-century US textbook on journalism practice, *Handbook for Newspaper Workers* by Grant Milnor Hyde, published in 1926, contained a detailed thirty-eight page chapter on 'Applied Ethics' with maxims, homilies and principles that remain the engaging issues concerning the ethics of journalism in 2009. (Hyde 1926: 204–42) Norman J. Radder's seminal *Newspaper Make-up and Headlines*, published in 1924, had chapters devoted to 'The Law of Libel' and 'The Ethics of the Headline'. Journalism ethics were being widely taught in US universities with degrees in journalism through the 1920s and 1930s, and texts such as *Ethics and Practices in Journalism* by Albert F. Henning (1932) were prominently cited on reading lists.

The US and UK media industries in 2009 were straining under the ravages of recession, and the crisis in media ethics fused with the crisis language of economics when a media analyst reported to a UK House of Commons committee that up to half of the country's 'local and regional newspapers could shut within the next five years as revenues continued to decline.' (Brook *Guardian* 2009)

But Jonathan Coad warned British MPs not to be deceived by the apparent woes of media recession into emasculating a civil law cost remedy (conditional fee agreements) which enabled the poor as well as the rich to sue for libel:

> The total cost of CFA claims is under £5 million. Set against Paul Dacre's £1.2 million package, the Fleet Street turnover of £6.5 billion and profit of £1 billion and advertising revenue alone of £1.8 billion, this hardly merits any serious consideration on the part of Parliament to change the law.
>
> (Coad written evidence to House of Commons 2009)

The Press Complaints Commission Code of Ethics

Unlike the USA, the UK has a national system of print media regulation administered by the Press Complaints Commission (PCC). The PCC is charged with enforcing the Code of Practice, which was framed by the newspaper and periodical industry. The Code appears to be subject to a continual process of change and evolution. There have been more than thirty versions since the first was published in 1991. But the PCC does not have a particularly good press. Geoffrey Robertson QC has been scathing:

> The deal that has been done allows Britain to snigger over what people are like in bed rather than worry about what they are like in their bank accounts or business dealings. The apogee of this state of hypocrisy is a body called the Press Complaints Commission (formerly the Press Council), funded by newspaper proprietors as an insurance policy against the advent of privacy laws. Every time there is an outrageous invasion and it is said that the press are 'drinking in the last chance saloon', the Commission is there to find an excuse for the saloon never closing. It will promote endless amendments to its 'code of conduct' which everyone knows will be ignored by editors in the interests of circulation, because breaches involve no fines or payments of compensation to victims.
>
> (Robertson 1999: 350–1)

The distinguished media historian James Curran has also conferred a negative judgment on the role of the PCC and its predecessor, the Press Council. When it was set up in 1953 it bore very little relation to 'The General Council of the Press' advocated by the Royal Commission on the Press four years earlier. Curran writes that these good intentions promised 'a well-funded and widely respected public body concerned not only with investigating complaints but also with such matters as the recruitment and education of journalists and the promotion of substantial research into the press.' (Curran and Seaton 1991: 287) But it became enfeebled by compromises. The 1977 Royal Commission on the Press, for which Curran served as an academic researcher, made twelve recommendations for reform. Nine were ignored, and he argues that public and political confidence continued to decline:

> The Press Council continued much as before. Its central weakness remained unchanged: It was a toothless watchdog, which was not taken seriously by the papers, which it most often criticized. In 1981 the National Union of Journalists, which had been pressing for reform of the Council, withdrew from it as a mark of the union's lack of confidence in the Council's proceedings.
>
> (Ibid.)

In June 2004 the PCC began implementing a programme of 'permanent evolution' – a policy conceived by its then chairman Sir Christopher Meyer. This means that the PCC's Code Committee conducts an annual 'audit' or 'health check' of the Code. It takes submissions from the print industry, members of the public and the Commission itself.

The preamble was changed and expanded:

> to re-emphasise that editors and publishers have the ultimate duty of care to implement the Code; to stress that its rules apply to all editorial contributors, including non-journalists; to make clear that it covers online versions of publications as well as printed copies; and to insist that publications which are criticised in adverse adjudications include a reference to the PCC in the headline.
>
> (PCC 2004)

New editions since June 2005 have tried to respond to a combination of change in media law, fashion in media moral panics and issues raised by pressure groups, political pressure in Parliament and changes or patterns in the nature of complaints.

The print industry funds the PCC annually with a budget of more than £1.5 million. The PCC has been criticized as a body dominated by the interests of print industry proprietors and members of the political and state establishment. Although it claims to be a 'voluntary' and self-regulatory body it can also be seen as an expedient industry buffer between the freedom of the press, its independent responsibility and state control and regulation.

The chair of the press scrutiny charity MediaWise, Louis Blom-Cooper QC, said Lord Devlin's warning that a Press Council body should 'never allow itself to become mostly a tribunal which convicts or acquits' has come to pass. (Blom-Cooper 2004: 6)

Non-media representation tends to be dominated by academics. The PCC took over from the old Press Council in January 1991, after the first highly critical parliamentary report on Privacy and Related Matters by David Calcutt QC. Calcutt believed the PCC, unlike the old Press Council, should not be involved in press freedom issues. Transgressions of the Code can lead to dismissal and unemployment. The control is therefore surrogate and privatized in the work arena. The evaluation of journalistic conduct is also undertaken without the basic standards of due judicial process. Complaints are evaluated on the basis of paper submissions. There is no apparent provision for individual journalists to separate their position and argument from that of their employing organization. Professor Chris Frost offers a detailed analysis of the origin and operation of the PCC in the first and second editions of his book *Journalism/Media Ethics and Self-Regulation*. (Frost 2000: 205–11; 2007: 204–33)

There is a continuing debate focusing on the justice and effectiveness of the remedies available to readers who believe they have been wronged by newspapers. The debate engages significant empirical research into the operation of the PCC by Professor Chris Frost in his article 'The Press

Complaints Commission: a study of ten years of adjudications on press complaints' in *Journalism Studies*. (Frost 2004: 101–14)

Robertson and Nicol highlight the PCC's obvious weakness in not having any powers to financially penalize offending publications, which Ofcom has. It shares with the statutory regulator of broadcasting, Ofcom, the impotence of not being able to award compensation to people wronged by misconduct. As a result, powerful media celebrities are increasingly bypassing the PCC and seeking media privacy remedies in the courts. (Robertson and Nicol 2008: 757–815)

In the 2009 House of Commons Select Committee enquiry the leading media law firm Schillings identified four key PCC failings in: not being able to make findings of fact or declarations of falsity of allegations; not making a monetary award of compensation in appropriate cases; not compelling witnesses or ordering disclosure; and not dealing effectively with pre-publication disputes. The firm also said there was a general public perception that the PCC is 'too favourable to the media; accordingly there is a lack of public confidence in using this route to resolve serious complaints against the media.' (H of C Select Committee 2009, Schillings)

The solicitor Jonathan Coad, with eighteen years' experience in media law practice, submitted a paper to the Select Committee that was also highly critical of the PCC's constitution and performance:

> The PCC's structural and institutional lack of independence, which is evident from its constitution, personnel and practice, fatally compromises any regulatory role it has.
>
> The power of the press to wreck lives is no small issue. I have acted for clients who have had nervous and physical breakdowns, seen their marriages destroyed and even attempted suicide in the face of press onslaughts. [...]
>
> A Commission which has been set up by the press, administering a Code written exclusively by the press, which is funded by the press and whose staff members are ultimately employees of the press is not likely to inspire confidence.
>
> If you add to this that 7 of the 17 commissioners are newspaper editors, no right for complainants to attend adjudications, and no substantive right to appeal then inevitably alarm bells ring. [...]
>
> It is inconceivable that a body of commissioners can both lobby and campaign on behalf of the press, and also form disinterested judgments on whether it has abided by the terms of its Code, a Code which of course the Commission itself has also written via a committee which has no lay members.
>
> (Coad written evidence House of Commons 2009)

The Press Standards Board is the body which manages the PCC and it publishes a codebook of PCC precedents. *The Editor's Codebook* was first published in 2005, with a second edition in 2009 (Beales 2009) that brings together the PCC Code of Practice and its 'case law.' It is intriguing that the PCC should legitimize its decisions as 'case law' when there are no oral hearings and forensic examination of issues in either the inquisitorial or the adversarial model, and no system of appeal. The Press Standards Board was upbeat about PCC efficacy:

> The PCC itself has proved to be an efficient and accessible regulator. Numbers of complaints – a sign not of declining press standards, but of ever increasing public awareness of the PCC – have grown steadily over the years, as has the Commission's record in resolving them. The latest statistics show that over 80% of possible breaches of the Code were resolved.
>
> Furthermore, the system has shown that it has the ability to adapt not just to the public's expectations – as happened in the wake of the death of Diana, Princess of Wales – but crucially to changes in technology. In 2007, the PCC's remit was extended by the industry to include on-line audio-visual material in a speedy and flexible manner that would have been impossible under any form of statutory system.
>
> (Press Standards Board 2009: para 6–7)

In deciding to regulate Internet content, the PCC has been more pioneering than either Parliament or the statutory broadcasting regulator, Ofcom. But such optimism cannot displace a growing argument that the PCC Code is no longer a buffer between the operation of the legal system and ordinary citizens. The Judiciary is now obliged by statute to treat the Code as a jurisprudential reference point in a growing number of media legal disputes. The claim by the newspaper industry that the PCC is the only way to check the introduction of more reporting restrictions and oppressive media law can be shown to be wrong in the face of an avalanche of new case law and legislation affecting journalists since 1980. The argument that the PCC provides the only remedy to poor people who cannot afford to seek redress in the courts has been challenged by the operation of conditional fee agreements.

Abolitionists say perhaps it is now time to liquidate the PCC and dismantle this complex framework of regulatory harassment for journalists. Genuine grievances would be resolved by the existing legal system with due process of law and proper representation. Working journalists would be spared the burden of gratuitous complaints. Most genuine complaints would be able to seek proper redress in the courts. Abolition would halt the growth of secondary media law.

302

But the PCC Code and its decisions have spawned a canon of jurisprudence and this represents another body of knowledge and training for the working journalist. It cannot be ignored. Media lawyers now see it as significant ordnance in the armoury of tactics and redress for their clients. Unlike the situation with the predecessor Press Council, complainants are not obliged to sign away their litigation rights. This means that the PCC is a good trial run for regulatory transgressions that overlap with existing law. Where primary law does not provide an avenue in the courts, the PCC process does provide a speedy opportunity for a potential right of reply and formalized declaration of correction. It is becoming increasingly apparent that solicitors are representing more PCC complainants. This is another sign of the growing transformation of the PCC into a quasi-judicial body.

The US public does not have this facility. Retraction statutes in some states certainly offer a compromise position between a complaint of defamation that is ignored and one that might eventually get to court. The False Light tort fills the vacuum that in British law is not covered by the media legal remedies of libel and privacy, and offers a refuge for those damaged by a highly offensive portrayal written with reckless disregard for the truth. Yet this is a legal process and involves the cost of litigation. Unlike the British PCC route it is not cost free.

The US media also have a long-established professional culture of readers' ombudsmen and fact checkers, and a popular media that is judged by some to be more deferential towards politicians and less aggressive in the pursuit of the sordid and tawdry subjects of life. And Zelezny reports on the existence of bench/bar/media committees that recognize the need for media publishers and key people in the justice system to resolve friction, mitigate disputes and reach understanding about each other's role in society: 'These groups of judges, lawyers, police officers and newspeople meet periodically to discuss problems, and, ideally, build cooperation.' (Zelezny 2004: 257) Zelezny reproduces the joint declaration of the bench, bar and news media committee in California. The American practice is something the British judiciary and media could certainly learn from. (Ibid.: 284–7)

Journalist associations, societies and newspaper publishers have been enthusiastic framers of ethical codes from as early as 1910, as in the case of the Kansas Editorial Association's Code of Ethics for the Publisher. (Frost 2007: 281) Apart from enthusiastic support for a Minnesota News Council, dedicated to the promotion of media fairness by encouraging the public to insist on responsible reporting and editing (ibid.: 282), there is little evidence of the American media industries rallying to establish stateside or federal press council bodies.

303

Regulatory secondary media law for UK and US broadcasters

From 1927, when Congress passed the Federal Radio Act, the US broadcast media have been subject to federal regulation that the print media has never experienced. Furthermore, Supreme Court cases such as *Red Lion Broadcasting v FCC* 1969 have made it clear that the scarce nature of the broadcast medium requires the federal government to license and regulate the broadcasting spectrum, despite the free press imperative of the First Amendment. The 1934 Federal Communications Act set up the Federal Communications Commission (FCC), which reigns supreme over broadcast licensing and regulation to the present day. Cable television is also regulated on a federal and state level.

The FCC applies government policies on broadcast licensing and content regulation. This applies legal restraints on station ownership, encouraging diversity of ownership, applying equal opportunity rules and policies that reflect the socio-economic politics of the time. For example, the Telecommunications Act of 1996 was seen as deregulatory in nature and encouraged acquisitions, mergers and multiple ownership across city markets. At one time all licensed US broadcast stations had to run a news service, but this requirement was withdrawn in the 1980s. Up until 1987 the FCC managed the content control, known as the 'fairness doctrine', which imposed a duty on each broadcast licensee to ensure that the full range of political viewpoints was always represented.

Complex rules and obligations still apply to the use of the airwaves by political candidates and include an 'equal opportunities rule' that can be triggered when a candidate is performing a broadcasting role outside the usual frame of news coverage. There are strict rules relating to advertising during children's television programmes.

Congress has prohibited indecency and obscenity in licensed broadcasting, and the FCC has a track record of imposing heavy fines as sanctions for transgression, particularly if it is judged that the material has been broadcast at a time when significant numbers of children have been listening or viewing.

The FCC and Ofcom face similar difficulties over the transition of broadcasting from analogue to digital spectrums. They share the experience of media group consolidation since the introduction of deregulatory policies, which have created a tension between the demand for more locally orientated broadcasting and the development of large conglomerates such as Clear Channel in the USA, with over twelve hundred radio stations, and Global Radio in the UK. However, Ofcom in the UK has shepherded the development of a community radio network that has some of the characteristics and ethos of the public radio stations and low-powered FM radio stations introduced in the US 1996 Telecommunications Act.

Broadcast media regulation in the UK has been wrapped up in the single statutory body called Ofcom since December 2003, when it took on the supervisory powers of the Broadcast Standards Commission (BSC) over taste and decency and privacy in relation to all broadcasters. But it also acquired sharper teeth, in that it had the power to fine the BBC for non-compliance with its regulatory authority on these matters. The BBC was a broadcasting monopoly until 1955 and has always tried to regulate itself. The UK did not establish a formal process of broadcast regulation until the inception of ITV regional companies in that year, and licensed independent radio in 1973.

British broadcasting has seen an accelerated process of centralization and privatized monopolization of regulation, production and transmission. A single commercial company now controls all of the licensed areas of television broadcasting in England. This must surely be a mockery of the principle of localized licensing. There is very little competition or diversity in the supply of television news and current affairs to the independent television networks. A similar trend has developed in the ownership and control of UK independent radio, with most of the power of news and programming in 2009 being in the control of a handful of large radio groupings, such as Global Radio. ITN and Sky are only the realistic alternatives for supplying commercial news to commercial television and radio broadcasters in the UK.

This centralization of control and capital is reflected in Ofcom's quasi-judicial and statutory controls over independent television, radio, advertising and, to some extent, BBC broadcasting.

The centralization of media regulatory power in Ofcom means that the prospect of its remit being extended to the print media has turned it into a sword of Damocles hanging over the newspaper and magazine industry. During the passage of the Communications Bill in 2003 the New Labour government was heavily lobbied to make Ofcom enforce the code of practice issued by the Press Complaints Commission. Junior Media Minister Lord McIntosh of Haringey rejected the call, saying:

> If you start to have a Government-inspired organisation like Ofcom imposing fines, the immediate reaction of the worst end of the press is that they will opt out of the Press Complaints Commission. Where is Ofcom going to be then? I cannot see why an editor would voluntarily sign up to a code that is meant to epitomise self-regulation if the code were to be enforced by Ofcom, a state regulator. The commission was under a constant obligation to itself and the people of this country to improve the code and its enforcement. There are lessons to be learned and I believe the commission's chairman, Sir Christopher Meyer, is learning them.
>
> (*Media Lawyer* July 2003: 44)

The idea of Ofcom regulating the print media as it does the broadcasting media is an ever-present threat, and the minister's comments above indicate how politicians expect the threat of legislative regulation of the print media to galvanize the PCC into invigorating the process of voluntary self-censorship.

Powers and penalties – the quasi-criminal sanctions for broadcast breaches of privacy, taste and decency

The BBC, as the UK's main public service broadcaster, has tried to establish its own sophisticated structures of codes and compliance on standards and ethical conduct. It could be said that its 'Editorial Guidelines' amount to the most detailed and transparent document on public broadcasting responsibility in the world.

It was clear that the BSC and its predecessor bodies had been given a duplicated regulatory control over the BBC under the 1990 and 1996 Broadcasting Acts. The BBC sought to challenge the jurisdiction of these bodies by way of judicial review in the High Court. The problem with judicial review is that it can involve only a legal assessment of the process of regulation rather than the merits of the regulatory decision.

Rulings by the BSC had no financial impact on the BBC. But fines have accompanied rulings by Ofcom. This development sprang from the recommendations of a joint House of Commons and Lords committee chaired by the filmmaker Lord Puttnam. The committee said that the BBC should be subject to the fines in order to demonstrate a level playing field between the BBC and other broadcasters and make the BBC 'more accountable' to viewers and listeners. It can be argued that there is disturbing reverse logic to these points.

If the penalty system operating against independent broadcasters is flawed from the point of view of freedom of expression and due process, how can progress be achieved by extending it to the BBC? Furthermore, accountability to its audience is hardly achieved by fining the BBC through the licence fee. The fining system becomes an ad hoc additional level of taxation. Licence fee payers are footing the bill for mistakes made by the BBC.

Ofcom has become a punitive body with statutory powers against British electronic communicators breaching laws on taste, decency, fairness and privacy that have been constructed by non-elected bureaucrats. The BBC Editorial Guidelines remain an orbit of self-regulation administered by the BBC Trust, itself a replacement for the BBC's Board of Governors in order to create the appearance of more distanced and independent accountability. The penalties for BBC staff and freelancers who transgress the Guidelines rise as far as dismissal, and denial of future employment and commissioning.

The Ofcom code is enforceable throuh statutory powers of financial penalties and licence suspension and withdrawal. The intention of Ofcom was that its new supercode (introduced in July 2005) would be 'proportionate, consistent and targeted.' (Ofcom 2004) But the pattern of fines has been on a scale that is disproportionate in relation to those imposed in the criminal courts. It started with one of Ofcom's predecessor bodies, the ITC (Independent Television Commission), imposing a fine in 1998 of £2 million ($3.4 million) on Carlton Television for a documentary, *The Connection*, about cocaine smuggling from Colombia. Originally broadcast in 1996, the programme contained non-signposted dramatization. A short summary of the narrative is set out in Table 6.1.

Table 6.1 Who's to watch the watchdog? The story of *The Connection* and the *Guardian*

October 1996: ITV broadcasts *The Connection*, a documentary that claims to expose a new heroin route from Colombia to the UK. The film presented a rare documentation of the way drugs are smuggled: being swallowed by a 'mule' and then carried on a plane, straight to the streets of London, in just 24 hours. The documentary, produced by Carlton TV, was sold to fourteen countries, won eight international prizes and was described by the Royal Television Society as 'an exceptional journey into the world of drug-trafficking'.

May 1998: *The Guardian*, in a two-part investigative article, claims that the film 'is an elaborate fake ... the true story of Carlton's programme is one of lies, broken promises and the lust for ratings and prizes'. This is a result of 6 months' investigation carried out by Michael Sean Gillard and Laurie Flynn.

Some of claims against *The Connection*:

1   It was not a 24-hour journey; the sequences were filmed in two legs, six months apart.
2   The 'mule', therefore, did not carry drugs in his stomach when he flew to the UK.
3   The man described as the No. 3 in the Colombian cartel is a retired banker with low-level connections to the drugs underworld.
4   The production paid for the flight of the 'mule' from Colombia to the UK.
5   The main source for the story was the researcher of the film, an inexperienced freelancer, originally from Colombia, who had a financial dispute with Carlton.

Later in 1998: *Hard News* on Channel 4 asked: did the *Guardian* stand up for its own professional standards? *Guardian* editor Alan Rusbridger defended his reporters, and it could be argued that their robust approach to interviewing was appropriate when dealing with media professionals who were themselves well-practised in the rituals of news gathering.

The ITC, following the *Guardian*'s story, decided to fine Carlton 2 million pounds for 5 breaches of the ITC Programme Code exposed by the paper.

Source: Summary by Anat Balint

The Channel 4 programme *Hard News: Did you Fake this Film Marc?* investigated the ethical inadequacies of the documentary and the *Guardian* newspaper's exposé of the programme's fakery and deception. *Hard News* questioned the style of interviewing adopted by the *Guardian* reporters and the fact that one of them had worked previously with an interviewee, but these complaints were not on the same scale as the reporters' exposé of fakery that the then television regulator, ITC, described as a 'wholesale breach of trust' with the viewers. Even if there had been a complaint to the PCC, any remedy, if proven, would have amounted to no more than a critical adjudication. The facts that no retributive remedies apply to PCC rulings, and that the ITC, like Ofcom, had the power to fine a broadcasting company millions of pounds, demonstrate a discrepancy in the comparative justice being meted out to unethical broadcasters on the one hand, and print publishers on the other.

Ofcom has imposed fines ranging from several hundred thousand pounds and up to £2 million on television and radio broadcasters that are found to have defrauded and deceived listeners and viewers who have taken part in fake or terminated competitions. In 2009 it collected £150,000 from the BBC for offensive prank calls made by leading comedy artists Jonathan Ross and Russell Brand to an elderly actor. ITV was fined £220,000 for failing to meet its quota for programme spending outside London.

It could be argued, at a time when independent broadcasting has been struggling to fulfil its public service obligations in relation to news provision, and when the only real victims of huge fines on the BBC are the viewers and listeners who fund it through the licence fee, that such penalties would serve a better social purpose by being compensatory in nature. Would it not be more constructive to divert the money for investment in the fund available to community radio broadcasters or public service broadcasting projects outside the BBC? In the USA, the FCC has a similar track record of large-scale fines, including $550,000 imposed on CBS for Janet Jackson's 'wardrobe malfunction' during the broadcasting of her appearance at the Super Bowl in 2004, and $3.6 million in 2006 on more than one hundred television stations which transmitted an episode of the missing persons drama *Without A Trace* that was judged to be indecent.

Restorative justice – a proposed solution for media content regulation and law

Restorative justice originated from the largely left-wing, pacifist and feminist field of 'policy entrepreneurs'. They were part of an intellectual and political movement that critiqued the inadequacies of punishment structures in Western criminal justice. In short, the restorative justice movement advocates alternative methods of social control, faith/religious based approaches to criminal justice, the abolition of existing criminal justice institutions, structures and practices, and their replacement with feminist and peacemaking criminology and the development of communitarian forms of social control.

Nils Christie is regarded as the leading proponent of the European critical criminological abolitionist tradition that seeks to challenge the criminalization and penalization paradigm. (Christie 2003: 21–30) Christie argues that there should be a substitution culture of compensatory solidarity so that victims receive material and status restitution for their suffering, and new communal rituals of grief, forgiveness and sorrow are engaged to deliver symbolic compensation. (Ibid.: 29) The ethics of care and solidarity have also spawned the concepts of participatory justice and redress. (Ibid.) Christie and other theorists proselytize the rhetoric of 'progressive transformative agendas' in the context of peacemaking and feminist ideologies.

The emergence of restorative justice as a criminal justice policy concern occurred because theorists such as Christie problematized the criminal justice process by alleging that the professionals participating in the system functioned as self-interested occupationalists, so that the state's overarching and centralized power deprived citizens of their powers of conflict resolution by dominating the control of conflict. (Ibid.: 22–3) He argued for a recentring of the victim, largely because the state had effectively ventriloquized and colonized the victim's role in the criminal justice process. (Ibid.: 27) Restorative justice offered an opportunity for victims to be more than mere evidence, to understand the nature of the criminal justice process, and to participate in the process and represent their own character. (Ibid.)

Could it not be argued that, given the fact that media law offences in terms of crime, civil torts and regulatory transgression deal mainly with victims' damaged emotions, restorative justice procedures would be a more effective remedy in resolving disputes?

Peacemaking criminology dances at the opposite end of the spectrum to retributive vengeance. It could be argued that delinquent media behaviour is increased rather then decreased by the process of legal and regulatory stigmatization and labelling. The standpoint is welfarism rather than penality. Progress can only be achieved by engaging with democratic, non-violent, non-oppressive forms of human society. This is the language of caring, reintegration, healing and compassion rather than indifference, marginalization, an eye for an eye, and pitiless deterrence. The theorist John Braithwaite advocated restorative justice as a way of resolving the problem of adversarial systems' removing, diluting and distorting shame and responsibility on the part of offenders. (Braithwaite 2003: 55) He argued that state-centred structures were anti-democratic. The due process model is adversarial and impersonal instead of consensual and human. (Ibid.: 62–3) Braithwaite's concerns parallel the feminist reading by Tauri and Morris that the male punitive paradigm is preoccupied with rationality and neglects the affective and emotional nature of most crimes. (Tauri and Morris 2003: 45)

Restorative justice is also underpinned by faith-based principles of reconciliation, in the context of forgiveness and tolerance as discoursed in the religious traditions of Buddhism, Hinduism, Islam, Judaism, Sikhism, Chinese religions and Christianity. (Muncie and McLaughlin 2005: 68)

Fundamentally, restorative justice has grown up as a result of seeking alternative solutions for the long-standing mainstream institutional players in crime and punishment. The doctrine is idealistic, but where there is a perceived need to deal with the chilling effect on freedom of speech and media content resulting from the overly retributivist nature of media laws, it offers a solution that could deliver more meaningful justice to media victims. The advocates hanker after the restorative methods of conflict resolution that dominated pre-state and proto-state societies. This could be described as the anthropological tradition of restorative justice. The inspiration often comes from the community practices of indigenous pre-colonial cultures such the Maoris of New Zealand, Aborigines of Australia and First Nation peoples of Canada and the USA. (Ibid.: 69)

The restorative justice movement seeks to contextualize its legitimacy in a communitarian aspiration at a time when liberal capitalist theory and practice are critiqued as discredited and morally bankrupt. Amitai Etzioni argues that the antidote to failed liberal market capitalism is a strengthening of civic order, moral virtue and community bonding. (McLaughlin et al. 2003: 3) The assertion of universal individual rights needs to be balanced by social responsibilities and obligations, a criticism often directed at powerful media publishers. The communitarian project therefore activates communal processes as the response to media 'crimes'. This is achieved by assisting victims and offenders by restoring shattered personal and social bonds. Media victims and offenders are encouraged to find ways of 'dealing with their trauma by re-establishing their community ties and reconnecting them to community values'. (Muncie and McLaughlin 2005: 70)

Restorative conferencing, media offence and the community

Restorative conferencing is the concept of restorative justice in practice. It requires face-to-face interaction between media offenders and victims, with community representatives acting as agents for reconciliation. This is what the UK PCC is not doing at present. Bazemore and Griffiths present a positive case for the restorative conference over courtroom adjudication. (Bazemore and Griffiths 2003: 83) The victims can represent themselves instead of being spoken for by barristers in the interests of the state or, in the case of PCC, complainants who feel disengaged by the adjudication through paper submissions that have no direct involvement in terms of human experience. They would have the opportunity of participating in a more personalized environment, disinvested with the trappings of courtroom ritual and formalities. (Ibid.: 79) The location and time is much more flexible and the conferences can be accommodated much sooner after an offending media publication. (Ibid.)

The absence of the rules of evidence enables the victims to release pent-up feelings of anger and hurt and they can feel much more confident about talking through the emotional harm of the media offence and its impact on their lives, and in this way they have a direct input into holding the publishers to account. (Ibid.: 83–4) At the same time the media offenders can make amends as a voluntary response that is not commanded by formal due process, they can express regret and apology without fearing the consequences in terms of damages, conviction and sentencing, they can accept responsibility for actions in the context of the wider community, and they can humanize their relationship with the victim. (Ibid.)

Restorative justice conferencing, therefore, offers a culturally appropriate ritual in which genuine shame, remorse and forgiveness can emerge as a harmonious communitarian trinity. However, such a ritualizing of the interaction between media offender and victim carries potential risks and disadvantages. Some media offenders may deploy the technique of neutralization, and such indifference would not only waste the victim's time, but plunge the victim into an experience of re-victimization. The media victim might also feel pressure to compromise by taking on too much responsibility for the event. The victim may have suffered a level of injury that far exceeds anything that the offender is capable of compensating for. (Ibid.: 90)

Existing restorative justice structure of the PCC

A close examination of the policies and ethos of the UK PCC suggests that its *modus operandi* and infrastructure of regulation supports the spirit of the restorative justice doctrine. In its written evidence to the House of Commons in 2009 the PCC observed that:

> Hardly any complainants ask the PCC for money, or for the publication to be fined. Rather, people seem to want problems dealt with quickly, sometimes privately, and in a meaningful way. The PCC offers a whole range of remedies to complaints about privacy intrusion, which would be lost if we moved to a formal, fines-based system of regulation.
>
> (H of C Select Committee 2009, PCC)

The PCC says that it can work to prevent media intrusion into perceived areas of privacy in the first place, and it has developed a range of restorative justice remedies set out in Table 6.2.

Table 6.2 The Press Complaints Commission's existing framework of restorative justice remedies in privacy

---

Quickly negotiate the removal of intrusive material from websites so that it does not get picked up elsewhere;

Organise legal warnings to be tagged to publications' archives to ensure private information is not accidentally repeated;

Encourage the destruction or removal of intrusive information from databases or libraries;

Obtain personal apologies from editors, and undertakings about future conduct;

Secure prominent public apologies;

Help negotiate agreed, positive follow up articles;

Use the power of negative publicity by 'naming and shaming' a publication's conduct in a critical ruling (which must be published in full and with due prominence by the editor);

Organise a combination of the above, or, depending on the circumstances, the purchase of specific items in order to make amends (a wheelchair, for example), ex gratia payments, or donations to charity.

Source: H of C Select Committee 2009, PCC written evidence

The PCC does have a declared restorative justice philosophy which is detectable in its lobbying for fewer statutory and state retributivist structures in media regulation:

> Clearly the globalisation and digitalisation of the media have presented new challenges to regulation. But these are surely powerful forces favouring deregulation of formal structures and a greater reliance on self-regulation, which is particularly appropriate with its emphasis on self-restraint, swift remedies, and collaboration.
>
> (Ibid.)

Recommendations for media law and regulatory reform in the UK and a model for the USA

If there is consensus that media freedom in the UK has been strangled by the combination of law that gives too much weight to rights cancelling out freedom of expression and to legal processes carrying costs that have a chilling effect on media investigation and expression, is there a solution that bridges the need for retributivist measures for extreme harm and transgression, and the restorative and compensatory framework envisaged in the restorative justice doctrine? I would argue that there is. Many of the problems addressed by all sides complaining about media abuse of power, oppressive and inhibiting libel and privacy laws could be achieved through a Media Freedom and Restorative Justice Act that would bring about the following:

1   Transfer all media law processes (criminal and civil) to a new system of 'Media Law courts' that would sit with single specialist judges to adjudicate on final disputes that could not be resolved through restorative justice/alternative dispute resolution conferences. The remedies would be fixed on the basis of published 'rights to reply' and a maximum compensation level of £10,000. Fines, imprisonment and damages would be struck from the lexicon of media law. The courts would address anything from libel and privacy, to contempt and breach of statutory reporting restrictions. I would suggest that the specialist Media Law courts would sit in first-tier High Court centres. This recognizes that the bulk of their business would probably take place in London, but regional centres would be able to operate to serve local media throughout the country. The compensation remedies would be available to identifiable 'victim' parties in the case of privacy and libel. In what were formally criminal matters, the compensation would be available for distribution on a discretionary basis, by the adjudicating judges, to victims of criminal cases which had been disrupted by irresponsible reporting. This could include defendants who had been the victims of miscarriages of justice, witnesses wrongly identified, or charities serving the interests of criminal trial participants where the targets for compensation were not so well defined.

2   Transfer all of the positive restorative justice functions of the existing Press Complaints Commission and the regulatory media content functions of the BBC and Ofcom to a single 'Media Law and Restorative Justice Commission' (MLRJC) constituted by Parliament in the form of an independent trust, jointly funded on a 50/50 basis by the broadcast and print/online industries and the state. The commission would perform the following functions:

3   Act as a law and ethical regulatory reform commission for evaluating and creating media law and regulation under a recognized constitutional principle established as a Rubicon in the Media Freedom and Restorative Justice Act:

'All media laws and regulatory procedures will apply a particular regard and importance to the freedom of information and freedom of the media in the United Kingdom.'

4   All complaints concerning media law and ethical transgression would at first instance go before the MLRJC for investigation and then potential consideration through restorative justice procedures of conferencing and alternative dispute resolution. The disputing parties would have an opportunity to meet, exchange views, agree to disagree and take no further action, and agree resolutions through private and/or public apology and compensation of up to £10,000. Public apology would be a remedy of apology and correction that would be agreed between the parties and appear on the media space of the offending publication. It would be limited to four hundred words in the case of online/print publication and two minutes in the case of broadcast publication. In the case of online publication, the apology/correction would be embedded on the web page of the offending publication after agreed deletions and changes had been carried out.

5   Where restorative justice processes have been unable to achieve a solution to the dispute, the cases would then go to the Media Law courts for trial. The remedies available to the Media Law courts would be no greater than those available in the restorative justice processes but they would be by order of the court. The courts would be constituted under civil jurisdiction so that their 'findings' would not amount to criminal offences. The Media Law courts would therefore have the status of the High Court. A right of appeal would be established to the Court of Appeal Civil Division and then to the Supreme Court. The higher courts would not be in a position to order higher remedies. However, they would have jurisdiction to try, under common law contempt, instances of deliberate flouting and refusal to comply with the Media Law court orders under the legislation.

6   The commission would be constituted in the proportion of 50 per cent of representatives from the print, broadcast and online publication industries, with 20 per cent (two-fifths) of representatives being nominated from unions representing members in the industries. The rest of the commission would include 10 per cent of media law specialist judges, 10 per cent democratically elected representatives from the Westminster Parliament, Northern Ireland Assembly, Scottish Parliament and Welsh Assembly, and 30 per cent of lay members. Each commission member would serve a term limited to three years and would be able to serve again after a gap of three years from the last time of service.

The commission plan would have some merits in relation to the reform of media law and regulation in the USA. It could standardize, on a federal basis, media self-regulation and the varying state remedies in media law. It would end the vagaries of the 'chilling effect' in US media law and the problem of strategic law suits against public participation. The Rubicon guiding the equivalent US congressional statute would, of course, be the First Amendment. The US specialist Media Law courts would be at federal District Court level and key media law jurisprudence development would use the existing federal appeals route to the US Supreme Court.

The seeds for developing a restorative justice infrastructure have already been planted in the media culture and legal systems of both countries. In evidence to the House of Commons Select Committee enquiry on 'Press Standards, Privacy and Libel' in 2009 a consortium of US publishers submitted:

> most US media organizations readily offer alternative dispute resolution. Many have ombudsmen who will make an independent investigation of any allegation of defamatory reporting and order corrections and apologies – sometimes after a very critical report on journalistic standards. Most internet services will be prepared to hyperlink the offending article to a letter of complaint, so that no-one will read it without being able to read the complainant's alternative presentation. Newspapers usually offer a right of reply by way of a letter to the editor.
>
> (US publishers written evidence to House of Commons 2009:
> para 7)

At the Times-Matrix Privacy Forum in 2009, the legal manager of Times Newspapers, Alistair Brett, argued in his personal capacity for the UK PCC to offer a form of 'bolt-on' arbitration service so that serious complainants would have the opportunity of negotiating compensation. He said that arbitration and alternative dispute resolution was a sensible answer to the legal costs problem generated by CFAs, where media legal disputes can run up costs of a million pounds and the damages amount to only £1,000. He advocated law reform so that 'some system of neutral mediation or arbitration' would be obligatory and CFA libel driven cases could go no further if the parties refused the option. (*Media Lawyer* May 2009: 18–19)

It is clear that mediation and arbitration are low-cost solutions to PCC, Ofcom and FCC media regulation, as well as in the UK and US media law systems, where sensible cost and compensation ceilings of £10,000 ($15,000) could bring to an end the problems of the chilling effect. In any new system each side should pay its own costs. Joint bench and media committees in the USA prove that journalists and judiciary can work together. Britain's Lord Chief Justice, Lord Judge, acknowledged this in October 2009 when writing the foreword to the second edition of the guide *Reporting Restrictions in the Criminal Courts*. He noted how media and judicial representatives worked together fully respecting each other's independence in order to address misunderstandings and problems caused by the imposition of reporting restrictions.

7

STATE AND NATIONAL
SECURITY LAW

Epithets on the intelligence world

In this chapter we investigate the meeting place between the worlds of
espionage and spying, and journalism. It could be said that this involves a
joint conference of two of the world's oldest and most reviled professions,
although law and prostitution sometimes compete in these bottom rank-
ings. Spies and journalists are somewhat alike in their skills, talents and
functions. They collect and analyse information. Journalists are supposed
to do so with transparency and an aspiration to impartiality. Spies, by
their very nature, dissemble, deceive, lie and cover up. The British writer
Malcolm Muggeridge had the privilege of being an outstanding exponent
in both professions and he advised that 'Diplomats and Intelligence agents,
in my experience, are even bigger liars than journalists, and the historians
who try to reconstruct the past out of their records are, for the most part,
dealing in fantasy.' (Muggeridge 1975: 163) He also warned that 'Secrecy
is as essential to Intelligence as vestments and incense to a Mass, or darkness to a Spiritualist séance, and must at all costs be maintained, quite
irrespective of whether or not it serves any purpose.' (Ibid.: 133)

The national security paradigm

All nation-states in the world define and preserve the notion of 'national
security' and 'national interest' with a range of draconian criminal laws
and civil legal powers to pursue breaches of confidentiality and attempts
to derive financial advantage from undermining it. It is also apparent
that international agreements setting out worthy rubrics on human rights
frequently qualify them in terms of national security. Articles 10 and 11
of the European Convention on Human Rights – Freedom of Expression
and Freedom of Assembly and Association are both subject to restrictions
'prescribed by law and necessary in a democratic society in the interests of
national security or public safety'. The ECHR in Strasbourg has a tendency
to give its signatory states more discretion or 'margin of appreciation' on

316

matters of national security than on matters of freedom of expression, privacy and reputation.

Fashionable theories about the death of the nation-state through globalization are not borne out by the robust legal measures taken by nation-states to preserve their security when it is threatened by publicity or information which is perceived to be harmful. The evidence suggests that the ideology of national security is, along with constitutions, currencies, military capability and language, part of the matrix of the nation-state. European unification did not prevent perceptions of national security justifying the detention without prompt trial of twelve British tourists on a plane-spotting holiday in Greece in 2001.

National security seems to be a motivating imperative that transcends the legal dignity of even friendly nations which are part of economic, political and defence alliances such as NATO and the EU. The intelligence agencies of national members spy on each other. A country's pursuit of its 'national interests' will override respect for the laws of its allies.

On the other hand, it has been said that without the security of the state no citizen would enjoy any rights or liberties. Niccolò Machiavelli, in his *Art of War*, *The Prince*, and *Discourses* always emphasized that a state has no real security without arms. A prince who attends to his pleasures more than he attends to his arms will soon find himself deposed. Machiavelli was in fact a supporter of government by the people, but even when its citizens ruled the Republic, he always emphasized that it needed to be secure.

Machiavelli also strongly linked the notions of good laws and strong arms. In *The Prince* he stated:

> The main foundations of every state, new states as well as ancient or composite ones, are good laws and good arms; and because you cannot have good laws without good arms, and where there are good arms, good laws inevitably follow, I shall not discuss laws but give my attention to arms.
>
> (Bull 1999: 38)

The case of Mordechai Vanunu

It has been alleged, and not necessarily proved, that Israel was prepared to pursue unlawful measures in foreign jurisdictions in order to kidnap Mordechai Vanunu and return him to trial in Israel for revealing to the *Sunday Times* the extent of Israel's nuclear weapons programme in the Negev desert. He was sentenced to eighteen years' solitary confinement. The summarized narrative of his case is set out in Table 7.1.

He was able to communicate the manner in which he had been deceived into a false romance by an Israeli woman agent, drugged and smuggled in

Table 7.1 The case of Mordechai Vanunu: from the Israeli nuclear research centre to the *Sunday Times* (to jail in Israel)

Mordechai Vanunu was working as a technician at the Israeli nuclear research centre in the Negev (southern Israel) between 1976 and 1985. He was fired and left Israel.

He moved to Australia and decided to convert to Christianity.

In 1986 he met the *Sunday Times* journalist Peter Hounam, flew with him to London and revealed to the paper many details on Israel's nuclear capability, including photographs that he had taken secretly while working in the research centre. The Israelis claim he was paid $75,000, but this was denied by the paper. Vanunu claims he was motivated by his anti-nuclear pacifist ideology.

In September 1986 he was captured in Rome by the Mossad (Israeli secret service) and was brought to trial in Israel. He was lured to Rome by a 'honey-trap' agent called 'Cindy', in order to avoid diplomatic tension between Israel and the UK.

A month later the *Sunday Times* published the story, which was considered to be the first solid proof of Israel's nuclear ability, and a breach of the country's policy of deliberate ambiguity.

Vanunu was charged with treason and espionage and was sentenced to 18 years in prison. He spent 11 years in isolation.

Even after his release in 2004, he has severe restrictions on his freedom, not being allowed to leave the country, nor to speak to journalists and foreign citizens. Security forces claim he can still reveal further state secrets.

He was sentenced to 3 months in prison for breaking the restrictions imposed on him by talking to foreign citizens on the Internet and contacting journalists.

In 1988 the identity of the Mossad agent 'Cindy' was exposed by the *Sunday Times*. This was published by an Israeli journalist (and an ex-intelligence officer), Uzi Mahnaimi.

Source: Compiled by Anat Balint

a crate, by sea, from Rome to Tel Aviv, only via ballpoint pen notes written in long-hand on his palm and pressed against the window of his prison van. His solitary confinement ended in 1998 after 12 years but, despite international human rights campaigns, he had to serve the full length of his sentence. On his release, he was subject to virtual house arrest and constant surveillance. His contact with foreign journalists has continued to expose him to legal jeopardy and further controls on his freedom of expression and association while he remains in Israel.

'National Security' had constructed Vanunu as a spy and traitor in Israel. Yet the globalizing nature of his ethical outlook, his opposition to nuclear proliferation, his belief that his own country was violating international arms control agreements, his deontological loyalty to the citizens of the

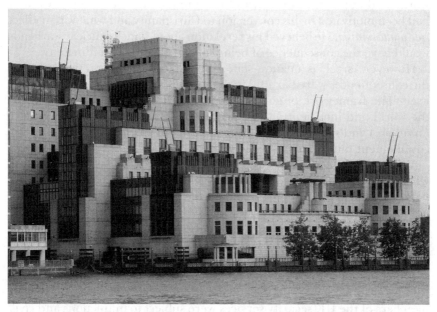

Plate 11 The headquarters of the British Secret Intelligence Service (MI6) at Vauxhall Cross, London. There is much less legislative and media scrutiny of the British intelligence services than of their equivalent bodies in the USA.

Plate 12 Anti-terrorism security on the River Thames, London. The growth of international terrorism, culminating in the attacks on America on 11 September 2001 and London on 7 July 2005, led to the governments in both countries passing laws said to curtail civil liberties.

world, and the democratic spirit of his country were no defence. Vanunu had been motivated by his conversion to Christianity and what was in effect *rule utilitarianism*. He believed his revelation about Israel's nuclear warheads would have the consequence of being for the benefit of all humanity.

However, Israel, as a nation-state, applied its own laws on the basis that the consequences were harmful to the greatest number of people in Israel itself. The framework of nation-state authority and law reached around the world and into neutral jurisdictions to seize him, try him in secrecy (*in camera*) and subject him to years of arguably disproportionate solitary confinement punishment.

Vanunu's alleged treachery was directly linked to his desire as an ethical whistleblower to reveal aspects of Israel's defence capability. However, national security is also constructed on the grounds of a *convicium* against national honour and economic interests.

The position for ethical secret service whistleblowers in the United Kingdom would appear to be somewhere between that of the USA and Israel. It attracted criticism from the UN Special Rapporteur on Freedom of Opinion and Expression in 2000 (Mendel 2000: 7) and the UN Human Rights Committee in 2008. A growing number of journalists and former members of the UK security services were subject to injunctions and civil/criminal prosecutions, and blocks to publication. In 2009 the British Court of Appeal said that it had no power to hear the case of a former senior MI5 officer who wished to publish his memoirs. The Director of Establishments of the Security Services has insisted that the former officer could only argue his case before the Investigatory Powers Tribunal, which ordinarily sits in secret and from which there is no right to appeal. (A v B CoA Civ 2009; *Media Lawyer* March 2009: 47)

British law had to catch up with the same kind of public-interest shield and constitutional safeguards that may be perceived in countries such as the USA, the Netherlands and Germany. In these countries the courts can examine government claims that national security has been harmed. In France an independent commission has access to classified information and decides whether the courts can have similar access.

US Supreme Court case law would suggest that the bar and restrictions on US intelligence officers who sign the contract on national security are roughly the same as those applying to members of MI5 or MI6. The First Amendment was crushed under the heel of national security in the case *Snepp v United States* in 1980.

Frank Snepp could not be regarded as a renegade former spy prone to blowing secrets or the names of agents. His book about his experiences and views of CIA service, *Decent Interval* (1977), contained the thoughts of a critical though patriotic American who believed and continues to believe that the nation needs the CIA, even covert action, albeit under strict rules of accountability. (Snepp 2009)

As in Britain, there are few secret service dissidents. Former CIA analyst Victor Marchetti and ex-CIA officer Philip Agee could be described as such. Agee was accused of writing books with the assistance of Soviet and Cuban intelligence, but he denied revealing information that cost lives.

The 1980 Supreme Court ruling ordered Frank Snepp to hand over to the US Treasury all profits, past and future, from his book, imposed a permanent gag order, and obliged him to submit to the CIA censors anything he might write about his service in fictional or non-fictional form. The decision was hardly different from the order by the House of Lords in 2000 that all the royalties earned from the publication of the memoirs of British traitor and former MI6 intelligence officer George Blake must be given to the government.

Frank Snepp subsequently developed a successful and award-winning career as a writer and journalist and he was allowed to publish *Irreparable Harm*, which analyses his legal battles, the Supreme Court decision in 1980 and the implications for free speech in America.

The British ethos on secrecy

The British state has maintained espionage and secret intelligence services throughout history, as Alan Haynes' book on Elizabeth I's security service illustrates. (Haynes 2001: xi–xxii) The tactics of surveillance of communications (including intercepting mail), informants, agents provocateurs and deceptive propaganda have their roots in a past stretching as far back as ancient Greece and Rome.

In the modern world the essential matter at issue is whether, and in what manner, the powers accorded to government and the security services are compatible with individual liberties. This has assumed increased importance with the enactment of the Human Rights Act 1998; and the Regulation of Investigatory Powers Act 2000 was passed with a view to making regulation of national security compatible with European Convention rights. The US has engaged a similar debate during its history. In 1982 Congress passed the Intelligence Identities Protection Act (IIPA) to protect the confidentiality of CIA officers in the wake of the campaign of 'outing' by Philip Agee, whose book publications challenged the ethics of US secret operations abroad. The law featured heavily in the Valerie Plame scandal, when it was alleged that officials in the administration of President George W. Bush deliberately exposed her in order to embarrass and intimidate her husband, whose public utterances had challenged US policy justifications for invading Iraq. The passing of the controversial Patriot Acts and the revival of US 'state secrets privilege' suggest that the US policy on national security is becoming closer to that of the United Kingdom.

The exploration of this issue does require a focus on cultural history, and an interpretative approach which seeks to explain how power is distributed and exercised in British and other societies. The title of the legislation, 'Official Secrets', implies that there is information which ordinary citizens and their 'eyes and ears', in terms of the media, should not be entitled to have. The laws legitimize the concept of maintaining secrets from the people. The purpose propagandized in the political debates leading to legislative controls centred on the 'defence of the realm' and 'the security of the state'. But the question arising is: what constitutes the threat to state security and what should the state be defending itself from? Is the threat external or internal? The establishment of the UK's Security Service, MI5, to deal with the threat from within and the Secret Intelligence Service, MI6, to deal with the threat from without, indicates that the risks are beyond those posed by enemies overseas.

The dual approach implies that the state needs protection from its own citizens who may or may not be sympathizers of foreign states that are perceived to be in conflict with British 'national' interests. The operation of intelligence agencies in a democratic society raises the issue of how such organizations are monitored, scrutinized and regulated. What role should the media perform in this task? What are the issues that require journalistic focus? The operations of secret service agents are the continual focus of controversial journalism and book publication. They are also a significant fuel for conspiracy theorists.

The denial of former MI5 officer David Shayler's public interest defence

The legal pursuit of former British MI5 officer David Shayler and the alleged harassment of his journalist associates raise a number of key questions about the ideological motive for such actions. Shayler affirmed his loyalty to the United Kingdom state and his country, and asserted that he was motivated by the desire to improve competence and efficiency, as well as ethical rectitude, on the part of Britain's intelligence agencies. If Shayler's position is regarded as sincere, what has been the deontological reference of state prosecution? Shayler could argue that his position is based on utilitarianism and moral consequentialism. The prosecution could also point to its position on the basis of utilitarianism. A disincentive to intelligence officers to communicate professional concerns in the public domain maintains trust and honour for MI5. Shayler sought the support of human rights legislation and the Court of Appeal and House of Lords. They did not come to his rescue and he was jailed at the end of his Old Bailey trial. The jury had to decide on his culpability according to the prevailing law, and not any moral utilitarian argument he wanted to present to them.

It is argued that in Britain the Official Secrets Acts have been repeatedly used by governments to suppress revelations that were, and are, politically embarrassing rather than genuine threats to national security. It is difficult to be sure whether the law in this area has served to protect the country from the external threat of spying and espionage or whether its main purpose has been to protect executive government from the political embarrassment of journalistic scrutiny as the result of whistle-blowers revealing injustice, incompetence and matters of public interest. David Shayler was one of only a very few high-profile British intelligence officers who have tried to expose iniquity. Peter Wright was much more senior in MI5, having reached the rank of assistant Director General. The government's decision to slice off eighteen years of his pension benefits meant that he exiled himself to a farm in Tasmania, from where wrote and published his memoirs, *Spycatcher* (1987). Instead of offering him a settlement, the government spent millions of pounds of taxpayers' money to get the book suppressed. The mantra of national security meant that the government won in the domestic courts, but the common sense of international publication and distribution outside the UK meant that the government lost in Strasbourg.

Lord Griffiths, one of the Law Lords involved in the plethora of legal rulings on *Spycatcher*, made the obvious suggestion that secret service whistleblowers needed somewhere to go:

> Theoretically, if a member of the service discovered that some iniqui-tous course of action was being pursued that was clearly detrimental to our national interest, and he was unable to persuade any senior members of his service or any member of the establishment, or the police, to do anything about it, then he should be relieved of his duty of confidence so that he could alert his fellow citizens to the impend-ing danger.
>
> (Attorney General v Guardian Newspapers HL 1988)

The US Congress has a massive machinery of intelligence commu-nity oversight in Congress, as well as the executive Foreign Intelligence Advisory Board which answers to the President. The US has hundreds of staff devoted to oversight, including investigative attorneys who can be proactive, carry out independent enquiries and produce reports. The Congressional committees give priority to evidence and reports in public hearings. In contrast, the UK has a Cabinet Intelligence and Security Committee (ISC) that sits in secret and reports only to the Prime Minister. This is a non-parliamentary committee that consists of nine members drawn from both the House of Commons and the House of Lords and is appointed by the Prime Minister. It was established by the Intelligence Services Act 1994 to examine the policy, administration and expenditure of the Security Service, the Secret Intelligence Service and the Government Communications Headquarters. Its resources are minimal and its members of staff can be counted on the fingers of one hand. The disproportionate disparity of oversight is evident in the size and splendour of MI6 headquarters at Vauxhall Cross, on the south side of the River Thames. MI5, and presumably MI6, endeavour to provide ethics counselling to officers troubled by the immediate moral complexities of their tasks, and both agencies can call on considerable internal legal advisory expertise.

David Shayler worked in MI5 as a counter-terrorism officer. He had been recruited via a newspaper advert seeking a wider social diversity of new intake into the security service. Somewhat ironically, while a student journalist at Dundee University, he had sought to publish extracts from Peter Wright's *Spycatcher* memoirs, in contravention of a court injunction. A summary of the narrative of Mr Shayler's story is set out in Table 7.2.

The main weakness in David Shayler's case at the Old Bailey was the fact that he had been paid just over £40,000 for the information he provided to *Mail on Sunday* journalists. This substantially weakened his argument that he was motivated solely on behalf of the public interest. However, Shayler's criticism of MI5 management and his assessment of the training and operations of MI5 provided invaluable insight into and illumination of the operation of 'the Secret State'.

In a marathon legal case which went to the House of Lords, Shayler sought to argue a public interest defence under Article 10 of the Human Rights Act 1998. His QC, Geoffrey Robertson, argued before the Law Lords that there was a class of about 10,000 people whose lips are buttoned and who are banned from disclosing to outsiders any information. He mentioned that if a Mr James Bond were indeed licensed to kill members of al-Qaeda in the UK, that could not be disclosed, even though lives were at risk. Michael Tugendhat QC joined the appeal on behalf of the *Guardian* and other media organizations, and he pointed out that journalists faced charges, including incitement, if they investigated these areas of government operations.

Shayler was charged, under the Official Secrets Act (OSA), with disclosing documents and information to the press in 1997, including the information that MI5 held files on Jack Straw and Peter Mandelson because of their involvement in student politics. The information also included an allegation that MI5 had wrongfully tapped the phone of a *Guardian* journalist, had run a 'honey trap' operation against a potential informer, had an outdated Cold War culture, and condoned alcoholism among its staff.

Mr Robertson argued that the OSA was in conflict with Article 10 of the European Convention enshrining the principle of freedom of expression without interference by public authority and that Shayler should be able to argue in court that he had disclosed the information in the public interest and out of necessity. The overarching issue in the appeal

Table 7.2 The case of David Shayler: from MI5 to the *Mail on Sunday* (and then to jail)

David Shayler joined MI5 in 1991 and dealt with counter terrorism, including left-wing groups, terrorist activity in Northern Ireland and later, the Middle East. He left the service in 1996, together with his partner at the time, Annie Machon.

Through the *Mail on Sunday*, Shayler presented a series of stories about MI5 and MI6, revealed documents and was highly critical of the management and professionalism of both organizations. He was paid around £40,000 by the paper.

Among other things, Shayler claimed that:

1 Peter Mandelson and Jack Straw had been under surveillance and that MI5 maintained files on them;
2 MI6 had been involved in a failed assassination attack on Libyan leader Muammar al-Gaddafi and that a Libyan Islamic group, linked to Al-Qaeda, was paid to carry out the attack;
3 The 1994 bombing of the Israeli embassy in London had been known to the intelligence services before the event happened and could have been prevented;
4 The Security Service had information that could have prevented the 1993 Bishopsgate bombing in the City of London.

Shayler fled abroad a day before the first publication, was arrested in France, and was detained for a short time in a French prison, where he claimed to have had a brief conversation with the notorious 1970s terrorist known as 'Carlos'. A French court decided that the application for his extradition was 'political'. Shayler returned voluntarily to the UK in August 2000.

In his legal case, which went to the House of Lords, Shayler sought to argue a public interest defence under Article 10 of the Human Rights Act 1998.

Shayler was denied the public interest defence by five Law Lords in March 2002. They concluded that a former member of the Security Service, who was prosecuted under the Official Secrets Act 1989, was not entitled to rely on the defence that the disclosure was made in the public or national interest.

Shayler was sentenced to 6 months in prison, served 7 weeks and was then released with an electronic tag.

In 2008 it was reported that he claimed to be the Messiah and that he had divine hallucinations.

Source: Compiled by Anat Balint

was whether the legislation creating these offences was incompatible with Article 10. Shayler had revealed information not to an enemy, but to the press, which the European Court of Human Rights ruled had a watchdog role, with a duty to bark at misbehaviour by public authorities. Robertson added that Whitehall's practice of keeping secret dossiers on public and political figures touched a deep nerve in the British culture of liberty.

Robertson recalled that Cathy Massiter, a former MI5 officer, had disclosed in 1985 that the agency had files on Patricia Hewitt, who at the time of Shayler's appeal before the House of Lords in February 2002 was the Secretary of State for Trade and Industry, and Harriet Harman, who was the Solicitor General. Ms Massiter had not been prosecuted and the two politicians had been compensated after a ruling by the European human rights court which had forced the Tory government to place MI5 on a legal basis for the first time.

The Law Lords ruled that a public interest defence was not available to David Shayler. This shut the door on giving him an effective defence before the Old Bailey jury. They concluded that a former member of the Security Service who was prosecuted under the Official Secrets Act 1989 for unauthorized disclosure of information and documents which he had acquired by virtue of his position as a member of the service was not entitled to rely on the defence that the disclosure was made in the public or national interest. Furthermore, the provisions of the 1989 Act that restricted members and former members of the Security Service and Secret Intelligence Service from disclosing such information did not contravene their right to freedom of expression guaranteed by Article 10 of the European Convention for the Protection of Human Rights and Fundamental Freedoms.

Shayler's position was that he was appalled at the unlawfulness, irregularity, incompetence, misbehaviour and waste of resources in the service, which he thought was failing to perform its public duty. He believed that unless those failings were exposed and remedied, dire consequences would follow, and he therefore believed it in the public and national interest to make the disclosure that he did.

Shayler had argued that if Article 10 of the Human Rights Act could not provide him with a defence, he could rely on the common law defence of duress in that he was acting to prevent danger to life and limb. However, he had been whistleblowing about events from the past and, as the Lord Chief Justice James Woolf had said in the Court of Appeal:

> The difference between Mr Shayler's case and any other case where this defence has been regarded as being available is that Mr Shayler is not in a position to identify any incident which is going to create a danger to the members of the public which his actions were designed to avoid.
>
> (R v Shayler CoA Crim 2001)

The common law of duress remains a potential refuge and legal remedy for troubled intelligence officers which the UK secret state wants to close off, perhaps for obvious reasons. To date they have not been able to plug it. Could it be the escape route by which MI5 or MI6 officers could whistleblow if they were outraged by their knowledge of torture or threat to life, as a result of having to cooperate with allied agencies?

The scenario is still on the borderline of British judicial discretion. Lord Justice Moses had no hesitation in 2008 in ending a secrecy order attaching to High Court litigation by Iraqis alleging abuse by British soldiers in Iraq. He said there was ample material justifying the proposition that the proceedings should be in the public domain and that the Ministry of Defence had no basis for keeping secret the names of Army regiments subject to investigation. (*Media Lawyer* March 2008: 7) Lord Justice Thomas and Mr Justice Lloyd Jones made it very clear in 2009 that they were concerned about the US government suppressing evidence about the detention and treatment of a British resident, Binyam Mohamed, who alleges that he was tortured in Pakistan, subjected to extraordinary rendition, and further tortured in Morocco with the connivance and involvement of US government officials. The judges declared:

> In the judgement of the Foreign Secretary, there is a real risk that, if we restored the redacted paragraphs, the United States Government, by its review of the shared intelligence arrangements, could inflict on the citizens of the United Kingdom a very considerable increase in the dangers they face at a time when a serious threat still pertains. [...]
> How is this judgement of the Foreign Secretary in relation to the public interest in national security to be balanced against the public interest in open justice as safeguarding the rule of law, free speech and democratic accountability?
>
> (Binyam Mohamed v Foreign Secretary HC 2009)

On 6 November 2002 David Shayler was jailed for six months, after defending himself during his Old Bailey trial. He had not been entitled to representation by counsel because his defence of acting in the public interest amounted to an admission of the strict liability OSA offences. Barristers in England and Wales cannot represent clients who plead not guilty when they effectively admit the offences. This strategy limits the tactics and strategies available to defendants pleading not guilty to laws they have broken because they disagree with them on the basis of political and religious conscience.

Mr Justice Moses (as he then was) said he had been minded to sentence Shayler to eighteen months but had taken into account the three and a half months he had spent in a French prison after going on the run. He also accepted some of the mitigating circumstances outlined by his QC. The judge had praise for Shayler's then partner, Annie Machon, who convinced him in a witness statement that Shayler had not taken the documents as part of a deliberate ploy to begin a new career as a journalist. Miss Machon told the court that Shayler felt passionately about certain issues such as democracy and after leaving MI5 had given up a well-paid job with a management consultancy to make the disclosures, knowing that he risked being sent to prison.

The judge said he was prepared to accept that Shayler had been motivated by a desire to expose what he thought was wrong, not by a desire for money. The judge observed: 'Your own actions demonstrate a lack of any real insight into what you were doing or any intelligent foresight into its consequences [...] It is, contrary to your own belief, that blinkered arrogance which has led you into the dock today.'

Mr Robertson had asked the judge to consider a suspended sentence, on the grounds that the offences Shayler had committed were in the 'lower end' of the spectrum of offences covered by Section 1 of the Official Secrets Act. Shayler had handed the documents not to a 'criminal gang' but to two journalists, and had made sure that they were returned to MI5 in due course. The judge agreed that it was to Shayler's credit that he had returned the documents.

David Shayler considered taking his case to the European Court of Human Rights. He hoped to challenge his trial under several articles of the convention. At the Old Bailey, when conducting his own defence, he had to submit all the questions of his cross-examination to the prosecution and judge for prior approval.

The significance of the House of Lords ruling in *R v Shayler* 2002 is that David Shayler and any other British intelligence officer troubled by conscience, having no confidence in internal grievance procedures will always be denied a public interest defence, unless Parliament reforms the OSA or the courts declare its provisions incompatible with Article 10 of the Human Rights Act. Although no journalists were prosecuted for publishing anything Shayler told them, the prosecution of Shayler clearly sent the message to members of the intelligence services, and any other crown servants working in sensitive areas, that blowing the whistle on wrongdoing will meet with investigation and severe punishment.

The personal impact of that decision was made poignantly resonant in the BBC2 documentary broadcast in January 2003 within days of Shayler being jailed for six months by Mr Justice Moses. A talented and patriotic man who wanted to improve MI5 appeared to be broken and humiliated. The documentary followed Shayler and his partner prior to and during the trial. He revealed his frustrations, sense of state persecution and feelings of betrayal. Annie Machon wrote a feature article for the UK journalists' magazine *Press Gazette* castigating the way in which the British media had used Shayler and then abandoned him. A permanent injunction against David Shayler was sustained by the High Court in 2006 (Attorney General v Shayler HC 2006; *Media Lawyer* September 2006: 43) and he is permanently gagged from discussing anything further about his MI5 career either in public or with the media.

Richard Tomlinson is the only other well-known British intelli-gence dissident. He worked for the Secret Intelligence Service, and the apparent lack of any clear explanation for his dismissal from the service led to an employment dispute spiralling into an Official Secrets Act saga attended by global media publicity and considerable embarrassment to an organization whose motto *sempere occultus* means 'always secret'. His desire to publish a book, and stubborn refusal to be silenced, resulted in his willingness to be jailed for one year for an OSA offence in London's high security Belmarsh prison and join in a cat-and-mouse odyssey with his former employers, who pursued him with legal injunctions and the support of allied agencies from one country to the next. He published his controversial book, *The Big Breach*, in 2001. Its contents suggested that Mr Tomlinson was a talented and brilliant intelligence officer who should have been kept on the inside rather than cast adrift to be exploited by enemy agencies. It was reported in May 2009 that MI6 chief Sir John Scarlett had reached a settlement and the agency's prodigal son was at last coming in from the cold. (Leppard *The Times* 2009)

It cannot be said that the US is any more tolerant of or receptive to constructive and patriotic whistleblowers such as Wright, Tomlinson and Shayler have claimed to be. In the case of former FBI intelligence translator Sibel Edmonds, the shutters of secrecy have descended with a crashing sound of silence. The federal courts, up to the Supreme Court, have provided her with no remedy and accepted the US Attorney General's formal assertion of 'state secrets' privilege to protect certain classified, national security information that goes to the core of her allega-tions. US District Judge Reggie B. Walton explained:

> During the course of her employment with the FBI, the plaintiff asserts that she 'reported a number of whistleblower allegations to FBI management officials concerning serious breaches in the FBI security program and a break-down in the quality of translations as a result of wilful misconduct and gross incompetence.'
>
> (Edmonds v FBI US Dist 2003)

Congress will not hear her, nor will the courts. But, unlike Shayler and Tomlinson, up until the time of writing she has not experienced the same level of retribution. Indeed former CIA officer and intelligence analyst Philip Giraldi wrote in the *Dallas Morning News*:

> Sibel Edmonds makes a number of accusations about specific criminal behavior that appear to be extraordinary but are credible enough to warrant official investigation. Her allegations are documentable; an existing FBI file should determine whether they are accurate.
>
> It's true that she probably knows only part of the story, but if that

part is correct, Congress and the Justice Department should have no higher priority. Nothing deserves more attention than the possibility of ongoing national-security failures and the proliferation of nuclear weapons with the connivance of corrupt senior government officials.

(Giraldi *Dallas Morning News* 2008)

In this analysis of the intelligence agencies it might be useful to investigate whether they serve to protect the country from the external threat of 'enemies' in war or in peace. The first UK OSA, in 1889, legislated for a public interest defence, but from the time of the moral panic in 1911 over the Kaiser of Germany swamping Britain with spies, all future OSAs would exclude any such defence and, up until 1989, would impose strict legal liability on journalists who simply received official information.

The Public Interest Disclosure Act 1998 provides no protection for members of the intelligence agencies, as they are among the excluded categories. The legislation allows the existence of OSA offences to trump the exposure of exceptionally serious failures, and crown servants who sign the OSA will not count as people acting in good faith, without personal gain, and revealing information reasonably believed to be true. It is my belief that Dr David Kelly should have been accorded full protection under the Public Interest Disclosure Act. He was criticized by Lord Hutton for breaching the terms of his civil service employment. Whilst Lord Hutton recognized the outstanding contribution he made to the UK and the world in the investigation of chemical and biological weapons in Iraq, he did not accord him a posthumous defence under what is now seen as a worthless and impotent 'whistleblowers' charter'.

The English legal device of issuing a *contra mundum* (against the world) injunction on anything David Shayler might communicate to any media publication about his service with MI5 led to the prosecution of *Punch* magazine for contempt of court. The Court of Appeal had ruled in favour of the magazine's editor, who said that he had no intention of breaching the injunction because he genuinely believed that three pieces of information Shayler was going to include in his column about the Bishopsgate IRA bomb of 1993 and the shooting of PC Yvonne Fletcher outside the Libyan Embassy in 1986 could not be in breach of national security. But the Attorney General successfully appealed to the House of Lords in 2002. (Attorney General v Punch Ltd HL 2002) US journalists would have been astonished at the idea that a magazine editor in Britain had been obliged to submit draft articles by Shayler for scrutiny by the Attorney General's official solicitor so as to avoid being in breach of a prior restraint injunction that applied to everybody, everywhere, for all time. They would also be astonished that the editor appeared to have no discretion in ignoring what the government lawyer said could not be published. The accepted rule in the United Kingdom was encapsulated in the words of Lord Griffiths in the *Spycatcher* ruling:

> The Security and Intelligence Services are necessary for our national security. They are, and must remain, secret services if they are to operate efficiently. The only practical way to achieve this objective is a brightline rule that forbids any member or ex-member of the service to publish any material relating to his service experience unless he has had the material cleared by his employers. There is, in my view, no room for an exception to this rule dealing with trivia that should not be regarded as confidential. What may appear to the writer to be trivial may in fact be the one missing piece of the jigsaw by some hostile intelligence agency.
>
> (Attorney General v Guardian Newspapers No 2 HL 1988)

A further manifestation of the absence of a public interest defence for 'crown servants' resulted in the prosecution and conviction in 2007 of of Downing Street civil servant David Keogh and House of Commons researcher Leo O'Connor, for respectively leaking and receiving a high-level political memo. The contrasting position in the USA is, of course, best referenced by the Supreme Court case *New York Times Co. v United States*, 1971, generally known as the Pentagon Papers case.

The predicament of David Shayler and the legal actions faced by news-papers that had been covering his campaign of criticism of MI5 contrasts with the more liberal climate in the USA, where the First Amendment provides constitutional protection for matters of public interest even when they impinge on national security. The Pentagon Papers case demon-strated that the pendulum swung in favour of freedom of expression, but it cannot be said that the US media were not shaken by the experi-ence of prior restraint injunctions on the grounds of national security that effectively gagged the *New York Times* and *Washington Post* for a period of a fortnight.

New York Times v US: the Pentagon Papers

America's involvement in the Vietnam War of the 1960s and 1970s divided the nation and cost more than 60,000 servicemen and women their lives. An academic working with a government department had access to a forty-seven-volume internal and classified *History of the U.S. Decision-Making Process on Vietnam Policy*. Daniel Ellsberg had a PhD from Harvard and he believed that the material he was able to read convinced him that the US public had been deceived and lied to. He began to copy the material and decided to leak it to the *New York Times*, though he maintained the confidentiality of two of the volumes on the basis that he thought they were still national-security sensitive. The actions by Ellsberg were *prima facie* unlawful as a violation of the US Espionage Act and the theft of government property. In the political storm that followed the US administration's efforts to prosecute him and Anthony J. Russo, Jr., who helped in the photocopying, foundered. Nixon's Watergate 'plumbers' had committed burglary at the offices of Dr Ellsberg's psychiatrist and conducted illegal wiretaps against government critics and opponents between 1969 and 1971.

The decision by the *New York Times* in 1971 to analyse the material over several months – in a hotel protected by security guards – and begin publishing a day-by-day series was seen as classic First Amendment-protected journalism. What became known as the 'Pentagon Papers' told the inside intelligence, government and military story of the USA and Vietnam up until 1968.

In June 1971 President Richard Nixon ordered his Attorney General, John Mitchell, to injunct or 'prior restrain' the *New York Times* on the grounds of national security. He was successful. A District Court issued a temporary injunction and halted further publication of the stories. The media and the White House joined battle. The *Washington Post* received copies of the papers. The US has not adopted the English Spycatcher doctrine that an injunction against one newspaper binds all other media organisations if they have been notified about the order. Consequently the US administration had to seek a separate prior restraint order against the *Washington Post*.

The ensuing litigation over two weeks was messy and uneven. At trial the New York District Court upheld the *New York Times* newspaper's right to publish. The federal appellate court upheld the government injunction against the *New York Times*, but another federal appeals court would not restrain the *Washington Post* from unrolling its own exposé of 'The Pentagon Papers'.

On 30 June 1971, the Supreme Court Justices abandoned their weekend and voted to overturn the injunctions, but though the effect of the judgment was that the newspapers were free to publish, as a precedent it is arguable whether the First Amendment had been given a sharpened spear in matters of national security. (*New York Times* v US; US v *Washington Post* SC US 1971) The later ruling in Frank Snepp's case probably proved that.

In the future, US governments were going to have to demonstrate that media publication would cause immediate and irreparable harm before the federal courts would resort to prior restraint. The *New York Times* won a Pulitzer Prize for publishing the Pentagon Papers, the Attorney General John Mitchell went to jail for offences connected with the Watergate scandal that also forced President Nixon to resign in order to avoid the ignominy of impeachment.

The Supreme Court's 6–3 decision in favour of the newspapers included separate concurring and conflicting opinions and, Moore and Murray say, 'For those who awaited a strong reaffirmation [...] and a ringing victory for First Amendment rights, the Court's decision was a hollow win and, to many, a major disappointment.' (Moore and Murray 2008: 161) Zelezny observes that none of the newspapers was prosecuted, 'though under some federal statutes a case might theoretically have been fashioned. Also, several justices hinted in the Pentagon Papers case that subsequent punishment under appropriate criminal statutes might be constitutionally permissible.' (Zelezny 2004: 93) The subsequent national security row in 1979 over an injuncted proposed article for *Progressive* magazine that detailed the design and operation of a hydrogen bomb did not reach any legal resolution in the higher courts when similar articles were published elsewhere.

The position of the US and UK Supreme Courts in the battle between freedom of expression, the media and national security is more than likely to take a winding road in the future. Media interests will be competing in the tension of the separation of powers. So far the UK's highest court has challenged the executive and legislature on detention of terrorist suspects without trial, use of torture evidence, use of secret witnesses in criminal trials, and secret evidence in control orders/house arrests of terrorist suspects. Both Supreme Courts will have plenty of opportunity to address the conundrum of how to measure the importance of free speech against the acute imperative of national security. As this book went to press the efforts by a former senior MI5 officer to publish his memoirs were to be considered by the UK's new Supreme Court. The first step in greater disclosure could well be the identification of the parties so that the case listing of 'A v B' reveals the names of real people. Part of the difficulty for the UK state in balancing security with freedom of expression is that the internal Security Service, MI5, has changed from being an exclusively counter-espionage agency to taking on similar roles to that of the FBI in the USA. MI5 now operates as a national police force investigating counter-terrorism and organized crime. Parliament and the courts are trying to negotiate the extent of this migration in terms of accountability.

The British courts are also showing a willingness to challenge the claims of national security in the exercise of search and seizure powers against journalists. In the year 2000 the High Court refused an application by the police to order the Observer and the Guardian to hand over all files and records they held concerning a letter from David Shayler and an article by the reporter Martin Bright that had been published in the Observer.

8

MEDIA LAW AND ETHICS:
FOUR GENRES OF
JURISDICTION

Research agenda and potential problems

This chapter aims to be an introduction to the discipline of comparing media law systems in different countries, and the cultures of media ethics associated with self-censorship and external censorship of media conduct and content. A chapter of this length can only be a gateway to understanding and investigating the media laws of the countries and legal jurisdictions cited. More resources to assist further research are provided on the book's companion website.

Jago and Fionda categorize four key legal jurisdictions of the world: common law, civil law, socialist law and Islamic law. (Jago and Fionda 2005: 5) The first three are clearly secular and the last, Islamic law, is based on religious doctrine. Consequently Islamic media jurisprudence is determined more by natural than by positivist law. The focus of this book has been on the two main common law jurisdictions of the world, in the UK and USA. We shall be touching on the media law and ethics system operating in the common law country with the largest population – India. The socialist law jurisdiction with the biggest population in the world is China. Saudi Arabia's population is modest, but its power in terms of oil wealth and relations with the West is by a far greater proportion. The Saudi genre of Shari'a law has an influence that is pervasive and controversial. China and Saudi Arabia, according to the NGOs Amnesty International and Human Rights Watch, are authoritarian societies where the index of human rights is considered to be much lower than in France or India. We also reference what could be considered a hybrid or composite jurisdiction – Japan. It is a relevant model not least because of its being the second largest economy in the world and practising a unique blend of civil and common law doctrines and indigenous laws unique to its history and culture.

The real risk in analysing a foreign jurisdiction is in judging harshly the customs and practice of another society according to the standards and values of the society from which the researcher hails. The phenomenon of regarding the media law and ethics of one's home country as normative and superior is a form of ethnocentrism. The potential difficulty in research is that anything identified as being different is assumed to be abnormal and wrong. The researcher needs to freeze or discount stereotypical assumptions of how media law and ethics should work, and endeavour to investigate and understand the religious beliefs, history, constitution, social values and political system of a specific country. A failure to fully understand the origins and development of Islamic belief in Muslim countries and the way Muslim law is inspired by religious pronouncements could lead the researcher to conclude that the application of media law in Saudi Arabia is harsh, bizarre, anachronistic and an affront to international human rights standards.

The relativist perspective focuses on an understanding of a media law system by examining the differences and relationships within the cultural and social contexts of the country under investigation. By being rooted inside the social environment being studied, the ethical analysis could be blighted by moral relativism and, as a result, the objectives of seeking provincial and universal benefits from the research are somewhat limited. The provincial perspective would be posited on observation in relation to the researcher's own media law and ethics system. The universal perspective would be in relating the comparison in the context of transnational approaches in response to perceived media legal and ethical wrongs.

One of the advantages of positivistic research of media law and ethics in another country is that if the country under study shares a similar legal background ideas may be gained from the foreign jurisdiction that could be appropriately and effectively adapted and implemented in the researcher's home country. This is why close investigation of the US media law system might bring benefits and reform to UK libel, contempt and privacy law. A study of the less litigious approach to media wrongs in Japan, where there is a unique cultural tradition of public apology, offers a promising subject for analysis in view of the current debate in the UK about high media law costs creating a chilling effect on freedom of expression. But how appropriate would the transfer of the practice be, given the widely different history, religious, social and political background of Japan?

The researcher therefore needs to be wary of the pitfall of criminological tourism, where rose-tinted intellectual spectacles, combined with short-stay romantic and superficial observation, can result in skewed research conclusions combined with embarrassing cultural misunderstandings. Without the language skills and necessary time for qualitative and quantitative research as well as ethnographic observation, a researcher in comparative media law and ethics may be lured into a process of academic false consciousness and make ill-advised recommendations for the transplantation of media law and ethical practices.

Comparative law researchers would be wise to tread cautiously in the area of media legal and ethical definitions. *Diffamation* in France is not a direct and comparative equivalent of the English word 'defamation'. Comparative concepts in law have been categorized as representative, prototypical, deviant and archetypical comparators. Briefly, the subjects for investigation in comparative media law analysis are divided between concepts or features that are (1) distinctive to the legal system investigated, e.g. the absolutist First Amendment in US constitution for freedom of the press and religion; (2) pioneering or forerunners of new policy, e.g. abolishing common law of blasphemy in UK; (3) unconventional methods of dealing with defamation, e.g. the punishment in Shari'a Islamic law of eighty lashes for defamation; (4) a media law feature common to many countries, e.g. a remedy for breach of privacy or attack on reputation.

Media law of France

France was one of the first countries to assert freedom of expression as an inherent right of citizenship. It could be argued that it may be one of the more sluggish countries in ensuring that the principle is fully exercised in the democratic context. There is an absolutist and authoritarian tradition in French historical culture. The years of the *ancien régime*, the French Revolution and General de Gaulle's period as president during the Fifth Republic are characterized by the use of censorship to reinforce political power and define the French national interest.

France is in the civil law tradition and its legal culture is strongly influenced by the codes of Justinian and Napoleon. The purpose of codified civil law is that lawyers interpret the law for themselves rather than depending on *stare decisis*. A key difference from the common law tradition is that it stresses the obligations of citizens rather than simply proscribing conduct that will constitute criminal offending.

Raymond Kuhn, in *The Media in France*, observes that the functions performed by the French media generate different and contradictory interpretations. He sets out the leading opinions: the media are primarily ideological weapons which are manipulated for the purpose of social control; they are part of a process whereby the contradictions of power relations in society are resolved to the economic benefit of a power elite or ruling class; they are primarily independent actors in a political system characterized by electoral competition and the diffusion of power; they act on behalf of the electorate, keeping it informed of elite decisions and acting as a check on the abuse of power. (Kuhn 1995: 2)

Unlike the situation in the USA and the United Kingdom, France has affirmed a constitutional right to privacy in Article 9 of the French Civil Code, which states: 'the court may prescribe measures, such as sequestration, seizure and others, appropriate to prevent or put an end to an invasion of personal privacy; in case of emergency those measures may be provided for by interim order'. The French constitution sources a process of criminal law enforcement for both defamation and privacy. French defamation law seeks to protect any sphere of a person's public or private life. This means that an attack on a person's reputation may not involve disclosure of private facts, but the disclosure of private facts commonly also involves an attack on a person's reputation.

In French law, defamation is a criminal offence and civil wrong, which consists of 'every allegation or imputation of a fact which attacks the honour or reputation of the person [...] who is the subject of the imputation'. It is a defence to prove the truth of the allegations. However, one of the three exceptions is when the defamatory allegation relates to the private life of the person. In reality it is difficult to distinguish between private and public life. The restriction on the defence to truth in defamation has gestated considerable uncertainty.

Fundamentally, freedom of expression is not the trump card in French media law. There is a balancing of expression rights with privacy rights, and some might argue that privacy rights are accorded priority more often than not. Consent was originally the method of demarcating the border between private and public life. Anything public would be that which the individual consented to being non-private. However, how would this be reconciled with the recognition that the public had a right to know matters which a person did not consent to being published?

A clue to a collective desire to protect a zone of personal dignity and private memory may lie in the cultural sensitivity of representing French history through the content of its film output. Kuhn argues that the French state has maintained a post-war policy of media regulation to support the important entertainment/cultural function as a vehicle for the popular dissemination of 'high culture' and a feeling of pride in great works of French music, art, literature, theatre and cinema. France has special legislation making it obligatory for all television networks to invest in film production and imposing a broadcasting obligation to show films with at least 40 per cent original French-language content.

Filmmakers in France have succeeded in creating a distinctive national cinema by investigating and interrogating aspects of the human condition experienced in France's particular national history, engaging with national and Continental traditions of philosophy and dramatic styles of expression, and the intersection of significant financial and cultural agents of support for national filmmaking. It could be argued that this voice in film narrative content reflects or signposts an explanation for the tendency of French media law to fashion the mythologies of French history and protect the private worlds of political, economic and cultural elites.

France had a troubled social, political and cultural experience during the Second World War. The country experienced defeat, humiliation, occupation, collaboration and then liberation. In the immediate post-war period it engaged in a process of mythologizing resistance and covering up of the reality of the Vichy regime. France also had a direct experience of Hitler's 'Final Solution'.

In the post-war years France, through the Marshall Plan and European Common Market, Community and Union, has articulated and applied policies to define and protect her indigenous culture from outside domi-nance. This is particularly true of the way French film production has been insulated and protected from the global hegemony of Hollywood. It can be argued that these national dynamics have informed and inspired the narrative and preoccupation of French filmmakers.

Louis Malle's two powerful films set in France during the Second World War, *Lacombe Lucien* and *Au Revoir les Enfants*, were informed and influenced by Marcel Ophüls' ground-breaking documentary *Le chagrin et la pitié*. Ophüls had breached the self-delusion of post-war Gaullist French culture by attempting to confront the national psyche with the reality, truth and ironic paradox of collaboration, occupation and resist-ance. His programme was commissioned and made for French television in 1969, but not shown until 1981 because 'so shocking were its revela-tions thought to be.' (Ophüls 1971) Yet Malle's films were not censored. This may be due to the fact that the more immediate and controversial fictionalization of the past was more acceptable in the cultural frame of indigenous French cinema than the stark reality of documentary journalism.

One of the most powerful representations of actuality in *Le chagrin et la pitié* is the narrative of Jewish politician Pierre Mendès-France, who was framed, prosecuted and jailed in Vichy France, escaped to join de Gaulle in London, and therefore avoided being despatched to Auschwitz. Louis Malle may well have given the name of the character Albert Horn's daughter as 'France' to construct the irony of Mendès-France's story. Both were Jewish, both survived, and were eponymous with their troubled and tragic nation. This is an exquisite example of screen irony and intertex-tual inspiration.

Directors Louis Malle in *Au Revoir les Enfants* and *Lacombe Lucien* and François Truffaut in *Le Dernier Métro* sought to challenge the ugliness of anti-Semitism in France, the horror that collaborationist French nationals were even more enthusiastic than German Nazis in their persecution of Jews, and the paradox that the motivation for betrayal and collaboration could be so banal and pathetic. In *Lacombe Lucien* the central character is an immature adolescent country *paysan* whose road to eventual summary execution stems from a moody reaction to the crushing of his self-esteem and pride by the rejection of his resistance teacher, Robert Peyssac. 'Lieutenant Voltaire' is probably being fatherly when he says Lacombe Lucien is too young. But the young man feels patronized and he wheels his punctured bicycle to town, arriving after curfew, clumsily gatecrashes the indulgence and decadence of the French fascists at their luxurious hotel HQ, and willingly sells Voltaire for the price of a few cognacs.

Curiously, one of the key themes of Marcel Ophüls's documentary is Anglophobia, and there is little evidence of mainstream French cinema exploring the paradox and irony of this cultural phenomenon. Few people appreciate the fact that after British servicemen gave their lives in rescuing more than 130,000 French in the Dunkirk operation, all but 6,000 returned when Pétain agreed an armistice. In *Le chagrin et la pitié* a witness expresses his disgust when 15,000 French sailors turn their backs on French resistance and the Free French call of General Charles de Gaulle. More attention is given to the cruelty of perfidious Albion in killing more than 1,000 French sailors in the British raid at Mers-el-Kébir in July 1940. The ambiguous nature of the *Entente Cordiale* receives no more than gentle farce treatment in Bertrand Tavernier's *Laissez-Passer* when a resistance French film director is plied with tea and interrogative misunderstanding after being spirited over the channel by the Special Operations Executive.

French filmmakers have developed a distinctive and indigenous national cultural genre by concentrating on the self-delusional nature of memorializing the past and constructing a comforting dimension of national identity. Jacques Audiard's *Un héros très discret* (1996b) transforms the phenomenon into an extraordinary fantasy of Albert Dehousse, whose ability to perform the role of resistance hero leads to promotion to Lieutenant-Colonel and responsibility for hunting collaborators and processing prisoners of war in the German-occupied zone of France. Audiard mixes documentary style with self-conscious artistic technique to equivocate the agony of reality and theatre of the absurd in the narrative of a nation pretending that 'we are all Gaullists now' in the aftermath of liberation. Dehousse is a study of the creativity of reinventing the human character, and Audiard says in his interview with *Positif* (Audiard 1996: 20): 'Albert's psychological need to lie coincides with the need that France had of that same lie in the aftermath of the war.' (Miller 2003: 93)

The high cultural traditions of filmmaking have also been engaged with the only permitted moving picture representation of French court proceedings. A choice was made to avoid the surrender of the realities and dramas of French inquisitorial criminal proceedings to the vulgarities of US-style court television. Instead, the concession and commission was granted to an award-winning filmmaker, Raymond Depardon, who in *Délits Flagrants* (1994) and *Dixième chambre: instants d'audience* (2004) turned the representation of crime and punishment in Paris into an extension of film art.

Media law of China

China's media law is set in a socialist law system in which the law is subordinate to the political ideology of the state. The Chinese Communist Party was formed in 1921 and came to power under Mao Tse Tung in 1949. After the death of Mao the ruling Communist Party regime began to reform and develop a code of civil law procedure and by 1987 it introduced 'The Fundamentals of Private Law'. A Confucian-inspired system of alternative dispute resolution is encouraged through mediation and compromise. The National People's Congress (NPC) adopted a new criminal procedure law in 1996.

However, despite the exponential development of Chinese cultural, economic and military power, nothing can hide the fact that China is an authoritarian society. The constitution adopted in 1982, which established the Supreme People's Court, has no power to judicially review the executive or NPC. China's criminal justice system is protective of the collective public interest rather than of the rights of the individual. Consequently, law pertaining to media conduct and content in China, whether civil or criminal, is political. There is no definable 'media law' as such.

An example of this political quality lies in the 'China Law on Maintaining State Secrets'. The definitions are broad and go much further than what would be seen as national security categories in common law countries. Information which weakens 'the economic, scientific, or technological strength of the State' could be deemed 'secret'. (Wang and Davis 2006: 88) The Chinese government operates a system of direct controls on content that is supervised on a day-to-day basis. Journalists and publishers are given a list of 'prohibited articles' and 'restricted topics'. Anything which harms the morality of society or negates respected cultural traditions, as well as articles that 'deny the need for society to be guided by Marxism, Leninism, the system of thought of Mao Zedong, and the theories of Deng Xiaoping', are prohibited. (Ibid.: 99) Any publication that touches on the subject of the various peoples and religions of China has to be submitted for official approval.

By contrast, the media freedoms enjoyed in Hong Kong prior to the British colonial handover to China in 1997 have been largely preserved, so much so that the province in 2009 was able to play host to a huge political rally commemorating the 1989 deaths of students in Tiananmen Square. But in mainland China journalists and media communicators who defy state censorship and politics are harassed and jailed.

In its 2009 report on the country, Amnesty International complained that around thirty journalists and fifty other individuals remained in prison for posting their views on the Internet. During the 2008 Olympics, Amnesty International claimed that the authorities questioned and harassed numerous signatories of Charter 08, which proposed a blueprint for fundamental legal and political reform in China.

Human Rights Watch echoed Amnesty International in its 2009 report on China, although both organizations conceded that there had been some relaxation of the controls on international media reporting in the country: 'On October 17, 2008, the Chinese government permanently lifted certain restrictions on foreign journalists. However, the new freedoms do not extend to Chinese journalists and foreign journalists still have limited access to certain parts of the country, including Tibet.' (Human Rights Watch 2009a)

Media law in India

India maintains a common law tradition borrowed from the period of the British Raj, but improved and developed by its 1950 written constitution, that asserts the guarantees of equal human rights and prohibits discrimination on the basis of race, gender, caste, ethnicity and religion. There is also a constitutional guarantee of freedom of speech and expression, although this is qualified for the purpose of imposing reasonable restrictions to protect national security, friendly relations with foreign states, public order, decency and morality. To some extent its media legal culture follows the maxim of the American jurist Oliver Wendell Holmes that 'the life of the law has not been logic; it has been experience' and the higher courts in India give as much weight and respect to US jurisprudence as they do to British.

This is the way in which the country has developed a privacy law. Madhavi Divan writes:

> In India, the right to privacy is not a specific fundamental right but has nevertheless gained constitutional recognition. 'Privacy' is not enumerated amongst the various 'reasonable restrictions' to the right to freedom of speech and expression enlisted under Article 19(2). However, this lacuna has not prevented the courts from carving out a constitutional right to privacy by a creative interpretation of the right to life under Article 21 and the right to freedom of movement under Article 19(1)(d).

> (Divan 2006: 119)

In *Gobind v State of Madhya Pradesh* 1975, one of the judges of the Indian Supreme Court said that the 1950 Constitution guarantees the individual his personality, and those things stamped with his personality should be free from official interference. In the *State of Maharashtra v Madhukar Narayan Mandikar* 1991, it was held that even 'a woman of easy virtue' was entitled to privacy and no one can invade her privacy as and when he likes. In *State of Maharashtra v Prabhakar Panndurang* in 1966, an individual's right to write a book and get it published was upheld by the Indian

Supreme Court. The Supreme Court in *R. Rajagopal v State of Tamil Nadu* in 1995 held that the fundamental right of privacy was constitutionally guaranteed. In the case of *People's Union for Civil Liberties v Union of India* 1997, it was held that telephone tapping is a serious invasion of an individual's privacy. A citizen's right to privacy has to be protected from being abused by the authority of the day. (Anand and Duggal 2000: 240–4) The statutory Press Council established in 1978 regulates and enforces norms for journalistic conduct. This includes Provision 13:

> The Press shall not intrude or invade the privacy of an individual unless outweighed by genuine overriding public interest, not being a prurient or morbid curiosity. So, however, that once a matter becomes a matter of public record, the right to privacy no longer subsists and it becomes a legitimate subject for comment by Press and media among others.
>
> (Rai and Chandra 2006: 128)

Hakemulder, Jonge and Singh argued in their 1998 text, *Media Ethics and Laws*, that the media in India need to be more critical and questioning of authority. They complained that they operate, through self-censorship, as the agents of power and consequently maintain the status quo:

> They back the elite and powerful persons. [...] For that matter, the same section of people continue to live in poverty and starvation for generations together. This is possible because the media have implicitly maintained the status quo. They have not posed uncomfortable questions to the government, at least at a sustained level. You do not often hear of the media in India campaigning for the rights of people belonging to the scheduled castes and tribes, but you do hear of the media taking a stand on the issue of reservation of jobs for the scheduled castes and tribes. This stand, more often than not, is in favour of the elite castes and classes.
>
> (Hakemulder et al. 1998: 348–9)

Whilst Indira Gandhi's State of Emergency in 1975–76 has often been cited as a catastrophic failure of Indian democracy, the event should be contextualized in the larger timeline of Indian post-independence history. Foreign journalists were expelled, Indian journalists were jailed, and censorship and control of the media were exercised. On the other hand, the fact that this lasted for only two years is a testament to the strength of long-term democracy in the context of India's post-independence history. Attempts by ruling political parties in India to muzzle the media have in the end been negated. Hakemulder et al. argued that 'The mass media can generate a strong public opinion about human rights issues. [...] They can very well provide a strong network of communication to help propagate an informed opinion about human rights.' (Ibid.: 350)

Media law of Japan

Japan's legal system is difficult to pigeonhole into the civil or common law systems, as it draws on six key sources: the constitution; civil code; code of civil procedure; penal code; code of criminal procedure; and commercial code. The pursuit of justice is achieved through consideration of Japanese and international law. Defamation law, as in India and France, operates on a dual criminal and civil dimension.

The written constitution, determined by the US occupation in 1946, led to a constitutional guarantee against censorship, and support for media freedom. Paragraph 2 of Article 21 states: 'No censorship shall be maintained, nor shall the secrecy of any means of communication be violated.' The effect of this written guarantee is to discourage prior restraint, but indigenous cultural factors mean there is a greater tradition of self-censorship and regulation. The equating of journalism with confrontation and conflict is not so prevalent in Japan, particularly in large media companies. Journalism 'beats' are very much subject to the 'kisha club' system in which: the covered and coverers form a tight group, excluding all others; loyal group members do not tell tales out of the club or school – for example, print disloyal investigative stories; and even for those who are not members of a kisha, getting along with one's colleagues counts for more than self-aggrandizement, making waves, writing exposés or 'crusading for the public'.

A fundamental difference in the philosophy of defamation law between the UK, USA and Japan is that the UK and USA seek to protect harm to individuals from unprivileged, false and defamatory statements through the award of damages. In Japan greater emphasis is placed on protecting the value of a person's good name. Nakada and Shimada state: 'Japanese litigants are more interested in extracting an apology than in recovering damages, and the court has a discretion to order an apology or a correction.' (Nakada and Shimada 1995: 175)

Whereas British and American persons define reputation in terms of individual rights, the Japanese generally view reputation within the context of their membership in a family or group. The influence of the Confucian tradition is strong, so that a defamatory accusation is perceived more as a loss of face to the group rather than as harm to individual rights. Defamation under the civil code is defined as injuring 'the social reputation that a person enjoys due to his or her personal merits such as personality, character, fame and credibility.' (Iteya et al. 2006: 133) Freedom of expression is measured in defamation actions through the application of the principles of balance (*hikaku koryo*), honour and esteem (*meiyo*) and reputation (*meisei*). (Nakada and Shimada 1995: 174)

Article 13 of the constitution protects a right to individual happiness, which sets up the notion of a 'personality right' to privacy, which is circumscribed by the public interest. Privacy does not have a direct translation in the Japanese language. Japanese speakers usually use the expression *puraibashii*.

At the beginning of the 1990s libel suits were rare, compared to the USA and Britain, but there was a perception that more people in Japan were beginning to use the libel laws, with greater frequency, by the end of the decade. Culturally, Japanese journalism has not been as libertarian and questioning as US and British journalism. Loyalty is an important cultural imperative, and a vertical system of human relations still has considerable influence. In government bureaucracies and large companies, such as mass media organizations, employees have clear role obligations and defined places in the hierarchical structure. The three traits of harmony, groupism and hierarchy are central to an understanding of the relationship of the Japanese individual to his or her family, community and society.

The hybrid nature of Japan's legal system can be demonstrated by the introduction from May 2009 of lay judge-jurors in serious trials such as murder. Six randomly selected citizens serve as lay judges alongside three professional judges in a pioneering introduction of the jury verdict in a criminal justice system that had previously reserved rulings on fact and sentence to the professional judiciary. The reform has generated considerable debate about the issue of potential media prejudice in the coverage of serious crimes. Japan's Newspaper Publishers and Editors Association (NSK) has been lobbying for lay judges to attend post-verdict news conferences in order to deepen public understanding and trust in the justice system. (NSK 2009)

Media law of Saudi Arabia

Saudi Arabia's Islamic legal system, in the context of the kingdom's authoritarian society of around twenty-five million people is not representative of the complexity and variety of Islamic law practised around the world, which has seen a rise in use and practice in the twentieth and twenty-first centuries. Islamic legal roots are much older than the other three genres of jurisdiction. But Saudi Arabia is unique in the Muslim world for being the geographical and cultural cradle of Islam. Shari'a means 'the way' and reflects the desire of the Prophet Mohammed to unite his followers behind the idea that there is one universe united behind one God (*Allah*). Up until the 1970s Islamic law was evolving with modernity and codifying for commercial procedure, property and obligations, family law and succession. However, the Iranian Revolution of 1979 precipitated a reversal of the displacement of the more anomalous features of Islamic law as compared to the common and civil law doctrines – particularly in the dimension of punishment.

Islam, like Christianity and other monotheistic religions, is complex and varied in the interpretation and teaching of the two main sources of Islamic law: *Shari'a* and the *Sunnah*. The Muslim faith is expressed through the Sunni, Khariji, Murji'ah, Shi'a and Sufi doctrines. A common theme identifiable in all of the doctrines emphasizes respect for political rights, elections, social autonomy and freedoms. As Dr Said Ramadan wrote in 1970:

> all principles of good morals and human dignity are equally applicable to Muslim as well as to non-Muslim subjects of the Islamic State. The inviolability of the human personality is the foundation of the justice demanded by God for all men. Freedom of opinion, oral or written, of worship, association, choice of profession and of movement is guaranteed to all subjects, Muslims and non-Muslims alike. This right flows from the principle of every individual's complete responsibility to himself and to God. Says the Qur'an: 'Every person is held in pledge for what he does.' [Q. LXXIV: 38]
>
> Difference of opinion has been described by the Qur'an as a continuous aspect of human life and even as a purpose of creation: 'And if thy Lord had willed, He verily would have made mankind one nation, yet they cease not differing, save those on whom thy Lord hath mercy; and for that He did create them.' [Q.XI:118,119]
>
> (Ramadan 1970: 146–7)

Saudi Arabia relies on the Qur'an as the full basis of all its laws and this governs the relationship between the citizen and the legal system. Interpretation is undertaken wholly by clerics rather than by secular leaders, and this could explain why the doctrine of *Siyyasa Shar'yya*, a discretionary interpretation of Islamic law in the public interest, has not led to a wider and more noticeable imitation of Western laws and standards in human rights and media freedom. Saudi Arabia's court of last resort is the Supreme Judicial Council (SJC), and the King retains the power of final judgment. But the SJC does not have the power to judicially review the source and exercise of power inside the country. Law is subordinate to religion in Islamic law, in the same way that law is subordinate to the political ideology of the Communist Party in China. Andrew Hammond explains the political dynamic in Saudi Arabia as Crown Prince Abdullah was pushing forward with modernizations

> that would gradually roll back the influence of the clerical establishment while not tampering with the fundamentals of the relationship between Al Saud and al-Wahhabiyyah, where the royal family controls

the state policy while Wahhabi clerics take charge of society – the duality at the heart of the Saudi-Wahhabi polity.

(Hammond 2009)

Hammond argues that the Saudi media have played and may continue to perform a central role in this ongoing strategy. An effective modernization of Islamic law will be achieved in Saudi Arabia and other Islamic states when discretionary interpretation in the public interest removes the application of *Hudud* punishment for defamation, set at eighty lashes. In some Islamic countries the Shari'a penalty is combined with criminal secular procedure and terms of imprisonment. Trials in Saudi Arabia are usually held in secret and no juries are used, yet the anachronistic penalties are applied in public. Human rights organizations repeatedly chastise the Kingdom for its record on capital and corporal punishment.

Amnesty International, Human Rights Watch and Reporters Without Borders regularly protest against disproportionate punishment imposed on media communicators for trying to represent their rights to freedom of expression.

Like China, Saudi Arabia applies direct censorship to old and new media. In the case of the Internet, the state blocks access to overseas sites considered subversive and harmful. It persecutes bloggers deemed to be critical of, or a threat to, the state. The Media Charter of 1982 asserted that the mass media in Saudi Arabia had a duty to 'oppose destructive trends, atheistic tendencies, materialistic philosophies and attempts to divert Muslims from their faith.' (*Arab News* 1982) In 2001 the Council of Ministers issued a resolution directing that all Internet users in the Kingdom had to refrain from publishing or accessing data that contained 'anything contrary to the state or its system'.

In its report on Saudi Arabia for 2009 Amnesty International protested that human rights activists and peaceful critics of the state were being arrested and imprisoned. Others detained in previous years remained in prison:

> Shaikh Nasser al-'Ulwan, arrested in 2004 or 2005 in Buraida reportedly for refusing to issue a fatwa (edict), continued to be detained without charge or trial or any effective means of redress. He was reported to have been held incommunicado and in solitary confinement for much of the time. Prisoner of conscience Fouad Ahmad al-Farhan, an internet blogger arrested in December 2007 apparently for criticizing the government, was held incommunicado at Dhahban Prison, Jeddah, until his release in April.

(Amnesty International 2009b)

Comparative analysis of media law and ethics systems in different cultures is an inevitably complex and open-ended process. Language barriers present a considerable difficulty and where, as in the case of Saudi Arabia and China, the media jurisprudence is framed and dominated by natural law, religiosity and political ideology, the challenge to understanding texts and their context is all the greater. This book's companion website will endeavour to update the availability of research and publications in English related to the countries referred to in this chapter.

9

THE LEGAL PROBLEMATIZING
OF JOURNALISM

This chapter investigates how the social and political function of journalism is problematized by the operation of the legal systems in the UK and USA. The focus is first on a practice in Britain to construct a legal jeopardy for journalists and journalism that arguably damages the public interest. Next we consider how governments and judiciary harass the journalistic function of protection of sources and make the problem or issue one of stark and unpleasant choices for media communicators.

The jigsaw obligation in communication

Journalism students in Britain are all taught the phenomenon of 'jigsaw identification'. This is where a criminal offence is committed inadvertently through different publications lawfully reporting the details of a court case subject to reporting restrictions. But by different publications including different details it is possible for members of the audience, including the friends, acquaintances and relatives of individuals given anonymity, to piece together the information and recognize who it is that the court is seeking to protect. This could be the case where a husband was convicted of raping his wife. One newspaper might report the case as an identified man who had raped an unidentified woman, excluding reference to the fact they were married. Another might report the case as an unidentified husband who had raped an unidentified wife.

In the USA the First Amendment does not permit state or federal law to criminalize journalists who publish in good faith fair and accurate reports of court proceedings held in public. No journalist should be prosecuted for reporting information not proscribed by law. In the balancing of interests between freedom of the media and the private feelings of victims and participants in criminal trials US constitutional law accepts that sometimes there will be publication of public record facts that people would prefer not to be public and this will cause discomfort and embarrassment. However, the English courts have statutory and case law obligations to protect vulnerable people such as crime victims and children and it is considered jurisprudentially valid to prohibit publication of information that is likely to lead to the identification of individuals entitled to anonymity. In the practice of countries where such legal restrictions do not apply, as in the USA, the potential harm or distress to individuals is attenuated effectively by ethical discretion.

The journalist Caroline Godwin and I legally challenged this problem in 1994. Two parents were convicted of the manslaughter of their 15-month-old son. They were also on trial for cruelty to three of their surviving children, who were in council care and did not want publicity. The father was jailed for seven years. There was a major controversy over the involvement of social workers. The media would normally have prioritized the reporting of the manslaughter case and identified the parents and dead child. No reference would have been made to the lesser cruelty charges and surviving children. The manslaughter was the news angle and the centre of public interest.

But reporting by some national newspapers began by including information about the child cruelty charges and the surviving children. The parents and the dead child were not identified. This policy was adopted because of confusion about the nature of the reporting restrictions under the Children and Young Persons Act 1933. Did they relate to the deceased child, to the parents or to the alleged victims of child cruelty, the surviving children? The judges dealing with the case did not put their orders down in writing. They were not published. The power they had to make such orders did not include anonymizing deceased victims or adult defendants. They could only protect the surviving children from being identified as the alleged victims of cruelty.

It was accepted that in a democratic society with freedom of expression the identity of the child who had died through neglect and those of his parents should have been published. But they never were. We argued that we should not be seen to be breaking any law by reporting the case only in terms of the manslaughter and identifying defendants and the dead child. But the judge said: 'Publishing the names of the defendants or of the deceased child is, in my view, calculated to lead to the identification of those protected children. To suggest otherwise is to close one's eyes to the obvious.' (R v Central Criminal Court ex p Crook CoA Crim 1994) But it was never our intention to identify the surviving children and our actions were not 'calculated to identify' them.

The judge had a legal duty to protect the surviving children. The journalists believed the lesser of the two evils was reference only to the parents and their deceased child. A US judge's powers would have remained inside the walls of the courtroom and not been transferred to the media outside as a process of problematization. We did not believe our reporting in the manner envisaged would have had the effect of causing the surviving children any more distress by their parents' identification than did the existence of the trial itself. But the Court of Appeal

Plate 13 Electronic and print media representatives assemble to interview Gordon Brown at the Royal Society of Arts in London when he was Chancellor of the Exchequer in 2007. This scene is viewed as a legitimate process of public interest 'doorstepping', and would not be construed as media harassment.

agreed with the Old Bailey trial judge. The identities of the parents and the child who was killed have never been made public. There have been more cases like this where very young children killed in the most horrific of circumstances will never be identified because of similar reporting restrictions that give rise to potential jigsaw identification.

Some of the potential problems that I and Caroline Godwin warned the Court of Appeal about in 1994 came to pass with added vengeance in the notorious case of 'Baby P' in 2008–9 that was referred to in Chapter 1. US media-judicial culture prioritizes the socio-philosophical importance that homicide victims in the criminal justice system must have the basic dignity and status of a published identity in the public record. This is particularly important in relation to defenceless minors such as 'Baby P', who over a period of eight months suffered sixty separate injuries, including a broken back and ribs, and was shown by the evidence to have been failed by the state child protection system. Equally important is that adult defendants in criminal trials should always be named without exception. If this is not the case public confidence in the law and its institutions may diminish. The English courts were faced with the challenge of upholding open justice, the right to fair trial and privacy interests for vulnerable and living children.

Firstly, the anonymity attaching to the child's name, his mother and stepfather meant that any mainstream media coverage of the narrative deflected attention away from the adult defendants accused of conduct leading directly to the child's death and onto the adult professionals accused of the professional negligence in not intervening and preventing his death. As a result the public, media and political vitriol directed at the professionals may have been disproportionate and unfair.

Secondly, the nature and degree of the secrecy provoked considerable public disquiet about the purpose and reasoning behind the court orders. This information could not be published for the simple reason that such publication would defeat the proper legal purpose of the restrictions. The catch 22 situation undermined public support, confidence and trust in the legal system. The public vented their fury across the Internet by identifying the trial participants whose names the judges had banned the mainstream media from publishing, and calling for violent retribution. Social networking group sites raged 'Death is too good for Tracey Connelly [the mother of the dead child], torture the bitch that killed Baby P', and 'Baby P killers should be hanged Drawn and Quartered'. In August 2009 the *Independent* newspaper published the headline 'Internet hate campaign that made a mockery of the High Court' and the newspaper's law editor, Robert Verkaik, observed that there appeared to be:

> a double standard at work, where the law is incapable of punishing flagrant breaches of court orders by internet transgressors while imposing draconian sentences on the mainstream media for committing much less serious breaches. The internet was born into a lawless cyberspace and has little respect for the fusty orders of the High Court.
>
> (Verkaik *Independent* 2009)

Thirdly, the civil disobedience of the court orders on the Internet through vigilante journalism vitiated the purpose of the restrictions on mainstream media. When Baby P's stepfather, Steven Barker, appeared in court accused of a rape offence and Tracey Connelly for a further allegation of child neglect in their second trial the problem would have been dealt with in the USA through a voir dire of the jury panel. The London court had to adopt the creative solution of trying the couple under pseudonyms until all the verdicts had been returned. The prohibition orders on the mainstream media reporting of their real names and that of 'Baby P' remained. Verkaik advised: 'Judges should stop acting like King Canute by trying to curb every excess of the internet and instead trust the jury to be able to maturely distinguish between online gossip and hard evidence adduced during a trial.'

Fourthly, the actual nature of the reporting restrictions, the debate and motivation behind their issue and the complex struggle by media organizations to preserve the 'open justice' principle of accurate reporting cannot be fully reported. The High Court ruling by Mr Justice Coleridge that permitted the eventual identification of Peter Connelly, his mother Tracey and stepfather Steven Barker after midnight 11 August 2009 remains confidential at the time of writing. It is therefore impossible to discuss the full details of the media law issues surrounding this case.

Fifthly, the vengeful mob dimension to this case has raised the prospect of *contra mundum* anonymity orders on the adults convicted in these trials when they are eventually released, on the basis that their right to life and freedom from torture and inhuman treatment can only be protected by secrecy in perpetuity, combined with the considerable expense of relocation and new identities provided by state authorities. We are thus finding that, far from the Venables and Thompson, Mary Bell and Maxine Carr cases being 'exceptions to the rule', they may have opened the floodgates. Perhaps the media must take some responsibility for this trend since it is media coverage that defines the notoriety and cues the debate. A mature society must learn that crime met with punishment is the limit and full authority of criminal justice. Anything else is unacceptable. As the *Guardian* newspaper wrote in an editorial in August 2009, those adults convicted of responsibility for the death of Peter Connolly

> stand properly and thoroughly condemned and there is nothing to be gained in condemning them any more. It is now time to invert the cheap slogan John Major [Prime Minister at the time] used in the Bulger case – and to condemn a little less, in the hope of understanding just a little more about how such a monstrous thing could happen.
>
> (*Guardian* 2009)

In 1994 Caroline Godwin and I were unsuccessful in our attempt as journalists in person to persuade the Court of Appeal to identify two parents convicted of the manslaughter of their 15-month-old child and to ensure that the victim left this world at least with the dignity of a public identity. Since that case, the British media have had to engage the struggle to preserve open justice and the publication of truth with great legal complexity, legions of specialist media lawyers, and costs running into tens of millions of pounds every year. Is it any coincidence that there has been a concomitant deracination of reporters and journalists covering the legal system through economic rationalization of editorial budgets?

In our arguments we sought to rely on the speech of Lord Justice Hoffmann, as he then was, in *R v Central TV*:

> The motives which impel judges to assume a power to balance freedom of speech against other interests are almost always understandable and humane on the facts of the particular case before them. Newspapers are sometimes irresponsible and their motives in a market economy cannot be expected to be unalloyed by considerations of commercial advantage. And publication may cause needless pain, distress and damage to individuals or harm to other aspects of the public interest. But a freedom which is restricted to what judges think to be responsible in the public interest is no freedom. Freedom means the right to publish things which government and judges, however well motivated, think should not be published. It means the right to say things which 'right-thinking people' regard as dangerous or irresponsible. This freedom is subject only to clearly defined exceptions laid down by common law, or statute [...] It cannot be too strongly emphasised that outside the established exceptions [...] there is no balancing freedom of speech against other interests. It is a trump card which always wins.
>
> (R v Central TV CoA Civ 1994)

Lord Hoffmann was speaking like a federal US Justice of the Supreme Court. But British law is not underpinned by US First Amendment style constitutional law. The problematized jeopardy highlighted in the 1994 case was visited upon the unsuspecting editor of *Marie Claire* magazine, Marie O'Riordan, who in a review of the year 2003 had included the photograph and details of an underage girl who had eloped with an adult man. Full publicity was given in the search for her. But after the girl returned home, the adult man was arrested and prosecuted for criminal offences and the young victim became anonymous because she had become a sexual offence complainant.

The magazine editor was judged to have inadvertently committed the criminal offence of publishing information 'likely to lead to the identification' of the young girl. The editor was fined £2,500 and her appeal was unsuccessful. The magazine had not made any connections between the criminal case and the narrative of the inappropriate elopement. It was in complete ignorance of the existence of the criminal case against the adult man and the statutory reporting restrictions which included the 1976 Sexual Offences Amendment Act and the Children and Young Persons Act. They had not been on the circulation list of the police force that had distributed an email in August 2003 advising the media that identification of the man could lead to the identification of the alleged victim.

Whilst the maxim 'ignorance of the law is no defence' is widely accepted, how could it be applied to the circumstances of a women's magazine with no expertise or interest in covering criminal trials? *Marie Claire* and its editor were being punished for publishing the truth in the past that was lawful at the time of publication but that became retrospectively unlawful in republication because of criminal proceedings they would not ordinarily have been made aware of.

To compound the editor's sense of injustice, two months after she had been prosecuted and fined, the law was changed to give editors in her position a defence to 'prove that at the time of the alleged offence he/she was not aware, and neither suspected nor had reason to suspect, that the allegation had been made.' (Statutory Instrument 2004/2428)

The High Court imposed a duty of care and jeopardy that the First Amendment would block in the USA. However, Mr Justice Crane said it 'seemed to him that Ms O'Riordan's argument that [...] she had no reason to suspect that the girl might be the victim of a sex crime was "an argument wholly removed from reality [...] it seems very little to ask of the media that they take precautions to prevent publication which might affect [the young] victim."' (*Media Lawyer* July 2005: 22; O'Riordan v DPP HC 2005) British courts also did not see the word 'likely' to be equated with statistical probability. The expression 'likely to lead to identification' meant a 'real chance that it may lead to that dangerous situation.' (Ibid.) The courts are obliged by statute to apply a law that penalizes reports that are accurate representations of the truth and of the past, but may relate to facts prohibited from publication.

The last time a British newspaper editor went to jail for contempt of court actually related to a publication judged to be prejudicial because it was assumed there could be jigsaw identification by a potential jury. In 1949 Silvester Bolam, the editor of the *Daily Mirror*, went to prison for three months over three reports in successive editions, the first headlined 'Vampire-Man Held', which talked about an unnamed man who had been charged with several murders and who had committed others and took pleasure from drinking his victims' blood.

The paper tried to minimize the risk of contempt by publishing a separate report about the appearance of John Haigh on a single murder charge at Horsham Magistrates' Court. But they were one and the same man. The Lord Chief Justice of the time, Lord Goddard, said the *Mirror*'s reports were 'a disgrace to English journalism as violating every principle of justice and fair play which it had been the pride of this country to extend to the worst of its criminals.' (*The Times* 26 March 1949) Goddard jailed Mr Bolam and fined the paper £10,000 because, he said, the reports were 'pandering to sensationalism for the purposes of increasing the circulation of the newspaper.' (Ibid.) But can it not be argued that is what newspapers exist to do? The very idea of an editor being jailed in the US for the same reason would have been considered an outrage. The issue of whether potential jurors were able to 'put two and two together' and manifest prejudice against Mr Haigh was wholly speculative. Bolam was jailed for an imagined wrong. Haigh, also known as the 'acid bath murderer' because of the process he used to destroy his victims' bodies, unsuccessfully argued insanity at this trial. He did not dispute the facts. If there was a real risk of prejudice in jurors' recalling that he was linked to more than one murder, a limited *voir dire* enquiry could have secured a jury that was unaffected by the media coverage.

Problematizing journalism of speculation under the Official Secrets Act

In 2007 a civil servant working for the Cabinet Office, and a researcher for an MP, went to prison for six and three months respectively for breaching the Official Secrets Act. The civil servant, motivated by conscience, had leaked a memo of a discussion between Prime Minister Tony Blair and President George W. Bush. The judge ruled that any of the proceedings discussing the content of the memo had to be held in secret session, but one day during the trial at the Old Bailey a question-and-answer exchange accidentally took place in open court. The court had to ban publication of anything said in this open court proceeding.

The appeal court upheld the decision to prohibit reporting of that session even though it was in public, and that any publication of speculation as to the content of the evidence given *in camera* could amount to a contempt of court. The effect of the order was to ban publication of the content of newspaper reports published before the trial. The media argued that the orders by the trial judge and the appeal court were wrong because they prohibited publication of matters already in the public domain. They questioned the efficacy and legality of banning speculation about the content of secret proceedings that the media had no access to and for obvious reasons could not verify. (Times & Others and R CoA Crim 2007)

As this textbook is published in the British jurisdiction it is impossible to fully analyse the media law issues in this case, in itself a severe abrogation of the principle of academic freedom. The trial judge stopped the media from using a word that would have linked newspaper coverage arising out of the leak of the memo and the reporting of the trial. If it be a contempt of court to speculate that the newspaper coverage of the contents of the memo is an accurate representation of what the court *in camera* learned of the actual contents of the memo, then it is impossible in this book not only to discuss the public interest issues in the case but also to extend this discussion to ethical and legal issues of profound international importance. The censorship also ends any British debate and discussion of political decisions and policies debated globally and with great controversy. Yet this censorship endures, despite the fact that all the issues and details that these court orders have prohibited can be read in the content of Internet articles.

At a legal seminar at Doughty Street Chambers in May 2008 Andrew Nicol QC, as he then was, discussed the problems arising out of what would be described in the USA as media gagging orders. The trial judge had prohibited any publication of an article which would or might disclose what had taken place *in camera*:

> That would mean that if a newspaper published speculation about what had happened and proved to be wrong it would nonetheless be guilty of infringing the court's order because it would have published something which might, even though it had not in fact, disclosed what had taken place *in camera*.
>
> (*Media Lawyer* July 2008: 12)

The Court of Appeal said that if a newspaper published speculation in this way it would run the risk of attempting to frustrate the court's order and that in itself would be a contempt:

> Such publications would be attempts, albeit unsuccessful, to flout the order made by the court and would be seen by the public as a violation of the order of the court. We consider it likely that any such attempt would, itself, constitute a contempt of court at common law. [...]
>
> Should any publication allege that those reports [in the press] accurately represent the evidence that was given in camera they will, for the reasons that we have given, be at risk of constituting a contempt of court.
>
> (Times & Others and R CoA Crim 2007)

At the media law seminar Mr Nicol explained that the idea of attempted inaccurate speculation being a contempt of court 'appeared for the first time in the court's judgment, so there were no submissions on it.' (*Media Lawyer* July 2008: 12) He also explained that the offence of 'attempted contempt of court' had been abolished by the 1981 Contempt of Court Act. The effect of the orders given by the trial judge and the appeal court is to emasculate any representation of the context of the crime committed by the defendants, David Keogh and Leo O'Connor, and any discussion of a substantial and global public interest issue. The information is freely available in the public domain and had been strongly discussed and published in the USA. The application of the Official Secrets Act in these circumstances creates a law and philosophical conundrum that past reality previously published is censored retrospectively.

Section 8 of the 1920 version of the Official Secrets Act means that anything mentioned in court during an in camera hearing that is 'prejudicial to national security' can never be published. Problems arise if aspects of the case are sourced outside the courtroom. In January 2009 *The Times* was referred to the Attorney General for possible contempt prosecution by Mr Justice Ouseley for its reporting of the case of a Chinese dissident convicted of murdering a millionaire author at his villa in Hampstead, North London. Much of the trial was held in secret session. The trial judge was obliged by law to issue reporting restrictions about speculation and information that journalists could not access but might inadvertently guess:

> It is clear from orders I have previously made in this case that speculation, whether accurate or inaccurate, which purports to reveal the matters which were considered *in camera* or which are covered by Contempt of Court orders may itself be a contempt of court. [...]
>
> Assertions, whether accurate or inaccurate, to the same effect are equally, or arguably more so, a contempt of court. Repetition of previously published material, whether accurate or inaccurate, which speculates about or asserts what was considered in camera is arguably a contempt of court.
>
> Repetition of *The Times* article, in any publication of this statement, may equally therefore be a contempt of court. It is in any event far from clear to me that *The Times* is correct in so far as it claims merely to repeat previously published material. [...]
>
> Media organisations are reminded that the orders made by the Court to protect national security and the administration of justice remain in force. The Court of Appeal confirmed that without such orders no trial of Wang Yam for the murder of Allan Chappelow would have been possible. [...]
>
> (*Media Lawyer* March 2009: 36)

The Times argues that it had simply reported public domain information published before Mr Justice Ouseley began making reporting restrictions and that it could not be closed down. It is unlikely that US courts would have the legal power in their own jurisdiction to impose the kind of orders made in the unrelated English trials of Keogh and O'Connor, and Wang Yam. By being directed to the media they represent a further dimension of the legal problematization of journalism.

Problematizing journalists' sources

It could be argued that the other method by which the US and UK legal systems problematize journalism is through harassment and persecution over their use of confidential sources. It is known that the free media can only function effectively in a democratic society with the right of people to provide information to journalists confidentially and for journalists to be able to report without having their impartiality impugned through being subpoenaed to give evidence about the news events they cover and witness. Yet governments and courts continue to interfere and endeavour to undermine the protection of sources.

It might be argued that academics too do not fully understand the wider and complex pressures involved in negotiating and maintaining the channels of confidentiality required when the publications that arise have to involve open communication of people and events for the public record. A wider cultural and anthropological enquiry into the subject of 'Journalists and their sources' is discoursed by Isabel Awad in *Journalism Studies*, Vol. 7, No. 6, 2006:

> In journalism, in contrast, 'ethical quality' is a matter of *getting it right* rather than of treating the sources in the right way. The profession's take on ethics [...] is fundamentally related to the motto of 'the public's right to know;' [*sic*] the prevalence of a narrow definition of truth in terms of facticity; and of communication as transmission of messages rather than as constitution of the social world. In brief, it is an ethics constrained by the ideology of objectivity.
>
> (Awad 2006: 935)

In this regard the positions of the British and American journalist have more in common than they have differences. Table 9.1 sets out a summary of the legal situation and contrasts some of the key cases on either side of the Atlantic. You may think there was a strangely ironic parallel between the Andrew Gilligan/Dr David Kelly scenario in Britain and that of Judith Miller/I. Lewis "Scooter" Libby in America. In both cases the sources were pressured into the spotlight. One was judged to have committed suicide and the other was prosecuted and jailed and his sentence was then commuted to enable his release by Presidential order. In the case of the journalists, the intriguing contrast was that the British journalist was investigating the UK government's campaign to go to war. The ethical and legal issues arising out of the Andrew Gilligan and Dr David Kelly affair, investigated by Lord Hutton during the public enquiry, have been debated in great detail in a number of publications. (Crook *British Journalism Review* 2003: 7–12; Harcup 2007: 67–75; Keeble 2009: 89–128)

In the case of the *New York Times* journalist Judith Miller, the obligation of a journalist to protect her source was played out in the context of the invasion of Iraq and allegations of manipulative propaganda. Miller was prepared to go to jail in order to protect a senior White House official

Table 9.1 Protection of journalists' sources: UK and USA

United Kingdom	United States
Section 10 of the 1981 Contempt of Court Act states: 'No court may require a person to disclose, nor is any person guilty of contempt of court for refusing to disclose, the source of information contained in a publication for which he is responsible unless it is established to the satisfaction of the court that it is necessary in the interests of justice or national security or for the prevention of disorder or crime.'	The First Amendment constitutional protection for freedom of the press and freedom of expression means that most state and federal courts recognize that journalists have a constitutional privilege, but this is qualified in relation to the constitutional rights of other citizens. For example, the Sixth Amendment guarantees that an accused person 'shall enjoy the right … to have compulsory process for obtaining witness in his favour'.
Journalists are entitled to some protection against police powers of search and seizure. Under the Police and Criminal Evidence Act 1984 'excluded material' includes 'journalistic material acquired or created for the purposes of journalism'. Excluded material is information and writing (notebooks or computerized information) that is held in confidence.	Many states have passed state legislation called 'shield laws' which protect journalists against being compelled to reveal their sources. 'Shield laws' can be *absolute*, providing protection except in exceptional circumstances, or *qualified* so that disclosure can be ordered if there is a compelling need for the information.
Journalistic material not held in confidence is also protected in that the police have to use a special procedure to obtain it. Only a circuit judge can give the police permission to seize such material through a court application.	US police forces have tried to circumvent shield laws by using search warrants. In 1971 police were attacked and beaten by some demonstrators when trying to remove them from administrative offices at Stanford University Hospital.
Most photographic and film material acquired through reporting requires special procedure if the police wish to seize it. The police can override these shields when investigating serious criminal offences such as murder, terrorism and espionage.	The *Stanford Daily* (a student newspaper) published photos of the event and the police believed they had more unpublished images that could assist their investigation.
The Terrorism Act 2000 and Anti-Terrorism, Crime and Security Act 2001 have created new offences of 'withholding information on suspected terrorist offences'. A journalist faces prosecution if, during the course of his/her work, he/she fails to report the discovery of information about terrorism and 'he/	Police went in with a search warrant but found nothing. However, the newspaper sued for violation of First Amendment rights. It argued that the search process was physically disruptive, intimidating to news staff and a threat to cultivation of confidential sources. At the Supreme Court in *Zurcher v Stanford Daily*, (1978) the newspaper lost. The court ruled that as long as a search warrant is supported by the probable cause of

Continued overleaf

she knows or believes he/she might be of material assistance in preventing the commission by another person of an act of terrorism, or in securing the apprehension, prosecution or conviction of another person in the UK for an offence involving the commission, preparation or instigation of an act of terrorism'.

Guardian/Sarah Tisdall case 1983/84

Sarah Tisdall was a clerk who worked in the Foreign Office. She was opposed to the siting of US cruise missiles in Britain and leaked papers to the *Guardian* newspaper. She did this anonymously by dropping them through the letterbox of the newspaper at 119 Farringdon Road, London.

The *Guardian* published extracts from the papers, which revealed the date and time of the missiles' deployment at Greenham Common, which had become the site of a protest camp by women demonstrators. The *Guardian* avoided any reference to the documents, which were security sensitive. The government demanded their return but the newspaper refused, saying that this might reveal its source.

The House of Lords held that the value of the documents was negligible and since the purpose of the exercise was to enable the ministry to deduce the source, the paper could invoke section 10 of the 1981 Contempt of Court Act. The section applied even though there was only a reasonable chance (rather than a certainty) that the paper's source could be revealed. The burden of proof lay with the government to demonstrate that one of the exceptions applied. Although three of the five Law Lords were persuaded that national security

there being a reason to believe that evidence of a crime will be found, a search warrant is acceptable. Nothing in the constitution gave the press a special privilege to avoid the process.

In 1980 Congress legislated to protect the press from intrusive police searches. The Privacy Protection Act 1980 is a federal statute which prohibits newsroom searches and seizures unless:

1. The person possessing the materials is the criminal suspect.
2. Immediate seizure of materials is deemed necessary to prevent death or serious injury.
3. Serving a subpoena would likely result in destruction or concealment of the materials.
4. A subpoena and court order to comply have already been unsuccessful. If these exceptions do not apply, the police have to serve a subpoena (summons) rather than go in with a search warrant to seize material from news organizations.

Many more US than UK journalists go to jail in order to protect their sources against court orders (subpoenas). During the 1960s period of civil unrest there was an increase in media disclosure orders. During 1969 and 1970 three major US television networks were served with 150 such orders and it was recognized that there was a need for the Supreme Court to define any constitutional privilege that reporters might have in this area.

Branzburg v Hayes 1972

The Supreme Court justices decided to rule in four cases where news reporters had been subpoenaed to testify before a grand jury.

required the leaker to be identified, all of them stressed that this conclusion could not be reached merely upon the government's say-so. There had to be realistic evidence that national security was imperilled.

Although the *Guardian*'s then editor, Peter Preston, would have been prepared to go to jail to protect the identity of the anonymous source, his paper was faced with contempt fines and economic sequestration. He had kept the document because he had been advised that section 10 of the 1981 Contempt of Court Act afforded him a legal protection for his source. As a result of the handing over of the document, the leak was traced to Ms Tisdall, who was jailed for 6 months after pleading guilty, before Mr Justice Cantley at the Old Bailey, to breaching the Official Secrets Act.

William Goodwin, 1991

Bill Goodwin was a reporter on *The Engineer* who, in 1991, received a leak of a financial report produced by a computer software company, Tetra. When he made enquiries of the company it secured an injunction preventing publication of the story, which might have been commercially damaging, and an order to disclose the identity of the source. Tetra claimed that public exposure of its refinancing problems might cost hundreds of jobs. Goodwin refused and his employer, Morgan-Grampian Magazines (part of United News and Media) supported him.

The case went to the House of Lords (the highest UK court), with Goodwin losing at every stage. He refused to comply throughout. He was eventually fined £5,000 – not a high figure in comparison with other cases. Tetra claimed that the leak was theft and

Case 1. Reporter Paul Branzburg, writing for the *Louisville Courier-Journal*, described how two youths from Kentucky made money by converting marijuana into hashish. He observed the process first hand after promising anonymity to his informants. Branzburg refused to disclose who they were when ordered to by the grand jury.

Case 2. Paul Branzburg reported on the use and sale of illicit drugs and based his material on interviews with drug users. He again refused to identify them when ordered to do so by the grand jury.

Case 3. A TV reporter from Massachusetts was allowed into the HQ of the Black Panther party, regarded as a militant Black organization. He was allowed to observe what was going on, provided that he reported none of what he saw or heard. After being summoned before the grand jury he refused to answer questions about any events inside the building.

Case 4. A reporter for the *New York Times* wrote some stories about the Black Panthers in the San Francisco area. A federal grand jury investigating possible crimes by the Panthers ordered the journalist to answer questions and surrender notes and tape recordings.

The Supreme Court was divided. This is called a plurality opinion. It declined to recognize a special First Amendment privilege for journalists. Four justices said there was no first amendment privilege, four justices said there was. The swing voter took the middle ground. As a result of Branzburg, although the 5–4 vote was against the reporters, lower courts recognize that five of the judges agreed there should be a qualified

Continued overleaf

it therefore needed the identity so as to trace the culprit. (In fact this was not true, the informant being a person lawfully holding the document, though Bill Goodwin could of course never disclose that.) The courts accepted the company's argument and found that the 'interest of justice' exception overruled the journalist's right to protect confidentiality.

The ECHR stated in 1996: 'Protection of journalistic sources is one of the basic conditions for press freedom [...] Without such protection, sources may be deterred from assisting the press in informing the public on matters of public interest. As a result the vital public watchdog role of the press may be undermined and the ability of the press to provide accurate and reliable information may be adversely affected [...] such a measure cannot be compatible with Article 10 of the Convention unless it is justified by an overriding requirement in the public interest.' A contempt finding had to be 'necessary in a democratic society' in terms of a 'pressing social need' and the criminalization of the journalist had to be a proportionate response to the aim of protecting corporate confidentiality.

Following the ECHR judgment, the UK government should have amended the 1981 Act so as to strengthen the protection of journalists, but successive governments have failed to do so.

Dr David Kelly, Andrew Gilligan, the BBC and the Hutton enquiry, 2003

No legal case arose from this affair, but the BBC instituted an enquiry and produced the Neil Report which concluded:

In 2003 after the invasion/liberation of Iraq, Andrew Gilligan reported that a senior intelligence source (Dr David Kelly) had told him the 45

reporter's privilege.

Judith Miller, the Valerie Plame affair, and I. Lewis 'Scooter' Libby

Judith Miller wrote for the *New York Times* and was associated with the newspaper's controversial coverage and journalism leading up to and during the invasion of Iraq, and she left the paper in 2005. In July 2005, Miller was jailed for contempt of court for refusing to testify before a federal grand jury investigating a leak naming Valerie Plame as a covert CIA agent. Miller did not write about Plame, but was reportedly in possession of evidence relevant to the leak investigation. According to a subpoena, Miller met with an unnamed government official – later revealed to be I. Lewis 'Scooter' Libby, Vice President Cheney's Chief of Staff – on 8 July 2003, two days after former ambassador Joseph Wilson published an editorial opinion piece in the *New York Times* criticizing the Bush administration for 'twisting' intelligence to justify war in Iraq. (Plame's CIA identity was revealed in a column by conservative political commentator Robert Novak on 14 July 2003.)

Libby signed a waiver allowing journalists to testify about their conversations on this subject. Miller had reportedly refused to accept its validity on the grounds that it was coerced. On 29 September 2005, after spending 85 days in jail, Miller was released after a telephone call with Libby. He had reaffirmed the release of confidentiality.

In a second grand jury appearance, Miller produced a notebook from a previously undisclosed meeting with Libby on 23 June 2003, several weeks before Wilson's *New York Times* editorial was published. According to Miller's notes from that earlier meeting, Libby disclosed that Joseph Wilson's wife was a CIA employee minute weapons of mass destruction claim in a government dossier was part of a 'sexing up' of the case for war and government put it out probably knowing it was wrong. Hutton and the BBC agreed:

'At the Hutton Inquiry, the BBC acknowledged that the 6.07 a.m. report on the Today programme was inaccurate and that with hindsight it would have done a number of things differently.

'One: Although the use of a single anonymous source is consistent with the Producers' Guidelines, the BBC acknowledged the dilemmas involved in seeking to protect Dr Kelly's identity while giving clues as to his credibility.

'Two: The notes of the meeting with the source were not complete and did not support all the allegations that were reported on air.

'Three: The allegations made were not put to Downing Street on the night before the broadcast, nor were there adequate notes of the conversations with the MoD [Ministry of Defence].

'Four: There was an issue of fairness in not being clear about the nature of the allegations which prevented a proper opportunity to respond.

'Five: The 6.07 broadcast should have been scripted. However, the BBC has subsequently asserted that a core script was properly prepared and cleared by the programme editor in line with normal practices, but not followed by Andrew Gilligan.

'Six: The inquiries into the complaints should have been handled differently and more time should have been taken to investigate thoroughly.

'Seven: The rules about BBC journalists writing for the press should be tightened. *(New guidelines have already been issued in this area.)*'

involved in her husband's trip to Niger. Miller's notebook from her 8 July 2003 meeting with Libby contains the name 'Valerie Flame'. This reference occurred six days before Novak published Plame's name and unmasked her as a CIA 'operative'. Libby was later prosecuted, convicted and imprisoned, but President George W. Bush exercised his constitutional power to commute the sentence so that he did not go to jail.

who had revealed that a former ambassador, raising questions about the veracity of US claims that Iraq had weapons of mass destruction, was married to a CIA agent. The protection-of-sources principle in journalism is not supposed to be the preserve of counter-culture and politically oppositional reporting.

Leading US court rulings setting out the American legal position on protection of sources are *Branzburg v Hayes* 1972 and *In re: Grand Jury Subpoena, Judith Miller* 2005. More than three-fifths of US states have passed special 'shield' statutes setting out the legal framework for the protection of journalists' sources, but they do not hold to the immutable and deontological ethical position that most journalists have to adhere to on pain of fine or imprisonment. By 2005 Professor Tony Pederson was arguing for a federal shield statute that reached into every state and clarified the issue of the reporter privilege: 'independent journalism is at the point of being compromised unless a privilege is recognized for all reporters.' (Pederson *The News Media & The Law* 2005) And as the case of Judith Miller showed, American journalists do sleep in prison cells to protect the principle. It is rare in the UK because, as I wrote in *British Journalism Review*:

> In post-industrial capitalist societies the judiciary enforcing the will of the executive tends to avoid making martyrs out of journalists and editors, and will attempt to 'sequestrate the assets' of the employing media corporation. [...] Decisions will be based on the grounds of commercial reality rather than journalistic principle. The hyper and postmodernist state controls journalism economically through debt and market economic forces.
>
> (Crook *British Journalism Review* 2003: 8)

In the USA, the Supreme Court in *Cohen v Cowles Media Co.* 1991 even supported the right for a journalist's source to sue and collect damages if any agreed confidentiality has been negligently or deliberately breached by the journalist. (Zelezny 2004: 296–7; Moore and Murray 2008: 202–3) Youm and Russomanno opened their ten-year review of *Cohen v Cowles* with the sentence: '"Burning" a source is no longer the type of ethical or moral issue for the US news media to dismiss cavalierly in determining whether to honor or to break their confidentiality promises to their sources.' (Youm and Russomanno 2002: 69) The case concerned Republican Party activist Dan Cohen, who in 1982 provided four news reporters with potentially damaging information on an opposition candidate in a Minnesota election. The editors of the *Star Tribune* and *Pioneer Press* overrode their reporters' pledge of confidentiality. Cohen lost his job and sued for breach of contract and fraudulent misrepresentation. (Ibid.: 72–3) Justice White in the Supreme Court stated:

the truthful information sought to be published must have been lawfully acquired. The press may not with impunity break and enter an office or dwelling to gather news. Neither does the First Amendment relieve a newspaper reporter of the obligation shared by all citizens to respond to a grand jury subpoena and answer questions relevant to a criminal investigation, even though the reporter might be required to reveal a confidential source. [...] The press, like others interested in publishing, may not publish copyrighted material without obeying the copyright laws.

(Cohen v Cowles Media Co. SC US 1991)

The ruling was a jolt to the US news media in addressing the ethics of newsgathering as much as relying on the protection of the First Amendment for content. Youm and Russomanno conclude that whilst journalists 'more deliberately guard against granting promises of confidentiality, courts apply the decision in a way that is more accommodating to freedom of the press interests than initially anticipated.' (Youm and Russomanno 2002: 101)

British and American governments know that the very process of arrest, search and prosecution or the issuing of witness subpoenas is enough to dissipate the investigative ardour of journalists and their employing organizations. Whatever the rhetoric engaged by academics and politicians about media power, a global recession, combined with large-scale redundancies and the rapid loss of advertising income to the Internet means that the news media are soft targets.

By the time judges are compelled by law to stop prosecutions, as in the case of *Milton Keynes Citizen* journalist Sally Murrer, who was acquitted of unlawfully receiving information from a police detective, there is a risk that the damage in benchmarking the disincentives has already been done. The very fact that her lawyers, instructed by the NUJ, had won her an acquittal had been delayed by reporting restrictions in November 2008. She observed: 'It's been a very long, horrible, nasty and vindictive case and we are all exhausted.' (*Media Lawyer* January 2009: 1–3) Her solicitor, Louis Charalambous, issued a statement which described the harm that had been done:

The safeguards enshrined in law for the protection of journalists have been trampled upon by Thames Valley Police – both at the outset and when they chose to bug Sally's conversations under a warrant that failed to mention that she was a journalist, and later when she was arrested and brought to a police station, where following a strip search and a night in the cells, she faced a gruelling interrogation – while her home and office were searched, and all of her notebooks seized. [...]

365

Sally has endured eighteen months of waiting for the case to reach this stage. The charge she faced – aiding and abetting misconduct in public office – was nonsense, the stuff of Orwell. [...]

Journalists talk to police officials every day about cases, which is precisely how crime stories in newspapers get written. Had the case against Sally gone ahead, it would have signalled a lurch towards a police state, a situation which is abhorrent in the minds of right thinking people.

(Ibid.: 3)

We may cite other positive outcomes. In 2009 Suzanne Breen, northern editor of the Dublin-based *Sunday Tribune* did not have to disclose information to the police about the Real IRA and its involvement in the murder of two British soldiers. (Sharrock *The Times* 2009), as the Recorder of Belfast agreed that the journalist's right to life outweighed the great public interest in apprehending the murderers. But Ms Breen's right to life had already been threatened by the court application.

There was indeed a victory for journalism in the 1996 ECHR ruling in *William Goodwin v UK*. But that was not until after years of a young journalist's life being hijacked by writs, court orders, litigation and a criminal conviction and fine by the House of Lords. The Court of Appeal ruling in *Mersey Care NHS Trust v Ackroyd (No 2)* in 2007 can be studied as a more recent British case, confirming the right of journalist Robin Ackroyd to withhold the identity of his source on application by a public health authority. However, despite judges' paying lip service to the importance of protecting confidential sources, British journalists are used to hearing the following phrase '"But in these particular circumstances..." and an order for disclosure.' (*Media Lawyer* November 2007: 21) It happened in the case of Channel 4, which in October 2007 was ordered to reveal the identities of two confidential sources who had provided information for a documentary on the death of Diana, Princess of Wales. (Assistant Deputy Coroner for Inner West London v Channel 4 HC 2007) *Media Lawyer* observed that the litigation in Mr Ackroyd's case:

> ended his career as an investigative journalist. It is now clear that despite the ringing declaration of the European Court of Human Rights on the importance of protecting confidential sources, journalists and editors cannot rely on national courts to take the same view.
>
> (*Media Lawyer* November 2007)

It would seem that the Strasbourg court is just as fickle in its supervision of journalist source protection. Professor Dirk Voorhoof of Ghent University was critical of a seven-judge ECHR decision that supported a police demand for a magazine to hand over journalistic material gathered in the reporting of an illegal street race. (Sanoma Uitgevers BV v Netherlands ECHR 2009; *Media Lawyer* May 2009: 32–4)

Nick Martin-Clark was a British journalist who did break the deontolog-ical code of the NUJ that when a pledge of confidentiality has been agreed or implied, sources must be protected. He agreed to be the only prosecution witness in the murder trial of loyalist terrorist Clifford George McKeown, who had confessed to him that he had murdered Michael McGoldrick, a part-time Catholic taxi-driver, by pumping five bullets into the back of his victim's head from close range. This case history arose out of 'the Troubles' in Northern Ireland, a period of violent inter-community conflict between paramilitary Protestant/loyalist and Catholic/nationalist terrorist groups that lasted over thirty years. The loyalists campaigned for the preservation of union with the UK. The nationalists sought fusion with the Republic of Ireland. The police were only able to prosecute McKeown if Nick Martin-Clerk was prepared to take the witness stand and breach his pledge of confi-dentiality. Mr Martin-Clark wrote in *British Journalism Review*:

> After swearing me to silence about the killing, he then boasted about it to me. It would have been easier to keep his secret because my life has been disrupted – we have had to move house and I am now on a witness protection programme for the rest of my life. But despite the difficulty of going against the source this was a promise I eventually felt, after some agonising, that I could not keep.
>
> (Martin-Clark 2003: 35)

McKeown belonged to the Loyalist Volunteer Force (LVF) that had killed Martin O'Hagan, the first journalist to be killed in the Northern Ireland 'Troubles'. Despite the risks and sacrifices that Martin-Clark made, the court did not offer him any protection from an application for full disclosure of all the journalistic material he had on Northern Ireland, including all his notes, tapes, 'even completely irrelevant ones'. He said that it was for this reason:

> I could not recommend to any other journalist that they should go down the path I did without a change in the law. Had I known that the legal system was going to treat confidentiality in such a cavalier manner, I doubt whether I would ever have undertaken to help the police.
>
> (Ibid.: 39)

Tim Gopsill of the National Union of Journalists of Britain and Ireland said Martin-Clark's actions had caused considerable disquiet among journal-ists in Northern Ireland: 'The issue has been discussed widely in the union and in April [2003] the National Executive Council declared Nick Martin-Clark "not a fit and proper person" for membership.' (Gopsill 2003)

But the crossing of the deontological line on journalists' sources is not a rare occasion limited to the British experience. Exceptional circum-stances drive individual journalists to make decisions that are morally consequentialist. Matthew Pollack, in 'How to save a life', reported on how and why *Village Voice* reporter Tom Robbins decided to break his promise of confidentiality to save a former FBI agent from a life sentence. He was faced with a source he had interviewed ten years previously giving testimony in court that differed from what he had recorded with her. He decided to reveal the content in a news article for his newspaper and his reasons for breaking the pledge. After listening to the tape recordings, the prosecution decided to end its murder case against the former FBI agent. Robbins explained that his decision was a difficult one:

> At the end of the day, this was a guy who would have been convicted on what was clearly perjured testimony. [...] Those are the kind of high stakes that take precedence over contracts and vows of confidence, no matter how important they may be to the business of reporting, and regardless of how distasteful it may be to violate them. [...] The threat of a life sentence trumps a promise.
>
> (Pollack *The News Media & The Law* 2008)

Problematizing the war correspondent in international criminal courts

Journalists and NGOs who are witnesses to genocide and war crimes perform a vital function in history. But would their safety and ability to report and monitor from a conflict zone be undermined if the forces they are reporting on know that at some time in the future they can agree, or be subpoenaed to give evidence in trials for crimes against humanity? The *Washington Post* journalist Jonathan Randal refused to testify in the International Criminal Tribunal on Yugoslavia (ICTY) trial at The Hague of Radoslav Brdjanin. Mr Randal won a significant shield of international legal protection for war correspondents in a decision in December 2002. Prosecutors wanted him to testify about an article he wrote in February 1993 entitled 'Preserving the fruits of ethnic cleansing: Bosnian Serbs, expulsion victims see process as beyond reversal'. Brdjanin was quoted as saying 'those unwilling to defend [Bosnian Serb territory] must be moved out [...] to create an ethnically clean space through voluntary movement.' (note 1 Prosecutor v Brdjanin: appeal of Jonathan Randal ICTY Appeals Chamber 2002) He was also alleged to have said that Muslims and Croats 'should not be killed, but should be allowed to leave – and good riddance.' (Ibid.) The Appeals Chamber ruled that compelling war correspondents to testify would hinder their ability to gather and report the news and that trial chambers need to demonstrate a two-pronged test that the evidence sought is of direct and important value in determining a core issue, and the evidence could not be reasonably obtained elsewhere. (Ibid.)

Robertson and Nicol cite the importance of a decision of the Appeals Chamber of the Special Court for Sierra Leone in 2006 when it decided that human rights reporters were 'entitled, in the course of their testimony, to decline to answer questions directed to identifying the sources of their information.' (Robertson and Nicol 2008: 680; Independent Counsel v Brima Samura Special Court of Sierra Leone 2005)

These protections are not absolutist and the ethical question relating to the duties and responsibilities of war correspondents remains an enduring debate. Lindsey Hilsum of UK Channel 4 News did testify before the International Criminal Tribunal on Rwanda about what she witnessed as a freelance in 1994:

> I read some recent testimony of a peasant woman from the southern Rwandan town of Butare, identified only by her initials, S.U., who wept in the courtroom as she described how her baby was hacked to death on her back, her four other children were also killed, and she, badly injured, was partly burned and left for dead. I reported as best I could in Rwanda. I did not change the course of history. I did not save anyone's life. And then I returned home to my family and friends and career. I think the least I could do was to testify alongside the Rwandans who lost everyone and everything.
>
> (Hilsum 2003)

The journalism professions in the UK and USA seem rather divided on the question of whether journalists should volunteer their testimony to international criminal courts and tribunals prosecuting war crimes. Ciar Byrne reported in 2002 that the BBC's former Belgrade correspondent Jacky Rowland and the award-winning war correspondent Janine di Giovanni believed they had a duty to say what they saw if asked. But Roy Gutman of *Newsweek* said there was a concern that testifying journalists become active participants in their news stories. He accepted, though, that where a journalist's evidence made the difference between the conviction and release of a war criminal, the eventual decision had to be a matter of conscience. (Byrne *Guardian* 2002)

The ICTY Appeals Chamber in *Randal* set a high threshold in international law in deciding when a court could force the journalist/war correspondent to give evidence. Courts everywhere have a responsibility to avoid problematizing journalists as convenient witnesses and evidence gatherers for lazy state investigators. They also have a duty to prevent their harassment and punishment for being the unpopular messengers of whistleblowers and informants seeking through conscience to expose executive iniquity, abuse of power and incompetence. In 2007 it appeared the NUJ had modified its deontological obligation on sources by stating that journalists 'were expected to abide' by the principle.

10

HUMAN RIGHTS AND
INTERNATIONAL LAW FOR
JOURNALISTS

Journalism in conflict: the potential for reverse culpability

Can journalism kill? Is it possible that people whose communication encourages genocide and murderous hatred can be held responsible for their propaganda and journalism? What responsibilities do journalists have under the Geneva Convention? This chapter also considers the issue of protecting journalists when reporting conflict, as well as the extent to which people need protecting from journalists in time of war.

If history can be a narrative of progress it is certainly the case that there has been an increase in the speed and power of military ordnance. This has been accompanied by hypermedia and asymmetric dimensions in the speed and power of the media reporting of war events, and an intensifying of the propagandized binary struggle and representation of good and evil. The pressure for journalists and media communicators to take sides means that the ethical obligations and dilemmas are no less problematic. The Norwegian sociologist Johan Galtung argued that any attempt to analyse war/violence journalism merited a consideration of peace/conflict journalism. The authors Jake Lynch and Annabel McGoldrick in their text *Peace Journalism* (2005) identified the shortcomings in the reporting of the build-up to war in Iraq in 2003. They asked the question whether 'peace journalism' represented a remedy 'for systemic shortcomings or distortions in coverage, arising out of this pattern of omission and marginalisation.' (Ibid.: 7) The significance of this text and the phenomenon of 'peace journalism' are summarized in Table 10.1.

During the early stages of the Anglo-American invasion of Iraq in March 2003, global 24-hour TV news networks were accused of breaking the Geneva Convention by filming and broadcasting footage of barefoot Iraqi prisoners in their humiliation of surrender and detention. But it transpired that British Army and US Army camera/media operatives had gathered much of the footage. The accusation of *prima facie* breaches of the Geneva Convention should have been directed at the UK and USA governments. In fact the global news media were simply fulfilling their

Table 10.1 Ethical approaches to peace journalism

The concept of 'peace journalism' was first originated by the Norwegian sociologist Professor Johan Galtung, who set out a model for analytical and fieldwork methods (Lynch and McGoldrick 2005: 6).

According to this concept, the choices editors and reporters make on which stories to report and how to report them can create opportunities for society at large to consider and to value non-violent responses to conflict.

Two journalists, Jake Lynch and Annabel McGoldrick, attempted to translate this theoretical concept into the practicality of journalism and war reporting.

Their book, *Peace Journalism – A Global Dialogue for Democracy and Democratic Media*, was published in 2005 and Phillip Knightley described it as an important and long overdue text that could 'spark off a revolution in journalism' (ibid.: iii).

Some of their 'tips' to peace journalists:
- Don't portray a conflict as if it consists only of two sides pursuing one goal.
- Don't accept stark distinctions between the 'goodies' and the 'baddies'.
- Try to report less-visible effects of violence (such as trauma), beyond the immediate casualties.
- Try to relate to areas of common ground between the parties, instead of focusing only on the points of division.
- Don't focus exclusively on the suffering, fears and grievances of one side, but treat the suffering of both sides as equally newsworthy.
- Don't rush to use labels such as 'genocide' or 'massacre' if these are not precise.

The authors concluded that journalists had to be aware of operating in a context of communication between a majority world and a minority world. It is important to give space to new voices and, in the words of Galtung: 'Peace Journalism makes audible and visible the subjugated aspects of reality' (ibid.: 224).

In conclusion, journalists are advised to think of peace as much as war in the organization of reporting, adopt analytical tools to 'excavate hidden details', recognize the agenda in news, avoid the bias towards 'war journalism', resist propaganda, recognize the vulnerability of 'objectivity' to hidden bias, be aware of the predictable rituals in reporting conflict and study the nature of conflict theory.

Source: Compiled by Anat Balint and Tim Crook

traditional function in reporting the facts of Iraqi POWs surrendering and their treatment by British and US soldiers.

The generic term 'Geneva Convention' covers a number of treaties setting out rules on how combatants should behave towards each other and treat non-combatants. Failure to observe the 'Geneva Convention' leads to UN war crimes prosecutions. A summary of the way the Convention recognizes journalists in conflict zones is mapped out in Table 10.2.

Table 10.2 Journalism/media and the Geneva Conventions

The first, second and third Geneva Conventions extend to war correspondents (embedded in the armed forces of a country) all the protections due to combatants. They are not to be treated as spies and, even though their notebooks and film can be confiscated, they do not have to respond to interrogation. If they are sick or wounded, they must receive medical treatment and, if they are captured, they must be treated humanely. They also have the right to receive assistance from international relief agencies. The correspondents should possess authorization from the armed forces they are assigned to, confirming their status.

The 1977 Geneva Protocols explicitly recognize journalists to be civilians and entitled to all the civilian protections. This clearly relates to the situation of non-embedded journalists wearing civilian clothes, who are sometimes referred to as 'unilaterals'. Article 79 entitles journalists to immunity from military discipline and they should not be exploited or manipulated by opposing forces 'provided they take no action adversely affecting their status as civilians'. Again, the protection is enhanced by the possession of an identity card declaring the journalist's status.

The Protocols imply that journalists must not be deliberately targeted, detained or otherwise mistreated any more than any other civilians. This means that journalists now have an obligation to differentiate themselves from combatants by not wearing uniforms or openly carrying firearms. Journalists have a choice of being treated either as civilians or as prisoners of war under Article 79 when they have been accredited to and embedded with a military force.

Warring parties must obey the rules spelled out in the common Article 3 of the Geneva Conventions, which requires that prisoners of war and wounded combatants be protected from murder; discrimination based on race, religion, sex and similar criteria; mutilation, cruel treatment and torture; humiliating and degrading treatment; and sentencing or execution without a fair trial.

In addition, the following actions are forbidden toward any persons in an area of armed conflict and the protection applies to journalists as it does to non-combatants and prisoners of war:
- Torture, mutilation, rape, slavery and arbitrary killing;
- Genocide;
- Crimes against humanity – which include abduction and concealment of combatants and non-combatants and depriving them of humanitarian aid;
- War crimes – which include apartheid, biological experiments, hostage taking, attacks on cultural objects, and depriving people of the right to a fair trial.

Journalists and broadcasters have been prosecuted and convicted for operating as the high priests and priestesses of hate. The Allies hanged Julius Streicher, editor of Nazi newspaper *Der Stürmer*, following his trial at Nuremberg in 1946, although the Nazi head of German radio was acquitted. The British hanged William Joyce and John Amery for broadcasting for the Nazis during the Second World War. They had been

Plate 14 Bulgarian soldier giving water to a dying Turk, Adrianople 1912, during a war in the Balkans.

Plate 15 The macabre duty of identifying the dead on the battlefield at the end of the Great War in 1918. Images of conflict collected and edited by journalists covering war. What are the duties of the journalist in war and conflict, and are they entitled to any special status under the Geneva Conventions?

prosecuted for the crime of treason – an offence and statute created in the early Middle Ages. Many 'collaborators' of the Axis powers who fought with words, through propaganda and not bullets or bombs, received lenient sentences, particularly in the USA. The British made examples of Joyce and Amery probably to support the policy of *pour encourager les autres*.

A United Nations tribunal in Tanzania convicted and imprisoned three journalist/broadcasters in 2003 for their role in hate communication during the Rwandan genocide of 1994. This was hailed as a significant development in international law and as defining the responsibility of journalism during conflict and war.

Underpinning this debate is the general acceptance of the protonorm that the *a priori* ethic for human communication is an unqualified respect for the right to life. Human communication must not be directed towards the imperative command to kill.

It may also be significant that the United Nations engaged in a process of prosecuting participating journalists in the context of a general debate on why the world failed to intervene effectively when the genocide took hold of Rwanda. This retrospective process of holding people accountable for their words was an additional remedy to holding people accountable for their actions and omissions.

The history of the 2003 conflict in Iraq was punctuated with propagandist assertions that killing is necessary, either in a call for nationalist defence or in a paradoxical call for proportionate killing in order to check the potential for launching weapons of mass destruction or to topple an evil dictatorship, otherwise known as 'regime change'. The moral consequentialism of the latter position is a matter of degree, and problematically relativist.

The treatment of journalists and media personnel by warring nations and terrorist organizations is a war crimes issue. In the 2003 Iraq conflict and subsequent insurgency journalists were being killed in greater numbers. Even where there may not have been clear evidence of journalists being singled out for attack, there appeared to be less observance of the convention in war to avoid harm to journalists either as embedded correspondents or non-embedded journalists who have been labelled as 'unilaterals'. Some were killed in controversial circumstances. The US military was criticized for attacking the locations of Al Jazeera journalists in both Afghanistan and Iraq. There was global controversy about the nature of the policy of the USA and UK towards Al Jazeera. (Shoenberger *The News Media & The Law* 2006) The violence, deaths and injuries suffered by journalists became a distressing and tragic trend in the conflict, and a clear breach of human rights. The issue of whether these were war crimes is a matter of international law, context and the evidence of intention.

The case of ITN journalist Terry Lloyd

At a coroner's inquest in Britain in 2006 a jury returned a verdict that the ITN journalist Terry Lloyd had been unlawfully killed near Basra in 2003. In fact Robertson and Nicol go further in their book *Media Law* by saying that he was 'recklessly murdered by US troops.' (Robertson and Nicol 2008: 677) The inquest revealed that the forensic and military video evidence suggested he was shot in the head by a US-fired bullet just as he was being loaded onto the back of a truck to be taken to hospital for a non life-threatening wound inflicted when a small convey of ITN vehicles (clearly marked) had been caught in crossfire on 22 March.

Mr Lloyd was not the only ITN media casualty of that day. Translator Hussein Othman died in the incident and cameraman Fred Nerac was missing, presumed killed.

The Deputy Coroner for Oxfordshire, Andrew Walker, asked the Attorney General and DPP to take action. He said the minibus being used to take Mr Lloyd to hospital 'presented no threat to American forces.' (BBC 2006) The NUJ issued a statement that this was 'a very serious war crime. This was not a friendly fire incident, it was a despicable, deliberate, vengeful act, particularly as it came many minutes after the initial exchange.' (Ibid.) But the US Department of Defense said that it was never their intention to deliberately target non-combatants, including journalists: 'combat operations are inherently dangerous.' (Ibid.) In 2008 the UK's Crown Prosecution Service announced that there was insufficient evidence to prosecute any US soldier.

ITN, Reporters Sans Frontières (Reporters Without Borders) and other global journalist charities, and Robertson and Nicol argue that 'There should be an international crime of wilfully killing a journalist during an armed conflict, whether international or internal. Such a specific crime would stress the unique and essential role played by war correspondents.' (Robertson and Nicol 2008: 677) It is argued that journalists deserve direct and special protection. Armed forces and insurgent groups single out journalists for attack because they are soft targets – but larger prizes and sometimes a greater priority for elimination than enemy combatants and non-combatants.

ITN's head of compliance, John Battle, drew up a paper, supported by legal advice from Geoffrey Robertson QC, to lobby for a change of Articles 79 and 8(1) of the 1998 Rome Statute constituting the International Criminal Court, whose powers and remit are summarized in Table 10.3. In a letter to the Foreign Secretary, Mr Battle explained that the current statute was too ambiguous in providing 'adequate legal protection for the

Table 10.3 The International Criminal Court (ICC)

This is an independent, permanent court that tries persons accused of the most serious crimes of international concern, namely genocide, crimes against humanity and war crimes. The ICC is based on a treaty, joined by 108 countries.

The ICC is a court of last resort. It will not act if a case is being investigated or prosecuted by a national judicial system unless the national proceedings are not genuine – for example, if formal proceedings were undertaken solely to shield a person from criminal responsibility. In addition, the ICC only tries those accused of the gravest crimes.

In all of its activities the ICC observes the highest standards of fairness and due process. The jurisdiction and functioning of the ICC are governed by the Rome Statute of 1998.

The ICC prosecutes under:
Article 5 Crimes within the jurisdiction of the Court
1   The jurisdiction of the Court shall be limited to the most serious crimes of concern to the international community as a whole. The Court has jurisdiction in accordance with this Statute with respect to the following crimes:
    a   The crime of genocide;
    b   Crimes against humanity;
    c   War crimes;
    d   The crime of aggression.

---

killing of journalists, whose deaths were usually caused by the assassination of any individual, or the execution of a group or team.' (*Media Lawyer* November 2007) In particular, Mr Battle emphasized that 'Soldiers need to be left in no doubt that it is an international crime to kill an individual journalist. The most effective way of obtaining this protection is by an amendment to the Rome Statute.' (Ibid.)

The United Nations Security Council Resolution 1738 (2006) expressed deep concern at the 'frequency of acts of violence in many parts of the world against journalists, media professionals and associated personnel in armed conflict, in particular deliberate attacks in violation of international humanitarian law.' (UN Security Council 2006) The Security Council also urged member states to 'do their utmost to prevent violations of international humanitarian law against civilians, including journalists, media professionals and associated personnel' and emphasized their responsibility under international law 'to end impunity and to prosecute those responsible for serious violations of international humanitarian law.' (Ibid.) It was vital to respect the professional independence and rights of journalists and media professionals working to cover armed conflict. Reporters Sans Frontières has drafted a 'Convention for the Protection of Journalists', but Robertson and Nicol fear that it may take many years for the ICC (International Criminal Court) treaty to be changed and international law to provide the machinery to prosecute and to achieve deterrence. (Robertson and Nicol 2008: 678) Progress also required the US to sign the Rome Statute and accept the liability of the International Criminal Court.

The debate clearly invites the reader to determine whether this kind of crime is enforceable; whether this is a realistic possibility, given the hazards and nature of armed conflict; and whether it would be fair to place the role of the journalist above or separately from that of other non-combatants. Anyone with any military experience of conflict will be aware of how confusing and chaotic human perception and judgment are in war. Eighteen-year-old conscripts or volunteers, trained to use lethal force, even in a disciplined manner, have fractions of a second in which to make decisions that can inevitably lead to 'collateral damage'. If journalists choose to be present in conflict zones is it not common sense that they must bear the consequences?

Media accountability in propaganda as war

The debate clearly has room for the issue of whether the propagandist role of journalists means that there is every reason to place them in the same category as combatants. The reverse side of the argument is that, as journalists fight wars with words, the focus, in turn, should be on their culpability in war crimes and crimes against humanity. The debate could also approach the topic by academically analysing whether there should be a special international treaty on the use of propaganda and on 'information terrorism' deployed by combatants during war.

The debate probably requires a definition of what the reader might mean by propaganda as a weapon of war, and what is meant by 'information terrorism' as a weapon of war. Article 20 of the International Covenant on Civil and Political Rights (ICCPR) provides that any 'propaganda shall be prohibited by law' and law should also prohibit the advocacy of 'national, racial or religious hatred that constitutes incitement to discrimination, hostility or violence'.

Liz Harrop, in an article in *Ethical Space*, analysed and evaluated the international legal culpability of the media's role in war propaganda and suggested that one of the roles of a free media 'could be to educate the public about its role, particularly in a state of emergency, when freedom of information is threatened. In this way it may be possible to confront the prejudice encountered by the "voice of dissent."' (Harrop 2005: 20) The International Council on Human Rights Policy (ICHRP) showed awareness of how market pressures in mass media journalism were hardly capable of applying restraint factors in war reporting coverage: 'Driven by new technologies and the lure of lucrative mass markets, media owners are themselves guilty of upsetting the balance of interest between journalism as an instrument of democracy and its exploitation as a tradable commodity.' (ICHRP 2002: xv) Its 143-page study on *Journalism, Media and the Challenge of Human Rights Reporting* issued detailed recommendations to journalists, editors and media, governments, and international and human rights organizations to improve education on human rights and cooperation between reporters and correspondents working for different media to facilitate understanding of local conditions and promote better ethnic and gender balance, self-reflexive approaches to journalism, the elimination of official and political interference, and the protection and enhancement of the right of journalists to act ethically. The council advised that the media should 'pay particular attention to *context* and *terminology*.' (Ibid.: 120)

The journalism of hate – origins and theories of war by propaganda

The US First World War propagandist George Creel identified the foundation of destructive communicative nihilism in his book *War Criminals and Punishment* (1944). In the chapter entitled 'The High Priests of Hate' (194–207) he highlighted the influence and inspiration of the political demagogue Heinrich von Treitschke, whose late-nineteenth-century journalistic and political rhetoric generated 'hate of peace, hate of small weak nations, hate of democracy, hate of Christians and Jews.' (Ibid.: 194)

Creel argued that Treitschke was 'not one of many voices, but *the* voice of Germany. No English or American writer ranks with him in point of influence, neither Carlyle, Macaulay nor Emerson, all of whom, by the way, he derided and despised'.

There is no doubt that key components of twentieth-century Nazi ideology can be identified in Treitschke's speeches and writing. This is an indication that German expansionist, ruthless and predatory attitudes did not begin, in a year zero position, with Adolf Hitler's *Mein Kampf* and Nazi aspirations.

Similarly, President Saddam Hussein's desire to invade Kuwait in 1990 was the manifestation of an Iraqi national policy that saw Kuwait as a province of Greater Iraq with no right to self-determination. In fact a previous Iraqi government had planned an invasion in 1955 that was discouraged by the strategic arrival of British troops and naval forces.

Treitschke was an enthusiast of the philosophy of Hegel and Fichte that saw the state as all powerful and to be obeyed without question. He was also a follower of Clausewitz, who saw war as the one way to the greatness of the state. Treitschke glorified war, conquest and pillage:

> Let the sword be drawn! Sound the war drums! Was it not Frederick the Great who said, 'He is a fool, and that nation is a fool, who having the power to strike his enemy unawares, does not strike and strike his deadliest?' [...]
> War is just and moral, and the ideal of eternal peace is both unjust and immoral, and impossible.
>
> (Ibid.: 194–207)

Treitschke's rhetoric lacked any sense of humanity and respect for human life. He began whipping up German public opinion into a frenzy of racial intolerance, as a cover for his drive in 1879 against democratic heresies. He described Jews as 'a dangerous, disintegrating force' because they assumed the 'mask of any other nationality', and he warned they were a party of compromise that 'must bear the blame for any unsavoury wave of anti-Semitism which may arise.' (Ibid.)

Treitschke was to die many years before the Versailles treaty, the League of Nations and the United Nations sought to organize a reckoning for the consequences of hate, intolerance and violence. But his exhortations and ideology contributed to the decision of Germany in 1902 to issue a new manual for its army and navy officers on the code of war that stripped the soldier of humanity, compassion and pity:

> War is not to be regarded as a contest between armed forces, but has as its one and only purpose the destruction of the spiritual and material power of the enemy country.
> [...] It is not only permissible but ordered to destroy private

property, to devastate systematically evacuated regions, to terrorise the civil population of invaded districts, to deport them for compulsory service in the enemy country, thereby releasing its own men for the army, to compel them to aid the enemy in the construction of fortifications and to dig trenches.

(Ibid.)

It could be argued that this doctrine of military necessity was an application of moral consequentialism far beyond the exceptional category of behaviour envisaged by Niccolò Machiavelli as the ruthless means to an end.

Propaganda – defining the meaning of the word

Any discourse on the subject of propaganda has to overcome the first hurdle of determining what is actually meant by propaganda. The word has been fought over in the context of moral value. When the word is discussed in the context of journalism it has a pejorative charge. Journalists perceive the process of propaganda as a method of manipulating them. Governments and institutions that set out to persuade people perceive propaganda as an art or profession. They will tend to avoid using the word 'propaganda' as it has such a bad name. They will call their process public relations, promotion or 'government information.' Britain's Special Operations Executive, known as SOE and commissioned by Winston Churchill during the Second World War to fight by using terrorism and sabotage in occupied countries, defined propaganda as 'the art of persuasion with a view to producing action.' (Rigden 2001: 217)

One of the key roots of the word and concept appears to be the Vatican's *Congregatio de Propaganda Fide* (Congregation for the Propagation of the Faith), established in the seventeenth century. The Catholic Church wished to defend its idea of the true faith against the growing spiritual challenge of Protestant Reformation. In the context of the bitter and bloody religious wars that scarred the face of Europe at this time, it is no wonder that the idea of propaganda began to fluctuate in a struggle between good and evil. 'Propaganda' as a word seems to fit into the same frame of disrepute as 'Machiavellian'. Perhaps it is no coincidence that the moral legitimacy of Niccolò Machiavelli's ideas and writings has been bitterly contested in a propaganda war through the centuries since his death. This ideological war has engaged racism against Italians and the struggle between republicanism and the divine right of rule by princes and monarchs.

A number of writers who analysed information warfare during the First World War began to demonize the practice of propaganda as something that was reprehensible, deceptive and unethical. The most trenchant attacks came from Arthur Ponsonby in *Falsehood in Wartime*, published in 1928 and J.M. Read's *Atrocity Propaganda 1914–1919*, published in 1941.

Ponsonby was vituperative in his moral condemnation of the practice of propaganda and he condemned the injection of 'the poison of hatred into men's minds by means of falsehood' as 'a greater evil in wartime than the actual loss of life. The defilement of the human soul is worse than the destruction of the human body.' (Ponsonby 1928: 18)

The stigma of propaganda in the context of the British bourgeois desire for respectability manifested itself during the Second Gulf War when a British Army 'psyops' officer who specialized in designing cartoons for leaflets would only be interviewed for television with his face blacked out. He insisted that his hand-drawn caricatures with bubbled messages were 'definitely not propaganda'. He was filmed demonstrating his art in a desert tent festooned with aerials and banks of digital electronic equipment. This activity was described, somewhat incongruously given the blatant identification, as 'Britain's secret campaign of psychological operations'.

Resistance as journalistic ethic

Journalists such as Phillip Knightley, in *The First Casualty – From the Crimea to the Falklands: The War Correspondent as Hero, Propagandist and Myth Maker*, certainly evaluate propaganda in an ethical context. The argument centres on the problem that successful manipulation of journalists, particularly in wartime through the techniques of propaganda, exacerbates human suffering and prolongs the dynamics of destructive conflict. Knightley and the campaigning journalist John Pilger believe journalists who unmask the futility and brutality of war can reduce needless slaughter.

British Prime Minister David Lloyd George told the editor of the *Manchester Guardian* during the First World War: 'If people really knew, the war would be stopped tomorrow. But of course they don't know and can't know.' (Knightley 2000: xi) Knightley argues that the Australian journalist Keith Murdoch exposed the incompetence of strategy in the Gallipoli campaign and 'cost a general his job, [and] contributed to the decision to abandon the campaign.' (Ibid.: 106)

The desire by journalists to decode propaganda

A few hours before the beginning of the Anglo-American or 'coalition' invasion of Iraq in March/April 2003, I was invited by London's Foreign Press Association to provide a briefing on how journalists are manipulated for the purposes of propaganda in wartime. Some UK news organizations asked me to provide a running analysis of the struggle that journalists had in dealing with the propagandist agendas advanced by countries that go to war with each other. Would it be possible to determine the motivations, objectives and strategies of those waging the propaganda war and enable the news media to critically distance them from the authors of the information they were being supplied with? An attempt was therefore made to evaluate the apparent propaganda tactics being deployed, on the basis of research into previous historical models.

Unique features of propaganda operations in the Second Gulf War

A number of claims have been made about propaganda events, rituals and characteristics that are unique to the Second Gulf War. For example the media identified the system of 'embedded journalists' as a 'new feature' of war journalism in the age of 24-hour global television news networks. A study of media content suggested that during the developing war Britain and the USA had difficulties in delivering propaganda objectives in a variety of arenas of reception. Messages designed to persuade British public opinion had the opposite effect in the Middle East and Arab world.

Techniques of labelling and fashioning language by governments and military authorities seemed to follow the model of propaganda techniques in previous conflicts. There was also evidence that the Anglo-Americans had used the acceleration and amplification of hypermedia to transliterate suspicions and possibilities into the reporting of facticity by media organizations. There was evidence that traditional techniques of propaganda warfare boomeranged when exaggerations and unfounded claims quickly turned out to lack credibility.

Philip M. Taylor, in his study of the propaganda conflict in the first Gulf War, observed that 'propaganda requires skilful planning, especially if it is to appear as something else, as it must to be really effective. It is therefore by definition a covert activity, just as intelligence is.' (Taylor 1992: 270) Yet the Second Gulf War was marked by a surprising, almost boastful openness about propaganda strategy and psychological operations.

The *modus operandi* was revealed and advertised before and during its deployment. Significantly, it was also shown to fail. There was a dangerous point during the campaign when the apparent construction of military strategy dependent on the success of psychological operations exposed supply lines and defied widely briefed and publicized expectations of regime overthrow and surrender. An improvised propaganda operation had to be instituted to cover up mistakes in planning.

There was also evidence that some news organizations and their journalists engaged their anticipation and suspicion of propaganda techniques with regular columns and analysis. These were sign-posted as an attempt to evaluate propaganda, and claims and counter-claims. The UK *Guardian* newspaper maintained updated columns in hard copy and an online publication entitled 'When Are Facts Fact? Not in a war – Claims and counter claims made during the media war in Iraq'. Brian Whitaker also ran a daily column of analysis of news sources and propaganda messaging in the *Guardian*.

The key ethical concern of journalists appeared to be a fear that they are tricked or manipulated into purveying 'lies' during the course of the coverage of military conflict. In the Kantian deontological frame, the act of lying is a categorical human wrong. It is immoral. Moral consequentialist and utilitarian frames evaluate the act of lying in human communication with more relativist imperatives. Journalists such as Bob Woodward and Carl Bernstein may argue that the lies they deployed in investigating the Watergate cover-up by Richard Nixon's US administration were venial in the frame of exposing the greater evil of abuse of power at the White House. Peter Preston advanced a similar defence to forging a letter on British House of Commons notepaper in 1997 in order to obtain evidence that proved Jonathan Aitken had been lying in his pursuit of libel proceedings against the *Guardian* newspaper. The venial conduct argument underpins a range of legal and ethical wrongdoing by journalists and state investigators who operate under cover and misrepresent themselves when seeking to expose crime 'in the public interest'.

It does seem that journalists are less tolerant of the process of lying when they become the unwitting victims of a course of conduct by military communicators and government information agencies that willingly envelop distortion, dishonesty and deception in a cloak of moral rectitude.

The protagonists of propaganda bandy the concept of truth with ruthless pragmatism. Sir Winston Churchill is frequently credited with the aphorism: 'In wartime, truth is so precious that she should always be attended by a bodyguard of lies.' Sun-Tzu, in *The Art of* War, acknowledged: "Warfare is the Way (Tao) of deception. Thus although [you are] capable, display incapability to them. When committed to employing your forces, feign inactivity. When [your objective] is nearby, make it appear as if distant; when far away, create the illusion of being nearby.' (Sun-Tzu 1994: 168)

Who won the propaganda war?

Throughout the Iraq conflict there were signs of cyclical events and patterns of communication where propaganda succeeded in manifesting itself in journalistic media coverage with poor attribution and little analytical and historical mediation. The language of purpose was emblematized in media reporting. Hence the regular use of 'coalition', 'liberating' and 'Operation Iraqi Freedom'. Philip M. Taylor observed that in the first Gulf War, 'the conflict belonged to the coalition's armed forces, and to the victors went the spoils of the information war.' (Taylor 1998: 278) He also observed that the operations of 1991 'demonstrated that modern democracies could fight wars, or at least a war of this rather special kind, in the television age without too much of war's visible brutality to appear in the front rooms of their publics.' (Ibid.)

Taylor and Knightley both acknowledge the significance of a growing body of research that audiences 'appear to not want the truthful, objective and balanced reporting that good war correspondents once did their best to provide.' (Knightley 2000: 525) Television viewers did not seem to want television networks to allow wars to dominate their schedules. There was negligible demand for the media in Britain and the USA to show the brutal reality of war. Knightley advanced a theory that citizens of the Western democracies in wartime are co-conspirators in a fugue or syndrome of self-deception.

The degree of violent intimidation and killing of so-called 'unilateral' journalists increased, compared to previous conflicts. Many journalists and their editors believed that there had been unfortunate recklessness so that independent-minded newsgathering journalists were targeted by default. Lord Kitchener threatened to shoot the *Daily Chronicle*'s Philip Gibbs during the First World War for evading censorship arrangements. During the Vietnam War, Australian journalist Wilfred Burchett, who sought to report the conflict from the North Vietnamese and Vietcong side, said the American military authorities' reaction to his presence was to try to kill him. British photojournalist Tim Page was nearly killed by an American B-57 that mistook his US coastguard cutter for a Vietcong vessel. The proportionate level of media casualties from so-called 'friendly fire' in the invasion of Iraq in 2003 was unprecedented, as compared to previous conflicts.

There was a cyclical repetition of the pressures of patriotic consensus against journalists and news organizations that provided a platform for criticism and contradiction of the British and US government propagandist line. The *Independent*'s Robert Fisk endured the same treatment and response to his finding of serial numbers on missile fragments pointing to US and British culpability in the bombing of non-combatants. On 30 March 2003 he reported for the *Independent on Sunday*:

> The piece of metal is only a foot high, but the numbers on it hold the clue to the latest atrocity in Baghdad.
>
> At least 62 civilians had died by yesterday afternoon, and the coding on that hunk of metal contains the identity of the culprit. The Americans and British were doing their best yesterday to suggest that an Iraqi anti-aircraft missile destroyed those dozens of lives, adding that they were 'still investigating' the carnage. But the coding is in Western style, not in Arabic.
>
> (Fisk *Independent on Sunday* 2003)

The almost ritualized response to his basic act of front-line reporting was virtually identical to what happened in the Kosovo war. On 16 April 1999 he reported in the *Independent*:

> Nato did all this, say the Serbs, and it is true that US munitions litter the road and fields around here, sometimes within a few inches of corpses, body parts, human bones, smashed tractors and trailers, their pathetic contents of old clothes, pots and family snapshots lying around them. Clearly there were air strikes here. And Nato appears to be responsible for an atrocity. [...] The munitions parked along the road bore several American markings.
>
> (Fisk *Independent* 1999)

In these separate conflicts Robert Fisk's reporting was subjected to suggestions from official and unofficial sources that the civilians had been killed accidentally or deliberately by their own forces, that intelligence agents had planted evidence to incriminate the NATO, British or US air forces and that he had been made a stooge for 'the real enemy'. The reporting of collateral damage morphed into a predictable ritual of doubt and rebuttal, alleging the source of death and suffering was the enemy firing on their own citizens, their anti-aircraft missiles malfunctioning, and using civilians as shields for military command installations. The language of rebuttal was qualified along the lines of 'possibility', 'probability', and 'may be', in the knowledge that repetition and bias in the media might translate arguments into facts.

The process of demonization of 'the enemy' along the lines of 'evil', and analogies to Hitler and the Nazis were ever present in the Second Gulf War in Iraq in 2003. Between 1945 and 1948, during its mandate in Palestine, the British government and military propagandists would label the terrorist tactics engaged by the Irgun Zvai Leumi and Stern gang as the tactics of the Nazis. This was an intriguing irony when juxtaposed with the Holocaust and the revelation of the consequences of the 'Final Solution'. Jewish terrorists were 'thugs' and 'gangsters', a lexicon of description used to describe Saddam Hussein's so-called 'irregular fedayeen'.

The British and US media made a decision, based on 'sensibility and good taste', not to transmit images of the corpses of two British soldiers killed near Basra, in contrast to the cultural expectation of audiences and decisions of journalists and serving Arab-speaking news networks such as Al Jazeera and Abu Dhabi television. Yet the hanging of two British sergeants by the Irgun in Palestine in July 1947 resulted in the *Daily Express* running a front-page photograph of the corpses under the caption 'A picture which will shock the world'. Susan L. Carruthers writes that this editorial decision was 'censured in Parliament and a direct correlation made between the manner in which terrorism was reported and the rash of anti-Semitic riots in Britain.' (Carruthers 1995: 63) However, it could be argued that this style of reporting contributed to the public outrage over the consequences of Britain's involvement in Palestine, and hastened an early announcement of withdrawal.

Familiar propagandist mythologies were advanced during the 2003 conflict. The so-called 'killing fields of Iraq' and 'Saddam's charnel house' emerged. The brutal slaying of the innocent child who sought help and refuge from the courageous coalition soldier, 'the saving of Private Jessica Lynch', 'the execution of British prisoners of war', all provided resonant echoes of exaggerated atrocity claims from the past. When General Tommy Franks declared at his first press conference in Doha in 2003 that the assembled journalists would only hear the truth, the historical memory of war and journalism retorted, in the words of Phillip Knightley, 'the point is that in wartime official promises to tell the truth are worthless.' (Knightley 1989: 436)

The plight of 12-year-old Ali in Baghdad, whose family were slaughtered, whose body was covered in ghastly burns and whose arms were ripped off by a US missile also served another ritualizing mythology of media war reporting. The salvaging of moral conscience engendered by this phenomenon was present during the First World War, when *Daily Mail* journalist Captain F.W. Wilson was directed to find an atrocity or refugee story. He created the legend of the 'baby of Courbeck Loo' – rescued from the Hun in the light of burning homesteads. Thousands of letters offering to adopt the baby poured into the newspaper's offices. When Wilson was ordered to send the non-existent baby to London, he obtained quotes from a doctor working with refugees to declare that the child had died of some very contagious disease and so could not have a public burial. (Ponsonby 1928: 90) But non-fictional representations of the baby of Courbeck Loo have lived on in subsequent wars and served the interest of assuaging guilt.

Much has been made of the pioneering use of 'embedded' journalists using instant digital transmission technology on the frontline of battle. But history informs us that the 'embedded journalist' is simply a new name for an old phenomenon. They turned out to be no more reliable and significant in their representation of events than the time-honoured 'corporal's perspective' in military history.

In accounts of war the experience of the single soldier in one skirmish, his suffering, hunger and fears, assumes a significance and value because, inevitably, he wants to make his dramatic experience a matter of general importance. Certainly the nature of the 24-hour instant-news attention cycle increased the volume, amplification and reverberation of first-hand reporting and analysis and, by consequence, the process of propagandist response and rebuttal. This may have been a factor in the rapid acceleration to credibility fatigue and meltdown in regard to Anglo-American objectives and political messaging. It was certainly the case with every report on the possible finding of chemical and biological weapons and associated paraphernalia, which in every case turned out to be a false alarm, the news of which was communicated with less time, sense of alarm and emphasis. The damage to the credibility of military and government authority undoubtedly impacts on the credibility of the media messengers.

There were signs that the Anglo-American propaganda campaign boomeranged in some respects. There was clear ambiguity in objectives between the United Kingdom and the USA, symbolized perhaps by the draping of the Stars and Stripes on Saddam Hussein's statue by an American marine in Baghdad, and its removal and replacement with the Iraqi flag before Saddam's image was pulled to the ground. The US government advanced its initial war aim on the basis of regime change.

The British government advanced its war objective on the basis of eradicating Iraq's alleged weapons of mass destruction. The Anglo-American alliance had to fight a campaign with different propagandist objectives, and different cultures of journalistic practice. The emotional baggage of 9/11 undoubtedly had a bearing on a paradigm of patriotism over impartiality on some US broadcast networks. The British media were dealing with a different emotional and political context. There were different propagandist objectives for a complex nexus of arenas of reception. One message and style of communication would serve the arena of British public opinion, but rebound negatively for Middle East/Arab world opinion. In an inter-media age, the difficulty of putting five different plays on the same stage would have some confusing outcomes.

The technology and presence of broadcast journalists in the midst of dramatic battle provided entertainment footage, sound, visual and verbal language that sometimes exceeded the vocabulary of action and war films. British and American military commanders encouraged the emotional resonance of film narrative by cueing code-names from James Bond movies and transforming the rescue of Private Jessica Lynch into a spin-off of Spielberg's *Saving Private Ryan*. This was clear evidence that the invasion of Iraq in 2003 was also an infotainment war.

The obvious antidote to the surrender of journalism to the objectives of propaganda is memory, experience and independence. But unfortunately there were only limited signs of a critical approach to the deployment of the techniques of propaganda in the mainstream media coverage of the 2003 conflict. The wider discourse on the vocabulary, concepts, theories and objectives that motivate journalists in the reporting of conflict through peace journalism and the engagement and understanding of human rights is intelligent and constructive. The deaths of Terry Lloyd and all the other media personnel during this conflict have been a foundation for the campaign to create a more clearly defined international war crime recognizing and protecting the inviolable neutrality and right to life of journalists reporting in conflict zones.

11

RACIAL AND RELIGIOUS
HATRED

At the time of writing, the UK has in place the Racial and Religious Hatred Act 2006, which makes it a criminal offence to stir up hatred against persons on religious grounds, and terrorism legislation of 2006 which makes it a criminal offence to glorify the commission or preparation of any act of terrorism, whether in the past, present or future. These criminal sanctions against extreme speech do not exist in the USA. If passed by Congress or any of the state legislatures, they would, in all probability, be declared by the Supreme Court as unconstitutional.

Outside the USA, the First Amendment free speech tradition of tolerance that has underpinned the accommodation of extreme expression, sometimes referred to as 'hate speech' appears to be under intellectual, academic, political and military attack. One representation of the struggle is that First Amendment free speech absolutism, in itself always a minority position in jurisprudence, is some form of liberal fundamentalism that is in conflict with dialogic multiculturalism. One finds bundled up with the attack on US First Amendment rights a denunciation of the historicized values of the European Renaissance and Enlightenment, a debunking and misrepresentation of Voltaire, Adam Smith, John Locke and John Stuart Mill, although it is a matter of fact that Mill was a post-Enlightenment philosopher and writer and more contemporary with Karl Marx than with the American and French revolutions. There is the impression that Voltaire (1694–1778), whose real name was François-Marie Arouet, deserves to be condemned along with all the other members of that doubtful lodge of Enlightenment *roués* for his attributed aphorism 'I disapprove of what you say, but I will defend to the death your right to say it'.

Essentially, an enquiry into the concept of free speech is seen as the problem, and not as a solution. Professor Brian McNair's discourse on *Cultural Chaos: Journalism, News and Power in a Globalised World* (2006) has observed a confusion in sociological and cultural thinking in a debating environment characterized by political, geographical and ideological dissolution. It is said that the postmodernist world has no time or patience for grand narratives associated with the age of two superpowers in a Cold War. The contemporary Information Age is accelerating, and dispersing power in directions and strengths that are difficult to understand and measure. The paradigms have been shifting.

As British Prime Minister Tony Blair said in response to the carnage of Britain's first 'home-grown' suicide bombings in July 2005:

> Let no one be in any doubt, the rules of the game are changing. These issues will of course be tested in the courts [...] There will be new anti-terrorism legislation in the autumn. This will include an offence of condoning or glorifying terrorism. But this will also be applied to justifying or glorifying terrorism anywhere, not just in the United Kingdom.
>
> (Downing Street 2005)

The noble ideas of liberty and democracy being defended by a sword in one hand and a toga in the other, or of the late-eighteenth-century *philosophe* drinking coffee in Paris or London and examining natural law with the eye of scientific positivism have become passé and redundant. There is a self-questioning insecurity in the notion that perhaps it is arrogant to suppose that just because post-Protestant nations clustered in Northern Europe and North America reserved and continue to practise a doctrine of free speech, the rest of the world should be obliged to adopt it. If there had been a genuine grassroots desire for the free speech doctrine, surely these ancient and well-established societies and cultures in Africa, Asia and the Middle East would have discovered and asserted it by now? Such a debating position is somewhat challenged by the reality of India's success as a democracy, the enjoyment of media freedom by its one billion-plus population, and its expectation of becoming a significant world power in cultural influence and trade in the twenty-first century by adhering to the liberal free speech doctrine. India is a country rich in cultural and religious traditions that transcend and rival the European-centred Greco-Roman, Renaissance, Enlightenment and Modernist epochs of so-called historical progress. Yet it was also a country that banned distribution of Salmon Rushdie's novel *The Satanic Verses*.

Mr Blair may have suggested that the rules of the game in marking the boundaries of civil liberty would have to change in order to respond to the threat of terrorism, but crossing those boundaries is not meeting with the approval of the courts. Issues are being tested and decided in the highest UK courts: detention without trial is wrong; using evidence obtained by torture in other countries is wrong; using secret witnesses and evidence in trials that the accused cannot challenge is wrong. By 2008 the US Supreme Court had decided that Guantánamo detainees, even as non-US citizens, had a constitutional right to bring federal habeas corpus challenges to their detention as 'enemy combatants' (Boumediene v Bush SC US 2008) The courts are yet to rule on many other attempts by the executive in the UK and USA to change the rules of the game. Media law and ethics play a vital role in enabling the people to find out how the state has decided to be so arbitrary, morally relativist, and morally consequential with the so-called 'old rules'.

It might be wise to exercise caution over any temptation to trivialize, belittle and dismiss the rational certainties of the past with the metaphorical cry of the pigs in George Orwell's *Animal Farm*: 'Two legs good, four legs bad!' Orwell was constructing a parody of ironic observation on the politics of totalitarianism. The pigs had decided to ape the human beings they had replaced as rulers. Is it really the case that old media technology is imploding as a result of new media transformation by Internet, 'citizen-on-the-street' journalism, Twitter, YouTube and social forums on the World Wide Web? Might it not be prudent to appreciate Marshall McLuhan's view in the 1950s, that new media technologies generally add to the matrix rather than dissolve and replace those that have worked so well in the past? Is secularization really being replaced by religiosity? A more precise observation could be that the West is revisiting the debate about the merits of separating the role of church, synagogue, temple and mosque from legislature, executive and judiciary.

The repetitive mantra that we now live in a new world order of globalization is somewhat challenged by the theory that cultural world experience has always been influenced by a *bricolage* of globalized dynamics in economic, social, cultural and military directions of communication. This was the methodology of Roman imperial trade, expansion and influence, and the British Empire operated, prospered and sustained itself in a similar way. In the twenty-first century the speed of communications and transport is so much faster; their scale is greater and their direction longer.

The US First Amendment paradigm

In 1919 the US Supreme Court in *Schenck v US* sought to identify the fairest and most effective way of qualifying the First Amendment against speech and communication that threatened the security of the country. The Justices adopted the phrase 'clear and present danger' and equated the evaluation as being able to identify the difference between speech that hurt people's feelings and offended, and speech that was the equivalent of crying 'fire' in a crowded theatre and risked death and injury in the ensuing panic. The Justices were struggling to find a way of testing the First Amendment position of anti-war campaigners who were publishing pamphlets and leaflets inciting people not to answer the draft following US entry into the First World War in 1917. Justice Oliver Wendell Holmes

Jr. decided that the First Amendment should not protect Schenck. In a similar case in the same year, *Abrams v US*, he changed his mind. In his minority opinion Holmes asserted that the 'best test of truth is the power of the thought to get itself accepted in the competition of the market'. He was also applying the developing European concept of proportionality in jurisprudential analysis, for, as he said:

> Now nobody can suppose that the surreptitious publishing of a silly leaflet by an unknown man, without more, would present any immediate danger that its opinions would hinder the success of the government aims or have any appreciable tendency to do so.
>
> (Abrams v US, SC US 1919)

Justice Holmes's position was not a precedent. It was only a seed, and through the 1920s and 1930s US states passed statutes that criminalized political minorities which advocated the overthrow of government, radical defiance of the state and revolutionary violence as the solution to the problems of world capitalism. The Supreme Court affirmed convictions against individuals criminally prosecuted for publishing or associating with political opinion that advocated violence. (Gitlow v New York SC US 1925; Whitney v California SC US 1927) However, the jurisprudential approach conceptualized by Holmes did take root with Justice Brandeis in *Gitlow* when he said *obiter dicta* that he did not believe there had been any clear and present danger in Whitney's speech and that the 'remedy to be applied is more speech, not enforced silence.' (Ibid.) Twentieth-century jurisprudence in the USA was endeavouring to teach the jackboot of executive policing that democracy and liberty is not about breaking butterflies on wheels or cracking nuts with sledgehammers.

The 1940s and 1950s saw a consolidation of federal legislation and Supreme Court affirmations in the prosecution and conviction of political activists, particularly communists, who published opinions supporting the overthrow of the government by force. This was in spite of an acceptance that the speech content *sui generis* did not constitute a clear and present danger. The Supreme Court and Congress were preoccupied with an anticipation of the consequence of disseminating such views in terms of recruiting and persuading others to take up arms.

In 1957 Chief Justice Warren adopted a new approach by the Supreme Court, and quashed criminal convictions against fourteen communist activists because he decided that their speech did not present a clear and present danger that was likely to result in violent action against the state. (Yates v US, SC US 1957) In a significant development, he ruled that the prosecution had to prove that the call to arms was likely to happen.

The counter-culture age of the 1960s saw Chief Justice Warren's approach in *Yates* consolidated in the case of a Ku Klux Klan activist called

Brandenburg who called for the deportation of American Jews and Blacks to Israel and Africa and threatened 'revengeance' and a march on the nation's capital. In a Supreme Court ruling in 1969, the criminal conviction applied against him in the Ohio courts for this expression of extreme political rhetoric was overturned on the basis that the First Amendment meant that speech could only be punished if it were 'directed to inciting or producing imminent lawless action' and was 'likely to incite or produce such actions'.

The evolution of the clear and present danger rule in US political speech was developed in parallel with an adjustment of how to evaluate 'fighting words' that were offensive and abusive. In 1971 the Supreme Court demonstrated the move to tolerance when ruling that Paul Cohen should not be punished for walking around in a courthouse in Los Angeles and wearing a jacket bearing the words 'Fuck the Draft'. The phrase used by one of the justices, that 'One man's vulgarity is another man's lyric', sounded as though it had been borrowed from a Bob Dylan song, but it reflected the spirit of a jurisprudential approach that supported the right to express offensive speech and indulge in political vulgarity. The phrase did not constitute 'fighting words', as there was no likelihood that it would provoke violence or a breach of the peace. The ruling needs to be judged by the social and political context of the time. Is it likely that a US court would come to the same view if, in 2009, a white supremacist turned up outside a mosque bearing a similar insult to the Prophet Mohammed?

In 1972 the Supreme Court ruled that a statute passed in the state of Georgia prohibiting 'abusive language tending to breach the peace' was unconstitutional because only speech which had 'a direct tendency to cause acts of violence by the person to whom, individually, the remark is addressed' could not be protected by the First Amendment. (Gooding v Wilson SC US 1972)

In 1978 the Illinois Supreme Court ruled that the village of Skokie had violated the free speech rights of US Nazi sympathizers who wanted to march through a predominantly Jewish community in Nazi uniforms, displaying swastika symbols. The legal analysis by the court highlighted the fact that the marchers had given prior notice, thus forewarning the residents. It was decided that even though their symbolic political speech was abhorrent, it was still entitled to First Amendment protection and the risk of a violent reaction was only a possibility and not likelihood. The spirit of tolerance in this case was replicated in 1992, when the Supreme Court overturned a criminal conviction for expressing racial or religious hatred against a 17-year-old youth who had set a burning cross in the yard of a home belonging to African Americans. The Supreme Court observed that the First Amendment 'does not permit St. Paul [Minnesota] to impose special prohibitions on those speakers who express views on disfavoured subjects.' (R.A.V. v St Paul SC US 1992) Moves to prohibit hate speech on university campuses were attenuated in 1989, when a federal judge ruled that a speech code passed by the University of Michigan prohibiting anything that stigmatized or victimized people 'on the basis of race, ethnicity, religion, sex, sexual orientation, creed, national origin, ancestry, age, marital status, handicap, or Vietnam-era veteran status' had gone too far. (Doe v University of Michigan DC US 1989) Its net had been too wide. It created a chilling effect and left students in a state of anxiety about whether their discussion of controversial subjects might lead to sanctions under the code. Even flag desecration would be judged First Amendment-protected symbolic speech, despite strong evidence of public opinion believing that such behaviour justified criminal prosecution. In 1989 and 1990 Supreme Court Justices ruled in a narrow 5–4 ruling that burning the Stars and Stripes was offensive but not dangerous political action. Even in the face of the Flag Protection Act of 1989, the Supreme Court would declare that the government could not 'prohibit the expression of an idea simply because society finds the idea itself offensive or disagreeable.' (Texas v Johnson SC US 1989; US v Eichman SC US 1990)

However, the idea that the application of the clear and present danger doctrine depends on political and social context could be supported by the apparent adoption by the Supreme Court in 2003 of dialogic multiculturalism. In writing the majority opinion of the Court, Justice Sandra Day O'Connor explained why it was not prepared to quash the convictions of individuals convicted for cross-burning offences in Virginia. Her approach seemed to make it clear that First Amendment protection did not apply if there had been a historical context of cross burning that had generated a tradition of fear and intimidation. The Virginia statute had been passed to challenge 'cross burning's long and pernicious history as a signal of impending violence.' (Virginia v Black SC US 2003) It was, therefore, a symbolic action creating a clear and present danger of racial and religious violence that usually followed. The Supreme Court was also not prepared to allow the First Amendment to prevent the increase in sentencing for crimes motivated through racial or religious hatred. It upheld the imposition of longer jail sentences in the case of a group of African American youths who had violently attacked a 14-year-old white youth after watching the film *Mississippi Burning*. (Wisconsin v Mitchell SC US 1993) The decision equates with a UK statute giving criminal courts a longer tariff in sentencing for crimes proven to be racially aggravated.

Britain's Racial and Religious Hatred Act 2006

The Racial and Religious Hatred Act 2006 created the new criminal offence of stirring up hatred against persons on religious grounds, and augmented existing offences criminalizing the stirring up of racial hatred

392

under the Public Order Act of 1986. The new offence was made punishable by fine or by prison sentence of up to seven years. The new legislation made it a crime for anyone, including a company, to intentionally stir up religious hatred by using threatening words or behaviour, and by displaying, publishing, distributing or possessing material which is threatening.

The prosecution has to prove the *actus reus*, i.e. the actual behaviour and publication, that this was threatening to the extent that it was probable somebody would feel threatened, and that there was an intention to stir up religious hatred – known as the *mens rea* of the offence. The government backed down on a plan to introduce the much more controversial offence of abusive or insulting behaviour and words that were merely likely rather than intended to stir up religious hatred. It faced a successful campaign by opposition parties, rebellious MPs and comedians such as Rowan Atkinson, and in response added a free speech defence stating that the crime could not prohibit or restrict:

> discussion, criticism or expressions of antipathy, dislike, ridicule, insult or abuse of particular religions or the beliefs or practices of their adherents, or of any other belief system or the beliefs or practices of its adherents, or proselytising or urging adherents of a different religion or belief system to cease practising their religion or belief system.
>
> (s. 29(j) Racial and Religious Hatred Act 2006)

Robertson and Nicol make the interesting point that religion is a matter of choice, whereas race is a matter of reality: 'religions are wealthy and powerful and in some cases deserving of the strongest disapprobation and most scurrilous satire.' (Robertson and Nicol 2008: 262) The provisions of the Act also protect people who are without religion, such as atheists and humanists.

The crime of stirring up racial hatred remains derived from the Public Order Act of 1986. A key difference between the two crimes of stirring up religious and racial hatred is that the 1986 legislation relating to racial hatred offers the media some degree of protection through the phrase 'having regard to all the circumstances'. *Bona fide* journalistic coverage of racist meetings would compel the courts to consider the context of any publication. In 1987 the Attorney General said that any decision on prosecuting media organizations would involve consideration of the nature, circulation, and readership of the publication as well as any special sensitivity existing at the time of the publication. However, unlike the 2006 stirring up religious hatred offence, the 1986 racial hatred offence can be committed without any intent to cause racial hatred. Both crimes give the police search powers that override protections in the 1984 Police and Criminal Evidence Act against seizure of journalistic materials. But for obvious reasons no prosecutions can be brought against fair and accurate reports of parliamentary or court proceedings.

Abolishing the crime of blasphemy

The UK abolished its common law offence of blasphemous libel in 2008. It was seen as flawed and discriminating in a multi-faith society, as it allowed a remedy only to practitioners of the Christian religion. In 1990 the High Court ruled out a private prosecution over Salman Rushdie's controversial novel *The Satanic Verses*. Muslims had been offended to the extent of the Ayatollah Khomeini in Iran issuing a fatwa urging Muslims to kill Mr Rushdie. Rushdie had to have police protection and go into hiding, and the threat was so real that people associated with the book were murdered and attacked in other countries. Rushdie would have been in difficulties if the blasphemy crime had been available to the Muslim faith, since intention and literary merit were not available as defences to blasphemy. The prosecution would only have had to prove that the book was likely to insult and outrage believers.

The last occasion of a blasphemous libel conviction had been against *Gay News* and its editor in 1977, over publication of a poem that metaphorically explored the idea of Jesus Christ being homosexual and involved in a series of sexual acts before and after his crucifixion. The editor's suspended prison sentence was quashed on appeal, but fines totalling £1,500 were upheld. The last unsuccessful attempt to seek a private prosecution for blasphemy concerned the BBC's broadcast of *Jerry Springer: The Opera* in January 2005. A Christian group objected to a scene depicting Jesus dressed as a baby and admitting to being 'a bit gay'. The High Court supported the decision by magistrates in Westminster that the law did not apply to stage productions.

Though few Americans know of their existence, unenforceable blasphemy laws are still on the books of several US states, including Massachusetts, Michigan, Oklahoma, South Carolina and Wyoming, but a Supreme Court judgment in 1952 rules out any potential revival. (Burstyn Inc. v. Wilson SC US 1952)

The extent and intensity of protest and complaint directed at anyone associated with Salman Rushdie's novel *The Satanic Verses*, the BBC's decision to transmit a television version of *Jerry Springer: The Opera*, a play written by the Sikh playwright Gurpreet Bhatti (withdrawn in 2004), the publication in September 2005 of satirical cartoons of the Prophet Mohammed in the Danish newspaper *Jyllands-Posten*, and the publication of the novel *The Jewel of Medina* by Sherry Jones in 2008 demonstrate a new phenomenon in social media that is globalized and is more complex than 'moral panic'. Each of the sagas or narratives mentioned involves the profound engendering of fear. This manifests itself in different ways and is connected with a perception of religious insult and outrage. In different degrees the problem for the authors of the original publication is that the reaction is disproportionate to the measurement of tolerable insult and offence set by the legal system of the contextual society. In the global context, one country's degree of toleration is another country's criminal offence.

In Austria the British historian David Irving can be jailed for three years for the criminal offence of holocaust denial. In the UK he was allowed to unsuccessfully sue the American academic Deborah E. Lipstadt for alleging that he was a Nazi apologist and admirer of Hitler. (Irving v Penguin & Lipstadt HC 2000) In 2005 a chamber of seven judges at the European Court of Human Rights upheld a conviction for blasphemy against the Turkish publisher of a novel that included phrases deemed to be offensive about the Prophet Mohammed. (Robertson and Nicol 2008: 66) The majority judges, including one from Turkey, saw the decision as a balancing exercise between Article 10 freedom of expression and Article 9 that everyone has the right to freedom of thought, conscience and religion. But the ruling can be criticized for an assumption that Article 9 protected the right of Muslims to have respect shown for their religion. (IA v Turkey ECHR 2005)

UK and US law allows satire, parody, criticism and offensive attacks and insulting depictions of any religion, particularly in the context of literary and artistic expression, because it is recognized that nobody is obliged to buy or read a novel. It is perhaps intriguing that Kenan Malik should write in 2008 that although Salman Rushdie's critics lost the battle, they won the war against free speech: 'The trouble with multicultural censorship, and self-censorship, is not just that it silences dissenting voices. It is also that it often creates the very problems to which it is supposedly a response.' (Malik 2008: 119) The writer Bernard-Henri Lévy wrote: 'Multiculturalism. Differentialism. Moral relativism and, should the occasion arise, assassin. That is the other legacy of the Rushdie affair.' (Lévy 2008: 129) He argues that the fatwa against Rushdie marked the new era of a retreat from the ideal of tolerance and the spirit of the Enlightenment.

Fear seemed to be the word and emotion that could not be addressed in the wide and global discourse about the so-called Danish cartoons of the Prophet Mohammed. Very few newspapers in the West chose to print them in order to provide the evidence and source for the discourse and debate taking place, yet they were always accessible 'virtually' over the Internet. The Internet was something that could not be firebombed or assassinated. The reception of the cartoons in Islamic countries was distorted and propagandized by the 'deliberate invention of some seriously revolting cartoons of the Prophet which had nothing to do with the originals and were allegedly disseminated by radical Muslim fundamentalists.' (Barnett 2006: 115)

Even an intelligent debate hosted by the Communication and Media Research Institute at the University of Westminster in February 2006, titled 'Press Freedom and Religious Respect', seemed to be disinclined to put them on display and prompted the observation by one of the speakers, Anthony McNicholas, that 'it would simply have been sensible to have been able to see them in order to determine whether or not we agreed with the interpretations given.' (McNicholas 2006: 120)

Indeed in 2008 Nordicom published a 270-page volume of academic analysis of *The Mohammed Cartoons and the Imagined Clash of Civilizations* in which the subject of the entire book's purpose was absent. Chapter after chapter interrogates and seeks to explain the transnational media event. A common factor in the West was restraint and self-censorship, yet the published explanations in editorials were criticized as cultural hypocrisy or false consciousness. Angela Phillips emphasized that the debate in Canada included views from comment writers 'who opposed the publication of the cartoons on principled, rather than merely pragmatic grounds.' (Phillips 2008: 112) She argued that Canada's Multiculturalism Act, passed in 1988, and a social context of 44 per cent of the population being foreign-born meant that 'the voices of the Muslim community were not subaltern voices unable to be heard, but rather representatives of a community elite which happened to be Muslim rather than Christian.' (Ibid.)

At the University of Westminster debate Rania Al Malky explained that the global situation has 'unfortunately played into the hands of authoritarian regimes and religious radicals who manipulated the emotions of understandably distressed Muslims for their own political gain.' (Al Malky 2006) She explained that Western reactionary forces jumped on the bandwagon and exploited the cultural chaos to say 'I told you so.' (Ibid.) Ajmal Masroor of the Islamic Society of Britain observed that 'Respecting what is sacred to Muslims isn't to compromise on freedom of speech, nor press freedom, it is merely respecting that which others consider sacred.' (Masroor 2008: 112)

The debate continues within a plethora of cultural and political dislocation, and widely differing perspectives of power. It is unlikely that the West, with all of its so-called enlightenment hubris, will ever surrender Salman Rushdie to the justice of a Shari'a court. Mohammad Hashim Kamali, author of *Freedom of Expression in Islam*, believes that he should answer to the charge of blasphemy, which:

> against the backdrop of his persistent defence of the book, whether for financial gain or a moral claim to righteousness, needs to be determined (if only on grounds of procedural propriety) by a competent judicial tribunal. The court that adjudicates this case must exercise full judicial authority and be able to issue a binding decision. It is one

thing for Rushdie to make statements in the knowledge that he does not have to comply with a binding order, and quite another when he knows that he would have to face the consequences of his conduct.

(Kamali 1997: 301)

Yet, while the civilized discourse is being played out in polite forums and academic monographs, McNicholas reminds us that to 'hound BBC executives and their families because they had the temerity to put on a musical [*Jerry Springer: The Opera*] which no one was forced to watch is disproportionate, unjust and bullying.' (McNicholas 2006: 120–1) The play *Behzti* and its gentle and thoughtful playwright, Gurpreet Bhatti, were run out of Birmingham by 'religious-inspired thuggery and abject cowardice.' (Ibid.) And the Hungarian academic Miklos Haraszti sounds a note of global warning about the spread of the law of defamation of reli- gion. He regretted the decision in March 2009 by the UN Human Rights Council to pass a resolution condemning defamation of religions as a human rights violation, because it could be used 'to justify curbs on free speech.' (Haraszti 2009: 109) Haraszti complained that in Russia the crisis around the Danish cartoons 'was used to get tough on critically minded outlets and journalists.' (Ibid.: 112) He argues that combating defamation of religions is the wrong fight and the wrong criminalization:

I do not see any moral difference between ordering a contracted killing of investigative reporters like Anna Politkovskaya and issuing fatwas that call for murdering writers or journalists. Both punish writers for doing their job. And, by the way, the fatwas also offer financial rewards, just like the *zakazchiki* in Russia.

(Ibid.: 114)

Glorifying terrorism

Legislation passed in 2006 created a new vista in British criminal law: communication and distribution of information offences in the context of supporting and endorsing the strategy of terrorism. The Terrorism Act 2006 came into force on 13 April 2006 and extended the period by which the police could detain terrorist suspects without charge up to 28 days. These would be steps too far in the context of US constitutional law. Whilst the US has followed the UK strategy of using administrative immi- gration laws to secretly detain and restrain overseas nationals, anyone arrested under US federal law has to be brought before a court within 48 hours. (Russell 2007: 9)

In 2008 the existence of the crime drew criticism from the United Nations Human Rights Committee (see Chapter 1), largely because the terms of the crime are so wide and vague. The crime does not require any evidence that anybody was in fact encouraged or induced by the terrorism-glorifying statement to commit, prepare or instigate any such offence, one of the requirements of 'clear and present danger' in US jurisprudence.

There is no public interest defence available for these offences, and trial and conviction at the Crown Court attracts a maximum sentence of seven years' imprisonment or a fine, or both. However, the prosecution has to prove that an individual intended the statement to encourage or otherwise induce the commission, preparation or instigation of acts of terrorism. There have been few prosecutions, and two men convicted and jailed in 2008, Abdul Rahman and Bilal Mohammed, had their prison sentences substantially reduced. The Lord Chief Justice observed: 'Section 2 of the 2006 Act is a complex and lengthy section. This is not surprising, for it imposes restrictions on freedom of expression.' (R v Rahman & Mohammed CoA Crim 2008) Lord Phillips also said that 'Care must, however, be taken to ensure that the sentence is not disproportionate to the facts of the particular offence.' (Ibid.) Reference has been made in Chapter 1 to the conviction and sentence of six years on Atif Siddique in Scotland for possession and distribution of terrorist materials under the Terrorism Act 2000 and 2006. His solicitor, Aamer Anwar, believed his client had been convicted of thought crimes: 'it is not a crime to be a young Muslim angry at global injustice.' (Re: Aamer Anwar HCJ 2008)

Disquiet remains that the law will be used disproportionately to crack down on confused and idealistic young people caught up in and intoxicated by the romanticism and radical fervour of revolutionary doctrines in the realms of politics or religion. British criminal law had adequate remedies to deal with 'hate preachers' such as the former controversial Imam of the Finsbury Park Mosque, Abu Hamza, jailed for seven years in 2006, who, as in the previous case of preacher El Faisal in 2004, was convicted of the existing criminal offences of incitement to murder and stirring up racial hatred. In February 2008 the Court of Appeal quashed convictions under section 57 of the Terrorism Act 2000 against five students for downloading from the Internet and sharing material alleged to have been terrorism related. (R v Zafar & Others CoA Crim 2008) The appeal court has been emphasizing that intention to possess material for a terrorist purpose is required and the presence of mere propaganda in materials is not enough. A staff member and a graduate student at Nottingham University were detained for six days before being released without charge after investigation into their possession of a document freely available on the Internet entitled 'The Al Qaida Manual' (Human Rights Watch 2009b)

There could be long-term problems associated with the 'glorifying terrorism' law. The definition of terrorism is so expansive that prosecuting the offence could lead to legitimate protest being undemocratically suppressed. Offences designed to combat 'preachers of hate' and individuals who indirectly incite terrorism by carrying placards inciting murder and praising terrorist bombers have the potential to be abused by the state in order to silence protesting groups calling for armed struggle against totalitarian regimes and governments waging genocide through domestic and foreign policy. The offences could stifle the letting-off of steam through language communication before the ideology of violence is reified and materialized into terrorist action, thereby producing the very opposite effect of what was intended. The offences have the potential to effectively criminalize praise and advocacy of any group using political violence anywhere in the world. At the time of publication the UK parliament was developing the nature, scope and defences for a new criminal offence of stirring up hatred on the grounds of sexual orientation. The crime would be available against persons who use threatening words or behaviour, display, publish, distribute or broadcast information that is threatening and intended to stir up hatred against homosexuals and bisexuals. However, the legislators were still debating whether there should be a statutory defence declaring that discussion or criticism of sexual conduct or practices or urging persons to refrain from or to modify such conduct is not, in itself, to be taken to be threatening or intended to stir up such hatred.

The UK could be seen to be creating necessary protections against minorities through its legislative innovations in this area. On the other hand, it could be criticized for criminalizing offensive and subversive speech that is best attenuated by social admonition, education and cultural enlightenment.

12

COPYRIGHT AND INTELLECTUAL PROPERTY LAW

Source philosophy

This chapter aims to analyse the world's two systems of intellectual property law, their differences and similarities, and how in the course of media history they have merged to share each other's benefits. The common law system in the UK and USA is generally known as copyright because, as a doctrine, it has emphasized the rights inherent in anyone having control of the copy of publication. The main body of current UK copyright law is to be found in the Copyright, Designs and Patents Act 1988 and subsequent amendments through statutory instruments applying European Union law, such as SI 96/2967 which extended the duration of literary, dramatic, and artistic copyright to 70 years after the death of an author. Similarly, US copyright law is set out in the Copyright Act 1976, followed by further legislation such as the Berne Convention Implementation Act 1988, and Copyright Term Extension and Digital Millennium Copyright Acts of 1998. The civil law system, exemplified for the purposes of this chapter in the law of France and Germany, has emphasized authors' rights with a focus on the creation and artistic presence in the original publication and how those rights are recognized in distribution and duplication. The social philosophy underpinning authors' rights is that, as literary and artistic creation are socially beneficial, everything should be done to ensure that the copying of an author's work could provide the means to subsistence and production of more creativity.

The common law system has appeared to be more concerned with preserving the trading interests of whosoever owned the copying rights in literary and artistic works and their availability in the public sphere for the purposes of entertainment, information and education. The social morality of protecting the interests of the original creator was not so important.

The focus for comparative analysis will be the contrasting approaches of the UK, USA, French and German jurisdictions to the issue of parodying original literary and artistic works. The deployment of ironic

400

representation that mocks, admires, imitates and entertains by its very nature raises intriguing issues of attribution, promotion, intellectual property and copyright. Where are the lines drawn between legally permissible derivation and harmful plagiarism?

The philosophers John Locke and Immanuel Kant provide inspiration for the essential elements of the legal concepts of copyright and intellectual property. In his *Second Treatise on Government* (1690) Locke reflected that the labour of a man's body and the work of his hands belonged to him in conjunction with the land and fruits of the earth that he toiled in. This was a divine and natural right in the creation of goods and assets. He implied that the concept of identity was fused in the creation of property and that property could be defined by the value of labour: 'Thus labour, in the beginning, gave a right of property, wherever any one was pleased to employ it, upon what was common.' (Sterling 2003: 106–7) Locke's reflections tended to stress the creation of property through the concept of labour and deployment of substantial skill, the foundation principles of common law copyright. Kant wrote a study 'Von der Unrechtmässigkeit des Büchernachdrucks' (On the lawfulness of unauthorized printing of books). He discoursed on the idea of the personality of the author speaking to the public through his book and therefore having the right to control the process of printing and distribution. Authorial speech and a book are in fact the actions of the writer. Sterling argues that Kant's reflection can be equated with the European-based doctrine of the moral rights of divulgation, attribution and integrity. (Ibid.: 1280–1)

In civil law countries the paradigm turned on the author's personality. In common law countries the fulcrum of legal concern lay with the public's interest in having access to copies of the author's work. It is the difference between subject and object. This is mirrored in the contrast between *droit d'auteur* and copyright.

Differences and similarities

André Françon, in his lecture 'Authors' rights beyond frontiers: a comparison of civil law and common law conceptions', finds the source for the differing socio-economic philosophies in the charters and documents arising out of the American and French revolutions of the late eighteenth century. The US constitution of 1787 conferred on Congress the power 'to promote the progress of science and useful arts by securing for limited times to authors and inventors the exclusive right to their respective writing and discoveries'. In the French decree of 1791 Le Chapelier said 'the most sacred, the most personal of all properties is the work, the fruit of a writer's thought.' (Françon 1991: 6) In the decree of 1793 Lakanal would write that of all the properties owned by man 'the least open to dispute is unquestionably that of productions of genius; and what should surprise us is that it has been necessary to recognize this property and secure its exercise by means of a substantive law.' (Ibid.)

At the beginning of the seminal work *World Copyright Law* by J.A.L. Sterling a short poem 'dedicated by the author to Valerio de Sanctis' makes play with the idea that the work of the cobbler produces the shoe whereas the work of the author produces literature and art, and the difference adheres to the fact that the shoe is made for the foot that walks to the tomb and literature is made for the spirit that walks into infinity. (Sterling 2003: v)

The common law system originated in the first British copyright act of 1710, which is known as the 'Statute of Anne' and granted the author 'the sole right and liberty' of printing his/her books for an initial period of 14 years, with an option to extend this for another 14 years. Publishers could easily gain ownership of the copyright by getting it assigned to them from the writers in the printing contracts. The US Congress passed the first American copyright act in 1790 and, although strongly influenced by the British model, this excluded any protection for foreign works and positively encouraged piracy of non-American writers such as Charles Dickens in the nineteenth century. Nothing was allowed to 'prohibit the importation or vending, reprinting or publishing within the United States, of any book etc. written, printed or published by foreigners in places outside the United States.' (Ibid.: 11)

Sterling argues that in addition to the *author's right* and *copyright* systems the world also accommodates a third *composite* system which combines elements from the common and civil law jurisdictions and adds distinctive features indigenous to the cultures of those countries with composite intellectual property law doctrines. China and Japan are examples of countries operating composite systems of intellectual property. (Ibid.: 15)

Françon suggests that the trading of intellectual property products across frontiers, over time, and the influence of international conventions and treaties have inevitably resulted in an exchange and interpenetration of legal doctrines. A selective summary of the respective copyright and intellectual property systems of the UK and USA is set out in Tables 12.1, and of France and Germany in Table 12.3. A chronology of transnational influences is provided in Table 12.2.

There has certainly been a harmonizing of duration rights. Prior to the USA's joining in the Berne Convention in 1988 and the UK's becoming subject to European Union directives, the two countries' common law jurisdictions allowed original authors much more limited exploitation of copyright interests prior to their expiration into the public domain, as compared with Continental jurisdictions such as France and Germany. In the USA, with fixation and registration requirements, the rights could be renewed for an additional 28 years after the first 28 years from publication. In Britain, works became public domain 50 years after the death of the author.

Table 12.1 Common law copyright jurisdictions compared: the UK and USA

United Kingdom	United States
Copyright protects the *expression* of an idea and not the idea itself. It is in the substantial labour in the work. Copyright is a right of commercial nature, so that the owner can make money out of the copying and distribution of the work.	Copyright protects original works of authorship and is determined by the *idea/expression* dichotomy. There is no protection for 'any idea, procedure, process, system, method of operation, concept, principle or discovery'. Protection extends to a non-exhaustive list of eight categories including:
Literary works, including: • Tables or compilations other than databases • Computer programs • Preparatory design for computer programs • Databases Musical works Dramatic works Artistic works, including: • Graphic works, sculpture and collage • Works of architecture • Works of artistic craftsmanship Films Sound recordings Broadcasts Typographical arrangements	Literary works: • Compilations are protected (Section 103, Copyright Act 1976) Musical works, including accompanying words Dramatic works, including accompanying music Pictorial, graphic and sculptural works Motion pictures and other audiovisual works Sound recordings Pantomimes and choreographic works Architectural works
Legislation • Copyright, Designs and Patents Act 1988 • Copyright and Trade Marks (Offences and Enforcement) Act 2002 • Directive 2001/29/EC of the European Parliament and of the Council of 22 May 2001	*Legislation* • Copyright Act 1976 • Berne Convention Implementation Act 1988 • Copyright Term Extension Act 1998 • Digital Millennium Copyright Act 1998

Continued overleaf

United Kingdom	United States
Key defence for media communicators	*Key defence for media communicators*
• Fair dealing	• Fair use
For the purpose of	Unlike the UK fair dealing defence, fair use is an open-ended doctrine. It includes the purpose of criticism, comment, news reporting and teaching but can be extended by judicial discretion on the basis of four factors:
a research or private study;	
b Criticism or review;	
c Reporting current events.	
This defence is not open-ended and so is restricted by the statutory construction in sections 29–30 of 1988 legislation.	1 Purpose and character of the use, including whether such use is of a commercial nature or is for non-profit educational purposes;
Courts normally consider the extent of the extract copied and used, whether it was necessary for the purpose stated in the Act, the economic consequences for the owner of the copyright and the nature and degree of any sufficient acknowledgment.	2 Nature of the copyright work;
	3 Amount and substantiality of the portion used in relation to copyrighted work as a whole;
Research and private study defences relate only to literary, dramatic and musical works. Criticism and review defences relate to all categories of work. Reporting of current events defence applies to all categories except photographs. Courts are flexible in interpreting criticism and review, but less so in considering the word 'current' in current events.	4 Effect of the use upon the potential market for or value of copyrighted work.
	Other factors deemed by court to be relevant can be applied. Fair use is considered more liberal than UK fair dealing but is not a licence for copyright infringement. US jurisprudence promotes more innovation and free speech, particularly in the area of parody.

Table 12.2 Intellectual property and copyright transnational agreements

---

Berne Convention for the protection of literary and artistic works. Original in 1886, latest text agreed in 1971

Phonograms Convention for the protection of producers of phonograms against unauthorized duplication of their products, Geneva 1971

Rome Convention for the protection of performers, producers of phonograms and broadcasting organisations, 1961

TRIPS – the international agreement on Trade-related Aspects of Intellectual Property Rights, Marrakesh, Morocco, 1994

UCC – Universal Copyright Convention, Paris 1971

WCT – World Intellectual Property Organization's World Copyright Treaty, 1996 agreed by member states in Geneva. WIPO is a specialized agency of the United Nations established in 1967

WPPT – WIPO agreed World Performances and Phonograms Treaty, Geneva, 1996

Table 12.3 Authors' rights jurisdictions of France and Germany

France	*Germany*
Dualistic theory distinguishing between physical or material intellectual property and immaterial property.	Monistic theory fuses codification of personality and economic rights but recognizes the source of author's creation. Intellectual property is a unity of economic and immaterial-moral interests. This means that economic rights always retain moral underpinning and the author can only assign commercial rights.
Moral rights belong to the individuality inherent in the work.	
Economic rights in the products of the author.	
Test of intellectual property ownership is whether the work contains the author's personal intellectual creation.	German law requires the work to contain the author's personal creation in a three-step analysis:
French law protects 'works of the mind' irrespective of type, form of expression, value or determination and issues of aesthetic quality and artistic level. It has to have originality separate from its functional character and the degree of expression must be materially perceptible.	• intellectual subject must be expressed • work expressed must be in perceivable form • work must display originality and be the result of individual endeavour.
Protected categories are indicated and non-exhaustive and include literary, artistic, scientific and dramatic as well as functional forms such as computer	German law is more detailed about protected subject matter and includes works of literature, science and art and a non-exhaustive list of categories that depend on the key value of constituting the author's personal

Continued overleaf

programs, databases, graphical and typographical works. Choreographs and pantomimes are protected if fixed on a carrier.

- Adaptations, translations, compilations
- Cinematographic works
- Computer programs

Related rights (*droits voisins*):

- Performing artists, phonogram/ videogram manufacturers and audio-visual communication enterprises.

1957 Author's Rights Act on the Protection of Literary and Artistic Property (No. 57–298) codified previous body of law, droit moral and confirmed jurisdiction and modern scholarly opinion.

1985 Parliamentary Bill (No. 85–660) implemented new provisions on royalties for private copying of records and visual works, the function of collecting societies, and contracts. Neighbouring rights introduced for performers and for manufacturers of audio-visual communications.

Law No. 92–597 (1992) and Intellectual Property Code (1994). Further regulation on law of intellectual property, patent and trademarks.

Moral rights in French law precede consideration of economic rights and can be inherited. They include:

- *Droit de divulgation* or right of publication – the right to decide if, where and when the work is published
- Right to be named as author
- Right of integrity of the work
- Right to revocation of the contract
- Right to waiver of rights.

Economic rights include:

- *Droit de représentation* – public communications of the work (non-physical)

intellectual creation. Speeches are protected from the time of creation, but this does not apply to interviews.

- Works of music and drama
- Photographs, film and television works
- Works of fine art
- Adaptations and free uses (instances of parody and imitation)

Neighbouring rights:

- Performing artists, publishers of new editions, non-original photographs, phonograms, broadcasters, databases, films.

1965 German Copyright Act, modern consolidating law abbreviated as UrhG standing for Urheberrechtsgesetz. Regulates authors' rights in modern media.

Implementation of Directives from European Union on intellectual property to adjust requirements of the law to the needs of the information society. These include directives on computer programs (1991), rental/lending and related rights (1992), satellite broadcasting and cable retransmission (1993), harmonizing terms of protection (1993), databases (1996) and information society (2001).

2002 Copyright Contracts Act, introduced to strengthen the bargaining position of authors.

As the German legal approach is monistic there is no hierarchy between moral and economic rights and sometimes they are indistinguishable, but they can be recognized as:

- Publication right – author can determine exclusively if, when, how and where the work is published
- Acknowledgement right
- Integrity right
- Access right and resale right – physical access to the original work and the right of an artist for a percentage of resale.

France	Germany
• *Droit de reproduction* – physical fixation of the work to facilitate communication to the public • *Droit de suite* – artist's resale right in the case of fine artists to claim royalty on each individual sale, further resale or any copies by public auction or other commercial sale.	Economic rights are non-exhaustive and include: • Reproduction • Distribution • Public performance • Broadcasts • Public communication.

France

Defences for media communicators or limitations on intellectual property ownership:

• Private copying in all categories, except in fine art where the copying would substitute the original.
• Reproduction for the purpose of analysis, press clippings and for the benefit of information in the media.
• Parodies, imitations and caricature.
• Government works.
• Private performances – where an entrance fee is not charged in private surroundings.

Germany

Defences for media communicators or limitations on use of intellectual property are more extensive:

• Individual uses: time shifting in the private sphere e.g. DVD, CD and video copying from television; scientific and academic use; using broadcasts to provide information about current events; professional and commercial purposes; where work has been deleted by publisher for more than two years; use of small parts of the work in school education.
• Limitation for trade benefits: demonstrating playback media appliances to customers; insignificant or incidental use of the image of a sculpture in the filming of a public street; exhibition catalogues and internal archives of museums.
• Limitations for the benefit of cultural discourse: using portions of a work in citation, education and in churches.
• General access to information: for the benefit of freedom of information, there is no protection for publication of laws and parliamentary debates, public speeches on current issues in public gatherings; electronic media clippings similar to newspaper articles; mixed news items of a factual nature and daily news published by press or broadcasting services.

Note: Rights are based on the original author's personality and cannot be transferred. Intellectual property as an economic investment is less important. Jurisdictions stress the concept of originality rather than 'skill and labour'. They originated the Continental civil law tradition of 'moral rights' that have been absorbed by UK and, to a lesser extent, US copyright law. Both French and German law in this area is determined by civil law code.

At the time of writing the standard duration in the majority of categories of protected work has now become 70 years after the death of the author. The question of when works are public domain has become rather complicated and necessitates complex tabulation in specialist textbooks on copyright. For example, harmonization has meant that a standard concept that all photographs publicly published in the UK prior to 1940 became public domain no longer applies where photographer's rights have been asserted, particularly in images that could be argued to be 'artistic.' EU harmonization meant that the copyright in the literary works of a writer such as George Orwell became extended from the year 2000 to 2020.

The US requirement for the registration of copyright at the Library of Congress is no longer a qualification for the proof of copyright ownership. Françon argued that the US copyright tradition relegated the bond of the work and its creator to the background: 'The author's spiritual interests can be safeguarded only by having recourse to other techniques outside copyright, such as that of personal rights, for example, or protection against defamation or consumer protection.' (Françon 1991: 14)

The distinction and differentiation between the civil law and common law systems of copyright and authors' rights appears much less clear on examination of Tables 12.1 and 12.3. But Table 12.1 does not indicate that moral rights are now explicitly part of the UK copyright law system and this penetration, as Françon so rightly observes, is the result of participation in the Berne Convention. But it is also a fact that the UK, as a founder member in 1888, did not absorb moral rights into its copyright legislation until 1988. British moral rights are interpreted with typical Anglo-Saxon terminology and are defined as right of paternity (right of attribution), right of integrity, right not to have a work falsely attributed and the right to privacy of certain photographs and films.

The USA joined the Convention by passing the Berne Convention Implementation Act of 1988 that came into force in the United States on 1 March 1989, but has legislated for only limited assertion of moral rights in the Visual Artists Rights Act of 1990. However, harmonization with the Berne Convention can be recognized in the USA's abolition of its stipulated conditions of protection through copyright registration, and the extension of ownership and duration rights. The moral rights protection guaranteed to visual artists is very narrow in scope and applies only to paintings, drawings, prints, sculptures and exhibition photographs, and only if they exist in a single copy or in limited editions of no more than two hundred copies.

The rights are limited to artists being known as the creators of their works and the right to prevent the use of their names on modified representations of their work if they believe such modifications can harm their reputation. They can also prevent intentional distortion or mutilation of their works. Further evidence of an American cultural distancing from the Continental philosophy of *droits d'auteurs* is that these moral rights last only for the life of the artist and cannot be inherited. This contrasts rather starkly with the metaphor conjured by the German copyright scholar Eugen Ulmer, who saw authors' moral rights rooted in the tree trunk which supported and controlled the branches of economic aspects and moral interests emanating from it.

Françon argues that common law copyright has invaded the authors' rights system of France and Germany through the commercial development of the cultural industries, digitization and the expansion of neighbouring producer rights from businesses that take the financial risks of investment. In 1985 France had to concede copyright protection in computer software 'in spite of the great differences that exist between a computer program and a work of the classic type.' (Françon 1991: 26) Sterling acknowledges the influence of civil law authors' rights concepts in the developing case history of higher US and UK courts. For example, in a US Supreme Court opinion in 1991 the judges were looking for a 'modicum of creativity' rather than evidence of the 'sweat of the brow.' (Feist Publications Inc v Rural Telephone Service SC US 1991; Sterling 2003: 17) UK courts apply the skill, judgment and labour approach to evaluating copyright in literary, dramatic, musical and artistic works, but reserve the test of 'the author's own intellectual creation' when identifying the necessary criterion of originality required in the copyright in databases. (Ibid.)

Cultural nuances in the privilege of parody

An interesting source for identifying contextual differences in the approach to intellectual property infringement can be found in the varying defences of parody. Civil law countries such as France, Belgium and Spain specifically protect parody as a respected and social art form. There may be an association with or inspiration in the tradition of social carnival in those countries, in which case there is an opportunity to discourse the defence in the context of Mikhail Bakhtin's theory of the carnivalesque in *Rabelais and His World*. The participation of the people in Carnival is understandably ambivalent and provides the audience with an arena of participation that circumvents the representation of the original. It is the opportunity to subvert the economic hegemony of law and, in the destruction of the original, give rise to a new creativity in the same way that symbolic carnival masques of death represent rebirth.

Article 39 of the Spanish Law on Intellectual Property 1996 states that parody does not require the consent of the author, provided there is no confusion with the original work and the pastiche does not damage the original work or its author. Germany does not mention parody as a limitation but it does provide for transformations of original works. The French legal code of 1992, article L. 122.5(4) specifically asserts that authors are not permitted to forbid 'parody, pastiche and caricature, taking account of the laws of the genre.' (Sterling 2003: 522) The French law protects the moral rights of the original author by excluding parody motivated by malice, and economic rights are protected through the requirement of connection and purpose elements. The public must be able to recognize the connection between the two works and that the parody is not the original. The purpose has to be comic or satirical, and malicious derivation producing *diffamation* of the first author vitiates the defence.

The German courts had to deal in 1993 with two actions against attempted parodies of the *Asterix* cartoon series and conjured new figures named Alcolix and Isterix. The German judges approached the question by assessing 'the difference maintained between the new work and the borrowed creative personal features: free use requires that the borrowed creative features have faded, so that these features become (mere) incentive. An "inner distance" is necessary.' (Sterling 2003: 523–4)

No special defence of parody is articulated in British statute law. US copyright jurisprudence has been much more adventurous, perhaps because of the elasticity and open-ended nature of the fair use defence. Zelezny explains how the freedom to parody was confirmed by the Supreme Court in 1994 in a dispute over rap group 2 Live Crew's parody of the 1964 Roy Orbison hit 'Oh, Pretty Woman' (Zelezny 2004: 337–9) It was a model of a four-step fair use analysis in evaluating whether the parody had commercial objectives, was highly expressive of the original, copied the original to a substantial extent and negatively affected the market for the original. (Campbell v Acuff-Rose Music, Inc SC US 1994)

In 2009 lawyers for the reclusive author of *Catcher in the Rye*, J.D. Salinger, succeeded in obtaining a preliminary injunction in a copyright suit before US District Judge Deborah Batts against the novel *60 Years Later: Coming through the Rye* by Fredrik Colting, writing under the name of John David California. Salinger alleged that Colting's character Mr. C was an infringement on his character Holden Caulfield. Judge Batts held that Holden Caulfield was sufficiently delineated in Mr. C, that Fredrik Colting had access to *The Catcher in the Rye* and that there were 'similarities that are probative of copying between the works', and there was 'a substantial similarity' between the two novels.

On the issue of parody Judge Batts was unconvinced by the defendant's argument that the novel contained sufficient commentary and criticism of Salinger to justify the defence:

> Defendant's use of Salinger as a character, in order to criticize his reclusive nature and alleged desire to exercise 'iron-clad control over his intellectual property, refusing to allow others to adapt any of his characters or stories in other media', is at most, a tool with

which to criticize and comment upon the author, J.D. Salinger, and his supposed idiosyncrasies. It does not, however, direct that criticism toward *Catcher* and Caufield themselves, and thus is not an example of parody.

(Salinger v Colting and others US DC 2009: 18–19)

The fourth factor in assessing the US defence of fair use cited by Judge Batts was that *60 Years* would harm the potential market for sequels or other authorized derivative works based upon *Catcher*. The judge concluded that the claimed parodic content is not reasonably perceivable and that 'the limited non-parodic transformative content is unlikely to overcome the obvious commercial nature of the work.' (Ibid.) However, this interesting case was likely to rise through the federal courts, as Mr Colting said he would appeal. If a similar case had been heard in France the courts would have examined the parody to evaluate its comic or satirical effect. There would have been a consideration of any allegation that the work had been malicious in injuring the honour or reputation of the author of the original work. The courts would also be looking to determine the connection element in terms of any evidence of a recognizable proximity between the original and parody.

Commodification of information

The jurisprudential osmosis between common law and civil law copyright and intellectual jurisdictions, combined with global harmonization through international treaty, raises the economic prospects and potential profits in the trade in human expression. However, the extension of the opportunity in moral and material rights 70 years beyond the death of the author has the potential to limit the public interest in free and low-cost access to information, art and culture. Furthermore, the limitation on reproduction could, in the passage of time, reduce the chance of public domain preservation. There is also the politico-economic issue of hyper-intensive profits in expression that have already returned remuneration to the original authors and associated/neighbouring publishers as a guarantee of continued creative development and expression in human society. Should there be a ceiling on such profits? Richard Haynes discussed the decision by singer George Michael in 2004 to distribute his new music free, via his dedicated website, on the grounds that, having been remunerated well for so many years, he hardly needed any more of the public's money. (Haynes 2005: 139) The ruthless pursuit by national and global anti-copyright-infringement agencies of free Internet music, video and literature exchange idealists has given rise to a fertile debate and the development of 'creative commons' rights and concessions.

13

FREEDOM OF INFORMATION LEGISLATION

US citizens have had the benefit of a federal freedom of information (FOI) act since 1966. All fifty states had either already passed legislation guaranteeing qualified access rights to public body documents and information before Congress legislated or did so afterwards. The United Kingdom passed its first FOI Act in the year 2000. Scotland introduced similar legislation through its own Parliament in 2002, and FOI campaigners say its provisions are somewhat stronger than are those of the legislation south of the border: 'The Scottish Information Commissioner is more powerful ....' (Brooke 2006: 34) But the legislation did not come into force in Scotland and the rest of the United Kingdom until January 2005. Was this a sign of the insecurity, lack of preparation and perhaps cultural reluctance inherent in the body politic?

A comparison of FOI laws indicates that they differ widely in detail and scope. However, there are some common factors. An underlying or central principle is asserted that the people have a right of access to government information. Inevitably, that right is qualified by exemptions that enable governments to refuse disclosure of information on the grounds that specific harm will be caused by publication. It is possible to identify common categories in FOI exemptions: formulation of executive policy, relations with other countries, investigation of crime and administration of justice, national security, privacy of citizens, and commercial secrets. The majority of FOI legislative machineries allow for a right of appeal to an independent body, usually known as an information commissioner, and this process of appeal is more often than not embedded into judicial review or referable up the ladder of the country's judicial system.

Discussions of the subject usually include the almost mythological fact that Sweden was the first country in the world to enact an FOI-style law, in the age of the Enlightenment in 1766. But the power to demand government documents could not in practice be used by Swedish citizens until some 43 years later. There was little enthusiasm to follow the model. More than a hundred years would pass before similar laws would be voted in elsewhere. The chronology of FOI law making around the world is set out in Table 13.1.

Table 13.1 Freedom of information legislation – unfolding internationally

Country	Date
Sweden	1766 – enacted 1809
Finland	1951
USA	1966 and 1967
Denmark	1970
Norway	1970
France	1978 and 1979
Netherlands	1978 and 1991
Australia	1982
Canada	1982
New Zealand	1984
Greece	1986
Austria	1987
Italy	1990
Spain	1992
Portugal	1993
Belgium	1994
Ireland	1997
Japan	Legislated 1999, enacted 2001
India	2005
United Kingdom	Legislated 2000, enacted 2005

One might be forgiven for detecting a lack of critical focus or contemplation over whether 'freedom of information' legislation is necessarily a good development in law or constitutional reform. Campaigners have an almost evangelistic zeal. One thing cannot be denied, and that is that FOI has become a transnational distinguishing mark of democracy and freedom. A two part series of BBC World Service documentaries, *The Right to Know*, broadcast in 2008, reported that more than seventy countries now have FOI, and another fifty are planning to join the club. At the time of writing Saudi Arabia and China have not joined, and it may well be more than a coincidence that both these countries are seen as authoritarian. But the academic and chronicler of freedom of information around the world David Banisar was in a position to write in 2006: 'The previous two years have been an exciting time for those promoting and using the right of access to information. Countries on every continent have adopted laws.' (Banisar 2006: 6)

The term 'freedom of information' is something of a misnomer. The legislation adopted in the USA and UK does not amount to an absence of restrictions on the voluntary disclosure of information. It does not involve the unqualified right to demand information, and the phrase does not appear in the language of the European Convention on Human Rights. We are not dealing with absolutes here. It is another case of relative freedom and attenuated rights. It certainly involves the bureaucratic legalization of the flow of information from governments to their citizens and it attaches a price and process to that flow. There is, consequently, a decline in the exercise of discretion and ethical negotiation, and an increase in legal process and litigation.

It might be argued that the FOI culture that requires public authorities and bodies to legally and constitutionally calculate the balancing of rights in disclosing information has seeded the developed cult of anonymity and a slowing down or delay in the dissemination of information. In practical terms I can cite two examples of how this change in culture directly affects the methodology and content of journalism.

In the 1970s, as a young reporter for media organizations, I would ordinarily be given the name, age, marital status and address of anyone involved in a public event recorded by the police and this could be an arrest, charge or accident. There was no legislation saying that the police should not provide this information; equally there was no legislation saying that they should. The practice was custom and had been established in the context of an open, liberal and democratic society that supported the idea that public events involving the police and emergency services should be reported with transparency and that when ordinary people got caught up in these events their named participation was part of the public record.

In the FOI culture this is no longer the case. Enveloped in the FOI process is normally some kind of data protection law rooted in the concept of privacy. The police in Britain will not ordinarily reveal the details of people arrested or charged with criminal offences. The issue of identification is usually left to the ritual of a first court appearance. If they decide to release any information before a court appearance it may be limited to a name and age, perhaps profession, but most rarely will this involve any address details. The identities of individuals involved in accidents that the police attend to will not be released except with their permission or with that of next of kin. The release of the identification of the victims and locations of crime will be determined by issues of privacy and by the anticipation of the consequences of that information's being used by other people to commit further crimes.

These developments are seen as representing progress. But there are consequences. Murders and serious crime incidents are sometimes not reported for 24 hours; sometimes days after the event. The nature of the representation of the event becomes the deep focus of controversy and enquiry, as was the situation with the deaths of Mr Jean Charles de

Menezes at Stockwell underground station in London in 2005 and of Mr Ian Tomlinson in the City of London in 2009. Both incidents involved investigation of the behaviour of police officers. Both incidents revealed contradictions in the release of information by the police in the immediate aftermath of the events and subsequent revelations of the actual narrative provided by witnesses.

In 1980 I was assigned to cover the case of a private aeroplane that had ditched into a heavy sea swell off the coast of the north-east of England. The pilot had been rescued by coastguards and was recovering in a local hospital, but the passenger had died from exposure. Both the police and the coastguard gave me the names, ages, addresses and professions of the two men in the plane. I simply rang up the local hospital, asked to be put through to the pilot, who I stated was a patient there, and was put through to his ward and was able to speak to him. I explained who I was, expressed my condolences and sympathy and asked whether he would be prepared to be interviewed. He invited me to visit him so that I could record an interview. He wanted to explain what had happened and pay a tribute to and make a spoken obituary of the passenger, who had been a close friend. He wanted to express publicly sorrow and condolence to the family of the man who had died. I walked into the hospital as a visitor, the radio station's large tape recorder, emblazoned with the station's logo, around my shoulder and was directed to the ward. Nobody challenged me. Afterwards the hospital authorities complained that I had trespassed, breached the pilot's privacy, failed to seek the permission of the hospital administrator, and tricked the pilot into giving an interview because he thought I was an air accident investigator. It is true that I had not sought the permission of the hospital administrator, as I had not thought this was relevant when the patient had invited me to visit him during advertised and public visiting times.

The same situation in 2009 would have had a different outcome. It is unlikely that the details of the pilot and his passenger would have been released until many days after the plane crash. The pilot would probably have been advised against the release of his personal details. Some kind of official liaison barrier would have been placed between the pilot and the media. No media reporter would be allowed on hospital premises without first reporting to hospital security and administration. It is highly unlikely that a reporter would be able to phone a recovering patient directly unless the details of the patient's personal mobile phone were known. Many would argue that this is all for the best. The circumstances in which the British actor Gordon Kaye was interviewed and had his photograph taken by a reporter and photographer who had walked into his private room at the Charing Cross Hospital in London in 1990 resulted in a notorious court case in 1991 and a ruling of malicious falsehood against the newspaper they worked for. (Kaye v Robertson HC 1991)

However, if it is accepted that everything connected with the aeroplane crash into the sea was bona fide, voluntary and without subterfuge, can it not also be argued that a method and spirit of openness in communication and journalism present in 1980 may well be absent in 2009? The difference in these journalistic time cultures could be accounted for by the differences in standard information-release and -retention cultures, separated by nearly three decades of history and the resulting changes in social and moral values. The campaigners for FOI legislation would argue that the powers given to citizens to apply for information create a freer and more liberal environment in which to discuss and debate the setting of those values.

By establishing statutory obligation to communicate public information as well as to release it on application, central government is fostering a more open climate for the exchange of official information. This is reflected in the optimism of long-standing FOI campaigner Heather Brooke, who believes passionately that secrecy on the part of government gestates injustice and disaster because it acts as a host for bad practices that cannot be challenged: 'One reason government officials hate openness is that it highlights their mistakes, and that's embarrassing. However, avoiding embarrassment should not be the guiding principle of any government; running an efficient and well-run system should be.' (Brooke 2005: 5)

David Banisar sets out four essential benefits arising from FOI laws: democratic participation and understanding; protecting other rights; making government bodies work better; redressing past harms. Banisar perhaps states the self-evident when he explains that 'Democracy is based on the consent of the citizens and that consent turns on the government informing citizens about their activities and recognizing their right to participate.' (Banisar 2006: 6) He was echoing US President Lyndon Johnson's resonant declaration when approving the 1966 Freedom of Information Act with the words: 'I signed this measure with a deep sense of pride that the United States is an open society in which the people's right to know is cherished and guarded.' But it has been debated whether President Johnson's mentality was in accord with his rhetoric. His successor, President Richard Nixon, struggled to use the Act's exemptions to block access to his White House tape recordings during the Watergate scandal. Supreme Court rulings thwarted the process of presidential cover-up and led to the threat of impeachment and his eventual resignation.

Banisar is by no means naive about the potential 'fig leaf' characteristics of FOI laws, which can easily camouflage arbitrary dictatorship and authoritarian oppression. There is always the risk that they will become as redundant and meaningless as superficially exercised constitutional articles on freedom of expression and free and democratic elections, and that the culture of secrecy will remain locked into the system: 'Many of the laws are not adequate and promote access in name only. In some

416

countries, the laws lie dormant due to a failure to implement them properly or a lack of demand.' (Banisar 2006: 6)

FOI legislation generates a scale of expenditure and bureaucratic infrastructure that can be exponential and cost inflationary. In 2006 the UK Department of Constitutional Affairs reported that FOI requests were costing government £24.4 million a year. (Welsh et al. 2007: 374) An initial wave of 13,000 requests were made to central government in the first three months of 2005 and by the end of the first year there was an estimated total of between 100,000 and 130,000 requests across all bodies, including 38,108 requests to central government bodies. (Banisar 2006: 156) The UK's Campaign for Freedom of Information sought to measure the cost qualitatively by publishing *500 Stories from the FOI Act's First Year* and the journalistic benefits from exercising rights to information from more than a thousand public bodies and authorities. There is clearly a disparity in proportionate costs, requests and results between the UK, with a population estimated at 60 million, and the USA, with a population of 300 million. In 2004, the US processed 4,047,474 requests at a total cost of $330,175,513.

Banisar reports that US FOI law may well be more established than its UK counterpart, but age does not necessarily bring the benefits of wisdom and maturity: 'The FOIA has been hampered by a lack of central oversight and long delays in processing requests. In some instances, information is released only after years or decades.' (Banisar 2006: 159) A review by Associated Press in 2006 found that nearly all executive departments had increasing delays ranging from three months to over four years; national security-related agencies were releasing less information; and 30 per cent of departments had not submitted their annual reports on time. The National Security Archive found that the oldest request on record was 17 years old. Banisar was critical of the Bush administration and he highlighted the issuing in 2001 of a memo by Attorney General John Ashcroft declaring that the Justice Department would defend in court any federal agency that withheld information on justifiable grounds. (Banisar 2006: 159–60)

In 2009 the Obama administration appeared to signify a change in policy; particularly with the release of the so-called 'torture' memos indicating the legal and political approval for the policies of water-boarding in interrogation of terrorist suspects. However, at the time of writing, the decision to pursue a defence against the American Civil Liberties Union's FOI disclosure request for Iraq and Afghanistan prisoner-abuse photographs and videos seems set to rise through the federal legal appeals system as far as the Supreme Court.

There is growing evidence that FOI laws generate transnational dimensions of empowered disclosure, so that liberty and democracy in non-FOI countries are seeded and inspired by disclosure achieved in others. In

417

1979, British Prime Minister Margaret Thatcher revealed in the House of Commons that the former Keeper of the Queen's Pictures, Sir Anthony Blunt, had been one of a group of home-grown spies recruited by the Soviet Union at Cambridge University in the 1930s and had been given immunity from prosecution. Her decision to expose the arrangement was against the advice of the Security Service, MI5. The political pressure on the government had been generated by Andrew Boyle's book *The Climate of Treason*, in which he had analysed the history and damage without actually naming Blunt as the 'fourth man' who assisted and protected the defectors Donald Maclean, Guy Burgess and Kim Philby. Some of the information in Boyle's book could only have been obtained under the US Freedom of Information laws. (House of Lords Select Committee 1998: note 32)

The historian Alasdair Roberts seems to argue in *Blacked Out: Government Secrecy in the Information Age* (2006) that the overriding question remains whether the drive for transparency has successfully stemmed the desire for government secrecy and effectively challenged overreaching presidents and secretive government agencies. Has the bureaucratic ritualizing, tracking and costing of information request and release simply served to educate government elites and state apparatchiks into ways of frustrating, concealing and offsetting 'freedom of information'? Have they learned to minute less and to shred more efficiently? Some of the drawbacks of British Freedom of Information Act culture are set out in Table 13.2

Table 13.2 Freedom of information: drawbacks for journalism

The end of exclusives?
The response to your FOI request will be publicly available – normally on the public body's website. This means that the rest of the media will be able to benefit from your investigative journalism.

Increased self-censorship by public bodies
Civil servants are avoiding the minuting of key information during meetings and administration so as to minimize embarrassing data trails. As well as circumventing the aims of the FOI Act, this will impair the quality of historical records.

Putting a price on information
The FOI Act has created a bureaucracy for releasing information, which has a price – that can be increased at any time.

The emergence of FOI specialists
There is a danger that the bureaucracy and time/labour requirements of FOI usage will divide journalists between the processors/churnalists and the interrogative investigative elite who have the status, resources and time to be given the privilege of FOI access.

At the beginning of his book Roberts playfully juxtaposes Jeremy Bentham's words from 1785: 'The eye of the public makes the statesman virtuous. The multitude of the audience multiplies for disintegrity the chances of detection', with Donald Rumsfeld's comment in 2004: 'Our country has forgotten how to keep a secret.' (Roberts 2006: v)

Ruling elites and government apparatchiks all realize that power is determined and exercised by the skill and methodology of concealing corruption, incompetence, human rights abuses and environmental degradation. Roberts highlights the impotence and limited reach of FOI laws in checking the records and paper trail of decision making by supranational corporations and bodies that are designated as either private or quasi-public. And in the future the key difficulties will be 'extracting and manipulating digitised data' and 'equity in access to government information.' (Ibid.: 227)

Practical guidance on using FOI laws

There is no shortage of excellent books published in the UK and USA providing 'how to' kits on using FOI laws for journalism, research and political campaigning. The laws in both countries are complicated, as the attempt to contrast them in Table 13.3 tends to demonstrate. However, in Tables 13.4 and 13.5 I have attempted to provide guidance tables with gate-keeper advice on online resources that were available as this book went to press.

By 2009 the United Kingdom had the benefit of nearly four years of Freedom of Information Act culture and process. It has transformed the nature of professional journalism by providing a focus and mechanism for investigative enquiry. In some respects this is very much counter to the tenor of the popular book by Nick Davies, *Flat Earth News: An Award-winning Reporter Exposes Falsehood, Distortion and Propaganda in the Global Media* (2008), in which he states 'I'm afraid that I think the truth is that, in trying to expose the weakness of the media, I am taking a snapshot of a cancer. Maybe it helps a little to be able to see the illness. At least that way we know in theory what the cure might be. But I fear the illness is terminal.' (Davies 2008: 397) Notwithstanding his discourse on 'churnalism' in newsrooms, the recycling of ideologically narrow sources of news agency, government and corporate public relations press releases, and the stretching of journalists into an overworked conveyor belt of over-production in high-pressured news factories, the Freedom of Information Act has led to the introduction of workshops and courses on the subject at universities that teach journalism. Training sessions and workshops have also been provided within the professional media and journalistic workspace. It has provided an opportunity for the news media to allocate and ring-fence resources and expertise for investigative enquiries into government information beyond the 24/7 time sequence.

419

Table 13.3 Comparison of UK and USA freedom of information operations and exemptions

United Kingdom	United States
Legislated for in 2000 and 2002 but operational January 2005 at UK and Scottish levels	Legislated for in 1966 but operational in 1967 in relation to federal bodies. Some states had legislation operating FOI-equivalent laws before 1966, but most was enacted afterwards.
Applies to all public authorities at national and local level. A legal right of access to information held by public authorities: 1(i) Any person making a request for information to a public authority is entitled: a to be informed in writing by the public authority whether it holds information of the description specified in the request and b if that is the case, to have that information communicated to him.	Applies to federal government bodies, but excluding Congress. The Act states that the public has a right of access to most existing government documents but does not provide a definition of 'record'. The federal agencies include 'the executive branch of the government and its departments; all regulatory agencies, such as the FCC and the FTC; cabinet-level agencies such as the Defense Department and the FBI; and government-controlled corporations, such as the U.S. Postal Service'. As in the UK there should be a response to a request within 20 working days, but in practice shortages of staff and resources can lead to long delays.
Two classes of exemption apply: Absolute exemptions and qualified exemptions. Authorities also have the right to refuse 'vexatious requests'. Public authorities normally have 20 days (four working weeks) in which to reply after receiving a request.	Nine categories of exemption apply; they are not divided into absolute and qualified classes. They are all discretionary, although there are 142 different statutes that legislate for concealment, including the 2003 Homeland Security Act, which prohibits the disclosure of voluntarily provided business information relating to 'Critical Infrastructure'.
Absolute exemptions mean that the public body does not have to confirm or deny that it has the information. They are set out in section 2(3) of the legislation: 1 information reasonably accessible to members of the public by other means (s.21(1))	The legislation has been substantially amended, including the Electronic Freedom of Information Act in 1996, which sought to update the law in the context of the Internet and digital age. The US lacks the infrastructure of an Information Commissioner or federal ombudsman. Broadly

United Kingdom	United States
2 information supplied by, or concerning certain security bodies (s. 23) 3 information contained in court records (s. 32) 4 disclosures that would infringe Parliamentary privilege (s. 34) 5 personal information (s. 40) 6 personal information the disclosure of which would constitute a breach of confidence (s. 41) 7 disclosure otherwise prohibited (s. 44(1)) See Robertson and Nicol (2007: 684) and Wadham et al. (2001: 74–87)	speaking the US shares with the UK exemptions relating to defence, security and international relations, internal discussion and advice, law enforcement and legal proceedings, effective management and operations of the public service, the privacy of the individual, third-party commercial confidences, information given in confidence and statutory and other restrictions. No exemptions are defined for public employment, public appointments and honours, unreasonable or voluminous requests, publication and prematurity in relation to publication.
Qualified exemptions mean that the denying authority must notify the applicant of its reasons and at the same time confirm existence of the information, which would fall under the following categories: 1 Information intended for future publication (s. 22) 2 Information the suppression of which 'is required for the purpose of safeguarding national security' (s. 24) 3 Information likely to prejudice the defence of the United Kingdom etc. (s. 26) 4 Information likely to prejudice foreign relations or the UK's foreign interests (s. 27) 5 Information likely to prejudice the economic or financial interests of the United Kingdom (s. 29) 6 Information likely to prejudice the protection or detection of crime, the administration of justice and law enforcement. etc. (s. 30 and s. 31) 7 Information relating to the development of government policy (s. 35) 8 Information which would prejudice the conduct of government and public affairs (s. 36)	Exemptions: 1 National defence and foreign policy secrets 2 Material relating solely to federal agency internal personnel rules and practices 3 Information specifically exempted by other federal statutes (a catch-all exemption) 4 Trade secrets and commercial or financial information obtained from businesses in confidence 5 Internal agency memos and policy discussions 6 Personal information, such as medical reports, personnel files and employment 7 Law enforcement investigative information 8 Federally regulated financial institutions. This is designed to protect the US banking and financial system from any catastrophic loss in confidence 9 Oil and gas well data of private companies

Continued overleaf

United Kingdom	United States
9 Information relating to communications with the monarch etc. (s. 37) 10 Information likely to endanger the physical or mental health, or the safety, of any individual (s. 38) 11 Information covered by legal privilege (s. 42) 12 Information relating to trade secrets (s. 43)	Zelezny observes that state open records laws tend to be more complicated: 'This is particularly evident in the lists of exceptions to required disclosure – the kinds of information that agencies may or must keep confidential. Whereas the federal law lists nine exceptions, state statutes often list twenty or more' (Zelezny 2004: 247).
See Robertson and Nicol (2007: 687–8) More detailed guides to and definitions of the absolute and qualified UK FOI exceptions, as well as advice on using the Act, can be found at: Brooke (2005: 27–33); Welsh, Greenwood & Banks (2007: 370–81) and Quinn (2009: 361–9).	More detailed guides on the operation of the exemption categories can be found at: Sadler (2005: 395–422); Zelezny (2004: 234–52) and Moore and Murray (2008: 616–35).

Table 13.4 Guidance table on using the British Freedom of Information Act 2000

Resource/advice	Details
Campaign for Freedom of Information (CFFI) (key resource)	www.cfoi.org.uk/ www.freedominfo.org/ 'is a one-stop portal for critical resources about freedom of information laws and movements around the world'. It is managed and primarily authored by the academic David Banisar, who edits and publishes *Freedom of Information Around the World 2006: A Global Survey of Access to Government Information Laws*.
What Do They Know (Supports, advises on and tracks FOI requests to UK 'public bodies')	www.whatdotheyknow.com/ The 'What Do They Know' website is a voluntary resource set up to help people use the FOI Act and to keep the site's visitors informed about the progress of requests and the information obtained. It has an extensive help guide at www.whatdotheyknow.com/help/about. This explains: 'You choose the public authority that you would like information from, then write a brief note describing what you want to know. We then send your request to the public authority. Any response they make is automatically published on the website for you and anyone else to find and read.' The Information Commissioner says requests must 'be made in writing (this can be electronically e.g., fax, email); state the name of the applicant and an address for correspondence; and describe the information requested.' (www.ico.gov.uk/what_we_cover/freedom_of_information.aspx)

Resource/advice	Details
Guardian Unlimited (guide to FOI)	www.guardian.co.uk/politics/freedomofinformation
Guardian (specific 'how to' FOI guide)	www.guardian.co.uk/politics/2004/dec/30/freedomofinformation.uk2
Open Secrets (an FOI blog by the BBC's Martin Rosenbaum)	www.bbc.co.uk/blogs/opensecrets/ Mr Rosenbaum was the producer of a two-part documentary series for the BBC World Service, *The Right to Know*, which is downloadable as a podcast from www.bbc.co.uk/documentaries/index.shtml
Your Right To Know (by Heather Brooke, FOI campaigner)	www.yrtk.org/ Brooke, Heather (2006) *Your Right to Know*, 2nd revised edition, London: Pluto Press. The book is a comprehensive kit and guide on using FOI laws for the purposes of private citizen, NGO and journalistic research. The author is a visiting professor at City University and provides courses and consultancies to organizations such as the UK National Union of Journalists.
Requesting information personal to you	Has to be done under Data Protection Acts 1984 and 1998
Requests to 'public bodies'	What is a 'public body'? Guide at: www.dca.gov.uk/foi/yourRights/publicauthorities.htm
Sample request letter	The *Guardian* has produced a sample request letter which can be posted, emailed, hand-delivered or faxed: http://image.guardian.co.uk/sys-files/Guardian/documents/2004/12/29/Public_info_lettera_new.doc
Replies to requests	Public bodies are supposed to have an 'FOI officer' and/or a 'publication scheme'. They are supposed to reply to you within 20 days. For an example of a publication scheme see the Goldsmiths College website: www.gold.ac.uk/foi/.
Complaints	If you are unhappy about the response you can complain to the Information Commissioner: www.ico.gov.uk/. The Information Commissioner provides detailed briefings and guidance notes on FOI law and a growing body of jurisprudence is developing from decisions of the Information Tribunal. The Scottish Information Commissioner provides a similar resource of information and guidance at: www.itspublicknowledge.info.
Appeals	The next stage in the appeal process is the Information Tribunal: www.informationtribunal.gov.uk/

Continued overleaf

Resource/advice	Details
Refusal of requests	There are twenty-three exceptions to enable public bodies to refuse your request for information. The key ones are: public interest in confidentiality is greater than public interest in disclosure; commercial interests; absolute exceptions (e.g. intelligence agencies and national security); information is accessible by other means; prejudice to effective conduct of public affairs; legal professional privilege; information is intended for future publication; cost is too much.
Cost	Ministers have claimed that most requests for information will be free. If the cost of answering your request is less than £450 (or £600 for central government) it will be free. Officials may ask you to pay for the cost of photocopying and postage. If a request costs more than these limits, a public body can refuse outright to answer your request.
Tips on making journalistic FOI requests	Matt Davis of John Connor Press Associates provides the following tips for journalists making FOI requests: • Think of the story before you think of the question. • Immerse yourself in the statistics and language of the organization. • Will the data you want be releasable? • Avoid overcomplicating the question. • The best questions are short and simple. • Ask for comparative data, to put your figures in context. • Ask for an index/chapter head so you can easily find what you're looking for. (Davis *Press Gazette* 2008)

Table 13.5 Guidance table on using US Freedom of Information Act 1966 and Electronic FOIA Amendments of 1996

Resource/advice	Details
Detailed briefings on FOIA in leading textbooks	Most of the standard textbooks on media law in the USA contain detailed chapters outlining the background, history and *modus operandi* of freedom of information research at the federal and state levels. See: Zelezny (2004: 234–54); Sadler (2005: 395–422); Moore and Murray (2008: 615–39).
Contacting public information or FOIA officer at relevant agency	A polite request for the records sought will sometimes result in the information's being supplied. The agency's website should disclose FOIA policy and contact details, and sometimes the fee schedule for copying documents.

Resource/advice	Details
FOIA request letter	Zelezny and Sadler provide sample letters. The USA does not have a federal Information Commissioner to provide advice to citizens on how to make FOI requests and to act as a first level of appeal should a request be denied.
Campaigning resources	Visit the Freedom of Information Service Center at www.rcfp.org/foia. This journalists' support organization provides booklets and templates as well as a telephone hotline: 1-800-336-4243. Another comprehensive web resource is offered by the Brechner Center for Freedom of Information based at the University of Florida at http://brechner.org/. The National Freedom of Information Coalition campaigns for the protection of the public's right to oversee its government and provides annual grants totalling $220,000 to foster and develop state FOI coalitions: www.nfoic.org/. Resources are also provided by the US Society of Professional Journalists at www.spj.org/foi.
Recommended handbook	The *Federal Open Government Guide* (formerly known as *How to Use the Federal FOI Act*), now into its 10th edition (2003), is published by the Reporters Committee for Freedom of the Press and can be viewed and downloaded at the Freedom of Information Service Center website or obtained from RCFP, 1101 Wilson Blvd., Suite 1100 Arlington, VA 22209.
Advice on making FOIA requests	Make the request precise by identifying records by name, number and date. Accurate descriptions will assist any federal employee who has to search for it. Check if the agency has indexed the records requested, and use this information. Identify the relevant federal agency by using the *United States Government Manual* (Zelezny 2004: 241).
Advice from Russell Carollo (2006)	Russell Carollo, special projects reporter with the *Sacramento Bee*, provides these seven tips:

Russell Carollo, special projects reporter with the *Sacramento Bee*, provides these seven tips:
1. File FOIAs months and even years before you expect to start on a project.
2. Always use certified [registered] mail and keep a record of everything.
3. Clearly identify the records by doing some research before you file.
4. Every time a FOIA officer contacts you by telephone, make a record of the call, and in that record indicate that you told the FOIA officer at the beginning and end of the conversation: 'I'm not agreeing to any changes during this conversation'.

Continued overleaf

Resource/advice	Details
Advice from Russell Carollo (2006) *continued*	5 Make changes and modifications in your request only through certified [registered] mail.
	6 Appeal. You stand at least a 33 per cent chance of getting more information.
	7 Always ask for a record layout (data dictionary) when you request a database, and tell them you want the complete record layout, naming all fields – including denied fields. Without such a record, it's impossible to know what they left out and impossible to file a real appeal.
	(See www.rcfp.org/foia/foia411.html)
Agencies' legal obligations	Agencies have 20 working days in which to reply, although delays are not uncommon, particularly if there are complex and multi-document requests. Where there is a compelling need for the information (i.e. for the purposes of journalism) the request can stipulate expedited processing. An entire document cannot be withheld if only small portions are exempt. Many federal agencies will allow journalists to visit their offices to inspect the requested records. News organizations, non-commercial scientific and educational organizations can be charged only for the costs of copying and not for employees' time in conducting the search. A waiver or reduction in fees can be applied for if it can be shown that 'disclosure of the information is in the public interest because it is likely to contribute significantly to public understanding of the operations or activities of the government and is not primarily in the interest of the requester' (Zelezny 2004: 241–2).
Appealing denied requests, non-response	A formal appeal letter should be sent to the principal, president or head of the agency, and the agency chief has 20 working days in which to reply. Template letters are provided by Zelezny in his textbook and are also downloadable at the Reporters Committee for the Freedom of the Press Internet FOI Service Center. Applicants for federal records are entitled to a legal explanation of denial. This explanation is known as a Vaughn Index as it was taken from a 1973 case (Vaughn v Rosen, D.C. Cir. US 1973) in which a federal appeals court declared that agencies are obliged to issue legal reasons for the withholding of each document (Sadler 2005: 399).

Resource/advice	Details
Suing	Russell Carollo accepts that although there is a cost in going to law, 'if you can, sue. It really gets their attention.' The next step after having no success with the federal agency is to make an appeal to the nearest federal District Court. The agency would have to persuade the court that the records asked for fall within one of the FOI Act's nine exceptions. A study by the Coalition of Journalists for Open Government reported that only about 6 per cent of all FOIA requests came from the media. Many reporters complained that the requests take too long to be processed, public records are getting progressively harder to obtain, and a media industry in recession in 2009 does not have the financial resources to combat a growing culture of FOIA denial – even where the grounds of appeal are unlikely to hold up in court.

The 2009 parliamentary expenses scandal in the UK certainly arose out of FOI activity and litigation, though the scale of public outrage and enlightenment on how British MPs exploited their system of allowances was the result of the data's being leaked in the old-fashioned way, probably for money. When the official FOI release was made it became apparent that the blacked-out documents obtained through the legislation would have covered up exactly what the *Daily Telegraph* was able to expose from the non-redacted and uncensored documents.

The BBC's FOI expert Martin Rosenbaum reminded everyone that the drive to transparency in the expenses story was not assisted by the Information Commissioner, who had ruled: 'It is not necessary for fully itemised amounts to be disclosed in order to meet the legitimate interest of members of the public in knowing how public money has been spent.' (Rosenbaum 2009)

Rosenbaum, though, was sure that 'freedom of information is now in a stronger and more established and entrenched position' and that 'politicians in the UK will now find it very difficult to propose any curbs on freedom of expression.' (Ibid.) The outgoing UK Information Commissioner in 2009, Richard Thomas, said that FOI had come of age and needed more money and that the public 'expect to be treated like grown-ups, with ready access to what is going on.' (Thomas *Guardian* 2009) But the newspaper publishing his article was having to fight for the release of information on the disciplining of 170 judges. In 2008 the Information Tribunal had turned down its request, saying that judicial authority would be undermined and individual judges would be distressed. It was four years since the original FOI application had been made. British media groups are going to have to be long on patience and to carry deep pockets in legal costs.

In the USA it is not uncommon for federal FOIA legal battles to result in rulings against media interests. In the 2004 case of *National Archives and Records Administration v Favish*, the Supreme Court ruled unanimously that ten death-scene photographs of Clinton White House counsel Vince Foster should not be released. The 9/11 terrorist attacks in the USA were followed by federal arrests and the detention of around 1,000 suspects, and civil liberties and media campaigning groups sought their identification under the FOIA. The federal courts supported the government's position that such information could endanger the lives of the detainees, give terrorists valuable insight into the conduct of investigations and jeopardize ongoing enquiries and grand jury proceedings. The *New York Times* request under the FOIA for a copy of the recording of the seven crew members of the space shuttle *Challenger* who were all killed shortly after take-off in January 1986 was rejected by a federal court in 1991 (Sadler 2005: 402–4)

But the UK *Daily Telegraph* parliamentary expenses scandal highlights the fact that FOI(A) blocks do not amount to closed censorship. If the information is leaked by whistleblowers it cannot be stopped from getting into the public domain. The existence of a democratic consensus emboldens whistleblowers, who can feel the consent and approval.

In 2009 it seemed likely that the battle by the American Civil Liberties Union (ACLU), with the support of media organizations, to secure the release of all photographs and moving images of the prisoner abuse by US soldiers in Iraq and elsewhere was likely to be heard by the Supreme Court. ACLU et al. had been successful before US District Court Judge Alvin K. Hellerstein in 2005 and the US Court of Appeals in Manhattan (2nd Circuit) in 2008, but in May 2009 President Barack Obama directed his legal team to fight the court-ordered release of the photographs because he was concerned they might 'inflame anti-American opinion and put our troops in greater danger'. The BBC reported a Pentagon official as saying: 'The president had been advised against publication by Defence Secretary Robert Gates, Centcom commander General David Petraeus and the commander of US forces in Iraq, General Ray Odierno.' (BBC 2009)

If the case is heard by the Supreme Court, it is possible that the US media will find its most acute test of the citizen's right to know provided by the FOIA. Previous Department of Defense attempts to resist the release of the photographs of Abu Ghraib images were outmanoeuvred by leaks to the media.

In order to win its case the US government will have to defeat the force of analysis represented in the conclusion of Judge Hellerstein's District Court ruling:

Suppression of information is the surest way to cause its significance to grow and persist. Clarity and openness are the best antidotes, either to dispel criticism if not merited, or, if merited, to correct such errors as may be found. The fight to extend freedom has never been easy, and we are once again challenged, in Iraq and Afghanistan, by terrorists who engage in violence to intimidate our will and to force us to retreat. Our struggle to prevail must be without sacrificing the transparency and accountability of government and military officials. These are the values FOIA was intended to advance, and they are at the very heart of the values for which we fight in Afghanistan and Iraq. There is a risk that the enemy will seize upon the publicity of the photographs and seek to use such publicity as a pretext for enlistments and violent acts. But the education and debate that such publicity will foster will strengthen our purpose and, by enabling such deficiencies as may be perceived to be debated and corrected, show our strength as a vibrant and functioning democracy to be emulated.

In its most recent discussion of FOIA, the Supreme Court commented that 'FOIA is often explained as a means for citizens to know what "their Government is up to." The sentiment is far from a convenient formalism. It defines a structural necessity in a real democracy.' (Favish 541 US at 171–2) As President Bush said, we fight to spread freedom so the freedoms of Americans will be made more secure. It is in compliance with these principles, enunciated by both the President and the highest court in the land, that I order the government to produce the Darby photographs that I have determined are responsive and appropriately redacted.

(ACLU et al. v Department of Defense DC US 2005)

SELECT GLOSSARY

a posteriori   After experience.

a priori   Before experience.

absolutism, ethical   The belief that moral and ethical values are always compulsory and true within all human communities and across the timeline of history. As a result protagonists of ethical absolutism can monopolize the idea of moral truth and legitimize and aggrandize the power of their culture over others.

accused   The individual accused of a criminal offence and usually sitting in the dock of a criminal court. This person is also known as 'the defendant'.

acquittal   Based on a Norman French word for a declaration of not guilty as the result of a criminal prosecution. Sometimes a lexicographical distinction is made between the ideas of being found 'innocent' and being 'acquitted'. This is based on the belief that some juries in England and Wales will acquit because they are not convinced beyond reasonable doubt. The Scottish legal system provides a middle-way verdict of 'not proven'. This clearly does not amount to an affirmation of innocence. The 'not guilty' verdict can arise on the direction of the court, e.g. when a judge decides as a matter of law that there is no case to answer, or by the verdict of jury as the result of a full trial.

actus reus   The guilty act in crime that can involve the conduct of the accused, the circumstances in which it has occurred, and the consequences of the act.

adversarial   A style of legal proceeding and advocacy. It is a feature of common law legal systems by which the parties to a dispute present evidence and argue their respective cases. The judge or tribunal's role is to decide matters of law and apply the rules of evidence. It could be argued that this tradition is derived from the ancient/medieval ritual of trial by battle. Adversarial systems are supposedly the opposite of inquisitorial – the civil law approach in Continental jurisdictions. However, the dichotomy is not as simple as it seems. On close analysis adversarial systems have inquisitorial dimensions and *vice versa*.

431

advocate   Another word for the lawyer in court. In England and Wales this could be a barrister or solicitor. In Scotland 'advocate' is the official description of the representing lawyer. In the USA lawyers are more popularly known as attorneys, whether as practitioners in court advocacy or lawyers who specialize in preparing litigation.

alienation   A term frequently associated with Marxist criticism of capitalism. People and societies are deprived of their intrinsic independence and control over their own lives. In essence it is the giving of oneself into the power of another.

alternative dispute resolution (ADR)   This is an agreed method of resolving disputes outside the arena of legal litigation and can include conciliation, mediation or arbitration.

anarchism   An anarchist society is one which is devoid of state infrastructure and power. The political philosophy of an anarchist regards the exercise of political power as an oppressive infringement of human freedom. Anarchists believe that equality and freedom are achieved without any form of domination. The doctrine was the inspiration for terrorism in the late nineteenth and early twentieth centuries. Anarchists would be responsible for political assassinations and indiscriminate bombings, including the detonation of the first 'car bomb' in Wall Street, the financial district of New York City's Lower Manhattan, on 16 September 1920. Thirty-eight people died and four hundred were injured by the device, which had been loaded onto a horse-drawn carriage.

appeal   Challenging the result of a legal case to a higher court. Legal systems sometimes limit the grounds on which appeals can be raised. In other words, only procedural matters can be challenged, or any decision on the facts can only be appealed with the adducing of new evidence that the lower court had not received.

appellant   The individual making an appeal. The opposite of the appellant would be the respondent. In English and Welsh Court of Criminal Appeal cases the respondent is usually the Crown, which brings state prosecutions. However, there are situations when the Crown can be the appellant, e.g. when challenging lenient sentences.

appellate courts   In the US legal system, these courts review the decisions of the trial courts, using a panel of judges to decide whether the court below made errors of law and whether those errors require the decisions to be reversed. If an appellate court agrees with the lower court decision, it *affirms* the judgment.

applicant   The description of an individual in whose name a legal applying process is undertaken. This would be the situation where a person is applying for leave to appeal or making an application for judicial review.

Aquinasian natural law theory   St Thomas Aquinas (1224–74) sought to integrate rationalist and religious approaches to natural law by

432

articulating four categories of legal authority: 1) eternal law – God's rational guidance for all created things; 2) divine law – revealed in the scriptures; 3) natural law – discovered through human reason; 4) human law – the essence to be just: *lex injusta non est lex* – an unjust law is not law.

Aristotelian law and ethics There is a purpose or goal of happiness common to all human beings. Natural justice would be achieved by the attainment of a state of goodness. Conventional justice varies from state to state in the context of the history and imperatives of their respective societies. The ultimate meaning of all things can be understood from an examination of their different ends. Aristotle (384 to 322 BCE) is famous for his lecture notes 'The Nicomachean Ethics', named after his son, in which he set out his theory of the Golden Mean for moderate living and moral responsibility. By avoiding extremes we learn to discover what is morally right for us in each problematical situation. Aristotle seemed to suggest that ethics was more of an approximate science determined by context.

ASBO An acronym standing in England and Wales for 'Anti-social behaviour order'. Introduced in the 1998 Crime and Disorder Act, it is a highly controversial method of effectively injuncting an individual from pursuing a course of conduct that is said to be 'anti-social'. In a sense, it is a civil court order, but it has quasi-criminal implications. ASBOs are imposed by magistrates as a result of an application by the police and local authority. Breaching an ASBO is a criminal offence. To this extent, ASBOs resemble the contempt of court powers available to the civil courts for breaching court orders. However, there is a civil rights debate that the criminal sanction on breaching a civil order effectively criminalizes people for conduct that does not amount to a crime. The measure was described in the media as a naming and shaming process to target juvenile/youth crime, but ASBOs are now increasingly being imposed against adults. Islington council in London has used ASBO procedures to combat fly-posting. Another local authority imposed an ASBO on a woman for persistently feeding seagulls.

authoritarian tendency A response of governments to ruthless tactics of global and extreme home-grown and global political groups prepared to use nihilistic suicide tactics in terrorist campaigns. This leads to a cycle of the breaking down of liberal and democratic traditions and laws, the attenuation of human rights, and the breach of international law through aggressive and militaristic foreign policies. A reductionism in understanding the conflicts of the world so that they are simply represented as a struggle between good and evil or 'the good guys and the bad guys'. Authoritarianism is a doctrine that requires acceptance of an individual, institution or text as privileged guidance and power.

bad conscience   Nietzsche coined the term after analysing the genealogy of morals in human history. He predated Freud in theorizing on the damage that a sense of guilt from frustrated instincts and inward self-torture can have on an individual. Bad conscience can manifest itself through asceticism, self-denial as a way of existence and altruism, being helpful to other people for their own sakes.

bias, ethical   A preference in expression, communication and editing that interferes with 'objective judgments'. Being economical with the truth (Lord Armstrong at the Australian *Spycatcher* hearings). Being economical with the actualité (Alan Clark at the Matrix Churchill trial). Oscar Wilde somewhat poignantly observed about the alleged objectivity of the critic as artist: 'The man who sees both sides of a question is a man who sees absolutely nothing at all.'

binary oppositions   Derived from the writing of the French anthropologist Claude Lévi-Strauss, who postulated that narratives are often shaped in terms of 'binary oppositions', e.g. virtue versus evil, good versus bad, or old versus young.

bona fide   A Latin legal expression meaning acting in good faith and with good intentions.

bricolage   A historical method of evaluating the process of cultural history in terms of choosing to absorb and reject foreign/alien influences. The process is regarded as a creative reception of influences. A term also used in postmodernism to mean a collage or recycling of previously copied cultural messages, icons and symbols so that the referentiality has constructed a new meaning.

carceral   Pertaining to imprisonment and penal punishment. A word associated with the discourse of twentieth-century philosopher Michel Foucault.

case law   Pertaining to the law of precedent. In essence, case law is the body of court decisions that apply to a specific legal issue or concept. Adversarial lawyers rely on law reports to support their arguments. They are looking for precedents where the facts are similar to the material circumstances constituting the case in dispute.

categorical imperative   Immanuel Kant's argument for the existence of God was built around the idea that there is a central moral obligation to everyone's being.

celebrocracy   A word to denote the existence of an elite of celebrities who self-perpetuate their interests and power in nation-states and the globalized realm of market economics. It is contended they have become an elite that is dependent on the oxygen of media communication and at the same time wish to exercise controls to enhance profitable representation.

certiorari   An old-fashioned term for an English and Welsh High Court order quashing the decision of a lower court or tribunal so that the matter can be investigated by the Queen's Bench Division. In Latin *certiorari* means to be informed. This order can be used to correct legal errors, secure an impartial trial, nullify a court decision that is contrary to natural justice, challenge a court accused of acting beyond its powers (*ultra vires*) and review an excess of jurisdiction. As a result of Lord Woolf's reforms into civil justice and his recommendations to make legal procedure more 'user friendly' a statutory instrument has abolished the Latin descriptions of *certiorari* and *mandamus* so that the three key higher court legal orders are now known as a quashing order (replacing *certiorari*), a mandatory order (replacing *mandamus*) and a prohibiting order (replacing prohibition). A number of US state jurisdictions continue to use the original Latin terms in their procedures and jurisprudence.

cognitivism A view that it is possible to understand the absolute truth about things such as justice, right and wrong. This is a meta-ethical theory and many if not most cognitivists are moral realists in the sense that they believe that moral properties are part of the world and constitute real facts. Immanuel Kant divided moral understanding between noumena and phenomena, with moral knowledge constituting pure noumenal (*a priori*) reason.

communism A development of Marxism that envisages that common ownership of production, distribution and exchange will ensure the eradication of inequality and injustice. Land, factories, machinery and banks are nationalized or taken into social ownership.

communitarian ethics The idea that moral values are derived from consensus principles propagated by the community.

communitarianism Political power is engaged to support the distribution of shared values and social practices, where the paradigm is respect for and allegiance to community values rather than individual autonomy. It is the 'we' rather than the 'I' in terms of subjectivism, more respect for the plural pronoun rather than the single in politics.

contractarianism A social and political philosophy based on the idea of the social contract between civilians and their governments and thereby presuming a framework of agreed social civility.

convention In constitutional law, a generally accepted custom or an established rule.

convergence In media, the coming together of different technologies or organizations. In ethics and philosophy it can also represent the intertwining of religious, ideological and philosophical doctrines.

cult of the courtier Developed by Renaissance writer Baldassare Castiglione, whose *Book of the Courtier* defined the behaviour and expectations of the courtier in relationship to his prince. It is a manifesto for advancement and survival in an authoritarian environment and remains relevant to the contemporary media professional working in corporations that are controlled and managed along authoritarian lines in an environment replete with totalitarian surveillance.

cultural chaos   The academic discourse about the crisis of belief and ethics in a confusing world of moral, religious and ideological uncertainty and relativism. The struggle to find meaning and identity in a post-Holocaust world of repetitive genocide and ethnic cleansing, where there is a doubt about the value of individual choice and consequence. The British academic Brian McNair published a book with the title *Cultural Chaos* (2006) in which he investigates journalism, news and power in a globalized world. He argues that the analytic focus of media/cultural studies and sociology should abandon the idea that the media materialize control and domination. In the twenty-first century, the greater scale of asymmetric global hypermedia produces an emerging cultural chaos of 'dissent, openness and diversity'. Fundamentally, McNair is a theoretical optimist and wishes to challenge the reigning pessimism of evaluating media institutions and their content as cultural mechanisms for 'closure, exclusivity and ideological homogeneity'.

cultural imperialism   The domination of one culture by another through exposure and status.

cyber ethics   The discourse on ethics in cyberspace, the virtual environment created by the links between computer users and systems.

cyclical notion of ethical chaos   Repetitive discourse in human history about a state of moral decline. In recent decades it has manifested itself in the terms 'back to basics', 'moral mission statements', descriptions of uncertainty and moral chaos, lack of respect for authority. Nowadays it is sometimes blamed on postmodern relativism. In fourth-century Athens, Plato thought the city-state was doomed because of the ethical scepticism of the Sophist philosophers. Certainly at the time of writing there is a growth in the idea that institutions and social groups should determine their ethical role in contemporary society.

damnum sine injuria   A Latin legal expression describing the most damage and harmful conduct you can do before breaching the law. The literal translation is 'damage without injury'.

Decalogue   The ten Judeo-Christian commandments.

deconstruction   The intellectual task of taking apart and breaking down media texts in order to achieve an understanding of how they communicate meaning.

deductive conclusion   An argument derived from logical principles rather than observation and collection of evidence.

democracy   Government by the people and for the people. It is direct when all citizens participate in the rule of any society and indirect or 'representative' when power is delegated to elected representatives in a congress or parliamentary body.

deontological A philosophical term that concerns duty to absolute values and concepts. Deontology is the science of duty or moral obligations. This is a normative moral theory judging an action by the properties of the action itself rather than its consequences. The duty is morally obligatory action.

descriptive ethics Describing the moral choices that are made, and their circumstances.

dialectic approach A thesis or view is challenged by an antithesis or counterview leading to a synthesis or third view. A Platonic method of discourse developed by Friedrich Hegel and Karl Marx. Dialectics is derived from the Greek *dialego*, meaning to debate or discourse.

difference principle In John Rawls's *A Theory of Justice* he argues that any social or economic inequality can only be tolerated on condition that it brings the greatest benefits to the most disadvantaged.

discretion A process of judicial decision making that exercises a quasi-legislative function by creating new law. Discretion operates where there is no clear rule of law, an irresolvable conflict of applicable rules forcing judges to base their decisions on personal individual conceptions of right and wrong, and in the context of public policy or social interest.

dualism The doctrine that two different substances lie at the root of existence. These could be material, in the sense of the body, and spiritual, in the sense of the soul.

efficacy Efficiency and efficacy in law and ethics. Asking the question what is the capacity of a legal and ethical measure, structure or process to achieve the desired result.

egoism Being guided by self-interest, and the opposite of altruism, which is being guided by concern for other people and treating them as ends in themselves rather than as means for personal advancement and self-gratification.

empirical approach Depending on the gathering of sense experience as the foundation of knowledge and expression of argument. Knowledge is gained from sense experience that also includes experimental scientific investigation.

empiricism, legal and ethical Rejecting all judgments of value and only taking into account statements that are objectively verifiable. An inductive process of reasoning that requires the empirical observation of facts and the formulation of a hypothesis that is then applied to the facts.

Enlightenment A cultural movement of the late seventeenth to early nineteenth centuries, when educated members of the intelligentsia in European countries perceived that they were engaged in a new way of judging nature and human society according to reason. The shadowy and dark world of tradition was metaphorically brought into light through empirical study and a consideration of the rights of the individual.

epistemological   Based on the construction of knowledge.

ethical imperialism   The hegemony of one outlook and framework of ethics on foreign cultures through military and economic power.

ethicology   The description of an academic approach to studying journalism and media communication by concentrating on the ethical process of decision making. The core of the subject is knowledge of ethics and morals in human communication and how they link in a more complex and comprehensive approach to media that takes into account history, politics and economics. The word is inspired by the French noun *l'éthicologie* and the work of Professor Pierre Fortin at Université du Québec à Rimouski in Canada.

eudaimonia   Aristotle's concept, which could be the origin of the concept of the pursuit of happiness. This idea is that there is a supreme good for human beings in the context of natural law. *Eudaimonia* is a flourishing of harmonious virtues within an individual over the course of a lifetime.

ex parte   Latin phrase referring to court applications where only one side is represented. This is common in relation to emergency English and Welsh High Court applications for injunctions. The injunction may be granted, but usually on condition that it would be reviewed on the representation of the parties affected and not represented. The US courts as a general rule do not permit the hearing of prior restraint applications without representation by the media party.

existentialist ethics   Jean-Paul Sartre (1905–80) argued that ethically we are totally free to make ourselves. The individual cannot be derived from a notion of Aristotelian purpose, Kantian rationalism or utilitarian equation on pain/pleasure teleology. Morality depends on the freedom of choosing rather than on what is chosen. Sartre and other existentialists acknowledged that the freedom to choose in desperate human circumstances can promise only a life of anguish, absurdity and despair.

Existenz   A German word from the school of phenomenology and existentialism which denotes, according to Karl Jaspers, 'the non-objective actuality of self-being, true self-hood, existential freedom, undetermined moral decision, or the genuine and authentic self'.

fairness   A critical multiplier in ethical evaluation, and similar to the notions of power and toleration. Fairness is a value that encompasses ideas of social and economic justice and equality. It is central to the twentieth-century American philosopher John Rawls's *A Theory of Justice*. Most of the great philosophers have interpolated the idea of fairness with justice. Aristotle stated that doing injustice is getting more than one ought and suffering injustice is getting less than one ought. Justice was therefore equity. To do justly was simply to be fair. This is transcending the idea of luck and social status and undermines the trite contemporary proverb articulated by many people who exercise power in the capitalist world that 'life is unfair'. Whilst positivists can rationally argue that you cannot derive an ought from an is, it is certainly possible to derive an is from an ought. To do unfairness is a choice and is not acquiescence to an obligation in nature.

false light   A legal tort available in US state jurisdictions where plaintiffs can seek damages for false and highly offensive media representations. It can be seen as a hybrid between libel and privacy, since the information must be false, published with reckless disregard for the truth or the knowledge that it was false (actuated by malice), but the information does not have to be defamatory. Unlike in privacy litigation, false light claimants can only obtain a remedy for publication that is inaccurate/untrue. The socio-political mischief of privacy law is that the remedy involves the suppression of the truth.

felicific calculus   A political equation conjured by the philosopher Jeremy Bentham to measure the extent to which laws can promote pleasure and prevent pain. As a result, there would be a science of legislation so that the state could meaningfully predict the consequences of new laws. The greatest happiness of the greatest number would be evaluated by the balancing of pleasure/good (riches, power, friendship, good reputation and benevolence) and pain/evil (privation, fear, enmity, bad reputation and malevolence). These factors would be measured according to purity, extent, duration, intensity, certainty, fecundity and propinquity.

feminist ethics   The attempt to distinguish a feminist discourse on ethics that is capable of identifying specific female virtues. The criticism of the ethical patriarchy that can be said to view women as intuitive, irrational, gentle, passive, selfless and sympathetic. As a result, the discourse of politics and ethics confines a moral role for women in the domestic sphere. Martha Nussbaum argues that men fictionalize elaborate systems of ethical belief to impose on others, including women. Mary Wollstonecraft (1759–97) wrote that the definition of female nature is an ideological construct whose objective is to legitimize male supremacy in the public sphere.

fetishizing   A process of taking a principle, idea, object or person and irrationally reverencing and overvaluing it. By paying the object too much undue respect it takes on imagined spiritual and magical properties.

formalism   Moral philosophy should be concerned with the purely formal characteristics of values that are prescriptive, overriding and universalizable. There must be a specific recommendation directed at the self and others on how to act in certain circumstances. The

439

moral judgment must take precedent when in conflict with any other recommendation. The moral judgment must also apply to all similar cases.

fortuna A concept developed in Machiavelli's writing which is an acceptance of the reality of a world in which the fate of the individual is as much determined by the actions of others and the fortunes of the state as by the exercise of human free will.

freedom, negative and positive Negative freedom is freedom from interference; positive freedom is the right to pursue ideals and interests; or 'freedom from' and 'freedom to'. Thomas Hobbes supported the concept of negative freedom, so his version of liberty was the application of rule of law to enable people to live together in peace, with law being a necessary evil and restraint on individual freedom.

gate keepers Individuals and media organizations in a position of power to determine what will be printed, broadcast, produced and consumed in the mass media. The exercise of power is the practice and activity that determines the ethical relationship between communicators and their audiences.

Golden Mean Aristotle's belief that to achieve happiness, people must act moderately, and so strive for the mean between two extremes. Therefore, the right action lies between two extremes and this means that in certain circumstances to act moderately is not necessarily making judgments in reference to the Golden Mean.

hedonism Happiness is the only good normative value, or happiness is pleasure with the absence of pain. Jeremy Bentham used these definitions to found his hedonic theory of utilitarianism.

hegemony A theory of ideology as ideas, beliefs and values established by the dominant culture in society or in the global context of the world.

higher pleasure John Stuart Mill argued that higher pleasures, i.e. intellectual pursuits such as reading philosophy or literature had more value than 'lower pleasures' such as gastronomic and sexual desire or the pleasures of the body. The exercise of the creative imagination, thoughts and feelings contributed more to individual and social happiness.

historicist Analysing the idea that historical texts are constructed and determined by the social and cultural context of their time.

Hobbesian ethics Surrendering to the imperatives of absolute power in order to live in a society with order and to ward away the impact of selfish and egoistic human nature in a life that is 'solitary, poor, nasty, brutish and short'. The political philosophy of Thomas Hobbes (1588–1679). The authoritarian dimension of contractarian ethics.

humanitas A German philosophical concept derived from the Latin word used by Kant, Husserl, Heidegger, Jaspers, Arendt and other thinkers and writers. Arendt said that *humanitas* was public space and spiritual realm for the individual. It is the valid human personality that never leaves the man or woman. *Humanitas* is achieved by an individual venturing life and personality into the public realm of human society.

idealism A system of belief where reality is dependent on mental consciousness.

ideology A collection of attitudes, values and beliefs held by a group of people. Marx believed that social being determined consciousness. If all ideologies are reflections of social existence, then it follows that politics, science, religion, art and morality are representations of ideology.

imperative A conception that regards law as a body of commands, orders or coercive actions from specific, powerful persons or organizations in society. Imperative positivism in jurisprudence has been advanced by Jeremy Bentham and John Austin, who saw law as a set of general commands of the sovereign power backed by the threat of actions, and by Hans Kelsen, who saw law as a system of conditional directives (primary norms) obliging officials to apply sanctions.

inductive approach A method of reasoning and argument based on setting up conclusions as the result of gathering evidence to support them.

intuitionism A meta-ethical theory situated in cognitivism. Our understanding of right and wrong is derived from intuition rather than from the exercise of reason or experience of senses.

Jaspersian ethics The ethical philosophy of Karl Jaspers (1883–1969), who posited an existential equilibrium or *humanitas* that can be achieved by seeking courage without self-deception, personal responsibility for the consequences of actions, respect for the personal freedom and self-realization of the Other, the avoidance of exploitation, and intellectual integrity and open-mindedness.

Kantian ethics Based on the deontological teachings and writings of Immanuel Kant (1724–1804). Human motive is more important than obeisance to law on the basis of obligation. He originated the concept of the categorical imperative: 'Act only on that maxim whereby thou canst at the same time will that it should become a universal law.'

lex injusta non est lex The maxim of St Thomas Aquinas that an unjust law is not God's law and therefore no law at all.

liberalism A political doctrine that prioritizes individual freedom, but not necessarily to the extent of absolute power of the individual over the 'Other'.

libertarian Giving priority to the concept of liberty or the specification, attainment and protection of basic freedoms. Libertarianism stresses free choice and opposes constraints on free choice imposed by political

441

institutions. The individual is to be given unrestricted scope for action without any institutional restraints by state government.

liminality A concept in social anthropology where a social/cultural media event shifts the ground of consensus and public opinion in terms of ethical values.

Locke's ethics John Locke (1632–1704) argued for the rule of law so that no one ought harm another in his life, health, liberty or possession. Equal treatment before the law and due process in the application of the law. The foundation of a democratic and representative social contract.

mandamus The literal meaning of this Latin word is 'we command'. It relates to a category of Queen's Bench Divisional court orders that directs a person or body to perform a legal duty. It is used to enforce administrative duties by local authorities, or legal duties by lower courts such as tribunals and magistrates' courts. The word for or description of this court order has been changed from 'an order of *mandamus*' to 'a mandatory order'.

Marxian ethics The idea of fairness and justice being privileged over materialistic and class-based deprivation. Challenging the depersonalizing of human relations by the dynamics of the profit motive and unbridled capitalism. Basing morality on human values rather than machine values. Karl Marx (1818–83) offered a ground of ethical philosophy as well as the political philosophy that carries his name, Marxism.

materialism Constructing the nature of being and existence according to the idea that reality is material rather than idealistic, a creation of the mind. Dialectical materialism and historical materialism in Marxist theory are based on the assumption that there are ongoing associations and contradictions between various social, technical, economic and political phenomena that determine the historical development of society.

maxim Essential to Immanuel Kant's moral theory. These are principles that guide individual choices and explain the moral duties and obligations determining right or wrong behaviour. Maxims are morally acceptable only if everyone can live by them.

maximum principle In John Rawls's theory this is the idea that human society should maximize the minimum, which is the option in political economics that gives people the best deal in the worst case.

McDonaldization An analogous term that takes the brand name of a US global fast-food corporation and attempts to define the idea of formal rationality, Weber's *The Iron Cage* and alienation. The marathon McLibel case is an ideal narrative focus of the struggle by two individual and apparently disempowered civil rights activists against an attempt by corporate power to silence their campaign of criticism.

442

A discourse on *The McDonaldization of Society* is the title of a seminal book on the subject by George Ritzer (California: Pine Forge Press, 2000).

media ethicism Studying the belief systems, moral doctrines and ideology of media communicators.

media jurisprudence Studying the process and history of making media laws.

mens rea The mental element in criminal behaviour often determining the nature of intent in criminal law.

meta-ethics Examining the claims made in normative ethics. Producing theories about the nature of ethical language. An approach pioneered by the Scottish philosopher David Hume (1711–76), who questioned whether moral knowledge has any validity. By studying the meaning, function and certainty of moral language (meta-ethics) he concluded that logic and reason cannot prove the truth of moral beliefs. It is not possible to prove moral beliefs by using logic and it is not possible to prove moral propositions by multiplying the assertion of facts. If moral knowledge cannot be established from empirical observations, then utilitarianism can be neither scientific nor provable. Ethics are, therefore, psychological rather than logical or empirical things. As a result of his writing meta-ethics is a distinct branch of ethical philosophy which debates whether morality is objective or subjective and whether there can be knowledge of right and wrong, or good and bad.

metaphysics Branch of philosophy which explores the structures of reality by looking at first principles such as being, substance, space, time and causality.

minimum content theory A convenient compromise between natural law and legal positivism advanced by H.L.A. Hart, who recognized that morality can be objectively identified and empirically analysed to assist in the survival of human society. These basic principles include protection of life, property and promises.

moral panic An intense and potentially irrational debate in the media in response to the behaviour of an individual or group of people, or a social event that challenges the dominant hegemonic ideology of any given society.

moral realism A meta-ethical theory that moral knowledge and moral values are part of existence and the real world. 'Good' and 'bad' are values that can be ascribed to situations and people. 'Right' and 'wrong' are values that can be ascribed to actions. As a result, if moral values/properties can be true or false, there must be moral facts.

moral relativism (also ethical relativism) The recognition that there will always be a wide variety of ethical beliefs and practices existing between cultures, subcultures, nations, classes and tribes and across the timeline of history. This is a meta-ethical theory which focuses on the idea that moral values are the constructions of human society. Consequently, media ethics – whether publications are right or wrong – will be relative to the contextual culture and society. There can be no truth about media ethics which is morally independent of the cultural and social context.

natural law The philosophy of law and ethics that assumes that law and moral rules are a social necessity based on the moral perceptions of rational persons. Any law which violates certain moral codes is not real law and lacks validity. Human law is therefore derived from certain universal principles, discoverable through reason or revelation. These are eternal, immutable and ultimately based on the nature of human beings. Practical reason has been laid down by God and can be recognized from the facts of human nature and the physical world around us. Islamic law is a natural law doctrine.

neo-conservatism A US political ideology emanating from University of Chicago political studies inspired by the academic Leo Strauss. It is said to be the antithesis of twentieth-century liberalism. It condemns the destructive force of liberal individualism for inevitably leading to nihilism, a world where nothing is true and everything is permitted.

new Aristotelianism An attempt to leave the internecine and proverbial warfare between deontologists and utilitarians and investigate issues of community, moral health and welfare. This move from individualism and private moral dilemmas to discuss the people we ought to be is known as 'virtue theory' and has been advanced by the philosopher Alasdair MacIntyre and others. He argues that instead of following Classical, Renaissance, Enlightenment, modernist and postmodernist debates that deracinate the certainties and confidence in subjectivist and objectivist moral values, we should recognize the unstoppable communitarian tradition of human society. Hope lies in Aristotle's central idea that people should be habituated into good dispositions towards each other so that moral behaviour becomes instinctive rather then determined by systems of ethical doctrine.

new natural law In the twentieth century the inadequacies of positivist jurisprudence and criminology resulted in a retrieval of natural concepts from Classicism in order to provide answers in a world that was experiencing a general decline of social and economic stability. There was an overwhelming expansion of the role of the state in the private lives of citizens through the legislation of behaviour in domestic and public space; the development of nihilistic weapons of mass destruction and the use of war to solve disputes in the global context; a collapse in confidence in the empirical sciences for determining and resolving the problems of the human condition.

nihilism This is a meta-ethical theory which argues that morality is a fiction and/or deception because there are no moral facts or values.

The approach is associated with the thinking of Friedrich Nietzsche and his book *On the Genealogy of Morality*. Nihilism is a non-cognitivist theory.

non-cognitivism   A meta-ethical theory that argues that there can be no ethical knowledge because morals are not capable of being true or false. They are simply emotional and attitudinal concepts. They are values and not facts. At most, moral concepts are prescriptions on how to behave.

normative ethics   Evaluating whether an action should be considered good or bad, right or wrong. The 'ought' rather than the 'is' of ethics.

noumenal   Apprehended by intellectual being. An imagined experience as opposed to a material experience. A thing in itself pertaining to the mind rather than a physical action or sensation pertaining to phenomena or the body.

obiter dicta   Legal comments made by a judge in a precedent that are by the way and do not arise from the reason for the decision. The Latin literally means 'sayings by the way'.

obligation   The legal philosopher H.L.A. Hart argued for a distinction between 'being obliged' to act or forbear and being 'under an obligation' to act or forbear. The former involves being motivated by the fear of sanction and the latter involves an internal and external motivation to act from a sense of moral duty. His approach is primarily Kantian.

ontological   Based on a construction of being or existence. A more purist philosophical position predicates ontological as arguing for the existence of God without empirical evidence to support it.

phenomenology   The study and branch of knowledge concentrating on the experience of life rather than existence. The exteriority rather than the interiority of being.

Platonic ethics   The idea of good and justice is an absolute thing in itself, having qualities of truth and reality that are higher than those of positive law. Positive law is a mere shadow of real justice, hence the philosophical parable of the shadow and the cave. This truth is anterior, *a priori* before monotheistic and polytheistic deity. Law and ethics must constantly strive to represent the absolute idea of justice, and ideal justice can only be achieved in the ideal state that is ruled by philosopher kings, who, through education, are the only people in society capable of understanding the absolute idea of justice.

plurality or plural opinion   In US law this constitutes a legal opinion held by more justices on an appeal panel than any other opinion. However, the sum total of justices supporting the opinion does not constitute a majority. As a result, the case law lacks the potency of precedent. However, it is legally more influential than the equivalent *obiter dicta* of dissenting judges in an English and Welsh ruling.

445

policy A statement of a social goal aimed at improving the welfare of people in society. This may be pursued even when it leads to the restriction of individual rights. The jurisprudential theorist Ronald Dworkin distinguished between policy and principle and the need for justice and fairness in maintaining a balance between these two concepts.

politics, applied ethics The argument that, given the conceptual inadequacies of absolutism and relativism, in the end ethics is merely a political discourse on rights and wrongs in the context of society, culture and time predicated by the power relationship between individuals. It can also be argued that the moral conundrums of humanity pivot on the same issues and consider similar dilemmas, whether you analyse human choice in terms of private or public space.

positivism An approach that only recognizes positive facts and observable phenomena. The idea is that every intelligible proposition can be verified or falsified using scientific analysis. In media jurisprudence positivism involves: 1) law defined as command of the sovereign power; 2) a conceptual and analytical study of law as it is; 3) a theory of judicial process in which correct decisions are deduced from understanding the relevant legal rules and the facts of a case; 4) no necessary connection between law as it is and law as it ought to be; 5) moral judgements not able to be established by rational argument, evidence or proof; 6) an unconditional obligation to obey the law, whatever the content.

post-Marxist critical theory Twentieth-century thinkers emphasize that personal morality is in fact a political conceit and construction and there is very little of individual moral autonomy and authenticity. Antonio Gramsci (1891–1937) argued that capitalist classes and governments control populations by persuading them that political and economic establishments are natural and commonsensical. Ideological superstructures such as media, churches, schools and families manufacture the consent of ordinary people in their own oppression. Herbert Marcuse (1898–1979) argued that capitalism makes people see themselves as one-dimensional isolated consumers with false needs and controlled by closed forms of discourse. Ideology is secreted in societies as the very element and atmosphere indispensable to their historical respiration and life. Roland Barthes (1915–80) said that those who control the dominant discourse in any society determine moral views of reality, a process of naturalizing the idea of common sense. Michel Foucault (1926–84) discussed in *Discipline and Punish* how ethical dissenters are categorized as mad or irrational so that critical discourse on morality is marginalized and disempowered. Human knowledge is an ideological construct used by the powerful to oppress the weak.

postmodernism A rejection of the modernist concepts of a self-conscious, authentic and creative being or the Cartesian ego. The rejection of grand theory narratives in ethics. The fragmentation of belief and ideas so that it is no longer possible to rely on Descartes when he said *cogito ergo sum* (I think, therefore I am). The idea that the world can only be explained by appreciating the role of language and symbols. It can be argued that postmodernist ethics is the road to accelerated disillusion and uncertainty. If ethics cannot be epistemological, are beyond empirical verification, cannot be guaranteed by logic, then they become pseudo-propositions. Ethical knowledge becomes a tautology. In the nineteenth century Friedrich Nietzsche (1844–1900) had challenged the legitimacy of metaphysics and criticized the attempts by philosophers to provide a rational foundation for morals.

power The key multiplier in the ethical relationship between human beings.

power of nightmares A discourse advanced by writers and academics such as Adam Curtis (the writer and producer of a three-part BBC television series bearing the same name and broadcast in 2004) that democratic politicians in the West are increasingly using fear and an exaggerated threat of global terrorism to enhance and aggrandize their power, instead of advancing the promise of building a better world in the post-Cold War, 9/11 era.

practical ethics A dimension of ethical philosophy concentrating on debating whether an action in real life is right or wrong. This is also known as 'applied ethics'. Obviously, in the field of communication that would be the debate about the morality of speech and publication in social situations.

prima facie Meaning on the face of it, or at a first viewing. A Latin legal expression normally used in the context of a criminal case where the police and prosecuting authorities need *prima facie* evidence of a criminal offence in order to start an enquiry. W.D. Ross described 'prima facie duties' as those we ought to perform unless they conflict with something more important.

principle A statement or proposition which describes the rights individuals may hold apart from those which are specified in the legal rules of a community.

public/private space A theory in ethics that there is a different scale and moral dynamic when evaluating the ethical outlook in the private and public arenas of social being. Private ethical space involves greater adherence to natural and absolutist values, whereas public ethical space involves greater flexibility in the application of a relativist and morally consequentialist approach to decision making. It can be argued that the state hypocritically applies morally consequentialist policies but demands private absolutist standards from journalists in their coverage of the polity. Journalists must abide by private ethical doctrine in their public behaviour and communication. This could be seen as the price they pay for condemning, ridiculing and criticizing the public conduct of politicians according to private ethical values.

qualitative altruism   John Stuart Mill's attempt to attenuate the utilitarianism of Jeremy Bentham with an antidote to quantitative hedonism by refining utilitarian theory to maximize the value of individual liberty, evaluate justice in terms of a harm principle, acknowledge social goals, but define utility as qualitative altruism.

radical Islamism   A genre of radical religious politics articulated by the Egyptian Sayed Kotb and based on the idea that US liberal democracy is a decadent, imperialist and perverted doctrine centred on vulgarity, corruption, selfishness, lustful materialism and immodesty. His writing and activism in Egypt inspired the Islamic Brotherhood and later informed the ideology of Ayman Zawahiri, Osama Bin Laden and Al Qaeda.

ratio decidendi   In the law of precedent, the part of a court's ruling that sets out the reason(s) for the decision. The point of law that decides the case in the light of the material facts and constitutes the reason for the court ruling.

rationalism   The theory of knowledge rooted in the actions of the human mind. Rationality is the ability to use one's reason or mental faculties generally to evaluate alternative courses or action.

realism, ethical   The belief that there are ethical and moral rules that represent a true genre of human knowledge. Also a philosophical approach which emphasizes objectivity over sentiment and idealism in the investigation of phenomena. The perception of phenomena is an experience of objective things independent of private sense data.

realpolitik   Politics based on pragmatics rather than ideological and moral considerations. Emphasizing the practical over the idealistic. The US Secretary of State during the Nixon administration, Dr Henry Kissinger, was regarded as an amoral pragmatist in his advancement of US foreign policy.

realreligiosity   Adapted by the author from realpolitik to introduce the concept that an understanding of ethics and moral thinking necessitates an acknowledgment of the practical influence and pervasiveness of traditional religions in the belief systems of people in contemporary society.

Renaissance   A period of history between the fourteenth and seventeenth centuries during which European people perceived themselves as absorbing and reviving the art and literature of Classical antiquity.

ressentiment   In *Genealogy of Morality* Friedrich Nietzsche wrote about the power and strength of resentment experienced by the oppressed.

The French word *'ressentiment'* means an imaginary revenge visited upon the powerful by the powerless as their idealistic way of fighting oppression.

restorative justice   A theory of punishment that advocates restoring the just order of relationships that have been disrupted by the committing of a crime. It is welfarist rather than retributivist and supports the idea of criminals meeting their victims to apologize and give emotional restitution. It is an alternative to prison/carceral methods of punishment and has its most practical application in the field of youth justice and petty or property crime.

Spinozan ethics   Ethics is a setting of values within a determinist and relativist world so that the individual will only know real happiness when prepared to accept the limits of human power. Based on the writing of philosopher Baruch Spinoza (1632–77).

sprezzatura   Careless grace or studied nonchalance cultivated by courtiers in the Renaissance age.

stare decisis   Latin name for the doctrine of precedent. Let what is decided stand.

strict liability   An important concept in criminal law where liability can be proved without the need to demonstrate *mens rea*. The term is critical to understanding media contempt in the 1981 Contempt of Court Act. Intention is not a relevant consideration. The fact that the editor and journalists did not mean to publish something that created a substantial risk of serious prejudice would not be considered by the court. However, the court would have to be convinced beyond reasonable doubt that the editor and publication had been responsible for the *actus reus*.

teleological   A philosophical term meaning a course of conduct based on goals, ends or final causes. An action is judged ethically on its consequences. Similar to utilitarianism.

toleration, ethical   An ethical attitude to wrongdoing by individuals whose behaviour and even existence generates disapproval or chastisement. Extended in the New Testament doctrine of the Christian faith that the individual should love his/her enemy. It is recognized that peace and harmony within and without human communities can be dependent on a willingness to forgive people whose words and actions have resulted in emotional and/or physical harm. Toleration and forgiveness are the antidotes to hatred and bitterness. Toleration is a quality that can be both utilitarian and Kantian.

tort   A civil wrong in law resolved by litigation, as opposed to a crime against the state, resolved by criminal prosecution.

universalism, ethical   The belief that there are moral/ethical rules and values that are universal throughout all human communities and the history of humanity.

utilitarianism Basing a judgment on predicted results. In the ethical context evaluating the consequences from the point of view of the greatest good for the greatest number of people. Utilitarianism is a goal-based approach to the problems of justice in the distribution of the benefits and burdens of society. It gives precedence to the advancement of the collective good or welfare, even if this requires extinguishing the political rights and liberties of the individual. In America some teachers of philosophy describe utilitarianism as a teleological doctrine of ethics.

veil of ignorance In the theory of John Rawls, this is the experiment conducted by human society in which people choose not to know what their position in that society will be. Rawls uses the metaphor of the concealing veil. Therefore our original position in this society would be ignorance of our place and position.

virtù Strength or loyalty of will to publicly serve the state. The virtue of public service, an idea discoursed heavily by Niccolò Machiavelli in his books. The exercise of prowess on the part of a ruler in order to serve the interests of the state – and this may involve ruthless and effective deployment of violence and bloodshed. This means that the amoral or immoral can be deployed in exceptional circumstances to ensure the survival and security of the state.

virtue/virtuous ethics Judging morality according to the value of the person rather than the action. By deciding on a virtuous being and then practising virtue in terms of action, the good life may be lived. This approach is regarded as Aristotelian. The doctrine focuses on the cumulative harmony of an individual's morally good traits and involves experiencing desires and emotions well at the right times, towards the right people, with the right motive and in the right way, rather than badly. The purpose of virtue theory in ethics is to answer the question 'What is the good person?' rather than 'What should I do in order to lead the good life?' An action would therefore be judged as right or wrong if it can be determined as an action which a virtuous person would do.

voir dire In the US system *voir dires* are detailed court investigations of the jury panel by prosecutors and defenders/plaintiffs and claimants in order to decide the composition of the jury trying the case/action. In England and Wales the term is understood as a 'trial within a trial' and is usually a hearing heard in the absence of the jury to decide the admissibility of evidence.

BIBLIOGRAPHY

Books and articles

Allen, John (2003) *The BBC News Styleguide*, London: British Broadcasting Corporation.

Al-Malky, Rania (2006) in *Westminster Papers in Communication and Culture*.

Amnesty International (2009a) 'Report on China 2009', available at http://report2009.amnesty.org/en/en/regions/asia-pacific/china.

Amnesty International (2009b) 'Report on Saudi Arabia 2009', available at http://report2009.amnesty.org/en/regions/middle-east-north-africa/saudi-arabia.

Anand, Pravin and Duggal, Gitanjli (2000) 'India', in Michael Henry (ed.), *International Privacy, Publicity & Personality Laws*, London: Butterworths.

Aristotle (2003) *Ethics*, trans. J.A.K. Thomson, London: Folio Society.

Armstrong Nick (2005) 'Maxine Carr', London: *Press Gazette*, 18 March.

Audiard, Jacques (1996a) *Positif*, 423, May, pp. 16–17.

Austin, John (1832) *The Province of Jurisprudence Determined*, reprinted 2000, New York: Prometheus Books.

Awad, Isabel (2006) 'Journalists and their sources: lessons from anthropology', *Journalism Studies*, Vol. 7, No. 6, pp. 922–39.

Bakhtin, Mikhail (1984) *Rabelais and his World*, Bloomington: Indiana University Press.

Banisar, David (2006) *Freedom of Information Around the World 2006*, London: Privacy International, available at www.privacyinternational.org/foisurvey.

Barendt, Eric, Lustgarten, Laurence, Norrie, Kenneth and Stephenson, Hugh (1997) *Libel and the Media: The Chilling Effect*, Oxford: Clarendon Press.

Barendt, Eric (2005) *Freedom of Speech*, 2nd edn, Oxford: Oxford University Press.

Barendt, Eric (ed.) (2009) *Media Freedom and Contempt of Court*, Aldershot: Ashgate.

Barnett, Professor Steven (2006) in *Westminster Papers in Communication and Culture*.

Bazemore, Gordon and Griffiths, Curt Taylor (2003) 'Conferences, circles, boards, and mediations: the "new wave" of community justice decision making', in McLaughlin, Eugene et al. (eds), *Restorative Justice Critical Issues*, pp. 76–93.

BBC (2005) 'The New Al-Qaeda: jihad.com', 20 July. Available at http://news.bbc.co.uk/1/hi/programmes/4683403.stm, accessed 10 January 2009.

451

BBC (2006), 'Iraq reporter unlawfully killed', 13 October, available at http://news.
bbc.co.uk/1/hi/uk/6046950.stm, accessed 1 January 2009.

BBC (2009) 'Obama defends abuse photos U-turn', 14 May, available at http://
news.bbc.co.uk/1/hi/world/americas/8048774.stm.

Beales, Ian (2009) *The Editor's Codebook*, rev. 2nd edn, Edinburgh: The Press
Standards Board.

Berlins, Marcel (2003) 'More equal than others', *Index on Censorship*, Vol. 32, No.
4, pp. 34–43.

Blom-Cooper, Louis (2004) 'Time to look again at the role of the press and its
regulation', in Cookson, Rich and Jempson, Mike (eds), *Satisfaction Guaranteed?
Press Complaints Systems Under Scrutiny*, Bristol: MediaWise, pp. 5–6.

Bok, Sissela (2005) 'Dirty hands', in Honderich, Ted (ed.), *The Oxford Companion
to Philosophy*, p. 216.

Bonnington, Alistair, McInnes, Rosalind and McKain, Bruce (2000) *Scots Law for
Journalists*, Edinburgh: W. Green/Sweet & Maxwell.

Booker, Christopher and North, Richard (2003) *The Great Deception: The Secret
History of the European Union*, London and New York: Continuum Books.

Borrie, Gordon J. and Lowe, Nigel V. (1973) *The Law of Contempt*, London:
Butterworths.

Boyle, Andrew (1980) *The Climate of Treason*, London: Coronet Books.

Braithwaite, John (2003) 'Restorative justice and a better future', in McLaughlin,
Eugene et al. (eds), *Restorative Justice Critical Issues*, pp. 54–65.

Braithwaite, Nick (ed.) (1995) *The International Libel Handbook: A Practical Guide for
Journalists*, London: Butterworth Heinemann.

Brooke, Heather (2005) *Your Right To Know*, London: Pluto Press.

Brooke, Heather (2006) *Your Right To Know*, 2nd edn, London: Pluto Press.

Bruschke, Jon and Loges, William E. (2004) *Free Press vs. Fair Trials: Examining
Publicity's Role in Trial Outcomes*, London and New Jersey: Lawrence Erlbaum
Associates.

Bull, George (trans.) (1976) 'Introduction', in *Baldassare Castiglione: The Book of the
Courtier*, London: Penguin Books, pp. 9–19.

Bull, George (intro. and trans.) (1999) *The Prince by Niccolò Machiavelli*,
Harmondsworth: Penguin Classics.

Bunyan, T. (1999) *Secrecy and Openness in the EU*, London: Kogan Page.

Burckhardt, J. (1990 [1858]) *The Civilization of the Renaissance in Italy*, trans.
Middlemore, S.G.C., Harmondsworth: Penguin.

Burgess, Susan (2006) 'Cases without courts', *The News Media & The Law*, Vol. 30,
No. 3, p. 32.

Burke, Jason (2007) *Al Qaeda*, 3rd edn, London: Penguin Books.

Burke, Peter (1995) *The Fortunes of the Courtier*, London: Polity Press.

Campaign for Freedom of Information, The (2006) *500 Stories from the FOI Act's
First Year*, London: Campaign for Freedom of Information. Also available at
www.cfoi.org.uk/pdf/foistories2005.pdf.

Carollo, Russell (2006) 'Q&A with a FOIA requester', Freedom of Information
Service Center, available at www.rcfp.org/foia/foia411.html.

Carruthers, Susan L. (1995) *Winning Hearts and Minds – British Governments,
the Media and Colonial Counter-Insurgency 1944–1960*, Leicester: Leicester
University Press.

Cathcart, Brian (1995) 'Reporting restrictions have been lifted – by the Internet', London: *Independent*, 19 February 1995.

Christie, Iain and Tugendhat, Michael (eds) (2002) *The Law of Privacy and the Media*, Oxford: Oxford University Press.

Christie, Nils (2003) 'Conflicts as property', in McLaughlin, Eugene et al. (eds), *Restorative Justice Critical Issues*, pp. 21–30.

Clark, Stephen (2005) 'Epictetus', in Honderich, Ted (ed.), *The Oxford Companion to Philosophy*, pp. 256–7.

Clayton, Richard and Tomlinson, Hugh (2009) *The Law of Human Rights*, 2nd edn, Oxford: Oxford University Press.

CMLPC (Programme in Comparative Media Law and Policy Centre for Socio-Legal Studies) (2008) *A Comparative Study of Costs in Defamation Proceedings Across Europe*, December, Oxford: University of Oxford.

Cohen, Stanley (1973) *Folk Devils and Moral Panics: The Creation of the Mods and Rockers*, St Albans: Paladin.

Collins, Matthew (2005) *The Law of Defamation and the Internet*, 2nd edn, Oxford: Oxford University Press.

Cottingham, Matt (2005) 'The new al-Qaeda uncovered', 21 July. Available at http://news.bbc.co.uk/1/hi/programmes/4700911.stm, accessed 10 January 2009.

Couldry, Nick (2006) *Listening Beyond the Echoes: Media, Ethics, and Agency in an Uncertain World*, Boulder, CO: Paradigm Publishers.

Creel, George (1944) *War Criminals and Punishment*, New York: National Travel Club.

Critcher, C. (2003) *Moral Panics and the Media*, Maidenhead: Open University Press.

Crone, Tom, Alberstat, Philip, Cassels, Tom and Overs, Estelle (2002) *Law and the Media*, 4th edn, London: Focal Press.

Crook, Tim (2003) 'Is your source ever really safe?', *British Journalism Review*, Vol. 14, No. 4, pp. 7–12.

Curran, James and Seaton, Jean (1991) *Power Without Responsibility – The Press and Broadcasting in Britain*, 4th edn, London and New York: Routledge.

Dacre, Paul (Editor-in-Chief, *Daily Mail*), (2008) Conference speech to Society of Editors, 9 November, available at www.pressgazette.co.uk/story.asp?storycode=42394.

Davies, Nick (2008) *Flat Earth News: An Award-winning Reporter Exposes Falsehood, Distortion and Propaganda in the Global Media*, London: Chatto and Windus.

Davis, Matt (2008) 'How to get the most out of the Freedom of Information Act', London: *Press Gazette*, 11 July.

Denniston, Lyle W. (1992) *The Reporter and the Law*, New York: Columbia University Press.

Denyer, N.C. (2005) 'Diogenes the Cynic', in Honderich, Ted (ed.), *The Oxford Companion to Philosophy*, pp. 215–16..

Dew, Walter (1938) *I Caught Crippen: Memoirs of Ex-Chief Inspector Walter Dew, C.I.D. of Scotland Yard*, London: Blackie and Son Ltd.

Divan, Madhavi Goradia (2008) *Facets of Media Law*, Lucknow, India: Eastern Book Company.

Drury, Shadia B. (1999) *Leo Strauss and the American Right*, London: Palgrave Macmillan.

Durham Peters, John (2005) *Courting the Abyss: Free Speech and the Liberal Tradition*, Chicago and London: University of Chicago Press.

Eady, Sir David and Smith, A.T.H. (2005) *Arlidge, Eady & Smith on Contempt*, London: Sweet & Maxwell.

Eady, Sir David and Smith, A.T.H. (2008) *Arlidge, Eady & Smith on Contempt – First Supplement to the Third Edition*, London: Sweet & Maxwell.

Eastburg, Rory (2008) 'Behind closed courtroom doors', *The News Media & The Law*, Vol. 32, No. 4, p. 5.

Economist, The (2002) 'Whose life is it anyway?', US edition, 9 March.

Eide, Elisabeth, Kunelius, Risto and Phillips, Angela (eds) (2008) *Transnational Media Events: The Mohammed Cartoons and the Imagined Clash of Civilizations*, University of Gothenburg: Nordicom.

Farrell, Mike (2008) 'Ethical dilemmas, issues, and concerns in mass communications', in Moore and Murray, pp. 105–42.

Fenwick, Helen and Phillipson, Gavin (2006) *Media Freedom under the Human Rights Act*, Oxford: Oxford University Press.

Finnis, John (1979) *Natural Law and Natural Rights*, Oxford: Clarendon Press.

Foster, Steve (2007) 'Interesting or in public interest?', London: *Press Gazette*, 24 August.

Foucault, Michel (1991) *Discipline and Punish: The Birth of the Prison*, trans. Alan Sheriden, Harmondsworth: Penguin.

Françon, André (1991) 'Authors' rights beyond frontiers: a comparison of civil law and common law conceptions', *Revue Internationale du Droit d'auteur*, 149, available at www.la-rida.com/english/.

Freedman, Des (2006) in *Westminster Papers in Communication and Culture*.

Frost, Chris (2000) *Journalism/Media Ethics and Self-Regulation*, London: Longman.

Frost, Chris (2004) 'The Press Complaints Commission: a study of ten years of adjudications on press complaints', *Journalism Studies*, Vol. 5, No. 1, pp. 101–14.

Frost, Chris (2007) *Journalism Ethics and Regulation*, 2nd edn, London: Longman.

Gandy, Oscar H. (1993) *The Panoptic Sort: A Political Economy of Personal Information*, Boulder, CO: Westview Press.

Gauthier, Ashley (2001) 'Are secret courts in the best interest of the child?', *The News Media & The Law*, Vol. 25, No. 1, p. 15.

Glasser, Charles J. Jr. (ed.) (2006) *International Libel and Privacy Handbook: A Global Reference or Journalists, Publishers, Webmasters, and Lawyers*, New York: Bloomberg Press.

Golden, Thomas H. and Vogel, Stephen B. (2006) 'United States', in Glasser, Charles J. Jr. (ed.) *International Libel and Privacy Handbook*.

Goldstein, Norm (ed.) (1998) *The Associated Press Stylebook and Libel Manual*, Reading, MA: Addison-Wesley.

Gopsill, Tim (2003) 'Protection of journalists' sources', National Union of Journalists of Britain and Ireland, May, available at http://europe.ifj.org.

Griffiths, D. (ed.) (1992) 'New journalism', in *Encyclopedia of the British Press 1422–1992*, New York, USA and Bath, England: St. Martin's Press, p. 434.

Guest, S.F.D., Geary, A., Morrison, W.J., Penner, J.E. (2004) *Jurisprudence and Legal Theory*, London: University of London Press.

Hakemulder, Jan R., de Jonge, Fay A.C. and Singh, P.P. (1998) *Media Ethics and Laws*, New Delhi: Anmol Publications PVT. Ltd.

Hales, Michael (2007) 'Privacy rights in the picture', London: *Press Gazette*, 31 August, p. 18.

Hall, Stuart et al. (1978) *Policing the Crisis: Mugging, the State, and Law and Order*, London: Macmillan.

Hammond, Andrew (2009) 'Reading Lohaidan in Riyadh: media and the struggle for judicial power in Saudi Arabia', *Arab Media & Society*, January, available at www.arabmediasociety.com/?article=702, accessed 3 June 2009.

Hansard (2008) 17 December, cols 59WH–71WH, 74WH, www.publications. parliament.uk/pa/cm/cmhansrd.htm.

Haraszti, Miklos (2009) 'In God's Name', *Index on Censorship*, May, pp. 108–15.

Harcup, Tony (2007) *The Ethical Journalist*, London: Sage.

Harrop, Liz (2005) 'Human writes: the media's role in war propaganda', *Ethical Space*, Vol. 2 No. 3, pp. 15–21.

Hart, H.L.A. (2002) *The Concept of Law*, 2nd edn, New Delhi: Oxford India Paperbacks.

Haynes, Alan (2001) *The Elizabethan Secret Services*, Gloucestershire: Sutton Publishing.

Haynes, Richard (2005) *Media Rights and Intellectual Property*, Edinburgh: Edinburgh University Press.

Heilbron Rose, Justice (1975) *Report of the Advisory Group on the Law of Rape*, December, Cmnd 6352, London: Home Office.

Henning, Albert F. (1932) *Ethics and Practices in Journalism*, New York: Ray Long & Richard R. Smith, Inc.

Heydt, Colin (2007) 'John Stuart Mill', *The Internet Encyclopedia of Philosophy*, www. iep.utm.edu/m/milljs.htm, accessed 24 December 2008.

Hilsum, Lindsey (2003) 'Deciding to testify about Rwanda', *Nieman Reports*, Spring 2003, pp. 78–9.

Hoffmann, Lord (2009) 'The universality of human rights', London: Judicial Studies Board Annual Lecture, 19 March.

Honderich, Ted (ed.) (2005) *The Oxford Companion to Philosophy*, new edn, Oxford: Oxford University Press.

Hooper, David (2001) *Reputations under Fire: Winners and Losers in the Libel Business*, London: Warner Books.

Hughes, Frank (1950) *Prejudice and the Press: A Restatement of the Principle of Freedom of the Press with Specific Reference to the Hutchins-Luce Commission*, New York: The Devin-Adair Company.

Hume, David (1854) *An Essay on Human Understanding*, London: Hayes & Zell.

Human Rights Watch (2009a) 'Report on China 2009', available at www.hrw.org/ en/node/79301.

Human Rights Watch (2009b) 'Report on European Union, including United Kingdom, 2009', available at www.hrw.org/en/world-report-2009/european-union#_United_Kingdom.

Human Rights Watch (2009c) 'Report on Saudi Arabia 2009', available at www. hrw.org/en/node/79258.

Hyde, Grant Milnor (1926) *Handbook for Newspaper Workers*, New York and London: D. Appleton and Company.

ICHRP (International Council on Human Rights Policy) (2002) *Journalism, Media and the Challenge of Human Rights Reporting*, Versoix, Switzerland: ICHRP.

Iteya, Yoshio, Fujimoto, Tomoya and Marumo, Akira (2006) 'Japan', in Glasser, Charles J. Jr. (ed.) *International Libel and Privacy Handbook*.

Jaconelli, Joseph (2002) *Open Justice: A Critique of the Public Trial*, Oxford: Oxford University Press.

Jago, R. and Fionda, J. (2005) *Comparative Criminal Justice Policy Section B*, London: University of London Press.

Jurisprudence (2002) 3rd edn, Cavendish Law Cards Series, London: Cavendish Publishing Ltd.

Jurisprudence (2008) 5th edn, Law Cards Series, Oxford: Routledge-Cavendish.

Kamali, Mohammad Hashim (1997) *Freedom of Expression in Islam*, Cambridge: Cambridge University Press.

Kant, I. (1997) *Immanuel Kant – Lectures on ethics*, trans. Heath, P. and Schneewind, J.B., Cambridge: Cambridge University Press.

Keeble, Richard (2009) *Ethics for Journalists*, 2nd edn, London: Routledge.

Kelsen, Hans (1946) *General Theory of Law and the State*, reprinted 2005, New Jersey: Transaction Publishers.

Kepel, Gilles (2009) *Jihad: The Trail of Political Islam*, London: I.B. Tauris.

Klug, Francesca (2000) 'In the footsteps of H.G. Wells', *New Statesman*, 9 October.

Knightley, Phillip (1989) *The First Casualty – From the Crimea to the Falklands: The War Correspondent as Hero, Propagandist and Myth Maker*, 1st edn, London: Pan Books.

Knightley, Phillip (2000) *The First Casualty – The War Correspondent as Hero and Myth-Maker from the Crimea to Kosovo*, 2nd edn, London: Prion Books.

Kristol, Irving (1995) *Neo Conservativism: The Autobiography of an Idea*, US: The Free Press.

Kuhn, Raymond (1995) *The Media in France*, London and New York: Routledge.

Lévy, Bernard-Henri (2008) 'Emblem of Darkness', *Index on Censorship*, November, pp. 127–30.

Locke, John (1986 [1690]) *The Second Treatise on Civil Government*, New York: Prometheus Books.

Lynch, Jake and McGoldrick, Annabel (2005) *Peace Journalism*, Gloucestershire: Hawthorn Press.

Machiavelli, Niccolò (1990) *The Art of War*, trans. Farnworth, Elis, New York: Da Capo Press.

Malik, Kenan (2008) 'Shadow of the fatwa', *Index on Censorship*, November, pp. 112–20.

Mansfield, F.J. (1943) *Gentlemen, The Press! Chronicles of a Crusade: Official History of the National Union of Journalists*, London: W.H. Allen & Co.

Margach, James (1978) *The Abuse of Power: The War between Downing Street and the Media from Lloyd George to Callaghan*, London: W.H. Allen.

Martin-Clark, Nick (2003) 'When a journalist must tell', *British Journalism Review*, Vol. 14, No. 2, pp. 35–9.

Masroor, Ajmal (2006) in *Westminster Papers in Communication and Culture*.

Mayes, T. (2002) 'Restraint or revelation? Free Speech and privacy in a confessional age', 22 October, available at www.spiked-online.com, accessed 22 October 2002.

McCormick, Matt (2006) 'Immanuel Kant (1724–1804) Metaphysics', *The Internet

Encyclopedia of Philosophy, www.iep.utm.edu/k/kantmeta.htm, accessed 12th December 2008.

McLaughlin, Eugene, Fergusson, Ross, Hughes, Gordon and Westmarland, Louise (eds) (2003) *Restorative Justice Critical Issues*, Milton Keynes: The Open University.

McNair, Brian (2006) *Cultural Chaos: Journalism, News and Power in a Globalised World*, London and New York: Routledge.

McNicholas, Anthony (2006) in *Westminster Papers in Communication and Culture*.

Media Law Resource Centre (1999) 'Annual study sees six media trials in 2008: half won by defendants', 9 March, available at http://medialaw.org.

Mediawise (1997) 'Child exploitation and the media forum', forum panel enquiry, summary by Denise Searle, 11 March, available at www.mediawise.org.uk.

Meiklejohn, A. (1948) *Free Speech and its Relation to Self-Government*, New York: Harper.

Melville-Brown, Amber (2006) 'The emergence of privacy as a claim in the UK: theory and guidelines', in Glasser, Charles J. Jr. (ed.) *International Libel and Privacy Handbook*.

Mendel, T. (ed.) for Article 19 and Liberty (2000) *Secrets, Spies and Whistleblowers – Freedom of Expression and National Security in the United Kingdom*, London: The Guardian.

Merrill, John C. (1997) *Journalism Ethics: Philosophical Foundations for News Media*, New York: St Martin's Press.

Metcalf, Eric (2009) *Secret Evidence*, London: Justice.

Miles, Hugh (2005) *Al-Jazeera: The Inside Story of the Arab News Channel that is Challenging the West*, New York: Grove Press.

Mill, John Stuart (1859) *On Liberty*, London: John W. Parker and Son.

Miller, Ann (2003) 'Units 17 and 18: French Cinema from 1974 to 2000', in *European Cinemas – AA310 Book 4 Film and Television History*, Milton Keynes: The Open University.

Moore, Roy L. and Murray, Michael D. (2008) *Media Law and Ethics*, 3rd edition, New York and London: Routledge.

Morgan, Piers (2004) *The Insider – The Private Diaries of a Scandalous Decade*, London: Ebury Press.

Morrison, Wayne (1997) *Jurisprudence: From the Greeks to Post-modernism*, New Delhi: Cavendish & Lawman (India) Private Ltd.

Morton, James (2001) *Gangland: The Lawyers*, London: Virgin.

Mostyn, Trevor (2001) 'Saudi Arabia', in Jones, Derek (ed.) *Censorship: A World Encyclopedia, Volume Four*, London and Illinois: Fitzroy Dearborn, pp. 2146–50.

Muggeridge, Malcolm (1975) *The Infernal Grove: Chronicles of Wasted Time, Vol. II*, London: Fontana.

Muncie, J., McLaughlin, E. et al. (2005) *D315: Crime, Order and Social Control Course Guide*, Milton Keynes: The Open University, pp. 66–101.

Nakada, Koichiro and Shimada, Makoto (1995) 'Japan', in Braithwaite, Nick (ed.), *The International Libel Handbook*, pp. 174–82.

Nietzsche, Friedrich (2006) *Genealogy of Morality*, 2nd edn, Cambridge: Cambridge University Press.

News Media & The Law, The (2002a) 'Supermodel's privacy victory in England would have ended differently in the U.S.', Vol. 26, No. 2, p. 30.

News Media & The Law, The (2002b) 'Government urges CBS, web site host to refrain from airing Pearl murder video', Vol. 26, No. 3, p. 44.

NSK (The Japan Newspaper Publishers and Editors Association) (2009) 'NSK calls for lay judges to attend news conferences after verdicts', March, available at www.pressnet.or.jp/newsb/0903b.html.

Odle, E.V. (1938) 'W.T. Stead: a champion of victims of white slavery', in Huson, R. (ed.), *Sixty Famous Trials*, London: Daily Express Production.

O'Neill, Brendan (2005) '"Repugnant" Britain lures libel tourists', London: *Press Gazette*, 30 September.

O'Neill, Onora (1998) 'Kantian ethics', in E. Craig (ed.), *Routledge Encyclopedia of Philosophy*, London: Routledge. Available at www.rep.routledge.com/article/L042, accessed 26 May 2009.

Örnebring, Henrik (2006) 'The maiden tribute and the naming of monsters', *Journalism Studies*, Vol. 7, No. 6, pp. 851–68.

OSCE (Organization for Security and Cooperation in Europe) (2005) *Libel and Insult Laws: A Matrix on Where We Stand and What We Would Like to Achieve*, Vienna: OSCE.

Pakes, Francis (2004) *Comparative Criminal Justice*, Cullompton, Devon: Willan Publishing.

PCC (Press Complaints Commission UK) (2001) 'Attard and The Manchester Evening News', PCC Adjudication, 15 June (Report 55).

PCC (Press Complaints Commission) UK (2004) Code of Practice. Accessed 14 October 2004; current (2007) code available at www.pcc.org.uk/cop/practice.html.

Pederson, Tony (2005) 'Warming up to the idea of a shield law', *The News Media & The Law*, Vol. 29, No. 1, pp. 8–9.

Penner, J. et al. (eds) (2002) *Jurisprudence and Legal Theory: Commentary and Materials*, London: Butterworths LexisNexis.

Petley, Professor Julian (2006) in *Westminster Papers in Communication and Culture*.

Phillimore, Lord (1974) *Report of the Committee on Contempt of Court*, Cmnd 5794, December, London: HMSO.

Phillips, Angela (2008) 'Who spoke and who was heard in the cartoons debate?', in *Transnational Media Events: The Mohammed Cartoons and the Imagined Clash of Civilizations*, Göteborg, Sweden: Nordicom.

Pilger, John (2000) 'Introduction', in Phillip Knightley, *The First Casualty – The War Correspondent as Hero and Myth-Maker from the Crimea to Kosovo*, London: Prion Books.

Pollack, Matthew (2008) 'How to save a life: A reporter breaks his promise of confidentiality to save a former FBI agent from a life sentence', *The News Media & The Law*, Vol. 32, No. 1, p. 24.

Ponsonby, A. (1928) *Falsehood in Wartime*, London: George Allen and Unwin.

Popkin, Richard H. and Stroll, Avrum (1998) *Philosophy*, Oxford: Butterworth-Heinemann.

Potter, Deborah (2001) 'Witnessing the final act' *American Journalism Review*, July–August, p. 76, available at www.ajr.org/Article.asp?id=691, accessed 10 June 2009.

Pring, George and Canan, Penelope (1996) *SLAPPs: Getting Sued for Speaking Out*, Philadelphia: Temple University Press.

Quinn, Frances (2009) *Law for Journalists*, 2nd edn, Harlow, Essex: Pearson Longman.

Radder, Norman J. (1924) *Newspaper Make-up and Headlines*, London and New York: McGraw-Hill Book Company.

Rai, Janmejay and Chandra, Barunesh (2006) 'India', in Glasser, Charles J. Jr. (ed.) *International Libel and Privacy Handbook*.

Ramadan, Said (1970) *Islamic Law: Its Scope and Equity*, Geneva: Islamic Centre; 1st edn (1961), London: P.R. Macmillan; 1992 edn, Kuala Lumpur: Muslim Youth Movement of Malaysia.

Rawls, John (1971) *A Theory of Justice*, Cambridge, MA: Harvard University Press.

Rawls, John (1996) *Political Liberalism*, New York: Columbia University Press.

RCFP (Reporters' Committee for the Freedom of the Press) (2008) 'Abu Ghraib photos must finally be released', 22 September, available at www.rcfp.org/news-items/index.php?i=7028, accessed 25 May 2009.

RCFP (2009) 'Brief of Amici Curiae', in support of Appellees in the appeal from the United States District Court For The Southern District of New York, The Honourable Alvin K. Hellerstein, in the case of ACLU and others v Department of Defense and others, May, p. 26.

Read, James Morgan (1941) *Atrocity propaganda, 1914–1919*, New Haven and London: Yale University Press, Oxford University Press.

Rich, R. Bruce (1995) 'The United States of America', in Braithwaite, Nick (ed.), *The International Libel Handbook*.

Rigden, Dennis (2001 [derived from 1943]) 'Introduction', in *SOE Syllabus – Lessons in Ungentlemanly Warfare, World War II*, Surrey: The Public Record Office.

Ritzer, George (2000) *The McDonaldization of Society*, California: Pine Forge Press.

Roberts, Alasdair (2006) *Blacked Out: Government Secrecy in the Information Age*, Cambridge: Cambridge University Press.

Robertson, Geoffrey (1999) *The Justice Game*, London: Vintage Books.

Robertson, Geoffrey and Nicol, Andrew G.L. (1984) *Media Law: The Rights of Journalists and Broadcasters*, London: Oyez Longman.

Robertson, Geoffrey, and Nicol, Andrew (1992) *Media Law*, 3rd edn, London: Penguin.

Robertson, Geoffrey, and Nicol, Andrew (2002) *Media Law*, 4th edn, London: Penguin.

Robertson, Geoffrey, and Nicol, Andrew (2008) *Media Law*, fully rev. 5th edn, London: Penguin.

Rose, Andrew (2007) *Lethal Witness: Sir Bernard Spilsbury, Honorary Pathologist*, Stroud, Gloucestershire: Sutton Publishing.

Rose, David (2004) *Guantánamo: America's War on Human Rights*, London: Faber & Faber.

Rosenbaum, Martin (2009), 'The state of FOI', 20 May, www.bbc.co.uk/blogs/opensecrets/2009/05/the_state_of_foi.html.

Russell, Bertrand (2004) *History of Western Philosophy and its Connection with Political and Social Circumstances from the Earliest Times to the Present Day*, London: Folio Society.

Russell, Jago (ed.) (2007) *Charge or Release? Terrorism Pre-Charge Detention: Comparative Law Study*, London: Liberty.

Sack, Robert D. (2003) *Sack on Defamation: Libel, Slander and Related Problems, Volume 1 and Volume 2*, 3rd edn, New York City: Practising Law Institute.

459

Sadler, Roger L. (2005) *Electronic Media Law*, Thousand Oaks, London, New Delhi: Sage Publications.

Salamun, Kurt (1998), 'Jaspers, Karl', in E. Craig (ed.), *Routledge Encyclopedia of Philosophy*, London: Routledge. Available atwww.rep.routledge.com/article/DD031, accessed 26 May 2009.

Seaton, Jean (2005) *Carnage and the Media: The Making and Breaking of News About Violence*, London: Allen Lane.

Sereny, Gitta (1998) *Cries Unheard: The Story of Mary Bell*, London: Macmillan.

Shoenberger, Heather (2006) 'Secrecy across the pond: British journalists feel the chill under the Official Secrets Act, and a bill in the Senate could have similar effects in the United States', *The News Media & The Law*, Vol. 30, No. 4 , pp. 9–10.

Skorupski, John (1998, 2005), 'Mill, John Stuart', in E. Craig (ed.), *Routledge Encyclopedia of Philosophy*, London: Routledge. Available at www.rep.routledge.com/article/DC054SE, accessed 26 May 2009.

Slattery, Jon (2004) 'Family court lifts ban on press after legal challenge', Croydon: *Press Gazette*, 20 February, p. 10.

Slote, Michael (2005) 'Utilitarianism', in Honderich, Ted (ed.), *The Oxford Companion to Philosophy*, pp. 936-9.

Smartt, Ursula (2006) *Media Law for Journalists*, London, Thousand Oaks, New Delhi: Sage Publications.

Snepp, Frank (1977) *Decent Interval*, New York: Random House.

Snepp, Frank (2000) *Irreparable Harm*, New York: Alfred A. Knopf. See also www.franksnepp.com.

Snepp, Frank (2009) 'Frank Snepp's Official Home on the World Wide Web', available at www.franksnepp.com/, Accessed 3 May 2009.

Soley, Lawrence (2002) *Censorship, INC: The Corporate Threat to Free Speech in the United States*, New York: Monthly Review Press.

Stanhope, John (1962) *The Cato Street Conspiracy*, London: Jonathan Cape.

Sterling, J.A.L. (2003) *World Copyright Law*, London: Sweet & Maxwell.

Sullivan, Ceri (2000) 'Britain's renaissance of letters', in David Mateer (ed.), *Courts, Patrons and Poets*, London and Milton Keynes: Yale University Press in association with The Open University.

Sun-Tzu (1994) *The Art of War*, trans. Sawyer, Ralph D., New York: Barnes and Noble.

Sweet & Maxwell (2008) 'Are media companies becoming more reluctant to defend themselves against defamation claims?' press release issued by Mattison Public Relations, available at www.sweetandmaxwell.thomson.com.

Tauri, Juan, and Morris, Allison (2003) 'Re-forming justice: the potential of Maori processes', in McLaughlin, Eugene et al. (eds), *Restorative Justice Critical Issues*, pp. 44–53.

Taylor, Philip M. (1992) *War and the Media*, Manchester: Manchester University Press.

Taylor, Philip M. (1995) *Munitions of the Mind – A History of Propaganda from the Ancient to the Present Day*, Manchester: Manchester University Press.

Taylor, Philip M. (1998) *War and the Media – Propaganda and Persuasion in the Gulf War*, 2nd edn, Manchester and New York: Manchester University Press.

Temkin, Jennifer (2002) *Rape and the Legal Process*, Oxford: Oxford University Press.

Tomlinson, Richard (2001) *The Big Breach*, Edinburgh: Cutting Edge Press.

Trestrail, John H. III (2007) *Criminal Poisoning: An Investigational Guide for Law Enforcement, Toxicologists, Forensic Scientists and Attorneys*, 2nd edition, New Jersey: Humana Press.

von Clausewitz, Gen. Carl (1949) *On War*, introd. and trans. Graham, Col. J.J., London: Routledge & Kegan Paul Ltd.

von Eckardt, Wolf, Gilman, Sander L. and Chamberlin, J. Edward (1988) *Oscar Wilde's London*, London: Michael O'Mara Books.

Wadham, John, Griffiths, Jonathan and Rigby, Bethan (2001) *Blackstone's Guide to the Freedom of Information Act 2000*, London: Blackstone Press Ltd.

Walkowitz, Judith R. (2000) *City of Dreadful Delight: Narratives of Sexual Desire in Late-Victorian London*, London: Virago Press.

Wang, Vincent and David, Edward J. (2006) 'China', in Glasser, Charles J. Jr. (ed.) *International Libel and Privacy Handbook*.

Warburton, Nigel (2003) *Philosophy: The Basics*, London, New York: Routledge.

Warburton, Nigel (2006) *Philosophy: The Classics*, 3rd edn, London, New York: Routledge.

Warren Commission (1964) *Report of The President's Commission on the Assassination of President Kennedy*, Washington, DC: United States Government Printing Office.

Warren and Brandeis (1890), 'The Right of Privacy', *Harvard Law Review*, 4 Harv. L. Rev. 193–220.

Wells, H.G. (1940) *The Rights of Man*, Harmondsworth: Penguin Books.

Welsh, Tom, Greenwood, Walter and Banks, David (2007) *McNae's Essential Law for Journalists*, 19th edn, Oxford: Oxford University Press (20th edn published in July 2009).

Westminster Papers in Communication and Culture (2006) '"Press freedom and religious respect": a debate hosted by the Communication and Media Research Institute at the University of Westminster, 22/2/2006', Vol. 3, No. 2, pp. 103–21; ISSN 1744-6708 (print), 1744=6716 (online).

Whyte, Frederic (1925) *The Life of W.T. Stead in Two Volumes, Vol. 1*, London: Jonathan Cape Limited.

Wright, Peter (1987) *Spycatcher: The Candid Autobiography of a Senior Intelligence Officer*, Toronto: Stoddart Publishing.

Youm, Kyu Ho (2006) 'Recent rulings weaken neutral reportage defense', *Newspaper Research Journal*, Vol. 27, No. 1, pp. 58–73.

Youm, Kyu Ho and Russomanno, Joseph (2002) '"Burning" news sources and media liability: Cohen v Cowles Media Co. ten years later', *Communications and the Law*, September, pp. 69–101.

Young, Filson (ed.) (1920) *The Trial of Hawley Harvey Crippen*, London: Butterworth & Co.

Zarek, Corinna (2006) 'Abu Ghraib appeal dropped', *The News Media & The Law*, Vol. 30, No. 2, available at http:/rcfp.org/news/mag.

Zelezny, John D. (2004) *Communications Law: Liberties, Restraints, and the Modern Media*, Belmont, CA: Thomson, Wadsworth.

Zelizer, Barbie (1992) *Covering the Body: The Kennedy Assassination, the Media, and the Shaping of Collective Memory*, Chicago and London: The University of Chicago Press.

Zylinska, Joanna (2005) 'Ethics and moral panics', in *The Ethics of Cultural Studies*, New York: Continuum Books

Media Lawyer

'£450,000 settlement in e-mail libel case', No. 11, September 1997.

'Sue where you download – court', No. 44, March 2003.

'Communications Bill: no role for Ofcom in press code', No. 46, July 2003.

'Manslaughter appeal anonymity', No. 49, January 2004.

'True ricin story could not be told', No. 57, May 2005.

'Declaration of falsity after "serious allegations"', No. 58, July 2005.

'Editor loses appeal over sex offence victim', No. 58, July 2005.

'Naming of mother with HIV banned', No. 59, September 2005.

'Galloway story "in public interest"', No. 60, November 2005.

'Shayler order to stay silent on MI5', No. 65, September 2006.

'Terrors suspects remain anonymous', No. 66, November 2006.

'Judges explains sex case identity ban', No. 68, March 2007.

'Protecting your sources? Do not look to the courts for help', No. 72, November 2007.

'ITN demands war law change', No. 72, November 2007.

'Iraq case gag order overturned', No. 74, March 2008.

'Contempt warning is a problem', No. 76, July 2008.

'Media are fighting fewer cases', No. 78, November 2008.

'Lawyer battles against libel ban', No. 79, January 2009.

'Police bug "a breach of rights"', No. 79, January 2009.

'Ex-MI5 man's book "must go to tribunal"', No. 80, March 2009.

'Judge protests over court story', No. 80, March 2009.

'Times loses Brunswick attack', No. 81, May 2009.

'Family hearings open up – but ...' No. 81, May 2009.

'Judge bans press from naming killer', No. 81, May 2009.

'Open courts are pointless unless there is also proper reporting', No. 81, May 2009.

'Watchdog should offer arbitration service – lawyer', No. 81, May 2009.

'Decision "a threat to sources"', No. 81, May 2009.

'Bill will change reporting laws', No. 82, July 2009.

Newspaper articles

Aaronovitch, David (2008) 'I'll eat my hat if Dr Crippen was innocent – ok?' July 1 2008, London: *The Times*.

Arab News (1982) 'Saudi Arabia Media Charter: Adopted by Council of Ministers 1982', 19 October. Excerpt available at www.al-bab.com/media/docs/arabcodes. htm#SAUDI.

Berlins, Marcel (1994) 'Writ large', London: *Guardian*, 5 April.

Bennett, Alan, quoted in Fiddick, Peter (1988) 'Alan Bennett says "gutter press" set up Russell Harty', London: *Guardian*, 12 October.

Brook, Stephen (2009) 'Half UK local and regional papers could shut by 2014, MPs are told', 16 June, London: *Guardian*.

Burke, Jason (2004) 'Theatre of Terror', London: *Observer*, 21 November. Available at www.guardian.co.uk/theobserver/2004/nov/21/features.review7/ print, accessed 10 May 2009.

Butterworth, Siobhain (2004) 'A risky libel defence', London: *Guardian*, 1 March.

Byrne, Ciar (2002) 'Di Giovanni: I would testify', London: *Guardian*, 25 October.

Campbell, Duncan, Dodd, Vikram, Norton-Taylor, Richard and Cowan, Rosie (2005) 'Police killer gets 17 years for poison plot', London: *Guardian*, 14 April.

Clarke, Liam (2006) 'American stars queue to sue in libel-friendly Belfast', *Sunday Times*, 25 June.

Cleland, Gary (2008) 'BBC film of mother losing child is halted', London: *Daily Telegraph*, 12 April.

Cohen, Nick (2004) 'Thousands of children may have been snatched from families because of evidence given in camera', London: *Observer*, 25 January.

Dixon, Cyril (2008) 'I am not the red light killer of five vice girls', London: *Daily Express*, 15 January.

Doward, Jamie (2004) 'Ministers told child harm theory was flawed', London: *Observer*, 25 January.

Duodu, Korieh (2007) 'Not the end of the story', London: *Guardian*, 13 August.

Dunlop, Emma (2002) 'Teacher wins website libel case', *Yorkshire Post*, 21 May.

Dyer, Clare (2004) 'Care case review follows cot death ruling', London: *Guardian*, 21 January.

Dyer, Clare (2005) 'Maxine Carr gets anonymity for the rest of her life', London: *Guardian*, 25 February.

Dyer, Clare (2007a) 'Inquiry into criminal cases after expert witness's secret patient files revealed', London: *Guardian*, 21 February.

Dyer, Clare (2007b) 'Court halts screening after official solicitor intervenes', London: *Guardian*, 23 July.

Elliott, Christopher (1994) 'Aitken knew of forgery which led to Ritz Hotel bill story six months ago, says Al-Fayed', London: *Guardian*, 3 November.

Engel, Matthew (1999) 'The day the sword of truth struck home', London: *Guardian*, 9 June.

Evans, Rob (2009) 'Justice should be seen to be done', London: *Guardian*, 15 June.

Expenses (2009) grouped articles on this topic in the online archive of: www.telegraph.co.uk/news/newstopics/mps-expenses/ and www.guardian.co.uk/politics/mps-expenses, accessed 25 May 2009.

Fisk, Robert (1999) 'This is a horror story and there is no other way to describe it', London: *Independent*, 16 April.

Fisk, Robert (2003) 'War on Iraq: In Baghdad, blood and bandages for the innocent; Robert Fisk reports on carnage in the market', London: *Independent on Sunday*. 30 March.

Flintoff, John-Paul (1998) 'Media: sleazy, tasteless and proud of it; The Daily and Sunday Sport's blend of sex and schoolboy humour is a success story of tackiness over taste', London: *Independent*, 15 September.

Foley, Michael (1998) 'Limits on right to privacy clarified', *Irish Times*, City edn, 9 October, p. 6.

Ford, Richard (2009) 'The Times fined £15,000 for contempt of court', London: *The Times*, 23 May.

Fresco, Adam (2005) 'Carr wins cloak of secrecy for life', London: *Times*, 25 February.

Gibb, Frances (1998) 'Human rights go to court', London: *The Times*, 3 November.

Gibb, Frances (2005) 'Fear grows of privacy law by stealth', London: *The Times*, 25 February.

Gibb, Frances (2009) 'Arcane laws of sedition and criminal libel scrapped', London: *The Times*, 15 July.

Gibb, Frances (2009) 'Should Wendell Wilberforce Baker be tried again for rape?', London: *The Times*, 28 July.

Gillan, Audrey (2004) 'Defeat for Blunkett as judges free detainee', London: *Guardian*, March 19.

Giraldi, Philip (2008) 'What FBI whistle-blower Sibel Edmonds found in translation: why is her story being covered up?', *Dallas Morning News*, 17 February.

Guardian, The (2009) Editorial, 'Baby P: Names, shame and a child', 11 August.

Hodgson, Martin (2007) '100 years on, DNA casts doubt on Crippen case', London: *Guardian*, 17 October.

Independent, The (2005) 'Maxine Carr has the right to be left alone', leader, 1st edn, 25 February, p. 30.

Jack, Ian (1994) 'Onwards, upwards, sometimes downwards', London: *Independent*, 10 July.

Joseph, Joe (2009) 'Like the student in Tiananmen Square, Neda has become a tragic icon,' London: *The Times*, 23 June.

Kent, Paul (2007) 'Mobs attack innocents: women lookalikes run out of town', Melbourne: *Herald Sun*, 29 December.

Laville, Sandra (2009) 'Judge lifts ban on identification of baby P's mother', London: *Guardian* 11 August.

Leppard, David (2009) 'MI6 tempts rebel ex-spy back home', London: *The Times*, 31 May.

Morning Star (2005) 'Mr Galloway goes to Washington', London, 19 May.

Murray, J. 'Victory, yes, but at a high price', Letters, *Grimsby Evening Telegraph*, 6 June.

Pannick, David (1994) 'No logic behind gagging terrorists' empty rhetoric', London: *The Times*, 2 August.

Peek Laura, Kennedy, Dominic and Charter. David (2004) 'Coroner ready to open new Kelly enquiry', London: *The Times*, 22 January.

Rozenberg, Joshua (2005) 'Maxine Carr wins anonymity for the rest of her life', London: *Daily Telegraph*, 25 February.

Sanders, Jo (2004) 'When editors need to take note', London: *Guardian*, 29 November.

Scotland, Baroness (2008) 'Law on contempt is a fine balancing act', Letters, London: *The Times*, 18 September.

Seaton, Jean (2009) 'NightJack blog: how the Times silenced the voice of valuable frontline reporter', London: *Guardian*, 17 June.

Sharrock, David (2009) 'Journalist Suzanne Breen need not disclose Real IRA contacts', London: *The Times*, 18 June.

Stead, W.T. (1876) *Northern Echo*, 3 April.

Stead, W.T. (1885) *Pall Mall Gazette*, 10 July.

Thomas, Richard (Information Commissioner) (2009) 'Freedom of information has come of age', London: *Guardian*, 11 June.

Times, The (1820a) 'High Treason Trial of James Ings', Issue 10914, 22 April, p. 2, col. D.

Times The (1820b) 'High Treason Trial of Brunt', Issue 10916, 25 April, p. 3, col. B.

Times, The (1820c) 'Editorials/Leaders' Issue 10920, 29 April, p. 2, col. E.

Times, The (1949) 'Contempt of court editor committed to prison, company fined £10,000', 26 March, p. 3.

Tomlinson, Hugh (2009) 'Censored version of MPs' expenses will break the law QC warns', London: *Guardian*, 25 May. Available at www.guardian.co.uk/politics/2009/may/24/mps-expenses-freedom-information, accessed 25 May 2009.

Townsend, Mark (2009) 'Appeal judges asked to clear notorious murderer Dr Crippen', London: *Observer*, 7 June.

Travis Alan (2005) 'Met chief wants ban lifted on terrorism reporting', London: *Guardian*, 7 February.

van Slambrouck, Paul (2003) 'Galloway papers deemed forgeries', *Christian Science Monitor*, 20 June. Available at www.csmonitor.com/2003/0620/p01s03-woiq.html.

Verkaik, Robert (2004) 'Terror laws in disarray after Woolf frees Libyan', London: *Independent*, 19 March.

Verkaik, Robert (2008) 'Britain's libel laws are stifling free speech, says UN', London: *Independent*, 14 August.

Verkaik, Robert (2009) 'Internet hate campaign that made a mockery of the High Court', London: *Independent*, 11 August.

Wainwright, Martin (1988) 'The media: the haunting of Harty – Russell Harty's last days brought out the press pack in full cry, but their tactics could now put them on a tighter leash', London: *Guardian*, 27 June.

Webb, Andy (2008a) 'Did the press play a part in Crippen's downfall?' London: *Guardian*, 30 June.

West Briton (2007) 'Police act to quash rumours Maxine is in Penryn', 18 January.

Films, TV and radio broadcasts

Audiard, Jacques (1996b) *Un héros très discret*, France: Studio Canal.

BBC Radio 4 (2003a) *File on Four*, rep. Allan Urry, prod. Liz Carney, London: BBC Radio 4, 11 and 16 March, programme no. 03VY3010LHO. Pdf transcript was available at www.bbc.co.uk.

BBC Radio 4 (2003b) *File on Four*, investigating the Family Courts Service, rep. Jenny Cuffe, prod. Ian Muir-Cochrane, London: BBC Radio 4, 8 and 13 July, programme no. 03VY3027LHO. Pdf transcript was available at www.bbc.co.uk.

BBC Radio 4 (2004) *File on Four*, reporter Allan Urry, prod. Andy Derwood, London: BBC Radio 4, 17 February.

Burke, Jason (presenter) (2005) *Channel Terror*, dir. and prod. David Akerman, exec. prod. Farah Durrani, London: BBC2 and BBC4.

Curtis, Adam (narr. and prod.) (2004) *The Power of Nightmares: The Rise of the Politics of Fear*, prod. Stephen Lambert, London: BBC2. Available at www.news.bbc.co.uk/1/hi/programmes/3755686.stm.

Depardon, Raymond (dir) (1994) *Délits Flagrants*, France: Arte Video EDV 236.

Depardon, Raymond (dir) (2004) *Dixième chambre: instants d'audience*, France: Koch Lorber KLF-DV-3072.

Ginnane, Maxx (dir) (2007) *First Cut: Being Maxine Carr*, prod. Joel Wilson, London: Renegade Pictures and Eleven Films for Channel 4 TV, 14 December.

Malle, Louis (dir) (1974) *Lacombe Lucien*, France: DVD Optimum World, OPTDO318.

Malle, Louis (dir) (1987) *Au Revoir les Enfants*, France: DVD Optimum World, OPTDO318.

Maltby, Clive (dir) (2004) *The Last Secret of Dr Crippen*, London: Justabout Productions for Channel 4 TV.

Nugus/Martin Productions (1992) 'Justice in Time', the case of Dr Sam Sheppard in *Great Crimes and Trials, Series One*, Columbia Tristar. DVD (2004), C822 8655.

Ophüls, Marcel (dir and prod.) (1969) *Le chagrin et la pitié*, France: ORTF. DVD (2004) Arrow Films B0002PC2OK.

Rosenbaum, Martin (presenter) (2008) *The Right to Know*, two-part documentary series, London: BBC World Service. Podcasts available at www.bbc.co.uk/worldservice/documentaries/2008/08/080807_right_to_know1.shtml.

Snoddy, Raymond (presenter) (1998) *Hard News: Did you fake this film Marc?*, dir. Eric Hawthorne, prod. Sam Bagnall and Oliver Wilson, London: Channel 4 TV.

Tavernier, Bertrand (dir.) (2002) *Laissez-Passer*, France. DVD: Artificial Eye, B0000800Q43.

Taylor, Peter (writer and presenter) (2005) *The New Al-Qaeda*, three-part series prod. Sandy Smith, London: BBC2, 25 July, 1 August, 8 August.

Truffaut, François (dir) (1980) *Le Dernier Métro*, France: Cinema Club. DVD B000LMPFPC.

Webb, Andy (dir and prod.) (2008b) *Was Dr Crippen Innocent?* London: Film of Record for Channel 5 TV, 1 July.

Official records and documentation

CPS (Crown Prosecution Service) (2009) 'Decision on prosecution – Mr Christopher Galley and Mr Damian Green MP', 16 April, Para. 33, available at www.cps.gov.uk/news/articles/decision_on_prosecution_mr_christopher_galley_and_mr_damian_green_mp/, accessed 25 May 2009.

Downing Street (2005), Downing Street Press Conference, 5 August, available at www.number10.gov.uk/Page8041.

Ofcom (2004) 'Consultation on the proposed Ofcom Broadcasting Code', 14 July, available at www.ofcom.org.uk.

Ofcom (2005) The Ofcom Broadcasting Code, London: Office of Communications (May). Also available at www.ofcom.org.uk.

Scott-Baker, Lord Justice (2008) 'Coroner's ruling on the verdicts', www.scott-baker-inquests.gov.uk, accessed 10 February 2009.

UN ICCPR (1996) International Covenant on Civil and Political Rights, United Nations Treaty Series, 1966 993 UNTS 171. Available at www2.ohchr.org/english/law/ccpr.htm (also Caddell, Richard and Johnson, Howard (2006) Blackstones Statutes on Media Law, Oxford: Oxford University Press, p. 15).

UN ICCPR (2006) UN Human Rights Committee, Eighty-seventh session, 10–28 July, United States of America.

UN ICCPR (2008) UN Human Rights Committee, Ninety-third session, Geneva, 7–25 July, United Kingdom of Great Britain and Northern Ireland.

UN Security Council (2006), Resolution 1738 (2006) Adopted by the Security Council at its 5613th meeting, on 23 December 2006, S/RES/1738 (2006).

UK Parliamentary papers

House of Commons Select Committee on Home Affairs (2003) Fifth Report.
House of Lords Select Committee on Draft Freedom of Information Bill (1998) First Report, 27 July, available at: www.publications.parliament.uk/pa/ld199899/ldselect/ldfoinfo/97/9701.htm.

House of Commons Select Committee on Culture, Media and Sport, Enquiry into Press Standards, Privacy and Libel, 2009

Uncorrected evidence:

Memorandum submitted by Advance Publications, Inc et al. (US Media/Publishers)

Memorandum submitted by Jonathan Coad, Swan Turton Solicitors 'The Law of Libel and Conditional Fee Arrangements'.

Memorandum submitted by PCC (Press Complaints Commission).

Memorandum submitted by Press Standards Board.

Memorandum submitted by Russell Jones & Walker, Solicitors.

Memorandum submitted by Schillings.

Memorandum submitted by Sir David Eady (Speech on Privacy to TIPLO (The Intellectual Property Lawyers' Association) House of Lords, 18 February 2009.)

Memorandum submitted by Society of Editors.

Memorandum submitted by Swan Turton Solicitors (Jonathan Coad, February 2009)

Memorandum submitted by the Master of the Rolls Sir Anthony Clarke.

Supplementary written evidence from DCMS (Department for Culture, Media and Sport)

Archival records

The National Archives, Kew, London (TNA)

Papers in the case of R v Crippen 1910:
DPP 1/3
HO 144/1718/19542/sub-file 38
HO 144/1718/19542/sub-file 86
MEPO 3/198

Table of statutes

UK statutes

Administration of Justice Act 1960
Anti-social Behaviour Act 2003
Anti-Terrorism, Crime and Security Act 2001
Broadcasting Act 1990

Broadcasting Act 1996
Children Act 1989
Children (Scotland) Act 1995
Children and Young Persons Act 1933
Communications Act 2003
Constitutional Reform Act 2005
Contempt of Court Act 1981
Copyright Act (Statute of Anne) 1710
Copyright, Designs and Patents Act 1988
Copyright and Trade Marks (Offences and Enforcement) Act 2002
Crime and Disorder Act 1998
Criminal Justice Act 1925
Criminal Justice Act 1988
Criminal Justice and Public Order Act 1994
Criminal Law Amendment Act 1886
Criminal Procedure (Scotland) Act 1995
Criminal Procedure and Investigations Act 1996
Data Protection Act 1984
Data Protection Act 1998
Defamation Act 1996
Education Act 1870
Freedom of Information Act 2000
Freedom of Information (Scotland) Act 2002
Human Rights Act 1998
International Criminal Court Act 2001
Judicial Proceedings (Regulation of Reports) Act 1926
Magistrates Court Act 1980
Mental Health Act 1959
Official Secrets Act 1911
Official Secrets Act 1989
Police and Criminal Evidence Act 1984
Protection from Harassment Act 1997
Public Interest Disclosure Act 1998
Public Order Act 1986
Racial and Religious Hatred Act 2006
Regulation and Investigatory Powers Act 2000
Serious Organised Crime and Police Act 2005
Sexual Offences (Amendment) Act 1976
Sexual Offences (Amendment) Act 1992
Sexual Offences Act 2003
Single European Act 1986
Social Work (Scotland) Act 1968
Terrorism Act 2000
Terrorism Act 2006
Youth Justice and Criminal Evidence Act 1999

US federal statutes

Berne Convention Implementation Act 1988
Communications Decency Act 1996
Copyright Act 1790
Copyright Act 1976
Copyright Term Extension Act 1998
Digital Millennium Copyright Act 1998
Domestic Security Enhancement Act of 2003 [Patriot Act II]
Electronic Freedom of Information Act 1996
Espionage Act 1917
Federal Communications Act 1934
Federal Radio Act 1927
Flag Protection Act 1989
Freedom of Information Act 1966
Homeland Security Act 2003
Intelligence Identities Protection Act 1982
Privacy Protection Act 1980
Provide Appropriate Tools Required to Intercept and Obstruct Terrorism (PATRIOT) Act [Patriot Act I] 2001
Sedition Act 1918
Telecommunications 1996
Visual Artists Rights Act 1990

Table of case law citations

A v B (a company) and another [2002] EWCA Civ 337.
A v B [2008] EWHC 1512 (Admin) (4 July 2008).
A v B ECWA [2009] Civ 24 (18 February 2009).
A Local Authority v W.L.W. and T&R (By the Children's Guardian) [2005] EWHC 1564 (Fam).
Aamer Anwar – Opinion of the Court delivered by Lord Osborne in Remit by a Trial Judge of an Issue of Possible Contempt of Court [2008] HCJAC 36 IN932/06.
Abrams v US 250 US 616 (1919).
ACLU et al. v Department of Defense S.D.N.Y., Index No. 04, Civ. 4151 (AKH) (direct) (2005).
Ackroyd v Merseycare NHS Trust No 2 [2007] EWCA Civ, 101 (21 February 2007).
Al-Fagih v HH Saudi Research & Marketing (UK) Ltd [2001] EWCA Civ 1634.
Al-Megrahi (Abdelbasset Ali) v Times Newspapers Ltd, 2000 J.C.22; 1999 S.C.C.R. 824.
Ambard v Att-Gen of Trinidad and Tobago [1936] 1 All E.R. 704.
Applause Store Productions Ltd and Matthew Firsht v Grant Raphael [2008] EWHC 1781 (QB).
Ashdown v Telegraph Group Ltd (2001) The Times, 1 August 363.
Assistant Deputy Coroner for Inner West London v Channel Four Television [2007] EWHC 2513 (31 October 2007).
Attard v Greater Manchester Newspapers Ltd, Fam 14/15 June 2001, Bennet J.

Attorney General v BBC [2007] EWCA Civ 280.

Attorney General v Express Newspapers, Queen's Bench Division (Divisional Court) [2004] EWHC 2859 (Admin), CO/1131/2004.

Attorney General v Guardian Newspapers Ltd et al. (No.2) [1988] 1496, HKHL 6 (13 October 1988).

Attorney General v ITN [1995] 2 All E.R. 370; (1995) 1 Cr. App. R. 204.

Attorney General v MGN Ltd and others, Queen's Bench Division [1997] 1 All ER 456, [1997] EMLR 284.

Attorney General v Punch Ltd and another [2002] UKHL 50.

Attorney General v Pelling, Queen's Bench Division (Divisional Court) [2005] EWHC 414 (Admin), CO/1406/2004 (Transcript).

Attorney General v Shayler [2006] All ER (D) 436 (Jul).

Attorney General v Michael Alexander Seckerson and Times Newspapers Limited [2009] EWHC 1023 (Admin).

Author of a Blog v Times Newspapers Ltd [2009] EWHC 1358 (QB).

Binyam Mohamed v Secretary of State for Foreign and Commonwealth Affairs [2009] EWHC 152 (Admin) (4 February 2009).

Bonnard v Perryman. [1891 B.735] – [1891] 2 Ch. 269.

Boumediene v Bush 553 US ___ (2008).

Brandenburg v Ohio 395 US 444 (1969).

Branzburg v Hayes 408 US 665 (1972).

Bridges v California, 324 US 252 (1941).

Burstyn Inc. v Wilson 343 US 495 (1952).

Bush v Gore 531 US 98 (2000).

Campbell v Acuff-Rose Music, Inc., 510 US 569 (1994).

Campbell v MGN Ltd [2004] UKHL 22.

Carr (Maxine) v News Group Newspapers Ltd [2005] EWHC 971 (QB).

Cohen v California 403 US 15 (1971).

Cohen v Cowles Media Co. 501 US 663 (1991).

Corporate Officer of the House of Commons v Information Commissioner & others [2008] EWHC 1084 (Admin).

Cox Broadcasting v Cohn, 420 US 469 (1975).

Craig v Harney, 331 US 367 (1947).

Doe v University of Michigan 721 F. Supp. 852 (E.D. Mich. 1989).

Dow Jones & Company Inc v Gutnick (2002) 210 CLR 575.

Duke of Brunswick v Harmer (1849) 14 Q.B. 185.

Edmonds v Department of Justice et al., US Court of Appeal District of Columbia Circuit, 74 U.S.L.W. 3321 (2005).

Edwards et al. v Audubon and New York Times 556 F.2d. 113 (2d Cir. 1977).

Feist Publications v Rural Telephone Service Co. 499 US 340 (1991).

Florida Star v B.J.F. 109 S. Ct. 2603 (1989).

Galloway (George) MP v Telegraph Group Ltd [2004] EWHC 2786 (QB)

Galloway (George) MP v Telegraph Group Ltd [2006] EWCA Civ 17 (25 January 2006).

Guardian News & Media Ltd v Information Commissioner & Ministry of Justice, Information Tribunal EA/2008/0084 (10 June 2009).

Gertz v Welch, 418 US 323 (1974).

Gitlow v New York 268 US 652 (1925)

Gobind v State of Madhya Pradesh AIR 1975 SC 1378.

Godfrey v Demon Internet Ltd (2001) 1QB 201.

Gooding v Wilson 405 US 518 (1972).

Goodwin (William) v United Kingdom 7488/90 ECHR 16 (27 March 1996).

HM Attorney General v Pelling [2005] EWHC 414 (Admin) (08 April 2005).

Hustler Magazine v Falwell 485 US 46 (1988).

IA v Turkey 42571/98 [2005] ECHR 590 (13 September 2005).

In re: Grand Jury Subpoena, Judith Miller 397 F.3d 964 (2005).

In the Matter of W.I. Clement, Court of Exchequer, (11 June 1822) 11 Price, 68–95, 147 Eng. Rep. 1220-1865.

Irving v Penguin and Lipstadt [2000] EWHC QB 115 (11 April 2000).

It's in the Cards v Fuschetto 535 N.W.2d 11 (Court of Appeals of Wisconsin 1995).

Jameel v Wall Street Journal [2006] UKHL 44.

Kaye v Robertson [1991] FSR 62. CA.

Kemp v Glasgow Corporation, 1918 S.C. 639.

Lawson v Dixon 512 U.S. 1215 (1994).

Lillie and Anor v Newcastle City Council and Others [2002] EWHC 1600 (QB) (30 July 2002).

Loutchansky v Times Newspapers Ltd [2002] QB 783; [2002] 1 All ER 652.

MacAlister v Associated Newspapers Ltd, 1954 S.L.T. 14, HCJ Appeal.

Maxine Carr v News Group Newspapers Limited & Others, [2005] EWHC 971 (QB).

Murray (David) (by his litigation friends Neil Murray and Joanne Murray) v Big Pictures (UK) Ltd, [2008] EWCA Civ 446. Case No: A3/2007/2236.

McKennitt v Ash [2005] EWHC 3003 (QB).

Mosley v News Group Newspapers [2008] EWHC 1777 (QB) (24 July 2008)

Murray v Spencer, 2002, District Judge Andrew Maw, Lincoln County Court. This case is unreported.

National Archives and Records Administration v Favish 124 S. Ct. 1570 (2004).

New York Times v Sullivan [1964] 376 US 254.

New York Times Co. v United States, 1971, 403 US 713. Together with No. 1885, United States v. Washington Post Co. et al. New York Times v NASA 782 F. Supp. 628 (D.D.C.1991).

Oklahoma Publishing v District Court, 430 US 308 (1977).

P., C. and S V United Kingdom ECHR 2002 No: 56547/00 Judgment of the Court 16 July 2002 [Section II].

Olmstead et al. v US 277 US 438 (1928).

O'Riordan (Marie) v DPP [2005] EWHC 1240 (Admin) (19 May 2005).

Pennekamp v Florida, 328 US 331 (1946).

People's Union for Civil Liberties v Union of India (1997) 1 SCC 301.

Press-Enterprise v Superior Court (P-E 1) 464 US 501 (1984).

Press-Enterprise v Superior Court (P-E-II) 478 US 1 (1986).

Prince of Wales, The HRH v Associated Newspapers Ltd (No. 3) [2006] EWHC 522 (Ch).

Prosecutor v Brdjanin: appeal of Jonathan Randal ICTY judgment of Appeal Chamber, December 11, 2002.

Prosecutor v Brima, Appeals Chamber of the Special Court for Sierra Leone, Case Number SCSL-2004-16-AR73, judgement May 16, 2006.

Red Lion Broadcasting v FCC 395 US 367 (1969).

Reynolds v Times Newspapers [1999] UKHL 45.

R v Abu Hamza (No. 2) [2006] EWCA Crim 2118 (28 July 2006).

R v Angela Cannings [2004] EWCA Crim 01.

R v Burrell, Central Criminal Court 17 December 2004, Mr Justice Aikens, 'Reasons for refusing the Crown's application for reporting restrictions on aspects of the complainant's evidence'.

R v Central Criminal Court ex part Crook, Court of Appeal Criminal Division, 10 November 1989, case reported: Re Crook [1992] 2 All ER 687 at 689.

R v Clarke, ex parte Crippen (1910), 103 L.T. 636.

R v Clement Court of the King's Bench, (28 January 1821) 4 B. & ALD. 219–233, 106 Eng. Rep. 918 1378-1865.

R v Central Criminal Court, ex p Crook (1984) Times, 8 November.

R v Central Criminal Court, ex p Crook and Godwin [1995] 1 FLR 132.

R v Central Independent Television [1994] Fam. Law 500, CA (Civ Div).

R v El Faisal [2004] EWCA Crim 456 (4 March 2004).

R v New Statesman (Editor), ex parte Director of Public Prosecutions (1928), 44 T.L.R. 301.

R v Rahman & Mohammed, [2008] EWCA Crim 1465 (8 July 2008).

R v Shayler [2001] EWCA 1977 (28 September 2001).

R v Sherwood, ex parte The Telegraph Group & others, Court of Appeal, Criminal Division, Times Law Report June 12 2001.

R v Socialist Worker, ex p A-G [1975] QB 637.

R v Solicitor General ex parte Taylor and Another, Queen's Bench Division (Divisional Court) The Independent 3 August 1995, The Times 14 August 1995.

R v Wilkinson (1930), Times, July 16.

R v Zafar and Others [2008] EWCA Crim 184.

R. Rajagopal v State of Tamil Nadu AIR 1995 SC 264.

R.A.V. v St. Paul 505 US 377 (1992).

Re Crook's Appeal [1991] 93 Cr. App R 17 CA.

Re: D and the BBC, Attorney General's Reference No. 3 of 1999: Application by the British Broadcasting Corporation to set aside or vary a Reporting Restriction Order [2009] UKHL 34.

Re S (A Child) (Identification: Restriction on Publication), [2004] UKHL 47.

Revell v Lidov, 317 F.3d 467 (5th Cir. 2002).

Richmond Newspapers Inc v Virginia 448 US 555 (1980).

Roberts v Searchlight Magazine Ltd [2006] EWHC 1025 (QB).

Salinger v Colting & Windupbird Publishing 09 Civ. 5095 (DAB) US District Court Southern District of New York (July 1 2009).

Sanoma Uitgevers BV v The Netherlands ECHR Third Section, no. 38224/03, March 31 2009.

Schenck v United States 249 US 47 (1919).

Scott v Scott [1913] AC 417.

Sheppard v Maxwell, 384 U.S. 333 (1966).

Smith v Daily Mail 443 US 97 (1979).

Snepp v. United States, 444 U.S. 507 (1980).

Spink v HM Advocate, 1989 S.C.C.R. 413.

State of Maharashtra v Prabhakar Panndurang AIR 1966 SC 424.

State of Maharashtra v Madhukar Narayan Mandikar AIR 1991 SC 207.

Steel & Morris v United Kingdom [2005] ECHR 68416/1.

Stirling, Petr v Associated Newspapers Ltd, 1960 J.C. 5.

T (by her litigation friend the Official Solicitor) v BBC [2007] EWHC 1683 (QB).

Texas v Johnson 491 US 397 (1989).

The Secretary of State for the Home Department Appellant v M [2004] EWCA Civ 324.

Thorgeirson v Iceland; sub nom. Thorgeir v Iceland App. No. 13778/88; Series A, No. 239 (1992) 14 E.H.R.R. 843.

Time, Inc. v Hill, 385 US 374 (1967).

Times Newspapers Ltd and Others, Court of Appeal, Criminal Division, [July 31, 2007] Times Law Reports.

Times Newspapers Ltd v Secretary of State for the Home Department Re: AY, [2008] EWHC 2455 (Admin).

Times Newspapers Ltd (Nos 1 and 2) v UK, ECHR, Fourth Section, Applications 3002/03 and 2367/03, March 10 2009.

Turkington and Others (Practising as McCartan Turkington Breen) v Times Newspapers (Northern Ireland) [2000] UKHL 57 (2 November 2000).

US v Eichman 496 US 310 (1990).

Venables (Jon) & Thompson (Robert) and News Group, Associated Newspaper & MGN Ltd [2001] EWHC QB 32 (8 January 2001).

Village of Skokie v National Socialist Party 373 N.E.2d 21 (Ill. 1978).

Virginia v Black 123 S. Ct. 1536 (2003).

Von Hannover v Germany – 59320/00 [2004] ECHR 294 (24 June 2004).

Wainwright v United Kingdom [2006] ECHR 807.

Western Provident Association v Norwich Union Healthcare HC 1997. This case is unreported.

Whitney v California 274 US 357 (1927).

Wisconsin v Mitchell 508 US 476 (1993).

Yahoo! Inc v La Ligue Contre Le Racisme Et l'Antisemitisme, 169 F. Supp. 2d 1181, 1186-87 (N.D. Cal 2001).

Yates v US 354, US 298 (1957).

Young v New Haven Advocate, 315 F.3d 256 (4th Cir. 2002).

X v Sweeney, 1982 S.C.C.R. 161.

X, A woman formerly known as Mary Bell and Y and Stephen O'Brien and News Group Newspapers Ltd and MGN Ltd [2003] EWHC QB 1101.

INDEX